MORAL REASONING

Rediscovering the Ethical Tradition

Louis Groarke

OXFORD

UNIVERSITY PRESS

OXFORD
UNIVERSITY PRESS

8 Sampson Mews, Suite 204, Don Mills, Ontario M3C 0H5
www.oupcanada.com

Oxford University Press is a department of the University of Oxford.
It furthers the University's objective of excellence in research, scholarship, and education by publishing worldwide in

Oxford   New York

Auckland   Cape Town   Dar es Salaam   Hong Kong   Karachi   Kuala Lumpur   Madrid   Melbourne
Mexico City   Nairobi   New Delhi   Shanghai   Taipei   Toronto

With offices in

Argentina   Austria   Brazil   Chile   Czech Republic   France   Greece   Guatemala   Hungary   Italy   Japan   Poland
Portugal   Singapore   South Korea   Switzerland   Thailand   Turkey   Ukraine   Vietnam

Oxford is a trade mark of Oxford University Press
in the UK and in certain other countries

Published in Canada
by Oxford University Press

Library and Archives Canada Cataloguing in Publication

Groarke, Louis
Moral reasoning : rediscovering the ethical tradition / Louis Groarke.

Includes index.
ISBN 978-0-19-542561-1

1. Ethics—Textbooks. I. Title.

BJ1012.G76 2011   170   C2010-906160-8

Cover image: Melissa King/iStockphoto

This book is printed on permanent acid-free paper ∞.
Printed and bound in Canada.

1 2 3 4 – 14 13 12 11

Contents

Preface   ix

Acknowledgements   xiii

CHAPTER 1 INTRODUCTION

What Is Ethics?   1

To Whom Is This Book Addressed?   9

This Book Presents an Alternative Account of Moral Philosophy   12

This Book Is an Account of Virtue Ethics in the Spirit of Aristotle   15

What Is the Purpose of Ethics?   19

Questions for Study and Review   22

CHAPTER 2 MORAL EPISTEMOLOGY: WE CAN REASON ABOUT MORALITY

What Is Moral Epistemology?   23

How Do We Reason?   24

Challenges to Moral Epistemology   27

The 'Is–Ought' Fallacy   43

Why Should I Be Moral? A Self-Interested Challenge   52

Moral Philosophy Requires Objectivity and Subjectivity   55

Questions for Study and Review   58

Suggestions for Further Reading   59

CHAPTER 3 THE EARLY TRADITION: FROM CONFUCIUS TO JESUS AND BEYOND

Introduction   60

Master Kong (Confucius): *Dao*   61

Heraclitus: The *Logos*   67

Democritus: Pleasure, But Not Too Much   68

Diogenes the Cynic: A Man and His Barrel   70

Epicurus: Refined Hedonism   75

Epictetus: Things Within Your Power   81

Pyrrho: Skepticism and Peace of Mind   90

Protagoras: *Nomos* and *Physis*   97

Jesus: Love   101

Questions for Study and Review   109

Suggestions for Further Reading   110

CHAPTER 4 SOCRATES AND PLATO

Introduction   111
Socratic Teachings   112
Plato's Teachings   124
Questions for Study and Review   145
Suggestions for Further Reading   146

CHAPTER 5 UNDERSTANDING MORAL THEORY: ARISTOTLE

Introduction   147
On Happiness (*Eudaimonia*)   149
On Virtue (*Arete*)   151
On Practical Reason   157
On Means and Ends   158
On External Goods   162
On the Good Life   163
On Three Kinds of Life   164
On Virtue as Habit   165
On the Golden Mean   167
On Morality and Choice   174
On Two Moral Faults: Weakness of Will and Ignorance   177
On Six Character-States   181
On Five Kinds of Intelligence   187
On Two Minor Intellectual Virtues   191
On Moral Induction and Moral Deduction   192
On Moral Approximation   196
(More) On First Moral Principles   197
On Slaves and Friends   198
Questions for Study and Review   201
Suggestions for Further Reading   201

CHAPTER 6 UNDERSTANDING MORAL THEORY: THOMAS AQUINAS

Introduction   202
On Religion and Morality: The Euthyphro Problem   203
On Virtue: Theological and Cardinal   206
On the Cardinal Virtues   209
On the Definition of Law   218
On the Four Kinds of Law   219
On the Principle of Double Effect   232
On the Internal and External Structure of Voluntary Action   236
On the Three Moral Criteria of a Good Action   240
On Voluntary, Involuntary, and Non-Voluntary Acts   242
A Thomistic Account of Ignorance   247

Questions for Study and Review 253
Suggestions for Further Reading 254

CHAPTER 7 THE CONTRACTARIANS: THOMAS HOBBES, JOHN LOCKE, JEAN-JACQUES ROUSSEAU, AND KARL MARX

Introduction 255
Ancient Contractarianism: The *Anonymous Iamblichi* 256
Thomas Hobbes and the Beginnings of Modern Contractarianism 258
John Locke and Two-Tiered Contractarianism 271
Jean-Jacques Rousseau and the State of Nature 278
Karl Marx: Rousseau's Legacy 286
On Hypothetical Agreement 288
On Contractarian Virtue 290
Questions for Study and Review 291
Suggestions for Further Reading 292

CHAPTER 8 KANT: DUTY AND MORAL LAW

Introduction 293
Kant and the Enlightenment 294
On Reformation Theology 295
On Duty 295
Morality Derives from Pure, A Priori Reason 299
On Happiness 301
On Good Will 302
On Imperatives: Categorical and Hypothetical 305
On the Categorical Imperative: Five Universal Formulations 307
On Autonomy 331
Criticisms of Kant's Deontological Approach 332
Questions for Study and Review 337
Suggestions for Further Reading 338

CHAPTER 9 UTILITARIANISM AND LIBERALISM: JEREMY BENTHAM AND JOHN STUART MILL

Introduction 339
Jeremy Bentham: Original Utilitarianism 340
John Stuart Mill: Moral *and* Political Philosophy 348
Questions for Study and Review 387
Suggestions for Further Reading 388

CHAPTER 10 CONTEMPORARY MORAL THEORY

Anti-Theory: A Paradigm Shift in Ethics 390
Kierkegaard's Transcendental Subjectivism: Becoming Yourself 392
Personalism: Persons as the Most Fundamental Moral Reality 395

A Feminist Ethics of Care: Nel Noddings   396
Human Rights: Looking at Duty Backwards, Punishment   401
Divine Command Morality   406
Ecumenical Global Ethics: Agreement between Religions   408
Environmental Ethics: Beyond Deep Ecology   410
Contemporary Contractarianism: Rational Agreement   414
Epilogue   420
Questions for Study and Review   421
Suggestions for Further Reading   421

Glossary   422
Notes   435
Index   449
Credits   462

Preface

The present book was born of a frustration with current offerings in ethics. There are several widespread problems with contemporary textbooks. Let me list them quickly here.

To begin with, most textbooks on the market seem remarkably uninformed on the history of ethics. Several generations of students (both philosophy majors and thoughtful non-majors) have passed through the university system without gaining any careful familiarity with the moral wisdom bequeathed to us by an army of talented authors in the Western philosophical tradition. This is nothing short of a tragedy. When we leave aside the usual prejudices and look carefully at earlier sources, we find a rich and eminently practical source of moral reflection. This book is intended to improve critical skills in moral analysis by introducing the contemporary student and general reader to the richness of this tradition.

I myself have come to feel the need for a broad but reasonably detailed critical source on Western ethics, both for teaching and for general consultation. Standard fare is meagre, to say the least. In standard textbooks one finds, perhaps, a little on the historical origins of deontology and utilitarianism and—if one is lucky—on Aristotelian virtue ethics. There is almost no treatment of a major author like Thomas Aquinas (someone who summarized hundreds of years of medieval moral speculation) and little or no comment on a series of early thinkers, ranging from epoch-making individuals like Jesus and Socrates to long-lived schools like Stoicism, Epicureanism, and Ancient Skepticism. Even modern movements such as liberalism or contractarianism are presented with insufficient historical depth.

Trying to organize a course around a hodgepodge of individual books—some older, some newer, some no longer available, all at different prices, all standing in need of selective abridgement—is not a practical solution to teaching needs. The present volume gathers and makes accessible a broad range of major and minor writers in moral philosophy in one, easy-to-read, moderately priced volume. I know of no other text that deals with such a comprehensive range of sources. An instructor may, of course, pick and choose which authors are most appropriately discussed in a particular pedagogical context. (There is no need to engage with every author presented here.) But they are here, available for use, inside or outside the classroom as need be.

What we ignore, we misunderstand. Even in the specialized academic literature, one encounters embarrassing errors in treatments of historical theories and figures. Books aimed at a more general audience tend to 'dumb down' historical arguments almost to the point of caricature. The following volume is intended as an introductory treatment; everything possible has been done to make the material readily accessible to readers with no prior familiarity with moral philosophy. At the same time, the analysis is not simplistic or cursory. I do not skim over important theories but describe them in substantial detail. Although I have taught ethics to hundreds of students in practical disciplines like business or nursing, I have met with little resistance. Young adults, who are trying to establish goals and careers for themselves, find the material intrinsically interesting. When properly introduced to the requisite vocabulary and technical points of dispute, they are discerning enough to understand the import of even recondite discussions and come to navigate through the complex world of moral philosophy on their own.

We cannot come to properly evaluate the wisdom in the moral tradition by reading solely secondary sources. At the same time, it seems obvious that primary sources (especially those from a distant era or culture) present peculiar problems for interpretation. This book tries to incorporate the best of both worlds. I have tried to expose readers to the most important and representative texts while explaining as clearly as possible their meaning. Reading these original sources is an introduction to the history of ideas itself. This book could be easily incorporated into a great books program or a liberal arts curriculum.

There is a second series of problems with standard treatments of ethics. Contemporary authors tend to provide a very thin account of morality. Morality is depicted as a matter of narrow rules rather than individual self-affirmation. This tends to enlarge the range of what we are allowed to do but it does not provide for a fulfilling account of human aspiration. This is in sharp contrast to the traditional view that sees morality as the central theme in human life and even the supreme human accomplishment.

It is hard to take seriously something we doubt. Sociological factors have led to an unexamined infatuation with moral skepticism. Historical authors do not attempt to provide an absolute proof for morality but neither do they acquiesce to a self-indulgent skepticism that is really an excuse for moral nonachievement. Standard modern treatments do not do enough to distinguish knee-jerk, doctrinaire skepticism from rigorous moral inquiry. There is some sort of mean to be struck between close-minded dogmatism and an uncritical acceptance of all views as equally valid. I do, of course, discuss challenges to morality, but the general viewpoint taken throughout the book is that morality is something we have a general sense of while being confused about details, something we tend to rationalize away when it thwarts our desires but something we all return to when our own interests are at stake.

One of the guiding principles of this volume is the idea that courses in moral philosophy should inspire moral excellence without giving up on the scrupulously critical nature of good philosophy. After several years of teaching ethics, it seemed to me that ethics courses undermined rather than bolstered my students' moral sensibilities. It is not simply that so much textbook writing seems decidedly uninspiring. It goes deeper than that. The philosophers and texts investigated in the following pages take morality seriously; they offer a deep perspective on human nature and the human condition; they ponder what makes life worth living; they view moral philosophy as a force for good in the world, and as something that has direct practical application. Their words still strike a chord today.

A third problem with many contemporary textbooks is the almost single-minded emphasis on moral disagreement. There may be strong disagreement on *some* of the *details* of morality, but there is also overwhelming consensus on general issues. Any prolonged, careful reading of the history of moral philosophy indicates that individual authors are puzzled by similar problems, make similar arguments, and appeal to similar kinds of moral evidence. Unfortunately, the impression the beginning reader gets from reading most contemporary textbooks is just the reverse. Clearly, morality can be viewed from many different perspectives. I try to use these different perspectives in a constructive manner, to build up to one coherent, larger view.

In teaching morality to students, many books begin with the most difficult, divisive, and controversial issues. This is like trying to teach someone how to count beginning with the transfinite (infinite) numbers. As historical authors all recognize, applying general principles to specific situations is a challenge; hence, the emphasis on casuistry. (The modern preoccupation with rule-morality and the neglect of casuistry has contributed to some of the theoretical problems that plague recent approaches to moral philosophy.) As the tradition teaches, one needs to understand how to apply general principles to straightforward cases before tackling more complex situations.

The almost single-minded emphasis on the most controversial issues and problems in standard textbooks is counterproductive. This is not to say that we should be uncritical about historical authors and their texts. Acquaintance with the moral tradition does not smother—indeed, it *fosters*—critical reflection; it forces us to think hard about seminal issues, to develop views and positions than go far beyond what peer pressure or ideology can offer. I find students come to appreciate the opportunity for an in-depth look at issues, whatever their personal agreement or disagreement with the positions raised in readings and discussion. They often adopt opposing positions in class discussion, particularly when it comes to specific examples. There is also room for a

more single-minded focus on problematic issues in actual discussions and in student papers.

I do not adopt any narrowly partisan position in the forthcoming pages. To the best of my ability, I have tried to make room for as many different views, historical and modern, as possible, without, however, refraining from criticism when necessary. Clearly, not all arguments are good arguments; not all theories are good theories. In critiquing particular views, I always attempt to recuperate whatever is good or insightful in each position presented. Some readers will inevitably disagree with some of what I say, but I hope that I provide at least the opportunity for vigorous discussion of alternatives. And, no doubt, some of the readers of this book will push the principles and arguments presented here to new conclusions and insights that I have missed or inadequately commented on.

If I take a substantive position in this work, it is that the general import of the mainstream tradition is largely correct although it can always be improved upon. Those who persist in dismissing earlier philosophers and schools as unforgivably naive or primitive or somehow misguided will disagree with the presentation here. (Such opinions, it seems to me, are on the wane.) The advent of modern skepticism and moral relativism has not diminished the importance or the usefulness of these sources. (My experience is that such prejudices are invariably fuelled by a lack of familiarity with or by egregiously uncharitable readings of the primary sources.) I hope that my efforts will reach those with little access to the moral tradition and convince them that there is something of lasting value here.

I should perhaps add a word about a hotly contested topic: religion. This is a book for religious believers, for agnostics, for atheists, and for so-called secular humanists. I have never thought that it was my job to ridicule or contest my students' religious (or a-religious) views. Because religious influences of one sort or another have had a determining influence on the moral tradition and because this text aims at historical accuracy, it deals with religious questions in passing. Clearly, one cannot understand a major moral thinker like Thomas Aquinas without explaining his religious views. One does not have to be religious or 'unreligious' in precisely the same way that Thomas Aquinas was in order to profit from his moral wisdom. But then again, one cannot understand certain Enlightenment views without understanding views on the opposite side. One cannot fairly capture what these authors are saying without exploring, in as charitable a way as possible, the religious content of their views. This is not a book on philosophy of religion, or political philosophy, or philosophy of human nature, or epistemology. But I do discuss these (and other issues) when they bear on the moral tradition.

There is one final problem with conventional treatments that needs to be mentioned. Ethics revolves around the study of what human beings do. In truth, human beings do all sorts of strange things: some of them wonderful, some of them woefully disturbing. As someone who has always read newspapers—my father was a teacher and journalist—I have been surprised at the lack of pertinent, vivid examples in so many introductory treatments. Yes, we need to discuss general principles, but we also need to test our theoretical assumptions with concrete cases. The growth of the Internet has, in particular, put a smorgasbord of interesting and challenging information within easy reach. To be a good ethicist is, first of all, to be an attentive student of human behaviour. I have, therefore, tried to pack the text with singularly appropriate, probing, or puzzling examples by introducing short, boxed citations, mostly from newspaper articles. These cases should provide plenty of fodder for classroom discussion.

In an age of specialization, it is easy enough to disparage introductions to any subject matter as overly simple simulacra of the real thing. If, however, the technical literature is inaccessible to ordinary readers, I believe that we can capture the development of moral philosophy in a manner that is open to anyone who wants to take the trouble and the effort to investigate these matters. This effort may perhaps, in its own small way, contribute to scholarship on these issues. Thomas Aquinas, in composing his enormously influential *Summa,* intended it as an *introduction* for students in theology. I have more modest aims. Still, within these pages I have tried to provide a compelling and insightful synthesis of a long tradition of moral reflection in Western philosophy.

The present book is intended, then, to fill a gap. Hopefully, it will provide readers with a useful alternative to what is presently available.

Louis Groarke
Antigonish, Nova Scotia
2010

Acknowledgements

I wish to extend my deep gratitude to Oxford University Press, especially developmental editor, Jennifer Mueller; copy editor, Colleen St. Marie; acquisitions editor, Stephen Kotowych; and managing editor, Phyllis Wilson. They have all been a pleasure to work with. ✌

For Marie-Andrée Glen-Groarke

Patience et longueur de temps
Font plus que force ni que rage.

— 'Le Lion et le Rat,' Jean de la Fontaine

Chapter One

Introduction

♋ Chapter Objectives

After reading this chapter you should be able to:
- Describe how historical and modern authors view the purpose of the discipline of ethics (or moral philosophy).
- Describe, using examples, how moral standards differ from other ways of evaluating human behaviour.
- Explain the relationship between humanity, rationality, freedom of choice, and morality.
- Explain, in a preliminary way, what the history of ideas teaches us about morality and why moral skepticism is unconvincing.
- Explain (a) the difference between virtue ethics and moral law; (b) what hermeneutics has to do with morality; (c) Auguste Comte's law of three stages; (d) Derrida's notion of *différance*; (e) the logical principle of charity; (f) the relationship between personal autonomy and morality.

What Is Ethics?

This is a book on ethics, or **moral philosophy**. But first a quick note on terminology. I will use the terms *ethics* and *moral philosophy* interchangeably throughout this text. Although some contemporary authors continue to distinguish morality from ethics, to specialists in the field this dichotomy will seem slightly dated. It is certainly misleading. Authors who separate ethics from morality usually view morality as a restricted set of basic rules that society enforces on all its members without exception. Ethics is alleged to be more personal: it is said to consist of those private beliefs and aspirations that motivate our personal endeavours. Some of these authors make a distinction between evaluating behaviour (morality) and evaluating character (ethics). But this book will not use this problematic distinction. Suffice it to say that even on this reading of philosophical terminology, moral and ethical values are so closely associated and interdependent that we cannot make any clear distinction between the two. As we shall see, morality develops out of ethics. But more on this topic later in the book.

So, then, the first question to be asked is 'What is ethics'? Or, expressed otherwise, 'What is moral philosophy'? There are two ways of answering this question, and both may surprise the unsuspecting reader:

1. Modern philosophers think of ethics as the most rigorous way of evaluating human behaviour.
2. Historical authors present ethics as the secret to happiness.

Modern View: Ethics Is the Most Rigorous Way of Evaluating Human Behaviour

Most contemporary authors would claim that ethics has to do with one special kind of evaluation: how humans evaluate their own behaviour. As common sense, shared experience, literature, and even science indicate, we are all able to evaluate the world in relation to various standards of beauty, usefulness, goodness, truth, and happiness. We all approve and disapprove of certain things; we praise and condemn; we accuse and congratulate. Collectively, we celebrate human achievement and we lament human failure. We do this constantly and hardly give it a second thought. Our evaluations run the gamut from the mundane to the grandiose; they touch on many different aspects of reality and human experience. For example, we value physical beauty, intelligence, wealth, and political power, but we also value generosity, courage, patience, and cheerfulness. Sometimes our evaluations

seem to reinforce one another; sometimes they seem strangely out of step with what we believe or what we do. Ethics can be construed then as a rigorous attempt to understand this everyday business of evaluating human behaviour.

Morality Is Obligatory

Many contemporary thinkers distinguish sharp-ly between moral and non-moral evaluation. Historical authorities prefer broader categories. Still, moral judgment seems to be the most important way in which we evaluate human behaviour. First, morality is *obligatory*. You may be a bad tennis player. I may criticize your lack of skill. I may even dislike you because of your ineptitude on the court. But you are not *morally* required to be a good or even an average tennis player. There are other ways of succeeding that are more important than tennis. Morality is about what you *must* do in order to qualify as an acceptable example of human individuality. Tennis is optional; morality is not. You can be a good human being and a bad tennis player, but you cannot be a good human being and an immoral person.

Today, many philosophers try to evaluate morality by means of universal rules: Do not kill. Do not steal. Do not commit adultery. These rules are, in a strict sense, obligatory. (More on this later.) The historical tradition suggests a different emphasis. Many of these older authors focus on the notion of virtue. But virtue, like moral law, is also obligatory. We cannot be minimally decent human beings without being virtuous. That is, we must be honest, courageous, patient, fair (etc.) or we fail, in some important way, at the human project.

Moral thinkers—those we call 'ethicists'—propose authoritative criteria for the evaluation of humans. When a Hollywood tabloid ranks best-dressed actresses or the sexiest eli-

---

ꙮ Applied Philosophy Box 1.1 ꙮ

'Real Heroes vs. Sports Heroes' by D.C. Copeland

Today *The Miami Herald* ran their annual pro and college football special edition. It was an amazing thing to see and hold—it could easily replace light dumbbells for a workout. It had 6 sections, 74-pages with full color/full depth covers of serious, stoic players. Only one guy was frowning this time— probably because he was a college player and wasn't getting paid copious amounts of money yet. . . . Now don't get us wrong, the staff at MVB loves football. We believe it is the nearly perfect game that combines suspense, action, brute strength and violence with athleticism and balletic beauty. But that doesn't mean we aren't tired of seeing athletes made into heroes. It is our contention that our commu- nity should also allocate time and media space for the unsung heroes, the ones 'who live lives of quiet desperation,' who get up every morning to go to work to make ends meet, who struggle to keep a family together despite working for minimum wage. ABC News recognizes the worthy in their Friday 'Person of the Week.' *The Miami Herald* and local TV could do the same. These kinds of awards and recognition are not only good for the spirits of those being honored, they're good for us too because they remind us, if nothing else, that someone a lot like us—maybe even someone who is worse off than we are—can make the effort to not only keep on keeping on but takes it a step further by giving something back to the community.

Notice what is going on here. Showering attention on athletes is another way of presenting them as role models of human behaviour. This author is complaining that sports evaluation has taken on so much im- portance that it crowds out and obscures a more important form of evaluation, namely, moral evaluation.

Source: D.C. Copeland, 'Real Heroes vs. Sports Heroes.' *EzineArticles.com*, http://ezinearticles.com/?Real-Heroes-vs.-Sports- Heroes&id=287017, 31 August 2006.

---

gible bachelors or the richest people in show- biz, this is a kind of evaluation. When a politi- cian wins an election by a landslide or when a student receives an A in calculus, these, too, are kinds of evaluation. But non-moral evalua- tion schemes are often superficial. They do not provide the key to what is best (or worst) about human nature.

Morality Is Fundamental

So morality is, first, obligatory; second, it is *fundamental*. Getting an A in calculus, being polite to an older person, making money (in an honest way)—these behaviours may be im- portant ethical achievements. But these issues

must be understood in light of a deeper theory of what human beings are and what is worth- while for them to accomplish. Ethics is an at- tempt to develop a more basic theory of right and wrong that we can use to evaluate more specific cases of human achievement.

Life is complicated. At first glance, you might not think that it is *morally* required to practise holding your breath under water. And gener- ally speaking, you would be right. If, how- ever, you are a lifeguard, you may be morally required to practise holding your breath under water so that you will be able to save someone from drowning. Now this may seem to be a very special situation—it is—but the requirement relating to lifeguards derives, on closer inspection, from a logically prior moral principle: that human life is intrinsically valuable and ought to be preserved. Morality may apply differently to the endlessly variable individual circumstances of human life, but it does this by tapping into root principles that underlie these surface differences. Being aware of these deeper principles is part of what morality is all about. Ethics collects and investigates the principles and concepts that can stand as the ultimate reference in our evaluation of human success and failure. Exploring these most fundamental principles and applying them to particular situations is what this book is about. We will try to discover and articulate the most basic criteria for determining what makes one a good human being and what makes a life worth living.

Perhaps an analogy from physics might help. If someone lifts a set of keys in the air and then releases those keys, they fall to the ground. This is what all physical objects do, whether they are keys, baseballs, rocks, raindrops, snowflakes, chairs, or plates: they move from a position in the air to the ground unless they are somehow held up in the air by some applied force. Newton was able to explain this in terms of a single fundamental law: the universal law of gravity. Ethicists try to do something similar. They propose, in effect, the moral equivalent of a concept of gravity or a universal law of gravitation. That is, they try to explain, in a rigorous, consistent, and probing way, the ultimate principles that lie behind our everyday moral evaluations. They try to explain, at the deepest level possible, the difference between right and wrong.

Morality Is Comprehensive

Not only is morality obligatory and fundamental, it is also *comprehensive*. Because morality provides the most basic understanding of human behaviour, it is also provides the most general standard of evaluation. For morality applies not only to lifeguards, but also to forest rangers and nurses and engineers and politicians and monks and mothers and uncles. Morality applies, not because we are employed at a particular job, but because we are human. It derives from our own nature. As such, the moral imperative is inescapable. Of course, there are special circumstances where morality does not apply. If, for example, you are asleep, or in a coma, or drugged, or mentally ill, or still a baby, morality does not apply. But more on these special circumstances later.

Morality is also comprehensive in another way. As human beings, we could not make sense of our attitudes without assuming that morality holds in different times and places. Yes, accepted standards of moral behaviour change through time (though not as much as we sometimes assume). Still, we often do pass judgment on earlier eras and on other cultures as well as on our own. One could not argue, for example, that the way slaves or women were treated in the past was cruel or unfair or wrong unless we took some implicit standard of morality and applied it to the time period in question. There is no need to be embarrassed or defensive about this. As we shall see, the popular idea that morality is purely subjective or relative does not hold up to close scrutiny.

Morality Is Authoritative

One final characteristic separates morality from other types of evaluation: morality is *authoritative*. Moral standards are absolutely urgent and compelling. When it comes to deciding what we should do, they rank higher than other considerations. As a perspective on human achievement, morality is more commanding.

To use a technical-sounding phrase, we might say that morality has normative priority. Most ethicists would argue that moral considerations always override other considerations. In point of fact, people do not always put morality first. They sometimes have understandable and pressing reasons to ignore or even transgress moral codes. But morality is not about what people do; it is about what they should *ideally* do or about what they are obliged to do.

Consider a case in point. Imagine the law tells you to do one thing, but morality tells you to do something else. Suppose you live in a Nazi society. Do you obey the law of the land and turn in the 11-year-old Jewish orphan cowering in your basement to the Gestapo? Or do you obey the moral imperative that obliges you to protect the innocent and the weak? Surely, the moral injunction that we must protect the weak takes precedence over an inhumane law that all Jewish children be handed over to the perpetrators of the Jewish genocide. Granted, individuals might, for various reasons, be unable to obey this imperative, but a vast majority of ethicists would argue that if there is a serious clash between morality and human law, it is morality that provides the true measure of human achievement. As a general rule, then, moral evaluations take priority over other evaluations.

There are perhaps a few contemporary authors who argue that moral evaluations are not normatively prior to all other evaluations. But any such view is problematic. To argue that our actions should be guided by more important principles than morality is not to oppose morality but to propose a different morality. Whatever our most basic reasons for acting, these values and principles constitute our own morality. In the following pages, we will investigate not only what passes for morality, but also the belief systems that, rightly or wrongly, motivate ordinary human behaviour.

What Are Other Ways of Evaluating Human Behaviour?

When we say that morality is obligatory, fundamental, comprehensive, and normatively authoritative, we do not mean to overlook other ways of evaluating human behaviour. Some of these ways are, in effect, quasi-moral. We might say of a professional athlete that 'he has guts' or that 'you can depend on him' or that 'he is a disciplined player'. We are commenting on, in each instance, how this person is a good athlete, but there is a moral overtone to such comments. Courage, perseverance, and reliability are also moral qualities. Many ways we use to evaluate ourselves and others overlap with morality. Consider, then, the case of that quasi-moral type of human evaluation we call etiquette, that system of observances and customs that regulate behaviour in so-called polite society.

Emily Post (1872–1960), who became the great twentieth-century American maven of etiquette, tells her readers how to properly address civil and religious dignitaries:

> A doctor, a judge, a bishop are addressed and introduced by their titles. The protestant clergy are usually called Mister unless they hold the title of Doctor, of Dean, or Canon, in which case the surname is added: 'Dean Wood,' 'Doctor Starr,' 'Canon Cope.' A Catholic priest is 'Father Kelly.' To call him Mister is an inexcusable offense. An introduction to a Catholic archbishop, 'Your Grace, may I present _____?' A senator is always introduced as 'Senator Davis,' whether he is in office or not. But the President of the United States, once he is out of office, is merely 'Mr.' and not 'Ex-President.'[1]

Clearly, Post proposes a right and a wrong way of doing things. But this is not morality.

Why? Because these polite rituals do not define in any necessary, fundamental, comprehensive, and authoritative way what it means to be a good human being. Knowing these rules might be an example of good taste and worldly sophistication, but one could be a good human being without understanding anything of these social conventions. Etiquette is, in comparison to morality, trivial. The moral rule 'Thou shalt not kill', for example, carries normative weight; the rule of etiquette 'A senator is always introduced as Senator' pales in significance. The latter injunction must be understood relative to a very specific circumstance. In many societies, there is no political official who is formally called a senator. Even in American society, the custom could, in principle, change over time. But the commandment 'Thou shalt not kill' (properly understood and qualified) is timeless.

If morality and etiquette are distinguishably different, moral philosophers tend to overlook the inevitable connection between the two. Post's book, which became the American bible of good manners, begins with an introduction by Richard Duffy entitled 'Manners and Morals'. Duffy begins with a reference to the Ten Commandments and the 'Chinese sage, Confucius', who viewed etiquette and virtue as 'inseparable'. He compares 'the structure of etiquette . . . to that of a house, of which the foundation is ethics and the rest [is] good taste, correct speech, quiet, unassuming behavior, and a proper pride of dignity'.[2] 'Selfishness,' he explains at further length, 'is at the polar remove from [old-style] manners . . . according to which . . . others were preferred to the self, pain was given to no one, no one was neglected, deference was shown to the weak and the aged, and unconscious courtesy extended to

---

❧ Applied Philosophy Box 1.2 ❧

Etiquette Changes

Emily Post tells her readers how to properly take leave from a formal dinner. She explains:

'That the guest of honor must be the first to take leave was in former times so fixed a rule that everyone used to sit on and on, no matter how late it became, waiting for her whose duty it was to go! More often than not, the guest of honor was an absent-minded old lady, or celebrity, who very likely was vaguely saying to herself, "Oh, my! Are these people never going home?" until by and by it dawned on her that the obligation was her own. But today, although it is still the obligation of the guest who sat at the host's right to make the move to go, it is not considered ill-mannered, if the hour is growing late, for another lady to arise first. In fact, unless the guest of honor is one *really*, meaning a stranger or an elderly lady of distinction, there is no actual precedence in being the one first to go.'

Etiquette changes with society. This formality may now be dispensed with. Many earlier authors in the Western tradition would argue that morality is not like this. Murder is always wrong; cruelty is always a vice; breaking promises is never acceptable; we must always love our neighbour. The most basic principles (morality) never go out of date.

Source: Emily Post, *Etiquette: The Blue Book of Social Usage* (New York and London: Funk and Wagnalls Company, 1937), p. 227.

all inferiors.'[3] Post herself comments, 'Etiquette must, if it is to be of more than trifling use, include ethics as well as manners'.[4] Ethics is more than manners, but insomuch as etiquette is, at its best, a way of showing respect, deference, and consideration to other people, it has, at a deeper level, a basis in morality.

There are many different ways in which we evaluate human behaviour. Ethicists try to elaborate, at the most *fundamental* level possible, a *comprehensive* and *authoritative* theory for evaluating human behaviour. They try to define and establish those concepts, principles, arguments, rules, and theories that can best determine the criteria we *must* meet if we are to be good human beings. And they try to apply what they learn to the wrinkles and complications of everyday situations and to the controversial issues of the day.

Historical View: Ethics Is the Secret to Happiness

There is another, time-honoured way of describing what ethics is about. Past philosophers have claimed that ethics, or morality, must be understood, first and foremost, as the means to happiness. They argue, in short, that the best way to find an enduring, satisfactory sense of happiness is by acting morally. Ethics is the 'happy art' or the 'happy science'. Because we all want to be happy, ethics is everybody's business.

So we are left with two definitions of ethics. First, moral philosophy is an attempt to evaluate human behaviour at the most basic and comprehensive level possible. Second, moral philosophy is about how to be happy. This book will accept both definitions. We have to consistently evaluate human behaviour, but the pursuit of happiness, properly understood, provides the most basic criterion

for this business of evaluation. To some readers, it may seem strange to connect morality and happiness. In contemporary Western society, the idea that morality is an attractive, engaging ideal has been severely criticized and held up to ridicule. Morality, to borrow a phrase from the vernacular, 'gets a bad rap'. In a popular culture that celebrates rebellion, non-conformism, individual freedom, and even eccentricity, to insist on morality is to be straightlaced, old-fashioned, judgmental, uptight, or simply unimaginative and obtuse. According to a clichéd way of thinking, moral people lack that spark of imagination or creativity or self-initiative that separates the bold and the hip from the run-of-the-mill and the ordinary. This view sees moral people as submissively doing what the rules tell them to do. Even those contemporary authors who argue for morality often talk about it as if it were like a tablespoon of bitter medicine we take, not because we like it, but on the doctor's orders. We grimace as the unpleasant stuff goes down, but we swallow because it is supposed to be good for us. Yes, we have to be moral, but do not expect us to enjoy it! A famous modern moral philosopher like Kant, for example, views morality as a muscular and almost painful expression of pure willpower.

However, these are distinctly modern attitudes. Earlier philosophers in the Western tradition equate morality with happiness. It is not just that they claim that morality is the best way to achieve happiness. They maintain that it is the *only* way. To use a logical term, morality is a necessary condition for happiness. If we hope to find happiness, it is necessary to be moral. These authors sometimes go so far as to suggest that morality may even be—to use another logical term—a sufficient condition for happiness. In other words, morality may be enough—by itself—to produce happiness. If this suggestion seems odd or even outrageous, then this book is for you.

What, then, is the alleged connection between morality and happiness? Historical philosophers offer different explanations: only moral people experience self-esteem; only moral people avoid guilt and remorse; only moral people can successfully deal with the hardship and suffering that is an inevitable part of the human condition; only moral people win the trust and friendship of their colleagues; only moral people benefit their friends and the rest of society; only moral people understand the true meaning of love; only moral people get to Heaven; and so on. Explanations differ, but traditional philosophers, in one manner or another, tend to see morality as the means to happiness and personal fulfillment. In comparison, modern commentators, given to a mindset that derives from historical Puritanism, tend to focus on the bad that people may do. They view morality as a warning that, in effect, tells us what we should feel guilty about.

Historical authors are not naively optimistic; they are well aware of the importance of avoiding evil. At the same time, they also see morality as something that helps us to discern the good things in life. For traditional philosophers, morality is not just a warning as it is to more recent commentators; it is a way of identifying what makes us happy and brings us peace of mind. If there are times when we should feel guilty about things we do, moral philosophy is as much about eliminating a misplaced sense of blame about innocent behaviour as it is about determining what is truly deserving of moral censure.

However we decide to approach moral philosophy, in our daily lives we cannot escape the need for ethics. Contemporary anti-moralists, those thinkers who loudly dismiss morality as overly conventional and restrictive, are really moralists in disguise. After all, to complain that the moral individual is a dinosaur, a prude, a conformist, a busybody, or a bigot is, after all, to engage in the business of human evaluation. Even anti-moralists are committed to some sort of underlying value system. They have views about what is admirable and what is not, about what counts or does not count as human achievement. This book is intended to push the ordinary reader into a deep consideration of some of the most basic concepts and principles of morality. To cite Socrates's well-worn dictum, 'the unexamined life is not worth living'. Either we give in to a mindless reliance on stereotypes and borrowed judgments, or we thoughtfully reflect on the principles that underlie this daily activity of human evaluation. Either we sleepwalk through life or we begin thinking.

Anything that contributes to our evaluation of human beings and anything that contributes to human happiness has moral or ethical content. As we have already mentioned, we evaluate human behaviour on many grounds, some of which are trivial, confused, or simply wrong. Clearly, some ways of being good or bad are momentous; others are hardly worth serious consideration, at least when looked at in terms of a whole life or in terms of what humans, at their best, are capable of accomplishing. Part of the job of morality or ethics is to elucidate the most important issues in some detail. This book will show that if we look carefully at Western intellectual history, a deep consensus emerges about human morality. This is what this text is all about.

To Whom Is This Book Addressed?

This book is addressed, in the first instance, to students of moral philosophy, whether they are enrolled in formal classes or not. Although the chapters presuppose no previous knowledge of the discipline, the reader who masters the material presented in the book will come away with an advanced understanding of the concepts of morality as they have been developed in the Western intellectual tradition.

Historical authors typically associate morality with human nature. They believe that we cannot be fully human—that is, we cannot be truly ourselves—unless we obey a moral impetus that has its origin deep inside us. What is it about human nature that is so special? Aristotle, in his *De Anima* (Latin for *On the Soul*), the first full-length treatise on psychology, defines human beings as 'rational animals'. This became a traditional definition. What does it mean?

To be a rational animal is to be able to think. It is to possess a high level of intelligence. In the present age, we tend to associate high levels of intelligence with technical or scientific or mathematical knowledge. Someone who is extremely smart knows differential calculus, works for NASA, wins the Nobel Prize for Physics. But traditional philosophers also associate intelligence with morality. Morality is itself a way of being smart. Because human beings are smart animals, they are moral animals. Morality and smartness, in a way that needs to be explained, are inextricably connected.

We can use the term morality to refer to moral standards or to the behaviour that conforms to these standards. Only rational beings can act morally. Why? Because only rational beings possess free will. To be moral is to choose to do the right thing. But we cannot choose to do the right thing unless we are smart enough to possess a concept of right and wrong; that is, unless we are rational beings. Aristotle, as we shall see, observes that 'choice is not common to irrational creatures'.[5] Yes, your dog Fido can 'choose' to walk over to his bowl and take a drink of water. But this is not enough for morality. Fido is not smart enough to have a concept of good, so he cannot knowingly choose to do something because it is good. He is incapable of the kind of deliberate choice that is necessary for morality.

It does not follow, according to the traditional view, that morality is restricted to human beings. It depends on whether or not there are other intelligent creatures out there in the world. In John Milton's (1608–74) poem *Paradise Lost,* Lucifer—an angel, not a human being—possesses free will. Lucifer knows the difference between right and wrong and in choosing to do what is wrong is punished by God. This explains, in Milton's Christian account, the introduction of evil and suffering into the world. Milton's God, foreseeing the first sin of Adam and Eve, declares bitterly, 'I made him just and right, Sufficient to have stood, though free to fall'.[6] Whatever their theological convictions, this is how ethicists view human beings: as capable of good but free to choose evil. Immorality, like morality, presupposes free will, understood as the ability to knowingly choose between right and wrong.

If irrational animals lack the ability for morality, even so-called rational animals may be excluded, permanently or temporarily, from the moral game. Children before they acquire proper use of reason, the criminally insane, the senile, the comatose, those who sleepwalk, those who have been drugged: these individuals exist outside the moral arena. They deserve appropriate respect, but they themselves are not (in such circumstances) actors in this drama we call morality. They have, so to speak, stepped off the stage. Or perhaps they never stepped onto the stage in the first place. Indeed, they are not even in the audience. They may see others acting morally or immorally, but insomuch as they are unconscious of the difference between good and evil, they cannot comprehend what is going on. The moral knowledge we use to evaluate our own actions is the moral knowledge we need to evaluate other people's actions.

There is another way in which morality requires a high level of intelligence. As contemporary philosophers in what has come to be known as the Continental tradition maintain, morality must include *self*-consciousness. Moral agents need to be able to critically reflect on their actions. This knowledge does not have to be expressed in words, but it has to be a part of what is going on in moral behaviour. Ask yourself, how does the human mind work? European philosopher Franz Brentano (1838–1917) noticed that human consciousness is always directed toward some aim or idea or object of interest. We do not just think—we are always thinking about something. Consciousness is not like a cloud hovering aimlessly in a vacant sky: it is more like an arrow or a gun pointed toward a target. This aspect of human awareness is called *intentionality*. Moral behaviour, then, must be accompanied by some kind of moral intentionality. It must include some kind of critical self-awareness. It is not that we have to spend all our time consciously thinking about morality. As a philosopher like Aristotle argues, moral awareness comes naturally. It is an integral aspect of the human disposition. But the conscious awareness that we are aiming toward the good must form the basic framework of our decision making.

Aristotle writes, 'on voluntary passions and actions praise and blame are bestowed'.[7] Although we will provide no argument for free will in this book, simply note that we could not make sense of human life without free will. If we did not possess freedom to choose, this business of praising or criticizing human behaviour would be empty pretence. It is no use blaming a rock for where it falls. It, so to speak, has no say in the matter. Insomuch as people cannot choose how they act, they cannot be blamed or congratulated for what they do. But this is what morality is about: evaluating, negatively or positively, human beings.

Moral freedom is notoriously difficult to extirpate. This is the basic human predicament: you are free—what are you going to do about it? Psychiatrist Viktor Frankl (1905–97), in a book of reminiscences about his life as a prisoner in a Nazi concentration camp, insists that we are each responsible for our destiny:

> Nothing conceivable [could] so condition a man as to leave him without the slightest freedom. . . . What [man] becomes—within the limits of his endowment and environment—he has made out of himself. In the concentration camps, . . . in this living laboratory and on this testing ground, we watched and witnessed some of our comrades behave like swine while others behaved like saints. Man has both potentialities within himself; which one is actualized depends on decisions but not on conditions.[8]

At one of the darkest moments of human history, this was the choice that prisoners faced: to behave like pigs or to behave like moral heroes. Our own fate may be less dramatic, the choices more mundane or ordinary, but in the details of our daily routines we all have to choose between right and wrong. This is why human life matters so much. This is what it means to possess free will.

<hr>

✎ Applied Philosophy Box 1.3 ✎

On Concentration Camps

Viktor Frankl said this about his prison camp experience:

'We needed . . . to think of ourselves as those who were being questioned by life—daily and hourly. Our answer must not consist in talk and meditation, but in right action and right conduct. Life ultimately means taking responsibility to find the right answer to its problems and to fulfill the task it constantly sets for each individual.'

Source: Viktor Frankl, *Man's Search for Meaning* (New York: Washington Square Press, 1963), p.122.

<hr>

Frankl's view that we are 'inescapably free' is echoed in existentialist Jean-Paul Sartre's (1905–80) famous phrase that we are 'condemned to be free'. Sartre argued, like Frankl, that the only thing that limits our capacity for choice is choice itself. We cannot choose not to choose, for to choose not to choose is itself a choice. We must accept complete responsibility for our own actions. This is the beginning of morality.

Of course, we are not completely free. As the ancient Stoics suggest, we cannot always choose the external circumstances that frame our everyday lives. We are hemmed in by things over which we have no control. We can choose, however, how we respond to unchosen circumstances. This is what ethics is about: what is the best way to respond to the predicament—however modest—we happen to find ourselves in. We all have lives to live; we all are confronted with decisions to make, promises to keep, truths to be told, values and beliefs to be adhered to. It follows that moral philosophy is supremely relevant; it has something important to say to anyone who is intelligent and free. And that includes almost all of us.

The truth is that some readers will be leery of moral philosophy. The more practically minded may distrust any book with the word philosophy in the title. They may be suspicious of intellectuals. They may be turned off by the prospect of dry, technical prose. And they may dismiss philosophy as highly speculative, irrelevant, and impractical. They may prefer to turn their minds instead toward more basic preoccupations. But this would be unfortunate. There is no need to be intimidated by the study of ethics.

During his trial for treason in Athens, Socrates, perhaps the most famous philosopher, declared, 'I have nothing else to tell besides the truth, after the fashion of the ordinary man'.[9] Socrates eschewed the fancy rhetoric, clever dissembling, and verbal manipulation common in ancient (and modern) courtrooms. He spoke simply, even when his life was at stake. His homey, everyday speech can provide us with something of an ideal to which we can aspire. Advanced moral reasoning does require a certain amount of technical mastery; later generations of philosophers pushed ethical inquiry further, in directions Socrates only hinted at. Still, the basic principle that we should express ourselves as simply and as plainly as possible is a worthwhile aspiration for philosophers and students alike.

Moral philosophy is not as esoteric or as abstract as other fields in philosophy. It deals with how we act. It boils down to a critical study of human behaviour, a fascinating (and, at times, distressing) subject. This book makes a constant attempt to connect theory to lived experience. It grounds ethical theory in everyday problems and in real situations. Using examples from newspaper reports, from court cases, from this author's own life experience, and occasionally from world literature, the following pages investigate the most important issues while avoiding the temptation to rely solely on tired tropes and unrealistic thought experiments. We need to begin out in the world where life happens and move from there to a considered reflection on what it means to be a decent human being. To adapt a famous line from William James, moral philosophy is nothing more than an 'unusually stubborn attempt to think clearly'. This is what authors in the tradition were trying to do. This book is written in a similar vein.

Some readers, more used to abstract or formulaic modes of presentation, may find this approach startling, even offensive. The point is to be realistic. We need to study human behaviour as it actually occurs. When gothic novelist Flannery O'Connor was asked why she insisted on writing about such distressing subject matter, she retorted that an author has to write in very large script when writing for the half-blind. We all have our blind spots. But even if we can see very well, great failure, like great success, illuminates, in the most conspicuous way, what morality is all about. Although there is a curiosity about the bad things people do that has more to do with titillation than moral understanding, we cannot adequately grasp the full extent of good and evil or test our theories without examining unsavoury, unwholesome, disturbing cases of serious immorality. We should not be squeamish. We may take heart from Aristotle's comment, in a biological work, that studying the lowest and ugliest parts of nature is noble activity.[10] If Aristotle's specific comment is about biology, his plea in favour of a healthy inquiry into all aspects of life and nature applies to moral philosophy as well.

In a discussion of the role of memory in moral judgment, medieval philosopher Thomas Aquinas makes a sensible recommendation. He writes, 'When a man wishes to remember a thing, he should take some suitable yet somewhat unwonted illustration of it, since the unwonted strikes us more, and so makes a greater and stronger impression on the mind.'[11] The Latin word translated here as 'unwonted' might also be translated as 'unusual', or 'unaccustomed', or 'unfamiliar'. This text will use memorable examples to capture the issue at hand. As Thomas points out, 'the reason for the necessity of finding these [striking] illustrations or images, is that simple [mental] impressions easily slip from the mind, unless they be tied as it were to some corporeal image, because human knowledge has a greater hold on sensible objects'.[12]

This book is addressed, then, to the avid student of human behaviour. The theory discussed is grounded in what happens around us: the good and the bad, the ordinary and the extraordinary, what we read about in newspapers and what we observe right in front of us at the supermarket, in the workplace, at school. The subject matter will be of interest to the theoretically inclined as well as to those whose principle concern is getting on with the business of living a good life.

This Book Presents an Alternative Account of Moral Philosophy

A conventional way of teaching undergraduate ethics seems to undermine instead of bolster the moral impetus in students. Using this all-too-familiar approach, the teacher provides rival theories, focuses on highly controversial and problematic issues, develops arguments for and against a particular position, and leaves it to students to choose sides. Students are left with the impression that philosophers have shown that you can come up with an equally valid reason for or against anything.

None of us believe, however, that anything goes. Rape, murder, genocide, bestiality, cruelty, child abuse, pedophilia, racism, lying, stealing, cheating, breaking promises: these are only a few obvious examples of moral wrongs. We know we should tell the truth; we should keep our promises; we should tend to the sick; we should love one another. We know, too, that impatience is a weakness; cowardice is shameful; being a bully is base. And we also know that generosity, kindness, compassion, empathy, and forgiveness are admirable. Yes, human life is complicated: decision making is messy; there are strange circumstances, mitigating and excusing factors, puzzles that defy easy solutions, terms that need re-defining, and subtle distinctions to make. But there is no reason to begin moral philosophy by doubting everything we already know about morality. In moral philosophy we begin with something like moral common sense, which we then try to clarify and refine and improve and extend in some coherent way. We strive for consistency. We do not try to create morality from nothing.

Modern philosophy often focuses on the very issues that produce the sharpest disagreement while ignoring issues and themes on which there is widespread consensus. Add to this the modern prejudice that moral reasoning is inevitably soft, a matter of vague feelings rather than logic, and we have an approach that spawns an

---

✎ Applied Philosophy Box 1.4 ✎

Vlad the Impaler and Morality

A popular source informs us about the ruler who was allegedly the inspiration for the vampire legend:

In the West, Vlad III Tepes has been characterized as a tyrant who took sadistic pleasure in torturing and killing his enemies. The number of his victims ranges from 40,000 to 100,000. . . . He also had whole villages and fortresses destroyed and burned to the ground. . . . The atrocities committed by Vlad in the German stories include impaling, torturing, burning, skinning, roasting, and boiling people, feeding people the flesh of their friends or relatives, cutting off limbs, drowning, and nailing people's hats to their heads. His victims included men and women of all ages, religions and social classes, children and babies. One German account includes the following sentence: 'He caused so much pain and suffering that even the most bloodthirstiest persecutors of Christianity like Herodes, Nero, Diocletian and all other pagans combined hadn't even thought of.'

These stories are likely exaggerated. But whatever the truth, we can all agree that it would be absurd—not to say monstrous—to argue that such behaviour could be moral. Cases like this are so clear-cut that there is no room for disagreement.

Source: 'Vlad III the Impaler.' *Wikipedia*, http://en.wikipedia.org/wiki/Vlad_III_the_Impaler.

uncritical skepticism. Of course, there are hot-button issues in any age, controversial topics that spawn vehement dispute. Still, it does not follow that there is no agreement about morality. Underneath the bewildering surface array of opinions, there are common principles, concepts, and procedures that can be rigorously applied to diverse human situations. If we cannot eliminate all disagreement about specific issues, we can—and we must—develop a methodology based on a broad consensus that uses reason to think carefully about morality.

Those who attack morality often end up contradicting themselves. Moral skeptics complain that dogmatism (commitment to one moral view) leads to intolerance. But this is to presuppose that tolerance is good and intolerance is bad. In other words, skeptics, whether they admit it or not, are committed to a moral view. Some modern libertarians argue that we should not impose moral views on others. But in telling us not to impose our moral beliefs on others, they are telling us what we *ought* to do; that is, they are imposing their moral views on others. Doubtless, it is easy to pretend that morality does not matter when we are safely ensconced in the comfort of our living-room or when we are drinking cold beer in a local tavern or when we are discussing with classmates on a full stomach in a safe classroom far away from violent conflict. But deal harshly with those who like to play the moral skeptic and they will complain that they have been treated unfairly. The same person who flippantly said that morality does not matter will vociferously complain to the professor that the mark she got on her final exam was too low, that it was an unfair indication of her abilities. But fairness is a moral concept. You cannot consistently claim that morality does not matter and that fairness does. And so on.

The taking-sides-on-controversial-issues approach makes moral philosophy more difficult than it has to be. Rightly or wrongly, specific issues become focal points of disagreement at particular times and in particular places. There are difficult, complex cases—cases where there is room for reasonable people to disagree. But this is not the place to start our ethical inquiry. When we want to teach children mathematics, we begin with simple arithmetic. It is better to start ethics with simple, glaring examples of moral goodness and badness, with blindingly clear cases. In articulating aloud why these examples so forcefully strike us as right or wrong, we can come to identify and isolate precise aspects of moral judgment. Faced with an unimpeachable moral conclusion, it may be easier to argue back to the reasons that give it intuitive support. We can graduate to more difficult cases later.

The adversarial approach to ethics also lends itself to abuse. The temptation is to contrive arguments after the fact, to rationalize so as to defend the unexamined views we already hold. The point of ethics education is not to encourage a smug, anything-goes cleverness that contrives arguments in support of predetermined prejudices. We do not need an ethics of excuses, but an ethics of honest self-scrutiny. This is hard, but morality demands a constant effort to test ourselves and our own beliefs. We must attentively and objectively examine difficult issues. Consulting great thinkers from the past, understanding the larger themes in their work, and coming to grips not just with specific arguments but with their overall world views can lead us away from contemporary disagreement to a more dispassionate consideration of perennial human values.

Contemporary thinkers often assume not only that there is no present agreement about morality, but that philosophers in the past presented radically different theories that contradict and undermine each other. It does not matter how ubiquitous such assumptions are—they are simply untrue. Any in-depth, rigorous study of philosophical history demonstrates that despite important differences, there is a wide consensus among authors in many different epochs and cultures about the basic points of morality. The moral theories of apparently divergent authors are, to a very large extent, reconcilable. A lack of historical erudition exaggerates unexamined opinions about the prevalence and extent of moral disagreement. Perhaps part of the problem here has to do with the division of labour in philosophy departments.

In teaching, there are courses that introduce students to the history of philosophy and courses that discuss contemporary issues in ethics. And—it sometimes seems—'never the twain shall meet'. This textbook is intended to bridge the gap. Attitudes are slowly changing, but much contemporary ethical discussion ignores, misconstrues, or caricatures the historical tradition. In this treatment we will take insights from every period of philosophy and use them to illuminate contemporary issues. Great thinkers in the past thought long and hard about such seminal concepts as virtue, duty, happiness, friendship, freedom, and so on. We tend to forget that the concepts we use in ethical discourse all came from somewhere—we all owe a real debt to past thinkers, a debt that is not always acknowledged. The aim here is to synthesize a great wealth of Western philosophical theory into a succinct but comprehensive system that can be used to direct moral belief and everyday decision-making. Many modern theories unknowingly repeat much earlier arguments about morality.

Academic philosophers understandably focus on very small points and deal in razor-sharp distinctions. But we professionals sometimes lose sight of the forest for the leaves. Commentators often divide themselves up into various schools of thought that compete with one another for intellectual supremacy. In this clash of world views, ideology pushes participants to exaggerate differences. (A common tendency is to favour one aspect of ethical understanding to the exclusion of other aspects.) We need a broader approach. There is a proper place for specialized disagreement but there is also a need for theoretical synthesis. Opposing views must be understood and reconciled within a larger view of things. Where schools and authors disagree, we will use the strengths of one theory to supplement and rehabilitate the weaknesses of the other theory. The aim is to produce a highly versatile methodology for contemporary moral thinking.

This Book Is an Account of Virtue Ethics in the Spirit of Aristotle

This volume will present an account of ethics largely in the spirit of Aristotle. Although the book surveys a wide group of theories, both ancient and modern, the overall approach resembles Aristotle's in that we will focus on what has come to be known as *virtue ethics*. There are two ways of construing morality. In explaining the moral impetus, previous philosophers tend to focus on one of two key concepts: virtue or moral law. An exclusive emphasis on law as an expression of moral sensibility leads to a very impoverished account of what morality is all about. We shall indeed discuss the Decalogue, natural law, Kant's categorical imperative, utilitarianism, and so on. But the view taken here sees law as deriving from a prior, deeper concept of virtue. The ultimate questions are as follows: What are the character traits (the virtues) that make up a good person? What are the habits and attitudes (vices) that I should avoid? Or more simply, what kind of a human being should I be? We may look to moral law for invaluable guidance but moral laws cannot, as is sometimes supposed, stand on their own. They rest on a deeper virtue ethics foundation that needs to be explored.

For the most part, the book is organized chronologically. Very briefly, we will begin, in Chapter 2, with some discussion about moral reasoning and the nature of moral knowledge. Chapter 3 turns to very early thinkers in the ethical tradition, considering Confucius, various Greek and Roman philosophies, and Jesus. Then, Chapter 4 focuses on Socrates and Plato; and Chapter 5, on Aristotle. Chapter 5 presents a detailed, state-of-the-art account of Aristotle's moral philosophy, while Chapter 6 expands his view, using the medieval synthesis of Aristotle elaborated, in particular, by Thomas Aquinas. Chapters 7, 8, and 9 consider important traditions in contractarianism, deontology, utilitarianism, and liberalism, while Chapter 10 finishes up with a succinct treatment of modern movements, such as feminism and environmentalism, and of specialized topics, such as punishment and human rights. The later chapters also incorporate some material from modern continental philosophy. In addition to this step-by-step treatment of the historical tradition in ethics, the book contains a helpful glossary of Greek and Latin words and of technical terms.

Moral Reasoning: Rediscovering the Ethical Tradition aims at a comprehensive treatment of ethics. But the book could also be used for a broad humanities course. Readers will come away with a better sense of the history of ideas as well as of ethics. This is not merely a text about great ethical ideas: it is also a compilation of wise words and carefully selected passages taken from the authors themselves. Reading lengthy selections from historical texts is an exacting art, so the chapters rely on short citations and standard translations, supplying a historically sensitive explanatory apparatus that synthesizes and clarifies the intended meaning. The book works on the presumption that there is at least a large grain of truth in major historical doctrines. Each theory and argument is discussed in the best possible light. Without avoiding necessary criticism, we try to show how divergent theories provide valuable insights into ethics. The goal is to set up an overarching, historically informed system that leaves room for different kinds of moral understanding: virtue ethics, deontology, utilitarianism, liberalism, religious and secular ethics, existentialist ethics, and so on.

There is a great deal to say about the ethics tradition. *Moral Reasoning* is divided into self-contained chapters and sections so that readers or teachers can use or omit parts of the book in accordance with their own requirements. The division into sections with subtitles should make it easy to find or revisit specific parts of the text dealing with individual issues.

Morality As Seen through the Lens of the History of Ideas

We live in an age that emphasizes progress, innovation, change, novelty, and difference. (It was not ever thus.) Arthur Schopenhauer (1788–1860), not one to mince words, writes, 'There is no greater mistake than to suppose that the last work is always the more correct; that what is written later on is in every case an improvement on what was written before; and that change always means progress'.[13]

This book looks at ethics through the lens of the history of ideas. Hermeneutics is the art and science of interpreting original texts. The Jewish religious tradition provides a particularly striking example of the hermeneutic mindset. If we look at a page from Jewish biblical commentaries, what we see is an original citation from the Hebrew Bible in very large letters, surrounded by the commentaries of rabbinic scholars down through 900 odd years of development. Note that the original Scriptural verse, revered as the definitive word of God, is not the end of the story. Thinking does not stop there. It carries on. These later authors expand on the original text; refine its message; interpret it in innovative ways; connect it to other texts; apply it to new situations; include additional examples; and so on. The rabbinic commentators can disagree with one another, even vehemently, but they carry on an intelligent conversation focused on perennial themes important to this group. The original text provides a way of approaching the problem of human life, a program and project that allows for an insightful discernment into the human predicament.

This book is premised on the idea that seminal texts in the philosophical tradition provide a similar function in moral thought. The intellectual work does not end with the original texts of Aristotle, Thomas Aquinas, Immanuel Kant, or John Stuart Mill. These texts are not the revealed word of God. They do not claim to be definitive in the way that Hebrew Scripture is held to be definitive. They are human products, pieced together by careful but fallible reasoners. They are incomplete, inconclusive, obscure, complex, inconsistent, and, because they are historically situated, open to serious misunderstanding. But they are, at the same time, works of genius,

which is why we study them. These texts provide an impetus for deep thought, a starting point, not a terminus, for moral reflection. They introduce the themes and questions that compose the Western cultural heritage none of us can escape. Even intelligent disagreement is not possible without some common understanding of whatever it is we are disagreeing about.

Great philosophical texts play an important role in the kind of moral philosophy we are proposing here. Whether they realize it or not, contemporary thinkers are part of something larger. The myth of the cultural, ethical, and philosophical Robinson Crusoe is only that, an appealing straw man, a noble lie, a caricature. Our own thoughts and moral perceptions have been implicitly shaped and modified by a long succession of thinkers and schools of thought. Inquiring into what past philosophers have said about morality inevitably turns into a voyage of self-discovery, a way of understanding where our own ethical ideas come from.

In this book we will approach the history of philosophy first as philosophers and only second, as historians. We have to get the history right. Much of the contemporary criticism of historical authors is based on an erroneous reading of the historical context within which those authors worked. At the same time, we study past masters so as to be able to subject their arguments to further refinement and critical evaluation. In looking at the past we should expect to find helpful insights but also error. There is no need to read earlier authors in a subservient, uncritical way. In sorting through the rich interplay of ideas, we can, in a spirit of *philosophia perennis* (perennial philosophy), sort through moral problems and ideas that recur again and again throughout human history. We can make our own contributions to a thoughtful conversation

---

✍ Applied Philosophy Box 1.5 ✍

There is No Escaping Tradition

To submit ourselves to certain traditions—say liberal individualism or market capitalism—on the premise that in doing so we are escaping submission to tradition is self-deceiving. Certain beliefs, stories and traditions can of course be destructive. But that does not make belief, story and tradition per se destructive. In fact they turn out to be the basis of our human identity and life. We are not only stuck with them. We only thrive because of them.

As Christian Smith, a modern philosopher, points out, it is an abject illusion to think that we can escape all influence and somehow think in a vacuum. 'Liberal individualism' and 'market capitalism'—to use Smith's examples—are part and parcel of a tradition. The ideas they revolve around came from somewhere. So it is with other moral and political vocabularies.

Source: Christian Smith, *Moral Believing Animals* (Oxford: Oxford University Press, 2004), p.155.

---

about values that are always relevant and even timeless.

We must address two principle objections to the historical approach. One is the still influential idea that thinkers from past ages are somehow primitive, naive, clumsy, simplistic, inferior. The idea that earlier generations are philosophically gullible has a history and is one of the more disappointing legacies of the Enlightenment. Auguste Comte's (1798–1857) infamous law of three stages is an obvious restatement of this familiar theme. Comte, sometimes considered the father of sociology, posited three chronological periods in human history: the theological, the metaphysical, and the positive. To explain the main thrust of his theory, thinkers at the theological stage are religious— that is, credulous, superstitious, and uncritical; those at the metaphysical stage are philosophical—that is, abstruse, unempirical, mystical, and hair-splitting; and finally, those at the positive stage are scientific—that is, empirical, realistic, mathematical, and, of course, enlightened.

But this grotesque caricature cannot be sustained by any close reading of older texts.

Achievements in science and technology have clearly progressed, but the basic impression one gets from a thorough reading of the history of philosophy is that human beings have been facing, more or less, the same dilemmas throughout their recorded history. To simply assume that earlier writers did not know what they were talking about is little more than a disguised bias against those who happen to be different from us. Clearly, older philosophies are not always right (that would be Comte's 'positivist' bias in reverse). But they are generally interesting, insightful, and useful. They offer a refreshingly new point of view—new to us because their views have been widely misrepresented and caricatured. What they say can be used to solve problems in modern ethics, problems that have sometimes arisen because of what has been largely forgotten.

The second objection we need to address holds that any precise interpretation of historical texts is fatally problematic. Authors of this persuasion insist that even if past wisdom could be used to solve modern-day ethical problems, such distant wisdom is irretrievable. Contemporary post-modern philosopher Jacques Derrida's (1930–2004) concept of *différance* is one expression of this attitude. The central point of Derrida's analysis is that the original, essential meanings of texts can never be fully recuperated because language changes over time. Whenever we interpret a text, *différance* results: a difference, or gap, between our understanding of the text and the original meaning. Such ideas are not all wrong, but Derrida takes them to extremes. It would be better to claim that although *some* meaning gets lost, a good deal is passed along to the attentive, historically informed reader. Human beings at different periods of history all have to face similar problems: death, hunger, loneliness, disappointment, betrayal, failure, etc. And presumably they experience similar triumphs and joys as well. It strains the imagination to suggest that language is useless in passing along thought from one human being to another. Reputable scholars spend much time going over the ways in which specific words are used by previous authors. In our discussions here, we will follow their lead.

Derrida's concerns about the misinterpretation of the intended meaning of original sources should serve as a warning. Many contemporary accounts of older philosophy tend to be anachronistic; scholars who lack sufficient erudition read modern meanings into old texts in such a way that they caricature and disfigure the original source. At the same time, a thorough knowledge of an entire corpus (that can be built up only over a long period of time) provides a way into the mind of the author. This is why this book is more than a simple anthology of disjointed primary texts. Citations are accompanied by an explanatory apparatus that attempts to bridge the gap for those who have not had the time or the opportunity to acquaint themselves thoroughly with these authors on their own.

This book aims to inspire students. It presents morality as the central human project, as something demanding but ennobling while, at the same time, leaving open room for discussion and strong disagreement about specific issues. The idea is not merely to recuperate these older authors but to take a previous understanding and refine it, adding to it in ways that make it more complete. Without a doubt, there are historical blind spots and mistakes. Earlier thinkers (like their present-day counterparts) are eminently fallible. Nonetheless, an unbiased, careful reading of the classical tradition in ethics reveals an uncommon breadth and depth of insight. If moral philosophy is a daunting subject, we do not need to start from scratch, all over again. We can begin with the moral wisdom we have inherited and work from there.

Logicians sometimes refer to the principle of charity. When we deal with a difficult text, especially one we disagree with or have a hard time understanding, we ought to strive to interpret the author's arguments in as fair a manner as possible. Think of moral philosophy as a group project. We need to enter into a conversation with great thinkers from the past. Dealing with such intelligent interlocutors should give us pause. They, like us, were struggling to make sense of the meaning of morality in a consistent, logical way. We do not have to agree with all they say, but the idea that their discussions enclose key insights should guide our interpretation.

What Is the Purpose of Ethics?

One important issue remains. Aristotle writes that the aim of moral philosophy 'is not knowledge but action'.[14] 'The purpose . . . is not to know what virtue is, but to become good.'[15] Does moral philosophy make us better people? Some people seem to lead morally responsible and even heroic lives without moral philosophy. When a maniac murderer broke into a small Amish school in Pennsylvania in October 2006, 13-year-old Marian Fisher, one of the slain girls, apparently asked to be shot first, hoping that the killer would then let the younger girls go free.[16] Marian knew very little about moral philosophy. She did not know about Aristotle or Kant or John Stuart Mill. She knew about Jesus (whom we discuss in a later chapter). And she cared about other people. Perhaps she remembered Jesus's teaching about giving one's life for one's friends. In any case, she displayed supreme courage. And generosity. She died for those who were more vulnerable than her. So, to ask a hard question, do we need moral philosophy in order to be moral?

Moral philosophy, as we shall understand the discipline here, is only an extension and a refinement of the moral understanding we all begin with. Learning the names and doctrines of this or that philosopher or school is a useful and worthwhile tool. But moral philosophy is, in the first instance, about gaining moral wisdom. Even a child, insomuch as he or she thinks about what it means to be a decent human being, starts to philosophize. Great thinkers develop this line of inquiry with inimitable power and insight, which is why we study them. But academic pretensions aside, they are doing nothing more (or less) than other human beings do when they try to make sense of human endeavour and achievement. Socrates thought that this was the central human project.

Imagine track-and-field athletes. You see them running on the track, which is an impressive sight: they run fast; they keep it up a long time; they have beautiful strides. But running is not just for the experts. Someone who runs to catch the bus is also running. We all run from time to time. Moral thinkers may be experts at moral reasoning. But even if one could live one's entire life without running, no one could live a normal human life without making moral decisions—and on a regular basis. Moral reasoning is unavoidable. Moral philosophers make us wake up and take notice. They communicate knowledge that is useful to have. Ideally, they help us make sound moral decisions. They are like coaches, but they coach an event in which we all participate.

Still, do we need to know moral philosophy in order to be moral? Does better philosophy result in better morality? Immanuel Kant, a very different sort of thinker than Aristotle, suggests that moral wisdom is not a matter of book learning. It 'consists more in doing and not doing than in knowing'.[17] Clearly, theoretical knowledge of morality is not enough to make us moral. Still, this book is premised on the idea that ethics does have the potential to make us moral people. Indeed, at this moment in history, we need moral philosophy more than ever.

Many ordinary people think of philosophical argument as a kind of verbal trickery that slips all too easily into a disguised kind of rationalization. Academic philosophers split hairs; they quibble. On this account, a philosophical mindset dilutes the requirements of morality. A humble heart, simple, straightforward rules, good intentions—compared to moral philosophy, these are a better guide to human decency.

Those of us with university degrees need not ridicule these anti-intellectual views. As is usually the case, there is a grain of truth here. Words and arguments are often used to obscure the truth. But a carefully constructed moral philosophy recognizes this possibility. Good philosophy—rigorous, consistent, persistent, critical philosophy—works to expose rhetorical excess and deceit. To use a traditional metaphor, it pierces appearances and gets to the reality of the matter. In some sense, this is the whole point of philosophy: to cut through lazy, self-indulgent, self-interested thinking that obscures and disguises what is—on the most fundamental level—false, unreasonable, implausible, unsound, or evil. We can make moral mistakes because we contrive self-serving arguments that excuse our own immorality, but we can also make moral mistakes because we lack the intellectual penetration and logical acumen that develops from serious academic study. Moral philosophy explains how to apply moral generalities to the endlessly complicated circumstances that make up our individual lives. It throws further light on what rigorously follows from deeply held beliefs.

Ethics has now become part of a regular university and college education. It would seem strange that society should embrace education in chemistry and calculus and art history and German and not embrace education in moral philosophy. A university degree would be incomplete without some serious consideration of morality. We cannot present ourselves as truly educated without some formation in the history of moral philosophy.

Academic training in ethics is a particularly urgent need given the erosion of the usual channels of moral education in contemporary society. The young Amish martyr Marian Fisher mentioned above was part of a closely knit community. She received her moral training from a dedicated band of believers bent on preserving a set of treasured values. This is not the case for most of us in the modern world. Individualism, pluralism, secularism, and a legitimate liberal emphasis on freedom of choice have set us adrift. The rejection of the moral wisdom of the past threatens to leave us without any definitive moral guidance. Such moral amnesia is a recipe for disaster. We need to reclaim the moral heritage that is fundamental to the Western philosophical tradition—not blindly or uncritically but in a way that challenges us and makes us better. Recuperating our own philosophical past is the first step to a meaningful public debate that can preserve and expand on what has lasting moral value.

We live in a society that emphasizes personal autonomy. To be autonomous is to govern yourself (from the Greek, *auto*, which means 'self', and *nomos*, which means 'government'); autonomous individuals make their own decisions when it comes to determining the kind of life they will lead. The rise of liberalism as the prevailing political conviction has produced a popular culture that views individual freedom as the ultimate value. There are various historical events behind this noticeable shift in values: the Enlightenment, the Protestant Reformation, the rise of democracy (and so on). Contemporary authors, with some moral justification, focus on a pivotal issue: making sure that citizens are able to choose for themselves. (We discuss related moral issues in the chapter on John Stuart Mill.) But it makes no sense to set people free to decide for themselves unless we also supply them with the moral resources they need to make good decisions. Suppose we were to throw someone who does not know how to swim into the deep end of the pool, leaving them free to do whatever they want. This is not a recipe for human flourishing but for disaster. We must first teach them how to swim;

then they can navigate freely their way through the water. The purpose of moral philosophy is not to interfere in other people's decisions but to develop their natural intelligence so that they can decide for themselves in an intelligent way. Moral philosophy explains the whys and wherefores of moral consensus, but mostly, it teaches a way of intelligent thinking that can hopefully keep us afloat in confusing times.

Moral philosophy is not didactic or moralistic in any simple sense. Ethics leaves it to the student to find the ultimate answers, not in any arbitrary way, but by following through some disciplined, rigorous method of reasoning. Still authors in the tradition conceive of moral philosophy as an aid to morality. We are all prey to prejudice, to hearsay, to blind loyalty. We need logic and argument to delve into the details and

avoid extremism. We need to analyze our moral beliefs, to test them rigorously to see which ones are worth keeping. Contrary to what is sometimes assumed, consulting the historical tradition contributes to autonomy and resourceful, independent thinking; it makes us question our lazy, present-day assumptions; it compels us to critically defend what we believe and, in the process, to arrive at some critical understanding of the challenges inherent in the subject matter. Perhaps most importantly, it forces us to break through the straitjacket of peer-group pressure as it manifests itself in one narrow location in space and time. Rather than relying on trendy or clichéd ideas, we may find that in grappling with perennial ideas treated by the tradition we come, for the first time, to truly think things through ourselves.

✍ Questions for Study and Review ✍

1. How is morality different from other ways of evaluating human behaviour?
2. What is the relationship between happiness and morality?
3. How are human beings different from other animals? What does this have to do with morality?
4. Why does free will, understood in a moral sense, presuppose reason?
5. What does the term *intentionality* mean? How does it connect to morality?
6. What does most modern moral philosophy focus on? What does virtue ethics focus on?
7. What does the term *hermeneutics* mean? Explain how the Jewish rabbinic tradition presents a good example of the hermeneutical method.
8. What does the term *philosophia perennis* indicate?
9. Explain Comte's law of three stages.
10. What does Derrida mean by the term *différance*?
11. What is the principle of charity?
12. What is personal autonomy? How do personal autonomy and moral philosophy complement one another?   ·

Chapter Two

Moral Epistemology:
We Can Reason about Morality

ᔓ Chapter Objectives

After reading this chapter you should be able to:

- Explain the role of moral understanding (i.e., intuition or conscience) and logic.
- Respond to major criticisms of moral reasoning: moral skepticism, sociobiology, noncognitivism, prescriptivism, the 'is–ought' fallacy, economic views of decision-making, and psychological egoism.
- Explain associated concepts and principles, such as the principle of sufficient reason, the burden of proof, unfalsifiability, the argument from queerness, supervenience, the traditional notion of evil, impartial spectator theory, empathy, and bad faith.
- Contrast the roles of practical and theoretical reason while explaining the importance of the former.
- Explain anthropological and realist answers to the is–ought problem.

What Is Moral Epistemology?

Moral philosophy unravels, so to speak, the logical ramifications of what we believe. It does this through reasoning—hence the title of this book. Great philosophers in every historical age have thought long and hard about morality: they have analyzed concepts; they have induced first principles; they have followed through the consequences of particular beliefs; they have made claims about what is morally sound or unsound; they have advanced and criticized arguments; they have sifted meticulously through a great deal of evidence. They have also expended considerable energy examining the ways in which we arrive at moral judgments or principles. In fact, interesting and insightful commentary on the process of moral reasoning can be traced to every period of moral philosophy.

This chapter, in contrast to later chapters, does not focus on one particular era, school, or philosopher. Instead, it considers, in a general way, the epistemological status of morality. **Epistemology** is that branch of philosophy that inquires into the nature of human knowledge. Moral wisdom presupposes, for reasons that will become evident, a highly contested sort of knowledge. Indeed, there are philosophers in the tradition who go so far as even to argue against the possibility of moral knowledge. Various groups, particularly in the modern age, have argued that we cannot reason about morality, that moral claims are neither true nor false, or that nothing could convince rational agents to be moral. This chapter presents, as befits a book on moral philosophy, a defence of moral reasoning. Following the viewpoint of mainstream authors in the Western tradition, the following sections will do the following:

- Show how and why moral knowledge is possible;
- Elucidate the relationship between reason and morality;
- Describe how we can approach ethical issues logically and fairly.

Moral philosophy must be inserted into to a larger context. Philosophy, in general, could be described as the art or science of reasoning. Philosophers not only study various subject matters and questions, but also study the method of reasoning itself. What does it mean to *reason* about something? This is not an easy question to answer. Although some contemporary philosophers equate reasoning with **logic**, which is understood roughly as the study of argument, this definition is too narrow. Argument does play an important role in philosophy, but, as historical authors repeatedly acknowledge, argument is not the only way that we reason.

How Do We Reason?

Let us begin our analysis by identifying reasoning, very broadly, with the successful operation of human intelligence. (Whether and to what extent animal species have reasoning is beyond the scope of the present discussion.) If reasoning means using human intelligence well, we can immediately think of two ways that reason influences moral understanding. First, we need a basic sense of discernment, which allows us to come up with moral ideas and concepts expressed properly in sentences according to the most basic laws of evidence-gathering and grammar. Second, we need logic; we need to be able to make moral arguments, to arrange premises and conclusions in the right order so that they support or derive from each other. Both these operations require an active intelligence; that is, they both can be considered as integral aspects of moral *reasoning*.

We Use Logic

We can then distinguish roughly between these two phases of moral thought. Most textbooks on moral philosophy emphasize the importance of moral arguments. Keep in mind that philosophers use the word **argument** in a somewhat specialized way. For philosophers, arguments are not primarily about agreeing or disagreeing with other people. To argue is to provide reasons for a claim. It is to explain and support one's own beliefs with evidence.

An *argument* can be defined as a collection of one or more statements called premises that lead logically to another statement called a conclusion. The premises in an argument give us reasons to believe in or assent to the conclusion. If, for example, I say, 'It's raining outside, so you need to bring your umbrella', that can be considered, informally, as argument. The conclusion is 'bring your umbrella'. The premise, 'It's raining outside', gives you a reason to bring your umbrella. We can, of course, have moral arguments. I could say to my son, 'Stop teasing your sister; you wouldn't want someone teasing you, would you?' The conclusion of this argument (which, in this case, is listed before the premise) is 'stop teasing your sister'. The premise that logically leads to the conclusion is that you should not treat other people in ways that you do not want to be treated (which is, in fact, a more specific version of the 'Golden Rule' we will discuss later).

Logic is usually defined as the ability to make good arguments. We use logic when we properly move from the premises in an argument to the conclusion that really follows from those premises. We can say that the premises *entail* the conclusion. Or that we *derive* the conclusion from the premises.

Philosophers admire logic, in part, because it requires serious mental work. Logic is an incremental, step-by-step process. It involves pulling ourselves up the ladder of knowledge rung by rung. Thomas Aquinas, an important ethicist and a medieval theologian, believed that **angels**—pure spirits who are *more* intelligent than human beings—know all things immediately, through intuition. Human beings, on the other hand, need logic because we are *not smart enough* to figure things out without laboriously piecing together the evidence. Although human beings do not immediately understand all there is to understand, logic allows us to extend the scope of reasoning, to come to conclusions about new issues that confront us. Using properly formulated arguments, we can move from the knowledge we already have to new insights about things, moral and otherwise.

Logic is, in the first instance, about making good arguments, and in the second instance, about evaluating arguments that have already been made. Good arguments are composed of properly ordered premises that provide relevant, sufficient, and acceptable reasons for establishing a conclusion. However, as we mentioned, moral philosophy is more than argument. This is only half the picture.

We Need Understanding

There is more to reasoning than logic and argument. Before we can even start to arrange sentences in the proper order, we must be able to construct truthful, properly ordered sentences that are themselves composed of even more basic concepts and ideas distilled from human experience. We cannot argue until we have premises but the very first premises cannot come from logic (for that would lead to an infinite regress). Before human beings can make use of arguments, they first must use intelligence to make sense of the world and to translate that discernment into beliefs, actions, mathematics, and language. The power of discernment that allows us—not through feeling, but by some mental acuity—to intelligently accomplish these tasks is what we will refer to as **understanding**. (Some authors use the term *intuition* to refer to this power of first intelligence. The problem is that people often use the word intuition to refer to vague feelings or hunches that turn out to be correct or even allow one to predict the future. This is not what epistemologists are referring to when they speak of *intuition* as the original source of knowledge.)

All human knowledge begins with understanding; argument develops only later. This is true for science as well as for ethics. Of course, we are primarily interested in *moral* understanding, in how we first arrive at the most basic moral concepts. There is much that could be said in this connection. Simply note that we can immediately know that something is right or wrong without elaborate explanation or argument. When, for example, I nonchalantly tell my students that I am considering taking up serial killing as a hobby, they immediately react in horror. But when I press them for an argument, they are mostly at a loss for words. Many are unable to give any adequate explanation as to why killing other human beings is wrong. They just *know* that it is wrong. They know this not because some-

one has given them a convincing argument but through moral intuition. Moral philosophers may usefully inquire into the wrongness of serial killing, but, clearly, people who have never studied moral philosophy already know this.

An analogy from agriculture may help here. It is a matter of some importance for farmers to be able to differentiate between male and female chicks, which are virtually indistinguishable. Farm workers who specialize in this task are unable to explain how they do it. By carefully looking at a chick they can determine its gender, classifying upwards of

---

ఴ Applied Philosophy Box 2.1 ಌ

Intuitionist Laura Day Predicted the Credit Crunch—Now Big Business Is Paying Her Big Bucks

Who'd have thought that the strictly secular swarmis of Wall Street would employ a psychic to direct their business dealings?

Laura Day is the leading light of a new business breed dubbed 'intuitionists.' Day, a 49-year-old New York mother with no business training, says she has earned $10m (£5m) advising everyone from hedge fund managers to Hollywood movie stars. Her psychic hunches have influenced billion-dollar business deals . . . Her clients are lauding her abilities—and paying $10,000 a month to employ them.

Day . . . took part in research studies into the power of the human mind. 'I came to intuition from science,' she explains, 'not from spirituality. I describe myself as an intuitive. Basically, I'm a psychic.'

When a hedge fund manager friend first started paying for her stock tips in the early 1990s, Day admits her business knowledge was negligible. 'I couldn't even balance my credit card,' she says, yet her instincts were impeccable. Soon her personal finances were less of a problem. 'Intuition,' she argues, 'works best in the absence of information.'

Authors in the moral tradition do not situate the beginnings of morality in any sort of psychic, supernatural ability. Notice this statement: 'Intuition works best in the absence of information.' It is one thing to observe that we can size up situations quickly (without using actual arguments); it is another to think that we have magical powers to arrive inexplicably at true conclusions. Compare the way the authors of this article use the term intuition to the way logicians and moral philosophers use the term intuition (or understanding).

Source: Tim Walker, 'Intuitionist Laura Day Predicted the Credit Crunch—Now Big Business Is Paying Her Big Bucks.' *Independent.co.uk*, www.independent.co.uk/news/business/news/intuitionist-laura-day-predicted-the-credit-crunch--now-big-business-is-paying-her-big-bucks-859021.html, Thursday, 3 July 2008.

20,000 chicks a day. Chicken-sexers do not rely on bare feeling; there is a cognitive element to what they are doing. Because they respond to the visual evidence wordlessly, without explicit method, it does not follow that their judgments are based on a pure, magical hunch. Likewise, the moral agent has good reasons for believing that certain types of behaviour are cruel, murderous, or self-centred. The moral philosopher tries to tease out and explain what is going on. But, in conspicuously clear cases, moral people understand this intuitively.

Here, then, is a basic model for moral reasoning: we first need moral understanding; second, logic. Both moral understanding and logic are forms of reasoning; both are examples of the successful operation of human intelligence. Human beings can perceptively discern the difference between right and wrong, and they are able to use logic to extend this capacity for moral discernment to a wide range of sometimes puzzling cases. Logic depends on a prior moral understanding. Unless we are first able to discern moral ideas and then correctly combine them to produce proper sentences, moral argument would be impossible.

Challenges to Moral Epistemology

Unfortunately, because modern authors focus so determinedly on logical argument, they often fail to acknowledge the importance of understanding. But we can err in the other direction as well. If we can reason without argument, it surely does not follow that every time we arrive at a moral opinion we judge things correctly. Nor does it follow that this intuitive ability can never be corrupted by

group-think, by laziness, by self-indulgence, or by insincerity. People can misunderstand an issue; they can jump to conclusions; they may give in to peer-group pressure; they may even slip into self-deception. We will explore these possibilities later.

Modern philosophers have, for these reasons and others that will be discussed, grown skeptical about understanding in general and about moral understanding, or what we familiarly call conscience, in particular. This attitude has, moreover, filtered down to popular culture. So we come to the first major philosophical problem associated with moral epistemology: the problem of moral skepticism.

Moral Skepticism: A Philosophical Challenge

We can define moral skepticism as a radical rejection of moral judgment. Moral skeptics do not question particular instances of moral judgment; they question moral judgment *in general*. They dismiss moral claims *in principle* as hopelessly weak, unverifiable, unprovable, or subjective. They question the validity of *all* moral arguments and dismiss moral reasoning and moral philosophy as less than compelling. In some cases, moral skeptics point to empirical science as the perfect model of rationality. Because moral knowledge is not scientific, they dismiss it as somehow soft, unreliable, or defective.

We must not confuse this generalized moral skepticism with skepticism about a particular moral position or world view. People who denounce one version of morality in favour of another have already committed themselves to a moral point of view. Once they begin to offer reasons for their opinions, they are already doing moral philosophy. To be a radical skeptic is to refrain from all moral judgment. It is to believe, in some thorough-going sense, that there is no way of determining who is right or wrong.

Although skepticism was influential in early Greek philosophy, we must not link this ancient world view to the more recent radical questioning of all morality we are discussing here. Ancient Greek skeptics believed in practical moral knowledge and questioned scientific knowledge. They viewed skepticism as an attractive moral option that makes us better people. We will discuss their views in detail in Chapter 3.

Radical moral skepticism often surfaces as an implied attitude rather than as a formal sequence of arguments. The idea that moral knowledge is not possible is, at best, a hypothetical possibility that no one ever truly embraces in day-to-day living. Those who raise the possibility of a general moral skepticism are quick to reassure the rest of us that they, too, believe in morality; that is, in being honest, in keeping their promises, in not murdering their companions, in not cheating on their taxes, and so on. They usually insist that they want to use skepticism as a method of philosophical clarification. This approach can be traced back to René Descartes (1596–1650), the seminal French philosopher, who introduces radical skepticism as a method of searching out *theoretical* truth in his famous *Meditations*. Descartes writes, 'I will proceed by casting aside all that admits of the slightest doubt . . . and I will continue always in this track until I shall find something that is certain'.[1] Descartes never proposes his own method of complete doubt as a guide for moral philosophy, but the idea that one can (legitimately) question anything seems to have set the tone for much of later philosophy. If, of course, comprehensive doubt is legitimate, then comprehensive moral doubt is, by extension, legitimate. What, then,

can we say to someone who insists, for whatever reason, on taking an entirely skeptical view of morality? How would historical authors answer these radical skeptics?

It may come as a surprise to realize that most mainstream historical authors believe that skeptical concerns, pushed to this kind of extreme, are largely irrelevant. As these authors see it, the principle problem of ethics is not how to convince someone who has no moral beliefs how to be a good person, but how to explain to someone who has confused moral beliefs how to be a good person. Moral philosophy is not generally viewed as a cure for the absence of all moral belief but as a cure for wrong or inconsistent moral belief. We can construct an answer, nonetheless, to those Doubting Thomases who, somewhat disingenuously, throw into question the validity of all moral judgment. Surely, the first thing to say to moral skeptics is that reasonable people do not doubt something unless they have a good reason for doubting it. People who believe need reasons, but doubters need reasons, too. Otherwise their doubt is just obstinate willfulness. There is nothing rational about such questioning.

Old logic textbooks refer to the **principle of sufficient reason**, which can be expressed as a general rule of thumb: do not believe in something unless you have a good reason. But the reverse seems equally plausible: don't doubt something unless you have a good reason. We need reasons for believing; therefore, we need reasons for disbelieving. It is easy to say, 'I don't believe in something', but skepticism becomes a serious philosophical option only when it is backed up with reasons. The fact that we can doubt something does not, in itself, amount to much.

A second way of challenging moral skepticism relates to the notion of the **burden of**

proof. You have probably heard the term used with respect to what happens in a courtroom. The criminal-justice system in place in the United Kingdom and the Americas is based on an adversarial model. The prosecution argues, in effect, 'here are the reasons why the accused should be convicted'. The defence argues 'here are the reasons why the accused should not be convicted'. The familiar principle 'innocent until proven guilty' places the burden of proof on the prosecution. Whoever has the burden or onus of proof has to establish their side beyond a shadow of a doubt. If the reasons pro and con are of equal weight, the prosecution loses. The defence does not have to prove that the accused is innocent; it only has to show that the prosecution is unable to prove its point. This is enough to win the case.

When it comes to the case of moral skepticism, we can likewise raise this question: Who has the burden of proof—the person who believes in morality or the person who argues against morality? If neither the believer nor the skeptic provides a completely convincing case—if there is, so to speak, a tie—who wins the argument? It would seem that the burden of proof lies not with those who believe in morality but with moral skeptics. We should not accept their position at the outset, for it clashes with the bulk of human experience, with human sentiment, common sense, social practices, religion, and tradition. The sensible thing, surely, is to believe in morality *unless it can be proven otherwise*. We can listen to the arguments of moral skeptics, but the onus is on them to prove their point. To date, however, they are far from proving their case.

Indeed, moral skeptics cannot *prove* their point. Looked at from the viewpoint of the burden of proof, moral skepticism is an indefensible position. The skeptic has to prove beyond a reasonable doubt that there is no morality. How could anyone do that? Human experience is fraught with morality. To make matters worse, rigorous skeptics will have to be skeptical about everything (including being skeptical about skepticism!—something the ancient skeptics, to their credit, quickly realized). If, therefore, the burden of proof is on the skeptic to *prove* that there is no genuine morality, and if rigorous skeptics themselves believe that proof of anything is impossible, moral skeptics cannot—by their own admission—win their argument against moral believers. Skeptics are good at undermining other people's arguments, but that's about it. To say that someone else's argument is wrong—or more carefully, that it *may* be wrong—is not to prove that your position is right.

A final reason why moral skepticism is not an attractive philosophical position is that radical moral skepticism is unfalsifiable. To say that a theory is falsifiable is to say that proponents accept that there is some evidence that could, in principle, disprove their position. But moral skeptics discount all conceivable sources of evidence: conscience, common-sense belief, psychological factors, the moral tradition, the conclusions of the greatest thinkers, and indeed an almost universal consensus on the most basic issues, a consensus even moral skeptics abide by in their daily lives. This is to subscribe to an unfalsifiable belief system, one that is impervious to counter-evidence by ruling out all counter-evidence beforehand. Many epistemologists would argue that such a belief system cannot count as knowledge. It is an unmovable conviction, a matter of disposition or personal preference, not of evidence-based rational belief.

These three charges against moral skepticism—(1) that it violates the principle of sufficient reason, (2) that the burden of proof is on the skeptic, and (3) that skepticism is unfalsifiable—revolve around a similar concern. Moral skeptics take an offensive strategy. They busy themselves attacking other people's opinions, but that does not divest them of the epistemological responsibility of backing up their own theory with positive evidence (the principle of sufficient reason), of accepting the onus placed on them by the radically un-intuitive nature of their account (the burden of proof), and of indicating clearly what available evidence would, in principle, defeat their own position (unfalsifiability).

When it comes to offering positive arguments in support of skepticism, radical skeptics mostly emphasize the pervasiveness of moral disagreement. They point to vehement disagreement about many moral issues and claim that we can never agree about morality—that moral consensus simply is not possible. As the subsequent chapters of this book demonstrate, any such claim is tendentious. Skeptics tend to exaggerate disagreements between competing schools and historical periods while overlooking obvious commonalities. (Even if there

were insurmountable disagreement about moral belief, this would not prove the skeptics' point as we discuss in the section on the Greek Sophists in Chapter 3. Moral disagreement shows, at most, that morality can be a confusing, fallible affair. But that is hardly surprising.)

Moral skeptics throw out a challenge to moral philosophers: defeat skepticism before undertaking moral philosophy. But radical moral skepticism seems largely irrelevant. There is no need to set out in search of an impossible solution to an unfalsifiable theory. Morality is all around us. We see people striving after happiness, making promises, giving money to charity; we see them complementing and sometimes vehemently criticizing one another; sometimes they are proud of what they do, sometimes they feel horribly guilty, and so on. The traditional attitude is that morality is what people already do: let's try to be intelligent about it. Radical moral skepticism is un-helpful insomuch as it gives us speculative reasons to disenfranchise the moral convictions we inevitably live by.

Moral reasoning is a search for consistency. We need to start with our own moral beliefs

---

↷ Applied Philosophy Box 2.2 ↶

Life is Short. Have an Affair.™

This is an advertisement from a specialized Internet dating service designed for people who want to cheat on their spouses. In a question-and-answer sheet directed at some of their customers, the company advises this:

'Take your time to build an additional level of trust with attached people you wish to meet.'

Can one consistently follow this advice and cheat on one's spouse? If morality requires consistency, what does this tell us about such behaviour?

Source: Affair Guarantee Program, The Ashley Madison Agency®, www.ashleymadison.com/app/public/guarantee/detailsform.p.

and attitudes and extend them outward, correcting as we go, paying attention to possible falsehoods, hidden contradictions, and imprecise distinctions. Suppose someone were to say, 'I only care about myself; be my friend.' This is inconsistent. You cannot care only about yourself and have friends. Or suppose someone were to angrily complain to a political opponent, 'You shouldn't lose your temper.' Again, this is inconsistent. These are very simple examples but they indicate a general method for moral philosophy. Thinking through our own moral beliefs leads to a process of self-correction that deepens moral understanding.

Logic is objective. It does not bend to our own peculiar whims and caprices. Faced with moral claims that just do not feel right, you need to follow through the logical implications of this way of thinking. Two strategies may be of help. First, ask yourself, what are the basic principles that motivate this way of thinking? Second, sincerely try to apply these principles to parallel cases, and be vigilant. Seemingly small modifications to our basic ways of thinking may lead to glaring moral errors.

Sociobiology: A Scientific Challenge

While moral skepticism is primarily a philosophical challenge to morality, some partisans of contemporary science propose a scientific challenge. Sociobiologists such as Edward O. Wilson, Michael Ruse, Steven Pinker, and Richard Dawkins try to explain human behaviour through an exclusive appeal to the process of biological evolution, understood as a byproduct of Darwinian natural selection. Sociobiologists argue that it is a mistake to view moral conduct as a free-will response to rational, social, and/or religious imperatives. We act morally because we have been genetically programmed to act in a co-operative

manner. In a natural world composed of competing species, co-operation is a useful adaptation in the struggle to survive. Individual specimens that co-operated in the past passed on their genes to their progeny. We have inherited these co-operating tendencies. Whereas moral philosophy presents morality as a product of rational choice, sociobiology presents it as an instinctive drive and as, ultimately, a product of random genetic mutation. We act morally, sociobiologists believe, not because we freely choose to do good but because 'morality' is 'in our genes'. According to this new allegedly scientific perspective, ethics is nothing more than 'a *shared* illusion of the human race',[2] 'an illusion fobbed off on us by our genes to get us to cooperate'.[3]

We will not investigate the biological background to these theories here. Instead, let us focus on the moral issues they confront. Sociobiologists believe in science. They want a *scientific* account of morality. They first reduce morality to sociology and then reduce sociology to biology. Both steps in their reductionist methodology can be challenged. First, morality cannot be equated with social behaviour, at least not in any simple way, for morality may require antisocial behaviour (if, for example, you found yourself in a Nazi society). Second, to explain rationality as mere biology gives short shrift to reason. It downplays the distance between humans and other animals. Many if not most philosophers accept that there is an important biological component to moral behaviour, but they investigate other aspects of human nature as well. Aristotle, one of the most respected authors in the tradition, was himself a biologist. He, along with other historical authors, described humans as 'rational *animals*'. But Aristotle never tried to reduce morality to *mere* biology. As we shall see, morality transcends biology insomuch as it proposes a model for human behaviour that moves beyond blind instinct to rational enlightenment and free will (notions we all subscribe to in our ordinary, everyday lives).

We should point out that this recent 'biological' challenge to morality is not unprecedented. Not so long ago, Freudian psychologists traced the details of moral behaviour to our subconscious sexual identity, and Marxists traced them to the power structures of a bourgeois society. We need not deny that these (and other) factors play a role in human behaviour; they clearly do. But none of these explanations provides an adequate account of how human reason operates in the moral arena. Return to the sociobiological example.

In a paper entitled 'Why Men Rape', evolutionary psychologists Randy Thornhill and Craig T. Palmer use the sociobiological model to trace the moral problem of rape to hidden biological drives. (The paper is an adaptation of their book-length treatment of the subject, *A Natural History of Rape: Biological Bases of Sexual Coercion*, 2000). Thornhill and Palmer write this:

> We fervently believe that, just as the leopard's spots and the giraffe's elongated neck are the result of aeons of past Darwinian selection, so also is rape. . . . From a Darwinian perspective, every kind of animal—whether grasshopper or gorilla, German or Ghanaian—has evolved to produce healthy children that will survive to pass along their parents' genetic legacy. . . . Rape can be understood as a third kind of sexual strategy: one more way to gain access to females. . . . For example, men might resort to rape when they are socially disenfranchised, and thus unable to gain access to women through looks, wealth or status. Alternatively, men could have evolved to practice rape when the costs seem low—when, for instance, a woman is alone and unprotected.

> . . . Over evolutionary time, some men may have succeeded in passing on their genes through rape, thus perpetuating the behaviour.[4]

There was a public outcry at the publication of these views. Why? Because this kind of explanation seems to transform a serious moral fault into a useful biological adaptation—not that the authors suggest that rape is good. After introducing their explosive theory, they go on to declare that 'We must hasten to emphasize that by categorizing a behaviour as "natural" and "biological" we do not mean in any way to imply that the behaviour is justified or even inevitable'.[5] However, such reassurances provide cold comfort, for it is hard to see how a consistent sociobiologist could come to any other conclusion: men who rape are doing only what they have been genetically programmed to do. If human reason is only a product of a blind drive for genetic replication, the proper moral conclusion is not merely that rape is good, but also that rape is even better if the victim falls pregnant!

Sociobiology reduces rationality to a mere expression of biological drives. But human reason is not equivalent to these drives but transcends and evaluates them. Consider birth control, rightly or wrongly pervasive in modern society. Sociobiologists can ingeniously try to explain how the drive to reproduce becomes a drive not to reproduce. But this misses the point. If something other than the 'drive to reproduce' is, for whatever reason, in control, then an exclusive focus on sociobiology will inevitably fall short of any adequate account of human decision-making. What is missing from the theory is an understanding of reason as a distinctive viewpoint that supplies an idea of the good as somehow separate and superior to the mere drive to reproduce.

Within the sociobiological model, human beings are not 'rational animals' but 'reproduc-

---

✍ Applied Philosophy Box 2.3 ❧

Animals that Kill Their Young

For India's langur monkeys, infanticide works. . . . In 1965, a naturalist wrote that the long-tailed black and gray langurs were 'relaxed' and 'nonaggressive.' Now, a Harvard researcher has shown that the langur society operates more like the House of Borgia, complete with kidnapping, constant sexual harassment, group battles, abandonment of some wounded young by their mothers, and the regular practice of infanticide. In her new book, *The Langurs of Abu*, Harvard Anthropologist Sarah Blaffer Hrdy, 31, portrays langur life as a 'soap opera' that revolves around the struggle between the sexes. As in other species, the strongest males compete for control of each troop. What makes the langurs different is that the winner tries to bite to death the young offspring of his predecessor. The mothers resist the infanticide until the struggle looks hopeless, then pragmatically present themselves to the new ruler for copulation. . . .

Any attempt to reduce human beings to mere animals will be unable to account for our negative assessments of such behaviour. How would you explain the difference between human beings and langur monkeys?

Source: 'Animals that Kill Their Young.' *TIME.com*, www.time.com/time/magazine/article/0,9171,912086-1,00.html, Monday, 9 January 1978.

---

ing animals'. The ultimate point of human behaviour is (species) survival. Seen from a moral point of view, survival is the raw material from which something noble and beautiful is built, but it is not the goal of human life. Many authors in the moral tradition argue that it is better to die than act immorally. It is better indeed that the entire human race go extinct than that one person act immorally. Whether one agrees or not, sociobiology cannot explain how anyone could come up with such an idea in the first place. Clearly, we are not just biological automatons driven to reproduce as much and as often as possible. There are other factors at work. It is equally important—no, it is *more* important—to treat each other with dignity, to love our neighbour, to uphold justice, to comfort the suffering, to tell the truth, and so on. These activities are not valuable because they help us to reproduce; they are valuable because, well, they are valuable. Reason, wherever it came from, is the mental power that enables us to see that these ideals are in themselves valuable.

Many academics who critique sociobiology insist that it is both unverifiable and unfalsifiable. But there is no need to enter into such debates here. Sociobiology, to whatever degree true, does nothing to address the urgency of the moral dilemma. Imagine you go on a long journey and end up at a fork in the road. We might try to describe the journey you had to follow to reach this point: that is what sociobiology is about. Moral philosophy addresses a different question: now that you are standing at the point where these two roads diverge, what choice should you make? Which road should you take? Understanding how we got to the point where we can decide between right and wrong may have repercussions for morality, but it is not the central issue of ethics.

Noncognitivism: A Rational Challenge

There are other contemporary challenges to even the possibility of moral reasoning. The awkward term **noncognitivism** designates an orientation in contemporary moral philosophy that is also referred to as emotivism, intuitionism, or, more recently, expressivism. We shall use the term *noncognitivists* to broadly refer to philosophers who, whatever their differences, argue that ethics is not cognitive, that it is *not* a matter of reasoned thought or genuine knowledge. Noncognitivists generally claim that morality is about *feeling*. Moral language, they insist, expresses how we *feel* about things.

A.J. Ayer (1910–89), the British positivist, distinguishes between facts and values in a familiar way. On this noncognitivist account, science is about facts; ethics is about values. Facts tell us what is true about the world; values tell us what we ought to do. Facts are observable; values are not. If you say 'it is raining outside', I can go outside and see for myself. If you say 'don't steal because stealing is wrong', how in the world could I ever *observe* whether that particular statement is true? Ayer concludes that 'statements of value are simply expressions of emotion which can be neither true nor false'.[6]

Ayer's noncognitivist account seems to drain the meaning out of moral language. As he explains it, ethical statements play a role similar to an exclamation mark: they serve to place an emotional stress or slant on certain properties of existence without, however, telling us anything that is true or logical. As Ayer maintains,

The presence of an ethical symbol [or word] in a proposition adds nothing to its factual content. Thus if I say to someone, 'You acted wrongly in stealing that money,' I am not stating anything more than if I had simply said, 'You stole that money.' In adding that this action is wrong I am not making any further statement about it. I am simply evincing my moral disapproval of it. It is as if I had said, 'You stole that money,' in a peculiar tone of horror, or written it with the addition of some special exclamation marks. The tone, or

the exclamation marks, adds nothing to the literal meaning of the sentence. It merely serves to show that the expression of it is attended by certain feelings in the speaker. If now I generalise my previous statement and say, 'stealing money is wrong,' I produce a sentence which has no factual meaning—that is, expresses no proposition which can be either true or false. It is as if I had written 'Stealing money!!'—where the shape and thickness of the exclamation mark show, by a suitable convention, that a special sort of moral disapproval is the feeling which is being expressed. It is clear that there is nothing said here which can be true or false. Another man may disagree with me about the wrongness of stealing, in the sense that he may not have the same feelings about stealing as I have, and he may quarrel with me on account of my moral sentiments. But he cannot, strictly speaking, contradict me. For in saying that a certain type of action is right or wrong, I am not making any factual statement, not even a statement about my own state of mind: I am merely expressing certain moral sentiments. And the man who is ostensibly contradicting me is merely expressing certain moral sentiments. So that there is plainly no sense in asking which of us is in the right. For neither of us is asserting a genuine [logical] proposition.[7]

This mindset can be traced back to historical authors such as David Hume, the famous Scottish skeptic (1711–76), who comments that morality 'is the object of feeling, not of reason'.[8] According to Hume, 'when you pronounce any action or character to be vicious [or wrong], you mean nothing, but that from the constitution of your nature you have a feeling or sentiment of blame from the contemplation of it'.[9] We will not, however, examine the precise historical development of this view here. Let us focus rather on these issues in the context of contemporary philosophy.

Although the influence of noncognitivism has waned slightly in contemporary Anglo-

American philosophy, it is still a dominant force. If noncognitivism were correct, mainstream ethics of the sort presented in this book would be based on a fundamental error. Although historical authors recognize that there is a 'feeling', or better yet, a motivational component to moral discourse, they generally maintain that ethics also has a cognitive aspect. We use *reason* to arrive at moral conclusions. Moral philosophy, traditionally construed, requires a logical examination of issues and the correct presentation of evidence. Although historical authors do believe in what we now somewhat misleadingly call intuition, this capacity for first understanding is not, as we have seen, a matter of feeling but, rather, a form of intelligent discernment.

The traditional project of moral philosophy is motivated by the idea that if we think very hard about things, we can find the correct answers to many moral questions. We can use logic to progress in moral knowledge. If, in contrast, noncognitivism were correct, moral reasoning would be impossible. We could not, in any meaningful sense, argue about morality. There are, however, good reasons for rejecting anything but the most benign form of noncognitivism. In the following section, we show that noncognitivists misunderstand what moral language refers to, that morality does not depend uniquely on feelings, that morality is objective, and that historical authors *correctly* view moral philosophy as an empirical discipline. We will finish by considering prescriptivism, an important historical response to noncognitivism.

Morality Is Not an Object in the World

Noncognitivism is, in large part, spurred by **positivism**, the idea that science, and science alone, produces true knowledge. Imagine someone who believes fervently in modern science, indeed, who thinks that science counts as the ultimate achievement of human rationality. This is a common theme in contemporary thought. Most of us, to some degree, share in these sentiments. But why do we think that science is so impressive? The idea is that science shows what is really out there in the world; it alone gives us a reliable description of reality.

Faced with a lack of physical evidence for morality, noncognitivists come to think of morality as something in our heads, something we project onto the world. Morality is something we make up—not necessarily a figment of our imagination, but a kind emotional overlay or colouring that comes from our minds, not from outside reality. It is not something 'out there' but something that resides purely in the mind.

This positivist stance is aptly captured in the work of British philosopher J.L. Mackie (1917–81), who uses 'an argument from queerness' to suggest the implausibility of objective values. Mackie thinks like a scientist. In science, if we want to know if something exists, we search for a specimen. If, for example, we want to know if the Higgs Boson (the 'God particle') exists, we build a high-speed particle accelerator that will allow us to observe it. We can't know for sure it exists until we observe one. Following the same logic, it would seem that we could only know that objective right and wrong exist if and when we find the moral objects to which they correspond. But moral ideas like objective right and wrong are not observable physical objects or properties in the universe. So, Mackie claims this:

> If there were objective values, then they would be entities or qualities or relations of a very strange sort, utterly different from anything else in the universe. Correspondingly, if we were aware of them, it would have to be by some special faculty

of perception or moral intuition, utterly different from our ordinary ways of knowing anything else.[10]

But most of us (particularly those of us who take science as the ultimate truth) do not believe in anything like an extrasensory power of paranormal perception that allows us to 'see' invisible, immaterial moral properties or objects. So, according to Mackie, it is preposterous to claim that there are objective moral properties or values. In short, 'There are no objective values'.[11]

Mackie's argument from queerness is itself a very strange argument. It is based on an obvious category mistake: the morality or immorality of a human act is not an object or property like an appendage that sticks out of those acts we observe. (One contemporary British philosopher, George Moore, comes close to arguing this.) We can agree with Mackie that we do not possess any extraordinary powers of paranormal perception. But so what! It does not follow that because there are no invisible moral objects in the world, there are no objective moral values. Suppose I say that Tom loves Betty. Love is not a physical object in the world. Does that mean that love is not real? That it is not objectively present in the world?

Noncognitivists like Mackie want to claim that we cannot make true or false claims about morality. Surely, however, it may be true or false that Tom loves Betty. We can even make an argument: 'He stood by her when she lost her inheritance, even when she had cancer; he must love her.' It seems very odd to suggest that this kind of discourse is somehow illogical or unreasonable. But this is what morality is like. Indeed, some authors argue that morality is rooted in love (but more on that later.) For the moment, simply note that there is no rea-

son to believe that knowledge is restricted to statements about which physical objects exist in the world. Because morality is not a piece of physical furniture in the universe, it does not follow that morality does not, in any sense, exist or that moral statements do not provide true descriptions of reality.

Even science uses nonphysical concepts to account for reality. Think of numbers. No one has ever seen the number seven. (We see invented symbols or words representing the number seven; we see a row of seven cars or seven oranges; but we never see the number seven by itself.) Yet numbers can be correctly (or incorrectly) applied to the world. It makes sense to say, 'It's true; there really are only seven oranges left'. Numbers are not illogical. In a similar way, even if moral concepts do not represent any special class of physical objects, this does not mean that they cannot be correctly (or incorrectly) applied to the world, or that they are somehow illogical or arbitrary. Moral terms like right or wrong and good or bad are not names for a new class of invisible objects or properties. But historical philosophers never argued that they were. They claim, instead, that moral terminology serves a useful purpose when it comes to describing and evaluating what goes on in the world.

Morality Is Not Only a Matter of Feelings

Clearly, morality evokes feelings. We *feel* bad when we do something wrong; we *feel* proud of our accomplishments. We angrily condemn evil-doers; we warmly applaud heroes. Moral knowledge is not something abstract, cold, and distant. It stirs our emotions and pushes us to act. Still, noncognitivists base morality *purely* on feeling. And this is going too far.

Hume, who uses the old-fashioned term *passions* to refer to feelings, explains:

Since morals, therefore, have an influence on the actions and affections, it follows, that they cannot be derived from reason . . . because reason alone . . . can never have any such influence. Morals excite passions, and produce or prevent actions. Reason of itself is utterly impotent in this particular. The rules of morality, therefore, are not conclusions of our reason.[12]

Hume immediately adds, 'No one, I believe, will deny the justness of this inference'.[13] But most authors in the historical tradition would indeed challenge this line of reasoning.

Hume thinks that people *never* act according to reason. But what could it mean to say that we act only on feelings, never on reasons? I *believe* that the Bible is the word of God, so I obey the Ten Commandments. I *believe* that these two people are my parents, so I support them in old age. I *believe* that money makes people happy, so I buy a lottery ticket. I *believe* that a sedentary life leads to illness, so I exercise. In each case, I have identified a reason that makes me act in a certain way. You can agree or disagree with my reasons. The point is that these reasons, which I may hold with a certain emotional intensity, are beliefs, not mere emotions. A belief may provoke or elicit an emotion, but it is an exercise in thoughtful intelligence, not a mere outpouring of sentiment. Beliefs can be true or false, and true beliefs are the main component of rational knowledge.

Hume assumes that there are only two mutually exclusive alternatives: reason pushes us to act, or emotion pushes us to act. But there is a third possibility. Mainstream authors identify a mental capacity Hume overlooks, a form of intelligence somewhere between the extremes of pure theoretical reason and pure unthinking feeling they call **practical reason**. Practical reason has an affective, motivational compon-

ent. It is not cold, aloof theoretical reason, but neither is it naked emotion. Loosely described, practical reason is reason mixed with feelings. This, then, is the sense in which moral judgments are rational: they include a thoughtful and an emotional component. They involve, so to speak, reasoned or intelligent emotion: feeling that is motivated by sound thinking about the world. The standard account that believing is one thing and acting is another is overly simple. Our actions depend crucially on our beliefs. The same human being feels *and* believes and, contrary to what Hume suggests, these two aspects of the same mental awareness overlap and interact with one another.

Morality Is Objective

Noncognitivists generally argue that morality is subjective. What they mean is that because morality is based on feeling, it must vary in a nonrational way from individual to individual. If, of course, there were no agreed-upon standard for behaviour, this would doom the project of moral philosophy, which is, in part, to build consensus through argument. Even assuming, however, that morality was based purely on feelings, the idea that a healthy individual could feel *any* feelings about *anything* is highly exaggerated.

There is a meaningful sense in which moral judgments are subjective. Yes, we believe that serial murder is wrong because psychologically and emotionally, even instinctively, human nature pushes us in this direction. But that does not mean that killing others is immoral only because it inevitably makes us feel bad. Moral philosophers down through history generally argue that there is an objective standard outside ourselves, which stays the same from person to person, according to which our actions and our lives must be judged.

Believing in objective morality may clash with certain popular prejudices, but it is more faithful to human experience. I cannot arbitrarily decide that scratching one's nose is the height of evil and that murdering tots is a pleasant pastime. Morality is not like that. The world is, at the deepest levels, unmovable; at the very least, it resists modification. Try changing your moral view about serial killing—it just does not work. We do not *decide* that serial killing is wrong, for if we did, we could decide that it was not wrong. Serial killing is wrong because of its nature, because the wanton destruction of innocent human life is objectively evil—not just because disapproving of serial killing suits our fancy.

Moral values have persistence, staying power. People with integrity do not change their moral beliefs at will, even when doing so would be to their own advantage. For example, moral business people do not suddenly start believing that stealing is legitimate, even virtuous, even though stealing might be a useful way of profiting from their business transactions. They do not rearrange their moral beliefs for their own benefit. In fact, people who do end up stealing (at least in small amounts) do not usually declare that stealing is morally good behaviour. When confronted with the wrongness of their own behaviour, they make exceptions for themselves: 'Well, in *my* case, it wasn't really stealing because the company didn't have any use for it anyways'; 'Everybody helps themselves, it's understood'; 'They owed me the money'; and so on. These people do this to protect their self-esteem—they do not want to see themselves as morally inadequate or inferior. This strategy in itself shows the importance of objective morality. To say that morality is objective is not to overlook the human element in morality. The noncognitivist may insist that morality is a human artifact. Without humans there would be no morality. This might very well be true. But it does not show that morality is not objective. Suppose all human beings and indeed all living beings were colour blind. Firetrucks would still be red. Seeing red is an artifact of our retina, our optical nerves, and the brain stem (etc.), but it does not follow from this that red firetrucks are not red in some objective sense. We do not see red in any arbitrary way; the sensation of redness is somehow forced upon us by the nature of the world. It would appear that something similar happens with morality.

Scientific theories and mathematical calculations are as much artifacts of the human mind as moral judgments are. Does that mean that they have no objective validity? That there is no criterion for correctness or error in these disciplines outside our own personal opinions? To privilege one form of human intelligence over another is inconsistent. Mathematics is no more real than morality, at least not on any unbiased account of human intelligence. It is the very same human mind that produces both mathematics and moral philosophy.

There is one final reason why it is important to maintain that moral judgments are objective. Recognizing the *objective* nature of morality *is an acknowledgement of human fallibility*. If moral judgments really were subjective, any person's moral judgments would be as good as any other person's. This would mean, in effect, that no one could make a moral mistake. If there were no outside standard, if all that mattered was what I happened to feel about an issue, my view of morality could never be improved upon or corrected. But this seems pretentious. Human beings are eminently *fallible*; they make mistakes. A rejection of moral objectivity is more like a license for smug, uncritical belief than anything else. Someone might legitimately worry that if we think our beliefs are objectively true, we will try to force them on other people. Tolerance is a serious ethical (and political) concern. But the idea of tolerance itself must be an *objectively* valid moral ideal, otherwise someone who felt like being intolerant would have no compelling reason to alter their own behaviour. To claim that morality is objective is not to claim that our own moral views will always, after critical reflection, turn out to be correct. It is to claim rather that the *correct* moral beliefs—whatever they happen to be—are objectively true. Knowing that we are rational but fallible beings who are capable of discovering the truth about things but also liable to error, we can never complacently assume that we have the right opinions about everything.

Moral Philosophy Is an Empirical Discipline

Scientific knowledge derives from sense perception, that is, from observation. As we have seen, noncognitivists maintain that moral knowledge is unempirical; it derives from feeling, not from observation. This is an exaggeration. In fact, historical philosophers base their ethical theories on a persistent, thorough observation of human behaviour. Aristotle, to cite only one example, approaches ethics as a biologist would. In the same way that we learn about lions, and polar bears, and rainbow trout—by watching them and talking to people who watch them—Aristotle suggests that we should do the same thing when investigating humans. Ethics, the study of human behaviour, is not biology, but it is *like* biology. If the ornithologist goes out into the field to study red-tailed hawks, the ethicist needs to do the same thing when it comes to studying

humans. For Aristotle, this is a large part of what moral philosophy is all about.

Studying different animal species has its challenges. But in the case of ethics, we can access human experience rather easily. First because we *are* humans: we can be introspective; we can investigate our own reasons for acting or not acting. We can study when we are happy and when we are disappointed in ourselves. And we can reasonably assume that we are not so radically different from other people. Second, humans are articulate: we keep records; we have mastered speech; we communicate with one another. Ethicists can, therefore, ask other people questions; they can catalogue other people's opinions and even study the correspondence or lack of correspondence between what other people say and what they actually do. Even a religious ethicist like Thomas Aquinas does not think that morality just falls from the heavens. It resides deep in human nature. Morality is something human beings do. It follows, then, that morality is open to empirical inspection.

Is this observational approach to ethics absurd? Hume, the father of noncognitivism, argues in favour of this approach. He writes:

> It is universally acknowledged that there is a great uniformity among the actions of men, in all nations and ages, and that human nature remains still the same, in its principles and operations. The same motives always produce the same actions: the same events follow from the same causes. Ambition, avarice, self-love, vanity, friendship, generosity, public spirit: these passions, mixed in various degrees, and distributed through society, have been, from the beginning of the world, and still are, the source of all the actions and enterprises, which have ever been observed among mankind. Would you know the sentiments, inclinations, and course of life of the Greeks and

Romans? Study well the temper and actions of the French and English: You cannot be much mistaken in transferring to the former most of the observations which you have made with regard to the latter. Mankind are so much the same, in all times and places, that history informs us of nothing new or strange in this particular. [History's] chief use is only to discover the constant and universal principles of human nature, by showing men in all varieties of circumstances and situations, and furnishing us with materials from which we may form our observations and become acquainted with the regular springs of human action and behaviour. These records of wars, intrigues, factions, and revolutions, are so many collections of experiments, by which the politician or moral philosopher fixes the principles of his science, in the same manner as the physician or natural philosopher becomes acquainted with the nature of plants, minerals, and other external objects, by the experiments which he forms concerning them. Nor are the earth, water, and other elements, examined by Aristotle, and Hippocrates, more like to those which at present lie under our observation than the men described by Polybius and Tacitus are to those who now govern the world.[14]

Wise words, eloquently said. If Hume is right, we can base morality on empirical observation. To begin with, we can study human nature; we can understand how and why human beings act, which is at least a preparation for understanding how they *should* act.

The critic may protest that it is easy to observe what people do, but how do we observe what people *ought* to do? Imagine the following scenario. You see a group of people in different uniforms with batons in their hands, running as fast as they can around an oval. They complete a lap, pass the baton to a team member in the same uniform, and then that group of runners takes off as fast as they can around the track. You notice that the runners are out of breath; some are at the point of exhaustion; they are sweating profusely. The lead runner keeps looking over his shoulder to see how far ahead he is; the second runner is madly trying to catch up. The crowd is yelling encouragement. The second runner passes the leader just before the finish line and breaks into a large smile. The other runner looks dejected. Could you figure what was going on? Of course, you could. They are in a relay race and the goal is to come in first. But notice: there is a criterion of human success implicit in this activity. The team that wins succeeds; the other teams fail. With a little bit of intelligent analysis, one can figure out what those teams that failed—even the team that came in last—were all trying to do. In scrutinizing failure, we can come to understand success. Likewise, even if most of us sometimes fail, or indeed fail repeatedly at less momentous pursuits, we can still come to an understanding of the admittedly more complicated goals and requirements imposed by morality.

Moral reasoning is an inextricable aspect of human experience. We can derive knowledge of morality, then, through a careful study of what we do. If, for example, you watched figure skating long enough, you would begin to understand what is going on and could, with time, start to explain, in great detail, the difference between a good and bad performance. This is how empirical knowledge of morality arises. In some sense, we are competing against our own expectations of ourselves. There are objective standards we strive to live by, standards that are so important that our self-esteem falters when we fail to achieve them. Ethics looks into what those standards are.

As I have already explained, historical authors believe that morality is all about happiness. One way to figure out what morality requires is to observe what makes people happy. The basic perspective here is that morality is what makes us deeply satisfied, pleased, fulfilled, content, tranquil, and proud of ourselves. Immorality is what makes us inevitably frustrated, unsatisfied, ashamed, guilty, worried, restless, and disappointed. This may sound as if moral philosophy is just a branch of modern psychology. But there are important differences. If modern psychology strives to be an objective account of what people do without value judgments, this is precisely what moral philosophy is about: making value judgments about our own and other people's actions. Whereas psychology studies how people behave, ethics, in contrast, is about how people *ought* to behave. If we evaluate how our children are doing in school, how well the economy is performing, the chances of our favourite baseball team going to the World Series, or whether the latest movie deserves two stars or four stars, it would be very odd not to evaluate ourselves. Ethics is about doing this fairly, thoroughly, and logically.

Morality Is Made Up of Universal Prescriptions

British analytic philosopher R.M. Hare (1919–2002), in responding to certain noncognitivists, such as Ayer, developed an influential position that came to be called universal prescriptivism. According to this account, morality is made up of universal prescriptions or commands that apply equally to everyone in the same circumstances. We will not discuss all the details of his position here, but it is interesting to note how Hare's intended alternative is, on closer inspection, another expression of some of the noncognitivist attitudes and assumptions we have been criticizing.

Hare points out that morality involves imperatives or commands. Moral statements are not true or false. They tell us to do something; they do not describe the nature of the world. Hare tends to favour a highly technical approach, but consider how he defines *prescriptivism*. Read the following statement slowly. (Don't worry, the general idea can be readily explained.)

> *Universal prescriptivism*, [focuses on] what has been called the *universalizability* of 'ought'-sentences and other normative or evaluative sentences. . . . One cannot with logical consistency, where *a* and *b* are two individuals, say that *a* ought, in a certain situation specified in universal terms . . . to act in a certain way, . . . but that *b* ought not to act in a similarly specified way in a similarly specified situation. This is because in any 'ought'-statement there is implicit a principle which says that the statement applies to all precisely similar situations.[15]

In Hare's account, moral commands have two logical properties: universalizability and prescriptivity. First, they must be applicable to a universal class of situations, and second, they must be authoritative. They must *prescribe* what anyone caught in a similar situation is obliged to do. An example may help. Suppose I claim that because you are wealthy *and* my best friend, you are morally obliged to pay my way to law school. Hare claims that for this to be a legitimate moral rule, it would have to apply to anyone who finds himself in the same situation. If, for example, the positions were reversed, if *I* were your wealthy best friend and *you* needed to go to law school, *I* would be obliged to help *you* pay your debts. When I say that you are *morally* obliged to do something, I am claiming that *all* individuals must do the same thing when they find themselves in precisely the same circumstance. (There are some difficulties determining what counts as the *same* situation but leave those aside.) Hare succeeds in imposing a consistency requirement on morality. As it turns out, there is a logic to morality. It applies universally—without exception—to everyone across the board.

Like the noncognitivists, Hare believes that moral judgments are not true or false. At the same time, he provides a logical structure for moral claims in that there is a consistency requirement that moral rules must satisfy: they must apply to all individuals in the same situation. This sounds right, but there is an underlying problem: Hare is unable to explain where moral rules come from. The best he can say is that they originate in our personal preference. But *preference* here is only a code word for a certain kind of emotion: we *prefer*, we *desire*, we *want*, or we *feel* that people should act in certain ways in certain situations. That is all. Our feeling (however misguided) is the basis of morality. But this is only to return to Hume's original argument that morality is ultimately not a matter of reason but of emotion.

'I prefer strawberry ice cream'; 'I prefer hockey to basketball'; 'I prefer names that begin with *M*'. Even if I could wish my preferences on other people—even if I believe that everyone should prefer names that begin with *M*—that would not turn my preference into morality. *Preference*, then, is too weak a term to capture what is going on in ethics. A moral *imperative* cannot be true or false, but it can be reasonable or unreasonable. What makes morality compelling is that it is based on reasonable beliefs about the world. Mainstream historical authors, in contrast to Hare, do not base morality on mere emotion but on *intelligent emotion*—in other words, on practical reason. It is not any preference that counts; it is only reasonable preferences that count. The fact that I consistently want something—that

all men (including me) should be tattooed with a serial number on their right cheekbone—is not enough for morality. How do we determine what preferences are reasonable? By thinking long and hard about the world. And which preferences are those? Well, the rest of this book explores them at length.

Hare claims that morality is ultimately based on nothing more than preference. But this is highly implausible. I may feel like doing (or not doing) many things. But in many cases, I ignore or even actively suppress my preferences. Why? Because they are inappropriate or unworthy or—worse yet—evil. If my behaviour were motivated only by feelings, the strongest *feeling* would always win. But this is not the case. I do not necessarily act on my strongest feelings; I may not *feel* like doing what I *ought* to do and do it anyways, even though I do not feel like it, out of a sense of duty. Duty is a sense of obligation that compels me to act in certain ways regardless of my feelings. I listen to the voice of duty because it has more authority than ordinary feeling and because it is more in keeping with what is reasonable to believe about the world. In other words, duty has a *cognitive* element.

There is a second way in which Hare reiterates the noncognitivist doctrine. Hare claims that moral properties *supervene* on natural properties. He explains his meaning by way of an example:

> [L]et us take that characteristic of 'good' which has been called its supervenience. Suppose that we say 'St. Francis was a good man.' It is logically impossible to say this and to maintain at the same time that there might have been another man placed in exactly the same circumstances as St. Francis, and who behaved in exactly the same way, but who differed from St. Francis in this respect only, that he was not a good man.[16]

Hare is re-expressing here the same requirement of logical consistency discussed above. Identical cases of human behaviour must be evaluated identically. If St. Francis is good and if St. Dominic and St. Francis behave in exactly the same way, St. Dominic must be equally good. This seems uncontroversial—except that this use of the concept of **supervenience** is problematic. In Hare's account, there are two sets of properties: natural (or physical) properties and moral properties. Moral properties supervene or ride piggyback on natural properties. Let us explain.

Suppose St. Francis gives a loaf of bread to a beggar. We can describe the natural (or physical) properties that characterize his actions: here is the loaf of bread in his sack; here he is taking it out and giving it to the beggar; here he is walking away. Or we can describe the moral properties that (so to speak) attach to his actions: he is being generous, kind, and compassionate. Hare tells us that the same natural properties must always possess the same moral properties. If St. Dominic gives a loaf of bread to the poor (in exactly the same way), St. Dominic must be equally generous, kind, and compassionate.

Insomuch as we must award the same moral status to the same kind of behaviour, Hare's principle seems incontrovertible. But what an odd way of making the point! In rescuing morality from logical inconsistency, Hare posits the existence of invisible, immaterial moral properties that supervene on physical properties in the world. This sounds like Mackie's argument discussed earlier. When we say 'That was a very good act!' we are not claiming that there is an extra, invisible property called goodness that is somehow attached to this person's behaviour. We mean two things: (1) that the act meets the criteria of a very good act, and (2) that other intelligent people will see how good it is. These are meaningful assertions that may be either true or false. But there is no need to posit the existence of a second set of invisible moral properties out in the world somehow floating above human behaviour.

The 'Is–Ought' Fallacy

Although opinions have slowly started to shift, many present-day philosophers still believe that there is another logical problem with moral reasoning: what is familiarly referred to as the **is–ought fallacy** (also called the naturalistic fallacy.) According to this standard view, arguments are composed of 'is statements' and 'ought statements'. 'Is statements' are scientific; 'ought statements' are moral. 'Is statements' describe the world; 'ought statements' tell us what to do. It is a logical mistake, on this account, to move from an 'is statement' to an 'ought statement' in an argument. Here is a simple example of a moral argument:

> **Premise:** Gloria is not feeling well.

> **Conclusion:** We ought to do something to help Gloria.

The premise here is an 'is statement'; it tells us what *is* the case for Gloria. But the conclusion is an 'ought statement'; it tells us what we *should* do. So the argument jumps from an 'is statement' to an 'ought statement'. There is no 'ought' in the premise: it somehow pops into existence in the conclusion without any explanation or justification. Some logicians insist that this is a fundamental mistake in logic.

The classic statement of this problem is found in David Hume's *A Treatise of Human Nature*. Hume makes a simple observation:

In every system of morality, which I have hith-erto met with, I have always remarked, that the author proceeds for some time in the ordinary way of reasoning, and establishes the being of a God, or makes observations concerning human affairs; when of a sudden I am surprised to find, that instead of the usual copulations of proposi-tions, is, and is not, I meet with no proposition that is not connected with an ought, or an ought not. This change is imperceptible; but is, how-ever, of the last consequence. For as this ought, or ought not, expresses some new relation or affirmation, it is necessary that it should be ob-served and explained; and at the same time that a reason should be given, for what seems alto-gether inconceivable, how this new relation can be a deduction from others, which are entirely different from it.[17]

Hume demands a reason for the 'ought' and goes on to recommend that authors avoid this kind of logical move. But he is inconsistent. Only *two paragraphs* after introducing the no-tion of an is–ought fallacy, he himself admits that we all make the same jump when think-ing about morality. Hume discovers the ori-gins of the moral impulse in 'particular pains or pleasures', which, he explains, 'sufficiently explain the vice or virtue'.[18] Simply put, he argues that we know something is evil be-cause it hurts; we know something is good because it provides pleasure. To express his line of reasoning as a formal argument:

Premise: X causes pleasure/pain.
Conclusion: Therefore X is moral/immoral.

But the premise here is an 'is statement', whereas the conclusion is really a disguised 'ought statement', for to say that act X is moral/immoral is to say that we *ought* to do or not to do X. We could rewrite Hume's argument:

Premise: It *is* the case that X causes pleasure/pain. (A simple fact about the world.)

Conclusion: Therefore, we *ought* to do/not to do X. (A normative recommendation.)

So according to Hume, all moral reason-ing begins with an unaccountable jump from a statement about 'is' to a statement about 'ought'. Hume is as human as the rest of us. If this is how human beings come up with moral judgments, he too must come up with moral judgments in the same way. That is, he must commit the 'is–ought' fallacy whenever he thinks about morality. This is not really very surprising, for morality would not be possible unless human beings were able to somehow move from our beliefs about the world to ideas about the way we should act.

But the is–ought problem is not restricted to morality. Consider the statement, 'as soon as you have finished browning the meat, you ought to add the onions and garlic'. Here is a jump from 'is' to 'ought'. When the meat *is* brown, you *ought* to add onions and garlic. But a recipe is not a moral statement. (Although the act of cooking may have moral implica-tions, the point here is that the statement 'Add onions and garlic when the meat is brown' is not a moral imperative.) A little reflection should convince you that we make this kind of leap all the time. We do it without realizing what is happening.

Many philosophers who take this line of attack on moral reasoning champion science at the expense of morality while complete-ly overlooking the fact that science also moves from an 'is' to an 'ought'. Science moves from claims about what *is* the case to claims about what we *ought* to do. Consider the following:

- When you mix these chemicals together, you get a white residue, heat, ash, and smoke.

- Therefore, you *ought* to believe this scientific hypothesis.

This is a scientific argument. The premise is a mere statement of fact; the conclusion is an 'ought statement': you are obliged to do something: believe! Believing is a kind of doing. So science also depends on a normative jump that takes reasoners from certain 'is statements' to 'ought statements'.

Is there any logical way of bridging the 'is–ought' gap? There are two basic answers to this question. We can call the first approach, which centres on the idea of human nature, the anthropological view. We can call the second approach, which focuses on the idea of the good, moral realism. We can associate the former approach with Aristotle; the latter, with Plato. Although many commentators treat these two approaches as opposing theories, it is better to think of them as complementary rather than contradictory accounts. Morality involves human nature, but it also involves whatever embodies the good. In the next section, we will look at moral reasoning from an anthropological perspective; in the section after that, we will consider it from the perspective of the idea of the good.

The Anthropological View of Moral Reasoning

Let us return to the argument on page 43 about helping Gloria in her illness. What is the missing premise here? What unspoken piece of information allows us to move from premise to conclusion? It should be obvious that this reasoning hinges on an unspoken assumption: 'We ought to help people who are not feeling well.' We can rewrite the argument with the missing premise:

> **Premise:** Gloria is not feeling well.
>
> **Hidden Premise:** We ought to help people who are not feeling well.
>
> **Conclusion:** Therefore, we ought to help Gloria.

This argument does not commit the 'is–ought' fallacy because there is an 'ought' in the premises from which we derive the 'ought' in the conclusion. Where does this 'ought' come from? Many philosophers claim that it comes from human nature. Human beings are intelligent enough to understand that we *ought* to help people who are not feeling well. This moral insight derives perhaps from an awareness of the demands of logical *consistency*, or from

---

◦ Applied Philosophy Box 2.4 ◦

Dog Food Recipes

'Never ever give bones to dogs. Bone fragments can actually become lodged in the throat or alimentary tract of the dog and cause trauma or even death.'

This is a very simple, inverted argument (beginning with the conclusion) that moves from 'is' to 'ought':

Premise: It is the case that bone fragments can . . . cause trauma or even death.
Conclusion: Therefore, you ought not give bones to dogs.

Is this a good argument? What is the hidden idea that supplies the 'ought'?

some intelligent exercise of compassion or empathy, or from some conception of virtue and vice. But however it arises, historical authors locate its origins deep inside human nature.

Hume complains that authors forget to mention this step in moral reasoning. But there is a good reason why this step goes unmentioned. Who makes moral arguments? Human beings. Who are those arguments addressed to? Other human beings. So the role of human nature is typically presupposed whenever we engage in moral argument. When I argue that 'Gloria is not feeling well; we ought to do something to help Gloria', I am, in fact, arguing that *because we are human beings*, we ought to help Gloria. It is understood where the 'oughts' come from. They come from ourselves. In bringing our humanity along with us when we argue, we also bring along the necessary 'oughts' that are located inside human nature, and we naturally assume that our listeners can supply the same 'oughts' because they are human beings as well.

Pre-modern authors do not commit the naturalistic, or 'is–ought', fallacy. They know what they are doing. They make it very clear that morality derives from human nature. Much of their reasoning, in fact, focuses on this point. They argue that morality requires us to be true to our own humanness. One might conclude, at first glance, that they share an account of human nature like the account we find in sociobiology (discussed on pages 31–33). But there are important differences. In sociobiology, the 'ought' buried in human nature is to 'replicate my own genes as much as possible'. In moral philosophy, the 'ought' buried in human nature aims at the higher good: love, honesty, justice, courage, and moderation. In the first case, we seek to preserve our genes through blind impulse. In the second, we freely choose

to do good. The sociobiological view is fatally self-centred. We feel the need to replicate our genes, not because they are good but because they are our *own*. The moral view adopted by most philosophical authors claims that we possess the cognitive abilities needed to recognize a common good that embraces other people. Reason supplies a higher criterion we can use to judge what we are about. These are, therefore, different views. In sociobiology, human beings operate according to a biological 'ought'. In moral philosophy, they operate according to a biological *and* a moral 'ought'.

We may wonder why earlier philosophers were not bothered by Hume's is–ought problem. It is because they developed a rich account of practical reason. Hume is stumped by the 'is–ought' problem because he only thinks of reason in theoretical terms. Consider an example of pure theoretical reason. Suppose you were to carefully calculate the value of pi to 50 places: 3.14159 26535 89793 23846 26433 83279 50288 41971 69399 37510. This accurate theoretical result does not give us any reason to act morally. To go from a theoretical fact like this to the idea that we should be moral would require a real leap from 'is' to 'ought'. We would need to embrace some sort of 'ought belief' to move from this 'is statement' to an 'ought conclusion'. (It is hard to imagine what it could be.) But practical reason does not work in this way.

Aristotle, writing in the fourth century BC, claims that 'Intellect itself [i.e., purely theoretical reason] moves nothing, but only the intellect which aims at an end and is practical'.[19] We do not care about the exact value of pi to 50 decimal places. (Well, most of us, anyway.) But we do care about other things: human life, for example. The same practical *reason* that tells me you are splashing about in the deep end of the pool because you cannot swim also tells me that your life is valuable. The same power of intelligent discernment provides an understanding of the situation *and* the emotional response that stirs me to action. When I dive into the water and pull you to safety, my behaviour is a *conclusion* that I reach through reason.

Our beliefs—even though they are beliefs and not mere emotions—are not all neutral. Nor should they be. We are participants; we look at the world from the viewpoint of someone who has a role to play. Sizing up what has to be done is intelligence. If moral agents always had to move from theoretical reason to action, they would have to inexplicably jump from 'is' to 'ought'. But this is not what happens, at least in a moral individual. Moral agents do not jump from pure theory to pure emotion. In practical reason, the two are mixed together. Moral agents intelligently desire and emotionally believe. When necessary, practical intelligence takes the lead and pushes them to act.

The Idea of the Good: The Moral Realist View

We have introduced the idea that human nature supplies the 'ought' in moral reasoning, but there is another way of understanding what is going on. Instead of focusing on human nature, we can contemplate whatever we desire. That is, we can focus on the good understood as an objective reality—not as something that comes from within us but as something outside ourselves that attracts our attention and loyalty.

Moral realists argue that some things in the world really are good, some things really are bad, and that we are intelligent enough to understand the difference. We are duly attracted to good things and repulsed by bad

things. On these mainstream accounts, we *discover* what is good or bad; we don't invent it. Consider simple arithmetic. We don't decide that two plus two equals four or that the value of pi will be equal to 3.14. Using our intelligence, we discover that this *must* be the case. Moral realists believe that things such as love, friendship, honour, truth, health, and prosperity are good in their own right; they would be valuable even if we were too confused to desire them. It is our intelligent attraction to these things that supplies the ought in moral reasoning. Perhaps, for example, we understand that it is good to help those who are ill because we understand the goodness of health and the badness of disease. Perhaps we understand that suffering without help is bad and being cared for is good. And so on.

Authors who adopt the anthropological view (see pages 45–50) claim that human nature supplies the 'ought' in morality. In contrast, moral realists assert that the good in things supplies the 'ought'. Why not say then that the 'ought' comes from both these sources: from human nature and also from the nature of things? Morality means two things: (1) being true to our nature and (2) being true to the nature of the world. These are two different sides of the same coin. Let us, turn, then to a more focussed consideration of moral realism.

On this moral realist account, clear-thinking humans are attracted to what is really, truly good: not because they happen to view it as good but because of some property inherent in its nature. This clashes with some modern attitudes we have been considering. Contractarian author Thomas Hobbes (1588–1679) famously writes, 'whatsoever is the object of any man's appetite or desire that is it which he for his part calleth good'.[20] Moral realists flatly reject this idea. In their account, we find out what is good through the use of reason, not by following mere appetite or desire. Those things that really are good are good in themselves, separate and apart from our sometimes uncritical tastes and judgments.

Let us consider carefully what moral realism is telling us. Many people (with serious justification) believe, for example, that health is a good. Moral realists argue that health is not a good because we desire it. Rather, we desire it because it is a good. The person who does not value health is a confused individual. That is all. The nature of things in the world, not the nature of our beliefs, provides the correct criterion for the good. When our desires do not match up properly with the nature of things in the world, we fall into error.

Without some kind of robust commitment to the idea that there are good things in the world—just as there are red things, heavy things, and things that can be counted—we end up with a moral theory that amounts to little more than rationalization. We invent reasons to show that what we desire is good. But this does not seem to be true to moral experience. As contemporary philosopher Michael Sandel writes, 'Values and ends must have a sanction independent of the fact that I happen

---

๑ Applied Philosophy Box 2.5 ๑

Elicitors of Disgust

This is from a scientific paper on the origin of the human experience of disgust:

> We suggest that the objects or events which elicit disgust can be placed in the following five broad categories: 1. Bodily excretions and body parts 2. Decay and spoiled food 3. Particular living creatures 4. Certain categories of 'other people'. 5. Violations of morality or social norms. Bodily secretions are the most widely reported elicitors of the disgust emotion. Feces appear on all of the lists, while vomit, sweat, spittle, blood, pus, and sexual fluids appear frequently. Body parts, such as nail clippings, cut hair, intestines, and wounds, evoke disgust, as do dead bodies. . . . Spoiled food, especially meat and fish, and other decaying substances, such as rubbish, are disgusting to many respondents. . . . Material that is seen to be 'dirty' or contaminated, such as a stained toilet, clothes, sheets, or teeth, or rubbish on a beach, also cued disgust. . . . Food leftovers that may have been touched by saliva, salad that has had insects in it, and food that has been cooked by a menstruating woman can become disgusting by actual or imagined contact.

These medical researchers go on to argue that humans naturally feel repugnance toward those things that lead typically to infection and disease. Moral realists, in a somewhat parallel way, claim that we can use our intelligence to identify beneficial and harmful features of the world. Certain things (such as virtue, love, friendship, fairness, pleasure, beauty, and knowledge) are objectively good; other things (including disease and infection) are objectively bad. We are smart enough to realize this—and this is the beginning of morality. (Note, however, that the mere experience of disgust is not quite a moral category. To be moral is to feel disgust at the appropriate objects—but more on this and related issues in later chapters.)

Source: Valerie Curtis and Adam Biran, 'Dirt, Disgust, and Disease: Is Hygiene in Our Genes?' *Perspectives in Biology and Medicine* 44.1 (2001): 20-22-31. Available online at *Project MUSE*, http://muse.jhu.edu/journals/perspectives_in_biology_and_medicine/v044/44.1curtis.html.

to hold them with a certain intensity'.[21] If I am passionately attached to particular aims, this does not necessarily mean that these aims are legitimate, commendable, or valuable. Moral vision, on the moral realist account, provides a standard, a measuring stick by which our desires are to be evaluated.

Moral realists do not have to adopt the kind of crude realism noncognitivists like Mackie deride. We can claim that there are things in the world that are inherently good without asserting that moral goodness is an invisible, immaterial object. Nor does the realist have to argue for an exclusive realism, as if the goodness in the object is only in the object and not, in any sense, in the mind. Obviously, there is an interior aspect to moral cognition; we have an inner experience of the goodness of things. It does not follow from this that there is no sense in which goodness resides in the world. Let us return to our example of the red firetruck. It makes sense to say both that the firetruck really is red and that an experience of redness somehow enters the mind. It is not red because we have decided to see it as red; it is red because redness (properly understood) is an objective feature of the world that *causes* the mental state we call red.

Likewise if certain things are objectively good—if they are good in themselves, the way the firetruck is red—that does not mean that our knowledge of this goodness is not dependent on moral understanding. Moral realism requires a belief that the judgments of goodness in our mind, properly made, correspond, more or less accurately, with the objective goodness of things in the world. We access the firetruck's redness through perception, whereas we access the goodness of things either through direct understanding, or sometimes—when we reflect on things, for example—through argu-

ment. One way or another, it is intelligence or reason that allows us to 'see' the goodness of things in the world.

Sometimes, debates about moral realism converge on one speculative issue: if there were no human beings in the world, would good and evil exist? From the perspective of moral realism, the answer seems relatively straightforward. Without humans—that is, without animals who can distinguish between right and wrong—there still could be bad things in the world, such as disease or suffering, and there could be good things, like the beauty of a rainbow. But there would be no one to appreciate such goodness or badness. And there would be no one who could deliberately act in a good or a bad manner.

Moral realists understand that the evaluation of the goodness and badness of things is complicated, especially because many things are sometimes good, sometimes bad. Having your legs cut off, for example, is normally a very bad thing, but if you are suffering from gangrene, it may be a good thing as it is the only way to save your life. (You can think of other examples.) When moral realists refer to the good things in the world, they are usually trying to identify those things that have enduring value, those things that are valuable on their own account and thus valuable in all (or most) circumstances. For example, I might argue that health is an objective good. We may have to make a choice between health and a more important good (say, loyalty to a cause), but health derives its value from what it is, not from the specific circumstances. Alternatively, I might argue that love is an objective good. Insomuch as we love one another, it is good. Love may even be the most important good, but one way or another, it is something that *reason* correctly values *independent of the circumstances.*

Philosophers, in discussing such issues, naturally attempt to identify the most fundamental good of all. Different authors offer different answers: pleasure, happiness, human flourishing, inner peace, truth, love, loyalty, duty, religious salvation, and morality itself. Some claim that 'the good' is irreducible to other properties. Most famously, Plato argues that there is a metaphysical reality he calls 'idea of the good' that transcends all the particular instances of goodness we encounter in the world. In this mystical doctrine, individual good things in the world participate in a universal idea of the good. This is the source of their goodness.

Plato is an extreme moral realist. He does not claim simply that the good exists outside us, but that weak human nature is not powerful enough to catch a glimpse of the good on its own. It is the idea of the good that gives 'the power of knowing to the knower'.[22] We can only discern the good because it opens our minds to the unchanging, invisible reality of itself. If Plato's description of the good as a nonphysical, unobservable entity seems too antiquated to be taken seriously, note that a *modern* British thinker such as G.E. Moore (1873–1958) comes to similar conclusions. Moore uses his 'open question test' to prove that the good is an undefinable, nonnatural, simple property that cannot be further analyzed into anything more basic.[23] His proof revolves around a simple point of logic. Consider this strange-sounding pronouncement: 'the good is good.' This is like saying 'green is green'. Nothing could be more obvious. Of course, the good is good! This kind of statement, which is always true, is what is called, in logic, a **tautology**. It makes no sense to deny or even question a tautology. Moore noticed, however, that something very odd happens when we substitute different definitions of the good into the question 'Is the good, good?'

Suppose we try to define the good in terms of some natural property like pleasure. If the good is pleasure, then the question 'Is pleasure good?' should mean the same thing as the question 'Is good, good?' But the question 'Is the pleasure good?' is not (unlike the latter question) an obvious tautology. We can legitimately question whether pleasure is good. Moore concludes that pleasure cannot be the good. Indeed, he believes that we cannot come up with a satisfactory definition of the good in terms of any other property or feature of existence, for we can always meaningfully ask, 'Is this feature of existence good?' Suppose we define the good as 'that which we desire', or even as 'that which we desire to desire'. We can legitimately ask, 'Is that which we desire good?' or even, 'Is that which we desire to desire good?' Try other examples yourself. Whenever you substitute a new term into the question 'Is the good, good?' you will end up with something that is not a self-evident tautology. Moore concludes that the good is an unanalyzable, self-sufficient notion that cannot be defined in terms of anything else. His compatriot Iris Murdoch (1919–99) further develops these ideas in a suggestive way.

Moral Realism: Evil

It is important to point out that moral realists believe that evil does not have the same metaphysical status as the good. It is not that the term **evil** does not indicate something true about the world. Any keen observer of human behaviour will have to confront the reality of evil (as evidenced by some of the examples in this book). Consider evil here as a wide term denoting both natural evil (including disease, suffering, death) and, more specifically, moral evil, the evil human beings deliberately do. Moral realists believe that evil generally is different from good in that the good has an independent, real existence whereas evil derives, in every instance, from some kind of imperfection or corruption of the good. The good can exist on its own, but evil cannot exist on its own, for the evil always has to do with a good thing that fails to achieve its full potential. It is this failure that we call evil. In this traditional view, evil is parasitic on the good.

This familiar account of evil as privation is most readily associated with St. Augustine of Hippo (354–430 AD), who derived it from earlier authors, such as the Roman philosopher Plotinus. Augustine compares evil to a wound or a disease. He writes, 'what is called evil in the universe is but the absence of the good'.[24] Suppose I take out a switchblade and gouge a piece out of your shoulder. The resulting injury is not something that naturally develops in a healthy muscle. The blood, the bruise, the searing pain, the infection, and the resulting lack of movement are genuine, objective features of the world. But they are, most fundamentally, caused by the *absence*, not the presence, of something. As Augustine explains,

> In the bodies of animals, disease and wounds mean nothing but the *absence* of health; for when a cure is effected, that does not mean that the evils which were present—namely, the diseases and wounds—go away from the body and dwell elsewhere: they altogether cease to exist; for the wound or disease is . . . but a defect in the fleshly substance,—the flesh itself being . . . something good, of which those evils [are] privations of the good which we call health.[25]

Augustine claims that evil happens when something good is somehow deformed, corrupted, or damaged. Evil is always dependent on a prior good. Let us turn to an Augustinian example. Lying is generally considered to be inherently bad. Without the good of truth-telling, however, there would be no lies. Lies happen when a being who is capable of telling the truth fails to realize this possibility. Likewise for liars. Liars are damaged human beings who fail to achieve their full potential as rational beings who are able to tell the truth. According to Augustine, at any rate.

In popular culture at least, we tend to view morality as a mere limitation, as something that holds us back from doing what we want to do. In the eyes of the tradition, however, this is to misunderstand our own goodness. Originality, creativity, telling funny stories, the power of exaggeration, and the art of embellishment (properly used) *are* positive human traits, while the actual telling of lies is a defect; it is like an injury to human rationality. Lying involves the frustration, not the development, of authentically human traits. Although Augustine's concerns are largely theological, his view of the metaphysical nature of evil coincides with the general thrust of mainstream moral philosophy. The earliest authors believe that morality is not, in any deep sense, a negative or destructive factor. Yes, morality may require self-discipline and self-sacrifice; it may require a positive shaping of human nature, much like the pruning of a diseased and overgrown tree. But understood in a more careful way, morality always means holding back from what injures and harms us. This traditional view avoids some of the problems associated with more recent accounts of morality, which we discuss in future chapters.

Why Should I Be Moral?
A Self-Interested Challenge

We will now turn briefly to a different kind of challenge to moral reasoning. Some philosophers argue flatly against morality on the grounds that it is *not* in our self-interest to be moral. If morality means, roughly, doing good to others, these philosophers ask an awkward question: What is in it for us? This challenge may strike the moral person as self-centred. Nonetheless, this why-should-I-be-moral question requires some answers.

The most famous exposition of the why-be-moral problem can be found in Plato's *The Republic*. We will discuss his answer to the puzzle in Chapter 4. Contemporary philosophers, investigating the same issue, express similar concerns in economic language. Consider what happens in a market setting. I buy at the best price I can get; you sell at the best price you can get. You do what is good for you and I do what is good for me. This free-market approach to politics and society has won a large following who argue, with some plausibility, that this is the most efficient way to organize a prosperous society. We need not debate the issue here. What is important for our purposes is that this economic model works efficiently when rational agents *maximize* their self-interest, that is, when they do what is best for themselves. But how do we square this with morality, which often requires that we transcend self-interest and selflessly focus on what is best for *other* people? Historical authors offer different answers to this question. Let us briefly consider the general problem here.

Traditional Criticism: Wrong Question

First, many earlier philosophers would insist that this is not a properly formulated question.

The problem is not with the question itself (which traditional authors, such as Plato, spend considerable time answering). The problem is that the kind of answer contemporary philosophers are looking for is not available, and for several reasons.

Contemporary authors who ask this question (such as Jan Narveson and David Gauthier, for example) view ethics as a logical puzzle. The goal is the resolution of an apparent paradox. We need to be able to show that, despite appearances to the contrary, morality is in our self-interest. These authors posit the existence of a hypothetical amoral person: a person who has no ethical commitments and is purely self-interested. The idea is that this person is neither moral nor immoral but, rather, neutral, unbiased. If morality really is good for us, we should be able to convince this impartial judge that it is in his or her self-interest to act morally. Ethics, seen in this light, is a matter of successfully convincing (hypothetical) amoral agents that they should be moral. However, historical authors would reject this method of doing ethics.

As we have already mentioned, historical philosophers have a much wider conception of morality than modern theorists do. In the older view, anyone who operates according to a coherent value system embraces some form of morality. These philosophers never set about showing amoral people that it is in their best interest to be moral. Why? Because they believe that there are no amoral people! Doubtless, there are confused people, people who believe falsehoods, and people who act in ways we justly condemn. But even the most immoral people have some grounding in basic morality. Everyone is moral to some extent. The project of moral philosophy is to clear up this moral confusion. Historical philosophers

---

∽ Applied Philosophy Box 2.6 ∾

The New Economics and the Pursuit of Happiness

Neoclassical economists had insisted upon the primacy of self-interest only in order to model human behaviour, but the way rational choice theory developed (at the University of Chicago in particular) suggested that self-interest was not just a fact for these thinkers, but also an ideal: not just how people do act but also how they should act. Their relentless advocacy of market-based public policies was finally ideological—and, by my lights, ideologically wrong.

Alan Wolfe questions the 'ideological bent' of the free-market economics of self-interest: the idea that (1) people always act so as to maximize self-interest and that (2) this is how people should act. What do you think?

Source: Alan Wolfe, 'The New Economics and the Pursuit of Happiness'. *The New Republic*, 9 July 2008.

---

are not in the business of convincing people who do not believe in anything ethical that they should be moral. They would view this effort as a red herring, a logical distraction. They want to iron out the wrinkles in the morality most of us already have.

A Narrowly Economic Account of Rationality

A second overlapping problem with contemporary treatments of the why-be-moral problem is the extreme narrowness of the modern, economic model of rationality. The term *rational animal* suggests a penchant for the pursuit of knowledge. But the pursuit of knowledge is its own reward. Indeed, it requires a *selfless* devotion to the truth. If I want to find out what is true about science, should I focus on doing what is in my self-interest? No, what is in my self-interest is beside the point. So if I want to discover the truth about ethics, why should I always be asking myself 'Is this in my self-interest?' or 'Am I acting *economically*?' This is a distraction. Of course, these are legitimate questions about appropriate behaviour in the

marketplace, but all of life does not take place in the marketplace. Ethics is a form of rationality; it is, in the first instance, about the pursuit of knowledge; even practical reason requires a larger understanding of the world and human nature. Authors discussing the why-be-moral problem tend to reduce the traditional notion of practical reason to modern economic notions of self-interest. Practical reason includes but is not limited to notions of self-interest. *Homo economicus* ('economic man') is at best a crude simplification. Human beings do not always act out of economic motives. The baker has the right to expect a fair price for his bread, and he deserves a good living from what he does. At the same time, most moral philosophers would argue that the baker must give his bread away for free in times of famine. Why? Because people are starving. What this shows is that there are times and occasions when market calculations are out of place. It is not that such calculations are inherently wrong. It is that the market rationality and market practices must be situated within a much larger picture of human aspiration. Traditional authors are not against self-interest, but self-interest needs to be informed by ethical considerations.

Selflessness as Essence of Morality

The third problem with posing the why-should-I-be-moral question in terms of whether or not I can profit from morality is that it undermines the selflessness that great thinkers in the past locate at the heart of morality. Even if I could convince you that you would profit, in some nonmoral sense, from morality, any such strategy would be self-defeating. Morality must be motivated by a disinterested commitment to goodness. If you are doing what is right, not because it is right but because it is to your own advantage, you are not, in the best sense of the word, acting morally.

Morally Neutral Agents Do Not Know

One final problem with the why-be-moral approach is the unexamined assumption that a neutral, amoral judge, someone who is not already committed to morality, would be in the best position to evaluate moral arguments. Suppose there were people who had never tasted food. Imagine they had survived on an intravenous drip all their lives. Would we run to them for advice about gastronomy? In the traditional view, morality is a form of intelligence. Even if human beings could exist apart from all morality (and they cannot), morally neutral agents would not be objective judges of human behaviour. They would be obtuse—brazenly, blindingly stupid. Why on earth would we run to such people for advice? If morality is a joy, how would they ever know? Only those who are truly moral over an extended period of time can understand the sense of interior well-being and self-esteem that accompanies morality. They have a personal experience that philosophical arguments cannot replace.

Human beings who have no experience of morality cannot know what these people are talking about. This would be reason enough to discount their 'neutral' views, not to appeal to them.

Psychological Egoism

The predominance of economic thinking has fueled a widespread cynicism about the possibility of moral selflessness. Naysayers about morality like to appeal to **psychological egoism**, which is mostly a theory about human nature. Proponents of psychological egoism argue that all our actions are motivated by self-interest. When we seem to act out of a selfless concern for others, we are really seeking our own psychological self-gratification. We act morally only because we want to feel good about ourselves. Fernande, the lady next door, may think that she gives generously to charity without expecting anything in return, but she really gives to charity only because it makes her feel good about herself. On this view of human nature, all this fine moral talk about giving and expecting nothing in return is only a cover for the narcissistic pleasures of thinking we are something grand. We do what is right for the psychological reward—so that we can secretly congratulate ourselves on our own good deeds.

The main problem with psychological egoism is that it is entirely unfalsifiable. We can never get inside other people's heads. So how could we ever prove that psychological egoism is right or wrong? We can always read self-interest into other people's motives, correctly or incorrectly. To explain human behaviour through an appeal to secret, invisible motives that all people hide from themselves is more like an unverifiable assumption than a genuine scientific hypothesis. One could respond to those who brandish psychological egoism as an argument against all morality that they are only reading their own self-centred motives into other people.

It certainly seems that some people genuinely do good things without expecting anything in return. People give up their lives for moral causes and for loved ones. Suppose, however, that psychological egoism is true. Suppose your neighbour, Fernande, does give large sums to charity in order to feel good about herself. Proponents of this theory still cannot explain *why* practising charity makes her feel this way. The moral realist, however, might say, 'She *should* feel good because charity is a genuine accomplishment'. Because traditional authors associate morality with self-esteem, it doesn't follow that psychological egoism is correct.

Psychological egoism confuses the results of an activity with its aim. Because we feel good about ourselves when we act morally, it does not follow that we act morally *in order to* feel good about ourselves. Suppose I spend a lot of time doing manual labour on my farm, which causes me to grow physically stronger. Because this farmwork makes me physically strong, it does not follow that I work on the farm *in order to* become physically strong. I may enjoy feeling physically strong—it may even increase my sense of self-esteem. Still, it does not follow that boosting self-esteem is the main purpose of the work. Likewise for morality. It is definitely good for one's self-esteem, but it does not follow that this is why we act morally. It is a *good* thing to experience a (modest) sense of accomplishment, but this need not detract from the selfless spirit of morality.

In any case, psychological egoism seems a simplification. What does it mean to feel good about oneself. Self-esteem is not just a momentary matter of self-congratulation. Self-esteem encompasses decisiveness, authenticity, cheerfulness, peace of mind, integrity, consistency, and optimal functioning, all of which characterize the most successful human beings. At least this is how historical philosophers view self-esteem. Seen this way, you *should* aim for self-esteem—not for self-centred pleasure, but for a state of optimal human flourishing that produces and includes a healthy sense of self-respect. Self-esteem, in this sense, is not merely compatible with selfless behaviour; it is a requirement for selfless behaviour. Without inner strength and a consistent sense of self-worth, one would not be capable of noble deeds and true generosity.

In the mainline historical view, moral philosophy is, in part, about needling us and prodding us to be better. Philosophers who pose the why-should-I-be-moral question risk legitimizing an excessive amount of self-interest. To orient moral philosophy around the working assumption that we need a reward for being moral is already to slip into a self-centred attitude, which is less than ideal.

Moral Philosophy Requires Objectivity and Subjectivity

Moral philosophy, like any other philosophy, requires logic. In the following chapters, we will explain and critically examine examples of logical mistakes, such as begging the question (not offering any evidence for your position), contradiction (claiming that the same statement is both true and false), and equivocation (surreptitiously changing the meaning of a key term). Let us finish the present chapter, however, with a brief word about the intellectual virtues that facilitate and prompt successful moral reasoning. We can organize our discussion around the twin concepts of objectivity and subjectivity.

Objectivity is a virtue. Understood as an intellectual disposition, it can be roughly defined as the ability to distance oneself from any partisan personal perspective and fairly consider the evidence. As we have seen, some philosophers identify rationality with economic self-interest. But economic self-interest focuses on whatever is personally advantageous. This is not, in the most fundamental sense, what reason is about. Reason—understood as a power of intelligent discernment—tries to understand morality from an impartial point of view, irrespective of our particular place within the world.

Adam Smith, the famous Scottish economist and moral philosopher (1723–90), traces the origins of morality, not to human sentiment but to hard-edged reason—understood as the power to think objectively. Smith refers to the **impartial spectator** situated in the heart and mind of each human being. If we want to understand what morality requires, we need only to imagine how this 'inhabitant of the breast, the man within' would react upon seeing us act in a specified way. Smith, who views morality largely from the viewpoint of duty, identifies as the epitome of moral success 'the wise and just man' who has, with time and practice, come to fully identify with the judgments of the impartial spectator within himself. He explains:

> In success and in disappointment, in prosperity and in adversity, before friends and before enemies, . . . he has never dared to forget for one moment the judgment which the impartial spectator would pass upon his sentiments and conduct. He has never dared to suffer the man within the breast to be absent one moment from his attention. With the eyes of this great inmate [and interior companion] he has always been accustomed to regard whatever relates to himself. . . . He has been in the constant practice, and, indeed, under the constant necessity, of modelling, . . . even his inward sentiments and feelings, according to those of this awful and respectable judge. He does not merely affect the sentiments of the impartial spectator. He really adopts them. He almost identifies himself with, he almost becomes himself that impartial spectator, and scarce even feels but as that great arbiter of his conduct directs him to feel.[26]

Good moral reasoning requires a certain distancing from our own partisan feelings and preferences. If Smith's stern account of impartial reason will strike some readers as somewhat cold, there are other ways to describe the widening of personal perspective that objectivity requires. To cite one other example, the continental German author Edith Stein, who died in Auschwitz (1891–1942), speaks of **empathy** (*Einfühlung*) as the objective experience of crossing over and entering inside someone else. This is a kind of objectivity—an objectivity of feeling. Stein does not portray empathy as mere sympathy, or pity, or even imitation (you cry, I cry). It 'is the experience of foreign consciousness'.[27] Somehow, we enter into someone else and view their world as our own. Stein does not think that we can force this experience on ourselves. We feel empathy the way we fall in love—it just happens. All of a sudden, we understand the other person from the inside-out! That is, if we are open to others. Whereas Smith asserts the importance of strict impartiality, Stein paradoxically develops a notion of objectivity as feeling through a *different* observer. Empathy requires a similar movement outside ourselves, away from an exclusively self-centred perspective. This larger understanding of things seems a prerequisite for good ethical reasoning.

But life is complicated. While moral reasoning requires objectivity, it also presupposes the

✎ Applied Philosophy Box 2.7 ✎

Deep Down, We Can't Fool Even Ourselves

Two psychologists, Piercarlo Valdesolo and David DeSteno, tested people's reactions to the following situation. You show up for an experiment and are told that you and a person arriving later will each have to do a different task on a computer. One job involves a fairly easy hunt through photos that will take just 10 minutes. The other task is a more tedious exercise in mental geometry that takes 45 minutes.

You get to decide how to divvy up the chores: either let a computer assign the tasks randomly, or make the assignments yourself. Either way, the other person will not know you had anything to do with the assignments. Now, what is the fair way to divvy up the chores? When the researchers posed this question in the abstract to people who were not involved in the tasks, everyone gave the same answer: It would be unfair to give yourself the easy job.

But when the researchers actually put another group of people in this situation, more than three-quarters of them took the easy job. Then, under subsequent questioning, they gave themselves high marks for acting fairly. The researchers call this moral hypocrisy . . . [Later, they asked] some of these people . . . to memorize a list of numbers and retain it in their heads as they answered questions about the experiment and their actions. That little bit of extra mental exertion was enough to eliminate hypocrisy. These people judged their own actions just as harshly as others did. Their brains were apparently too busy to rationalize their selfishness, so they fell back on their intuitive feelings about fairness.

This experiment seems to show that 'bad faith' takes hard work. When these subjects were forced to expend significant mental energy on a separate task, they were unable to come up with the mental effort needed to keep up false appearances. This is a relatively minor case of immorality. One wonders how much energy must be expended on self-defence mechanisms in serious cases of bad faith.

Source: John Tierney, 'Deep Down, We Can't Fool Even Ourselves.' *NYTimes.com*, www.nytimes.com/2008/07/01/science/01tier.html?em&ex=1215316800&en=9d338334a2c1ca0b&ei=5087%0A, 1 July 2008.

right kind of relationship to ourselves. There is a subjective aspect to moral experience. We need, to borrow an overused expression, to remain in touch with ourselves, not only with our deepest emotions but also with interior reason, with the power for moral discernment that makes us human. We can be inauthentic, phony, hypocritical. This is a serious obstacle to moral achievement.

French existentialist Jean Paul Sartre (1905–80) uses the term **bad faith** (*mauvaise foi*) to describe a chronic condition of insincerity.

Sartre (who focuses on psychological description rather than moral judgment) points to the contradictory nature of such behaviour. When we tell an ordinary lie, we tell someone else a falsehood. When we practise bad faith, we try to tell ourselves a falsehood: 'The one to whom the lie is told and the one who lies are one and the same person.'[28] But this seems impossible. As Sartre explains, when I practise bad faith, 'I must know in my capacity as deceiver the truth which is hidden from me in my capacity as the one deceived. Better yet I must know the truth

. . . not at two different moments . . . but in the unitary structure of a single [moment]'.[29] People who practise bad faith know that they are deceiving themselves and yet they continue to try and believe in this self-admitted falsehood. Bad faith is a lie that inevitably fails. It keeps collapsing into an awareness of its own dishonesty. It results in a kind of split personality: in people who are divided against themselves. Yet Sartre suggests that bad faith pervades modern life: 'Even though the existence of bad faith is very precarious . . . it can even be the normal aspect of life for a very great number of people.'[30] If we believe what other people believe, we do not escape the problem. Our peer group may be practising bad faith as well.

Sartre's concept of bad faith can serve as a reminder of the importance of honest self-knowledge. There are other ways of describing what can go wrong with the relationship of the self to the self. Complacency, smugness, pretentiousness, insincerity, despair, and so on: these varied conditions all detract from any serious attempt to understand ourselves. We cannot come to moral knowledge unless we simultaneously embrace objective standards while honestly listening to what is going on inside ourselves. Morality is objective but it arises from some subjective experience of personal authenticity. Moral reasoning requires, in addition to logical argument, probing, forthright introspection.

❧ Questions for Study and Review ❧

1. What is epistemology?
2. What is logic?
3. What is intuition?
4. What is the difference between logic and intuition?
5. Explain what *the principle of sufficient reason* maintains.
6. Explain *burden of proof.*
7. Explain the concept of unfalsifiability. Why is an unfalsifiable theory less than rational?
8. Viewed from a sociobiological perspective, what is the purpose of marriage? Viewed from an ethical perspective, what is the purpose of marriage?
9. What is noncognitivism? Explain the basic tenets of this school.
10. What is theoretical reason?
11. What is practical reason?
12. Define *empirical knowledge*. What does this have to do with moral philosophy?
13. Give a *nonmoral* example of an argument or explanation that commits the 'is–ought' fallacy.
14. What is Moore's open question argument?
15. Augustine thinks that evil is like a hole in a boat. Explain.
16. Describe the doctrine of psychological egoism.
17. Describe Smith's theory of the impartial spectator. What necessary aspect of morality does he emphasize?
18. Describe Stein's account of empathy. What necessary aspect of morality does she emphasize?
19. Describe Sartre's account of bad faith. Why is this a puzzling condition?
20. How could we at least begin a cure for bad faith?

✒ Suggestions for Further Reading ✑

- A.J. Ayer, Language, *Truth and Logic* (New York: Dover Publications, 1946), see especially Chapter 6.
- David Hume *A Treatise of Human Nature*, David Fate Norton (Editor), Mary J. Norton (Oxford UK: Oxford, 2001). Book 2, 'Of the Passions', and Book 3, 'Of Morals', provide an accessible look at an early-modern emotivist perspective on ethics and the resulting epistemological issues. Hume is a good writer.
- For electronic version see: David Hume, *A Treatise of Human Nature* (original 1739 edition), ebooks@ Adelaide, 2006, http://etext.library.adelaide.edu. au/h/hume/david/.
- J.L. Mackie, *Ethics: Inventing Right and Wrong* (Harmoondsworth: Penguin, 1977).
- For something up-to-date, the beginner may find a bit technical, try: Antonio Marturano, 'Non-Cognitivism in Ethics', *The Internet Encyclopedia of Philosophy*, www. iep.utm.edu/non-cogn/.
- Also, Doris Schroeder, 'Evolutionary Ethics', *The Internet Encyclopedia of Philosophy*, www.iep.utm.edu/ evol-eth/#H3.

Chapter Three

The Early Tradition: From Confucius to Jesus and Beyond

✎ Chapter Objectives

After reading this chapter you should be able to:

- Explain the historical origins of moral philosophy in the ancient world.
- Identify the doctrines and principles of the major schools of ancient moral philosophy that flourished alongside Plato and Aristotle.
- Insert important individual thinkers, such as Confucius (Master Kong), Epictetus, Epicurus, Diogenes, and Jesus, into a larger historical context.
- Apply these doctrines to everyday problems in the contemporary world.
- Critically evaluate some of the shortcomings of these different moral philosophies.

Introduction

Although the discipline of philosophy tends toward careful arguments, rigorous theories, and comprehensive systems, this is not how moral traditions began. In both the East and the West, moral philosophy begins with exceptional individuals, sages, who make a reputation for moral understanding with wise words and sometimes dramatic acts. These early philosophers were as much role models as theoreticians. They were often known for their exploits and for their conversations and behaviour rather than for what they wrote down. Generally, they set a very high standard of behaviour, a virtuous ideal for others to follow. They used arguments but were not, for the most part, specialists in logical disputation. They did not strive to elaborate exhaustive, all-embracing logical systems in words; they bore witness, rather, through their individual gestures and remarks to a particular approach to life. It was often their later followers who collected their sayings and reported on the incidents of their lives, tying them together so as to elucidate the coherent pattern of belief and attitude that motivated them. What resulted is a wisdom literature, comprised of proverbs, witty remarks, personal advice, theoretical principles, outrageous stories, fables, and anecdotes. All this goes into the mix to produce what is, at times, some profoundly challenging and insightful moral theories.

We will consider, in order, the Chinese sage Confucius; the pre-Socratic thinkers Heraclitus and Democritus; a central figure in Cynicism, Diogenes of Sinope; Epicurus and his school; a prominent Roman Stoic, Epictetus; the skeptics Pyrrho and Sextus Empiricus; the most famous Greek Sophist, Protagoras; and finally, Jesus. Contemporary moral philosophers largely overlook these early thinkers. This is unfortunate for they left an indelible mark on future generations. Confucius was the mainstay of a proper Chinese education for centuries; Roman Stoicism ruled the philosophical world for a period of about five hundred years, and one can hardly think of a more influential individual in the Western tradition than Jesus.

If these thinkers have often been set aside, it is largely because they produced an unsystematic kind of philosophy. They were not, first and foremost, theoreticians and academics, but saints and sages. They did not construct the kind of comprehensive, technical logical systems attempted by synoptic philosophers like Aristotle, Thomas Aquinas, Immanuel Kant, or John Stuart Mill. They were content to propose practical philosophy as a way of life. There is no need to belittle their accomplishments for their insights still ring true. Indeed, we could argue that later philosophers only systematized and expanded on the moral understanding these earlier authors bequeathed to future generations. We can use these first

building blocks of moral theory as a foundation for our own understanding.

When we study the extant manuscripts from this period, a coherent picture emerges as to what morality is all about. We do discover important, even ferocious disagreements among some early authors, but seeing these differences through the lens of history allows us to get a better grasp on the underlying principles all these authors share. Although notions of moral law can be traced far back in history, early philosophers mostly did virtue-ethics, sketching out a picture of the ideal human being for followers to emulate. They discussed happiness at length, associating it, for the most part, with peace of mind rather than with joyful exultation. They acknowledged the suffering and failure that attends even the most fortunate human life and suggested ways for coping with human frailness and mortality. They agreed, in general, that we will not be happy unless we act in accordance with nature, often understood as the universe with all its laws to which we owe humble allegiance. Indeed, this might be taken as the most important principle of all: *act in accordance with nature*. In figures like Jesus and Socrates (whom we will discuss in Chapter 4)—even in Pyrrho, the skeptic—we see the beginnings of a morality that pushes us to transcend nature, not in a way that destroys or negates what is lower, but that completes, refines, and perfects it.

Master Kong (Confucius): *Dao*

Although we cannot explore the Eastern tradition at length, we should point out that early moral philosophy comes from a common fund of practical, everyday shrewdness that transcends distinct cultural, linguistic, and even religious barriers. East and West are not so different when it comes to the first stirrings of systematic moral thought. Consider, then, the ancient Chinese thinker Confucius.

The name *Confucius* is the Latinized version of '*Kong fuzi*' or 'Master Kong'. Master Kong is thought to have lived in the fifth century BC (traditionally, 551–479 BC), just about the time of the Greek philosophers we discuss beginning on page 67. Although we know very little about his life, there is one small book entitled *The Analects*, which consists of about 500 short anecdotes about Master Kong or his disciples.[1] This commentary ranges from very matter-of-fact descriptions of specific events to more enigmatic utterances. Although **Confucianism** developed into a complicated pedagogical tradition in later China, we will limit ourselves to the contents of this original prose source here.

In a conservative society based on class structure, Master Kong begins by associating moral merit with noble birth. His moral philosophy rests on a pivotal comparison between two types of characters: the '**gentleman**' or 'ruler's son' (*junzi*) and '**the small man**' (*xiao ren*). Master Kong uses these standardized types as foils to teach the difference between virtue and vice. As would be expected in a highly stratified, aristocratic society, the gentleman is presented as socially and morally superior; the small man is one of the uncouth masses. But social differences recede into the background as the ideal of the 'gentleman' increasingly takes on a moral meaning. The difference between the gentleman and the small man comes to represent, roughly, the difference between moral success and moral failure. Noble *behaviour* becomes more important than noble *birth*.

Master Kong tells us this:

1. 'The gentleman reaches out for what is above, the small man reaches out for what is below.'[2]

2. 'The gentleman is dignified but not arrogant. The small man is arrogant but not dignified.'[3]

3. 'The gentleman is familiar with what is right [i.e. with morality], just as a small man is familiar with profit.'[4]

4. 'The gentleman cherishes virtue, but the small man cherishes soil [i.e., property]; the gentleman cherishes the rigors of the law, but the small man cherishes leniency [i.e., being able to get away with things].'[5]

5. 'The gentleman is calm and peaceful; the small man is always emotional.'[6]

6. 'The gentleman has universal sympathies and is not partisan. The small man is partisan and does not have universal sympathies.'[7]

7. 'The gentleman brings to completion the fine qualities in others and does not bring to completion the bad qualities in others. The small man does the opposite of this.'[8]

8. 'The gentleman, although he behaves in a conciliatory manner, does not make his views coincide with those of others; the small man, although he makes his views coincide with others, does not behave in a conciliatory manner.'[9]

9. 'The gentleman remains firm in the face of suffering, but if the small man suffers, he is carried away on a flood of excess.'[10]

10. '[The gentleman] is in awe of the decree of Heaven, . . . in awe of great men, and . . . in awe of the words of sages. The small man, being unaware of the decree of Heaven, is not in awe of it. He is rude to great men and ridicules the words of sages.'[11]

11. 'The nature of the gentleman is as the wind, and the nature of the small man is as the grass. When the wind blows over the grass it always bends.'[12]

This is virtue ethics; indeed, it is morality through character sketch. The criterion for what we ought to do is not a set of rules but an ideal of superior character. We are to aim, not merely at wealth or power or social status, but at virtue. To be a true gentleman, then, it is not enough to have fine clothes, a magnificent house, property, many servants, a position in government, notoriety. To be a true gentleman is to be *morally* superior.

In Master Kong's mind, the individual and the society are inescapably intertwined. Indeed, Master Kong sees his principal role as preparing men for public office. Studying morality, i.e., studying the moral wisdom of the past, is a civic duty. As one of his disciples declares, 'If one has more than enough energy for office, then one studies; and if one has more than enough energy for study, then one holds office'.[13] So the active life and the thinking life, the life of politics and the life of moral philosophy are not opposed; indeed, they are inseparable.

Master Kong has been criticized for his conservatism, one reason why Communist leaders disapproved of his teachings in modern China. While Master Kong does accept the social hierarchy of the time (as part of the larger order of nature), he places added responsibilities on the shoulders of the nobles and upper classes. He explains their social role in an exchange with a student. The text narrates a story:

> Zilu asked about the gentleman. The Master said: 'He cultivates himself in order to show reverence'. 'Is that all he does?' asked Zilu. The Master said, 'He cultivates himself so as to bring tranquillity to others'. 'Is that all he does?' Zilu again asked. The Master said: 'He cultivates himself so as to bring tranquillity to the hundred surnames [i.e., to the mass of people]'.[14]

In other words, the gentleman cultivates himself so that there will be peace throughout the land.

Master Kong believes that morally good rulers inevitably produce prosperous, just societies. It is like a law of nature. 'If good men ran a state for a hundred years', he claims, 'they might therefore vanquish cruelty and abolish killing'.[15] When asked point-blank whether the ruler should kill those who are not moral, Master Kong responds that they must rule by example. If a ruler does his best to be good, his subjects will try to be good as well,[16] for 'Gentlemen are proud but not quarrelsome'[17] and 'The gentleman is correct but not inflexible'.[18]

We might be tempted to dismiss Master Kong's moral code as little more than court etiquette for civil servants and bureaucrats. But this would be hasty and unfair. Master Kong's moral wisdom strikes a very deep cord. If Jesus is credited with the Golden Rule, 'Do unto others as you would have them do unto you',[19] Master Kong comes up with a negative version of the same principle: 'Do not impose on others what you would not like yourself'.[20] Or, as he expresses the thought in a different passage, 'Do not inflict on others what you yourself would not wish done to you'.[21] This basic principle, often referred to as the **Silver Rule**, is largely self-explanatory. Master Kong equates morality with unfailing goodness: gentlemen 'repay hostility with uprighteousness and repay kindness with kindness'.[22] They *never* do evil to others. But reaching such heights is a strenuous achievement. When one of his disciples says, 'If I do not want others to inflict something on me, I also want to avoid inflicting it on others', Master Kong gently chides him: 'this is not a point you have yet reached'.[23] In other words, complying fully with the Silver Rule is such an extraordinary accomplishment, few people ever manage to do this consistently.

Master Kong believes that there is a larger design or order to reality and that morally superior individuals accept their role in the grander scheme of things. Although there are religious overtones to his teaching, **The Analects** is not explicitly or precisely theological. Master Kong does emphasize the importance of religious ritual (in part, as a way of keeping civilization and tradition intact), but he sees religious ceremony, as Jesus does, as an outward expression of an inner moral commitment. As he puts it, 'If someone is not humane in spite of being a man, what has he to do with [religious] ritual!'[24]

Figure 3.1 The Chinese Symbol for *Dao*

Central to Confucian teaching are notions of *Dao*, *ren*, rectification of names, moderation, and good reputation. We will begin our analysis of these five themes with the concept of *Dao*. (Figure 3.1 shows the corresponding Chinese character.)

The word **Dao** has two related meanings. First, it signifies the 'Way' with a capital *W*, meaning the interconnected structure or plan of the world that often hides behind the surface appearances of things. Second, it signifies the 'way' with a small *w*, the personal path we must follow if we are going to organize our lives in accordance with all things. Master Kong believes that the personal way we choose to live our lives must correspond to the larger Way of Nature. The wise temper their expectations and desires in accordance with the World. They do what is right and appropriate. We become sad because summer is over and

winter arrives, but the changing of the seasons is the Way of the world, and so we should accept the cold and snow without complaining. We become frustrated because we are getting old, but getting old is the Way of the world, and so we should ease into old age gracefully. We become too lazy to take good care of our children, but taking care of offspring is the Way of the World, so we should strive to be good parents. And so on. Morality requires humility. We must submit to what is greater than ourselves. We must understand how we fit into the larger picture and act accordingly.

Master Kong thinks that we must always act as if we are part of nature. At the same time, he is impressed with the special role reserved for human beings in the world. Ancient chemistry and physics focused on basic substances like water, fire, metal, wood, and wind. Master Kong believes that nature moulds humans out of these most basic elements, but he also insists that we are much more than this. If we can perish by coming into contact with physical elements, close contact with our own human nature keeps us morally alive. Master Kong declares, 'The people's connection with humanness is more important than [their connection with] water or fire. As for water and fire, I have come across people who have died through stepping on them, but I have never come across people who died through stepping on humanness'.[25]

Figure 3.2 The Chinese Symbol for *Ren*

Master Kong uses the Chinese word **ren** to refer to the supreme moral virtue. The corresponding Chinese character combines the symbol for *man* (like a two-legged stick) with the symbol for *two* (like an equal sign), so the word has something to do with the way *two human beings* should behave towards each other (see Figure 3.2). The term is variously translated into English as 'humanness', 'benevolence', 'reciprocity', 'mutuality', 'good-heartedness', or even 'love'. What makes us virtuously human is then the ability for benevolent, reciprocal, loving interaction with other human beings in particular.

Seen from the Confucian perspective, morality requires only that we act like human beings. Virtue is no further from us than our own humanity. If we really want to be ethical, we just have to be ourselves. Master Kong asks a rhetorical question: 'Is humanness [*ren*] really so far away?' And he immediately answers: 'If we ourselves wanted humanness, then humanness would arrive.'[26] Master Kong does not set out to elaborate a definition of *ren* (or humanness). He is more practical than philosophical. He tells his followers how to bring humanness into the world. The task is not complicated. The Master advises, 'Set you heart on the Way, base yourself on virtue, rely on *humanness*, and take your relaxation in the arts'.[27] Three simple virtues epitomize properly realized humanness: 'Courtesy in private life, reverence in handling business, loyalty in relationships with others'.[28] But we must be careful. We must not restrict humanness to family, friends, or even countrymen. Master Kong explicitly advises that virtue 'should not be set aside even if one visits the barbarian tribes'.[29] Humanness is to be our guide in our conduct with *all* human beings. Even distant foreigners are human by nature, and we must treat them accordingly.

Master Kong devises a strategy for good government that comes to be known by the phrase 'the **rectification of names**'. One of his faithful followers declares, 'For a long time those in authority have lost their Way and the people have become disorganized'.[30] Master Kong believes that the people will follow the Way and live virtuously *if* the rulers set a good example. When Duke Jing of Qi asks the Master about good government, Master Kong replies, 'Let a ruler be a ruler, a subject a subject, a father a father, and a son a son'. The Duke replies, 'Indeed, if a ruler be not a ruler, a subject be not a subject, a father be not a father, and a son be not a son [then society will collapse into such chaos and anarchy that], even if there is grain shall I manage to eat it?'[31] In other words, good government means acting in accordance with what we already are. Problems arise because we ignore our roles in the world: e.g., The ruler does not act as a ruler—he does not rule wisely. The father does not act as a father should—he does not raise his son with sufficient care. The son does not act as a son should—he is not obedient and respectful to his father. What results? Greed, anger, jealousy, ignorance, robbery, civil unrest, murder, and so on.

The solution to these social ills is the practice later Confucians call 'the rectification of names'. How can we restore peace and prosperity in the world? We must 'correct names'. That is, we must act so that the title we are called by corresponds to how we act. If we bear the name *ruler*, for example, we must act like a proper ruler: we must be wise, decisive, fair, merciful, and generous. If we bear the name *father*, we must act like a proper father: we must take good care of our children, supplying their needs, teaching them right from wrong, encouraging their natural talents, wisely providing for their future. If we bear the name *teacher*, we must act like a teacher; if we are a police officer, we must act like a police officer; and so on. In doing this, we will be 'correcting the names' we use to describe ourselves. In harmonious society, therefore, names correspond to reality: rulers are true rulers, fathers are true fathers, teachers are true teachers, and so on.

Master Kong, like Aristotle, recognizes the importance of **moderation**: 'If one does not get hold of moderation,' he warns, 'it is necessary to turn to either the impetuous or the [overly] cautious'.[32] The immoderate are either rash or overly careful. The impetuous try to do more than they are capable of, whereas the overly cautious do less. Neither condition is admirable. Opposite virtues and traits need to be balanced with one another: we should be neither too serious nor too silly, neither too precise nor too imprecise, neither too stubborn nor a push-over. When Master Kong reports that one of his disciples 'goes beyond' and that another 'does not arrive', and an interlocutor comments that the latter condition is better, Master Kong disagrees. Over-achieving is as much a failure as under-achieving, and doing too much is as bad as doing too little:[33] 'To go beyond is not different from not arriving.'[34]

Master Kong also connects happiness to **good reputation**. People fondly remember the good long after they are dead. He tells a story: 'Duke Jing of Qi possessed a thousand teams of four horses, but on the day he died the people had no opportunity to offer him praise. Bo Yi and Shu Qi starved at the foot of Mount Shouyang and the people praise them up to the present day.'[35] (Horses were expensive: having many horses is another way of saying that the Duke was extremely wealthy.) But the Duke did not do anything worthwhile. The brothers Bo Yi and Shu Qi, on the other hand, became recluses in order to avoid a quarrel over family inheritance, and they died penniless. Yet they were praised for their heroism. In death, the rich became poor and the poor became rich. Master Kong, like Aristotle (and many other authors), identifies human happiness with earning the good reputation that naturally follows from the death of good people. Death, as it turns out, can serve as an objective vantage point from which to judge the true worth of human beings.

Some of Master Kong's teaching amounts to shrewd, sensible advice about daily life. Even then, there is inevitably an ethical edge to his gestures and observations. We read, 'The Master used a line, but did not trawl for fish'.[36] Master Kong caught fish individually, not by scooping them en masse out of the water. Why? Because he was not greedy and wanted

---

∽ Applied Philosophy Box 3.1 ∾

What Is Overfishing?

Overfishing can be defined in a number of ways. However, everything comes down to one simple point: Catching too much fish for the system to support leads to an overall degradation to the system. Overfishing is a non-sustainable use of the ocean. . . . Fishing so much that the fish cannot sustain their population. The fish get fewer and fewer, until finally there are none to catch.

Relate this to Confucianism. What would Master Kong say about overfishing? Hint: relate to the central concept of Dao.

Source: Pepijn Koster, 'Overfishing: A Global Disaster.' http://overfishing.org/pages/what_is_overfishing.php, 9 November 2010.

to leave fish for others—advice contemporary commercial fishing interests could do well to heed. Master Kong also used 'a chorded arrow', an arrow with a string on it, so that he could retrieve it afterward.[37] He did not waste what could be used again, but lived frugally. And, out of a sense of sportsmanship, he 'did not shoot at sitting targets'.[38] He gave his quarry a fighting chance.

Heraclitus: The *Logos*

The first Western philosophers are called **pre-Socratics** (because they lived *before* Socrates). They are often thought of as the earliest scientists or 'nature-philosophers' because they tried to make sense of the material world in a systematic, logical way. But these early thinkers did not separate their scientific research from their moral commentary. What we encounter in their fragmentary writings is a combination of science and religion and metaphysics and morality all mixed up together. Consider, then, how Heraclitus and Democritus, two important figures in pre-Socratic philosophy, think about morality.

Heraclitus of Ephesus (c. 535–475 BC), was known as 'Heraclitus the obscure' because he wrote in **aphorisms**: short pithy sayings, like riddles, that are difficult to decipher. We can piece together his moral philosophy from these seemingly scattered observations. More of a metaphysician and less a dispenser of moral advice than Master Kong, Heraclitus adopts, at first glance, a very different point of view. Master Kong sees virtue as a solution to war and civil unrest, whereas Heraclitus seems to have accepted war as an unalterable fact of human life. He tells us that 'War is common and strife is justice, and everything happens in accordance with

[them]'.[39] And, in another place, he declares that 'War is the father of all and king of all'.[40] Heraclitus even argues that war has a specific moral function, for 'souls slain in war are more pure than those which die through illness'.[41]

As we shall see, Heraclitus's glorification of war is meant as a comment on the deep nature of things. Nonetheless, his attitude is not particularly surprising. Ancient peoples had to engage in armed struggle with other ethnic and national groups to survive. War was an undertaking of epic proportions: the subject matter of poems and stories. Even the gods cared about war. Heraclitus is only giving voice to a common theme of the time when he writes, 'Gods and men honor those slain in battle'.[42]

If Master Kong focuses on the notion of *Dao*, Heraclitus, along with other early Greek philosophers, focuses on the philosophical notion of **logos**, a Greek term which can be variously translated as 'language', 'statement', 'discourse', 'opinion', 'reason', or even 'proportion'. In philosophical circles, this very rich concept came to refer to reason, understood as the ultimate explanatory principle for reality. To search for the *logos* was to search for the logical answer to metaphysical questions. (The English word *logic* derives from *logos*.)

Heraclitus, in his scientific writing, points to fire as the ultimate explanation for the world. Fire, then, is the *logos*. Whereas the other Greek elements (earth, water, and air) possess a fixed, permanent nature, fire is always changing. To say that fire is the most fundamental element of all is a poetic way of insisting that everything changes except for the unalterable fact of change itself. 'Everything flows and nothing abides. Everything gives way and nothing stays fixed.'[3] This is why Heraclitus believes that nature is at war: hot fights with cold; wet fights with dry; night fights with day; summer fights with winter; happiness fights with sorrow. War, understood as the conflict between opposites, is the underlying metaphysical reality of the universe.

Heraclitus (like Master Kong) bewails moral ignorance. People do not recognize the *logos*, the metaphysical principle according to which the universe operates. Even though 'everything happens in accordance with this principle [of change]', people act as if they had 'no familiarity with it'.[44] 'In their ignorance . . . [they] behave like the deaf.'[45] Most of us want to stop the world from changing. We want to 'freeze' reality in a way that satisfies our own self-centred desires. Consider, for example, the eternal war between happiness and sorrow. Most people want only the positive side of the equation: they want happiness. They want to be *always* happy and *never* sad. But this cannot be. Sometimes happiness conquers all; sometimes sorrow conquers all; sometimes happiness and sorrow mix. That is just the way it is. To aspire to 'total happiness' is to harbour false hopes; it is to set ourselves up for inevitable frustration and disappointment when our unrealistic expectations fail. The wise person accepts both happiness and sorrow as recurring features of human life.

In the modern world, we are inevitably taught that we will be happy if we realize all our desires. Heraclitus begs to differ. 'It is *not* better for men to get everything they want', he insists. Why? Not simply because privation teaches us to withstand adversity but because the bad times actually make the good times better. We enjoy food most when we are really hungry. We have the best sleep when we are really tired. And it is the person recovering from sickness who most appreciates health. Heraclitus writes, 'Disease makes health pleas-

ant and good, as hunger does being full, and weariness rest'.[46] The *logos* is greater than us; there is a wisdom to the way in which things are put together. We need to submit to whatever happens without complaining.

It turns out, then, that Heraclitus and Master Kong are not nearly so different as may first appear. Heraclitus believes that nature is warfare; Master Kong believes that nature unfolds harmoniously. But both philosophers believe that we must act as if we are part of a larger whole that operates according to its own inner logic. Whether we follow *Dao* or the *logos*, the underlying principle is the same: we must act *according to nature*. Call this basic idea the **nature principle**. As we shall see, early philosophers point to the nature principle as the fundamental axiom of morality. The wise use the power of reason to peer beyond appearances and discover the nature inherent inside the very structure of things. And they act accordingly. This is what morality is all about.

Democritus: Pleasure, But Not Too Much

Although Heraclitus presents a basic framework for morality, that is about it. Unlike Master Kong, he does not provide detailed ethical advice for day-to-day human behaviour. We turn, then, to a pre-Socratic philosopher who does moral philosophy in a more explicit fashion. Democritus of Abdera (460–370 BC), who is famous for his atomic theory of matter, actually lived at about the same time as Socrates but is included among the pre-Socratics because of the style and content of his philosophy.

Democritus, who was known as 'the happy philosopher', was an enthusiastic advocate of **hedonism**, the belief that pleasure alone is what is ultimately valuable. (The word *hedo-*

nism derives from the Greek term for pleasure: *hedone*.) If this seems, at first glance, an unusual stance for a moralist, Democritus believes, like Heraclitus and Master Kong, that the secret to the good life is acting in accordance with nature. To pursue pleasure and avoid pain *is*, in his mind, to act according to nature. It is to adhere to the nature principle.

Democritus observes, 'The guides to what is good and bad for people are pleasure and pain'.[47] If, however, Democritus believes that we should aim toward pleasure and away from pain, he does not believe that we should indulge in any pleasure we like. What he recommends is that we pursue pleasure thoughtfully and cautiously. The ultimate end is not joyous ecstasy—a transitory state accompanied by great risks—but a milder form of 'happiness, contentment, well-being, harmony, and also concord and composure'.[48] We should be satisfied if we achieve peace of mind, 'equanimity', or 'a mind freed from fear'.[49] This is, as we shall see, a recurrent theme in early moral philosophy.

Democritus does not think that the purpose of morality is to put a damper on pleasure. The goal is, on the contrary, to have *as much pleasure as possible*. To use a modern technical term, Democritus believes that we should 'maximize' pleasure. This is what he means by hedonism. But he also believes that we should *not* indulge in sexuality, drunkenness, drugs, or overeating. Why? Because this turns out to be a very poor strategy for maximizing pleasure. As Democritus explains,

All who derive their pleasures from their guts, by eating or drinking or having sex to an excessive and inordinate degree, find their pleasures are brief and short-lived, in that they last for only as long as they are actually eating or drinking, while their pains are many. For the desire of more of the same is constant, and when they

get what they desire, the pleasure passes rapidly. They get nothing good out of the situation except a fleeting pleasure—and then the need for more pleasure recurs.[50]

Democritus's point is that when we indulge in things like casual sex, pornography, drinking, overeating, or recreational drugs, we become dependent upon them. The sensual experience dissipates quickly, leaving us with a craving for more of the same. Our own desires may become, in the long run, a source of intense suffering and even torment.

Suppose those who are ignorant desire X. They are convinced that once they have X, they will be very happy. But suppose they want something they cannot obtain. When they realize they cannot have X, they will be unhappy. The more they want X, the more unhappy they will be. In this way, intense desires, left unfulfilled, can lead to intense disappointment, frustration, craving. So, Democritus thinks, we must limit our desires to what is realistically possible. We must practise *restraining* our desires in order to be happy. We must learn that 'contentment comes to men from a *moderate* amount of enjoyment'.[51] We can reduce Democritus's teaching to a simple rule of thumb: desire little and you will be easily satisfied; desire much and you will be tremendously disappointed. In this sense at least, 'Moderation increases pleasure and exaggerates enjoyment'.[52]

Democritus has some practical advice for the discontented. Instead of wanting more and more until you burn with unfulfilled longing, stop and think of those who are less fortunate. 'Consider the lives of those who are badly off, and bear in mind their terrible sufferings, to help . . . ease the mental torment that desiring more brings.'[53] This will make you satisfied with your own comparative good fortune.

Democritus continues, 'It is important to compare one's own life with the life of those who are worse off . . . appreciating how much better than them one is doing and faring. By sticking to this intention you will live with a greater degree of contentment and you will keep at bay quite a few things that can ruin a life—things such as envy, jealousy, and ill-will'.[54]

Democritus's account is a warning to those enamored with modern consumer culture. Money and material possessions do not bring happiness. It is not wealth but our outlook on life that determines how happy we are. Democritus agrees with Heraclitus that 'Happiness and misery are properties of the mind'.[55] If we want to be happy, we must train ourselves to be content with little. In this way, we can escape the suffering that wanting more and more inevitably begins.

We are faced with an apparent paradox. Democritus, a hedonist, believes that we should aim at *less* pleasure in order to experience *more* pleasure. Limiting our own desire for pleasure is the key ingredient to happiness. This is the only way to avoid unrequited desire. As we shall see, other ancient philosophers quickly seize upon this idea of happiness, understood as freedom from unfulfilled desire. The Epicureans, Stoics, and ancient skeptics, in particular, come to see this liberation from inner torment or unrequited longing as the ultimate goal of human striving.

Diogenes the Cynic: A Man and His Barrel

Diogenes of Sinope (c. 404–323 BC), a central figure in Cynicism, was once described by Plato as 'Socrates gone mad'.[56] Although Diogenes is alleged to have written a few works (dialogues and tragedies), none survive. We are left with more or less reliable reports of his unconventional behaviour, along with collected sayings. This material should be approached with caution, but it does throw light on the moral attitudes of this group of philosophers and the mood of the time. Consider, then, the legendary wisdom of Diogenes the Cynic, whom we might describe as philosopher-qua-homeless-man.

The first thing to notice is that ancient Cynics are not 'cynical' in the modern sense. Yes, they are often critical, but they are something more than sneering, pessimistic, grouchy old men. Teaching by example more than by word, they offer a positive philosophical program and a theory about how to be happy. Mostly, they insist on a return to bare biological instinct, proposing as a positive ideal animal-like (and even brutish) behaviour that frees itself from the artificial impositions of acquisitive, hierarchical society.

The word *cynic* derives from the Greek term for *dog* (*kuon*—the *ku* beomes *cy*). Diogenes and his colleagues were called Cynics (that is, dog-like or canine) because they tried to live like animals, ignoring to a sensational extent usual human codes of conduct. Originally intended as an insult, Diogenes and his group wore the 'dog-label' as a badge of honour. According to one story, when his followers buried Diogenes, 'Over his grave they set up a pillar and a dog in Parian marble upon it'.[57] As another ancient writer explains,

There are four reasons why the Cynics are so named. [The] first [reason is] because of the indifference of their way of life . . . for they . . . like dogs, eat and make love in public, go barefoot, and sleep in tubs and at crossroads. . . . The second reason is that the dog is a shameless animal, and they make a cult of shamelessness, not as being beneath modesty, but as superior to it. . . . The third reason is that the dog is a good guard, and they guard the tenets of their philosophy. . . . The fourth reason is that the dog is a discriminating animal which can distinguish between its friend and enemies. . . . So do they recognize as friends those who are suited to philosophy, and receive them kindly, while those who are not suited to philosophy, they drive away, like dogs, by barking at them.[58]

We are told that Diogenes 'would often insist loudly that the gods had given to men the means of living easily, but this had been put out of sight, because we require honeyed cakes, unguents and the like'.[59] And that he 'would ridicule good birth and fame and all such distinctions, calling them showy ornaments of vice'.[60] Diogenes believed that society teaches us to covet artificial wealth, political power, social prestige, and refined pleasure; we learn to pursue these things feverishly while ignoring the simple life of making do with what nature provides. No wonder we are so desperately unhappy: we do not act according to nature!

Diogenes laments the sad spectacle of human foolishness. He complains, 'Instead of useless toils men should choose as nature recommends, whereby they might have lived happily. Yet such is their madness that they choose to be miserable'.[61] How can we escape from human misery? We should live like dogs! Diogenes tells us to give up the comfort, the luxury, the artificial aspirations and restrictions of human society. He and his followers set an example: refusing to go to work, making do without money, sleeping outdoors, wearing rags, eating whatever came their way, satisfying their natural bodily desires outside without shame, paying no attention to social etiquette or custom.

Diogenes has been largely ignored by academic philosophers. This is hardly surprising. For the most part, he rejected books and philosophical arguments. He was converted to the Cynic way of life 'through watching a mouse running about, . . . not looking for a place to lie down, not afraid of the dark, not seeking any of the things which are considered to be dainties'.[62] Mice make do without fancy food, clothes, houses, carriages, or money. They just get on with the business of everyday living. And they thrive. How? By living in accordance with nature. And so, reasons Diogenes, the virtuous person must behave likewise.

Diogenes aims at simplicity of living. He embraced voluntary poverty, living like a homeless person at the edge of society. According to a famous story, he slept in an abandoned barrel (possibly an underground tank used for

---

๑๑ Applied Philosophy Box 3.2 ๑๑

Seductive Illusion

'That happiness is to be attained through limitless material acquisition is denied by every religion and philosophy known to mankind, but is preached incessantly by every American television set.'

What would Diogenes think about contemporary consumer culture?

Source: Robert Bellah, *The Broken Covenant*, 1975. From *Quotations on Consumerism /Overconsumption*, www.stthomas.edu/recycle/consume.htm, 9 November 2010.

storing cooking oil), spending most of his time outdoors, loitering, begging, and generally eking out a frugal existence at the edges of respectable society. Diogenes does not think of philosophy as a system of abstract logical thought, but as a way of life. Philosophy means putting your ideas into practice. He certainly does not hesitate to live up to his own ideals. We read, 'One day, observing a child drinking out of his hands, [Diogenes] cast away [his] cup . . . with the words: "A child has beaten me in plainness of living"'.[63] And again, he also 'threw away his bowl when . . . he saw a child who had broken his plate taking up his lentils with the hollow part of a morsel of bread'.[64] One does not need to drink and eat from cups or bowls to live a happy life in accordance with nature.

We might summarize three major elements of Diogenes's teaching. First, he conceives of philosophy as a practical rather than a theoretical occupation. Along with the other Cynics, he tries to emulate Socrates, a philosopher who wrote no books but gained a reputation for virtuous living. He has no patience for theory: 'He held that we should neglect music, geometry, astronomy, and the like studies, as useless and unnecessary.'[65]And he makes fun of Plato's pretensions to philosophical knowledge: '[When] Plato had defined Man as biped and featherless, and was applauded [,] Diogenes plucked a fowl and brought it to the lecture room with the words, "Here is Plato's man."'[66] It is not simply that Plato's definition is ludicrously wrong; the search for philosophical definitions is a ridiculous waste of time. Philosophy should be about a well-lived life, not about useless and inevitably inaccurate theoretical speculation. This is why some commentators brand the Cynics as anti-philosophical.

Diogenes's attack on theory is, in part, a moral attack on the hypocrisy of the learned who, in focusing on obscure details and on extraneous speculation, neglect their own moral development: Diogenes, we are told,

> would wonder that the grammarians should investigate the ills of Odysseus, while they were ignorant of their own. Or that musicians should tune the strings of the lyre, while leaving the disposition of their own souls discordant; that the mathematicians should gaze at the sun and the moon, but overlook matters close at hand; that the orators should make a fuss about justice in their speeches but never practice it; or that the avaricious should cry out against money, while inordinately fond of it.[67]

Moral wisdom is expressed in good decision making. The most important thing is not to be clever at using words but to lead a good life.

Second, Diogenes believes that virtue required strenuous training: 'As we read in one story, "He used to affirm that training was of two kinds: mental and bodily; . . . and [that] one half of this training is incomplete without the other. . . . He would adduce indisputable evidence to show how easily from gymnastic training we arrive at virtue."'[68] The point of training is to toughen up, to harden ourselves physically and mentally, so that we can do without luxury and comfort and excessive material goods. When asked why he begged alms of a statue, Diogenes replied, 'To get practice in being refused'.[69] The point is to become habituated to the hard things in life. Then one can find happiness in spite of them.

Diogenes maintains that 'Nothing in life . . . has any chance of succeeding without strenuous practice and this is capable of overcoming anything'.[70] The Cynics thought of themselves as philosophical athletes. The philosopher needs **askesis** (from the Greek verb *askeo*), which means 'exercise, practice, training'. Training does not mean studying

---

ᴈᴓ Applied Philosophy Box 3.3 ᴓᴐ

Visiting Parliament

Students from John Ferneley High School have been walking the corridors of power this week with a special visit to the Houses of Parliament. The 44 Year 9 students who went on the trip were met by Alan Duncan MP, and got the chance to explore the home of government in the UK, and learn more about how Parliament operates and governs the country. Mr Duncan, who met and spoke to the visiting students, said: 'It's always refreshing to have school children visit the commons as they are always keen to learn about politics and lacking in any cynicism. They were very inquisitive, and I was very impressed with their knowledge of Parliament'.

Compare this modern use of the word cynicism to the ancient use of the term. Diogenes would think that these students and the people who recognized the trip are not nearly cynical enough. Explain.

Source: Richard Bett, 'Visiting Parliament.' *Melton Times*, www.meltontimes.co.uk, 21 May 2008.

---

logic or grammar or learning how to make fine arguments. It means learning how to do without. Hence the English equivalent **asceticism**. Whereas civilization pampers and mollycoddles us so that we cannot withstand the rigours of a healthy, natural life, philosophy, by insisting on a life in accordance with nature, establishes a proper balance.

Third, Diogenes argues that we should ignore social custom as an artificial contrivance that separates us from nature. There is a political edge to his teaching. Legend has it that he was exiled (along with his father) from his homeland for counterfeiting money.[71] According to one (implausible) version of the story, the oracle at Delphi gave him a divine command that he was to adulterate the currency of his homeland. Still, one understands what those who told this story were trying to communicate. To counterfeit money is to flaunt a very important legal convention. It is to undermine the economic system on which a particular government depends. But the Cynics think money is an imposture. Looked at from the viewpoint point of nature, a one-hundred-

dollar bill is just another piece of paper. There is no reason to hoard it or to treat those who possess it with any special respect.

We are told that Diogenes 'allow[ed] convention no such authority as he allowed to natural right'.[72] Diogenes believed that we create a prison of artificial expectations and aspirations that frustrates our true animal nature; this leads inevitably to unhappiness. In Athens, for example, it was considered impolite to eat in the marketplace. Diogenes, of course, ate in the marketplace. When he was reproached for such behaviour, he responded, 'Well, it was in the market place . . . that I felt hungry'.[73] If you must choose between doing what society tells you or following nature, Diogenes thinks the answer is uncomplicated: the *virtuous* thing is to follow nature.

While ordinary Greeks felt an intense loyalty to their native city, Diogenes distanced himself from this local patriotism, famously declaring, 'I am a citizen of the world'.[74] Diogenes taught that there is only one country that is 'as wide as the universe'.[75] National boundaries are an artificial human construction. A dog does not care whether it is in England, the United States, or Canada. Wherever it happens to be, it gets on with the business of daily living. It gets on with being a dog.

In the most famous anecdote about Diogenes, Alexander the Great, 'the ruler of the whole world', goes to visit the famous Cynic, idly sunning himself by his barrel. When Alexander tells him he can give him anything he wants, Diogenes says simply, 'Move out of the sun'.[76] What is the point? Diogenes does not ask Alexander for money or a fine house or servants or women or employment. Like a dog sunning itself, Diogenes is perfectly content and perfectly independent; he needs nothing from Alexander to be happy. All he needs is the sun, which nature (not Alexander) freely provides.

In another story, Alexander tells him, 'I am the great king'. To which Diogenes responds, 'I am Diogenes the dog'.[77] Diogenes was *proud* of being a dog. If Alexander the Great had absolute authority over human affairs, Diogenes existed outside of human affairs. He belonged to nature. The Cynics argued that it is the natural world that matters; how human beings divvy up the world is mere pretending. Alexander was reported to have said, 'Had I not been Alexander, I should have liked to be Diogenes'.[78]

There are at least three problems with Cynicism. First, there is a basic inconsistency to the Cynic argument. Acting according to nature means, in the human case, acting like a human being. But emotional reactions like shame are an integral aspect of human nature. If, for example, dogs do their bodily functions in public, this is because they are dogs, not human beings. Negative attitudes like shame, regret, guilt, or embarrassment (as well as positive attitudes such as modesty, satisfaction, honour, or pride) are essential to the human

personality. Acting according to human nature means having these emotional reactions to the right extent, not disregarding them altogether.

Second, we should point out that Diogenes is seriously inconsistent. Like other Greek philosophers, he believes in valuing mind over body, the immaterial over the physical. Diogenes criticizes the party life;[79] rails against libertines;[80] complains that 'bad men obey their lusts as servants their masters';[81] calls prostitutes a 'deadly honeyed potion;'[82] and disapproves of ancient Greek homosexuality.[83] Observing a young man studying philosophy, Diogenes is said to have exclaimed, 'Well done, Philosophy, that [you turn] admirers of bodily charms to[ward] the real beauty of the soul'.[84] When he sees a young man blushing, he comments '[this] is the hue of virtue'.[85] As it turns out, even Diogenes believes that we should feel shame about some things. And he sternly criticizes those who, *like animals*, heedlessly satisfy all their physical desires.

Third, although Diogenes attacks society as an artificial convention, this is unfair. Diogenes himself does not retreat to a desert island. He sees himself as a gadfly sent to needle and prod the citizens of Athens into the practice of virtue. According to one story, when Plato invited friends of a rich king to his house, 'Diogenes trampled on his carpets and said, . . . "I trample on the pride of Plato," who retorted, "Yes, Diogenes, with pride of another sort."'[86] Diogenes's self-imposed role as social critic presupposes the importance of community.

Repudiating social conventions is not necessarily moral—it depends which conventions one is repudiating. Diogenes's attack on social customs is something of a caricature. The Athenian restriction against eating in the marketplace may be a trivial matter, but social restrictions against murder, incest, and cannibalism are of a completely different order of magnitude. We cannot uncritically ignore all social convention. In a *good* society, social attitudes will be legitimate guides to moral conduct.

There is a truth in Cynicism. We often assume that the conventional way of doing things is the right way of doing things. We uncritically give in to peer group pressure. This may be a mistake. Diogenes, with peculiar ferocity, exposes the superficiality of such thought. For Diogenes, *morality* means 'following nature'. If we have to choose, it is always nature over society!

According to one legend, Diogenes killed himself by voluntarily holding his breath.[87] This is, in fact, a biological impossibility—if you hold your breath long enough you fall unconscious and start breathing again—but those who told the story wanted to emphasize that Diogenes's mind was much stronger than his body. Even when he was old and decrepit, he was still able to use his will to overcome his bodily functions. Except that deliberately killing oneself to make a point seems to be acting *against* nature, not according to it. Self-preservation is one of the most basic instincts in animals. If we want a more consistent account of morality, we need a more careful account of what 'following nature' means.

Epicurus: Refined Hedonism

In the Western tradition, the popularity of individual thinkers whose reputation for wisdom garnered exceptional attention led naturally to the development of competing schools of philosophy. One of the most influential philosophical movements in the ancient world was founded by the Greek philosopher Epicurus (341–270 BC), who gathered a faithful circle of intimate companions around him in his house and gardens. This group of philosophers, commonly referred to as the Epicureans, managed to preserve and propagate their founders' teaching until the rise of Christianity in the Roman world. The Roman poet Lucretius (c. 99–55 BC) eloquently explained the Epicurean world view in scientific and moral terms in his famous Latin poem *On the nature of the Universe*.[88] In modern times, there is a noticeable upsurge of interest in Epicureanism. Notable historical enthusiasts include the Renaissance scientist Pierre Gassendi and the American president Thomas Jefferson.

Like the other philosophers we have studied, Epicurus believes that morality means acting in accordance with nature. But Epicurus is, like Democritus, an unabashed hedonist. He believes that pleasure is 'the alpha and the omega of a blessed life', the beginning and the end of moral success.[89] (The letters *alpha* and *omega* are, respectively, the first and last letters of the Greek alphabet.) Pleasure, according to Epicurus, is 'the starting point of every choice and of every aversion'.[90] In the Epicurean view, then, to act according to the nature principle is to be an intelligent hedonist. As one ancient historian explains, '[For] proof that pleasure is the end [Epicurus] adduces the fact that living things, as soon as they are born, are well content with pleasure and are at enmity with pain, by the prompting of nature and apart from reason'.[91] Even as children, before we think rationally, nature makes us pursue pleasure and flee from pain. Epicurus argues that if we do this intelligently, we will discover that moral virtue is the safest and surest means to pleasant living. (See Figure 3.3.) In aiming at pleasure, we will avoid immoral behaviours that, in the end, bring more suffering than happiness.

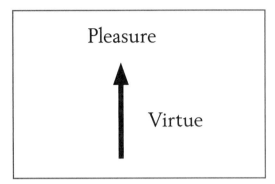

Figure 3.3 The Epicurean View of Life: The goal is pleasure; virtue is the means to pleasure.

The frank hedonism of Epicurus and his disciples certainly rankled his fellow philosophers. Wild rumours circulated that Epicurus was a glutton who vomited twice a day from over-eating, that he and his followers indulged in midnight parties with prostitutes, that he lived in luxury, that he openly preached a 'pig philosophy', and so on.[92] The modern English words **Epicurean** and **epicure** still carry these negative connotations. One contemporary dictionary defines the adjective *epicurean* as 'devoted to the pursuit of sensual pleasure, especially to the enjoyment of good food and comfort'.[93] But this contemporary usage is at odds with the picture Epicurus and his disciples present of themselves.

Epicurus attempts to reduce moral philosophy to a few very basic principles. If we are going to act in accordance with nature, we must first understand what nature is. Epicurus believes that science, and Democritean atomism in particular, provides the correct understanding of the world. According to the Greek atomist account, nature is made up of microscopic particles too small to see. These atoms inevitably collide, get tangled up together, and are arranged in various ways to produce the

macroscopic objects we perceive. Some objects are inert; some objects are alive. Living objects possess a soul made of thin, volatile atoms like fire. In this *materialist* account, there is no immaterial (non-physical) soul, just as there are no immaterial angels, spirits, or ghosts, and no immaterial gods. Everything that exists is composed of matter. (Epicurus does, in fact, believe that the Greek gods exist; he conceives of them as indestructible composites of material atoms, a point we briefly touch on, on page 79.)

Epicurus believes that if we are going to act in accordance with nature, we must base our morality on true scientific understanding of reality. There is no use complaining. We are short-lived conglomerates of atoms; there is no after-life; no Heaven or Hell, no immortal, immaterial soul; we are going to die soon and that will be the end of us. Our only salvation lies in temporary sensation: pleasure is good; pain is bad. Intelligent people organize their lives so as to obtain as much pleasure and as little pain as possible.

Epicureanism may seem, at first glance, like a recipe for extreme sensual indulgence, but Epicurus has modest aspirations. He does not argue that we should aim at a wealth of pleasurable stimuli. Given his rather bleak outlook on reality, he believes that it is enough if we do not feel pain. Unlike some Greek philosophers (for example, the Cyrenaics), he does not define pleasure as the dynamic, ecstatic gratification of appetites but as the tranquility that comes from a stable, unchanging condition of mental and bodily rest.[94] Epicurus observes, 'The magnitude of pleasure reaches its limit in the removal of all pain'.[95] In other words, the greatest pleasure is nothing more (and nothing less) than the absence of pain. If this sounds unduly pessimistic, Epicurus believes that it is foolish to hope for anything better.

Philosophical opponents criticize Epicurus's metaphysical definition of *pleasure* in three different ways. First, how could pleasure be nothing more than the 'absence of pain'? A stone is characterized by a complete absence of pain, but that is not enough for it to feel pleasure. Unaccompanied by agreeable sensation, the absence of pain would amount to mere unconsciousness. Pleasure must include, then, some positive component in addition to the absence of pain.

Second, the attentive reader can often catch Epicurus inconsistently using the word *pleasure* to refer to something more along the lines of pleasant feelings. And third, Epicurus devises his own negative definition of *pleasure* to deflect criticisms about the alleged Epicurean preoccupation with sensual gratification. As we shall see, Epicurus's opponents blasted Epicurus as a self-indulgent seeker of baser physical pleasures and maintained, instead, that the moral person should aim at **ataraxia**, a Greek term for 'unperturbedness' or 'peace of mind'. In defining *pleasure* as the absence of physical and mental pain, Epicurus is able to transform his own particular form of hedonism into a search for inner peace. As he insists, 'When we [Epicureans] say that pleasure is the end and aim, we do not mean the pleasures of the prodigal or the pleasures of sensuality, as we are understood to do so by some through ignorance, prejudice, or willful misrepresentation. By pleasure we mean the absence of pain in the body and of trouble in the soul'.[96]

One way or another, Epicurus recommends a Democritean approach to desire. He writes, 'He who has a clear and certain understanding of these things will direct every preference and aversion to securing health of body and tran-

quility of mind, seeing that this is the sum and end of a blessed life'.[97] The secret to happiness is not the continual satisfaction of every want or craving, but the proper management of desire. Epicurus observes, 'nature's wealth at once has its bounds and is easy to procure; but the wealth of vain fancies recedes to an infinite distance'.[98] There is no limit to undisciplined desire. If we do not learn to ignore and resist artificial and unnecessary desires, we will never be happy. We can always think of something more that we want. If, however, we strictly limit our desires only to what is natural and necessary, we can find happiness close at hand.

Epicurus distinguishes between three kinds of desires: those that are (1) natural and necessary, (2) natural and unnecessary, and (3) artificial and therefore illusory. If we want to be happy, we must focus on satisfying the first group of desires. We must satisfy our needs for such things as healthy food, simple drink, solid shelter, warm clothing, meaningful friendship, and meaningful intellectual stimulation. The problem is that we tend to get carried away and desire exaggerated amounts of food, expensive drink, large houses, fancy clothes, friendships with important people, and esoteric knowledge. Such desires are natural but unnecessary. Or, even worse, we desire things like wealth, political power, and immortality. These desires are artificial and illusory. They will lead to our ruin and downfall.

Here we come to the key insight of Epicureanism: the secret to happiness is desiring the right things. Epicurus writes, 'Since pleasure is our first and native good, for that reason we do not choose every pleasure whatsoever, but oftentimes pass over many pleasures when a greater annoyance comes from them'.[99] Let us illustrate Epicurus's meaning with a contemporary example. Suppose

---

◌❀ Applied Philosophy Box 3.4 ❀◌

Hangovers

Kingsley Amis, *Lucky Jim*

> Dixon was alive again. Consciousness was upon him before he could get out of the way; not for him the slow, gracious wandering from the halls of sleep, but a summary, forcible ejection. He lay sprawled, too wicked to move, spewed up like a broken spider-crab on the tarry shingle of the morning. The light did him harm, but not as much as looking at things did; he resolved, having done it once, never to move his eyeballs again. A dusty thudding in his head made the scene before him beat like a pulse. His mouth had been used as a latrine by some small creature of the night, and then as its mausoleum. During the night, too, he'd somehow been on a cross-country run and then been expertly beaten up by secret police. He felt bad.

Tom Wolfe, *The Bonfire of the Vanities*

> Something had happened last night. These days he often woke up like this, poisonously hung over, afraid to move an inch and filled with an abstract feeling of despair and shame. Whatever he had done was submerged like a monster at the bottom of a cold dark lake. . . . He had to look for the monster deductively, fathom by fathom. Sometimes he knew that whatever it had been, he couldn't face it, and he would decide to turn away from it forever, and just then something, some stray detail, would send out a signal, and the beast would come popping to the surface on its own and show him its filthy snout.

These are two descriptions of a hangover from modern novels. The first focuses on the resulting physical discomfort; the second focuses on the resulting mental discomfort (in the dreaded form of guilt or shame for something one did). Epicurus would argue that, given the consequence of such pleasures, they are self-defeating and even immoral.

Sources: Kingsley Amis (and David Lodge), *Lucky Jim* (Penguin, 1992), p. 61; Tom Wolfe, *The Bonfire of the Vanities* (Bibliolife, 2008), p. 165.

George is going to a party. Being a good hedonist, George is out to have some serious fun. He decides to get drunk and spends the whole night in a bout of non-stop drinking. What happens? He reaches his limit, but he resolutely keeps on drinking until things take a turn for the worse, and he begins to feel nauseous and gets sick in the washroom. He goes home feeling terrible and wakes up with a hangover. He is unable to study for his chemistry exam and fails the chemistry test he takes the next day. Epicurus would say that the momentary pleasure of getting drunk has been cancelled out by the prolonged pain and negative consequences that inevitably follow. So this kind of pleasure is more trouble than it is worth.

For Epicurus, as for Diogenes the Cynic, philosophy is a practical endeavour. The goal is not knowledge for knowledge's sake but knowledge for the sake of *ataraxia*, or inner peace. Still, Epicurus thinks that theoretical knowledge has an important role to play. In particular, he believes that a proper scientific understanding of nature removes the two worst causes of human anxiety: fear of the gods and fear of death. We are afraid that the gods will punish us after we die (or even during our lives), and we are afraid of ceasing to exist. Epicurus believes that correct philosophy rescues us on both accounts. Consider first his argument about the gods, and second, his argument about death.

Epicurus assures us, 'Verily there are gods, and the knowledge of them is manifest'.[100] Except that the gods, according to Epicurus, 'are not such as the multitude believe'.[101] Like everything else that exists, they are composed of atoms. What distinguishes them from other objects is that they are 'glued' so tightly together that they never come apart. The gods are, in a word, immortal.

What, then, from an Epicurean perspective, should the gods do? Because they are perfectly wise, they must act in accordance with a perfect understanding of reality. They must, in effect, act as perfect Epicureans. They must perfectly experience pleasure and perfectly avoid pain. It follows that the gods are wrapped up in their own pleasure and pay no attention to what happens on earth. Human history is filled with misery, failure, and wickedness. Sitting in the heavens and watching what happens on earth would be like sitting through a long and very bad movie—it would leave one sorely depressed. So, Epicurus believes, the gods simply ignore what happens on earth. They have better things to do. Because they take no interest in human affairs, we do not need to be afraid of them. They do not punish or reward human beings for that would require a rapt attention to the sad, sorry, and even boring spectacle of human life.

Epicurus thinks that this *scientific* understanding of the gods combats superstition and eliminates the dread that often accompanies religious belief. We need not fear angry gods, evil spirits, ghosts, or goblins, curses, or bad omens. There is no life after death and, therefore, no Last Judgment, as well as no Heaven or Hell. Epicurus believes that his scientific philosophy, in this way, removes one basic source of fear and suffering on earth: we need not fear the supernatural. But what about death? If, as Epicurus claims, there is no life after death, this means we will stop existing when we die. Most human beings find this to be a frightening prospect. Consider, then, how Epicurus tries to eliminate the other great human fear: our fear of death.

Epicurus devises a justly famous argument about why we need not fear death. The basic point is easily understood. Once we have ceased to exist, we are no longer capable of painful sensation. As Epicurus observes, 'on the departure of the soul, [the body] loses sentience'.[102] But, as we have already seen, Epicurus identifies evil with painful sensation. It follows that we cannot experience evil once we are dead. Once we are dead, we have been removed, so to speak, from the ambit of good and evil. As Epicurus puts it, 'Death is nothing to us; for the body, when it has been resolved into its elements, has no feeling, and that which has no feeling is nothing to us'.[103] (Epicurus argues further that even if something bad were to happen after death—which is impossible—it would not matter as we would no longer be there to experience it. As he puts it, 'death the most awful of evils, is nothing to us, seeing that when we are, death is not come, and when death is come, we are not'.[104])

What are we to make of Epicurus's powerful argument about death? Epicurus reasons: if Epicurean hedonism is right, death is no evil. Epicurean hedonism is right. Therefore, death is no evil. But an opponent could respond, 'If Epicurean hedonism is right, death is no evil. But death *is* an evil. (In other words, it is *not* "not evil".) Therefore, Epicurean hedonism must be wrong'. The first kind of argument is called *modus ponens*. (It has the logical form: if *A*, then *B*; *A*, therefore, *B*.) The second kind of argument is called *modus tollens*. (It has the logical form: if *A*, then *B*; not *B*, therefore, not *A*.) As one cheeky philosophical saying goes: one man's *modus ponens* is another man's *modus tollens*. Whether we find Epicurus's argument convincing depends on which belief we find to be the most convincing—the belief that Epicureanism is morally sound or the belief that death is something to be feared. To believe that Epicureanism is morally sound is to believe that good and evil are to be *exclusively* equated with pain and pleasure. That nothing else matters. This is what is at issue.

Epicurus claims that nothing can hurt a nonexistent being, but an opponent could claim that this is to spectacularly miss the point. What disturbs us about death is not the prospect of future pain after death but the change from existence to nonexistence. Even if we will not experience pain, it is the fact that we no longer exist that is disturbing. This is why we worry about death. We fear death because it means the elimination of everything that we are. The point is that we do not just value pleasure and pain; we also value the preservation of the individual person.

It need not be that hedonism is all wrong. We can accept that pleasure is, *caeteris paribus*, good, whereas pain is, *caeteris paribus*, bad. (The important Latin phrase *caeteris paribus* means for 'all things being equal'.) The problem is that hedonism is incomplete. It does not explain everything that needs to be explained. An analogy may help make the point. Imagine an artwork, say a Michelangelo sculpture. It makes sense to argue that that sculpture ought to be preserved, that something goes terribly wrong when it is destroyed. The human individual could be compared to a Michelangelo

sculpture. When an individual is destroyed, something of great value that can *never* be replaced is destroyed. This explains why we experience death as a negative event—indeed, as a calamity. Epicurus's attitude notwithstanding, it is entirely natural to feel disappointed, sad, even angry, when something of great value is destroyed. To acknowledge the reality of such feelings in the face of human death is to act in accordance with nature.

Epicurus is so busy acknowledging the importance of pleasure that he overlooks the value of the individual. This brings us to a central flaw in his theory. In arguing that we need friends to be happy, Epicurus comments, 'Of all the means [that] ensure happiness . . . by far the most important is the acquisition of friends'.[105] But Epicureanism seems incompatible with true friendship. The problem is that Epicurus is a hedonist and a **moral egoist**. He believes that we should pursue pleasure *for ourselves*. But true friendship requires that we should try to please our friends even when this entails serious suffering for ourselves.

Pericles, the ancient Greek statesman, once boasted in a famous speech that Athenians were more virtuous than other people because they 'make friends by doing good to others, not by receiving good from them'.[106] This was a familiar theme in ancient philosophy. But Epicurus seems to move in the opposite direction. His living assemblages of atoms egotistically pursue their own pleasures. But can they *selflessly* care for one another? Can they sacrifice their own well-being for someone else? This is what true friendship requires.

Epicurus tries to say the right things. He claims, for example, that the wise man 'will on occasion die for a friend' (a common theme discussed by early philosophers).[107] Suppose then I sacrifice my life so that my friend can live. Epicurus argues that death is harmless; so I am not saving my friend from harm. And in dying I am giving up future pleasures; I am settling for less pleasure instead of more. There seems to be no way to reconcile this with egoistic hedonism.

One ancient chronicler reports that the 'Epicureans do not suffer the wise man to fall in love. . . . Nor, again, will the wise man marry and raise a family. . . . Nor will he take part in politics.'[108] What is the problem with such conditions or activities? They all require a selfless devotion to others. Epicurus tells us to avoid these kinds of responsibilities so as to preserve our own happiness. But this inattentiveness to other people and larger causes seems more like selfishness or self-absorption than morality.

Epictetus: Things Within Your Power

We must turn now to the **Stoics**, an influential group of moral philosophers often overlooked in the contemporary literature. Zeno of Citium is generally identified as the founder of the movement, which grew up in Athens during the Hellenistic era (the period after Plato and Aristotle), around 300 BC. The name **Stoicism** comes from a famous painted porch or colonnade in Athens (the *stoa poikile*) that Zeno used for his teaching. The group is named, in effect, after the 'storefront' where members used to 'hang out'.

Zeno's fame quickly spread. During the next 500 years, Stoicism became the dominant philosophy and the unofficial philosophy of ancient Rome. Stoicism had famous adherents, including Cicero, the Roman Senator (106–43 BC); Seneca, the dramatist (4 BC–65 AD); and even the Emperor Marcus Aurelius (121–80

AD), who wrote a famous philosophical diary familiarly known as *Meditations*. In this short treatment, we will focus on Epictetus (c. 55–135 AD), a Greek Stoic who rose to fame and influence from inauspicious beginnings.

Although many details of his life are not entirely clear, we do know that Epictetus was a slave who was eventually freed. He was crippled early on—perhaps the result of harsh punishment by his master—and, later in his career (at some point between 89 and 95 AD), he was exiled along with the other philosophers from Rome by the emperor Domitian. During his exile, Epictetus founded a famous school in Nicopolis, Greece, that the later Emperor Hadrian visited.

No one knows what Epictetus's real name was. The name *Epictetus* is really a pseudonym that comes from the Greek word *epiktetos*, meaning 'newly acquired'. So when we refer to Epictetus, we are referring to the man who renamed himself: 'newly named'. Epictetus's desire for anonymity was intended as a gesture of humility. It was not who he or his family was that mattered; it was the content of his teaching. Epictetus himself recognizes that the moral doctrines he teaches did not originate with him but came from other Stoic philosophers as well.

At one point, Epictetus describes his modest existence: 'I have no house or city, property or slave: I sleep on the ground, I have no wife or children, no miserable palace, but only earth and sky and one poor cloak.'[109] This is not a complaint. Epictetus does not yearn after these things; he is quite happy to do without them. And there is a philosophical point to this pronouncement: we don't need these external things to be happy. Because they get in the way of happiness; we may be able to lead more successful lives without them.

As a philosopher, Epictetus is mostly concerned with the practical application of Stoic morality to everyday life. He sees himself as a role model who teaches by his actions, making fun of those who are 'philosophers only with their lips and without action'.[110] In fact, this master Stoic wrote nothing down. It was Arrian, his student, who recorded and paraphrased the content of his master's teaching in two books: the first, a series of public lectures called *The Discourses;* and the second, a more popular, shorter digest of Stoic philosophy entitled *The Enchiridion* or *Handbook.* Both books are written in a simpler, less sophisticated form of the Greek language called *Koine* (or common Greek).

Arrain describes the attitudes that reigned in Epictetus's school. In his interactions with his students, Epictetus took on the role of teacher, coach, personal trainer, military superior, and spiritual director. He championed military virtues like toughness, loyalty, duty, and perseverance. And he appealed to Roman religious principles. He was not in the business of teaching speculative philosophy but of exhorting people to become better. He believed that the point of moral philosophy is not to niggle about abstract points of doctrine but to produce noble human beings.

Arrian tells us that Epictetus compared himself to the famous Greek sculptor Phidias, who was known for his exceptional skill at carving marble statues. Just as Phidias shaped roughhewn blocks of marble into beautiful, well-proportioned human figures, Epictetus strove to shape morally lax students into virtuous human beings. As Epictetus was in the habit of telling followers, 'So now I am your teacher, and you are at school with me, and my purpose is this, to make you my completed [sculpture,] . . . a [Stoic] man molded to the [Stoic] pattern . . . in the same way as we call a statue Phidian that is molded according to the art of Phidias'.[111] Except that Epictetus believed that the good Stoic was a much more valuable work of art than 'the Zeus of Phidias or his Athena [made] of ivory and gold'.[112]

The English word *stoic* denotes someone who is physically tough, self-controlled, determined, serene, imperturbable. Epictetus prized such character traits. But Stoicism is more than a natural admiration for 'manly' virtues. Rather, it proposes a complete world view. Epictetus was, like Epicurus, a realist. He believes we live in a harsh, unforgiving world, where human life is punctuated by suffering. The Stoic aims at *ataraxia* or peace of mind. Ecstasy, joy, success are too much to ask for. It is enough if we achieve inner tranquility, and freedom from worry, bother, disappointment, frustration, and dissatisfaction.

Epictetus claims, like most ancient philosophers, that what makes us human is our ability to reason. He compares a human being to a coin that has the image of the emperor stamped on it. Reason, which is a reflection of the divinity, is the royal image stamped on the coin of human nature that makes us valuable. Epictetus explains that an unreasonable man 'lose[s] the qualities that make him a man, the distinctive stamp impressed upon his mind: like the stamp we look for on coins, [when] we find [this stamp] we [spend them], and if we do not, fling them away'.[113] Without reason, a human being is like a slug of base metal we throw away, like a worthless old coin after the royal stamp that makes it worth something has been rubbed off.

Epictetus equates human happiness with the life of reason. He looks to the natural world for inspiration: 'When is a horse miserable? When it is deprived of its natural faculties, not when it is unable to crow like a cock, but when it is unable to run. And the dog? Not when it cannot fly, but when it cannot follow a trail. On the same principle a man is wretched . . . when he has lost his rational and trustworthy faculty.'[114]

Morality is not about walking on two legs, or making human sounds, or possessing a human nose. It is not about having the external shape of a human being; it is about being human all the way through. Epictetus compares immoral individuals to mere animals. He continues:

> Is everything judged by its outward form alone? On that principle you must call your waxen apple an apple. No it must smell and taste like an apple: the outward semblance is not enough. So, when you judge man, nose and eyes are not sufficient, you must see if he has the judgement of a man. Here is one who does not listen to reason, who does not understand when his fallacies are exposed; he is an ass. Here is one whose self-respect is deadened: he is useless, anything other than a man. Here is one looking for someone he can kick or bite; it turns out he is not even a sheep or an ass, but some savage beast or other.[115]

Epictetus tells us that reason is the supreme human faculty, 'for this alone of all the faculties' comprehends everything, 'even its own nature'.[116] Reason is able to understand the world and can even understand itself through introspection. There are two kinds of reason: theoretical reason is the ability to evaluate logical arguments, and moral reason is the ability to make good decisions. Someone who is good at theoretical reason masters logic and physics, while someone who is good at moral reasoning lives a good life.

Epictetus complains that speculative philosophers tend to forget about moral reason because following it is hard. Their studies in logic and theoretical science are little more than an inane diversion: 'If a man studies logic . . . because he wants to show [off] at a dinner party', this is a waste of time.[117] We should instead consider logic as a tool that facilitates

---

꧁ Applied Philosophy Box 3.5 ꧂

Rex Accused of Acting Like 'an Animal'

Big Brother 9 contestant Rex Newmark has been described as acting like 'an animal' by a female clubber. Kerry O'Brien, 22, alleges that Newmark reacted angrily after she spurned his romantic advances, reports the *Daily Star*. Newmark ended up in a scrap with five men in Soho following his rejection, claims O'Brien. 'I was scared. He turned into an animal', she said. 'There was a group of five nice guys nearby, who we had been enjoying a friendly conversation with before Rex came along. Once Rex realised we weren't interested in him, he just went over and started punching one of them. He flipped. I don't know where Rex had been earlier, but he seemed pretty drunk . . . He caught one of the guys, whose name was John, between the eyes and blood started pouring out'.

The entertainment world is remarkably permissive; but even here, the Stoic view of human nature is not entirely out of place. What would Epictetus say about the incident?

Source: Alex Fletcher, 'Rex accused of acting like "an animal".' *Digital Spy Network*, www.digitalspy.com/bigbrother9/a132022/rex-accused-of-acting-like-an-animal.html, Tuesday, 7 October 2008.

and perfects the moral life: 'In so much as we study logic, we should do it for "the purpose of right living".'[118] Epictetus believes that if we hope to become good moral reasoners, we must begin by developing clearness of vision, what the Stoics call **apathy** (*apatheia* = 'without pathos or passion'). Stoic 'apathy' is not, in the modern sense, a lethargic, lazy indifference but a disciplined, *passionless* capacity for true judgment. Achieving **Stoic apathy** requires discipline and effort; we must master our emotions, putting aside partisan attitudes like self-pity and pride, and forcing ourselves to view the world as it objectively is. Good moral reasoners obey the nature principle; they act in 'perfect harmony with nature'.[119] They strive to 'understand nature and follow her'.[120] This is how they find *ataraxia*, or peace of mind.

Epictetus believes that human suffering comes about because we misunderstand our role in the universe: instead of serving the world, we act as if the rest of the world should serve us. But this is outrageous! It is overweening pride to think that the universe should bend itself to our every whim and fancy. Epictetus explains:

> All things obey and serve the Universe—earth and sea and sun and the other stars and the plants and animals of the earth; and our body too obeys it, enjoying sickness or health, and passing through youth and old age and other changes when the Universe wills. It is not reasonable then that . . . our judgement, should . . . be the only thing to strive against it. For the Universe is strong and superior to us and has provided for us better than we can. . . . And besides, to act against it is to side with unreason, and brings nothing with it but vain struggle, involving us in miseries and pains.[121]

The Stoics also believe that reason removes our fears. Much of what we are afraid of has to do with superstition and restless imagination. For example, we are afraid of ghosts or that we will lose our money in the stock market, or that we will not be invited to a lavish dinner, or that we will die. But reason tells us that there are no ghosts, that excess money is a hindrance to the moral life, that we can dine pleasantly on simple fare without noise and commotion, and that every creature has to die. Once we understand the world, we can settle down and calmly accept our role in history and in nature.

The Stoics propose a solution to the problem of human unhappiness. The Stoic solution is not to change the world to get what we want—which is plainly impossible—but to change ourselves so that what we want better corresponds to the world. Instead of trying to make reality fit our own expectations, we must strive to make our expectations fit reality. Epictetus advises, 'Ask not that events should happen as you will, but let your will be that events should happen as they do, and you will have peace'.[122] Stoic moral education consists of training the will to accept what happens. In Epictetus's words, 'Education is just this—learning to frame one's will in accord with events'.[123] When we simply accept that whatever happens to us is for the best, there is no room for disappointment, regret, dissatisfaction.

In contemporary times, we assume that the solution to our unhappiness is to get what we want. How? By changing the world so that it conforms, as closely as possible, to our desires. The Stoics believe that this is nothing short of lunacy. The world will never conform to precisely what we want, no matter how hard we try. We cannot rid the world of death, disease, pain, hunger, loneliness, unfairness, cruelty, poverty, and so on. These painful realities are an unmovable part of the way things are.

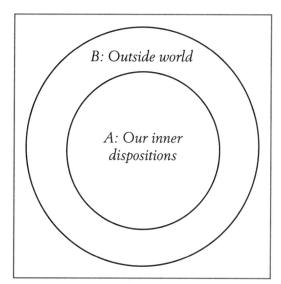

Figure 3.4 Stoics Claim We Should Be Concerned about *A*, not *B*

Epictetus differentiates between *things in our power* and *things outside our power*. This twofold distinction corresponds roughly to the distinction between what exists inside or outside the mind. Things in our power include our own thoughts, beliefs, attitudes, decisions, and desires. Things outside our power include events and circumstances determined by other people or by the nature of the external world. (See Figure 3.4.) The Stoics believe that we must focus on changing the things that are in our power and simply resign ourselves to those things that are outside our power. In other words, we must change our inner dispositions so as to accept what is beyond our control.

Epictetus explains: 'Things in our power are thought, impulse, will to get and will to avoid, and, in a word, everything which is our own doing. Things not in our power include the body, property, reputation, office, and, in a word, everything that is not our own doing.'[124] Suppose I decide to buy a lottery ticket. It is in my power to buy or not buy the ticket. But once I have the ticket, it is not in my power to decide whether I win the lottery. This is an example of the difference between things in our power and things outside our power. There is no point in focusing all my energies on winning the lottery. Once I have bought a ticket, I must simply accept whatever happens.

Epictetus believes that we can control our own thoughts and actions, but that is about it. If our body is injured in an accident, if our property is stolen, if our reputation suffers unfairly, if our careers end in failure—these things may depend on factors outside our control. We must accept our fate, whatever happens, without complaint, jealousy, or self-pity. Epictetus advises:

> Remember that you are an actor in a play, and the Playwright [Zeus—i.e., God] chooses the manner of it; if He wants it short, it is short; if [He wants it] long, it is long. If He wants you to act a poor man you must act the part [of a poor man] with all your powers; and so if it is your part to be a cripple or a magistrate or a plain man. For your business is to act the character that is given you and act it well; the choice of the cast is Another's.[125]

Epictetus believes that the secret to happiness is to keep the mind tightly focused on those things that are in your power and to ignore everything else. He advances a simple, practical rule for good living. Whenever you feel a desire, ask yourself this: "'Is it concerned with what is in our power or with what is not in our power?' And if it is concerned with what is not in our power, be ready with the answer that it is nothing to you.'[126] Suppose you want to be famous. As it turns out, fame is not within our power. People are fickle; taste changes; reputations are unfairly set aside, and what will happen in the future is largely unpredictable. Epictetus would recommend focusing your efforts, not on being famous, which is outside your power, but on changing your attitude toward celebrity, which *is* entirely within your power. Instead of hoping for fame, tell yourself that fame is nothing to you; regard fame with utter disdain, and you will not be frustrated if you live the most anonymous life.

Epictetus distinguishes between three categories of objects in the world: those that are good, those that are bad, and those that are neutral or indifferent. He writes, 'The virtues . . . are good, [the] vices . . . are bad, and all that comes between is indifferent'.[127] We should try to possess virtue; we should try to avoid vice, and we should not care very much about anything else. He concedes, however, that it is acceptable to prefer some '**indifferents**' over others. We naturally prefer health over sickness, life over death, pleasure over pain, wealth over poverty. There is nothing wrong with this. Even neutral things like health, money, reputation, or pleasure may be a means to virtue. Nonetheless, in the overall scheme of things, these are minor issues. We should not pay much attention to them, one way or another.

Epictetus teaches that morality is objective. Some things really are good; some things really are bad. Although most people mistake the bad for the good, Epictetus believes that when it comes to the basics, moral knowledge is close at hand. He writes, 'Everyone has come into the world with an innate conception as to good and bad, noble and shameful, becoming and unbecoming, happiness and unhappiness, fitting and inappropriate, what is right to do and what is wrong'.[128] Understanding the essence of morality is not that difficult; what *is* difficult is putting moral principles into practice.

Epictetus's lectures are filled with practical, earthy advice. In any situation, we can always construe things in ways that makes us more or less upset. Imagine, for example, a container that has two handles: one to the right, the other to the left. Epictetus advises, 'Everything has two handles, one by which you can carry it, the other by which you cannot. If your brother wrongs you, do not take it by . . . the handle of his wrong, for you cannot carry it by that, but rather by the other handle—that he is a brother, brought up with you, and . . . you can carry it by that'.[129] The best way to understand this situation is to focus on the fact that it is your dear brother that wronged you, so that you will be able to forgive him without exaggerating the extent of the harm.

We can translate this teaching into a modern idiom. Is the glass on the table half-empty or half-full? If we think it is half-empty, we will be disappointed and upset. If, on the other hand, we think that it is half-full, we will count our blessings. We cannot change the amount of water in the glass, but the wise person changes the way he or she understands the situation. We should approach every situation in a similar manner,

Epictetus also tells us not to be upset over trifles; accept them as unimportant and move on. When someone else suffers some minor setback, we do not make a fuss: 'For instance, when another man's slave has broken the winecup we are very ready to say at once, "Such things must happen"'.[130] And so we should have a similar reaction when the same thing happens to us: 'Know then that when your own cup is broken, you ought to behave in the same way as when your neighbor's was broken.'[131] Reason requires that we react to negative events in our lives in the same way that we respond to similar events in other people's lives.

As we have seen, Stoic moral philosophy is not primarily about talking (or writing). It is about *acting*. Epictetus advises, 'On no occasion call yourself a philosopher, nor talk at large of your principles among the multitude, but act on your principles. For instance, at a banquet do not say how one ought to eat, but eat as you ought'.[132] Epictetus thinks of philosophical truths as food that needs to be digested; comparing philosophical speeches to vomiting. He tells his students that philosophical training requires time and humility:

> So that if ever any talk should happen among the unlearned concerning philosophic theorems, be you, for the most part, silent. For there is great danger in immediately throwing out what you have not digested. And, if anyone tells you that you know nothing, and you are not nettled at it, then you may be sure that you have begun your business. For sheep don't throw up the grass to show the shepherds how much they have eaten; but, inwardly digesting their food, they outwardly produce wool and milk. Thus, therefore, do you likewise not show theorems to the unlearned, but the actions produced by them after they have been digested.[133]

Epictetus identifies three steps in education: 'To accuse others for our own misfortunes is a sign of want of education; to accuse oneself shows that one's education has begun; to accuse neither oneself nor others shows that one's education is complete.'[134] The ignorant blame others for their own misfortunes. Students blame themselves, for they have come to understand their own judgments are the source of their unhappiness. Those who have mastered virtue, in contrast, are not angry at themselves or anyone else; they have achieved *ataraxia*, and they are at peace with themselves and the world.

We might expect that a stern moralist like Epictetus would be a harsh judge of other peo-

ple, but when it comes to those who indulge in ordinary, run-of-the-mill immorality, he is remarkably patient and forgiving. Mostly, he tells his students to pity wrong-doers, not to be angry with them. This makes perfect sense for Stoicism takes away the target for our anger. Or rather, it makes *ourselves* the target. It is the way we react to what other people do that makes us miserable. 'When anyone makes you angry,' Epictetus concludes, 'know that it is your own thought that has angered you'.[135] When we feel anxiety or disappointment, it is because we have failed to make our own ideas correspond to the way the world is. We are the authors of our own misery. As Epictetus repeatedly insists, 'When we are hindered, or disturbed, or distressed, let us never lay the blame on others, but on ourselves, that is on our own judgments'.[136]

Epictetus's moral philosophy is remarkably democratic. It does not matter if one is a slave, a foreigner, a citizen, a general, or even the emperor. Moral distinctions matter; legal or political distinctions are secondary. Like Diogenes, Epictetus argues for **cosmopolitanism**. The good person is 'a citizen of the universe and a son of God'.[137] The true philosopher must 'do as Socrates did [and] never reply to one who asks him his country, "I am an Athenian", or "I am a Corinthian", but "I am a citizen of the universe"'.[138] Nature is the 'country' we should all serve, and we should act in accordance with nature's laws. This is what matters most of all.

All in all, Epictetus constructs an impressive moral theory. Stoicism is, nonetheless, liable to some serious criticism. Like Epicureanism, Stoicism preaches a virtuous **egoism** that is a serious obstacle to love and friendship. We are to concern ourselves solely with things within our power: our own ideas, beliefs, attitudes, and desires. But it is hard to see how this relentless retreat inside ourselves is compatible with the close identification with another person's interests that love and friendship require. The Stoic approach risks becoming an invidious self-absorption that pulls us away from other people.

Epictetus advises, 'When you see a man shedding tears in sorrow for a child abroad or dead, or for loss of property . . . Do not hesitate to sympathize with him so far as words go, and if it so chance, even to groan with him; but take heed that you do not also groan in your inner being'.[139] Epictetus tells us to keep our distance. We can make a show of sharing in other people's feelings, but we must not give in to feelings of deep sympathy. We must refrain from involvement in another person's misfortune so as to preserve our own peace of mind.

When it comes to human relationships, Stoicism seems aloof and distant. Again, Epictetus famously advises, 'If you kiss your child or your wife, say to yourself that you are kissing a human being, for then if death strikes . . . you will not be disturbed'.[140] This seems coldhearted in the extreme. The problem, as with Epicurus, is egoism. Stoicism is a noble egoism but an egoism nonetheless. Epictetus sets very high moral standards. Still, what motivates Stoic philosophy? 'I should be moral in order to escape from suffering.' Whose suffering? My own. Epictetus's advice seems to be, do not love your wife or child too much, or it will hurt when they die. But surely, one could riposte, 'it *should* hurt when they die'. If you manage to care so much for someone else that it hurts, this is in itself a noble achievement.

Epictetus provides ambiguous advice about the relationship between parents and children. On the one hand, he upbraids a student for his unnatural behaviour when he abandons his sick daughter.[141] On the other hand, he tells his students that they will not progress in moral philosophy unless they 'abandon' thoughts such as 'If I do not punish my [boy], he will be wicked', declaring that, 'It is better for your [boy] to be wicked than for you to be miserable'.[142] But is this moral advice? If disciplining a wayward son involves a lot of worry, headache, and trouble, perhaps it is better to have a good son than to have a peaceful life. We are too attached to many things: money, material possessions, prestige, political power, popularity, etc. But perhaps it is good to be intensely attached to *other human beings*. If you love your children, your spouse, your parents, your colleagues, perhaps this is worth a certain amount—even a lot—of misery.

Stoicism is a noble ethics and remarkably unsentimental in the way it faces up to the harsh realities of the world. But there is a cautious egoism at its logical centre that remains troubling. Although an admirably consistent and humane thinker, Epictetus leaves little room for deep commitment to larger causes. But noble achievements may necessitate deep commitment to something outside oneself. This attachment may be more effective, the stronger it is. While strong attachment can disturb a tranquil existence, perhaps the moral response is to accept the worry and perturbation for the sake of this greater cause.

Epictetus tries to justify egoism: 'It is natural to man as to other creatures, to do everything for his own sake; for even the sun does everything for its own sake, and . . . so does Zeus himself . . . and in general he has so created the nature of the rational animal, that he can attain nothing good for himself, unless he contribute[s] some service to the community.'[143] Epictetus insists that, 'to do everything for [one's] own sake is not unsocial'.[144] But, surely, such egoism may have disastrous consequences. And even if I do serve the community for self-interested reasons, isn't this selfishness rather than morality? If this is what motivates my community service, what will happen when it is no longer in my self-interest to help others? Morality requires that we do good things for others even when it is *not* in our own self-interest. We should do what is good for others, not because it is good for us, but because it is good for them. A fuller approach to morality requires that we move beyond egoism to mutual love.

We cannot finish this short discussion of Stoicism without commenting on the great philosophical rivalry that pitted Stoics against Epicureans. Epictetus is not uniformly critical of other philosophers and schools. In fact, he expresses great admiration for Socrates and for Cynics like Diogenes. In sharp contrast, he dismisses his Epicurean rivals as hardly human. 'Be off with you [Epicurus] and go to sleep', he exclaims, 'do as the worm does for this is the life of which you pronounce yourself worthy: eating, drinking, copulation, evacuation and snoring'.[145] Epictetus believes that the Epicureans are base hedonists, that they are intellectually dishonest. Although they claim that they are striving after *ataraxia* (pleasure, negatively defined), they are really interested in sensual pleasure. What they want is not the philosophical life but a life of ease, comfort, and self-satisfied sensation.

When it comes to the respective roles of virtue and pleasure, Stoics and Epicureans adopt contrary approaches. Epicurus believes that we should aim at pleasure and that virtue will follow; Epictetus claims that we should aim at virtue and that pleasure (understood as *ataraxia*) will follow. (See Figure 3.5 and compare to Figure 3.3.) Epictetus believes that Epicureans confuse the means with the end. They chase after pleasure; we should set our sights, instead, on virtue. If we practise virtue, *ataraxia* will come of its own accord. Epictetus asks, 'What does virtue produce?' and responds, 'Peace of mind'.[146]

If, however, Epictetus criticizes the Epicureans for their self-centred pursuit of pleasure, we might critique his Stoicism on parallel grounds. On many occasions, Epictetus talks as if we should be virtuous *in order to* achieve peace of mind. Later historical authors on ethics generally concur that we should do what is right because it is right, not because we get some advantage from it. Peace, tranquility, self-satisfaction, happiness, and contentment will *usually* follow. But morality is worthwhile regardless.

One final point: Epictetus had himself been a slave, and so we might expect that he has something important to say on the topic of individual freedom. Epictetus does describe, with feeling, how even caged animals yearn to be free:

> Men put lions in cages and rear them as tame creatures . . . [But] what lion if he got sense or reason would wish to be a lion of that sort? Look at the birds yonder and see what lengths they go to in striving to escape, when they are caught and reared in cages; why some of them actually starve themselves rather than endure that

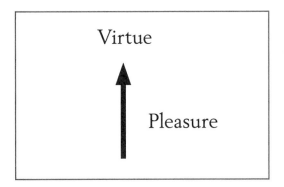

Figure 3.5 The Stoic View of Life

way of life; and even those that do not die, pine away and barely keep alive, and dash out if they find any chance of an opening. So strong is their desire for natural freedom, an independent and unhindered existence.[147]

Epictetus believes, however, that only Stoic philosophy makes us free. 'That man is free', Epictetus observes, 'who lives as he wishes'.[148] But only the Stoic lives as he wishes, for only the Stoic fully accepts what happens to him. If you want to be free, then, Epictetus has some advice: become a Stoic philosopher. Stop trying to change the world (which is impossible); change your desires so as to desire whatever happens to you, and you will always live as you wish. You will be free.

While most of us equate freedom with power over *others*, Epictetus equates freedom with power over *ourselves*. He plainly states, 'There is only one way to freedom—to despise what is not in our power'.[149] What happens in nature and what other people do is not in our power. This, then, is the secret to freedom: we must learn to desire whatever happens, and we will be free. We may readily accept that the Stoic emperor (Marcus Aurelius) is free. But even the Stoic slave is free. Neither is more free than the other.

But let us turn now to two other schools of moral philosophy: the skeptics and the Sophists.

Pyrrho: Skepticism and Peace of Mind

Some readers may wonder about the place of skepticism in a book on moral philosophy. If, however, contemporary skeptics focus on the possibility of knowledge, ancient philosophers viewed skepticism, primarily, as a *moral* alternative. They were convinced that the practice of doubting everything, done in the right way, was a reliable means to inner peace and freedom from anxiety. Eschewing hedonism, Stoicism and Cynicism, ancient skeptics chose disbelief as the surest route to *ataraxia*.

Who was the first skeptic? There is no easy answer to this question. Although Pyrrho (c. 360–270 BC) is generally identified as the founder of skepticism, many ancient authors express reservations about the veracity of human belief.[150] One Roman commentator goes so far as to identify Homer as the original skeptic, which is pretty much an ancient way of saying that skepticism began with recorded thought! As he expresses the thought, 'Some call Homer the founder of this school, for to the same questions he more than anyone else is always giving different answers at different times, and is never definite or dogmatic about the answer'.[151] One gets the basic idea that the Greek poet was a skeptic because he believed that there are no fixed, right answers to important questions and that what we call knowledge is inconstant and ever-changing.

The same authority suggests that other Greek philosophers, including Heraclitus, Democritus, Xenophanes, Zeno of Elea, and even Plato were skeptics in their own way.[152] If, however, philosophers are inevitably cautious when approaching knowledge-claims, Pyrrho, the philosopher we will study, embraced the skeptical outlook in an unusually consistent and conspicuous way, which is why later skeptics were often called Pyrrhonean skeptics.[153] Although the material relating to Pyrrho is (like the material relating to Diogenes) mostly composed of stories, one of his later followers, called Sextus Empiricus, produced detailed manuals that confirm and elucidate the belief-system and practices of the skeptics in a more systematic manner. Consider first Pyrrho and then the system of Sextus.

Like other philosophies we have studied, Greek skepticism is a direct response to the problem of suffering. At its origins, it may have borne some semblance to Buddhism. Pyrrho allegedly travelled the world with Alexander the Great and studied in India under the Gymnosophists (literally, the 'naked philosophers'—i.e., religious ascetics who dispensed with clothes) and with the Magi (wise men, magicians) in Persia. We are told that his travels 'led him to adopt a most noble philosophy . . . taking the form of agnosticism and suspension of judgement'.[154] It is this practice of suspension of judgment or **epoche** that is at the heart of Pyrrho's skeptical method.

Ancient skeptics pointed to Pyrrho as a moral hero, as someone who provided a virtuous example we should emulate and follow. The situation is somewhat complicated by the fact that two different stories about Pyrrho's life were circulated. In the literature of the period, we find, in effect, two Pyrrhos.

In the first instance, Pyrrho is presented as an absolute skeptic. In the second, he is presented, more realistically, as a mitigated skeptic. Absolute skeptics—in so much as absolute skepticism is possible—do not believe anything; they deny all claims to knowledge, both practical and theoretical. Mitigated skeptics, on the other hand, accept that we can 'know' things in a practical, everyday sense; what they doubt are larger philosophical claims to metaphysical and universal truth. They accept that we can have some 'knowledge' about how the world appears to us but claim that we have no way of knowing if this local knowledge is an accurate reflection of the way things universally or objectively are.

A consistent absolute skepticism seems impossible, but some ancient stories do depict Pyrrho in such terms. We read that Pyrrho doubted the reality of the external world, the existence of other people, and all the contents of sense perception. As one ancient historian reports,

> he led a life consistent with this doctrine, going out of his way for nothing, taking no precaution, but facing all risks as they came, whether carts, precipices, dogs or what not, and, generally leaving nothing to the arbitrament of the senses; but he was kept out of harm's way by his friends who . . . used to follow close after him.[155]

In other words, Pyrrho disbelieved sense perception to such an extent that he would have stepped off cliffs and stood in the way of galloping horses if his dedicated band of admirers did not take him by the hand, navigating him around such obstacles. Although such reports make for sensational reading, it is hard to believe that a real person could have ever lived like this. The stories about Pyrrho's complete disregard for sense perception seem to be 'tall tales', exaggerations intended perhaps to demonstrate where extreme skepticism logically leads.

In the second instance, Pyrrho is presented, more realistically, as a mitigated skeptic, as someone who relied on common sense and sense perception in everyday life but doubted larger philosophical claims to certain knowledge. The same historian tells us that 'Aenesidemus says that it was only his philosophy that was based on suspension of judgement, and that he did not lack foresight in everyday acts. He lived to be nearly ninety'.[156] Indeed, all the evidence indicates that Pyrrho lived a long and successful life, something that requires practical common sense. (Take it as a rule that absolute skeptics would die early!)

Pyrrho seems, then, to have proposed skepticism as a philosophical ideal without denying that we know enough to get by in an ordinary way. An insistent critic might complain, of course, that mitigated skepticism, if consistently applied, reduces to absolute skepticism. According to one story, 'When a cur rushed at [Pyrrho] and terrified him' [in other words, when Pyrrho was caught believing that he knew that something was true about the world] 'he answered his critic that it was not easy entirely to strip oneself of human weakness; but one should strive with all one's might against facts, by deeds if possible, and if not, in word'.[157] Pyrrho's position seems to be that there is something good about not knowing what is true or false and that we should aspire, *as much as possible*, to skepticism.

The skeptics called their philosophical opponents dogmatists because they (allegedly) maintained dogmatic or inflexible beliefs. Still, the dogmatist could protest in return that aiming at radical skepticism will lead to the most absurd and even evil acts. If I cannot know what is true about the world, how can I *know* that murder is wrong? Indeed, if I cannot trust sense perception, if logic is unreliable, if human intelligence inevitably leads me astray, how can I even know the difference between murder and charity? For all I can know, that bloody knife in the murderer's hands may be nothing more than a bouquet of red roses.

One ancient source describes the skeptics' response to the dogmatists:

> When the dogmatists argue that [the Skeptic] may thus live in such a frame of mind that he would not shrink from killing and eating his own father if ordered to do so, the Skeptic replies that he will be able so to live as to suspend his judgment in cases where it is a question of arriving at the truth, but not in matters of life and

taking precautions. Accordingly, we may choose a thing or shrink from a thing by habit and may observe rules and customs.[158]

Here again, the response is to propose a mitigated skepticism: you are to yield to natural habit and the social customs of your place and time, but when it comes to the practice of philosophy, you are to suspend your judgment.

In a modern world that cherishes science and education, it may seem little short of crazy to *aim* at ignorance, even at philosophical or theoretical ignorance. Shouldn't we be endeavouring to gain more and more knowledge? Isn't that why you are reading this text? What could be the point of doubting as much as possible? Why should we try to suspend judgment when it comes to theoretical and even practical questions?

The skeptics argue that knowledge, or rather claims to knowledge, disturb us. When faced with competing claims about the truth, we should not embrace one side of the issue. Instead of taking sides, fighting about intractable problems, and worrying ourselves half to death about finding the correct answer, we should simply accept that we cannot know. This intellectual modesty will put to rest our endless, useless questioning.

Pyrrho claims that learned ignorance leads to *ataraxia,* or inner peace. We are told that he 'would maintain his composure at all times'.[159] This state of absolute equanimity was, for skeptics, the highest virtue. A Stoic colleague of Pyrrho's tells a revealing story: 'When his fellow passengers aboard a ship were all unnerved by a storm, [Pyrrho] kept calm and confident, pointing to a little pig in the ship that went on eating, and telling them that such was the unperturbed state in which the wise man should keep himself.'[160] The little pig remained calm because it did not have an opinion about what was true or false about the storm. It did not presume to know what was going to happen. The human passengers thought they knew. They believed that they were all going to drown in a shipwreck. The pig did not believe—animals are not able to think—and so it went on happily eating. The skeptics recommend that we use philosophy to return to this state of blessed ignorance. We can then get on with the daily business of living, keeping our composure in the midst of the most terrifying storms.

Contemporary readers naturally tend to think of **agnosticism** in a religious context. Religious agnostics do not believe or disbelieve in God. They, so to speak, sit on the fence. Ancient skeptics, however, apply agnosticism to *all* knowledge claims. They sit on the fence on every issue. They claim that we cannot know for certain whether any claim is true or false. Why? Because there are as many reasons for not believing something as there are for believing something. The only solution to the resulting confusion is to simply accept that we cannot know for certain—i.e., to acquiesce to a generalized skepticism.

Ancient philosophers looked to Pyrrho as an example of outstanding moral achievement. His life was presented as the model for how a skeptic should live. It was left for later followers to synthesize and organize his thoughts in a more complete and coherent fashion. Sextus Empiricus, who lived some 500 years after Pyrrho in Alexandria, Rome, or Athens, systematically records skeptical arguments in his book *Outlines of Pyrrhonism*.[161] Although Sextus is less of an original mind and more a historian than Pyrrho, his text provides a very complete account of the skeptical mindset. Like Pyrrho, Sextus claims that skepticism is the surest way to attain peace of mind. He combats 'dogmatism', the idea that we can know certain truth.

At the same time, he moderates somewhat the skeptical position.

Sextus tells us that the skeptic aims at neutrality in intellectual debate and at as much equanimity *as possible* when it comes to the pains and discomforts, the ordinary ups and downs, of mortal life. In his words, 'The Skeptic's end, where matters of opinion are concerned, is mental tranquility; in the realm of things unavoidable, moderation of feeling is the end'.[162] Emotional detachment is here a virtue. 'When the Skeptic is disturbed', Sextus reports, 'it is by things which are unavoidable'.[163] If some things inevitably bother us, the skeptic is bothered less than the ordinary man.

Sextus admits that no life is 'altogether free from disturbance'.[164] Even the skeptic 'is sometimes cold and thirsty [and] suffers in other such ways'.[165] Nonetheless, skepticism is an attractive world view, for the skeptic minimizes suffering. When faced with hardship, the skeptic suffers from one evil, whereas the ordinary man suffers from two. Sextus explains: 'Two circumstances combine to the detriment of ordinary man: he is hindered both by the [negative] feelings themselves and not less by the fact that he believes these conditions to be evil by nature. The Skeptic, on the other hand, rejects this additional notion that . . . these things [are] evil by nature and thus he gets off more easily.'[166] The ordinary man who is wet and cold knows that he feels wet and cold and also knows that this is a very bad thing, whereas the skeptic in the same situation only knows that he feels wet and cold and reserves his judgment as to whether this is a good or a bad thing.

The skeptic aims at a kind of emotional indifference. If we hope to achieve *ataraxia*, we must leave aside whatever disturbs us. But what disturbs us most of all are fierce convictions about what is good and bad. If we accept that we cannot really know what is good or bad, we will avoid overly negative (or positive) judgments about things in the world. Sextus explains:

> The person who entertains the opinion that anything is by nature good or bad is continually disturbed. . . . [He flees from] those things which are by nature bad, and pursues what he believes to be the good things. But when he has acquired [good things], he encounters further perturbations. This is because his elation at [their] acquisition is unreasonable and immoderate, and also because in his fear of a reversal, all his exertions go to prevent the loss of the things which to him seem good. On the other side there is the [skeptical] man who leaves undetermined what things are good and bad by nature. He does not exert himself to avoid anything or seek after anything, and hence is in a tranquil state.[167]

To recommend that we temper our strongest convictions about what is good and bad may seem like startling (and even dangerous) moral advice. We need to base our moral judgments on some authoritative principles. Sextus follows Pyrrho's lead in recommending custom and law as moral guidelines. He confirms that 'we [Skeptics] follow a certain line of reasoning which indicates to us . . . how to live in accordance with customs, the laws, and the institutions of our country, and with our own natural feelings'.[168] Michel de Montaigne (1533–92), the famous French essayist, developed a Renaissance world view based on these principles.

Whereas Pyrrho taught mostly by example, Sextus outlines, in careful prose, the skeptical method of **antithesis** or opposing arguments. This involves balancing considerations pro and con so as to come to a state of indecision on an issue. Sextus defines philosophical skepticism as 'the ability to place in an antithesis . . . appearances and judgments, and thus—because

of the equality of force in the objects and arguments opposed—to come first of all to a suspension of judgment and then to mental tranquility'.[169] Whereas most of us want to know what to believe, Sextus tells us how to avoid belief altogether. Faced with competing claims about the same issue, he suggests that we use reason to contrive a stalemate. The point is not to determine who is right. The point is to find good reasons to believe *both* sides of an argument. Faced with an equally strong case for and against a position, we will be forced to retreat into agnosticism. The resultant psychological state of suspending judgment (what the Greeks called *epoche*) will, according to Sextus, bring us *ataraxia* or inner peace.

In closing, let us quickly review four objections to ancient skepticism. To begin with, a philosophical opponent might complain, not merely that emotional detachment is an unattractive option, but that it is mostly unachievable. Perhaps we cannot help feeling that certain things are good and bad, particularly when they affect us directly. Perhaps emotional disturbance is just an inevitable part of any proper human life. One ancient writer informs us that 'Pyrrho had pupils of repute, in particular one Eurylochus, who fell short of his professions; for once . . . he was so angry that he seized the spit with the meat on it and chased his cook right into the marketplace'.[170] There are also suggestions that Pyrrho himself lost his temper or reacted with lively emotion on different occasions.[171] If hardened skeptics fail at emotional detachment, we might conclude that a thoroughly consistent skepticism is practically impossible. (Clearly, we should not lose our temper over minor issues, but we do not need skepticism to come to that conclusion.) Emotional detachment also seems to stand in the way of friendship, which, it could be argued, requires the sharing of deep feelings and partisan commitment.

A second objection to skepticism could be that skepticism is not theoretically consistent. As we explained in earlier paragraphs, Sextus maintains that there is an equally good argument for and against any assertion. Call this the antithesis principle. If, however, the antithesis principle is true, there must be an equally good argument for and against the antithesis principle; that is, there must be an equally good argument for and against skepticism. So how can the skeptic so confidently assert (or assume) that the antithesis principle is sound or true? We are told by ancient writers that both Pyrrho and Sextus aimed at the 'absence of all determination, and withholding of assent'. So how could Pyrrho and Sextus *assent* to skepticism? These logical puzzles can be multiplied endlessly. Skepticism seems at odds with itself. Pursued rigorously, it ends in a series of logical contradictions.

Sextus distinguishes between academic skeptics, who dogmatically assert that knowledge is impossible and Pyrrhonean skeptics, who remain open to the possibility of knowledge but have yet to find it. He maintains that skeptical formulae are not to be interpreted as dogmatic assertions but as indications of an open-ended attitude of noncommittal. Members of the skeptical school went so far, at times, as to actually recommend skepticism about skepticism, comparing it to a medicine, a purge that ultimately purges itself: 'so that after destroying the [rival philosophical theories, Skepticism] turns around and destroys itself, like purge which drives the [bad] substance out, and then is itself eliminated and destroyed'.[172] As one fellow authority puts it, 'Thus in saying "We determine nothing", we

are not determining even that'.[173] This approach is arguably inconsistent. [174]

The third problem with skepticism is the way it ignores the evidence. Skeptics *assume* that there is equal evidence on both sides of every issue. This seems nothing short of preposterous. Sextus claims that even when we cannot come up with a reason for doubting a claim, we can still justify doubt by appealing to as yet unknown arguments. As he explains, 'Whenever [a philosopher] proposes an argument that we are not able to dispose of, we make this reply: . . . "It is possible, as far as nature is concerned, that an argument antithetical to the one now set forth by you is in existence, though as yet unknown by us"'.[175] But this is to justify doubt on any issue whatsoever, regardless of the evidence. Reasonable people do not doubt on principle; they weigh the evidence. The condition of having knowledge is generally taken to mean having enough evidence to convince a *reasonable* person. This is enough for moral knowledge, too.

The skeptics themselves recommend that we depend on laws and customs for moral guidance. But why would anyone respect these conventions unless they represented the accumulated moral *knowledge* of past generations? It seems inconsistent to argue that there are authoritative moral principles but that moral knowledge is impossible.

Finally, the dogmatist opponent could argue that skepticism encourages not mere peace of mind but downright passivity. In fact, skepticism breeds **quietism**, a passive acquiescence to whatever happens. (The term quietism is derived from a seventeenth-century religious movement that preached complete withdrawal from the world.) The American president John F. Kennedy was fond of quoting Dante: 'The hottest places in Hell are reserved for those who in time of moral crisis preserve their neutrality.'[176] (Kennedy gets Dante wrong, but one gets the point.) Virtue sometimes requires a vigorous response to pressing circumstances; it needs to be triggered by strong beliefs about what is right or wrong. It is hard to see how skepticism can provide sufficient motivation for any active resistance to evil.

Although the skeptics champion neutrality, nonpartisanship, and the suspension of belief, these attitudes are not invariably virtuous. In the face of serious evil, moral heroes know that something is wrong, and they strenuously try to fix the problem. (Or, alternatively, they know that something is right and try strenuously to preserve it.) Skepticism proposes neutrality as a way of life, but this may encourage acquiescence to unjust customs, laws, and institutions. How could skepticism provide an incentive for moral reform? At its worst, it seems to focus on academic hair-splitting: this is where the intellectual energy goes. But these mental gymnastics seem a distraction from the ordinary work of morality and may drain us of those robust moral convictions that spark moral heroism.

∾ Applied Philosophy Box 3.6 ∾

We No Longer Have a Moral Compass

In Hartford, Connecticut, indifference and apathy has reached a new high. Just recently, a pedestrian was hit by a car and lay in the middle of the road. Nobody came to the man's rescue.

Video footage taken on the streets of Hartford, Connecticut, has shown a new all-time high in regards to selfishness, apathy, and indifference. Recently, an elderly man had become a victim of a hit-and-run. He was hit by a car as it swerved to the side. After the man was hit, the driver of the car did not bother to stop the car let alone check on him.

The driver just left. 78-year-old Angel Acre Torres' head hit the side of the car and was slammed to the ground like a rag doll. Torres laid there in the middle of the street motionless. Still, nobody came to Torres' aid.

The video shows that the cars passed by and did nothing. Bystanders only stopped and looked at the man. The video reveals that nobody had bothered to help Torres out.

Hartford Police Chief Daryl Roberts said that: 'We no longer have a moral compass'. Roberts said that people seemed to have no regard for each other . . . It was by [luck] that the police officer arrived. If that was not the case, it is unknown what would have happened next. Also in the video, a man on a scooter circled the immobilized Torres before driving off.

The moral problem here is a failure to act. Morality requires more than mere passivity. This seems to be the Achilles' heel of ancient skepticism. The worry is that a skeptical attitude to moral and even physical truth will sap us of the robust conviction we need to act decisively in times of urgent need. How would the skeptics respond to this kind of objection? (Hint: What is mitigated skepticism?) How could one respond in turn to the skeptics?

Source: Susan Duclos, 'Police Chief: "We No Longer Have a Moral Compass" After Hit-and-Run Victim Is Ignored.' *Digital Journal*, www.digitaljournal.com/article/255730, 5 June 2008.

Protagoras: *Nomos* and *Physis*

Whereas the skeptics believed that they were advancing a specific moral point of view, another group of ancient thinkers, the **Sophists**, argued *against* morality. At times, they expressed open hostility to morality, at least as conventionally understood. Much of Plato's philosophy is a response to the Sophist point of view. Consider, now, the Sophist challenge to morality.

The term *Sophist* (in Greek, *sophistes*) is derived from the Greek word *sophia*, which means 'wisdom'. Contemporaries of Socrates, the Sophists or 'wise men' were itinerant teachers who were initially admired in Athens for their learning and eloquence until the movement fell into disrepute subsequent to Socrates's trial and execution. With the passing of time, the Sophists came to be seen as quibblers and demagogues who were interested in politics and public life largely for reasons of personal gain. Plato consistently portrays the Sophists as 'the bad guys', the morally sleazy political hacks whom the noble Socrates opposes. Although some modern scholars have criticized this view as one-sided, there does seem to be something to Plato's criticism.

The Sophists were a wide-ranging group, motivated by personal ambitions rather than by any strict allegiance to any clearly defined set of precepts. They wanted to make money by teaching; they valued prestige and celebrity. They were skilled at rhetoric, the art of persuasion. Slick and smooth-talking, they could defend either side of any issue. The common charge brought against them was that they often made the weaker argument appear stronger. At the same time, there were individual Sophists who were seriously interested in theoretical questions. They argued, first, that there is no objective morality; and second, that morality is not a matter of nature but only of human convention. Let us briefly consider Protagoras, the most famous Sophist, and the challenge the Sophists, in general, posed for moral theory.

Protagoras of Abdera (c. 490–20 BC) was almost universally acclaimed by his contemporaries as the first and most successful Sophist. Although he wrote at least one lost philosophical treatise on truth, he achieved renown as a teacher. Plato depicts Protagoras responding to a student: 'Young man, what will happen to you, if you associate with me, is that the first day of that association you will go home better, and the same thing will happen the next day, and each day thereafter you will make progress towards a better state.'[177] When Socrates asks Protagoras what he means by 'better', they both agree that he is 'talking about political expertise, and [is] promising to make men good citizens of their community'.[178]

Protagoras saw himself, then, as a teacher of civic virtue, as someone whose job was to form in eloquence and common values the next generation of political leaders. It is hard, however, to reconcile morality with Protagoras's well-known subjectivism: the idea that the truth is different for each individual and that no particular account of what is true is better than any other. To use the contemporary idiom, Protagoras believed that truth is relative and that morality is subjective, an account still favoured in some intellectual circles today.

Plato tells us that Protagoras's lost book on truth begins with the enigmatic observation that 'Man is the measure of all things'.[179] What this statement really means is open to question. Protagoras seems to argue that human beings, perhaps because they possess reason, are able to determine, in some authoritative sense, what ultimate reality is. They are able to determine 'of things that are, that they are, and of things that are not, that they are not'.[180] The later Aristotle carefully follows through the logical consequences of his views. He reports,

> Protagoras said that man is the measure of all things, by which he meant that any impression a person receives is also securely true. From this it follows that the same thing both is and is not the case, and is bad and good, . . . because it often happens that something can appear beautiful to one lot of people and the opposite to the other lot, but on Protagoras's view it is what appears to anyone.[181]

Protagoras argues that beauty is in the eye of the beholder. What makes something beautiful is not something in the object itself, but the opinion of the person looking at it. If I say that this is a beautiful painting, this means that beauty exists in this painting *for me*. If you say that this is not a beautiful painting, this means that beauty does not exist in this painting *for you*. If you say it is warm outside, it is warm *for you*. If I say that it is cold outside, it is cold *for me*. So the same thing can be beautiful and not beautiful, warm and cold, existent and non-existent. There is no objective or independent truth about such things. It all depends on the individual.

This seems to be the specific sense in which Protagoras taught that 'man is the measure of all things'. What Protagoras means is not simply that humans are able to describe the world but that their opinions somehow determine what is true and false about the world. Let us recast his famous phrase in more explicit language: The *individual* human, *not the objective world*, is the measure of existence and nonexistence, of what is and what is not the case, and

of good or bad. It is the opinions of the individual human being, not the objective world, that determine the nature of reality.

In other words, Protagoras believes in **relativism**. The truth differs from one individual human being to the next and, indeed, from one human society to the next. This kind of relativism has, however, worrisome repercussions for morality. It will follow that anything that anyone or any community thinks about morality is equally sound or true. But this is not only implausible, it seems a convenient way of rationalizing immoral behaviour, however intemperate, destructive, or self-interested. The Sophists' ambitious students often desired verbal eloquence as a means to ruthless political power. Moral relativism, in justifying any view whatsoever, served their purposes admirably. (Remember that Protagoras was a teacher. He did not champion a partisan moral or political point of view. He spent his time teaching students to argue eloquently and effectively. That was the point: to be able to argue effectively on *any* side of any issue.)

Socrates leads mainstream philosophical tradition in its reaction to these ideas. Simply put, philosophers like Plato and Socrates argued that morality is objective; it is a matter of ***physis***—the Greek word for *nature* (from which we get the modern word *physics*). The Sophists responded that morality is something made up or invented by human beings; it is not a matter of *physis* but of ***nomos***—the Greek word for 'human law' or 'custom'.

Herodotus, the famous ancient Greek historian, joined in, on the Sophist side of things, with a very famous example intended to demonstrate how different societies have divergent standards of behaviour. Herodotus points out how burial rites differ from society to society:

I will give this one proof among many from which it may be inferred that all men hold this belief about [the superiority of] their [own] customs. When Darius was king, he summoned the Greeks who were with him and asked them for what price they would eat their fathers' dead bodies. They answered that there was no price for which they would do it. Then Darius summoned those Indians who are called Callatiae, who eat their parents, and asked them (the Greeks being present and understanding through interpreters what was said) what would make them willing to burn their fathers at death. The Indians cried aloud, that he should not speak of so horrid an act. So firmly rooted are these beliefs; and it is, I think, rightly said in Pindar's poem that custom [*nomos*] is lord of all.[182]

This is a vivid example. The reader immediately sees the problem. The Greeks, who ritually burn their dead on a funeral pyre, react with horror at the idea that someone could be so uncaring as to actually eat their dead; the Indians, on the other hand, who ritually eat their dead, react with equal horror at the idea that someone should be so uncaring as to actually burn their dead. So what is the right way to dispose of the dead? Herodotus thinks there is no fixed answer to such questions. It just depends on who you ask. If you happen to be a Greek, burning is good and eating is bad; if you happen to be an Indian, eating is good and burning is bad. As Protagoras argued, it seems that our sense of right and wrong, of proper and improper, is purely relative, a matter of social custom, of where we come from, or of what group we belong to. Herodotus concludes, then, that human beings invariably believe that their own ways of doing things are true, and that foreign ways of doing things are false. It seems that the Sophists are correct. Virtue is purely a matter of *nomos* or custom.

When we study the history of ethics (as we will throughout the rest of this book), we encounter moral philosophers who, in many different ways, supply a detailed and thorough response to this kind of objection. Although there is no need to engage in a full-fledged rebuttal here, a few brief comments are in order. First, notice that despite his self-assured rhetoric, Herodotus does not prove what he sets to prove. It does not logically follow that cultural diversity *proves* that morality is relative. In fact, Herodotus uses **circular reasoning**. He *assumes* that moral relativism is correct; he does not prove this using logic.

Suppose that we are faced with two cultures: Culture *G* (for *Greek*) approves Practice *F* (for *fire*), and Culture *I* (for *Indian*) disapproves of Practice *F*. Herodotus (along with the Sophists) claims that this shows that morality is relative. But this follows only if Culture *G* and Culture *I* are both right about morality. One could just as easily argue that one group must be wrong and the other group must be right. Human culture is, after all, a fallible institution.

We can present the structure of the Sophist argument in the following way:

Fact: Culture *G* argues for Practice *F*, and Culture *I* argues against *F*.

Assumption: When it comes to morality, every culture is equally right.

Sub-Conclusion: So *G* and *F* must both be right.

Main Conclusion: Therefore, morality is relative.

This may appear to be a reasonable argument, but, in fact, it does no logical work. Examine carefully what we have called the assumption. To say that 'every culture is equally right when it comes to morality' is to say that 'morality is relative'. In other words, we arrive at the conclusion that morality is relative only because we have already assumed that morality is relative. But this argument proves nothing. This way of thinking may have the appearance of logic, but it *assumes* rather than logically demonstrates its point. To use an expression from logic, this kind of argument **begs the question**: that is, it gives no true support for the position and leaves us questioning whether or not the conclusion is true. It is, in the pejorative sense of the term, a mere sophism.

Herodotus uses his example of divergent burial rites to demonstrate an irreconcilable moral difference that separates two cultures. But here again, closer analysis demonstrates just the opposite. What it shows, in fact, is that these vastly different cultures agree on a very basic point of morality. Why are the Greeks disgusted at the thought of eating their parents? Because they think that it is disrespectful; it desecrates something sacred; it violates the remains of a loved one. Why are the Indians disgusted at the thought of burning their parents? Because they think that it is disrespectful; it desecrates something sacred; it violates the remains of a loved one. These cultures practise conspicuously different burial rights but the difference is only skin deep. Hiding underneath these differences is the same basic moral insight: one should not treat the body of the dearly departed disrespectfully. Only a superficial reading of the situation fails to see that these two groups share a common moral sense that includes an entire set of basic beliefs: parents ought to be honoured and respected; we should treat our dead parents the way they would have wanted to be treated; we should not dispose of their bodies in an undignified ways and so on. As we shall see, important authors in the tradition never argue that moral behaviour is entirely uniform and homogenous. They argue, instead, that

we share, at the most basic level, insights into moral principles that can be fitted to individual circumstances in different (and sometimes perplexing) ways.

If the 'morality is always relative' line of reasoning begs the question, one can also argue that the Sophists' position is ultimately inconsistent. Socrates catches Protagoras in a contradiction (the worst logical mistake). He disputes the opening line of Protagoras's famous book that 'man is the measure of all things'. As Socrates insists,

> Why didn't [Protagoras] start off [his book] by saying 'A pig is the measure of all things', or a baboon, or any sentient creature, however outlandish? That would have been a magnificently haughty beginning, showing that although we regard [Protagoras's own] wisdom as remarkable and almost divine, yet he is not better in fact than a tadpole, let alone another human being.[183]

A contradiction occurs when the same person argues that the very same claim is both true and false. Protagoras believes (1) that the truth is what anyone thinks it is. But he also believes (2) that he is a teacher who corrects and improves his students. If, however, whatever we believe about the world is true, how could Protagoras ever *correct* his students? He could correct his students only if they make mistakes, and if they make mistakes, then the truth is not what anyone thinks it is. So Protagoras believes (1) that the truth is what anyone thinks it is and (2) that the truth is not what anyone thinks it is. In other words, he contradicts himself.

Indeed, as Socrates points out, if what Protagoras and the other Sophists teach is true, there would be no room for teaching of any kind. After all, a teacher corrects errors. That is what a teacher does. If, however, truth is in the eye (or brain) of the beholder, there would be no errors to correct. An exasperated Socrates responds to another Sophist, 'If neither speaking falsehood nor thinking falsehood nor ignorance are possible, then surely it is impossible, in any action, to make a mistake, because the agent cannot go wrong in what he does? . . . If action, speech, and thought are not wrong, then who on earth have you come to teach?'[184]

If, as Protagoras claims, no version of the truth is more accurate than any other, there would be no way to distinguish between people in terms of their intelligence or moral success. But the Sophists present themselves as experts, as men who are wiser and more learned than ordinary people. As Socrates explains,

> [Protagoras claims that] each person alone makes up his mind about his own impressions, and all of them are correct and true; [but] if all this is so . . . how on earth are we to distinguish Protagoras, whose cleverness was such that he thought he was justified in teaching others for vast fees, and ourselves, who are less gifted and had to go and be his students, when each of us is the measure of his own cleverness?[185]

As we have already seen, ancient thinkers stipulated a basic rule for morality: 'follow nature'. In effect, the Sophists say that there is no nature and only opinion. Whatever we believe about nature, then, turns out to be true. This kind of permissiveness may initially seem to be tolerant, but it is so excessively tolerant (or loose) that it undermines the very foundation of morality. Morality makes distinctions between good and bad and all the degrees in between. To suggest that all positions are sufficiently truthful, wise, considerate, or beneficial is to remove the basis for morality. The logical conclusion of Sophism seems to be that no one can make a moral mistake. If all moral opinions are equally valid, attempts to differ-

entiate between better and worse actions are seriously misguided.

Although Sophism may seem, at first glance, like a more specific version of skepticism, one ancient source reports that Pyrrho, in fact, 'was . . . most hostile to Sophists'.[186] In some sense, skepticism and Sophism are at antipodes. The skeptics claim that we never have enough evidence to know if our opinions are true, whereas the Sophists claim that our opinions are always true. The skeptics are pushed to a state of equanimity or peace of mind, but the Sophists rush to a position that excuses all. Pyrrho aims at moral and even religious or spiritual enlightenment, whereas the Sophists were professional teachers who expected to be paid, and often handsomely, for their pedagogical services. They were more interested in political ends than in moral enlightenment.

But all is not lost. The philosophical tradition has a way of incorporating whatever is useful from any position and adding it to the fund of moral wisdom passed down to future generations. In one of Plato's dialogues, Protagoras tells a story of how Zeus, the chief god, orders Hermes, the heavenly messenger, to distribute 'justice and decency' to *all* human beings without exception.[187] Protagoras here insists that every human being has justice and decency located deep inside them. Understood in this more nuanced way, Protagoras's claim that man is the measure of all things could be interpreted as elucidating an important theme taken up in later moral philosophy: the idea that every human being (except perhaps for the mentally ill) has a trustworthy moral conscience.

Jesus: Love

We come finally to Jesus, with little doubt the most influential moral and religious thinker of the ancient world. As a historical figure, Jesus is so complex a personality, with so much having been written about him by such a wide variety of authors that we cannot attempt any kind of decisive treatment here. Instead, we will highlight some of the most influential elements of his teaching as they relate specifically to moral philosophy. Jesus's focus on other-centred love as the basis of the moral impetus has been enormously influential in the Western tradition.

Revelation

Jesus of Nazareth (c. 7–2 BC to 26–36 AD) was a Jewish religious prophet and not, strictly speaking, a philosopher. The story of his life as recorded in the four gospels is as much a theological and moral treatise as it is a biography. Jesus, the divinely appointed son of Mary and Joseph, comes from Galilee; spends three years of public ministry in healing and preaching; is baptized by John the Baptist in the Jordan River; and is crucified in Jerusalem, on the orders of Pontius Pilate—officially for sedition against the Roman Empire and also, according to the Gospels, for religious blasphemy.

Jesus is not someone who follows the Greek tradition of logical argument. He comes out of an explicitly religious Jewish tradition, one that emphasizes Scripture, prophets, preaching (as opposed to arguing), parables, and miracle-working. Still, one can draw an intriguing parallel between Jesus and Socrates (whom I discuss in the next chapter). Both men avoid technical jargon and sophisticated language, speaking about ordinary things using down-to-earth images and metaphors familiar to all. Both men are viewed as moral heroes, in life and in death, and both have been portrayed as martyrs who were unjustly executed and met death with bravery, refusing to modify their teaching or to grovel for mercy. Both suggest that the good will be rewarded and that the bad will be punished after death. And both seem to regard death as something not to be feared. But there is an important difference between them.

The difference between this Jewish prophet and this Greek philosopher boils down to the difference between Revelation and logic, religion and philosophy. The *Bible* is an example of **Revelation**. Revelation communicates truth through some sort of divine inspiration and operates through trustworthy divine pronouncement. Christians believe that the *Bible* reveals God's will through the written world. But Revelation is not restricted to Scripture. Jesus presents himself as the word spoken by God, as someone who reveals God's will through his way of life, words, gestures, and actions.[188] Socrates, unlike Jesus, does not claim divine parentage. He is not a prophet but a philosopher. His method is forensic. He is a Sherlock Holmes of human behaviour who carefully examines human aspiration in the light of *natural* human intelligence. He tests what people say to see if it holds up under the weight of logical scrutiny. As it turns out, Socrates does claim to have a supernatural aid (an angelic-like voice) that, on occasion, deters him from doing wrong. Nonetheless, in his role as a philosopher, he uses unaided human intelligence to investigate the nature of human life and aspiration.

Unlike Socrates, Jesus is not a constructor of arguments and a champion of natural reason. His teaching rests on supernatural authority. Jesus declares, 'I do nothing on my own, but I say only what the Father taught me'.[189] God speaks through Jesus. At least this is what the Gospels tell us. Although there is a logic to what Jesus says, he is more the religiously inspired sage who gives remarkable advice than the logician or the philosophy professor.

Jesus's Moral Claims

Jesus teaches about morality using various techniques: he preaches; he tells parables or stories; he comments on and interprets Scripture; he responds to pressing circumstances through memorable gestures; and he expresses deep moral insights in powerful, aphoristic-like, and often enigmatic utterances. We can give only a very brief summary of his moral doctrines here. Jesus makes four overlapping moral claims we will focus on: (1) we should act according to the Golden Rule; (2) we should judge ourselves by the same standards we use to judge other people; (3) we should be moral even to those who act immorally, and (4) we should regard personal love as the very core and origin of morality. Let us consider these in order.

'Do Unto Others What You Would Want Them To Do Unto You'

First, Jesus formulates, in explicit and uncompromising terms, the famous **Golden Rule**, 'Do unto others what you would want them to do unto you'.[190] After telling his listeners to comply with the principle, he immediately adds, 'for this is the Law and the Prophets'.[191] Jesus is not trying to teach us something new, nor is he is not trying to surprise us. He is trying to express in a brief and unforgettable phrase what he believes is already implicit in the Jewish tradition. What is remarkable here is the way Jesus is able to come up with a deft phrase that economically expresses what we already know deep in our hearts. On hearing the Golden Rule, the proper response is 'Of course: this *must be* what morality is all about!'

As we discussed at the beginning of this chapter, Master Kong articulates a Silver Rule according to which we are to refrain from inflicting the harm on other people we do not want them to inflict on us. The Golden Rule, however, goes further. It is not enough to refrain from hurting others; we must actively help them. We desire help from other people when we are in need, and so we must help other people when they are in need, even if they do not ask, and even if it is to our own disadvantage. This is a radical teaching, a lofty moral ideal. (Some contemporary authors refer to Golden Rule ethics as an ethics of reciprocity.)

Logical quibbles about the Golden Rule miss the point. The Golden Rule is *not* intended as an argument or a proof. It opens a window on moral knowledge that we already possess in some tacit form within us. It requires us to be consistent, not with some arbitrary, mechanical standard, but with a basic natural wisdom we already possess. The idea is that if we honestly look inside ourselves and sincerely try to understand what is at the centre of morality, we will discover this simple principle.[192]

One could, of course, misinterpret the Golden Rule. Clearly, if we have immoral desires, extending these desires to other people will not make us more moral. If I enjoy murdering other people, the Golden Rule is not about letting other people murder me. That is just silly. The thing is not to have immoral desires in the first place; then we can apply the Golden Rule properly.

As well, the Golden Rule is not a substitute for moral intelligence. Jesus directs his teaching toward good-willed (but imperfect) people who already have a basic sense of morality and an understanding of individual circumstances. If I would like to be fed a steak, given a beer, and brought to the hockey game, that does not mean that I should feed steak to vegetarians, give beer to teetotalers, or bring

◌ Applied Philosophy Box 3.7 ◌

Some Religious Expressions of the Gold and Silver Rules

Buddhism:
' . . . A state that is not pleasing or delightful to me, how could I inflict that upon another?'
—Samyutta NIkaya v. 353

'Hurt not others in ways that you yourself would find hurtful.'
—Udana-Varga 5:18

Hinduism:
'This is the sum of duty: do not do to others what would cause pain if done to you.'
—Mahabharata 5:1517

Islam:
'None of you [truly] believes until he wishes for his brother what he wishes for himself.'
—Number 13 of Imam 'Al-Nawawi's Forty Hadiths'

Judaism:
'...Thou shalt love thy neighbor as thyself.'
—Leviticus 19:18

'What is hateful to you, do not to your fellow man. This is the law: all the rest is commentary.'
—Talmud, Shabbat 31a.

'And what you hate, do not do to any one.'
—Tobit 4:15

Shinto:
'The heart of the person before you is a mirror. See there your own form.'

'Be charitable to all beings, love is the representative of God.'
—Ko-ji-ki Hachiman Kasuga

Taoism:
'Regard your neighbor's gain as your own gain, and your neighbor's loss as your own loss.'
—T'ai Shang Kan Ying P'ien.

'The sage has no interest of his own, but takes the interests of the people as his own.'
—Tao Teh Ching, Chapter 49

Yoruba: (Nigeria):
'One going to take a pointed stick to pinch a baby bird should first try it on himself to feel how it hurts.'

Zoroastrianism:
'That nature alone is good which refrains from doing unto another whatsoever is not good for itself.'
—Dadistan-i-dinik 94:5

'Whatever is disagreeable to yourself do not do unto others.'
—Shayast-na-Shayast 13:29

Source: Ontario Consultants on Religious Tolerance, 'Some "Ethic of Reciprocity" passages from the religious texts of various religions and secular beliefs.' *Religious Tolerance.org*, www.religioustolerance.org/reciproc.htm, 9 November 2010.

people who hate sports to watch hockey. Again, this is just silly. The Golden Rule operates on a more fundamental level. We would like other people to treat us like human beings, so we should treat them like human beings in return.

Judge Others as You Would Have Them Judge You

The second moral principle Jesus teaches has to do with how we judge other people and ourselves. In the Sermon on the Mount, Jesus declares,

Do not judge so that you will not be judged. For in the way you judge, you will be judged; and by your standard of measure, it will be measured to you. Why do you look at the speck that is in your brother's eye, but do not notice the log that is in your own eye? Or how can you say to your brother, 'Let me take the speck out of your eye', and behold, the log is in your own eye? You hypocrite, first take the log out of your own eye, and then you will see clearly to take the speck out of your brother's eye.[193]

When it comes to moral judgment, there are two associated problems: (1) we are too hard on other people; (2) we are too easy on ourselves. We see a tiny imperfection in our neighbour's eye and dwell on it without noticing that the very same imperfection is multiplied many times over in our own eye. We reprove our brother for the slightest errors as we tolerate much worse errors in our own behaviour without any hint of self-correction. Jesus tells us to be gentle in judging others so that God will be gentle with us at the Last Judgment.

Be Moral To Everyone

The third moral principle Jesus invokes is that we must be moral to *everyone*. It is not enough to benefit and respect those whom we like or who are good to us. We must care even for those who dislike or oppose us. We must do *good* things for *bad* people. In the Gospel of Luke, Jesus tells his disciples, 'Love your enemies, do good to those who hate you, bless those who curse you, pray for those who mistreat you. If someone strikes you on one cheek, turn to him the other also. If someone takes your cloak, do not stop him from taking your tunic. . . . If anyone takes what belongs to you, do not demand it back'.[194] In the Gospel of Matthew, he abounds in the same sense,

You have heard that it was said, 'An eye for an eye and a tooth for a tooth'. But I say to you, Do not resist one who is evil. But if any one strikes you on the right cheek, turn to him the other also; and if any one would sue you and take your coat, let him have your cloak as well; and if any one forces you to go one mile, go with him two miles. Give to him who begs from you, and do not refuse him who would borrow from you.[195]

The Old Testament law of *lex talionis*, of returning like for like—an eye for an eye, a tooth for a tooth—is overturned. Someone who returns hatred for hatred, violence for violence, fraud for fraud, stoops to the level of the wicked. Immorality is not, under any circumstances, an option. Even when dealing with immoral people, the moral person always acts morally.

This radical advice can, however, be misconstrued. Jesus is not excusing wrongdoing. He is not saying that we should stand idly by and watch evil being done. His point is that we must move beyond what is minimally required by the law and aim at moral heroism. Ordinary decency is not enough. Jesus upbraids his followers: 'If you love those who love you, what credit is that to you? Even sinners love those who love them. And if you do good to those who are good to you, what credit is that to you? Even sinners do that. And if you lend to those from whom you expect repayment, what credit is that to you? Even sinners lend to sinners, expecting to be repaid in full.'[196]

Jesus, conceived of as a moral philosopher, is a virtue-ethicist. The goal is virtue, excellence in the highest degree, even perfection. While presenting himself as the fulfillment and apotheosis of the Jewish religious tradition, Jesus raises the bar. It is not enough to be partially moral, to be moral to a middling degree, to obey the letter of the law. Jesus teaches the crowds:

You have heard that it was said to the people long ago, 'Do not murder, and anyone who murders will be subject to judgment'. But I tell you that anyone who is angry with his brother will be subject to judgment. . . . You have heard that it was said, 'Do not commit adultery'. But I tell you that anyone who looks at a woman lustfully has already committed adultery with her in his heart. . . . You have heard that it was said, 'Love your neighbor and hate your enemy'. But I tell you: Love your enemies and pray for those who persecute you.[197]

The message is clear and unequivocal. Go beyond ordinary human behaviour; go beyond what is expected or required; aim at moral perfection. Jesus informs his followers, 'You must be perfect as your father in Heaven is perfect'.[198] This is, needless to say, a strenuous ideal. Succeeding in the moral life is like climbing Mount Everest: the way is very narrow, very winding, and very steep.

Regard Love as the Core of Morality

The fourth moral principle Jesus subscribes to identifies morality with love. We read this in the Gospel of Matthew:

> Then one of them, a lawyer, asked [him a question], tempting him, and saying, 'Master, which [is] the great commandment in the law?' [And] Jesus said unto him, 'Thou shalt love the Lord thy God with all thy heart, and with all thy soul, and with all thy mind. This is the first and great commandment. And the second [is] like unto it, Thou shalt love thy neighbor as thyself. On these two commandments hang all the law and the prophets'.[199]

The lawyer in the story is trying to stump Jesus. Jewish religious law is a marvel of intricate legal thought. Again, Jesus cuts through the myriad qualifications. The heart of the moral project, the nub on which the entire wheel turns is love. Love God; love your neighbour.

By themselves, these two commandments tell us all we have to know, all we have to do to succeed at the moral life. All moral obligations derive, according to Jesus, from these two basic requirements.

Comparing Jesus to Other Moralists

How would we compare Jesus with other ancient moralists? We will dwell on four crucial points: (1) the importance of logical consistency; (2) the importance of morality; (3) the importance of inner peace; and (4) the importance of nature.

Regarding Logical Consistency

The first point that should be emphasized is that Jesus, like other moral thinkers, believes in using logic to sort out the difference between right and wrong. Despite the overwhelmingly religious orientation of his moral world view, the sage from Nazareth does not reduce morality to mere mysticism. Jesus insists on principles. We are to treat others the way we would want to be treated; to judge ourselves and others with equal severity; to deal morally with everyone without exception; and to make all our actions conform to the same principle of selfless love. These principles represent a demand for logical consistency. We are told to comply with basic normative standards; we are not free to just act on our unexamined feelings. We must rigorously apply the same ethical principles to our own and other people's actions without favouritism or self-indulgence.

Consider the second principle of Jesus: that we are to judge ourselves as we judge other people. Jesus is telling us that it is not the identity of the agent but what he or she is doing that is at issue. The nature of our moral evaluation must correspond to the nature of the act.

We must judge similar cases similarly. This is a logical not just a religious requirement for morality.

Regarding Morality

The second way in which Jesus's moral teaching resembles that of the moral philosophers is in his insistence on the momentous nature of morality. Like most of the other philosophers we have covered (except perhaps some figures identified with the Sophists), Jesus emphasizes the supreme importance of morality as a human aspiration. Jesus is not afraid of hyperbole. How important is it to avoid evil? 'If your right eye causes you to sin, gouge it out and throw it away. It is better for you to lose one part of your body than for your whole body to be thrown into hell. And if your right hand causes you to sin, cut it off and throw it away. It is better for you to lose one part of your body than for your whole body to go into hell.'[200] This is a manner of speech. Jesus is not recommending self-mutilation. He is trying to communicate the absolute *urgency* of the moral imperative.

We could express this teaching of Jesus as a logical argument:

> If you are going to act immorally, then you should cut off the part of your body that acts immorally.
> You don't want to cut off any part of your body.
> Therefore, don't act immorally.

(You should recognize this as the *modus tollens* pattern of argument referred to earlier: if *A*, then *B*, not *B*, therefore, not *A*.) Obviously, people do everything they can to avoid bodily injury. Jesus knows this. He is recommending that we regard evil in the same spirit. This way of expressing the thought drives home the message that evil is not something to be taken lightly. Morality matters.

Jesus does engage in some fierce rhetoric about the human propensity for sin. But his preaching is also about the virtue of hope. In the **Beatitudes**, Jesus consoles the innocent who are mistreated with the promise of future happiness. To paraphrase, he claims, that the poor in spirit, the grieving, the humble, those who hunger and thirst for righteousness, the merciful, the pure of heart, the peacemakers, and those who are persecuted for the sake of righteousness are 'blessed'.[201] The English term *blessed* is a translation of the Greek ***makarios***, which means 'divinely happy', 'fortunate', or 'rich'. Jesus is assuring his followers that those who suffer innocently will be, in the end, divinely happy. He does this using a manner of speech that deliberately flaunts the apparent contradiction. This sounds a lot like Socrates's affirmation that the good *must* be rewarded. Nothing else makes logical or religious sense.

Regarding Inner Peace

A third parallel can be drawn between Jesus's promise of peace (*shalom*) to his followers and the preoccupation with *ataraxia* in ancient moral philosophy. Jesus proposes interior peace as a reward for a life of righteousness. He tells his disciples, 'Peace I leave with you; my peace I give to you. . . . Do not let your hearts be troubled or afraid'.[202] The traditional Hebrew word for *peace* is **shalom**, which designates a state of tranquility and contentment associated with completeness, prosperity, health, and abundance of life. The Evangelists depict Jesus as the one who brings *shalom* to those who believe in him. Consider the story of the Samaritan woman at the well:

> [Jesus] came to a town of Samaria called Sychar, . . . Tired from his journey, [he] sat down there at the well. . . . A woman of Samaria came to draw

water. Jesus said to her, 'Give me a drink'. . . . The Samaritan woman said to him, 'How can you, a Jew, ask me, a Samaritan woman, for a drink?' (For Jews use nothing in common with Samaritans.) Jesus answered and said to her, 'If you knew the gift of God and who is saying to you, 'Give me a drink', you would have asked him and he would have given you living water'. The woman said to him, 'Sir, you do not even have a bucket and the cistern is deep; where then can you get this living water? Are you greater than our father Jacob, who gave us this cistern and drank from it himself with his children and his flocks?' Jesus answered and said to her, 'Everyone who drinks this water will be thirsty again; but whoever drinks the water I shall give will never thirst; the water I shall give will become in him a spring of water welling up to eternal life'.[203]

Jesus is not speaking of physical water but of spiritual well-being. Physical water quenches physical thirst. The truth Jesus brings quenches spiritual thirst. He assures his interlocutor, a woman from a lower caste, that anyone who believes in him will have an inexhaustible source of spiritual solace that opens up within them. The phrase 'living water' signifies 'running water' as opposed to 'stagnant water'. In the hot, arid land of Samaria, fresh running water was a priceless commodity. Mortal life depended on it. Jesus tells the Samaritan woman that life-giving religious truth is much, much more valuable.

As we mentioned above, we can draw intriguing comparisons between Jesus and Socrates. Socrates, as we relate in the next chapter, compares the soul of the immoral individual to a leaky jar that can never be filled. His point is that immoral people are always dissatisfied; it doesn't matter how much water you pour in, they are still thirsty. Jesus, on the other hand, claims that his followers are *never*

thirsty; they do not have to labour to find refreshment; there is a source of fresh, running water that opens up inside them. Even Jesus, in this sense, preaches a gospel of peace, not unlike Socrates, the Stoics, the Cynics, the skeptics, and even the Epicureans.

Regarding the Importance of Nature

We have touched on three parallels between Jesus and other ancient moral philosophers. If, however, other moral philosophers emphasize the **nature principle**, the idea that we should always act in accordance with nature, Jesus, in line with the rabbinic tradition, adds a higher supernatural dimension to social, political, cultural, psychological, or biological descriptions of human condition. Insomuch as there is a philosophy of human nature in the gospels, Jesus's teachings might be said to resemble that of the later Stoics: we are children of God and children of his creation; the merely political pales in comparison to the moral. If, however, the Stoics emphasize reason, Jesus emphasizes love. As later authors in the tradition came to realize, love need not exclude reason, and reason need not exclude love. Indeed, love and reason may be understood as different expressions of the very same thing. One might argue that this idea is already implicit in the moral thought of many early philosophers.

To the degree that Jesus has an account of nature, it is anchored in a wider story about God, Creation, Original Sin, the Last Judgment, Heaven and Hell, and the history of the chosen people. Jesus believes, first and foremost, that human beings are fallen and in need of salvation. Nature comes from God, but human happiness is not possible until we repair the broken relationship between sinful human beings and the Divine Source of all Creation. Human beings are capable of moral success, but moral success requires grace, God's unmerited help, which is available only through faith in God's Son.

Jesus is not alone in his view that we must act in accordance with not merely the natural, but also the supernatural. Early philosophers do make allusions to the divinity and the eternal. For example, Pyrrho's apparently mystical way of life and his contempt for the physical, perceptible world seems to have been motivated by deep spiritual values. With Jesus, however, the focus on religious truth takes a very explicit turn. Jesus believes that we can have religious knowledge. His morality, so to speak, derives from his theology. This focus on the supernatural need not hinge, however, on a repudiation of nature. Seen from a Judeo-Christian perspective, God did not create a bad world. The world was originally good and

still bears the potential to be fully good; it has, however, been debased by human sin. It is as if the cosmos is broken and stands in need of repair. The proper order of things needs to be restored by religion. A later Christian philosopher, such as Thomas Aquinas, does not deny the goodness of human nature but attempts to push moral striving to a higher level.

Jesus teaches us that morality begins with the basic requirement that we should love other people for their own sake. This insistence on the importance of other-directed, asymmetrical love has justifiably had an enormous influence on the history of Western ethics. Many of the arguments and moral principles formulated by later philosophers have their origins in the ancient period. In particular, Jesus and Socrates (whom we discuss in the next chapter) have had an enduring influence on later generations right up to the present day.

❧ Questions for Study and Review ❧

1. How did moral philosophy start?
2. Master Kong personifies moral success and failure. Explain.
3. Explain what the Chinese concept of *Dao* represents.
4. Why was Heraclitus called 'Heraclitus the obscure'? What is an aphorism?
5. Define *hedonism*.
6. Why does Democritus think that habitual sensual pleasure, say habitual use of drink or pornography, is a bad idea?
7. The English word *cynic* derives from the Greek word for _____. Explain. Compare the modern and ancient meanings of the term.
8. Why did Diogenes consider himself a citizen of the world?
9. What are the fundamental flaws in Cynicism?
10. Epicurus distinguishes between three kinds of desires. Explain.
11. Explain what moral egoism is. Why is Epicurus an egoist?
12. Epictetus distinguishes between two types of reason. Explain.
13. Explain the Stoic concept of 'apathy'. How does it differ from the modern concept of apathy? Relate it to the 'nature principle'.
14. The skeptics believe that we cannot have certain knowledge about morality. What, then, do they suggest we can rely on when it comes to moral judgment?
15. Explain the skeptical method of antithesis, *epoche*, and *ataraxia*.

16. What is a Sophist?
17. What is the difference between a philosophical approach to ethics and a religious approach to ethics?

18. What are some similarities between Jesus and Socrates?
19. In what sense is Jesus a virtue ethicist?
20. Explain the meaning of the story of the woman at the well.

∽ Suggestions for Further Reading ∾

Many of the relevant texts here are scattered in fragments but thankfully, many ancient sources are increasingly available (in translation) online for the general or introductory reader. To cite only three examples:

- 'Peithô's Web: Classical Rhetoric and Persuasion,' includes Diogenes Laertius, *The Lives and the Opinions of the Eminent Philosophers,* C.D. Yonge, trans.: http://classicpersuasion.org/pw/diogenes/.
- 'The Stoic Foundation' (maintained by Keith H. Seddon) includes references to a wide series of online texts: www.btinternet.com/~k.h.s/stoic-foundation.htm.
- And the *Epicurus & Epicurean Philosophy* website, hosted by Vincent Cook, again, presents a wide range of translations: www.epicurus.net/.
- Confucius, *The Analects*, Raymond Dawson, trans. (Oxford, UK: Oxford, 2000).

- *The First Philosophers: The PreSocratics and the Sophists,* Robin Waterfield, trans. (Oxford, UK: Oxford, 2000).
- Diogenes Laertius, *Lives of the Eminent Philosophers*, R.D. Hicks, trans. (Cambridge, MA; London, UK: Harvard, 2000). (Loeb Classical Library.)
- *The Bible: Authorized King James Version with Apocrypha*, Robert Carroll and Stephen Prickett, introduction and notes (Oxford, UK: Oxford, 1998).
- For online editions of the Bible, see BibleGateway.com: http://www.biblegateway.com.
- Cicero, *On Obligations*, P.G. Walsh, trans. (Oxford UK: Oxford, 2000).
- Marcus Aurelius, *Meditations of Marcus Aurelius Antoninus* and *A Selection from the Letters of Marcus and Fronto*, A.L. Farquharson, trans. (*Meditations*), R.B. Rutherford, trans. (*Letters*) (Oxford, UK: Oxford, 1998).

Chapter Four

Socrates
and Plato

---

৩ Chapter Objectives

After reading this chapter you should be able to:
- Describe who Socrates and Plato were and the historical relationship between them.
- Explain Socratic ideas and methods, such as *elenchus*, the teacher as midwife, the role of the philosopher as gadfly, the relationship between ignorance and immorality, the problem with hedonism, the logically necessary link between morality and happiness, and the asymmetrical nature of morality.
- Explain major themes in Plato's work, including the story of Gyges's ring, the Platonic notion of forms, the Divided Line, the form of the good, the analogy of the cave, the tripartite soul, the model of the human individual as chimera, and the close relationship between politics and morality.
- Illustrate and apply these key ideas to modern day events, such as those reported in the media.
- Explain some major lines of criticism directed at Plato's system.

Introduction

Socrates and his pupil Plato have had a long and pervasive influence on the progress of philosophy in the Western world. It is hard to imagine two more famous philosophers in any period of history. Because Socrates (like Jesus) never wrote anything down, we must mine Plato's texts for information about the original content of his teaching. This is not a straight-forward task as Plato, who is an excellent writer as well as a philosopher, undoubtedly availed himself of a certain poetic license in his retelling of events and situations. His dialogues are literary dramatizations rather than detailed journalistic reports of historical events.

Scholars often divide Plato's works into an early, a middle, and a late period. According to this tentative historical schema, Plato begins his career with short, literal reports of Socrates's actual practice of asking his interlocutors questions about virtue. In his middle period, he moves to construct a detailed metaphysical view, situating the practice of morality within wider questions about politics and the ultimate nature of reality. In his late period, he revisits the themes of his middle period, qualifying earlier arguments and revising some of his earlier conclusions. Much of the knowledge we have of the real, historical figure of Socrates is gleaned from Plato's so-called early dialogues.

In this section I shall discuss Socrates's viewpoint first and go on to examine Plato's mature moral philosophy. Although we cannot definitively distinguish between Socrates's and Plato's ideas, we can draw contrasting portraits of these two original thinkers. Socrates is the teacher; Plato is the student. Socrates looked the part of an ordinary citizen: he mingled with everyone, standing on street corners, talking non-stop to anyone who would listen. Plato was the son of a noble family and he became the headmaster of his own university. He was a famous intellectual and author who offered systematic treatments of the mysteries of metaphysics and epistemology. Early philosophical schools such as the Stoics, Cynics, skeptics, and Epicureans all claimed that they were emulating the way of life of their philosophical hero, Socrates. Plato's treatises came to have an overpowering influence on later philosophers that continues all the way up into the present day.

The contemporary reader may be unprepared for the orientation of Socrates's and Plato's moral philosophy. Both thinkers identify virtue with knowledge and associate vice with ignorance. Plato, in particular, believes that we first need to know what reality is before we can understand the nature of morality. Once we have come to an adequate understanding of the world and our place within it, we can come to a better understanding of what it means to pursue a truly moral life.

Socratic Teachings

As we have seen in the previous chapter, there were earlier philosophers than Socrates. Nonetheless, Socrates (469–399 BC) was such a powerful influence that he is often thought of as the father of philosophy. Indeed, early philosophers regarded him with such reverence that he could almost be called the patron saint of philosophy. Despite his important place in the history of philosophy, however, there is no definitive historical record of exactly who Socrates was. We have to piece together a picture of this famous Athenian from several historical sources.

Ancient authors report that Socrates was a modest stone mason and a loyal citizen of Athens; a good foot soldier who served his country in wartime; a father of three sons; and a man who devoted his later life to moral philosophy. He was a free man, a member of the lower aristocracy, who was described as walking around Athens bare-footed in a tattered old cloak. His wife, Xanthippe, was apparently dissatisfied with his lack of practical sense and his inattention to household matters, due probably to what she saw as his excessive enthusiasm for philosophy.

Although Socrates was widely seen by his contemporaries as an amateur teacher, he resolutely asserted that he had never taught anyone anything but simply set about searching for the truth. Unlike the Sophists, he never received money for teaching. Although Plato informs us that Socrates purposely avoided political life, his eventual trial and condemnation on charges of treason were, in large part, politically motivated. He was eventually executed—and, according to reports, forced to drink a cup of hemlock—for corrupting the youth. In death, he became something of a martyr for philosophy.

Although he must have been a riveting and charismatic conversationalist, legend has it that Socrates was ugly. Indeed, very ugly. He was described as short, pot-bellied, balding, thick-lipped, snub-nosed, with protruding eyes and a cadaverous complexion.[1] Such reports are, no doubt, highly exaggerated. Ancient authors seized on the plain-looking, poorly-dressed Socrates as a perfect illustration of the age-old idea that beauty is a property of the soul, not the body. They surely embellished their stories for better effect. Socrates's unimpressive looks drove home the general principle that it is moral and intellectual beauty that matters. (Socrates's infamous pupil Alcibiades, a traitor to Athens, was, in sharp contrast, reported to be physically handsome but morally shallow.)

Unlike later philosophers, Socrates did not write anything down. He was not the author of textbooks and treatises; he avoided monologues; he did not give public lectures. He is mostly someone who responds to objections and questions in the course of his conversations with other people. Given the scattered, complex nature of the primary source material, the best way to approach Socrates's philosophy is to break his teaching, life, and reputation into a list of individual assertions. The rest of this section is organized in the following manner: each subtitle makes a new claim about Socrates's influence, attitude, or world view. Taken together, these individual affirmations provide a comprehensive summary of Socrates's philosophical heritage. In the prose text following each subtitle, the relevant point is explained in greater detail.

A Perfect Mirror of Morality

Although the comic author Aristophanes pokes fun of Socrates in one of his plays, ancient philosophers looked to him as a source of moral inspiration. One main idea pervades philosophical discussions of Socrates: here is a moral hero! Here was a man we should emulate! Plato finishes the story of Socrates's death with a comment by his student Phaedo: '[So] that . . . was the end of our companion, a man who, among those of his time [was] the best, and the wisest too, and the most just.'[2] The best, the wisest, the most just. This is how Cynics, Stoics, skeptics, and Epicureans regarded Socrates in ancient times. They were impressed, not merely by his logical arguments, but by his example—by the way he lived and died, invariably demonstrating humility, good judgment, honesty, temperance, courage, and good humour. These different schools of philosophy all tried to emulate Socrates, taking his life to be a perfect mirror of morality.

On Religion

Socrates likely had unorthodox religious beliefs for his place and time, but there is no reason to doubt that he was a sincerely religious man. Like some of the earlier pre-Socratics, he was attracted to monotheism—which would have been shocking to ordinary, polytheistic Greek citizens who believed in a constellation of gods, including Zeus, Apollo, Athena, Dionysius, and so on. If, however, Socrates was mildly skeptical about details of Greek legend and mythology, he shows a genuine respect for religious practice and ritual, takes the idea of life-after-death very seriously, and argues that his own philosophical mission is divinely inspired. Indeed, Socrates even claims that he hears a supernatural voice that guides him in important decisions, and he goes so far as to insist that if he must choose between obeying the Athenians and obeying the god, he must obey the god.

While Socrates was intellectually critical of all belief, including religious belief, some modern commentators suggest that Socrates (and Plato) were hostile or at least indifferent to Greek religion. They base their accounts on a short dialogue called the *Euthyphro* in which Plato recounts a discussion between Socrates and a young man called Euthyphro, who could be aptly described as a religious fanatic. Euthyphro wants to have his father tried in court as a murderer because of the largely accidental death of a criminal slave. (Fathers were revered in Greek society, and ordinary Greek citizens would have considered any attempt to bring one's father to court on murder charges as almost insane.) Euthyphro, who does not lack confidence, insists that his actions are holy and that he is imitating the chief god, Zeus, who punished his own father (Cronos) for his evil deeds. Socrates, who is sincerely shocked, demands an explanation for his strange actions.

In the discussion that follows, Euthyphro presents an uncritical religious rationale for his actions, which Socrates duly deflates. Euthyphro, who is hardly a subtle theologian, argues that things are holy because they are loved by the gods. Socrates responds that Euthyphro has the relationship backward. It is not because the gods love something that makes it holy; rather, they love it because it is holy: '[It] is loved because it is holy, [it is] not holy because it is loved.'[3] Socrates does not dispute the idea that the gods love what is holy.

Still, this does not count as an explanation of what the good is. As he tells Euthyphro, 'And so, . . . when you are asked what the holy might be, it looks like you'd prefer not to explain its essence to me, but would rather tell me one of its properties—namely, that the holy has the property of being loved by the gods; but you still haven't told me what it is'.[4]

Socrates wants a definition of the holy, which Euthyphro is unable to give. Suffice it to say, without entering into the details of the argument, that Socrates is rightly understood as presenting a challenge to uncritical religious belief. If, however, Socrates is, like other philosophers, skeptical about some aspects of the Greek myths (which include the gods doing many unsavoury and immoral acts), it does not follow that all religious belief is uncritical. In Plato's eyes, the difference between Euthyphro and Socrates is not that one is religious and the other is not. The difference is that Euthyphro is out to harm someone for religious reasons, whereas Socrates is out to help others for religious reasons. Euthyphro may be a sincerely religious person, but he is gullible and unreflective. Clearly, Socrates believes that religion can be abused and that even religious belief must be open to rational scrutiny. It does not follow, however, that he is an irreligious figure.

We should be careful about attributing contemporary religious attitudes to Socrates. Plato's teacher was not, for example, Christian, or Muslim, or Jewish. But neither did he subscribe to a secular humanism that would banish religion from public life. Whatever our personal views about religion, this book is intended to provide a view of morality that is, in a philosophical spirit, open to religious and nonreligious readers alike. Socrates warns against religious complacency. It is not enough to smugly assume that the gods approve of our actions. But he is equally critical of complacency when it comes to unreflective moral and political beliefs. Whatever our deep views about things, Socrates believes that we must critically test our beliefs and actions in the light of reason.

On Morality as Human Aspiration

Plato reports that Socrates would not do something unjust at his trial (i.e., lie to the court) even to save his own life. As Socrates himself declares to the jurors, 'I would not submit to a single person for fear of death, contrary to what is just; nor would I do so, even if I were to lose my life on the spot'.[5] In other words, morality is more important than life; it is better to be good and die than to be bad and live.

But, for Socrates, even this is not strong enough. The moral individual does not simply consider morality as somewhat superior to many other good things; no, morality is so vastly superior to all other good things that, as a human goal, it stands supreme above all else. The biological fact of life pales in significance to the awesome responsibility of morality. Again, Socrates addresses his jurors: 'you are sadly mistaken . . . if you suppose that a man with even a grain of self-respect should reckon up the risks of living or dying, rather than simply considering, whenever he does anything, whether his actions are just or unjust, the deeds of a good man or a bad one.'[6]

Socrates believes that morality is not only worth dying for; it is the only thing worth living for. Not to understand this basic truth is to be less than human. In contemporary philosophy, the idea that morality is the most important human preoccupation is sometimes captured in the awkward phrase, 'the overridingness of morality'. If we have to choose between being moral and being wealthy or gaining polit-

ical power or having friends, we must always choose morality. Moral considerations *override* other considerations. In any competition with other human aspirations, morality always wins out. Some contemporary philosophers debate the issue, but Socrates would have scoffed at any suggestion to the contrary.

On Moral Philosophy

Moral philosophy is Socrates's primary preoccupation. At his trial, he makes fun of the idea that he is a scientific philosopher studying the secrets of nature. What he wants to learn about is virtue. As we shall see, Plato transforms Socrates's hints and suggestions about the ultimate nature of reality and life after death into a complicated metaphysics, but Socrates has a more practical bent. He firmly believes that the main purpose of philosophy is learning how to be a good person.

On Morality as an Irritant

Socrates presents himself as the gadfly sent by the god to rouse the great horse of Athens from its moral inertia. In the course of his trial, he boldly tells his fellow Athenians:

> I have been literally attached by God to our city, as if to a horse—a large thoroughbred, which is quite sluggish because of its size, and needs to be roused by some sort of gadfly. Yes, in me, I believe, God has attached to our city just such a creature—the kind which is constantly alighting everywhere on you, all day long, arousing, cajoling, or reproaching each and every one of you. . . . Perhaps you will heed [my accusers], and give me a swat: you could happily finish me off, and spend the rest of your life asleep—unless God, in his compassion for you, were to send you someone else.[7]

Socrates thinks that moral philosophy is supposed to make us feel uncomfortable.

Moral teachers succeed—they do not fail—when they irritate their students, for this intellectual annoyance will goad the students on to deeper reflection on the meaning of decency and virtue. Socrates also believes that his pursuit of moral truth is a divinely inspired mission and that it makes Athenians better people. He observes,

> Those are my orders from my god, I do assure you. I feel that no greater good has ever befallen you in our city than my service to the god; all I do is to go about persuading you, young and old alike, not to care for your bodies or for your wealth so intensely as for the greatest possible well-being of your souls.[8]

But persuading other people to act morally is a risky operation. None of us likes to be criticized. Plato suggests that it is annoyance and anger at Socrates's moral admonishments that brings about his execution. Socrates upbraids the Athenians: 'if you imagine that by putting people to death you will prevent anyone from reviling you for not living rightly, you are badly mistaken.'[9] The way to effectively silence moral criticism is to lead a good life, not to execute your enemies.

On Morality versus Immorality

Socrates believes that morality is a form of knowledge and that immorality is a form of ignorance. Socrates explains the motivations behind good and bad acts. In short, why do people do good? Because they are knowledgeable. Why do people do bad? Because they are ignorant. The connection he draws between knowledge and morality, ignorance and immorality, arises from a specific view of moral psychology.

Socrates believes that we all desire as much goodness and as little evil as possible. He insists, 'it is not in human nature . . . to go after what one thinks to be evil in preference to the good; and when compelled to choose one of two evils, nobody will choose the greater [evil] when he may [choose] the lesser'.[10] How, then, does immorality arise? Socrates has a straightforward answer: through ignorance and stupidity. We act immorally when we mistake the bad for the good. This is the origin of vice. There are two solutions to immoral behaviour: (1) obedience to enlightened authority; or (2) learning, for ourselves, what the good is. The best way to learn about the good is to do philosophy.

On His Own Ignorance

Socrates repeatedly claims that he has no knowledge. This is a hard teaching. How can this be? In his trial, he reminds the audience that the Oracle at Delphi (the mystic priestess who communicated with the Greek god Apollo) had once told a fellow Athenian that none was wiser than Socrates. But Socrates claims that he is wisest because he realizes that he is ignorant, that he knows absolutely nothing. The message from the god is that 'the wisest among . . . human beings is anyone like Socrates who has recognized that with respect to wisdom he is truly worthless'.[11]

So how can Socrates, the epitome of moral wisdom, be completely ignorant? Clearly, Socrates must know something. He knows, for example, that his name is Socrates, that he is an Athenian, that the accusations brought forward at his trial are false, and so on. Socrates even claims that he does know things about morality. For example, he tells his jurors, 'acting unjustly in disobedience to one's betters, whether god or human being, is something I know to be evil and shameful'.[12] How, then, can Socrates claim to know nothing and, at the same time, know something? Was this all a trick to avoid being found guilty? Was Socrates insincere? Was he pulling the wool over our eyes?

Scholars disagree, but perhaps we can best understand his position in the following way. Let's begin with an analogy. Suppose someone were to ask, is an elephant big or small? Surely, an elephant seems very big. But suppose we were to compare an elephant to a planet, to a star, or to the entire Andromeda Galaxy. All of a sudden, the elephant seems very small—indeed, tiny. Compared to a human being, an elephant is big; compared to the Andromeda Galaxy, it is miniscule. There are, then, two ways to assess Socrates's knowledge. First, compared to other human beings, Socrates is a tower of moral erudition, for he is much wiser than the ordinary, unthinking person. Second, compared to the god he claims to serve, Socrates knows very little for human knowledge is nothing compared to the divinity. We can now see how Socrates can be both wise and ignorant at the same time. It depends on the perspective. In one sense, Socrates does not know anything about morality; in another sense, he knows a lot. Measured in human terms, Socrates is morally wise; measured in terms of the divinity, Socrates's knowledge is, like the knowledge of all human beings, irretrievably inadequate, incomplete, and fallible.

Socrates' declaration of complete ignorance is intended as a fierce expression of humility. Socrates knows he is not divine. Some ancient philosophers did have divine pretensions. The followers of Pythagoras, for example, believed he had a 'golden thigh' (perhaps a birthmark on his thigh) that was viewed as a mark of divinity, while Empedocles, another pre-Socratic philosopher, declared himself a god.[13] Socrates, in contrast, reaffirms that he is entirely human. He is not a religious figure like Jesus. His knowledge is entirely human and counts as nothing compared to divine wisdom.

Socrates does not believe that he has the final answer to all moral questions, but he does believe that moral knowledge is possible. As he instructs a colleague, 'if you analyze [concepts] adequately, you will, I believe, follow the argument to the furthest point to which a human being can follow it up; and if you get that clear, you'll seek nothing further'.[14] Human understanding comes to an end eventually. Nonetheless, we can pursue an argument up to the furthest point that a human being can attain. This is what Socrates is about. We are rational beings, and so we must logically investigate the truth about morality. Although we may reach the point at which human powers fail, we need to advance as far as we can. As responsible human agents, we must set about improving and extending our knowledge about morality. This is what Socrates did; this is what this book is about.

On the Socratic Method

The Socratic method consists of a kind of cross-examination, in Greek *elenchus*. We do not begin with true belief but with false belief. The goal is to refute error. It is by disproving and discrediting false belief that we arrive at true belief. Refutation, then, produces affirmation. Socrates continually challenges his interlocutors, testing their beliefs to see if they can withstand rigorous scrutiny. He corrects their arguments as the discussion moves along. Some scholars argue that the method matters more than the results. This seems extreme, although it is true that all we learn from some dialogues is that we do not know something we thought we knew. But even this—to learn that we know less than we thought—is an advance in knowledge.

Socrates's persistent questioning of his interlocutors' claims to knowledge may resemble the practices of ancient skepticism, and, indeed, the skeptics thought of Socrates as one of their own. But this is going too far. Socrates rejects the skeptical method of antithesis outright, dismissing 'those who've spent all their time on contradictory arguments, who end up thinking they have become extremely wise [and that] they alone have discerned there's nothing sound or secure whatever, either in things or arguments'.[15]

Despite his willingness to question conventional belief, Socrates firmly believes in the power of logical argument. He complains bitterly about **misology**, a hatred of arguments that stands in the way of knowledge. The problem is not that logic cannot lead us to the truth; the problem is that we do not have sufficient patience or logical skill to arrive at the correct answer. Without logical argument, we cannot do philosophy, and without philosophy, we cannot discover deep truth. Socrates tells a student, 'It would be a pitiful fate, if . . . one blamed neither oneself nor one's own lack of skill, but finally relieved one's distress by shifting blame from oneself to arguments, and then finished out the rest of one's life hating and abusing arguments, and was deprived both of the truth and of knowledge of realities'.[16] If we have yet to find the right answer to moral questions, Socrates recommends that we redouble our efforts in philosophy to discover what we have failed to grasp. We must, he says, 'strive manfully to become sound'.[17]

◌ Applied Philosophy Box 4.1 ◌

Cross-Examination

'Cross-examination is the most difficult of the adversarial skills to acquire. Once mastered, however, it is also the most significant skill, since it is from the crucible of cross-examination that truth most often emerges.'

'[Cross examination] requires the greatest ingenuity; a habit of logical thought; clearness of perception in general; infinite patience and self-control; power to read men's minds intuitively, to judge their characters by their faces, to appreciate their motives; ability to act with force and precision; a masterful knowledge of the subject matter itself; and extreme caution; and, above all, the instinct to discover the weak point in the witness under examination.'

These two quotes are from the website of a law firm. Socrates uses the same basic technique of cross-examination in his philosophical practice. In some of Plato's dialogues, he successfully extracts the truth from unhelpful, even dishonest witnesses. After reading the next section, explain how Socrates's use of the method of cross-examination reinforces and compliments the maieutic [or birthing] metaphor he uses to describe his teaching. Also, what does this method of teaching have to do with Socrates's unpopularity at the end of his life?

Sources: Law Offices of Howard L. Nations, 'Cross-Examinations,' cited from: Francis L. Wellman, *The Art of Cross-Examination*, 1903, www.howardnations.com/crossexamination/ cross_ex.html.

On Teaching and Midwifery

Socrates recounts that his mother was a midwife and claims that he is following in her footsteps. Whereas his mother helped deliver babies, he assists in the birthing of new ideas:

> How absurd of you, [he tells the young man Theatetus] never to have heard that I am the son of a midwife, a fine buxom woman called Phaenarete! . . . My art of midwifery is in general like [that of ordinary midwives]; the only difference is that my patients are men, not women, and my concern is not with the body but with the soul that is in travail of birth. . . . Those who frequent my company at first appear, some of them, quite unintelligent, but as we go further with our discussions, all who are favored by heaven make progress at a rate that seems surprising, . . . although it is clear that they have never learned anything from me. The many admirable truths they bring to birth have been discovered by themselves from within. But the delivery is heaven's work and mine.[18]

In this **maieutic** model, the teacher supervises the learning process, using the method of *elenchus* to induce the labour. He may hold up the final product for public display, but the baby—the knowledge produced—comes from the student, not the teacher.

Socrates does not believe that teaching is a matter of conveying information to a student but of turning on a light inside the student's mind. As he points out, midwives in Greek society were generally older women past the age of child-bearing: 'they never attend to other women in childbirth so long as they themselves can conceive and bear children but only when they are too old for that.'[19] Socrates claims that he is a midwife in that he is philosophically infertile: he has no knowledge to impart to his students. As he puts it,

> I am so [much] like the midwife that I cannot myself give birth to wisdom, and the common reproach is true, that though I question others, I can myself bring nothing to light because there is no wisdom in me. . . . Heaven constrains me to serve as a midwife but has debarred me from giving birth. So of myself I have no sort of wisdom, nor has any discovery been born to me as the child of my soul.[20]

This is, of course, consistent with Socrates's repeated claims to ignorance.

∾ Applied Philosophy Box 4.2 ∾

The Montessori Method

A woman ahead of her time, Maria Montessori, MD, devoted her life to the advancement of education for children of all ages. She believed that the typical teaching method of teacher-lecturing-student was not a conducive learning environment, failing many students. It was from this dissatisfaction that the Montessori schools were born. Since the early 1900s, Montessori schools have provided a unique learning environment tailored to students of all capabilities from infancy to 18 years old. Teachers are not considered the centre of learning; rather, it is the student that is the master of their learning, and it is simply up to the teacher to assist them in exposing their true potential with challenging experiences to be completed uninterrupted in a nurturing environment.

This Montessori method could be compared to Socrates's maieutic method of teaching. Explain.

Sources: "Our Kids Go to School," Our Kids Media, http://www.ourkids.net/montessori-schools.php, 9 November 2010.

On Popular Opinion

Socrates is not a revolutionary or a rebel in a political sense. He strives to bring about the moral improvement of individuals in a society; he does not aim at rearranging the existing power structures. He believes that obedience to proper authority is a virtue; as a result, he submits docilely to unjust punishment at the hands of the Athenian court. At the same time, he questions received opinion as persistently lazy, credulous, uncritical, self-interested, and morally lax. The fact that the majority believe something does not make it true. What the majority believes may be false.

Socrates responds to a Sophist:

> The trouble is . . . that you're trying to use on me the kind of rhetorical refutation which people in the law courts think is successful. There too . . . people think they're proving the other side wrong if they produce a large number of eminent witnesses in support of the points they're making, but their opponent only comes up with a single witness or none at all. This kind of refutation, however, is completely worthless in the context of the truth, since it's perfectly possible for someone to be defeated in court by a horde of witnesses with no more than apparent respectability who all testify falsely against him. In the present dispute, if you feel like calling witnesses to claim that what I am saying is wrong, you can count on your position being supported by almost everyone in Athens. . . . Nevertheless, there is still a dissenting voice, albeit a single one—mine. You're producing no compelling reason why I should agree with you; all you are doing is calling up a horde of false witnesses against me to support your attempt to dislodge me from my inheritance—the truth.[21]

We might describe an argument from received opinion as an argument that conforms to the following pattern: most people believe X; therefore we should believe X. As a philosopher, Socrates heeds the voice of reason, not of popular opinion. The fact that most people in Athens believe X does not show that X is true. If X is true, it is true because it makes logical sense, not because most people believe it.

On Hedonism

One thing Socrates knows is that hedonism is wrong. Socrates has an answer to philosophers like Epicurus. Morality means more than doing the right thing; it means doing the right thing for the right reason. Those who do the right thing for their own pleasure subordinate morality to self-gratification. Even if they do what they are required to do, this focus on their own self-gratification contaminates the goodness of their actions.

Socrates claims that hedonists contradict themselves. He explains, 'It's because [hedonists are] afraid of being deprived of further pleasures, and desire them, that they abstain from [other pleasures]. . . . They overcome some pleasures because they're overcome by others. And that is the sort of thing just mentioned: . . . they achieve temperance because of intemperance'.[22] Temperance is a virtue; intemperance is a vice. The temperate refrain from immoderate pleasure; the intemperate indulge. Socrates believes that hedonists practise temperance with respect to some pleasures so that they can practise intemperance with respect to other pleasures. In other words, they practise a limited virtue so that they can indulge in a different vice.

For Socrates, morality is its own reward. Imagine that Monique does the right thing in order to procure more pleasure for herself. According to Socrates, this is to lose sight of what morality is all about. Monique has been sidetracked by extraneous considerations. Morality is not about 'exchanging pleasures for pleasures, pains for pains . . . like coins'.[23] Morality is about virtue. But good people do not aim at virtue in order to procure more pleasure or less pain for themselves. They aim at virtue because virtue is a praiseworthy and wonderful on its own account. In short, moral people aim at morality in order to be moral. This is enough in itself. Issues about pleasures or pains are a distraction.

In Socrates's account, those who act morally for extraneous reasons of any kind are not truly moral. They stop doing the right thing when it is no longer pleasurable, profitable, prestigious, or politically useful. They only appear to be moral: they play the part, but their morality is as changeable as the circumstances. Moral individuals always do the right thing, even in the face of great adversity, hardship, misery, and misfortune. They act like Socrates, who always told the truth, even at the risk of death.

On How Pleasure-seeking Equals Unhappiness

Socrates is not suggesting that we should be moral and miserable. On the contrary, he believes that hedonism backfires. Hedonism is not only immoral; it makes us miserable. Socrates believes, like Democritus, that when we indulge in pleasure, the desire for more and more pleasure takes over our lives, leaving us permanently dissatisfied. Socrates contrives three memorable images to illustrate this.

First, he compares the life of pleasure to a life spent scratching an itch[24]—except that the itch becomes itchier the more we scratch it. Pleasure-seekers keep on scratching, but instead of relieving their distress, they worsen their condition.

Second, Socrates compares the souls of pleasure-seekers to leaky jars.[25] Whatever amount of pleasure they pour into their souls, everything runs through and, in a moment, the containers are just as empty as before. Because pleasure is an ephemeral experience, pleasure-seekers can never be satisfied. They are always in need of a new pleasure as the old pleasure fades.

Third, Socrates says that the wicked are punished for their evil deeds in the afterlife—in Judeo-Christian terms, when they go to Hell—by being forced to carry water in a sieve.[26] Socrates, in effect, identifies Hell with pleasure-seeking. Obviously, no one can carry water in a sieve. A sieve is a variation on a leaky jar—the water runs through. So the wicked are to be punished for their evildoing by being forced into a life of unsatisfied pleasure-seeking. The life of endless craving is a logical extension of their lives on earth.

Socrates repeatedly identifies a link between evil and pleasure-seeking. In another striking image, he compares pleasure-seekers to cattle that butt heads with one another and gore one another to death:

> [Those] whose only interest is self-indulgence . . . are no different from cattle, [for] they spend their lives grazing, with their eyes turned down and heads bowed to the ground and their tables. Food and sex are their only concerns, and their insatiable greed for more and more drives them to kick and butt one another to death with horns and hoofs of iron, killing one another because [of the] leaky vessel they are trying to fill.[27]

Violence between individuals is a direct result of disordered appetite.

On the Happiness of Moral People

Socrates believes that moral people are always happy and that immoral people are always unhappy. This is another hard teaching. It conflicts sharply with what seems to happen around us. We see good people suffer and bad people prosper. Yet Socrates insists that it is illogical to think that good people could be unhappy or that evil people could be happy.

As a corollary to this claim, he maintains, even more outrageously, that it can *never* be the case that good people are punished and that bad people are rewarded. He lectures the jurors at his trial: 'Moreover, you too, gentlemen of the jury, should be of good hope in the face of death, and fix your minds upon this single truth: nothing can harm a good man, either in life or in death.'[28] Socrates, who is fully aware that he is about to be put to death on trumped-up charges, is adamant: *Nothing can harm a good man in life or in death*. The good *must* be rewarded and the bad *must* be punished. Nothing else, he believes, makes logical sense.

Socrates's claim gains some credibility from his belief in a final judgment when the good are rewarded and the bad are punished. But this is a secondary consideration.

Socrates would believe that the good must be rewarded and the bad must be punished even if there were no afterlife. Why? Because the good are rewarded insomuch as they receive virtue, the very best thing that there is, whereas the bad are punished insomuch as they receive vice, the worst thing that there is. So the good are invariably rewarded and the bad invariably punished by the nature of their respective choices.

Socrates assures us that 'life with an unhealthy mind—a mind which is unsound, immoral and unjust—is infinitely more wretched than life with an unhealthy body'.[29] Immoral people will, by definition, be saddled with infirmity. They will pass through life crippled and diseased, in mind and perhaps in body. Socrates concedes that the good may seem to be harmed and the bad may seem to benefit, but this is mere appearance, not real-ity. The external circumstances of fortune and misfortune draw our attention away from the moral good (or bad) that is actually happening inside the agent in question.

On Asymmetry as a Guiding Principle of Morality

Socrates takes a perspective on morality that foreshadows the heroic morality of Jesus. Jesus, of course, taught that we should turn the other cheek, love those who hate us, and do good to those who persecute us. Socrates comes to a similar position on his own, not by reading Scripture, but by following through the logical consequences of a line of thought. One useful way of describing the basic thrust of his moral thought is to invoke what we will call the **asymmetry principle**.

First, think of what moral behaviour would be like if it were symmetrical. We would treat people in the same way that they treat us. When they were good to us, we would be good to them. When they were bad to us, we would be bad to them. But Socrates, like Jesus, insists that morality is not symmetrical. Even if others treat us immorally, we must continue to treat them morally. Socrates is adamant: 'One shouldn't return injustice or ill-treatment to any human being, no matter how one may be treated by that person . . . Neither doing nor returning injustice is ever right, nor should one who is ill-treated defend himself by retaliation.'[30]

In fact, Socrates believes that morality is asymmetrical: 'It is never right to harm any-one.'[31] He proposes an absolutely rigorous standard for moral action: 'One must not act unjustly at all . . . Even if one is unjustly treated, one should not return injustice.'[32] Think of morality as a kind of equation that links us to other people. Put what we do to others on one side of the equation and what others do to us on the other side. If morality were symmetrical, this would give us this:

What we do to other people = What other people do to us

But this is what Socrates, like Jesus, contests. Socrates thinks the moral equation should look, instead, like this:

What we do to people = What good people do to us

Morality is, so to speak, a constant. It does not change according to how we are treated. When we deal with evil people, then, the moral equation will be this:

What we do to evil people ≠ What evil people do to us

This is the sense in which morality is asymmetrical. We must do good to those who do us good, but we must also do good to those who do us evil. We must always do good irrespective of the treatment we receive at the hands of others. We should return good for good and good for ill. We should benefit those who harm us. Morality is not, in this sense, about equality. It is about conformity to a greater ideal.

Socrates does not conceive of morality as an elaborate game of 'tit for tat', i.e., 'I'll be nice to you if you'll be nice to me'. Morality is, rather, about perfecting human nature. Why should the fact that other people fail miserably at human achievement motivate a similar lapse in us? Think of an ideal like beauty. Suppose you are surrounded by ugly people. Should you be ugly because they are ugly? How could we make sense of that? Likewise, if you happen to be surrounded by immoral people, why would that give you a reason to be immoral, too?

Socrates sets a very high standard for moral behaviour. If virtue is the height of human achievement, it retains its value independent of the circumstances. Socrates believes that we cannot excuse our immoral treatment of other people by complaining that 'they started it'. If other people act immorally, Socrates believes that the proper response is to treat them morally. What they do is to their disadvantage, not to ours.

We should not, however, misinterpret this doctrine of both Socrates and Jesus. Morality is not, to use a ubiquitous modern cliché, a matter of being nice to everyone. Nor is it a matter of being a moral doormat, of letting people— for immoral reasons—walk all over you. Doing the right thing may sometimes involve strenuous opposition to evil. It might involve taking arms against wrongful oppression. Socrates was no bleeding heart; neither was he a pacifist. He fought valiantly for Athens as a foot soldier in various campaigns. He also believed in punishment. As we discuss on page 143, he argues, in fact, that it is imperative that an immoral person be roundly punished. If excessive or unmerited punishment is clearly immoral, it is better to be harshly punished and so dissuaded from immorality than to be allowed to persist in evil, for becoming an evil person is the greatest misfortune that could befall an individual.

On the Moral Contract

Socrates posits a moral contract between the state and the individual citizen. In return for the benefits of living in a civilized society, the citizen promises to obey its laws. To disobey these laws would be a breach of moral obligation.

Although Socrates believes that he was unjustly punished by the Athenian court because of lies and false allegations, he meekly accepts the sentence of capital punishment, ignoring the very real possibilities of exile or escape. He argues that, as someone who has benefited from Athenian society all his life, he owes a debt of gratitude and obedience to Athenian law. If he breaks the law, he will become 'a subverter of laws' through bad example.[33] When friends urge him to escape, Socrates imagines the laws of Athens speaking to him:

> Please tell us, Socrates, what do you have in mind? With this action you are attempting, do you intend anything short of destroying us, the Laws and the city as a whole to the best of your ability? Do you think a city can still exist without being overturned, if the legal judgments rendered within it possess no force, but are nullified or invalidated by individuals?'[34]

For the sake of peace and social order, individuals must comply with the laws even when they disagree with the reasoning behind those laws.

Socrates believes that the just person is faced with two stark alternatives: if you disagree with society, 'you must either dissuade it, or else do whatever it commands'.[35] When society resists your arguments, you cannot do evil but you must submit to the penalty for noncompliance with the law whatever the cost. Socrates continues that 'if [the state] ordains that you must submit to a certain treatment, then you must hold your peace and submit to it; whether it means being beaten or put into bonds, or whether it leads you into war to be killed, you must act accordingly, and that is what is just'.[36] We have here the beginnings of a theory of conscientious objection.

In other words, morality has a social dimension: the good person has a patriotic duty. In his jail cell, awaiting execution, Socrates imagines the state of Athens lecturing him: 'In comparison with your mother and father and all your other forebears, your fatherland is more

precious and venerable, more sacred and held in high esteem among gods, . . . if it is sinful to use violence against your mother or father, it is far more so to use it against your fatherland.'[37] Socrates dies convinced that he has been unjustly convicted but, nonetheless, confident that he remains an ever loyal citizen to Athens.

Plato's Teachings

Plato (429–347 BC), Socrates's most famous student, was the son of a noble family in Athens, a brilliant writer, someone who travelled widely, and the director of the philosophical school called the Academy. The name Plato comes from a Greek word meaning 'broad' or 'wide'. According to one story, the athletic young man, originally named Aristocles, was dubbed 'Plato' by his wrestling coach because of his broad chest. Other authorities report that the name stuck because of the philosopher's broad forehead. Either way, the mature philosopher has passed down into history as Plato. The school of philosophy he developed and championed is known as Platonism or, in the case of later authors who revisited and revised his thought, as Neo-Platonism.

According to one story, the young Plato had set his heart on a career as a poet and playwright. When, however, he heard Socrates discoursing in the marketplace, he was so impressed that he immediately returned home, burned all his poems and plays, and decided on a philosophical way of life. He spent the rest of his life recording, retelling, and, no doubt, embellishing the intellectual adventures of Socrates.

Plato is not only a follower of Socrates but a remarkable philosopher in his own right. Scholars agree that in some of Plato's work, Socrates becomes the mouthpiece of Plato's own ideas. (Publishing your own opinions under the name of your teacher or master was a common ancient practice.) While it is sometimes very hard to discern where Socrates's views end and Plato's begin, we can say, generally, that Plato takes ideas that originate in Socrates's question-and-answer method, develops them further, and carefully inserts them into a consistent, highly organized system of thought that makes positive affirmations about both the nature of the world and the nature of morality. Socrates was a penetrating conversationalist given to flashes of insight, but Plato is more like an architect setting up, on solid foundations, a larger philosophical edifice. Still, the two thinkers are so intertwined we cannot make sense of one without the other.

In the following sections, we focus on the system of morality that Plato lays out in his famous political masterpiece, *The Republic*. We discuss, in turn, the story of Gyges's ring, the Socratic definition of pleasure, the form of the good, the Divided Line, the analogy of the cave, the tripartite soul, and Plato's model of the human individual as chimera. Plato would think it absurd to discuss morality without first gaining some very deep sense of what is true and real. So we cannot do justice to Plato's system without spending some time elucidating his metaphysical system. Although his metaphysical orientation differs markedly from modern treatments, it provides a framework within which we can better understand Plato's views about morality.

On Gyges's Ring

The Republic is an ostensible record of an extended dialogue between Socrates and a group of young men about the best form of government. It begins with a philosophical conversation that leads to a discussion of the question, 'Why should we be moral?'

Plato sets out the problem nicely by retelling the myth of Gyges's ring. (According to some reports, the story is about Gyges; according to other reports, it is about Gyges's ancestor. As Plato himself is inconsistent on this point, we will follow the usual custom and identify the ring as belonging to Gyges.) Glaucon, Plato's older brother, has just taken over the argument with Socrates from Thrasymachus, a particularly ruthless, violent Sophist. He recounts the following story:

> [Gyges] of Lydia . . . was a shepherd in the service of the Lydian ruler of the time, when a heavy rainstorm occurred and an earthquake cracked open the land to a certain extent, and a chasm appeared in the region where he was pasturing his flocks. He was fascinated by the sight, and went down into the chasm and saw there . . . among other artifacts, a bronze horse, which was hollow and had windows set in it; he stooped and looked in through the windows and saw a corpse inside, which seemed to be that of a giant. The corpse was naked but had a golden ring on the finger; he took the ring off and left. Now the shepherds used to meet once a month to keep the king informed of his flocks, and our protagonist came to the meeting wearing the ring. He was sitting down among the others, and happened to twist the ring's bezel in the direction of his body, towards the inner part of his hand. When he did this, he became invisible to his neighbors, and to his astonishment they talked about him as if he'd left. While he was fiddling about with the ring again, he turned the bezel outwards, and became visible. He thought about this and experimented to see if it was the ring that had this power; in this way he eventually found that turning the bezel inwards made him invisible, and turning it outwards made him visible. As soon as he realized this, he arranged to be one of the delegates to the king; once he was inside the palace, he seduced the king's wife and with her help as

saulted and killed the king, and so took possession of the throne.[38]

This then is Glaucon's story. The basic point
is that once Gyges realizes that he can make
himself invisible, he takes advantage of his
newfound powers and uses them to murder
the king and usurp the throne.

Glaucon believes that people are moral only
because they are afraid of being punished.
If, however, you knew how to make yourself
invisible, you could commit any crime you
want without getting caught. This is what happens to Gyges. As soon as he realizes he can
escape detection, he goes out and kills the
king. Glaucon goes on to claim that anyone—
moral or immoral—would do the same. He
continues:

> Suppose there are two [invisible] rings, then—
> one worn by our moral person, the other by the
> immoral person. There is no one . . . who is iron-
> willed enough to maintain his morality and find
> the strength of purpose to keep his hands off
> what doesn't belong to him, when he is able to
> take whatever he wants from the market stalls
> without fear of being discovered, to enter houses
> and sleep with whomever he chooses, to kill and
> release from prison anyone he wants, and gener-
> ally to act like a god among men. His behaviour
> would be identical to that of the other person;
> both of them would be heading in the same di-
> rection.[39]

Glaucon argues that 'the rewards of
immorality far outweigh those of morality'. It
follows 'that morality is never freely chosen.
People do wrong whenever they think they
can, [and] act morally only if they're forced
to'.[40] Indeed, Glaucon claims that only a fool
would act morally in the absence of any threat
of punishment. He appeals to popular opinion:
'the sight of someone [who could make himself invisible] refusing all those opportunities

for wrongdoing and never laying a finger on
things that didn't belong to him would lead
people to think that he was in an extremely
bad way, and was a first-class fool as well.'[41]

Is it better to be moral or immoral?
Glaucon argues that the immoral individual
can do everything and anything to secure
his ends; there is no limit to his capacities.
Most important, he can return aggression
for aggression. Other people will be afraid of
him and will respect his life and his property.
The moral hero is, in comparison, a vulnerable target. He must refrain from harming
others even when they harm him (remember
the asymmetry principle). But a man who is
unable to defend himself from immorality
by resorting to immorality is at a great disadvantage. He will have to patiently endure
the lies and the mistreatment of his enemies.
Glaucon, in a passage that strangely foreshadows the crucifixion story of the Jesus,
paints a gruesome picture of what will happen to the true moral hero: 'Even if he does
no wrong at all, . . . [he] must unswervingly
follow [the moral] path until he dies—a saint
[even if he has] a lifelong reputation for a sin-
ner, . . . [he must endure] flogging, torture
on the rack, imprisonment in chains, having
his eyes burnt out, and every ordeal in the
book, up to and including being impaled on
a stake.'[42]

Glaucon throws out this challenge to
Socrates: prove that morality is worthwhile *for
its own sake*, even if it means giving up the many
rewards and accepting many penalties. Show
that morality is something intelligent individuals would choose, even when they need not
fear any punishment or retribution—even if
they happen to possess a ring like Gyges! This
is the central problem Plato addresses in *The
Republic*. Although there are many interest-

✒ Applied Philosophy Box 4.3 ✒

Tolkien's Tale Bears Ring of Truth

There is little doubt that this ancient legend—of Gyges and his magic ring—was part of the inspiration for the dominant theme in J.R.R. Tolkien's epic masterpiece *The Lord of the Rings*. Plato's *The Republic* recounts the story of the ring of Gyges, as it was told by Glaucon to Socrates. . . . J.R.R. Tolkien, in focusing his tale on a magic ring like Gyges's, wrote perhaps the most brilliant and richly rendered portrayal of power and corruptibility ever conceived. Tolkien's ring, like Gyges', corrupts, and enslaves, even as it offers its owner invisibility and the temptation of unlimited powers. In both tales, the ring may be viewed as a metaphor for power and its corrupting influence, and the point may be summed up by Lord Acton's famous dictum. 'Power tends to corrupt and absolute power corrupts absolutely.'

There is, however, an important difference between Tolkien's and Plato's accounts. Frodo, the principle character in Tolkien's saga, has to destroy the ring to save the world. Plato believes that we do not need to destroy the ring; we need to achieve virtue. Even if there were such a ring, it would not make any difference to truly virtuous people like Socrates.

Source: Steve Bonta, 'Tolkien's Tale Bears Ring of Truth.' *The New American*, www.accessmylibrary.com/coms2/summary_0286-24993789_ITM, 28 January 2002.

---

ing side issues discussed throughout, this is the principle question Plato, in the guise of Socrates, sets out to answer.

On the Idea of the Good

As we discussed in the last chapter, the first philosophers generally argued that we should act according to nature. We called this general rule of thumb 'the nature principle'. Plato and Socrates carry on this theme in a way that expands and modifies the concept of nature to include a realm of immaterial ideas. We moderns tend to think that what is most real and trustworthy is the physical world that we perceive. This is what we have confidence in. Plato, in contrast, argues that the physical world is an illusory, transitory realm of shifting, unpredictable events. Behind the screen of murky, decaying appearances, there is a deeper, purer reality, made up of eternal, unchangeable ideas. If we want to be moral,

we should act in accordance with these higher ideas, and ultimately in accordance with the highest idea, with the supreme good that transcends the physical world.

Plato's views may strike some readers as startling. The best way to grasp his approach is through an example. Consider a triangle. We see many different triangular shapes in the world: mountains are more or less triangular, as are spruce trees, teepees, pyramids, and sails; sharks have triangular teeth; some plants have triangular leaves; and, of course, we are all familiar with triangles drawn on a blackboard or a piece of paper. Plato would argue that there is no perfect triangle in the world. Even the triangles we study in geometry (which already are an abstraction) are rough embodiments of the *idea* of the perfect triangle. (The sides are never perfectly straight; the angles never add up to exactly 180 degrees; and so on.) Plato believes that the imperfect triangular shapes

ᴖ Applied Philosophy Box 4.4 ᴖ

Beauty Speech from the *Symposium*

The proper way to go about this business . . . is for someone to start as a young man by focusing on physical beauty and initially . . . to love just one person's body. . . . He should realize next that the beauty of any one body hardly differs from that of any other body, and that if its physical beauty he's after, it is very foolish of him not to regard the beauty of all bodies as absolutely identical. Once he's realized this, and so become capable of loving every beautiful body in the world, his obsession with just one body grows less intense and strikes him as ridiculous and petty. The next stage is for him to value mental beauty so much more than physical beauty that even if someone is almost entirely lacking in the bloom of youth, but still has an attractive mind, that's enough to kindle his love and affection. . . . And this in turn leaves him no choice but to look at what makes people's activities and institutions attractive and to see that here too any form of beauty is much the same as any other, so that he comes to regard physical beauty as unimportant. Then after these activities he must press on towards the things people know, until he can see beauty there too. Now he has beauty before his eyes in abundance, no longer a single instance of it. . . . No longer a paltry and small-minded slave, he faces instead the vast sea of beauty, and in gazing upon it his boundless love of knowledge . . . gives birth to plenty of beautiful, expansive reasoning and thinking, until he gains enough energy and bulk there to . . . suddenly catch sight of something of unbelieveable beauty . . . which in fact gives meaning to all his previous efforts. What he'll see is, in the first place, eternal; it doesn't come or cease to be, and it doesn't increase or diminish. In the second place, it isn't attractive in one respect and repulsive in another, or attractive at one time but not at another, or attractive in one setting but repulsive in another . . . depending on how people find it. Then again, he won't perceive beauty as a face or hands or any other physical feature, or as a piece of reasoning or knowledge, and he won't perceive it as being anywhere else either—in something like a creature or the earth or the heavens. No, he'll perceive it in itself and by itself, and constant and eternal, and he'll see that every other beautiful object somehow partakes of it.

This famous speech from Plato's Symposium *gives some sense of his mystical account of learning. Knowledge of beauty comes gradually. One moves up the ladder of knowing, rung by rung, from one beautiful body to many beautiful bodies, to beautiful minds, to beautiful activities and institutions, to beautiful examples of knowledge, to all the beautiful aspects of things, and, finally, to the idea of perfect beauty in itself. For Plato, any beautiful object in the world is beautiful because it participates in this higher idea of perfect beauty. (In Plato's metaphysics, the idea of perfect beauty is more or less identical to the idea of the good).*

Source: Plato, *Symposium*, Robin Waterfield, trans. (Oxford: Oxford University Press, 1994), pp. 210a–211b.

we see with our eyes are more or less inadequate copies or reflections of a pure, immaterial idea: the idea of the triangularity-in-itself. It is only through participation in this universal idea of 'triangle-ness' that particular shapes are triangular. If we truly desire to know what a triangle is, we need to move beyond perception of inadequate particular triangles and think about the objective, immaterial, universal form of the triangle in itself.

Plato calls these perfect ideas after which physical things in the world are modelled the forms (in Greek, the plural is *eide*; the singular, *eidos*). Although he is frustratingly vague when it comes to determining which forms actually exist, Plato clearly indicates that existent forms are organized in a hierarchy from lower to higher. The lower forms are less general; the higher forms are more general. As we move from lower to higher, we move to increasingly larger ideas that incorporate and embody more and more reality. The lower forms would include such things as the idea of the perfect horse, the idea of the perfect human body, or the idea of the perfect triangle. The higher forms would include concepts such as the idea of perfect equality, the idea of perfect justice, the idea of perfect beauty, and ultimately, the most perfect and highest form of all, the idea of the good. Plato claims that the purpose of learning in general and of philosophy in particular is communion with the idea of the good, which fills and perfects all existent things.

What does all this have to do with morality? Plato thus explains the content of moral behaviour and also the motivation behind morality. Plato thinks that just as we catch a glimpse of the perfect idea of the good in acts of intellectual knowing, we also catch a glimpse of the perfect idea of the good in righteous behaviour. Seeing the good is a little like falling in love. Once we know and love the good, we will act accordingly. Our attraction to the idea of the good will invariably make us moral.

For Plato, morality is not a matter of following a set of prescribed rules. It is an issue of personal heroism. We must eliminate all physical and sensual distractions from our lives and focus single-mindedly on the pursuit of philosophy. There is, however, a serious obstacle to knowledge of the good, for Plato believes that the idea of the good is ineffable; it cannot be expressed in words. As one of Socrates's interlocutors chimes in, 'It's way beyond human comprehension'.[43]

Confronted with the impossibility of any adequate logical explanation of the good, Socrates suggests an analogy. He tells his friends, 'What I suggest . . . is that we forget about trying to define goodness itself. . . . However, I am prepared to talk about something which seems to me to be a child of goodness and to bear a very strong resemblance to it'.[44] Socrates goes on to compare the idea of the good to the sun, 'whose light makes it possible . . . for the things we see to be seen'.[45] Just as the sun illuminates the world of physical objects, the idea of the good likewise illuminates the world of ideas we apprehend with our minds. We could not think truthfully (which is a kind of 'seeing') unless the idea of the good shone the necessary light into our souls.

Socrates conceives of the idea of the good, not merely as a passive object of mental apprehension, but as an active power that helps us know. He explains, 'When our eyes are directed towards things which are lit up by the sun, then they see clearly. ... Well, here's how you can think of the mind as well. When its object is something which is lit up by truth and reality, then it has . . . intelligent awareness and knowledge. However when its object is permeated with darkness . . . [the mind] comes across as devoid of intelligence. . . . What I'm saying is that [the good] gives the things we know their truth and makes it possible for people to have knowledge'.[46]

We cannot discuss Plato's puzzling mystical doctrines further here. Suffice it to say that he believes that the idea of the good surpasses everything else in majesty and might. The good is not only responsible for making knowledge accessible, but also for the existence of everything there is. Socrates insists, 'it isn't only the known-ness of the things we know which is conferred upon them by goodness, but also their reality and being'.[47] Not surprisingly, some theologians identify this impersonal idea of goodness with God.

On the Divided Line (Education)

In Plato's mind, education and morality go hand in hand. In the case of the mediocre masses, morality means little more than obeying good rules set down by benevolent and intelligent superiors. But anyone who aspires to moral achievement needs to follow a step-by-step process of philosophical education. Plato describes this process using a diagram called the Divided Line, depicted in Figure 4.1.

Socrates instructs his listeners, 'Picture then a line cut into two unequal sections, and following the same [unequal] proportion, subdivide both the [lower and higher] section'.[48] The visual arrangement Socrates has in mind is a vertical (not horizontal) line divided unequally in two so that the top section is much longer than the bottom section, with each of these two sections divided unequally again so that the top subdivision is again, in the same ratio, much longer than the bottom subdivision. As Figure 4.1 indicates, the ratio of AB to CD equals the ratio of A to B, which again equals the ratio of C to D. To sum up, the relative proportions of these complementary divisions all mirror one another.

Situate the idea of the good at the very top of the line. Locate ignorance at the very bottom of the line. The purpose of education is to move the student from a condition of ignorance to union with and contemplation of the good. Each segment on the line represents a new stage of learning; the longer the segment, the more learning it encompasses. The higher we move up the vertical line, the more knowledgeable we become. The more

knowledgeable we become, the more moral we become.

Plato labels each section of the Divided Line according to the mental condition it represents. His terminology is not always consistent, but the general idea is clear.[49] Consider then the individual sections on the Divided Line in order.

The first segment (A) of the Divided Line represents the most distant and dubious form of knowledge, which we can call conjecture or imagination (*eikasia*). This segment deals with knowledge of images and pictures. (The English word *icon* comes from the Greek *eikon*, hence *eikasia* meaning, here, 'belief based on likeness or resemblance'.) The second section (B) represents the confidence, belief, or faith (*pistis*) we have in ordinary physical objects. The third section (C) represents science, mathematics, and natural philosophy (*dianoia*), all of which involve high-level conceptual analysis of physical things. (The word *dianoia* might be translated as 'discourse' or 'theoretical discussion'.) Finally, the top section (D) represents knowledge or understanding (*episteme* or *noesis*), which depends on a close familiarity with ideas in themselves. At the top of the line, this culminates in appreciation of the highest forms and ultimately, merges into an ineffable knowledge of the form of the good.

These four sections of the Divided Line are set up such that the two lower segments added together ($A + B$ = conjecture + confidence) represent our awareness of the visible (physical) world, whereas the two higher segments added together ($C + D$ = science + knowledge) represent awareness of the intelligible (non-physical) world of ideas. Plato calls our awareness of the visual world mere 'opinion', reserving the term 'knowledge' for the kind of cognition that he associates with the true world of ideas.

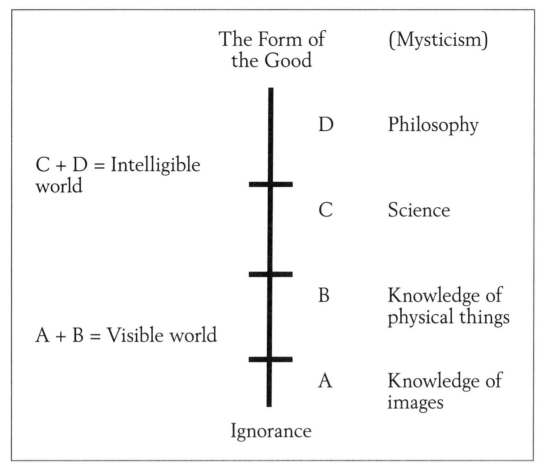

Figure 4.1 The Divided Line

We may well wonder what all this has to do with morality. The point is that the pursuit of knowledge pushes us ever upward toward a transcendental moral good that surpasses physical needs and preoccupations. As we shall see, Plato thinks that this exercise of knowledge-acquisition is the key to virtue.

An example will help illustrate what Plato is proposing. Imagine a modern student moving up the Divided Line. (We could imagine many different scenarios, but a simple, straightforward case illustrates the point.) Suppose young Jorge, who lives in a jungle, has never

seen a car. A visitor gives him a description of a car, shows him photographs of a car, and imitates the sound of a car. Jorge, who was originally ignorant about cars, has now gained some knowledge of what a car is. He has, so to speak, moved up the ladder of learning. Admittedly, he has a very tentative knowledge about cars, but it is at least something. This is like the first stage in the Divided Line; it consists of knowledge not of cars but of images and likenesses of cars.

Suppose, then, we were to take Jorge to the city, where he could see real cars, touch them, hear them, and ride in them. Perhaps he could get a driver's license and come to own and operate one. This first-hand knowledge of real, physical cars is like the second stage in the Divided Line, what Plato calls belief or confidence. Through sense perception, Jorge now *knows* what individual cars are like.

Now suppose Jorge becomes fascinated by cars and decides to become a car mechanic. He goes to college and studies not one car but all cars, so to speak; that is, he learns the general principles of car design and car mechanics. He graduates with an advanced knowledge of what a car is. He has now arrived at something akin to the third stage of learning, as indicated in the Divided Line. Jorge has mastered the science of cars; he knows the relevant concepts and general principles that apply to all cars, but he uses them to better understand and repair individual cars.

The transition from the third to the fourth stage of learning is more subtle. Suppose Jorge has to study physics and chemistry for his diploma in car mechanics. And suppose that he decides to return to school to study physics and chemistry, not for practical reasons but simply because he finds himself keenly interested in these subjects. He is no longer concerned about practicality. He just wants to learn in order to learn. And suppose that, at a certain point, he abandons physics and is attracted instead to the study of higher-level mathematics. It suddenly strikes him that the universal mathematical relationships that regulate the whole universe is based are beautiful and true and everlasting. (The Pythagorean theorem always has been and always will be true.) This moving up to ever higher levels of learning is the fourth stage of the Divided Line.

But Jorge's education is not quite finished. Plato thinks that the attentive mind will, at a certain point, move from mathematical accuracy to the *moral* realization 'this is good'. The knower comes to grasp—in some supreme and unexplainable sense—the goodness in things. He or she moves from simple mathematical cognition to an epiphany: 'Wow! This is true! This is beautiful! This is good!' Education ends with a moral illumination. The student comes to understand that goodness is at the heart of everything. Plato believes that this awareness will influence our behaviour. Once we see the goodness at the heart of things, we will want to make our conduct conform to a higher moral standard. We will want to live in harmony

---

◈ Applied Philosophy Box 4.5 ◈

Soap Operas

Here's a thought experiment: imagine someone stranded alone on a desert island with a television set. The only time the television works is every day at 5:00 for the duration of the same soap opera. This is the sole source of this person's knowledge of the outside world. He or she learns about human relationships by watching the soaps (which are images of real life). Make up a narrative, describing how the person leaves the island and slowly ascends up the Divided Line to the idea of the good. (Of course, this could happen in various ways. There is no one right answer—but all right answers will follow the same basic pattern.)

with what is truly good. A clear vision of the good will make us want to be good ourselves.

There is much more to say about the different stages in the Divided Line. Suffice it to emphasize that, in Plato's mind, the movement upwards represents both a progression from ignorance to an understanding of the good and a step-by-step movement toward higher and higher moral virtue. Socrates, Plato's moral hero, is simultaneously an outstanding philosopher and the most virtuous person in Athens. Plato does not believe that the link between his philosophical acumen and his moral integrity is happenstance. That is how it must be. The more we understand the world, the more we appreciate the goodness of the whole, the more we will strive to be moral. Moving up the ladder of knowledge is the same as moving up the ladder of morality. Once we grasp what goodness is and how it 'irradiates' the world, we will naturally shun evil. An intellectual appreciation of the good is, so to speak, the engine of morality. It is what motivates moral behaviour.

Although we will not explore the issue in great detail, we should point out that scholars generally agree that one can draw a direct parallel between the different stages in the Divided Line and Plato's famous analogy of the cave. Plato uses the cave analogy to describe the process of intellectual enlightenment that comes through philosophy. The story begins with a crowd of chained, immobile prisoners in an underground chamber watching shadows on a wall made by objects held in front of a fire burning behind them. In the next stage of the story, a selected prisoner is unchained, turned around, and forced to look at the objects held in front of the fire. He is then dragged from the cave into the outside world. Blinded by the sunlight, the dazzled prisoner

gazes first at shadows and reflections, then at physical objects, then at the moon and stars, and, finally, straight at the sun.

The allegory of the cave represents, in metaphorical form, the four stages of education represented in the Divided Line. The prisoners chained inside the cave represent the ordinary masses who uncritically accept unreflective stereotypes and common prejudices as true. They mistakenly think that the shadows or images on the wall constitute reality. The objects held in front of the fire represent physical things in the world. The world outside the cave represents the world of ideas. Once he has left the cave, the prisoner moves from a knowledge of shadows, the lowest ideas, to a knowledge of the stars, the higher ideas, to a knowledge of the sun, the form of the good. The prisoner leaving the cave moves from an awareness of images (Section *A* in Figure 4.1), to an awareness of physical objects (Section *B*), to an awareness of lower ideas (Section *C*), to an awareness of higher ideas (Section *D*), and finally to direct knowledge of the idea of the good (at the very top of the line).

There is a second, surreptitious echo of the Divided Line in Plato's account of what happens in the outside world where the prisoner contemplates first shadows and reflections (or images), then individual (physical) objects, then the moon and stars (ideas), and finally the sun (the idea of the good). Plato is clearly referring to Socrates when he describes the one who is 'able to discern and feast his eyes on the sun—not the displaced image of the sun in water or elsewhere, but the sun on its own, in its proper place'.[50] Socrates, unlike the rest of humanity, has escaped from ignorance and is alone fully able to comprehend and appreciate the idea of the good. This is why he is so virtuous.

On Immorality

If we agree with Plato's claim that virtue involves education, it will naturally follow that whatever is an obstacle to education is immoral. Plato believes, in a way that is no longer fashionable, that the main obstacle to philosophical and moral enlightenment is the lure of physical pleasure. Hedonism, the pursuit of pleasure, is the biggest moral problem that confronts us. Why? Because our appetites for food, drink, sex, and excitement distract us from what should be our main preoccupation: the pursuit of moral knowledge. Indeed, in addition to pursuing raw pleasure, we pursue things like power, money, and prestige as a means to pleasure. These desires drag us away from disciplined intellectual endeavours. We are so busy trying to satisfy ourselves that we no longer have the time, the energy, or the concentration required for serious, reflective study.

In the *Phaedo*, Plato depicts Socrates discussing the philosophical way of life with his friend Simmias:

> [Socrates begins:] 'Do you think it befits a philosophical man to be keen about so-called pleasures of, for example, food and drink?'
>
> 'Not in the least, Socrates,' said Simmias.
>
> 'And what about those of sex?'
>
> 'Not at all.'
>
> 'And what about the other services to the body? Do you think such a person regards them as of any value? For instance, the possession of smart clothes and shoes, and other bodily adornments—do you think he values them highly, or does he disdain them, except insofar as he is absolutely compelled to share in them?'
>
> 'I think the philosopher generally disdains them.'
>
> 'Do you think in general, then, that such a person's concern is not for the body, but so far as he can stand aside from it, it is directed towards the soul?'

> 'I do.'
>
> 'Then, is it clear that . . . the philosopher differs from other people in releasing his soul as far as possible, from its communion with the body.'
>
> 'It appears so.'[51]

Plato believes that our bodies and our physical appetites are a bad influence; they interfere with what is truly noble: the pursuit of philosophical knowledge. He even suggests that sense perception (because it deals with physical things) is a poor guide to knowledge. (This idea that perception is not to be trusted is a common theme in ancient thought. Ancient thinkers point to misleading experiences, such as mirages in the desert or optical illusions like straight sticks that look bent in water, as examples of erroneous perception.)

The conversation continues with Socrates questioning Simmias:

> 'And now, what about the actual gaining of wisdom? Is the body a hindrance or not, if one enlists it as a partner in the quest? This is the sort of thing I mean: do sight and hearing afford mankind any truth, or aren't even the poets always harping on such themes, telling us that we neither hear nor see anything accurately? And yet if those bodily senses are neither accurate nor clear, the others will hardly be so; because they are, surely, all inferior to those. Don't you think so?'
>
> 'Certainly.'
>
> 'So when does the soul attain the truth? Because plainly, whenever it sets about examining anything in company with the body, it is completely taken in [i.e., tricked] by [the physical senses].'
>
> 'That's true.'
>
> 'So isn't it in reasoning [i.e., by thinking rather than perceiving] that any realities become manifest to it?'
>
> 'Yes.'
>
> 'And it reasons best, presumably, whenever none of these things bothers it, neither hearing nor sight nor pain, nor any pleasure either, but

whenever it comes to be alone by itself as far as possible, disregarding the body, and whenever, having the least possible communion and contact with it, it strives for reality.'

'That is so.'

'So there again the soul of the philosopher utterly disdains the body and flees from it, seeking rather to come to be alone by itself?'

'It seems so.'[52]

Despite Simmias's hesitant assent, the conversation continues onward to an inexorable conclusion. Unlike modern authors who believe that empirical science (which is based on sense perception) provides us with reliable knowledge of the world, Plato believes that philosophical argument—logic itself—is the only sure way to knowledge. After mentioning the idea of justice, the idea of beauty, and the idea of the good, Socrates concludes as follows:

'[Knowledge] would be achieved most purely by one who approached each object with his intellect alone as far as possible, neither applying sight in his teaching, nor dragging in any other sense; . . . rather using his intellect alone by itself and unsullied, [the good student] would undertake the hunt for each reality alone by itself. . . . He would be separated as far as possible from his eyes and ears, and virtually from his whole body [because the body] it confuses the soul and wouldn't allow it to gain truth and wisdom when in partnership with it: isn't this the one, Simmias, who will attain reality, if anyone will.'

'What you say is abundantly true, Socrates,' said Simmias.

'For all those reasons, then, . . . as long as we possess the body, and the soul is contaminated by such evil, we'll surely never adequately gain what we desire—and that, we say, is truth. Because the body affords us countless distractions, owing to the nurture it must have; and, again, if any illnesses befall it, they hamper our pursuit of reality. Besides, it fills us up with lusts and desires, with fears and fantasies of every kind, and with any amount of trash, so that

really and truly we are, as the saying goes, never able to think of anything at all because of it. Thus it's nothing but the body and its desires that brings wars and factions and fighting; because it's over the gaining of wealth that all wars take place, and we are compelled to gain wealth because of the body, enslaved as we are to its service; so for all those reasons it leaves us no leisure to do philosophy.'[53]

Plato believes that the body is a prison that chains the soul earthward; physical pleasure and a reliance on sense perception bind the immaterial soul to the physical world so that it cannot escape into the higher realm of ideas. Socrates explains: 'Each pleasure and pain fastens it to the body with a sort of rivet, pins it there, and makes it corporeal, so that it takes for real whatever the body declares to be so.'[54] This is why Socrates teaches the strange-sounding doctrine that philosophy 'is nothing else but practicing how to die and be dead'.[55] In the pursuit of truth, we must die to the body. The soul must disengage itself from the material world and enter the realm of ideas. Those who live for and through the body only know the physical, visible world. They are dragged down into the mud of sensual immorality and physical unknowing. This is, in Plato's epistemology, to remain in the cave, to live like an animal, to fail as a human being. The whole point of education is to move into the higher sections of the Divided Line (*C* + *D*), where the mind communes with higher, immaterial ideas.

Plato has been severely criticized for his dualism, his doctrine of the absolute separation of body and soul. He was clearly influenced by Pythagorean ideas about reincarnation and believed in at least some kind of mental existence after death. Scholars offer various interpretations of his views. Suffice it to say that Plato sometimes suggests that it is a good and noble thing to believe that we will be punished or rewarded in the afterlife in some place like Heaven or Hell depending on the degree of morality (or immorality) we have achieved in this life.

On the Tripartite Soul

Plato believes that the goal of morality is a healthy intellectual life. If we take proper care of our minds, we will think good thoughts and will inevitably behave in an ethical way. In *The Republic*, Socrates (acting as the mouthpiece of Plato) contrives a logical argument to show that there are three different parts to the soul. He points out that something without parts could not simultaneously move in two different directions. The same physical projectile, for example, could not go backward and forward at the same time. It follows, by extension, that if the soul were made of only one part, it could not act in two opposite, mutually exclusive ways at the same time.

Socrates points to a situation in which a thirsty person refuses to drink a cup of water. Suppose, for instance, I am 'dying of thirst' on a hot day. My enemy offers me a glass of lemonade, but I suspect the lemonade may be poisoned. What will happen? My raging thirst will make me want to drink; my suspicions will make me not want to drink. I will be caught, then, between opposite desires. The dialogue progresses:

> [Socrates:] 'Imagine an occasion when something is making [the soul] resist the pull of thirst: isn't this bound to be a different part of it from the thirsty part, which is impelling it towards drink as if it were an animal? I mean, we've already agreed that the same one thing cannot thanks to the same part of itself simultaneously have opposite effects in the same context.'
>
> 'No, it can't,' [Glaucon said]. . . .

> [Socrates:] 'Do we know of cases where thirsty people are unwilling to drink?'
>
> 'Certainly,' [Glaucon] said, 'it's a common occurrence.'
>
> 'What could be the explanation for these cases?' [Socrates] asked. 'Don't we have to say that their mind contains a part which is telling them to drink, and a part which is telling them not to drink, and that this is a different part and overcomes the part which is telling them to drink?'
>
> 'I think so,' [Glaucon] said. . . .
>
> 'So it wouldn't be irrational of us to expect that these are two separate parts,' I said, 'one which we can describe as rational, and the other as irrational and desirous. The first is responsible for the mind's capacity to think rationally, and the second—which is an ally of certain satisfactions and pleasures—[is responsible] for its capacity to feel lust, hunger, and thirst, and in general, to be stirred by desire.'[56]

Socrates concludes that there must be at least two separate parts to the soul: **reason** or the mind (Greek: *logistikon*) and the **appetites** (*epithumetikon*). Reason tells us what to think; the appetites are the engine of desire. But, upon further reflection, Socrates decides that there must also be another part of the soul called the **spirit** or the honourable passions (*thumoeides*). Here, again, Socrates appeals to similar reasoning. He observes that there is sense of passionate feeling and integrity in the soul that is not quite reasoning but that conflicts, nonetheless, with the appetites. He retells a well-known story about Leontius, a fellow Athenian:

> [Socrates:] 'But there's a story I once heard which seems to me to be reliable, . . . about how Leontius the son of Aglaeon . . . saw some corpses with the public executioner standing near by. On the one hand, he experienced the desire to see them, but at the same time he felt disgust and averted his gaze. For a while, he struggled and kept his hand over his eyes, but

finally was overcome by the desire; he opened his eyes wide, ran up to the corpses, and said, "There you are, you wretches! What a lovely sight! I hope you feel satisfied!"'[57]

Although Leontius's appetites pull him toward the morbidly titillating sight of the fresh corpses, he is angry with himself. There is a sense of passionate, honourable, spirited feeling that resists the pull of his base, indecent appetites. But this means that his appetites and this element of high-spirited feeling cannot be the same thing for they simultaneously push him in opposite directions. Socrates makes the general point that the experience of feeling ashamed or repulsed by our own desires is a common experience.

> Socrates: 'And that's far from an isolated case, isn't it? . . . It is not at all uncommon to find a person's desires compelling him to go against his reason, and to see him cursing himself and venting his passion on the source of compulsion within him. It's as if there were two warring factions, with [honourable] passion [or spirit] fighting on the side of reason.'[58]

Socrates concludes that the spirit (or passions) must be different from the appetites. So the human soul must be composed of three parts: reason, spirit, and appetites.

Plato tailors his theory of virtue to this tripartite model of the soul. He associates a different virtue or excellence with each individual part of the soul. A moral person is wise, courageous, moderate, and just. The individual possesses **wisdom**, when reason does its job of governing behaviour well; **courage**, when the spirit, following the guide of reason, feels in the right passion about the right things; **temperance** or self-restraint (what the Greeks called *sophrosune*), when the appetites are well-ordered and obedient to the spirit in league with reason; and finally **justice**, when the different parts of the soul act together harmoniously. In the virtuous individual, reason rules; the spirit carries out its bidding, and the appetites remain obedient to higher authority. This group of four principle virtues—wisdom, courage, temperance, and justice—came to be known as the cardinal virtues and are discussed at length by later philosophers. (See, for example, Chapter 6 on Thomas Aquinas.)

Although Plato believes that reason has a special place of prominence among the virtues—knowledge is the path to virtue—he also stresses the importance of temperance or moderation. It is the appetites that pose the biggest challenge to morality. In another dialogue, Plato compares the soul to a warrior in a chariot pulled by two horses, one white, one black. 'Let's stick to the threefold division of the soul,' Socrates tells his friends, 'with each and every soul consisting of two horse-like aspects and a third like a charioteer.' The charioteer is, of course, reason; the white horse represents spirit or the honourable passions, whereas the black horse represents the appetites. Socrates continues:

> One of the horses [is] good and the other bad. . . . The one in the better position has an upright appearance, and is clean-limbed and high-necked, hook-nosed, white in color and dark-eyed; his determination to succeed is tempered by self-control and respect for others, which is to say he is an ally of true glory; he needs no whip, but is guided only by spoken commands. The other is crooked, over-large, a haphazard jumble of limbs; he has a thick, short neck, and a flat face; he is black in color, with grey, blood-shot eyes, and an ally of excess and affection, hairy around the ears, hard of hearing, and scarcely to be controlled with a combination of whip and goad.[59]

As these descriptions make clear, the appetites, represented by the ugly, hairy, squat

✎ Applied Philosophy Box 4.6 ✎

Nancy: The Story of a Kleptomaniac (Compulsive Shoplifter)

I will never forget Nancy, the first person with kleptomania that I treated. As she walked into my office late one evening, I was struck by how nervous she was. Perspiration covered her forehead, her voice was trembling, and her voice quivered as she introduced herself. . . . Nancy was certainly suffering from an anxious depression, but there also seemed to be something she wasn't telling me.

After the initial interview I received a letter from Nancy. In her letter she referred to herself as the 'devil's spawn'. 'I have been a horrible person so long, I can't bring myself to tell you these things in person. I'm a thief. I steal something almost every day. You probably won't believe this, but I don't want the stuff I take. . . . That's why I am depressed. How can I feel good when I am such an evil person? If you don't want to treat me any longer, I'll understand.'

Although she was somewhat reluctant, she agreed to come for another appointment. 'I was probably fourteen years old when I started stealing,' she said. 'I would go to stores with my mother. When I saw certain objects I would get urges to steal them. The odd thing was that the items I stole were so ridiculous. I remember stealing key chains for several months, maybe three or four times a week. I didn't use them. I am not even sure why I stole them. Then I went several months where I stole batteries—hundreds of batteries. Every time I stole something, I felt a sort of rush. The problem was that almost immediately after each theft, I felt guilty and ashamed. I wanted so much to tell my mother, but I couldn't. I was so afraid she would stop loving me.'

'When I got older, things got even worse. I continued to have urges to steal when I entered stores, but the items needed to be more expensive to make the urges go away. Also I was having the urges more often. I couldn't just steal batteries anymore. Instead, I began to steal vacuums or lamps. One time I stole seven blenders at the same time. I remember just walking out with them in a cart. No one stopped me.' Nancy started crying. Her pain seemed too much to bear. At the time I saw Nancy, she was contemplating suicide.

This excerpt from a book on impulse control disorders describes a condition that resembles what happened to Leontius. Nancy is ashamed of her behaviour. She is giving in to desires she strongly disapproves of. Explain how Plato would describe the situation. (Note that Plato thinks that appetites are irrational—left to themselves, they mutate and change, almost at random, growing ever stronger. More on this later.)

Source: Jon Grant, S.W. Kim, *Stop Me Because I Can't Stop Myself.* (New York: McGraw-Hill, 2003), pp.18–19. Reproduced with permission of The McGraw-Hill Companies.

---

black horse, are unruly and need to be kept in check. For Plato, the key to a good life is the reigning in of excessive and wrongheaded desires. Plato does not suggest gentle persuasion but forceful, manly command. He describes what happens when the morally good person restrains indecent desires in the case of carnal love (*eros*):

> [When the erotic appetites get out of control] the charioteer . . . recoils as if from a trap and even

more violently wrenches the unruly horse's bit back out of its teeth, splashing its curse-laden tongue and jaws with blood, pinning its legs and haunches to the ground, and causing it pain. Once the same thing has happened to it over and over again, the bad horse calms down, and now [that] it has been humbled it lets itself be guided by the charioteer's intentions.[60]

Moral self-restraint requires a very strong will, particularly in the case of sexual love. (Note that Socrates, in keeping with Greek aristocratic society, sometimes situates love in a male-to-male context, without approving of physical liaisons. If anything, Plato is at pains to present Socrates as someone who has entirely chaste relations with his young students. Although some Platonic passages are sexually tinged, Socrates inevitably directs any sexual or romantic notions toward a higher spiritual or philosophical goal. Physical beauty is a springboard to a higher, immaterial beauty that exists in the realm of forms.)

It is important to note that Plato believes that even the most decent, proper individuals may hanker after the basest physical things. Most of us are subject to indecent, exaggerated desire. Even if we manage to keep these ignoble desires in check during waking hours, they come to the surface when we let down our guard in sleep. Socrates explains:

> We probably all contain these [lawless] pleasures and desires, but they can be kept under control by convention and by the co-operation of reason and better desires. Some people, in fact, control them so well they get rid of them altogether or leave only a few of them in a weakened state, but they remain stronger and more numerous in others. . . . [They] wake up when we're asleep. . . . When all the rest of the mind—the rational, regulated, controlling part—is asleep, then if the wild, unruly part is glutted with food or

drink, it springs up and longs to banish sleep and go satisfy its own instincts. I'm sure you're aware of how in these circumstances nothing is too outrageous; a person acts as if he were totally lacking in moral principle and unhampered by intelligence. In his dreams, he doesn't stop at trying to have sex with his mother and anyone or anything else—man, beast, or god; he's ready to slaughter anything; there's nothing he wouldn't eat. In short, he doesn't hold back from anything, however bizarre or disgusting.[61]

Plato believes, like other ancient authors whom we have studied, that those who do not limit their desires end up desiring anything and everything. These misguided appetites, unless controlled by reason, will push the individual into an unreasoned and self-defeating search after mindless pleasure that ends in misery and bad reputation.

We will finish this section by noting that Plato's account of the cardinal virtues has both a political and an ethical side. *The Republic* is based on an analogy that Socrates makes between justice in the state and justice in the individual. Socrates suggests that understanding what justice is on a large scale in the political arena will make it easier to understand what justice is on a smaller scale in the individual human soul. The just city-state represents in LARGE LETTERS what is written in SMALL LETTERS inside the just soul. Socrates proposes the following scenario to his listeners: 'Suppose we were rather short-sighted and had been told to read small writing from a long way off, and then one of us noticed the same letters written elsewhere in a larger size and on a larger surface; I'm sure we would regard this as a godsend and would read them there before examining the smaller ones.'[62] This is how *The Republic* proceeds: Socrates begins with an analysis and observation of how

◦ Applied Philosophy Box 4.7 ◦

Hypersexuality

Sexual addictions are very real. Jennifer P. Schneider, MD, PhD states that 'addiction to sexual activities can be just as destructive as addiction to chemical substances'. Patrick Carnes, PhD, the researcher who first identified sexual addiction as a condition, has estimated that about 8 percent of men and 3 percent of women . . . in the US are sexually addicted. This constitutes over 15 million people in this country alone.

. . . The Mayo Clinic defines sexual addiction as a loss of control and utilizes the word compulsive. 'Compulsive sexual behaviour refers to spending inordinate amounts of time in sexual-related activity, to the point that one neglects important social, occupational or recreational activities in favor of sexual behaviour.' The Society for the Advancement of Sexual Health further illustrates this addiction by outlining several key components: 'Compulsivity, that is, loss of the ability to choose freely whether to stop or to continue; Continuation of the behaviour despite adverse consequences, such as loss of health, job, marriage, or freedom; Obsession with the activity.'

The above are the broad patterns of behaviour of sexual addiction. There are also a number of specific behaviours which are common to those who struggle with this addiction . . . includ[ing]: compulsive masturbation, compulsive sex with prostitutes, anonymous sex with multiple partners (one night stands), multiple affairs outside a committed relationship, frequent patronizing of sexually-oriented establishments, habitual exhibitionism, habitual voyeurism, inappropriate sexual touching, sexual abuse of children, and rape. In addition to these, fantasy sex, prostitution, pedophilia, masochism, fetishes, sex with animals and cross-dressing may also be behaviours of the sexual addict.'

There are many other examples of disordered appetites. In a book, a magazine, or on the Internet, find a different example of this kind of problem. How would Plato counsel such people?

Source: Kimberly Read and Marcia Purse, 'Sex Sex Sex and More Sex.' *About.com*, http://bipolar.about.com/cs/hypersex/a/aa_hypersex.htm, 5 March 2008.

justice manifests itself on a large scale between groups of people in a moral state and then uses this knowledge to explain what morality means for the individual human soul.

Socrates claims that an efficient political state will have to be organized according to one basic principle: 'that every individual has to do just one of the jobs relevant to the community, the one for which his nature best suit[s] him.'[63] He divides his republic into three different groups: rulers (what he calls 'the gold'), police and military ('the silver'), and the ordinary, working masses ('the bronze'). The basic idea

'that morality is doing one's own job and not intruding elsewhere'[64] becomes the defining theme for political and moral obligation. In a just community, smart rulers rule, loyal police and military enforce law and order, and the orderly workers busy themselves supplying all citizens with proper amounts of healthy food, drink, clothing, shelter, pottery, entertainment, and so on. Good rulers are well-trained in the study of philosophy; after a proper education that pushes them upward to the top of the Divided Line, they return as philosopher kings and govern benevolently.

The cardinal virtues then play a political and a moral role in Plato's system. Good rulers are chiefly characterized by wisdom; good police and soldiers are chiefly characterized by courage; good working people are chiefly characterized by temperance. In a good city-state, justice is embodied in the proper relations between these distinct classes. When everyone in every class does their proper work for the benefit of all—this is justice. The just individual is, thus, a microcosm of the just state.

In the case of individual human beings, morality means that each part of the soul does its proper work, without interfering in the specialized work of the other parts. Reason—the philosopher king inside the individual soul—is best equipped to make decisions; the passionate spirit—the policing-military element—is best equipped to put those wise decisions into effect; and the appetites—the ordinary working masses—are best equipped to provide for the physical, biological, and other needs of the individual. Inside the moral person, these different parts work harmoniously together for the benefit of all to produce just behaviour. Reason rules, the spirit restrains and guides the appetites, and the appetites promote the general well-being of the individual by engaging in properly ordered desire and practising self-restraint.

On the Chimera Model

Having devised a picture of what morality entails, Socrates is finally ready to answer the question posed by the story of Gyges's ring. Why should we refrain from immorality, even if we can get away with it? Why not pretend to be moral while taking advantage of other people? Socrates begins by proposing a colourful metaphor for the human soul:

[Socrates:] 'At this point in the argument, let's remind ourselves of the original assertion which started us off on our journey here. Wasn't it someone saying that immorality was rewarding if you were a consummate criminal who gave an impression of morality? Wasn't that the assertion?'

[Glaucon:] 'Yes, it was.'

'Well, now that we've decided what effect morality and immoral conduct have,' I [Socrates] said, 'we can engage him in conversation.'

'What shall we say,' he asked.

'Let's construct a theoretical model of the mind, to help him see what kind of idea he's come up with . . .'

'What sort of a model,' he asked.

'Something along the lines of those creatures who throng the ancient myths,' I said, 'like the Chimera, Scylla, Cereberus, and so on, whose form is a composite of the features of more than one creature.'

'Yes, that's how they described it,' he said.

'Make a model, then, of a creature with a single—if varied and many-headed—form, arrayed all round with the heads of both wild and tame animals, and possessing the ability to change over to a different set of heads and to generate all these new bits from its own body.'

'That would take some skilful modeling', he remarked, 'but since words are a more plastic material than wax and so on, you may consider the model constructed.'

'A lion and a man are the next two models to make, then. The first of the models, however, is to be by far the largest, and the second the second largest.'

'That's an easier job,' he said. 'It's done.'

'Now join the three of them together until they become one, as it were.'

'All right,' he said.

'And for the final coat, give them the external appearance of a single entity. Make them look like a person, so that anyone incapable of seeing what's inside, who can only see the external husk, will see a single creature, a human being.

'It's done,' he said.'[65]

Socrates's human being looks, from the outside, like an ordinary human being. But inside, it is composed of three different creatures: (1) a very large, many-headed **hydra**, that is, a hungry monster with multiple necks capable of growing innumerable new heads of any size and shape at random; (2) a smaller lion, the king of beasts, and (3) and an even smaller human being. The hydra represents the appetites; the lion represents spirit; the human being represents reason. So what happens in the case of the immoral person?

Socrates believes that, when we give in to wickedness, the appetites, assisted by the passions, come to control reason. In other words, the hydra takes over and, with the help of the lion, dominates the human being. Immorality effectively turns us into monsters: not on the outside, but on the inside. To practise immorality is to let our appetites multiply; it is to feed the ravenous hydra; to let it grow more wild, greedy heads that reach out insatiably craving everything imaginable. When the hydra is big and strong enough, it will use the lion as its ally to overpower and govern the interior human being. This leads to internal warfare. Without the calm, intelligent control of reason, the appetites and spirit will fight with one another, turning the conscious self into a battleground for conflicting desires and feelings. Whereas moral people use reason to govern their appetites in some sensible and coordinated way, immoral people, having forsaken reason almost completely, indulge in self-destructive and even contradictory behaviour.

Socrates continues:

'Now we had better respond to the idea that this person gains nothing from doing wrong, and loses from doing right, by pointing out to its proponent that this is tantamount to saying that we are rewarded if we indulge and strengthen the many-sided beast and the lion with all its aspects, but starve and weaken the man, until he's subject to the whims of the others, and can't promote familiarity and compatibility of the other two but lets them bite each other, fight, and try to eat each other.'

'Yes, that's undoubtedly what a supporter of immorality would have to say,' [Glaucon] agreed.

'So the alternative position, that morality is profitable, is equivalent to saying that our words and behavior should be designed to maximize the control the inner man has within us, and should enable him to secure the help of the leonine quality and then tend to the many-headed beast as a farmer tends to his crops—by nurturing and cultivating its tame aspects, and by stopping the wild ones growing. Then he can ensure that they're all compatible with one another, and with himself, and can look after them all equally, without favoritism.'[66]

So this is why immorality is both wrong and foolhardy: because it degenerates into a kind of violent slavery. It is not that other people enslave us, forcing us to their bidding. Immorality is a more subtle form of slavery that we perpetrate on ourselves. Socrates asks a question: 'The point is, if there's no profit in someone selling his son or daughter into slavery—slavery under savage and evil men—for even a great deal of money, then what happens if he cruelly enslaves the most divine part of himself to the vilest, most godless part?'[67] To aspire to immorality is to aspire to slavery; it is to want our soul to be chained and tethered to our most outrageous appetites; it is to use our spirit to force our soul to do the bidding of irrational, animal cravings; it is to make reason a slave of our baser selves.

Socrates elaborates a general moral principle: 'Things are [morally] acceptable when they subject the bestial aspects of our nature to the human . . . part of ourselves, but they're [morally] objectionable when they cause the oppression of our tame side under the savage side.'[68] Immorality turns us upside down. The ruling element serves; the serving element rules. The result is chaos and strife that we cannot escape for it is happening deep inside us, where we are most ourselves.

Glaucon, in telling the story of Gyges's ring, claims that the wicked are more fortunate than the good if they get away with their crimes. If criminals escape punishment at the hands of others, they will profit from immorality and lead the happiest life. Socrates responds that criminals who are caught and punished are more fortunate for they stand, at least, a chance of being forced to reform. This is the point of punishment: it is a kind of therapy. Evil-doers who escape detection are, in contrast, the most unlucky of all. Without outside help, they are doomed to unhappiness. Socrates lectures Glaucon:

> And how can it be profitable for a person's immorality to go unnoticed and unpunished. The consequence of a criminal getting away with his crimes is that he becomes a worse person. If he's found out and punished, however, then his bestial side is tamed and pacified, his tame side is liberated, and . . . his mental state becomes as good as it can be. [Remember] the mind is a more valuable asset than the body; it's more important for the mind to acquire self-discipline, morality, and intelligence than it is for the body to become fit, attractive, and healthy. . . . [So it is better if the reformed criminal will] put all his energies throughout his life, into achieving this goal.[69]

Plato views the law as an extension of morality. When people are unable to properly govern themselves, either because they are immature, or ill, or evil, they need to be governed from the outside—for their own good as well as for the good of the rest of society. Law and order,

social and familial discipline, are only a public reflection of the rule of reason that should, in the best of circumstances, derive from the inner person. Socrates explains:

> Subjection to the principle of divine intelligence is to everyone's advantage. It's best if this principle is part of a person's own nature, but if it isn't, it can be imposed from outside, to foster as much unanimity and compatibility between us as might be possible when we're all governed by the same principle. . . . It's also clear . . . that this is the function of law. . . . and it explains why we keep children under control and don't allow them freedom until we've formed a government within them, as we would in a community.[70]

Educating children and fellow citizens in morality is, then, the purpose of both law and parental authority.

Appraisal of Plato's Philosophical World View

Plato produces a monumental treatment of morality that is at odds with contemporary discussions both in its tone and in its literary form of expression. Contemporary moralists (still influenced by historical Christianity) tend to view morality as an issue of how to treat other people. Plato focuses on how we relate to ourselves. Justice involves an internal harmony between the different parts of our own nature. Roughly put, modern moralists focus on fairness or altruism, whereas Plato focuses on personal achievement. The contemporary critic may complain that the Platonic version of virtue is somehow self-centred or self-absorbed. In some important sense, it does not focus on how we treat others but on how we treat ourselves.

But this sort of criticism is unfair. Plato believes that the person who achieves the inner harmony engages in fair and even charitable behaviour toward other people. The virtuous would never steal, betray friends or country, break promises, commit adultery, abandon parents, or neglect religious duties. Their inner vision of the idea of the good and their self-discipline will lead necessarily to moral behaviour that is also directed outward at other people. Socrates tells his listeners:

'Take this [just] community of ours and a person who resembles it. . . . and suppose . . . we had to state whether . . . a person of this [virtuous] type would steal money which had been deposited with him. Is it conceivable to you that anyone would think our man capable of this . . . ?'

'No one would think that,' [Glaucon] said.

'And he could have nothing to do with temple-robbery, theft, and betrayal either of his personal friends or, on a public scale, of his country, could he?'

'No, he couldn't.'

'Moreover, nothing could induce him to break an oath or any other kind of agreement?'

'No, nothing.'

'And he is the last person you'd expect to find committing adultery, neglecting his parents, and failing to worship the gods.'

'Yes, of course,' he said.[71]

Plato believes the condition of having a well-ordered soul is intimately connected to the morality understood as an active disposition to treat others fairly and obey the moral law. A harmonious soul is the cause; what we call moral behaviour is the effect. The philosophically astute see the goodness in moral behaviour shining through, as a reflection of a higher good that is inside the moral individual.

Plato would think that contemporary authors miss the point. We moderns tend to focus on the distinction between moral and immoral behaviour. We use moral law as our guide. Consider the dictum, 'Thou shalt not steal'.

Assuming this rule is sound or true, we can know that shoplifting is a bad act and that returning a lost wallet to its owner is a good act. But Plato wants to ask a deeper question: why do people shoplift? They shoplift, he thinks, because their appetites, aided by their passions, control their reasoning; because they slip into the convenient rationalization that physical possessions are more important than spiritual achievement. Remember that Plato thinks that immorality springs from ignorance. People who shoplift are still in the cave. They are pursuing false goods; they mistake the shadows on the wall for true reality. Knowledge, then, is the route to moral behaviour. If we want to make these people moral, we must either push them outside the cave or we must make them obedient to someone who has already escaped the cave, someone like Socrates, someone who can be a philosopher king.

The modern critic might also complain that Plato has a confused notion of love. He clearly loved—the word is not too strong—Socrates. At the same time, Plato seems to emphasize the importance of a relationship not with other human beings, but with an impersonal idea of the good. Whether we can move easily from a focus on an abstract idea of the good to a focus on personal human relationships as the basis of morality is a legitimate question. Should we love Socrates as another human being or love Socrates only as means to philosophical enlightenment? Christian authors who explicitly base morality on Jesus's idea of a loving relationship have, in many instances, been deeply impressed by Plato's refined and otherworldly perspective. As we have seen in our discussion of the Divided Line, he describes an assent up the ladder of knowledge to a mystical embrace with an immaterial idea that some theologians identify as God. Seen from this perspective, the point of intellectual enlightenment is a relationship with an immaterial reality that is much larger than oneself. Still, this leaves open this question: should we focus on loving other people more than on loving an incorporeal idea? Note that Plato is not entirely consistent when it comes to questions about what happens after we are dead. I have mentioned Socrates suggests that there is individual survival along with reward or punishment after death. But there are other times when he talks as if the individuality of the good person will dissipate after death in a mystical union with the impersonal idea of the good. Considered from this latter perspective, morality is only a means to a kind of liberation from human selfhood, an idea akin to what some Eastern religions teach.

As I have already mentioned, contemporary authors have also criticized Plato for his metaphysical dualism: his neat separation of the physical from the immaterial. Plato emphasizes spiritual and intellectual values so much that he ends up denigrating physical, biological, psychological, and other aspects of human reality. He suggests that the physical body is only a prison for immaterial, angel-like souls. But this is to demean an important aspect of human nature. Is it not possible that our individual physical selves are good in themselves and an essential part of what we are? Although Plato is surely right to warn us about the dangers of unordered physical desires, it does not follow that we ought to live as immaterial minds detached from our bodies. It could be argued that our biological drives and our physical bodies (as well our concerns for theses aspects of the human condition) should be respected and valued as integral aspects of who we are, and that morality is not the elimination but the transformation of these traits into something more complete and noble. As we shall see in Chapter 5, Plato's student Aristotle reworks Plato's theory much along these lines.

✍ Questions for Study and Review ✍

1. Why is it difficult to separate out the views of Socrates and Plato?
2. How can we make sense of Socrates's claim of complete ignorance?
3. Describe the Socratic method of *elenchus*.
4. What, from Socrates's point of view, is the problem with hedonism?
5. Explain Socrates's asymmetry principle.
6. What, according to Socrates, is the relationship between the individual and society? What follows from that relationship?
7. How does Plato 'extend' the idea of nature?
8. How does Plato define *the good*?
9. Why does Plato think that philosophical education is a necessary part of moral training?
10. Describe and explain the analogy of the cave.
11. What is the problem with hedonism from Plato's point of view?
12. Plato, unlike many modern philosophers, thinks that sense perception leads us astray. It is not aid but a distraction. How, according to Plato, are we to arrive at the truth of the cave in relation to the Divided Line? Explain.
13. What is the difference between the physical and intellectual world for Plato?
14. According to Plato, what is better: that criminals be caught and punished or that they manage to commit their crimes without being detected? Explain Plato's reasoning.
15. Criticize the modern focus on moral and immoral actions from a Platonic perspective.

ᴇᴏ Suggestions for Further Reading ᴏᴇ

- One standard English translation of Plato's works is *The Collected Dialogues of Plato Including the Letters*, Edith Hamiltoon Cairns eds., (Princeton, NJ.: Princeton University Press, 1963).
- Plato, *Trial and Death of Socrates: Euthyphro, Apology, Crito, Death Scene from Phaedo*, G.M.A. Grube, trans.; John Cooper, revisions (Indianapolis: Hackett Publishing Company, 2001).
- Plato, *Defence of Socrates*, David Gallop, trans. (Oxford, UK: Oxford University Press, 2008).
- Plato, *The Republic*, Robin Waterfield, trans. (Oxford, UK: Oxford University Press, 1998).
- Plato, *The Republic*, Paul Shorey, trans. (London, UK: William Heinemann, Loeb Classical Library, 1956) vol. 5–6.
- Plato, *Gorgias*, Robin Waterfield, trans. (Oxford, UK: Oxford, 1994). Pay particular attention to the exchanges between Callicles and Socrates.
- Plato, *Symposium*, Robin Waterfield, trans. (Oxford, UK: Oxford University Press, 1998).
- For an excellent online collection of primary Greek and Roman sources (in original languages and translation), including the works of Plato and Aristotle, see: 'Perseus Digital Library,' Gregory R. Crane, ed.: www.perseus.tufts.edu.

Chapter Five

Understanding Moral Theory: Aristotle

ᴥ Chapter Objectives

After reading this chapter you should be able to:

- Define fundamental Aristotelian concepts, such as happiness (*eudaimonia*), virtue (*arete*), practical wisdom (*phronesis*), the good life, means and ends, instrumental and intrinsic value, involuntary acts mixed acts, and so on.
- Apply Aristotle's Mean to a wide variety of familiar virtues and vices.
- Elucidate Aristotle's understanding of moral failure in terms of moral ignorance, incontinence, and his schema of six related character types.
- Identify the major and minor intellectual virtues and describe Aristotle's inductive-deductive model of moral reasoning using examples.
- Explain Aristotle's account of the three types of friendship.

Introduction

The three most famous philosophers in the ancient world are undoubtedly Socrates, his student Plato, and Plato's student Aristotle (384–22 BC). Aristotle was a working biologist, historian, metaphysician, logician, psychologist, and literary critic as well as a moral philosopher. His father, who had been a doctor in the Macedonian court, may have played a role in directing his son's early interests toward science and biology. After the death of his father, Aristotle travelled to Athens to enroll as a student at Plato's famous Academy. (He was probably about 17 years old at the time.) After some 20 years at the Academy, he moved on, travelling and teaching in various regions around modern-day Greece and Turkey and eventually returning to Athens, where he founded a rival school called the Lyceum. At one point in his travels, he was summoned to the Macedonian court to tutor the teenage Alexander the Great, who later conquered Athens (along with much of the known world).

As a result, the older Aristotle, viewed as an associate of Alexander, was no longer welcome in Athens. Fearing for his life, he fled. According to one story, he explained that he did not want to permit the Athenians to sin a second time against philosophy (as they had already done by executing Socrates). He died a few months later at a country estate.

Aristotle's philosophical corpus is encyclopedic in scope. He was a greater collector and recorder of knowledge and interested in almost everything: from Greek mythology to the biology of birds, to sports, to the best way to win an argument, to different legal constitutions, to the nature of the human soul, and so on. His views on morality overlap with his views on politics. His very influential text the *Nicomachean Ethics* was named after his son Nicomachus.[1] Aristotle's followers were sometimes referred to as the **Peripatetics**, from a Greek word meaning 'to walk up and down, to walk about'. The name comes from Aristotle's alleged habit of walking to-and-fro as he lectured in his school. Although he wrote a great deal, Aristotle (unlike Plato) did not produce many complete and polished manuscripts. Mostly, we have his scattered lecture notes mixed perhaps with additions by his colleagues and students, arranged in rough sequence and pieced together at a later date by editors, most famously by Andronicus of Rhodes. Reading the original Aristotelian texts is, as a result, a daunting task. The beginner will find Aristotle's prose by turns disjointed, elliptical, obscure, repetitious, and even inconsistent. We need, then, to focus on his basic ideas rather than on individual passages.

We sometimes isolate great thinkers in our minds. We should not think of Aristotle, however, as a solitary thinker on a lonely mountaintop writing down his innermost thoughts.

Socially, he was well-connected. A famous thinker and lecturer, he travelled a great deal. In his writing, he displays great breadth of knowledge about other authors in the Greek tradition. His finished system of virtue ethics is, in many ways, a synthesis of the best moral ideas found in the Western world during Greek times. Perhaps more than any other author, Aristotle manages to combine common sense and the Greek moral tradition with the most sophisticated moral reasoning. Clearly, he does not say everything there is to say about morality, but he does provide a broad template that can still serve as the basis for an up-to-date moral theory.

It is easy to get lost in Aristotle: his unwieldy views are not always in line with modern attitudes; his prose style is difficult; his terminology is technical; he broaches a very wide range of topics; and arguments from one book or chapter of his expansive corpus sometimes depend on arguments from a different book or chapter. Aristotle does not summarize everything there is to know about morality in a few abbreviated rules. He devises a broad-ranging, somewhat rambling ethics that is intended to answer questions like these: What is the reason for human striving? What is human happiness? What is human excellence? How do human beings think about morality? What is the connection between morality and human society? What does it mean to be a good friend? And so on.

Aristotelian virtue ethics tries to make sense of what human life is about. Aristotle is not so much a religious thinker; he is more like a biologist, like a naturalist who observes animals in the field. Suppose you are a nature lover and you want to learn about lions. What do you do? You go out into the savannah and watch closely what lions do. You then try to explain, in general principles, the life and behaviour of lions. In his ethics, Aristotle does the same thing with human beings. He examines, in a scientific spirit, what human beings typically (or untypically) do, coming up with a comprehensive description of what is already going on in human behaviour. Morality is not biology, but (in Aristotle's view) it includes a biological, a psychological, a political, and even a religious component. Aristotle tries to elucidate, in the most comprehensive way possible, what human beings are trying to do with their lives and to supply natural standards of evaluation we can use to judge human behaviour in a rational, consistent manner.

There is no one right way to begin learning about Aristotle. Imagine you are visiting a new city. You can't take everything in all at once. You begin with a historical landmark; you familiarize with this or that street, and move on from there. We can approach Aristotle's moral philosophy in much the same way, familiarizing ourselves with one key concept, and then another, and another, until we begin to get a feel for his approach. A good place to start is with his account of human happiness. Aristotle believes that we all want to be happy and that we can only be happy when we are moral. Morality is a means to happiness.

On Happiness (*Eudaimonia*)

Aristotle begins his *Nicomachean Ethics* with a famous and much criticized argument: 'Every art and every inquiry, and similarly every action and pursuit, is thought to aim at some good; and for this reason *the good* has rightly been declared to be that at which all things aim.'[2] Critics of this argument misunderstand its logical structure. Aristotle reasons using syllogisms, arguments composed of three sen-

tences and three concepts. This particular syllogism is an enthymeme: an argument with a hidden premise. We can rephrase his line of thought while supplying the hidden premise. Premise 1: every (human) activity aims at some specific good; (Hidden) Premise 2: every specific good aims at the supreme good; Conclusion: so the supreme good is the aim of every activity. To express the logical structure of the argument more simply:

Premise 1: every activity → some specific good.

Premise 2: every specific good → the supreme good.

Conclusion: every activity → the supreme good.

Ethics is about understanding what human behaviour is all about. If, as Aristotle suggests, all human conduct aims at the supreme good, it is of utmost importance that we come to a proper understanding of what the supreme good is. Aristotle goes on to identify the supreme human good with happiness. He defines happiness in two different ways: first, with respect to what it is; and second, with respect to what causes it. We will, in this section, explain Aristotle's views about what happiness is. (We discuss what causes happiness beginning on page 151.)

Aristotle uses the Greek word *eudaimonia* to refer to happiness. The prefix *eu* means 'good' and the noun *daimon* means 'devil or invisible spirit'. To be happy is, literally, to be watched over by a 'good spirit'; it is, in Christian terms, to have a good guardian angel. The ancient Greeks believed that gods, demigods, and spirits (devils) watched over and influenced human history. To achieve happiness is to be blessed by the gods; it is to have a good destiny. The modern English word *happiness* has a related origin, for it derives from the archaic

---

✎ Applied Philosophy Box 5.1 ✎

How to Write Your Own Obituary

Advice from Obituary.com

'Summing up a life is an awesome responsibility', points out newspaper obituary writer Alana Baranick, on her website *Death Beat*.

Why not get started on writing your own obituary? This is your chance to say what you want others to know about you. Do it for yourself: for peace of mind knowing that you have had your say. And do it for your family and friends: that you have helped them cope with a difficult time.

Your best chance of having your wishes honored is to write them down. Writing your own obituary can be part of your life and end-of-life planning. The way you would like to be remembered is part of a careful arranging for yourself should you not be in the best of health or life.

We could say that Aristotle thinks that the end to a happy life is a good obituary. If you were to lead a successful life, what would your obituary say? What kind of life would you like to live? Write the obituary of an admirable life, a life well-lived.

Source: Alana Baranick, 'How to Write Your Own Obituary.' *Obituary.com*; www.obituaryguide.com/writeyourown.php, 3 January 2010.

English word *hap*, which means 'luck'. To be happy is to be lucky; it is, as in the Greek conception, to have a good fate. Happiness here is not about 'feeling good' but about living an admirable, enviable life.'

If happiness is good fortune; this leads inevitably to a second question. What counts as good fortune? Aristotle posits two requirements for such a life. First, we must be happy until the end of our lives, for, as he poetically says, 'one swallow does not make a summer, nor does one day'.[3] Human life has its ups and downs. Someone who is happy at 18 may be miserable at 46, and someone who is miserable at 18 may be happy at 46. In life, winners may become losers and losers become winners. When then can we safely declare that we are happy once and for all? Aristotle believes that we can only know this for certain at the end of our lives, 'since many changes occur in life, and all manner of chances, and the most

prosperous may fall into great misfortunes in old age'.[4] So the first requirement for happiness is that on your deathbed you must be able to look back on your entire life and honestly say, 'I have had a happy life'.

But there is a second requirement for happiness. Aristotle identifies *eudaimonia* with good reputation. The happy individual gains a good reputation, not among the ignorant but among those who are knowledgeable. It is not enough that you approve of your own life, for your judgment may be partisan and faulty. What matters is that someone who is a good judge of these things determines that your life was a happy one. To achieve *eudaimonia* is to leave this world with such a glorious reputation for goodness that *wise* people remember and admire you long after you are dead. To be happy is to achieve immortality, to be remembered because you have accomplished good and even great things.

On Virtue (*Arete*)

Aristotle's approach to morality is called **virtue ethics** because of the emphasis he places on key character traits. If happiness means good reputation, the best way to achieve such a reputation is through a virtuous character. It is important to emphasize from the outset that Aristotle has, like other ancient Greeks, a very broad notion of virtue. The Greek word he uses for virtue is *arete*, which can be translated, more simply, as (human) excellence. But there are many different kinds of human excellence. Yes, honesty is an excellence; courage is an excellence; kindness is an excellence. But being a good piano player, a good mathematician, a good doctor, a good football coach: these are excellences as well. Aristotle, clearly an aristocrat, favours some excellences over others. Still, the root meaning of *virtue* is human excellence of any sort. (We discuss the distinction between moral and intellectual virtues below. More on this later.)

We can use Aristotle's biological notions of **potentiality** and **actuality** to better explain what a virtue is. As Aristotle reports in his biological works, a caterpillar has the potential to become a butterfly. It realizes that potential when it enters the chrysalis and emerges as a mature butterfly. In a similar way, individual human beings have different potentialities that can be developed. This actualization of our best traits into an exemplary human personality is what Aristotle means by *virtue*. (Note that the word *personality* here and below does not denote superficial traits as in the stock phrase, 'she has a nice personality'. It means, as in psychology, the organized pattern of behavioural, attitudinal, and emotional characteristics that constitute a specific individual. Personality has to do with what a person *deeply* is, with the core settled traits that make each person unique. Aristotelian virtue ethics, it goes without saying, involves more than 'niceness'.)

Most basically, virtuous people actualize their talents. Someone who becomes a good hockey player, a good mathematician, a good teacher, a good concert pianist has, in this respect at least, achieved human excellence. Such people have actualized, or brought to completion, the talents they have. There is some kind of virtue here, on a very basic level. Of course, playing hockey is not all there is to the good life. If you are a great hockey player but a lousy father, you lack virtue in a crucial sense, for you have failed to actualize your ability to be a good parent. Still, virtue is all about developing our natural capacities to the utmost. This means, of course, developing our capacities for conspicuously moral things like mercy, honesty, generosity, good citizenship, fairness, friendship, and so on.

Aristotle goes on to elaborate a **functional argument** for the specific conception of virtue he favours. He writes, 'For just as for a flute-player, a sculptor, or an artist, . . . the good and the "well" is thought to reside in the function, so would it seem to be for man'.[5] The function of flute players is to play the flute well. We evaluate them according to how well they accomplish this musical task. Franz is not a good flute player because he makes the very best shoes but because he is adept at playing Mozart. It follows that if we could only determine what the function of a human being is, we could in the same way determine the degree to which a particular human being has (or has not) achieved excellence. Virtuous human beings will fulfill the human function admirably; bad human beings will fail signally at that function.

What then is the human function? Aristotle believes that there are three classes of living organisms: plants, animals, and human beings. Plants are characterized by nutrition and growth; animals are also characterized by movement and perception; human beings are also characterized by the capacity to reason. It is then the ability to reason that is the special characteristic that makes human beings human. (Hence the traditional definition of humans as **rational animals**.) Aristotle explains, 'Life seems to be common even to plants, but we are seeking what is peculiar to man. Let us exclude, therefore, the life of nutrition and growth. Next there would be a life of perception, but it also seems to be common even to the horse, the ox, and every animal. There remains, then, an active life of the element that has a rational principle'.[6] Only human beings are able to reason. This is, thinks Aristotle, the unique human function. Human beings read and write and do mathematics; they are capable of abstract thought and logic; they practise science and record history, and so on. But that is not all. In a book called the *Politics*, Aristotle observes, 'it is the peculiarity of man, in comparison with other animals, that he alone possesses a perception of good and evil, of the just and unjust, and other similar qualities'.[7] Humans can tell the difference between right and wrong. They possess moral judgment. A cat toys with a mouse without the least hint of moral guilt. Individual humans sometimes do terrible things, but they can also feel guilty about what they do. Humans evaluate their acts in accordance with higher standards; they are capable of a degree of moral self-consciousness that is not present in other animals.

If Aristotle associates virtue with reason, be careful! He is not equating reason with self-absorbed thought. There is more to the rational life than thinking! Aristotle understands this. The operation of human reason expresses itself in untold ways. Writing a novel, balancing chemical equations, playing chess, teaching yoga, arguing in court, raising children, doing moral philosophy (etc.) require the operation of human intelligence. All these activities can be considered virtuous insomuch as they require the actualization of intelligent human capacities. They all require mastery; they all require skill; they all require high levels of accomplishment. As we shall see, Aristotle does reserve a special place for mental activities such as philosophy and intellectual study. Nonetheless, we can extend his basic understanding of virtue to the most mundane human activities.

Are human beings like other animals? Suppose you go to the circus and see a trained bear riding a bicycle. You think to yourself, *That's just like a human being*! I will call this the bear-on-a-bicycle fallacy. In fact, a bear riding a bicycle and a human being riding a bicycle are *not* the same thing. Because human beings perform acts similar to other species—eating, grooming, reproducing, exercising, etc.—it does not follow that human purpose is identical with animal purpose. Perhaps I am riding my bicycle over to see my sick mother who is in the hospital. Perhaps I ride it because I want to lose weight. Or perhaps I am training for the Tour de France. The bear is not riding a bicycle for any of these reasons. We must beware then of superficial similarities. A human being riding a bicycle and a trained animal riding a bicycle are not the same thing.

Aristotle argues that human individuals develop virtue by participating in activities that represent or contribute to human excellence. There is no short-hand, formulaic, easy way to determine what counts as human excellence, but it goes without saying that we do admire certain people and criticize others.

☙ Applied Philosophy Box 5.2 ❧

Flow: A Modern Psychological Account of Happiness

The once-fuzzy picture of what makes people happy is coming into focus as psychologists no longer shun the study of happiness. . . . Life satisfaction occurs most often when people are engaged in absorbing activities that cause them to forget themselves, lose track of time and stop worrying. 'Flow' is the term Claremont Graduate University psychologist Mihaly Csikszentmihalyi coined to describe this phenomenon. People in flow may be sewing, . . . doing brain surgery, playing a musical instrument or working a hard puzzle with their child. The impact is the same: A life of many activities in flow is likely to be a life of great satisfaction, Csikszentmihalyi says.

Another description of the experience of 'flow':

Contrary to expectation, 'flow' usually happens not during relaxing moments of leisure and entertainment, but rather when we are actively involved in a difficult enterprise, in a task that stretches our mental and physical abilities. Any activity can do it. Working on a challenging job, riding the crest of a tremendous wave, and teaching one's child the letters of the alphabet are the kinds of experiences that focus our whole being in a harmonious rush of energy, and lift us out of the anxieties and boredom that characterize so much of everyday life. It turns out that when challenges are high and personal skills are used to the utmost, we experience this rare state of consciousness. . . . This state of consciousness . . . comes as close as anything can to what we call happiness.

This contemporary psychological description of happiness is very close to what Aristotle means by virtue. Aristotle sees virtue as activity done at a high pitch of mastery and skill. He would take exception, however, to the contemporary tendency to identify happiness with mere feeling. Aristotle views happiness as an objective state: it is not merely that the virtuous enjoy themselves; they are doing something that is truly good and noble. Not only do they themselves feel fulfilled, but this fulfillment derives from conduct that the rest of us can recognize as praiseworthy. (Aristotle believes that reason can objectively determine which activities are praiseworthy, as we discuss below.)

Source: Marilyn Elias, 'Psychologists Now Know What Makes People Happy,' *USA Today*, 12 October 2002. Reprinted online: www.biopsychiatry.com/happiness; Mihaly Csikszentmihalyi, *The Evolving Self*, pp. xii–xiv. Reproduced online: Rob Jellinghaus, 'Flow: What's Worth Living For?' www.unrealities.com/essays/flow.htm, 14 August 1995.

Aristotle's virtue ethics is an attempt to logically elucidate the criteria we rely on to make such all-round judgments and to set them up as an explicit basis for moral evaluation.

Criticisms of Aristotle's Notions of Virtue

Before going further, let's clear the air by quickly considering some of the typical criticisms of Aristotle's notions of virtue by contemporary philosophers. Examine briefly three familiar lines of criticism: (1) the idea that Aristotle's ethics is 'speciesist'; (2) the idea that there is no human nature, and (3) the idea that Aristotelian virtue ethics is self-centred.

That Aristotle's Ethics Is 'Speciesist'

Contemporary moral philosophers such as Peter Singer who argue for animal rights use the derogatory term 'speciesist' to denigrate a historical thinker like Aristotle. On their account, older thinkers were guilty of something akin to racism—what they call 'speciesism'—because they discriminated against animals, valuing members of our own species more than the members of other species. We will discuss these issues further in the very last chapter of this book. Simply note for the moment that Aristotle, who was, after all, a biologist, would probably retort that differences between species are a fact of nature. They are not arbitrary or made-up classifications. There are morally relevant differences that differentiate between organisms. Human beings do deserve a special kind of respect because rationality is an ennobling and praiseworthy capacity—indeed, Aristotle would claim, the most ennobling and praiseworthy capacity of all!

In any case, Aristotle is writing a morality for the human species. Some human beings—the very young, psychopaths, children brought up in the woods by wild animals, those with brain injuries, the senile—may lack rationality or moral intelligence. (As we discuss later in this chapter, Aristotle himself mentions these exceptional cases at some length.) But none of this discredits Aristotle's carefully qualified position that there is an essential connection between the human species and moral intelligence. When Aristotle calls human beings 'rational animals', he means that healthy human beings naturally develop rational capacities, including moral intelligence. Clearly, there are cases where such self-realization is blocked or hindered by all sorts of obstacles. But human beings typically possess rational and moral intelligence and the development of these capacities must be part of successful human self-realization.

That Belief in Human Nature Is Outdated

Some contemporary thinkers disparage what they see as an antiquated notion of a fixed or determinate human nature. To begin with, many of these criticisms are based on a modern misreading of ancient texts that fly in the face of common sense reality. Clearly, humans are not random aggregations of parts. They possess some sort of nature. A human being is not a cow, a fish, a pineapple, or a volcano. Humans share basic characteristics. There may be cases—even frightening cases—where we do not know if something is a human being. Would an embryo that develops from a monkey ovum and a human spermatozoa be a human being? Or would an extraterrestrial being with intelligent powers of speech be a human being? (In the first case, Aristotle would probably say no; in the second case, yes.) But these exceptional cases are beside the point. We do not progress in moral philosophy by allowing legitimate uncertainty about small details to cloud each and every issue. Humans, generally speaking, possess uniform traits. Their rationality, in particular, sets them apart. This means both that they should be treated with special respect but that they have to live up to a higher standard.

That Aristotelian Virtue Ethics Is Self-centred

Finally, some contemporary critics complain that virtue ethics promotes selfishness and self-absorption. Aristotle believes that we should devote all our energies to actualizing our own potential. But this makes morality sound like a project of self-aggrandizement. Isn't a life spent trying to develop our own talents less noble, less moral than a life directed to the selfless service of others? Is there any way to reconcile virtue ethics with, say, a morality of selfless, other-directed love?

There are several responses to such criticism. To begin with, it rests on a misunderstanding of Aristotle's position. Aristotle does not conceive of morality as the self-conscious pursuit of self-fulfillment. Self-fulfillment is a good thing; but the point of morality is not that I *feel* satisfied with myself. The point is to do something so praiseworthy that intelligent people ought to remember it for ages to come. Aristotle believes in objective moral standards. Either we achieve something worth remembering or we do not. What we ourselves feel about our achievements is a secondary issue.

In Aristotle's account, we may achieve happiness in the absence of any self-congratulatory feelings. Suppose you jump into a raging river to save a drowning person but suffer a stroke in the process. You manage to pull out the person, stagger out onto the bank, and collapse. You end up in the hospital in a coma. You have done a generous and a courageous act; you have been virtuous; you may have your name in the newspaper; people may talk about you for years to come; you have achieved happiness (*eudaimonia*). Still, you cannot feel self-esteem; you are unconscious, in a coma— still, for Aristotle, this is a kind of happiness, nonetheless. If self-esteem is a good thing to have, if it naturally accompanies virtue, it is, in the final analysis, virtue, not self-esteem, that we are after.

Aristotle tells us that we should focus on improving their *own* characters, but this is a good thing, not a bad thing. Suppose I tell you that you should strive to be as generous as possible. Is this morally objectionable? After all, I am telling you to focus on yourself, on what *you* should be like, on what *you* should do. But this is because we all have a particular responsibility for our own actions and character. It

---

༑ Applied Philosophy Box 5.3 ༖

Dad Drowns Saving Wife, Child

A hero[ic] Queens father drowned in the Rockaways yesterday after racing into the dangerous surf to rescue his wife and 10-year-old daughter, police and relatives said.

Jose-Luis Olivares, 36 . . . was in Jacob Riis Park around 7 p.m. when his wife and daughter got into trouble as they swam, according to officials and family.

Olivares dove into the water and managed to get his family members back to safety, but was swept out to sea himself, officials said . . . Olivares was rushed to Peninsula Hospital by helicopter and pronounced dead, police said.

'We're all feeling very bad right now because he was a hero today', said Olivares' brother Javier. 'He saved his daughter and his wife. He is a very good father—he loves his daughter. She is devastated.'

Paradoxically, perhaps, Aristotle would classify this as an example of 'self-love'. Explain. (He would also consider it an example of true friendship, which we discuss on page 199.)

Source: Philip Messing, Christina Carrega, Candace Amos, 'Qns. [Queen's] Dad Drowns Saving Wife, Child.' NYPost.com, www.nypost.com/seven/08152009/news/regionalnews/qns__dad_drowns_saving_wife__child_184682.htm#comments, 15 August 2009.

is up to us to make sure that we develop into moral human beings. This inevitably requires some sort of moral self-attention.

Contrary to what some would suggest, moral 'self-centredness' is not all bad. When Aristotle boldly asserts that 'a man is his own best friend and therefore ought to love himself best',[8] he is not arguing for any kind of unhealthy **narcissism**. Aristotle adds that in loving himself properly, a man 'will both himself profit by doing noble acts, and will benefit his fellows'.[9] Aristotle does not recommend selfish behaviour as a moral ideal. Wise lovers of self do not disregard morality, for moral achievement is (in Aristotle's mind) the very best thing there is. On the Aristotelian account, the true lover of self 'does many acts for the sake of his friends and his country, and if necessary dies for them'.[10] Self-lovers 'throw away wealth on condition that their friends will gain more'.[11] They 'throw away both wealth and honours [for the sake of] nobility'.[12]

One final point here is in order. It is true that Aristotle broadens the notion of virtue to bring under moral scrutiny many human occupations and behaviours that often escape moral notice. But this broader ideal of self-realization does not exclude narrower conceptions of morality. Traditional moral virtues, such as honesty, fairness, generosity, loyalty, courage (etc.), play a very large role in self-realization. We have a talent for hon-

---

ᴄ Applied Philosophy Box 5.4 ᴄ

Cheater, Cheater, Pumpkin Eater

From a high school newspaper:

> Cheating is unmistakably common in every school throughout the entire country. It has become a well-known fact that it is inevitable that if they are given the opportunity, then most students will cheat. But why? What makes our peers jump on the idea of cheating like it is the only way to success? . . . The majority of the adolescence [sic] of today is hooked on one thing: the media. Whether it be through TV, movies, music, advertisements . . . you name it, teenagers know all about it. One of the most famous false ideas that the media tries to push into the minds of today's children is that you have to be rich and famous to really succeed. And cheating your way to the top is the 'cool' way to do it. Plus, you have to figure that teenagers really look up and idolize the celebrities. If they see one of their favorite celebrities or 'role models' cheating in a show on TV or in a movie, or even hearing a song about it, than [sic] they are going to be convinced that it is a positive thing because that is what that famous person is doing. . . . Maybe if the media didn't try to convince that cheating is the only way to be rich and famous because it is 'cool', than [sic] it wouldn't be so common.

This high school journalist is complaining about a popular culture that identifies 'self-realization' with being 'rich and famous'. Aristotle would dismiss the idea of amoral wealth or fame as true self-realization as unbearably superficial and misleading. In his account, there is an inescapable moral component to healthy human development.

Source: 'Cheater, Cheater, Pumpkin Eater,' *South Western High Warrior News* (Somerset, KY), http://news.southwesternhigh.net/.

esty, and virtue means developing that talent. We have a talent for courage, and virtue means developing that talent. We have a talent for fairness; virtue means developing that talent. And so on. Someone might protest, 'I have a talent for dishonesty. Does virtue mean developing that?' But Aristotle would argue that honesty and dishonesty are not the same. What dishonesty really represents is a *lack* of effort and willpower. It is what happens when we do not try hard enough. Dishonesty is a nagging imperfection, not a human excellence.

Aristotle believes that what we now call conscience, the ability to determine what is good or bad, is part and parcel of human nature. (We discuss how we develop this moral knowledge on page 162.) He would insist that dishonesty produces shame, regret, and guilt in a well-formed, intelligent person. And these detract from self-realization. There is, no doubt, a bad kind of self-realization. There are those who lie, cheat, bully, scheme, and betray their way to success. If some contemporary authors want to suggest that such people have reached the pinnacle of self-realization, this is not Aristotle's take. The individuals in question may have achieved success of a certain restricted sort, but this is not what Aristotle means by virtue.

On Practical Reason

Aristotle conceives of morality, first and foremost, in terms of successful action. Ethics is a matter of doing. It expresses itself, not necessarily in words or in theory, but in right actions done at the right time for the right reason to the right effect. Imagine someone playing chess. Intelligent chess-players win games; that is how we know they are intelligent—because of the clever moves they make—not because they are good at speaking or writing about the game

of chess. In the same way, Aristotle believes that virtuous choices are a product of practical reason, what he calls **phronesis**. The ethically smart demonstrate their moral intelligence by the exemplary lives they lead. Honesty, sobriety, courage, patience, prudence (etc.)—these are not only moral choices but intelligent choices. This is enough for practical wisdom. The *phronimos*, the practically wise or prudent person, is able to get things done. Such people may or may not be able to express themselves efficiently in words, but this is a secondary matter. Insomuch as they possess practical wisdom, they manage to make good choices, to respond appropriately to varying circumstances. *Phronesis* = good choices.

Aristotle distinguishes between intelligence-in-thought and intelligence-in-action. Intelligence-in-thought gives us theory. Intelligence-in-action gives us morality. Practical wisdom is the successful exercise of intelligence-in-action. Aristotle succinctly writes, 'The end aimed at [in ethics] is not knowledge but action'.[13] Consider another example. Good basketball players know how to position themselves effectively, how to feint and jump, when to pass and when to shoot, and so on. A sports commentator or a coach might be able to explain in words what they are doing, but it is the athletes who act. In the heat of a basketball game, they make the right move quickly, in a split-second, without verbalizing what they are doing. They posses, we might say, basketball *phronesis*. Their play-making is a form of practical intelligence; it is intelligence expressed in and through action. This is what a moral person is able to do in the moral arena. They are able to respond—in a superior manner—to whatever befalls them.

Aristotle does not adopt a neutral stance towards morality. We study ethics 'not to know what virtue is but in order to become good'.[14] To be good is to be practically smart; to be bad is to be practically stupid. No enlightened person could purposely want to be stupid. So there is no room in Aristotle's theory for the clever criminal who is both evil and intelligent. This would be, for Aristotle, a contradiction in terms. A clever bank robber may be good at robbing banks but, for reasons we need to explore, he would inevitably fail when it comes to practical achievement.

On Means and Ends

If morality is about success at practical endeavour, practically wise people have the right goals and they are able to accomplish those goals by strategically choosing the right course of action. Aristotle uses the twin concepts of means and ends to analyze successful human behaviour. Consider a simple example. Suppose Abdul, an eight-year-old boy in Moose Jaw, Saskatchewan, wants to buy a brand-new bicycle. He decides to deliver newspapers so that he can save up enough money. What is this eight-year-old up to? Abdul has a goal: a new bicycle. This is the *end* he is aiming at. He delivers papers *in order to* make enough money to purchase the bicycle. Delivering papers is the *means* to this end. This fundamental distinction between our goals and how we go about realizing our goals is at the heart of Aristotle's understanding of ethics.

In his discussion of means–ends reasoning, Aristotle notes that we adopt the means we employ for the sake of our ends. The end is 'that for whose sake everything else is done, [and] it is for the sake of this that all men do whatever else they do'.[15] It follows that ends are more valuable than means. This makes good sense. Abdul, the newspaper boy, may hate getting up at five o'clock on frosty mornings to deliver newspapers; he may find going over the same route day after day boring and, considered for its own sake, a waste of time. But he does it anyway. Why? Because he values a brand new bicycle. He does not value the means; he values the end. Or, more accurately put, he values the means insomuch as it allows him to attain his end. If selling ice cream was a quicker and easier way of making the money he needs for the new bicycle, he would be selling ice cream. All things being equal, we change our means when we find a better way of attaining our ends. Aristotle suggests, then, a general principle: ends are logically and ethically prior to means. So the ultimate source of value must be our ends. Although some contemporary authors suggest that we choose our ends on the basis of mere feelings or arbitrary taste, Aristotle thinks that we can intellectually distinguish between ends that are objectively good or bad.

Aristotle differentiates between things that are 'good in themselves' and things that are merely 'useful'.[16] Things that are 'good in themselves' are valued as ends; they possess *intrinsic* value. Useful things are valued as a means to something else; they possess *instrumental* (or indirect) value. They derive their value from the end they allow us to obtain. (Aristotle does suggest, following Plato, that the very same thing may possess **intrinsic value**, **instrumental value**, or even a combination of intrinsic and instrumental value at the very same time.) We need to identify then which things possess what kind of value.

Which things possess instrumental value? Almost anything can be valued as a means to something else. Why do I value the shovel in my shed? Because it is a means to fresh garden tomatoes. I may value cod liver oil as a means to health. Or an undergraduate degree in Health Sciences as a means to get into med school. Or consider money. Aristotle makes the point that we value money not because it is 'merely useful'; we value it 'for the sake of something else'.[17] We value money because we can use it to buy what we want: money is a means to a house, to a car, to a bus ticket, to a meal, to a coffee. Some people—i.e., misers—mistakenly view money as something that is valuable in and of itself. Aristotle thinks that these people confuse that which is merely useful with that which is valuable for its own sake.

So, which things possess intrinsic value? Aristotle would include in this list things such as happiness, beautiful objects, health, pleasure, knowledge, truth, reputation, and virtue. We value these things in and of themselves, not merely as a means to something else, but on their own account. We may also value them instrumentally, as a means to something else. Suppose, for example, I own a beautiful painting by Vincent van Gogh. I value the painting simply because it is a beautiful painting. I value the painting for its own sake, irrespective of any further complications or consequences. End of story. But, of course, a painting by Vincent van Gogh also possesses instrumental value. Hanging the painting in my living room might be a useful way of impressing visiting royalty. Selling the painting would be a useful way of making money. And so on. Still, none of this detracts from the basic point that there is something about the painting that is intrinsically valuable.

Clearly, the value of something can sometimes change with the context. If I am dying of thirst in the desert, an ordinary glass of water will be an extremely precious item. If I am drowning in a raging flood, it will have no value at all. On closer inspection, the reason the value of the glass of water changes is because we are valuing it as a means to an end. In the first case, the glass of water is a much-needed *means* to survival. In the second case, it is useless as a *means* to survival. Instrumental value is then contingent on particular circumstances. When it comes to instrumental value, what is valuable in one circumstance may be worthless in another.

If, however, instrumental value may change, intrinsic value cannot. Intrinsic value is something fixed and unchangeable. Why? Because the worth of things that possess intrinsic value derives, not from their usefulness, but from what they are. It follows that as long as these things remain themselves, their value remains. Suppose I were to claim that scientific knowledge is intrinsically valuable, that it is an end worth pursuing for its own sake. If this is true, scientific knowledge will remain praiseworthy and commendable forever. It will always be valuable regardless of the circumstances. This follows logically. Consider: to say that scientific knowledge possesses intrinsic value is to say that scientific knowledge is valuable merely because it is scientific knowledge. But scientific knowledge must always be scientific knowledge (by definition) so if this is what makes it valuable, it must always be valuable. Aristotle believes that moral striving, in some very fundamental way, depends on a proper appreciation of intrinsic value.

Aristotle's practically wise person judges the true intrinsic value of things. The modern temptation is, of course, to say that all value is purely relative. Aristotle disagrees. He believes that reason provides a perspective from which we can determine what things are objectively praiseworthy and admirable. This is not, according to Aristotle, a matter of subjective opinion, but of proper evaluation. Aristotle's

---

๑๑ Applied Philosophy Box 5.5 ๑๑

Flow, Intrinsic Value

Mihaly Csikszentmihalyi

Artists are not the only ones who spend time and effort on an activity that has few rewards outside itself. In fact, everyone devotes large chunks of time doing things that are inexplicable unless we assume that the doing is enjoyed for its own sake. Children spend much of their lives playing. Adults also play games like poker or chess, participate in sports, grow gardens, learn to play the guitar, read novels, go to parties, walk through woods—and do thousands of other things—for no good reason except that the activities are fun. Of course, there is always the possibility that one will also get rich and famous by doing these things. The artist may get a lucky break and sell her canvas to a museum. The guitarist may learn to play so well that someone will offer him a recording contract. We may justify doing sports to stay healthy, and go to parties because of possible business contacts or sexual adventures. External goals are often present in the background, but they are seldom the main reason why we engage in such activities. The main reason for playing the guitar is that it is enjoyable, and so is talking with people at a party. Not everyone likes to play the guitar or go to parties, but those who spend time on them usually do so because the quality of experience while involved in these activities is intrinsically rewarding.

Aristotle would agree that certain activities are intrinsically valuable. But to contend that these activities are valuable only because they are fun—because they make us feel good—is, paradoxically, to attribute instrumental rather than intrinsic value to them. This is, for Aristotle, to put the cart before the horse: we enjoy these activities because they are valuable; they are not valuable because we enjoy them. Think of it this way. Aristotle believes that we experience a sense of thriving when we are participating in things that are objectively greater than ourselves. We find this pleasurable because we intelligently recognize that these activities are praiseworthy independent of whoever happens to be doing them. These are subtle issues, no doubt. Moral philosophy, thoroughly done, is an exacting science.

Source: Mihaly Csikszentmihalyi, *The Evolving Self*, pp. xii–xiv. Reproduced online at: Rob Jellinghaus, 'Flow: What's Worth Living For?' www.unrealities.com/essays/flow.htm, 14 August 1995.

---

position corresponds, perhaps surprisingly, with the common-sense view. When we come to think of it, we do believe that some things are objectively more valuable than others. Imagine someone picking up a handful of lint from the dryer and saying, 'I will trade you this dust-ball for your Vincent van Gogh painting'. We would think that he or she was plain crazy. A painting by van Gogh is more valuable than a shapeless lump of lint. It is not just that it has more instrumental value—it is worth millions of dollars on the open market—more import-antly, as anyone with artistic sensitivities will insist, it is valuable for its own sake. It possesses more intrinsic value than the dust-ball. We might imagine strange situations where the dust-ball happens to be very valuable: suppose, for instance, it houses a special, one-of-a-kind bacteria that would, if put in a Petri dish, produce an antibiotic that would cure all cancer. But this is to value the shapeless lump of lint as a *means* to something else. This does not detract from the view that some things are just more valuable in and of themselves.

All of this leads inevitably to the ultimate moral question. What is the most valuable thing of all? If ends are more valuable than means, which end is most valuable? What property or thing is the supreme human good? We already know the answer. Aristotle, without hesitating, responds,

> Now such a thing happiness, above all else, is held to be; for this we choose always for self and never for the sake of something else, but honour, pleasure, reason, and every virtue we choose indeed for themselves . . . but we choose them also for the sake of happiness, judging that by means of them we shall be happy. Happiness, on the other hand, no one chooses for the sake of these, nor, in general, for anything other than itself.[18]

People say things like, 'I want to be married so I can be happy', but it would be very odd to say 'I want to be happy so I can be married'. Marriage does have intrinsic value. But we also value marriage as a means to happiness. Happiness, on the other hand, is not the means to something else. We want to be happy simply because we want to be happy. That is all. Happiness is a first principle that does not need to be explained in terms of something else. It is, Aristotle thinks, the end that is above all other ends. Happiness is, he declares 'something in every way final'.[19]

In Aristotle's account, happiness does not possess instrumental value. We value it for its own sake, never as a means to any other end. All the value happiness has must derive, then, from its own nature. It can never lose its value—it must be, the ancient Greeks would claim, immortal and **divine**. Aristotle concludes, 'to us it is clear from what has been said that happiness is among the things that are prized and perfect. . . . It is a first principle; for it is for the sake of this that we all do all

that we do, and [because happiness is] the first principle and cause of goods [it] is, we claim, something prized and divine'.[20]

As we have seen, Aristotle recognizes that there are goods that are ends-in-themselves other than happiness: thing like beauty, health, pleasure, knowledge, and so on. But these goods also contribute to happiness. We value them for their own sakes but we also value them as a means to happiness. Happiness, on the other hand, is self-sufficient. Aristotle writes, 'the self-sufficient [is] that which when isolated makes life desirable and lacking in nothing; and such we think happiness to be'. Suppose you were as happy as could be. Suppose there was nothing that could be added to your life to make you happier. What would be missing from your life. Nothing! This is Aristotle's point. Other things that have intrinsic value are incomplete in themselves. If I have scientific knowledge but I am unhappy, I am still missing something. If I have health but I am unhappy, I am still missing something. Perfect happiness, in sharp contrast, is complete in itself. If I am as happy as I can be, if I could not be happier, then I have everything. There is nothing more to want.

I should point out that Aristotle believes that there must be an ultimate human end like happiness that we always value for its own sake and never as a means to another end. Why? For human motivation to make any sense, we must be able to strive towards a reachable goal. If, to return to our previous example, Abdul the newspaper boy knew that he would have to complete an infinite number of steps to obtain a new bicycle, he would have no reason to act on his desire. Obviously, no human being can complete an infinite number of tasks. But we do act on our desires. So we cannot 'choose everything for the sake of something else'.[21] If

I were to choose *A* for the sake of *B*, and *B* for the sake of *C*, and *C* for the sake of *D*, and so on to infinity, I would never be able to reach my goal. As Aristotle puts it, 'at that rate the process would go on to infinity, so that our desire would be empty and vain'.[22] It follows that there must be a goal that is valued, not as a means to something else, but for its own sake. Aristotle asserts that happiness is this final end and that happiness is attainable or we would never act.

On External Goods

Aristotle is undoubtedly a great moral philosopher, but his doctrine of happiness is not without its tensions. It is not so much that Aristotle is wrong but that human life is itself legitimately perplexing. As we have seen, Aristotle associates the best life with happiness. He identifies happiness with virtue (*arete*) and with a kind of glorious immortality (*eudaimonia*). Happy human beings do something so wonderful that people keep talking about them long after they are dead. But is this enough for perfect happiness? Aristotle seems to fudge the issue. At one point in his discussion, he adds a third requirement for human happiness. It is not enough that we have virtue and reputation. We also need a steady supply of what he calls **external goods**. Consider this issue more closely.

What are external goods? Aristotle loosely defines them as goods that are 'external . . . to soul or to body'.[23] More precisely, external goods are things we have no control over that are, nonetheless, conducive to human happiness. Imagine a complete stranger walks up to me and gives me a million dollars. I did nothing to deserve this. It just happened. This is an external good. Assuming that material wealth

is conducive to happiness, the money is something that contributes to my happiness that I obtained without any effort on my part.

Aristotle claims that external goods are an integral part of happiness. I have cited a spectacular, made-up example. But more usual things like mental and physical health, intelligence, good looks, a good upbringing, higher education, gifts, the opportunity for leisure and friends, lucky coincidences, (etc.), contribute to the good life even though they often depend on factors outside our control. Aristotle recognizes that these things contribute, nonetheless, to happiness, to a good life.

Recognizing the role of external goods in human well-being may seem trivial. But surely, Aristotle is making an important point. He maintains, 'there are some things the lack of which takes the luster from happiness, as good birth, goodly children, beauty; for the man who is very ugly in appearance or ill-born or solitary and childless is not very likely to be happy, and perhaps a man would be still less likely [to be happy] if he had thoroughly bad children or friends or had lost good children or friends by death'.[24] Virtue and reputation, as it turns out, may not be enough. 'Happiness seems to need this sort of prosperity in addition.'[25]

Aristotle is not suggesting that we should covet external goods because we are self-centered or self-seeking. He believes that external goods are a means to morality. The good life 'needs the external goods as well; for it is impossible, or not easy, to do noble acts without the proper equipment'.[26] Suppose I have a lot of money. This means that I can give a lot of money to charity. (Generosity is a virtue.) Or suppose I have political power. Perhaps I can use it to fight legal or political corruption. (Justice is a virtue.) Or suppose I am famous. Perhaps I can use my fame to promote important scientific research. (Knowledge is a virtue.) And so on. Aristotle writes, 'In many actions we use friends and riches and political power as instruments'.[27] Without friends or riches or political power, it is a harder to accomplish worthwhile goals. So external goods possess instrumental value. We can use them to make the world a better place. They may be an aid to virtue (*arete*) and to good reputation (*eudaimonia*).

On the Good Life

There is, however, a troublesome issue lurking in the background. Aristotle distinguishes between 'living well' and 'faring well'. Someone who lives well lives virtuously. Someone who fares well prospers. In a perfect world, being virtuous and prospering would always coincide. But this is not always the case in the imperfect world of human striving.

Aristotle acknowledges that one may win a reputation for virtue in the face of great misfortune. 'Nobility shines through', he observes, 'when [an individual] bears with resignation many great misfortunes, not through insensibility to pain but through nobility and greatness of soul'.[26] For example, a man who dies of leukemia at the age of 24 suffers a tragic fate. Yet, paradoxically, this man may, with his force of character, courage, perseverance, and good humour, provide a sterling example of how we should live. In fact, we may rightly look up to him as a moral hero. He may achieve virtue and long-lasting reputation and may, in Aristotle's terms, achieve happiness.

But we have to be honest. This is not the **good life**, the life a sensible person would choose. Good people cope with the suffering and unfairness and mishaps that come their way, but no one deliberately chooses a life of terrible misfortune. Aristotle explains that 'many events happen by chance' and that although 'small pieces of good fortune or of its opposite clearly do not weigh down the scales of life . . . a multitude of great events . . . if they turn out ill [do] crush and maim happiness; for they both bring pain with them and hinder many activities'.[29] It seems then that virtue is not enough for happiness; we need a bare minimum of good fortune as well. The good life means practising morality, but it also means prospering.

Popular culture has its own way of dealing with such issues. In trying to make sense of adversity, it proposes the 'happy ending', a familiar motif in literature. The protagonist passes through adversity to triumph in the end, and the ultimate victory is even sweeter because of the trials and tribulations encountered along the way. There is something immensely satisfying about this ordering of events; it appeals to our ethical sensibilities.

Aristotle has some fatherly advice:

[N]o happy man can become miserable; for he will never do the acts that are hateful and mean. For the man who is truly good and wise, . . . bears all the chances of life becomingly and always makes the best of circumstances, as . . . a good shoemaker makes the best shoes out of the hides that are given him; and so with all other craftsmen. And if this is the case, the happy man can never become miserable; though he will not reach blessedness, if he meet with fortunes like those of Priam.[30]

(Priam, a familiar tragic figure in Homer, met with many misfortunes and saw his beloved son Hector killed by Achilles in the battle at Troy.) Perhaps this is another way of saying that we can be happy but not perfectly happy if we are too deeply scarred by misfortune. Optimal happiness includes virtue (*arete*) *and* reputation (*eudaimonia*) *and* external goods. And yet, being provided with *all* external goods seems to leave little room for heroic achievement. Maybe the artistic answer, the happy ending, is the only solution. Most human beings must cope with some sort of suffering, with deprivation, with bad luck, with less than ideal circumstances. Overcoming such obstacles provides a test of moral character.

The good life is the life an intelligent agent would choose. Aristotle's teacher Plato, who believed in reincarnation, describes disembodied souls in the nether-world choosing new lives into which they will be reborn:

> Placed on the ground in front of [these souls were] sample lives. . . . Every single kind of human and animal life was included among the samples. . . . There were dictatorships, . . . and also male and female versions of lives of fame for one's physique, good looks and general strength and athleticism, or for one's lineage and the excellence of one's ancestors; and there were lives that lacked distinctions as well. . . . There was every possible combination of qualities with one another and factors like wealth, poverty, sickness, and health, in extreme or moderate amounts.[31]

Unlike Plato's souls, we cannot choose our lives at will. Our choices are highly restricted. Still, we do have to make important choices, and we have to be ready to answer tough questions about such choices from our children and from those we advise. Taking into account external goods—whether you will make enough money to live comfortably or to feed your family or to at least survive—these are legitimate aspects of those choices. The problem is, perhaps, that we place too much importance on external goods.

Aristotle does not supply any fixed, definitive answer to all these questions. Perhaps we simply have to accept that we can look at a life from two sometimes incommensurable perspectives: (1) that represented by the good life one would choose, and (2) that represented by the prospect of heroic moral achievement. One way or another, a successful moral life may require courageous acceptance or resignation in the face of troubles and hardships.

On Three Kinds of Life

There is another issue that arises in connection with the good life. Suppose we were able to choose between the three kinds of life Aristotle recognizes: the **life of enjoyment**, the **political life**, and the **contemplative life**. Which life should we prefer? One might think that Aristotle, being a philosopher, would prize the contemplative life, the life of study and thought, above everything else. He does, but the issue is somewhat complicated. Consider these three lives in turn.

Aristotle believes that the good man will find the virtuous life pleasurable. ('A good man . . . delights in virtuous actions . . . as a musical man enjoys beautiful tunes.'[32]) But a life devoted to *mere* pleasure-seeking is, for Aristotle, wholly superficial and morally trivial. 'Happiness,' he says curtly, 'does not lie in amusement.'[33] It is not that amusement is intrinsically wrong: 'to amuse oneself in order that one may exert oneself . . . seems right; for amusement is a sort of relaxation, and we need relaxation because we cannot work continuously.'[34] So, some amusement is healthy, but this should not be, for Aristotle, the most important activity in life.

This leaves us with the political and contemplative life to choose between. The political life is the active life, the life of doing things. The contemplative life is the life of study and philosophy. The political life involves social, political, legal, religious, and perhaps military activity. The contemplative life involves peace and quiet in order to facilitate thinking.

Down through history, the rivalry between proponents of the active and contemplative life has been a perennial theme in intellectual discourse. Medieval authors compared the relative merits of the *via activa* (Latin, for 'the active way') and the *via contemplativa* (Latin, for 'the contemplative way'). Many philosophers have championed the contemplative life, but there are notable exceptions. What then, does Aristotle say? It would seem, at first glance, that Aristotle firmly believes in the superiority of the contemplative life. The mental principle is, after all, the best human attribute. It follows that the contemplative life is better than the political life because it is devoted to the cultivation of the divine element in human nature. Aristotle writes, 'The activity of God, which surpasses all others in blessedness, must be contemplative; . . . [so] human activities [that are] most akin to this must [partake] most of the nature of happiness. . . . [Human] happiness, therefore, must be some form of contemplation'.[35]

Aristotle points to other advantages of the contemplative life. First, contemplation is self-sufficient; we don't need other people to think. 'Even by himself, the philosopher can contemplate the truth.'[36] Second, a life of pure thought does not require material wealth, at least not to any great degree. Third, contemplation is leisurely and unhurried. Fourth, we value knowledge for its own sake.[37] And finally, Aristotle thinks that thinking is the most enjoyable activity. 'The activity of philosophic wisdom is . . . the pleasantest of virtuous activities.'[38]

Still, things are not quite so clear as they seem. In a book called the *Politics*, Aristotle argues that 'man is a political animal, in a higher degree than bees or other gregarious animals.'[39] Aristotle claims here that humans *need* other humans. Hermits, who live alone, are no longer human. He strongly suggests here that associating with friends while pursuing the political life is humanly best.

It is very hard to reconcile Aristotle's claims about the superiority of a solitary life of contemplation with his enthusiasm for a political life of active involvement. There is no easy answer to these questions. Some later authors have tried to argue that the good life needs both elements; others have argued that the idea of a dichotomy between the two is to be resisted. But let us turn to Aristotle's account of virtue.

On Virtue as Habit

Aristotle's ethics is a kind of science. It is a search for causes. Aristotle focuses on the nature of overall character as the cause of specific actions. To consider only the act would be, for Aristotle, to miss what is really going on; it would be to judge the effect while ignoring the cause. We will consider an act-centred approach to ethics in later chapters.

Aristotle believes that people act in specific ways because they possess virtues or vices. This is what Aristotle is interested in. Suppose someone shoplifts. This is an immoral action. But why do people shoplift? Because they are dishonest, because they are lazy, because they are greedy. Or perhaps because they think that material possessions will bring them happiness (which would be the character flaw Aristotle identifies as moral ignorance). Aristotle thinks that we need to look at the kinds of people we are dealing with before we can understand their actions.

In Aristotle's account, to be virtuous is to exhibit good will. Virtue is neither mental capacity nor emotion. To think or to feel is not enough. As Aristotle puts it, 'Virtues are modes of choice or involve choice'.[40] The virtuous *choose* to do good over evil; the vicious *choose* to do evil over good. This is why the former are praised and the latter blamed. Ethics is about doing; thinking or feeling is not enough.

Aristotle defines virtue as good **habit**. (He points out that the Greek word for 'ethics'—*ethike*—derives from the Greek word for 'habit'—*ethos*.) We are not automatically good or automatically bad. 'Neither by nature, . . . nor contrary to nature do the virtues arise in us; rather we are adapted by nature to receive them, and [we] are made perfect by habit.'[41] Virtue is a dependable disposition, a constant character trait, something we build up through repeated acts. Aristotle observes, 'men become builders by building and lyre-players by playing the lyre; so too we become just by doing just acts, temperate by doing temperate acts, brave by doing brave acts'.[42] If you want to become a good guitar player, you have to practise playing the guitar. Likewise, if you want to become an honest person, you have to practise telling the truth. If you keep on telling the truth, it will become an integral part of who you are. Conversely, if you keep on telling lies, you will turn into a liar; lying will become characteristic behaviour.

Aristotle recognizes, then, the link between virtue and action: 'It is by *doing* just acts that the just man is produced, and by *doing* temperate acts, the temperate man: without doing these no one would have even a prospect of becoming good.'[43] Aristotle wryly observes that thinking about morality is easier than acting morally. In his words, 'Most people do not do these [virtuous acts], but take refuge in theory and think they are being philosophers and will

---

✍ Applied Philosophy Box 5.6 ✍

Virtue Still Matters to Some People. Police: Man Staged Robbery To Impress Wife

Edmond, Oklahoma – An Oklahoma man desperate to save his marriage by appearing like a hero to his wife ended up in police custody on suspicion of staging a crime. He hired 'burglars' and foiled their fake robbery attempt, police said on Friday.

Trent Spencer, 27, . . . was charged this week with the misdemeanor crime of filing a false report, said police spokeswoman Glynda Chu.

According to police, Spencer, a high school teacher, paid two students $100 each to break into his house and try to make off with a stereo.

The masked students tied his wife with duct tape and her husband was in the house just in time to foil the supposed crime, police said.

Police said Spencer attacked the two in a choreographed fight, even hitting one with a board that he had cut to break in half. The plan was going well until his wife freed herself and called police, something Spencer did not anticipate, police said.

What is going on here? Explain in Aristotelian terms. Why is this not true courage?

Source: 'Man Staged Robbery to Impress Wife.' *CNN.com* (Reuters), www.CNN.com, 11 October 2004.

become good in this way, behaving somewhat like patients who listen attentively to their doctors, but do none of the things they are ordered to do'.[44] It is not enough to think wonderful thoughts about ethics. At the end of the day we must go out and practise what we preach.

Although Aristotle believes that virtue is expressed through habitual action, he also points out that virtue entails *more* than the correct response to a particular situation. It is not enough to do the right thing accidentally, or for the wrong reason, or because one is forced to do it. To possess virtue is to reliably, deliberately do the right thing for the right reason. Aristotle explains:

> if the acts . . . in accordance with the virtues have themselves a certain character it does not follow that they are done justly or temperately. The agent also must be in a certain condition when he does them; in the first place he must have knowledge, secondly he must choose the acts . . . for their own sakes, and thirdly his action must proceed from a firm and unchangeable character.[45]

Aristotle contrasts morality with art. In art, we care about the finished work. In morality, we also care about the process that produced the finished work. A good act must be accompanied by the right state of mind. One must do it in the right way, for the right reason. Most importantly, moral behaviour must be an expression of a dependable set of stable character traits. Aristotle concludes, 'Actions, then, are called just and temperate when they are such as the just or the temperate man would do; but it is not the man who does these that is just and temperate, but the man who also does them as just and temperate men do them'.[46] Just and temperate men have just and temperate characters that give rise to their just and temperate actions; if we wish to be just and temperate, we must do likewise.

Aristotle's view of virtue as an expression of a firm and unshakeable character has one worrisome ramification. What about a bad person who suddenly turns around and embraces morality? The present author knew a homeless man who had spent years on skid row drinking himself into oblivion. One morning, he decided that was it and he never drank again. (This is a true story.) Aristotle seems unable to explain this kind of unhabitual behaviour. For our purposes, simply note that for any such change to be properly moral, it must be more than skin-deep. There has to be some deep transformation, a real change of *character*, however quickly it occurs. We discuss this possibility further below.

On the Golden Mean

Perhaps the most famous part of Aristotle's ethics is the 'Golden Mean', his idea that virtue is a middle between two extremes. There are antecedents for Aristotle's notion of virtue as a happy medium in Plato and Socrates and in Greek thought generally. Before explaining what the Golden Mean is about, some general comments are in order.

Modern critics have argued that the mean is circular: only moral people can figure out what the happy medium of a certain character trait is and they do not need the mean for they are already moral. This is to miss the point. Aristotle's **golden mean** (*mesotes*) is intended as a kind of measuring stick to evaluate virtue (*arete*). People who possess practical wisdom (*phronesis*) act according to the mean. They may act virtuously without consciously consulting it; indeed, it is only intended as a rule of thumb for figuring out what morality requires in a particular situation. The mean is not for the moral ignoramus. It is not intended as a proof of morality; nor is it a replacement for good judgment. It is an aid to good judgment. It is a mental tool that allows us to apply our ideas about morality to specific circumstances and to extend and sharpen the moral knowledge we already have. People who already have some basic knowledge of morality can use the mean to figure out more precisely what virtue consists of in specific cases. It is not a magic barometer that immoral (or **amoral**) people can use to determine what virtue is.

Aristotle proposes the mean as a solution to a problem. He compares morality to medicine and navigation. If general truths about morality are hard to express precisely, 'the account of particular cases is yet more lacking in exactness; for they do not fall under any art or precept but the agents themselves must in each case consider what is appropriate to the occasion, as happens also in the art of medicine or of navigation'.[47] A doctor modifies his treatment according to the condition of each patient, just as the captain of a ship modifies his route according to the topology of each harbour. In the same way, virtuous agents must constantly modify their behaviour according to the specific circumstances.

Aristotle proposes then the mean as a self-help device that we can use to adapt our moral understanding to each specific circumstance. Think of it as a kind of funnel: we throw heaps of something like dried beans into the wide end and they dribble out the narrow end just where we want them, inside the small-necked bottle. The mean is a focusing device. It shows us how to apply general concepts, like happiness and virtue and practical wisdom, to the narrow circumstances of our unique lives.

Aristotle himself provides (by way of illustration) a table of 14 virtues in a book called the *Eudemian Ethics*.[48] But we need more than a list. We need a schematic model of virtue we can apply to any virtue or situation whatsoever. The general idea behind the mean is easy enough to grasp. As Aristotle himself explains,

> It is the nature of such things to be destroyed by defect and excess, as we see in the case of strength and of health; . . . both excessive and defective exercise destroys the strength, and similarly drink or food which is above or below a certain amount destroys the health, while that which is proportionate both produces and increases and preserves it. So too is it, then, in the case of temperance and courage and the other virtues. For the man who flies from and fears everything and does not stand his ground against anything becomes a coward, and the man who fears nothing at all but goes to meet every danger becomes rash; and similarly the man who indulges in every pleasure and abstains from none becomes self-indulgent, while the man who shuns every pleasure, as boors do, becomes in a way insensible; temperance and courage, then, are destroyed by excess and defect, and preserved by the mean.[49]

One quickly appreciates the general picture. We can have too much or too little of something. When it comes to character traits, we should aim for the (approximate) middle. Aristotle's analysis of the virtue **courage** provides a good starting point. Aristotle writes, 'With regard to feelings of fear and confidence courage is the mean; . . . the man who exceeds in confidence is rash, and he who exceeds in fear and falls short in confidence is a coward'.[50] Courage is, then, a mean between rashness and cowardice.

We can schematically represent the mean as shown in Figure 5.1. The (approximate) middle of the vertical line in this figure—the mean—represents courage. The lower end represents not having enough courage, i.e., the vice of cowardice, which is the most common

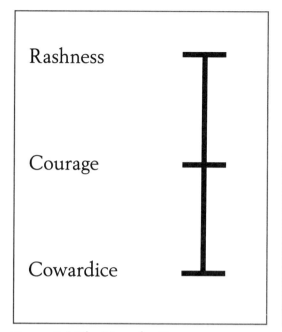

Figure 5.1 The Mean for Courage

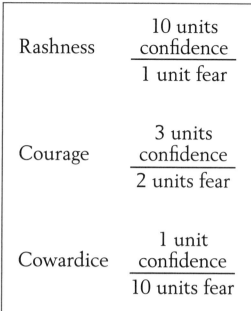

Figure 5.2 The Mean for Courage
Explained with Ratios

character fault. The upper, or opposite, end represents having too much courage, i.e., the vice of rashness. This, then, is the human predicament: we should aim at the (approximate) middle. We should face danger, risk, or threat the way a virtuous person would face them. The courageous stand up, in frightening circumstances, for some noble cause. The mousy personality who runs away from any hint of conflict is a coward. But there is also the opposite vice of rashness. The daredevil who dangles from the wings of a flying airplane for the thrill of it is rash. The rash take unnecessary (indeed immoral risks) for trivial reasons. They are not courageous but stupid. We may, then, fail at virtue through either deficiency or excess. It follows that we should neither aim too high nor too low. Most people do not put enough effort and energy into being courageous and end up being cowardly. But some people put so much energy and effort into being courageous that they end up being rash. The trick is to find the proper mean between the two: *le juste milieu.*

Aristotle defines courage as a mean with respect to feelings of fear and confidence. Courage, then, is the right balance of these two opposing states or feelings; indeed, he defines *courage* as the proper ratio of fear to confidence. Let us use numbers for the sake of illustration. (These numbers are not, of course, intended to be precise, but they help to make the point.) Assume that the ideal ratio of confidence to fear is, say, 3 units of confidence to 2 units of fear (3/2). Figure 5.2 illustrates this mean. Cowardice, as illustrated, is the condition of too much fear and not enough confidence (say 1/10), and rashness is the condition of not enough fear and too much confidence (say 10/1). As it turns out, cowardice is a *deficiency* of confidence but an *excess* of fear, whereas rashness is an *excess* of confidence but a *deficiency* of fear. True courage is neither deficiency nor excess.

However, we cannot truly measure the precise degree or quantity of a character trait. The numbers in Figure 5.2 are intended only to help us better understand these concepts. We can, in theory, locate people who are more or less courageous, more or less cowardly, or more or less rash at corresponding points on the vertical line. The closer they are to the bottom, the more cowardly they are; the closer they are to the top, the more rash they are; the closer they are to the middle, the more courageous they are. In point of fact, we do make rough quantitative and/or comparative judgments about the virtues. We think that Juan is *more* or *less* courageous than Ralph, that some cowardly acts are *worse* than others, that Maria has gained *more* self-confidence over the years, and so on.

We can use the kind of diagram illustrated in Figure 5.2 to depict almost any virtue. Suppose, for example, we want to investigate compassion, understood not as a mere feeling but as a virtue. A compassionate individual, therefore, has the right mix of sensitivity and toughness. The compassionate person cares about the ailing, the miserable, the suffering. Let us define, then, compassion as the proper ratio of 'sensitivity toward others' to 'toughness toward others'. The mean of compassion might be situated, in a diagram, between the vices of 'hardness' and 'softness'. Someone who is too hard has too much of a tendency to 'not relieve suffering'; they have too much toughness. Someone who is too soft has too much of a tendency to 'relieve suffering'; they have too much sensitivity. (These are both faults. Although the more common vice is hardness, softness

is a failure too. Imagine a professor who gives all his students As because he does not want to hurt their feelings. Or a parent who spoils a fat child by removing every source of physical discomfort. Or a doctor who is unable to perform a necessary medical procedure because it will cause pain. And so on.)

There is no one complete list of virtues in Aristotle. He is more the naturalist in the field jotting down notes about human behaviour than the academic theoretician who has produced a polished, complete system. Some identify as *the* Aristotelian virtues the following character traits: courage, temperance (or moderation), justice (having to do with our dealings with other people), proper ambition (aiming at small honours), magnanimity (aiming at greatness), liberality (properly distributing small amounts of money), magnificence (properly distributing great wealth), shame (having to do with desire), truthfulness, good temper, and wittiness. This is complicated by the fact that different virtues (and vices) overlap. Human behaviour can be cut up and examined from many different angles. We should not focus on terminology. Aristotle points out that many states of character do not have conventional names. In such cases 'we must try . . . to invent names ourselves so that we may be clear and easy to follow'. [51] If our terminology seems at times a bit strained, it is not eloquence itself that we are after but a clear understanding.

As it turns out then, virtue, most fundamentally, is the right balance between two opposing tendencies in human nature. Vice is the wrong balance. Note that the human propensities that combine to produce virtue in the right ratio are not, in themselves, bad or good. Confidence or fear, 'relieving suffering' or 'not relieving suffering', 'exposing the truth'

⌘ Applied Philosophy Box 5.7 ⌘

The American Dissident

The vague unwritten rule [of etiquette] with regards [to] 'not offending' evidently serves to encourage self-censorship and discourage free and open debate, [the] cornerstone of democracy. *The American Dissident* is a unique literary journal because it actually encourages the latter. In fact, it not only urges readers to openly criticize the journal and its editor, but will publish any such critique. The journal contains poetry, essays, literary letters, and cartoons of a caustic nature and will not hesitate offending if it means exposing reality and other such uncomfortable truths. . . . *The American Dissident* seeks to goad poets, professors, and artists to take that giant leap away from the herd and 'go upright and vital, and speak the rude truth in all ways'.

G. Tod Slone, the editor of this literary journal, borrows a slogan from Ralph Waldo Emerson: 'speak the rude truth in all its ways'. Slone is arguing that honesty is much closer to rudeness than conventional people think. Consult Figure 5.3 and explain in your own words. Do you agree?

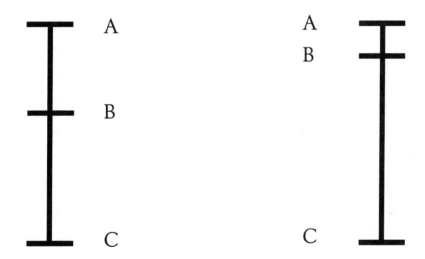

The mean for honesty according to conventional society

The mean for honesty according to *American Dissident*

Figure 5.3 The Mean for Honesty

Source: Advertisement for *The American Dissident*, G. Tod Slone, editor: www.theamericandissident.org/Flyer.htm.

or 'concealing the truth' (etc.) are neutral. Depending upon the circumstance, it may be appropriate to act in accordance with one or another of these human propensities. As we have seen in our discussion of courage, it is not simply a matter of fearing or not fearing. It matters how much one fears, what one fears, when and why. In Aristotle's words, 'The man who fears neither what, nor when, nor as he ought is [rash]; the man who fears what he ought not, and on the wrong occasions, and in the wrong manner is cowardly'.[52]

Aristotle does not believe that we can define virtue apart from the context. It is not as if courage is a fixed ratio of fear to confidence. What proportion of confidence and fear we should feel (and act upon) depends on circumstances. Aristotle writes, 'Both fear and confidence and appetite and anger and pity and in general pleasure and pain may be felt both too much and too little, and in both cases not well; but to feel them at the right times, with reference to the right objects, towards the right people, with the right motive, and in the right way, is what is both intermediate and best, and this is characteristic of virtue'.[53] There is no one mean for every circumstance; indeed, we could draw a mean for each group of like circumstances.

Aristotle recognizes that the mean is not the same for everyone. When it comes to our own lives, we are not trying to find a theoretical mean but the mean relative to us. If, for example, we should all practice moderation in food and drink, different amounts of food and drink are fitting for different people. Aristotle compares the moral person to a coach or fitness instructor:

> [i]f ten pounds are too much for a particular person to eat and two too little, it does not follow

that the trainer will order six pounds; for this also is perhaps too much for the person who is to take it, or too little—too little for Milo [a wrestler], too much for the beginner in athletic exercises . . . . Thus a master of any art avoids excess and defect, but seeks the intermediate and chooses this—the intermediate not in the object but relatively to us.[54]

We moderns, influenced as we are by the social science model, tend to think in statistical terms. If all your friends are pickpockets, you may think that stealing is normal. If you are a member of an online chat group for pedophiles, you may think that pedophilia is normal. Aristotle would insist that if you think that such behaviour is virtuous or even morally acceptable, you are sadly mistaken (Or, more likely, that you are hiding the truth from yourself). While in the statistical model, it is quantity that counts, in the Aristotelian model, the mean represents the height of virtuous achievement, not the average.

Indeed, Aristotle would not think that the average is a good indication of virtue, for he believes that most people are not virtuous, at least not to any noteworthy degree. Virtue is a signal accomplishment because it is so difficult: 'It is no easy task to be good'.[55] Aristotle explains, 'it is possible to fail in many ways (for evil belongs to the class of the unlimited, . . . and good to that of the limited), while to succeed is possible only in one way (for which reason also one is easy and the other difficult—to miss the mark easy, to hit it difficult)'.[56] Imagine an archer aiming at a target. To hit the bull's-eye—in other words, the mean—is very difficult. If there is only one way to hit the bull's-eye, there are a limitless number of ways in which one can miss it. That is why immorality is easy, while morality—hitting the mean—is very hard.

When it comes to the mean, the proper point of reference is the moral person. How do we determine what the virtuous person would think? There is no simple answer to this question. Aristotle believes that human beings share moral intelligence. We have within ourselves a capacity for moral understanding necessary for good judgment. We will discuss moral reasoning below. For the moment, suffice it to say that it would be mental laziness to simply assume that we are always thinking the way a virtuous person would. We need to strive toward objectivity, working through the details of a knowledge that Aristotle believes is already—at least in some latent, ambiguous, and undeveloped state—within the mind of the good person.

In light of how difficult morality is, Aristotle has some shrewd practical advice. Some vices are worse than others, and, depending upon our temperament, we naturally tend to one extreme or the other. For example, most of us tend toward cowardice instead of rashness. If those inclined toward cowardice want to become courageous, they might aim at being a little rash. And in trying to be a little rash, their natural tendency to be more cowardly will pull them back toward the mean. As Aristotle poetically explains, 'We must consider the things towards which we ourselves also are easily carried away; for some of us tend to one thing, some to another; . . . We must drag ourselves away to the contrary extreme; for we shall get into the intermediate state by drawing well away from error, as people do in straightening sticks that are bent'.[57] If I have a bad temper, for example, I need to aim closer to an excess of passivity so that I can straighten out the natural bent in my soul in the opposite direction.

Aristotle is careful to warn against simple-minded applications of the mean to any human characteristic whatsoever. 'Not every action nor every passion admits of a mean,' he observes, 'for some have names that already imply badness, e.g. spite, shamelessness, envy, and in the case of actions adultery, theft, murder; for all of these and suchlike things . . . are themselves bad, and not the excesses or deficiencies of them.'[58] Acts, like murder, theft, and adultery, are intrinsically evil—'the act is simply in itself wicked'[59]—so the mean does not apply to them. Conversely, some traits or inclinations seem intrinsically good—so good, in fact, that it is impossible to have too much of them. In Aristotelian ethics, practical wisdom (*phronesis*) is the supreme moral virtue. Someone who has practical wisdom has all the other moral virtues put together. So it seems that there can be no mean here; we can lack practical wisdom but we cannot have too much of it. That would be like complaining that someone is too moral, a complaint that does not make any sense (at least in Aristotle's ethical system). Perhaps this is what Aristotle means when he writes that 'there is no such thing as excellence [i.e., the virtuous mean] in practical wisdom'.[60]

Aristotle distinguishes between intellectual virtues (having to do with learning and knowledge), productive virtues (having to do with craftsmanship and art), and moral virtues. The mean is not thought to apply to the intellectual and productive virtues. Consider the intellectual virtue of being knowledgeable. Is having too much knowledge a vice? Shouldn't we try to know as much as we can? Or consider the productive virtue of being a skilful carpenter. The point is not to occupy a midpoint between not enough and too much of being a skilful carpenter. The point is to be as skilful a carpenter as one can.

Aristotle intends the mean as something of a simplification. (Hopefully, a useful simplification). It provides only a bare-bones analysis of virtues. Aristotle does present an in-depth analysis of important individual virtues. Let us consider once again his account of **courage**.[61] Aristotle thinks that the best example of courage is military heroism on the battlefield. He distinguishes true courage from five types of pseudo-courage: (1) *coercion*: those who are ready to do battle because they are afraid of being punished for refusing conscription; (2) *experience*: those who, because of experience, are not frightened by certain things that only *seem* to be dangerous; (3) *anger*: those who are not afraid because they fight in a blind rage; (4) *the sanguine*: those who have, through temperament or drunkenness, excessive self-confidence and who are not afraid to fight because they believe they can never be beaten, and (5) *ignorance*: those who accomplish dangerous tasks without knowing the risks involved. The main point is that what seems to be courageous behaviour, on closer inspection, may not turn out to be courageous at all. So we have to be careful. We have to investigate the motivation, the circumstances, and the precise nature of someone's conduct before coming to any precise judgment. Aristotle goes into many more details about individual virtues than we can report here. This ends, then, our discussion of the mean.

On Morality and Choice

Moral philosophy is about moral failure as well as about moral success. Aristotle identifies two basic moral faults that interfere with good decision-making: what he calls weakness of will and ignorance. We consider these moral errors next. As we shall see, ignorance is the most fundamental moral fault. But first, we need to get a better grip on the issue of moral responsibility. Let us examine then the role of will (or willpower) in morality.

To begin with, we need to dispose of the silly idea that the ancients did not believe in free will. True, beliefs in fate, destiny, and the influence of supernatural forces on human life were undeniably part of the ancient mindset. Still, moral philosophers believed in free will. As already mentioned, Plato suggests that souls facing the prospect of reincarnation in Hades choose new lives for themselves. In narrating the story of this event, he has the 'angel' in attendance tell the assembled souls: 'Let him who draws the first lot have the first choice, and the life which he chooses shall be his destiny. Virtue is free, and as a man [chooses] he will have more or less of her; the responsibility is with the chooser—God is justified.'[62] In other words, the soul who chooses a bad (or a good) life cannot blame God if they choose poorly. Whether they choose well or ill is entirely up to them.

Aristotle concurs. If many people believe 'that external advantages are the cause of happiness', Aristotle exclaims that 'one might as well say that a well-executed piece of fine harp-playing was due to the instrument, not the skill of the artist'.[63] Musical virtuosity does not happen by accident. In the same way, happiness does not happen by accident. Moral success takes deliberate effort and skill expended over a long period of time. Although Aristotle accepts that we need some external goods to succeed in life, the decisive factor is the virtue of the agent. Aristotle's view is that we may be lucky enough to have external goods—friends, education, money, good health, intelligence—but that these external goods are opportunities. Moral individuals take whatever opportunities come their way and make the most of them. Except in very unusual circumstances, 'it is in our power to be virtuous or vicious'.[64] Morality is ultimately a matter of free choice and hard work.

Aristotle argues that praise and criticism, like reward and punishment, only make sense if we assume that people have freedom to choose between right and wrong. He explains,

> Witness seems to be borne to this [fact] both by individuals in their private capacity and by legislators themselves; for these punish and take vengeance on those who do wicked acts (unless they have acted under compulsion or as a result of ignorance for which they are not themselves responsible), while they honour those who do noble acts, as though they meant to encourage the latter and deter the former. But no one is encouraged to do the things that are neither in our power nor voluntary; it is assumed that there is no gain in being persuaded not to be hot or in pain or hungry or the like, since we shall experience these feelings nonetheless.[65]

We try to encourage people to be moral only because we believe that people have within themselves a capacity for free choice. If their choices were forced on them by external circumstances or by fixed human nature, the regular human activity of praise and blame and reward and punishment would be useless and a waste of time.

Human beings are moral agents. An **agent** (from the Latin *agere*, which means 'to do') is the cause of its own behaviour. Agents alone are responsible for what they do; agents alone are an appropriate subject of praise and blame; agents alone can be held accountable for their actions. Consider the game of basketball, which is played with a ball. The ball is not an agent. It is an inanimate physical object: inert, passive, and an instrument of whoever happens to be throwing or shooting the ball. Basketball players, on the other hand, are agents. They move of their own accord—they *decide* where to run or jump, how to throw or pass the ball. They are not inert, passive objects, but willing, self-moving entities. We do not blame the basketball when our favourite team loses, just as we do not congratulate the ball when it wins. We blame or congratulate the players, for they are responsible for their actions.

Aristotle maintains that moral evaluation has to do with 'acts whose moving principles are in us'.[66] He writes, 'where it is in our power to act it is also in our power not to act'.[67] As agents, we are judged both on account of what we do and what we fail to do. Not acting is as much a choice as acting. We cannot hide ourselves under a rock, away from moral obligations. Morality imposes itself on human beings. Refusing to play the moral game is not an option.

Aristotle reserves the Greek word for **choice** (*proairesis*) for acts that are dignified by a certain intellectual intention. 'Both children and the lower animals share in voluntary action, but not in choice'.[68] A choice requires something more than selecting one alternative over another. A dog 'chooses' to walk over to the pond to take a drink of water. This is, for Aristotle, mere voluntary behaviour. It is the behaviour of a nonrational—i.e., unthinking—animal. Mature human beings do not act on mere instinct or on reflex; they know what they are doing and are aware of alternative possibilities. They choose in a much more thorough and intelligent sense. This is why we can hold them morally responsible for their actions.

As moral agents, humans are responsible for their own conduct, for whatever is under their own control. Aristotle draws a parallel between 'vices of the soul' and vices of the body. 'No one blames those who are ugly by nature', he reports, but 'we blame those who are so owing to want of exercise and care'. The same holds true, he observes, for 'weakness and infirmity; no one would reproach a man blind from birth or by disease or from a blow, but rather pity him, while every one would blame a man who was blind from drunkenness or some other form of self-indulgence'.[69] Those things that are really outside our control—external harms that afflict us—are not a fair target of moral criticism. But we can (and *should*) blame people for what they freely do.

Under usual conditions, moral agents must take responsibility for their own actions. None of us can easily divest themselves of moral responsibility. In a recent legal case, a man found guilty of assaulting his spouse claimed it was not his fault because he was too drunk to know what he was doing at the time. Aristotle writes, 'We punish a man for his very ignorance, if he is thought responsible for the ignorance, as when penalties are doubled in the case of drunkenness; for the moving principle is in the man himself, since he had the power of not getting drunk and his getting drunk was the cause of his ignorance'.[70] Being drunk is no excuse. This man made a free-will choice to be drunk in the first place; that is, he willingly put himself into a situation where bad things could happen. So he must be held accountable for the consequences.

Aristotle does, however, recognize that there are important exceptions when we cannot hold humans responsible for their actions. First, there are circumstances in which 'things . . . take place under compulsion . . . [when] the moving principle is outside, [and] nothing is contributed by the person who is

acting, . . . e.g. if he were to be carried somewhere by a wind, or by men who had him in their power'.[71] These are very straightforward examples of involuntary acts. Aristotle brings up a second example: 'if A takes B's hand and therewith strikes C, B does not act voluntarily; for the act was not in his own power'.[72] Suppose then I knock you over the head so you fall unconscious to the ground. I wrap your hand around a revolver aimed at Keisha, tie some thread around your index finger and make you pull the trigger. If the bullet kills Keisha, I am the murderer. You had nothing to do with it. This was clearly an **involuntary act**.

We cannot hold agents responsible for involuntary acts. The second exception to moral responsibility involves cases where individuals, through no fault of their own, are ignorant of the facts. In these cases, well-meaning agents do something wrong 'owing to ignorance'.[73] Aristotle explains: 'A man may be ignorant, then, of who he is, what he is doing, what or whom he is acting on, and sometimes also what (e.g. what instrument) he is doing it with, and to what end (e.g. he may think his act will conduce to some one's safety), and how he is doing it (e.g. whether gently or violently).'[74] He gives a number of examples: the person who passes on confidential information, not knowing that it was a secret; the person who (accidentally) gives someone poison to drink, thinking it is medicine; the person who accidentally triggers a loaded catapult when demonstrating how the machine works, and so on. Aristotle concludes that 'the ignorance may relate, then, to any of these things . . . and the man who was ignorant of any of these [circumstances] is thought to have acted involuntarily, and especially if he was ignorant on the most important points'.[75] This agent's ignorance must arise, of course, *through no fault of the agent*. Authentic cases of this sort must, furthermore, 'involve regret'.[76] A moral person who unintentionally does something wrong will inevitably feel bad about what happened.

To summarize Aristotle on free will: most human acts are voluntary, although some may be excused because the agents were acting involuntarily due to circumstances beyond their control or out of (nonculpable) ignorance of the particulars of the situation. Still, that leaves one problematic category of behaviour: what Aristotle calls **mixed actions**. These actions seem, paradoxically, to be both forced and voluntary. Aristotle mentions the ship captain who throws all cargo overboard in a storm to save the lives of his shipmates. Such actions are voluntary because the captain decides of *his own free will* to throw out the goods. On the other hand, the captain is responding to an extreme situation that, in some meaningful sense, leaves him no choice. Aristotle believes that, rigorously speaking, such acts are voluntary because the principle that moves the captain is inside him. After all, he makes the decision. He could decide to let everybody on the ship drown. On the other hand, the captain's acts are involuntary insomuch as 'no one would choose any such act in itself'.[77] In some meaningful sense, the captain is driven to do this thing *against his will*. His acts are then mixed; he is both free and unfree at the same time.

Aristotle introduces a second, more searing example. Suppose a tyrant were to tell you that he would kill your daughter if you did not go out and murder an innocent third party.[78] Would you commit murder to save your daughter? As a parent you might feel impelled to do whatever it takes to save her life. But murder is wrong. What then are you to do? Suppose you do carry out your side of the grisly bargain. Aristotle very sensibly points out that such acts are wicked. You are choosing to murder an innocent; this is clearly wrong. On the other hand, he recommends that we should treat someone who acts immorally under conditions of extreme duress with understanding and mercy rather than with blind punishment and hard criticism. He observes, 'On some actions praise indeed is not bestowed, but pardon is, when one does what he ought not under pressure which overstrains human nature and which no one could withstand'.[79]

On Two Moral Faults: Weakness of Will and Ignorance

Let us turn now to the two most basic moral faults Aristotle identifies: moral ignorance (or viciousness) and incontinence. Aristotle begins his investigation of these matters by considering Socrates's argument (discussed in the last chapter) that all immorality is due to ignorance. He initially disagrees with Socrates but, in the end, comes round to a position that is not entirely dissimilar. Let us begin, then, by revisiting Socrates's view.

Aristotle reports that Socrates believed that 'no one . . . acts against what he judges best'.[80] Suppose I rob a bank. Why do I do so? Because I want the money. But why do I want the money? Because I believe that having (stolen) money is better than not having poverty. I am doing what I (mistakenly) judge to be best. Socrates (and Plato) believe that the solution to immorality is education. If I come to see that stolen wealth does not equal happiness (money is, at best, an external good), I will stop robbing banks. Aristotle agrees that agents often act immorally because they are ignorant of what is truly good. But he also believes that there is, at least at first glance, another problem that surfaces in immoral behaviour.

Aristotle argues that although some immoral agents aim (as Socrates suggests) at false goods, other immoral agents fail because of 'weakness of will'. Aristotle uses the Greek term *akrasia* to refer to this problem. The term has been traditionally translated as 'incontinence', which suggests a lack of control. (Hence the medical use of the term to refer to the embarrassing condition of lack of control over one's bladder.) Those who display weakness of will cannot control themselves; they are unable to hold back when confronted with temptation; they lack the necessary backbone to do what is right.

Aristotle identifies, then, two moral mistakes that lead agents astray: **ignorance** has to do with a failure of understanding; **weakness of will** has to do with a lack of willpower. People who are ignorant are guilty of **vice** or wickedness (*kakia*); those who suffer from weakness of will are guilty of **incontinence** (*akrasia*). Aristotle writes that although the ignorant and the weak-willed both perform bad acts, their motives are different, for ignorance 'is in accordance with choice', whereas weakness of will 'is contrary to choice'.[81] Ignorant agents do something bad, thinking it is good, whereas weak-willed agents knowingly do something bad because they cannot control themselves. The ignorant (or vicious) pickpocket, for example, steals without realizing (or at least without admitting) that stealing is wrong. (These tourists are all rich, anyway!) The *incontinent* thief steals due to a lack of control. Imagine someone finds a wallet with three hundred dollars in it. She knows whose wallet it is; she can easily return the money,

and she also knows that stealing is wrong, but the temptation is too great. She steals the three hundred dollars and feels guilty about it. This is what happens to the weak-willed person who suffers from incontinence. The ignorant person wholeheartedly identifies with her choice (she thinks it is right); the incontinent person does not identify with her choice. It follows, then, that 'incontinence and vice are different [insomuch as] vice is unconscious of itself, incontinence is not'.[82]

Ignorant (i.e., vicious) people believe they are acting in an acceptable manner; they are unaware of their immoral state. Incontinent or weak-willed people, on the other hand, are painfully aware of their moral shortcomings; they are all too conscious of their immoral condition. They are, Aristotle says, half-good and 'half-wicked'.[83]

Aristotle compares the ignorant and the incontinent to two cities: The ignorant man 'is like a city that uses its laws, but has wicked laws to use'.[84] 'The incontinent man [is] like a city which . . . has good laws, but makes no use of them.'[85] A concrete example may serve to illustrate the difference. Suppose individuals have been brought up to think that revenge is an honourable duty. They kill an enemy—they commit murder—but they are convinced that what they did was right because it was an honour killing. This is vice. The person does wrong thinking it is right. Conversely, suppose individuals have been brought up to understand that human life is sacred and that murder is wrong. Caught in a dispute, they cannot control themselves. They kill an enemy in anger—they commit murder—but they know that what they did is wrong. In the aftermath, they feel guilty. This is weakness of will, or incontinence. These individuals knowingly do wrong because they are unable to control themselves.

Aristotle goes on to distinguish more precisely between two forms of incontinence: one involving lack of resolve; the other, impetuosity. In the first case, incontinence arises in conjunction with the appetites; in the second case, incontinence arises with respect to honour, wealth, gain, victory, anger. An example of the first kind of incontinence would be the weak-willed person who is unable to withstand the temptations of illicit sex, alcohol, or drugs. Examples of the second kind of incontinence would be the husband who loses his temper when someone offends his wife; or an athlete who, in trying to win the Olympic Games, cannot resist the lure of steroids. Aristotle thinks that the latter type of incontinence is more noble than the first. It is still a blameworthy excess, but it deals with noble goals and is at least half-rational, whereas the first type of incontinence reduces us to mere beasts.

Aristotle claims, more generally, that ignorance (or vice) is worse than incontinence. He believes that it is a bigger obstacle to the moral life, for 'the incontinent man is curable'[86] whereas the ignorant man is not. Because individuals who suffer from weakness of will know they are doing wrong, they lead lives of torment, racked with shame and guilt. This moral discomfort may prompt them to reform their behaviour. Ignorant individuals, on the other hand, are convinced of their own righteousness; they are not racked with guilt—they think they are acting correctly—so they have no reason to change. Only moral education could change the ignorant, but Aristotle, compared to Socrates and Plato, is not very optimistic about the possibility of morally educating the truly wicked through philosophy and argument. He writes,

Argument and teaching, we may suspect, are not powerful with all men, but the soul of the student must first have been cultivated by means of habits for noble joy and noble hatred, like earth which is to nourish the seed. For he who lives as passion directs will not hear argument that dissuades him, nor understand it if he does; and how can we persuade one in such a state to change his ways? . . . The character, then, must somehow be there already with a kinship to virtue, loving what is noble and hating what is base.[87]

One needs to be a minimally decent person to profit from moral philosophy. Because the ignorant have already formed vicious characters, it will be hard to convince them of the error of their ways even with the best reasoning in the world.

Curing ignorance is, in fact, doubly problematic, for there is a more specialized kind of ignorance Aristotle calls **akolasia** that is particularly difficult to extirpate. This Greek term is traditionally translated as 'self-indulgence', or 'licentiousness'. The self-indulgent person 'craves for all pleasant things or those that are most pleasant, and is led by his appetite to choose these at the cost of everything else'.[88] He is immoral because he delights 'in the wrong things;' he delights 'more than most people do', and he delights 'in the wrong way'.[89] Aristotle compares him to a spoilt child, 'since children in fact live at the beck and call of appetite, and it is in them that the desire for what is pleasant is strongest'.[90]

Aristotle at least hints, however, at another side of this character. Unlike the incontinent man, 'the self-indulgent man . . . has no regrets; for he stands by his choice'.[91] Self-indulgent individuals, it seems, rationalize what they do; in other words, they make excuses for their bad behaviour. Consider self-indulgent people who are unable to control their sexual appetites. These people are good at coming up with clichéd arguments to justify their loose behaviour: everybody does it; promiscuity is biological; morality is only subjective; self-restraint is unnatural; and so on. These kinds of arguments do not constitute a serious attempt at moral evaluation. What is really going on is that those giving in to their unreasonable appetites are simply covering up the fact that they are greedily seeking their own sexual pleasure. The self-indulgent do not honestly acknowledge what is going on. Instead, they spend their time trying to convince themselves of their own moral correctness until these rationalizations harden into self-righteous conviction. This is why Aristotle believes that self-indulgence is a permanent illness like 'dropsy or consumption'.[92] 'The self-indulgent man is incurable', for he has convinced himself of his own virtue and has become impervious to honest criticism.[93]

Moral self-scrutiny requires a kind of selfless objectivity that is hard to come by. The self-indulgent, particularly when they are clever arguers, are able to hide their immorality even from themselves. In the process, they save themselves from the discomfort of a bad conscience. They preserve their own sense of self-esteem but at an enormous cost. Their vice, their ignorance, may be invincible. (One could consider self-indulgence as a kind of moral cowardice; rather than facing up to their moral shortcomings, the self-indulgent find a strategy for looking the other way. This makes it easier on themselves. The incontinent, at least, face up to their own shortcomings. They are at least half-moral and, Aristotle thinks, less evil than those who are self-indulgent.)

Let us finish this section on the basic moral faults of ignorance and incontinence by mentioning an ingenious paradox (*aporia*) that Aristotle attributes to the Greek Sophists,

who argue that two wrongs *do* make a right! Suppose Alcibiades is simultaneously ignorant *and* incontinent (weak-willed). Because he is ignorant, he mistakes good for evil. He tries to refrain from doing good thinking it is evil. But because he is also incontinent, he is unable to control himself and so ends up doing good! As Aristotle explains, '[Sophists argue] that folly [i.e., extreme ignorance] coupled with incontinence is virtue; for [the incontinent] man does the opposite of what he judges, owing to incontinence, [and because he mistakenly] judges what is good to be evil, . . . [in giving into what he sees as evil] he will do what is good'.[94] What is the answer to the charming puzzle? There are at least two relevant issues. First, the paradox misrepresents the human predicament. Doing what is good is hard; it takes effort. Doing what is bad, on the other hand, is easy. Incontinent individuals do what is easy; they give in to temptation; they take the path of least resistance. It is hard to imagine someone losing control and acting morally. Acting morally generally requires control; it requires the active imposition of will.

Second, this puzzle only poses a problem for so-called consequentialists, whom we study in a later chapter. These modern theorists believe that the consequences of an act are morally all that matters. In this imaginary situation, the correct consequences may result, but Aristotle believes that morality is as much about intention as it is about consequences. It is about doing the right thing, for the right reason, in the right way, at the right time, and so on. As we discuss in the next section, Aristotle believes that ignorant agents must be held responsible for their own ignorance. The people in the puzzle are morally ignorant. This is, Aristotle would probably say, their own fault. So they are wicked people even if, by some strange coincidence, they end up doing an act that has good consequences.

On Six Character-States

Building on his account of ignorance and incontinence, Aristotle proposes a basic classification scheme for different types of morality and immorality. He points out that there are three 'moral states to be avoided . . . vice, incontinence, brutishness'.[95] And there are three opposite states we should emulate: continence, virtue, and superhuman virtue. The numbering in Figure 5.4 represents the relative merit (or, conversely, the relative blameworthiness) of individual states. So superhuman virtue is the best; virtue is the next best; continence is not quite as good, and so on. Aristotle divides these good and bad states into opposing pairs: brutishness opposes superhuman virtue, vice opposes virtue, and incontinence opposes continence. Let us begin, then, our analysis with the first pair of opposing moral states: brutishness and superhuman virtue.

Brutishness and Superhuman Virtue

Aristotle comments, 'to brutishness it would be most fitting to oppose superhuman virtue, a heroic and divine kind of virtue'.[96] Whereas superhuman virtue is the most noble state of all, **brutishness** is the most ignoble. But these are not, rigorously speaking, moral states; they are states of character that are so good or so bad that Aristotle places them above and below morality. To possess superhuman virtue is, in effect, to be like a god; to display brutishness is, in effect, to be like an animal. Aristotle comments, 'If, as they say, men become gods by excess of virtue, [superhuman virtue must] be the state opposed to the brutish state; for as a brute has no vice or virtue, so neither has a god; his state is higher than virtue, and that of a brute is a different kind of state from vice'.[97]

Moral endeavour presupposes that achievement and failure are possible. People who are superhumanly virtuous (if they exist) exist beyond the possibility of moral failure, whereas the brutish do not have a conscience. They cannot even try to be moral because they lack the moral equipment. Both groups exist outside the arena of normal human striving. It goes without saying that superhuman virtue and brutishness are exceedingly uncommon: 'It is rarely that a godlike man is found . . . so too the brutish type is rarely found among men.'[98] Most of us exist somewhere within a middle region; we are capable of moral success or failure depending upon the persistence of our own efforts.

Aristotle does not consider actual cases of superhuman virtue, but we might think of a saint or an exceptional philanthropist or a social reformer as a good modern example. Mother Teresa of Calcutta, tending to the dying and the homeless, provides an example of compassion, humility, perseverance (and holiness) that most

1. Superhuman Virtue	2. Virtue	3. Continence
6. Brutishness	5. Vice	4. Incontinence

Figure 5.4 Aristotle's Six Character Types

of us cannot follow. Someone might say that Mother Teresa exists in another realm; she qualifies as someone with superhuman virtue. Our own moral efforts inevitably pale in comparison. Still, even if we cannot quite live up to this kind of exalted standard, we can still manage to be moral. We can achieve a lower mean on a different line drawn for regular human beings.

Aristotle believes that brutishness is a more widespread phenomenon than superhuman virtue. In fact, he uses the term *brutishness* in several different ways. Brutishness 'is found', he tells us, 'chiefly among barbarians, but some brutish qualities are also produced by disease or deformity; and we also call by this evil name those men who go beyond all ordinary standards by reason of vice'.[99] Putting aside the idea of a sub-human, barbarian race, we are left with two types of brutishness: one caused by disease and deformity, the other by extreme immorality. Brutish people do monstrous things. Aristotle gives a number of examples: 'the case of the female who, they say, rips open pregnant women and devours the infants, or of the things in which some of the tribes about the Black Sea that have gone savage are said to delight—in raw meat or in human flesh, or in lending their children to one another to feast upon'.[100] He also mentions **Phalaris**, a Sicilian tyrant famous for his cruelty, who allegedly built a bronze bull with a hollow chamber so that he could burn his victims alive inside it while listening to their agonized shrieks.

Aristotle includes within the category of the brutish not only those who suffer from *extreme* moral ignorance, but those who are *extremely* incontinent. 'Every excessive state', he writes, 'whether of folly, of cowardice, of self-indulgence, or of bad temper, is either brutish or morbid'.[101] There are cases that are so extreme, they are barely understandable in normal terms. They involve a quantum leap to another frightening reality. Jeffrey Dahmer, the Milwaukee cannibal who tortured, murdered, and ate his young victims is a disturbing real-life example. Clearly, this kind of behaviour is beyond the bounds of ordinary moral failure.

We may then place psychopaths, sociopaths, serial killers, unrepentant pedophiles, the criminally insane, violent schizophrenics, and the extremely sadistic within the category of the morally brutish. Because the brutish are sick or morally deformed, they pose a serious problem for society. Should they be punished? We might argue that these people are criminally insane but the critic could argue, in response, that some of these people make decisions that eventually precipitate their disease or evil habit. So they bear some responsibility for their plight. We cannot consider such issues further here. Let us turn now to the next pair of opposite states: virtue and vice.

Virtue and Vice

Virtue and **vice** are situated somewhere between the two extremes of superhuman virtue (which is absolutely good) and brutishness (which is absolutely bad). The virtuous possess moral knowledge, not necessarily in a theoretical (or philosophical) sense but in an applied, practical, everyday sense. The virtuous make excellent decisions. Their exemplary lives demonstrate their moral wisdom. The vicious, on the other hand, are morally ignorant. They lack the fundamentals. They somehow do not understand that stealing, murder, assault, telling lies, adultery, etc., is wrong. They embrace greed, envy, cruelty, deceit, etc., as normal and acceptable. Imagine 'vicious' students who cheat on exams. It happens. When they are confronted by another student, they are not embarrassed; indeed, they think that they have out-smarted the professor. They are even proud of their achievement. This is moral ignorance. Not to understand the importance of honesty is to miss out on a key element of morality. Or imagine the hit man in a criminal gang who is proud of the number of kills he makes. Not to understand that murder is wrong is to misunderstand morality. Vicious individuals, in contrast to the virtuous, have lost sight of basic moral values. They suffer from moral blindness.

Aristotle believes that vicious people are responsible for their own moral blindness. He writes, 'Virtue and vice respectively preserve and destroy the first [moral] principle[s]'.[102] Virtuous people keep the window of moral conscience clear so that they can see through to the moral truth of things. The immoral, by their habits and their attitudes, cloud their judgment. They dull their consciences through bad behaviour until they no longer discern the difference between right and wrong. The mafia hit man has killed so many people, he has lost sight of the evilness of murder. He has become callous. Moral wisdom needs to be accompanied by virtue because 'wickedness perverts us and causes us to be deceived about the [moral] starting points of action'.[103] This is why, according to Aristotle, '[the moral] eye of the soul acquires its formed state *not without the aid of virtue*'.[104]

The relationship between virtue and vice is fairly straightforward. The reader can think of other examples of these conditions. Let us turn our attention now to the more complicated relationship between **incontinence** and **continence**.

Incontinence and Continence

As we have seen, the incontinent person is unable to resist temptation. The continent individual, on the other hand, is able to resist temptation. Aristotle explains: 'The incontinent man, knowing that what he does is bad, does it as a result of passion, while the continent man, knowing that his appetites are bad, refuses on account of his rational principle to follow them.'[105] Imagine two obese individuals. The first is tempted to eat a third piece of chocolate cake and gives in; the second experiences the same desire but resists temptation. The first agent is incontinent; the second agent is continent. So continence, being a form of self-control, is a form of virtue, although it is not the highest kind of virtue.

Readers may, at first glance, identify continence with morality. After all, what is morality other than resisting temptation? But this is a modern view. Aristotle's account is more subtle. Continence is not the same as virtue, for those who have virtue do not have bad desires to begin with. Continence means having bad desires we stoutly resist—this is a moral achievement—but it is not the ideal. Morally ideal people would not have bad desires in the first place, so ideally, they would have no need of continence. They will only have good desires, developed over time by good habit, and all they need to do is follow them.

Aristotle makes a point of distinguishing the Greek virtue of **temperance** (*sophrosune*) from continence. 'If continence involves having strong and bad appetites, the temperate man will not be continent . . . for a temperate man will have neither excessive nor bad appetites.'[106] Temperance means cultivating your appetites with such success that you no longer suffer temptation. Continence means suffering from but overcoming temptation. It is, at best, a partial success. The continent have excessive or disordered appetites which is bad; but they overcome them which is good. But it would be better not to have these disordered appetites in the first place.

Consider a very serious case of immorality: pedophilia, the sexual abuse of children. Aristotle associates pedophilia with brutishness. (He presciently suggests that it is caused by depraved habit or sexual abuse in childhood.) The brutish pedophile is hardly human. We might imagine, however, a pedophile with less extreme but still very immoral desires. In this latter case, we could differentiate between three possibilities: (1) A *vicious* pedophile would not regret what he does. (Perhaps he is self-indulgent.) (2) An *incontinent* pedophile would give in to temptation and feel regret afterward. (3) A *continent* pedophile would experience sexual attraction to children but stoutly resist this temptation. Although the continent pedophile is to be commended for his self-restraint, Aristotle would say that the truly temperate person would not feel such temptations in the first place.

We can use the case of pedophilia to illustrate Aristotle's six types of moral behaviour. The brutish pedophile is so extreme, he is less than human. The vicious pedophile is very immoral (he does not see the badness of his inclinations); the incontinent pedophile is a little better (he recognizes the badness of his inclinations), while the continent pedophile succeeds, within limits, at morality and does not give in to temptation. The virtuous person does not have such inclinations to start with and is even more moral. And, of course, the superhumanly virtuous are far beyond any such sordid possibilities.

We might question aspects of Aristotle's classification system. Of course, it is better not to feel temptation than to struggle against it. But a critic might complain that the continent person who successfully resists temptation may be a moral hero. In terms of effort and determination, they may have to work harder than someone who never has to face serious temptation. The chaste pedophile finds himself in a terrible predicament. The fact that he is able to resist this temptation qualifies as outstanding moral achievement. Still, Aristotle would counter that the virtuous person is a more exemplary specimen of humanity.

For Aristotle, morality is about evaluating the objective worth of human beings. Perhaps an analogy may help. Consider two paintings: one is a beautiful, superbly done work of art; the other is, at best, a mediocre treatment, not bad but not very good, either. Now suppose we learn that the mediocre painting is done by a right-handed artist who has just lost her right arm in an accident. This one-armed artist may have put much more effort into her work than the other artist. But this does not (in Aristotle's mind) improve the quality of the finished painting. This is still an inferior painting. Although incontinent individuals may have to struggle very hard to be good, Aristotle believes that the finished product is a less excellent example of humanity. His viewpoint seems to unfairly diminish their perhaps heroic efforts for the sake of the good. (Note that Aristotle concedes, morality is unlike art in that we do care about the process that led to the finished result.) Clearly, there is room for disagreement here.

Aristotle's six-fold scheme organizes his overall view of morality in a systematic, comprehensive way. But there is one last issue to explore. The classification scheme is based on a distinction between weakness of will and ignorance. As we shall see, however, weakness of will (incontinence) is, in fact, a form of ignorance. Consider more closely the cause of incontinence.

Weakness of Will: A Form of Ignorance?

Aristotle explains that 'outbursts of anger and sexual appetites and some other such passions, . . . actually alter our bodily condition, and in some men even produce fits of madness. It is plain, then, that incontinent people must be said to be in a similar condition to men asleep, mad, or drunk'.[107] Incontinent people are momentarily out of their mind. Aristotle believes that the moral intelligence of the incontinent man falls asleep, is pushed aside, or momentarily overshadowed by the pressure of temptation. It is only when the emotional disturbance subsides that his moral intelligence reawakens so that he becomes ashamed of his acts. As he explains, with enough time 'the [moral] ignorance is dissolved and the incontinent man regains his knowledge . . . as in the case of the man drunk or asleep'.[108] If the din of temptation momentarily drowns out the voice of conscience in the incontinent man, when the emotional disturbance dies down, he regains moral discernment and feels regret.

We can explain incontinence as dual consciousness. In one sense, the incontinent man knows what is wrong and in another sense he does not know what is wrong. Imagine an incontinent man who gives in to greed and steals when he has the opportunity. He knows that he should not steal: he can say out loud, 'I should not steal'. He can list the reasons why stealing is wrong. Why does he steal? Aristotle advises that 'The use of language by men in an incontinent state means no more than its utterance by actors on the stage'.[109] The incontinent have a kind of surface moral knowledge. They know about morality intellectually, but they do not have it in their hearts. Morality has some grip on them, but deep down there is something missing. Aristotle observes, 'The fact that men use the language that flows from knowledge proves nothing; for . . . those who have just begun to learn a science can string together its phrases, but do not yet know it; *for it has to become part of themselves, and that takes time*'.[110]

We have already mentioned that Aristotle cannot provide a good explanation of the way in which human beings can—on occasion—have a sudden change of heart. The emphasis in Aristotle is on character that develops gradually, the way a freight train gathers momentum. One cannot turn a freight train on a dime. In the case of the reprobate who turns over a new leaf, what happens is a kind of sudden conversion. Adapting Aristotle somewhat, one could perhaps explain this as a kind of incontinence in reverse. The moral knowledge is in such people but asleep. Then something happens—say, a riveting emotional experience—that wakes that knowledge up. It is as if they are drunk and then see something frightening, which suddenly sobers them up. These individuals somehow remember and recuperate the moral knowledge within them.

To summarize: it turns out, on closer inspection, that weakness of will, or incontinence, is a temporary form of moral ignorance. In fact, all three kinds of immorality—brutishness, vice, and incontinence—involve some kind of ignorance. Following is a summary of Aristotle's six moral (or immoral) states:

1. *Brutishness* involves extreme moral ignorance. This egregious lack of moral sensitivity is constitutional; it has become a part of the nature of the person. There may be some deliberate decision-making that contributes to such conditions, but by the time individuals have become brutes, they have morally forfeited their humanity.

2. *Vice* involves a serious but humanly comprehensible form of moral ignorance. It is dispositional, an issue of hardened character. Because of the poor decisions people make, they develop, over time, into morally ignorant agents. They lose sight of right and wrong. Vice is deliberate and may be culpable. These people may deserve punishment, for punishment, according to Aristotle, 'is a kind of cure'.[111]

3. *Incontinence* comes about through weakness of will. In the case of temptation, a counterfeit image of the good takes over; the will wavers; we acquiesce to what is happening. Weakness of will precipitates a bout of moral drunkenness; we give in to our baser desires. Incontinence is deliberate and culpable. It is an expression of free will. These people may also deserve punishment as 'a kind of cure'.

4. *Continence* or self-restraint comes from a steadfast focus on the good. It cannot occur without conscious intent. It is a refusal to acquiesce to temptation and is deserving of praise.

5. *Virtue* comes about through deliberate decisions that shape individuals into characters who do not even feel temptation, who are so truthful they could not imagine telling a lie. The virtuous are blessed—i.e., they achieve *eudaimonia*. They deserve praise. But their happy fate is a product of their own intelligent decision-making.

6. *Superhuman virtue* is divine. Perhaps human beings can turn themselves, through their deliberate choices, into something that seems to rank above human virtue. All cultures have moral heroes. This supreme virtue would be deserving of supreme praise.

Beware! Human life cannot be easily compartmentalized. It is not as if each life fits neatly into only one of these categories. Individuals may combine moral faults with

---

◌ Applied Philosophy Box 5.8 ◌

Woman, 86, Faces Shoplifting Charge in 61st Arrest

Authorities said a 86-year-old woman charged with shoplifting wrinkle cream and other items from a Chicago grocery store has been arrested 61 times since 1956. Ella Orko was arrested Sunday afternoon on the North Side after she allegedly stuffed $252 worth of groceries into her pants, including cosmetics, salmon, batteries and instant coffee. She was charged with felony shoplifting. Police said Orko has gone by as many as 20 aliases in the past. Court records indicate that she has now been arrested 61 times and has 13 convictions for shoplifting. She was arrested the first time in 1956 in Chicago for petty larceny and again in 1958 for grand larceny. She's being held on $10,000 bail.

This woman seems to be a good example of Aristotle's ignorant agent. Relate this to Aristotle's notion of virtue as a habit. Relate it also to Aristotle's notion of eudaimonia. *(Did this woman lead a successful life?) Explain your answers.*

Source: 'Woman, 86, Faces Shoplifting Charge in 61st Arrest.' *MyWay* (Associated Press), http://apnews.myway.com/article/20090806/D99TJEOO0.html, 6 August 2009.

moral accomplishments. Still, Aristotle's schema of six possibilities provides a useful reference point that can be usefully applied to individual cases.

One final point needs to be made about these different character states. Human life is a dynamic, changing event. The same individual may progress (or regress) through the different steps in this model toward virtue or toward vice. On a hopeful note, continent individuals who try very hard to be good despite wayward inclinations may, with time, come to develop a good habits and achieve virtue. In this way, continence may naturally develop into virtue. They may be freed of temptation. On a more worrisome note, continent individuals who do not make persistent efforts to be good may be dragged down by their wayward inclinations into incontinent behaviour. Incontinence is, however, an unpleasant condition that causes great psychic distress. The easy solution to this problem is self-indulgence, making excuses for our behaviour so as to relieve our guilty conscience. With time, self-indulgent individuals may lose sight of what morality requires and end up morally ignorant. Call this the **slippery slope problem** in ethics. Continence slips into incontinence; incontinence slips into vice; and in extreme cases, vice slips into brutishness. It is important to maintain virtue at all times or we may end up being more evil than we ever imagined.

On Five Kinds of Intelligence

Having completed an introductory account of the most basic moral concepts and a thorough survey of the different kinds of morality and immorality, we must now discuss the ways in which we learn, think, and reason about morality. Aristotle distinguishes between intellectual and moral virtue. He writes, 'we say that some of the virtues are intellectual and others moral, . . . for in speaking about a man's character we [say] that he is good-tempered or temperate; yet we praise the wise man also with respect to his state of mind; and of states of mind we call those which merit praise virtues'.[112] For Aristotle, intelligence is a human perfection, something we rightfully aspire to and admire. If moral virtue primarily has to do with being good; intellectual virtue has primarily to do with being smart. We gain moral virtue through habit; we gain intellectual virtue through education. As Aristotle explains, 'Intellectual virtue owes both its birth and its growth to teaching'.[113]

In contemporary accounts, there is a great divide that separates moral from intellectual virtue. But this is not Aristotle's view, for Aristotle believes that immorality is itself a form of ignorance or stupidity. It is best to think of intellectual virtue as a more specialized (but not separate manifestation) of human excellence. As we shall see, intellectual and moral virtues overlap and intersect. Still, we can make a distinction, *grosso modo*, between practical traits like honesty, courage, generosity, and fairness and the intellectual traits such as knowledge and judgment that make these and other aspects of the moral life possible.

As we have seen, Aristotle is a philosopher and a scholar but he does not believe that reading books and doing schoolwork is the only kind of intelligent activity. Human beings put their intelligence on display in many different ways. Aristotle believes that diverse human activities are all expressions of the very same power of human reason. He identifies five major intellectual virtues: understanding, science, art, philosophical wisdom, and practical wisdom. We will consider each in turn.

1. Understanding

Let us begin, so to speak, at the beginning. Aristotle believes that all intelligence depends on a power of first understanding that he calls *nous* (the Greek word for 'mind'). Translators sometimes render *nous* as 'intuition' or 'intuitive reason'. We will use the term **understanding** or 'intuitive understanding'. In the modern idiom, the word *intuition* denotes knowledge that comes to us through some sort of vague feeling or hunch. But Aristotle thinks of understanding as intelligent discernment. It is a matter of genuine cognition, not a matter of mere emotion.

Understanding is, then, the most basic intellectual category of all. It 'grasps the first principles'.[114] That is, it supplies the starting points of knowledge. Aristotle thinks that there are basic truths about science and morality we immediately apprehend; we know them, not through logic or argument, but through immediate discernment. We 'intuit' them. Observation of the world triggers an intelligent understanding that is able to discern the way the world works. We know, for example, that nothing happens without a cause. We do not know this because we have observed that every event in the history of the world has a cause. We know effects must have a cause from some intelligent grasp of the world. Something similar happens in the case of morality. We see human behaviour; we observe how good and bad people act, and we are somehow able to make sense of the world morally. We know, for example, that courage demonstrates strength of character, that justice requires that we treat other people fairly, that telling lies and hurting other people is wrong. Even children understand this. They do not need a logical demonstration, or a philosophical argument. They are—in the absence of neurosis or defect—somehow able to directly grasp the most basic moral truths.

Aristotle compares the intuitive understanding that grasps the first principles of morality to an eye. (The Greeks often associated intelligence with seeing.) He explains, 'one must be born with an eye, as it were, by which to judge rightly and choose what is truly good'.[115] People born without this moral eye—what we would call conscience—would not be able to *see* why morality matters. They would be impervious to moral persuasion. Aristotle observes, 'We cannot get or learn [this basic ability to discern the difference between right and wrong] from another, but must have just such as it was when given us at birth'.[116]

Understanding is the root source of both science and morality. It is what we start with; it gives us the first principles of moral knowledge. We cannot have too much understanding; we can only have too little. In this sense, the intellectual virtue of understanding does not obey the Golden Mean. Whether different people can possess more or less amounts of understanding is an open question. Aristotle does suggest that some individuals are quick-witted in that they have an intuitive knack for understanding practical things very quickly. But the most important thing to remember is that understanding is the first intellectual virtue upon which all other intellectual virtues depend.

2. Science

The second intellectual virtue Aristotle identifies is **science**, what he calls *episteme* (the Greek word from which we get an English word like **epistemology**). Aristotle's idea of science differs slightly from modern concepts. He includes within the domain of science such empirically based activities as physics, chemistry, biology, and astronomy, but also mathematics, and even theology. Science is knowledge of the most rigorously logical and theoretical sort. It produces exact laws or principles; it uncovers the necessary causes of things, and it proves—i.e., logically demonstrates—its conclusions. As Aristotle writes, scientific knowledge deals with 'things that are universal and necessary, and [with] the conclusions of demonstration'.[117]

All things being equal, more science is better than less science. We cannot have an excess of science. Unlike the moral virtues, science does not obey the Mean. It is, in this respect, like understanding.

3. Art

The third intellectual virtue is art, or **techne** (from which we derive English words like *technical* and *technology*). Aristotle writes, 'art is identical with a state of capacity to make, involving a true course of reasoning'.[118] Art, in this Greek sense, includes the fine arts, such as architecture, sculpture, painting, poetry, music, and theatre. But it also includes any instance of skilful or expert making. Making shoes, for example, is an art as is producing ceramics or sewing clothes. Any activity of that requires *technique* can be considered as art. Technique is reason applied to the activity of making. Aristotle writes, 'Art must be a matter of making, not of acting'.[119]

Aristotle believes that art is, in some ways, like science. Just as science produces knowledge, art produces an artifact, something crafted by human skill. Aristotle continues, 'All art is concerned with coming into being, i.e. with contriving and considering how something may come into being . . . whose origin is in the maker and not in the thing

made'.[120] The art-object is not a product of itself. It owes its existence to human ingenuity and is an expression of human intelligence. The artist (or craftsperson) constructs the artifact according to some rational method, i.e., by 'a true course of reasoning'.[121]

Clearly, we admire great artists and scientists of all sorts; to possess expert skill or to be a theoretical whiz is praiseworthy. The more we have of this kind of intelligence, the better. It follows that art, like the other intellectual virtues, is not something we can have in excess. Art does not obey the Golden Mean. Although art or science is not enough for a good life, art and science are different aspects of human excellence; i.e., they count as (intellectual) virtues.

4. Philosophical Wisdom

The fourth intellectual virtue is philosophical wisdom, which Aristotle calls **sophia** (as in the word *philosophy*, from the Greek *philia-sophia*: 'friendship-with-wisdom'). To be philosophically wise is not to be an expert in physics or chemistry or cellular biology; it is to be 'wise in general'.[122] People who are philosophically wise have knowledge of the highest things. Philosophical wisdom develops slowly over time. It is knowledge that 'has received as it were its proper completion'.[123] Old men and women, for example, are wise because they have spent a lifetime in reflection. Philosophical wisdom requires, then, an extended period of serious thought and study.

There is some truth to the familiar caricature of the starry-eyed philosopher who falls in a hole because he or she is too busy gazing at the heavens. (This is an incident related about Thales, a Pre-Socratic philosopher.) Philosophical wisdom *is* an impractical sort of knowledge. Aristotle observes, 'This is why we say that the great philosophers of the past have philosophical but not practical wisdom, when we see them ignorant of what is to their own advantage, and why we say that they know things that are remarkable, admirable, difficult, and divine, but useless, viz. because it is not human goods they seek'.[124] Philosophical wisdom is about developing a grasp of deep, eternal, unchangeable truths. This is the highest intellectual achievement. It aims, not at human knowledge, but at something truly divine. As is the case with the other intellectual virtues, one cannot have an excessive amount of philosophical wisdom. Aristotle believes that philosophical wisdom produces happiness, 'not as the art of medicine produces health, . . . but as health produces health'.[125] In other words, philosophical wisdom produces happiness because it is happiness. This is the highest activity of the soul in accordance with virtue. Philosophical wisdom produces happiness because achieving wisdom is what deserves the best, most enduring reputation. The activity of using our mental abilities to the utmost represents the highest level of self-fulfillment.

Philosophical wisdom does depend on the other intellectual virtues. Aristotle defines philosophical wisdom as understanding (or intuition) 'combined with scientific knowledge, of things that are highest by nature'.[126] It is, in other words, an acknowledgement of true first principles combined with logically rigorous theoretical knowledge.

5. Practical Wisdom

The fifth intellectual virtue is practical wisdom or *phronesis*. (We have already discussed this moral virtue earlier in the chapter.) Aristotle defines practical wisdom as 'a true and reasoned state of capacity to act with regard to the things that are good or bad for man'.[127] It is, he states, 'the mark of a man of practical wisdom to be able to deliberate well about what is good and expedient for himself, not in some particular respect, . . . but about what sorts of things conduce to the good life in general'.[128] When we measure practical wisdom, the reference point is not a particular specialized activity; that is, the question is not simply, Is this person a good car mechanic, a good cook, a good student? The question is, rather: Is this person a good human being? It is not the individual details that matter— this person liked broccoli, this person didn't; this person lived in Calgary, this person lived in New York; this person had three children, this person had four—it is whether these details add up to a good human life. When we stand back, can we admire this person's life taken as a whole? Was this individual an accomplished human being? Was this a life well-lived? The practically wise are virtuous, not merely with respect to the details of their lives; they are virtuous in general. Practical wisdom is, then, a generalized ability for good decision-making.

Aristotle associates practical wisdom with the Golden Mean. Practically wise people display moderation (*sophrosune*) for this is what it means to follow the mean. They think clearly and choose well. They possess all the moral virtues. Aristotle writes, 'One quality, practical wisdom [gives] all the virtues'.[129]

Aristotle distinguishes between 'natural virtue' and 'virtue in the strict sense'. 'From the very moment of birth we are just or fitted for self-control or brave or have the other moral qualities.'[130] But these positive natural inclinations do not amount to morality. 'For both children and brutes have the natural dispositions . . . but without reason these are evidently hurtful. . . . One may be led astray by them, as a strong body which moves without sight may stumble badly because of its lack of sight.'[131] In Aristotle's system, morality is not purely natural reflex. It requires some kind of vigilant moral intelligence. Aristotle explains, 'If a man once acquires reason, that makes a difference in action; and his state . . . will then be virtue in the strict sense'.[132]

Aristotle distinguishes *practical* wisdom from *theoretical* knowledge about morality. To be practically wise is to *act* morally. Theoretical understanding (what Aristotle calls *sunesis*) is not enough. As he explains, '[theoretical] understanding and practical wisdom are not the same. For practical wisdom issues commands, . . . but [theoretical] understanding only judges'.[133] Practical wisdom is an active, authoritative force inside the good person. It issues commands; it makes us do the right things; it orders us about. If someone who has theoretical understanding knows what morality requires; the person with practical wisdom does it.

Aristotle goes on to explain how practical wisdom is related to the other intellectual virtues. If practical wisdom depends upon intuitive understanding to supply it with the first moral principles, all the other intellectual virtues are dependent upon it. We cannot become skilful or theoretically smart or philosophically wise if we are lazy, intemperate, partisan, hot-tempered, distracted by sensual pleasure, and so on. Practical wisdom provides the diligence, perseverance, and discipline needed for serious study. Most importantly, Aristotle views practical wisdom as the *means* to the contemplative life of philosophical wisdom. Practical wisdom 'provides for [the] coming into being [of philosophical wisdom]; it issues orders . . . for its sake'.[134]

Like all the other intellectual virtues, practical wisdom is not subject to the mean. There is no mean for achieving the mean. If we were perfectly moral, we would achieve the mean all the time. We cannot achieve the mean too much, only too little. (Someone who had too much practical wisdom would be too moral.) Aristotle mentions other minor intellectual virtues, which we explore next.

On Two Minor Intellectual Virtues

Along with his treatment of the main intellectual virtues, Aristotle discusses a number of minor intellectual virtues in relation to practical wisdom. Consider here what he means by 'good deliberation' (in Greek, **bouleusis** or *eubulia*) and what I will call 'untheoretical judgment' (from Greek, *gnome*).

Aristotle writes, 'Excellence in deliberation [is] correctness with regard to what conduces to the end which practical wisdom apprehends'.[135] To deliberate is to ponder different ways of achieving a goal. After considering pros and cons, good deliberators choose the best course of action so as to readily achieve their moral goals. Suppose someone has to raise money for charity. There are many different ways of doing this. A good deliberator will consider alternatives so as to efficiently figure out the best way to collect the required amount of money. Good deliberation is particularly prominent when it comes to issues involving etiquette, diplomacy, personal relationships, business dealings, or political strategy. (As I mention below, good deliberation is only a particularly conspicuous instance of a moral reasoning procedure called deductive wisdom.)

Aristotle mentions a second minor intellectual virtue which I will call **untheoretical**

judgment. Aristotle advises, 'we ought to attend to the undemonstrated sayings and opinions of experienced and older people . . . not less than to demonstrations; because experience has given them an eye they see aright'.[136] Call this the 'good granny syndrome'. The advice of good, old people is as useful as arguments. Such people are naturally wise. Even if they have no theoretical education, even if they are not very good at arguing, we should pay attention to their moral opinions. People who live responsibly over long periods of time develop a instinctive and spontaneous sense of right and wrong. We can call this intuitive capacity for sound moral discernment 'untheoretical judgment'.

On Moral Induction and Moral Deduction

Aristotle adapts his model of scientific logic (with some modifications) to the activity of morality. In science, **induction** moves from particular cases to a general principle. To use a very simple example, we notice that this human being and this human being and this human being are mortal, so we conclude that all human beings are mortal. **Deduction** moves in the opposite direction: from a general principle to particular cases. For example, we know that all human beings are mortal and so conclude that Tom, a particular human being is mortal. There are two corresponding stages in moral reasoning: first, an inductive phase; and second, a deductive phase. In the first stage, we induce, or arrive at, general moral ideas. In the second stage, we apply these general ideas to the specific circumstances of our lives. Let us describe each stage in turn.

How do we arrive at the notion of virtue? Aristotle believes that we get it from natural

intelligence and a good upbringing. If I am intelligent enough, if I am trained properly, I will come to recognize the virtues as important human ideals. I will come to see them as ends I should strive toward, and I will *induce* a general idea of courage, of honesty, of fairness, of loyalty. This is the first half of moral reasoning. The second half of moral reasoning is about applying these general conceptions to particular situations. Aristotle calls the reasoning process that ends in a specific action a **practical syllogism**. Suppose I am a soldier defending my homeland. I reason: I should aim at courage; courage means standing my ground in battle; so I stand my ground in battle. This is a practical syllogism. It applies a general idea of virtue to a specific circumstance. It ends in an action: standing my ground in battle. Aristotle believes, then, that this is how moral reasoning operates. The moral agent induces a general idea of virtue as a goal and then deduces a specific application of that virtue using a practical syllogism.

We can refer to Aristotle's model of moral logic as an inductive-deductive model. Moral reasoning follows a characteristic up–down logical trajectory: we use induction to reason up to virtue, and deduction to reason back down to the specific application, as shown in Figure 5.5. In the previous example, morality begins with a ready intelligence that is able grasp the general idea of courage. We mentally move up to a general idea of courage and then down to a specific application. This up–down model can be applied to moral behaviour in general. Consider the virtue of generosity. As I am growing up, I come to understand that generosity is a virtue. As I walk past the subway station, a homeless man asks me for spare change. I reason: Generosity is a virtue; giving this homeless man two dollars is generosity;

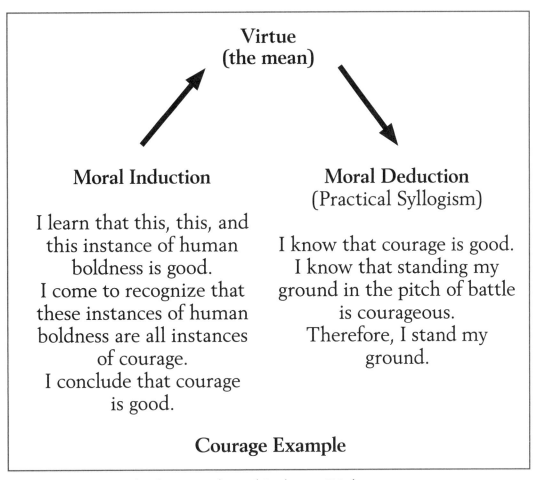

Figure 5.5 How Moral Induction and Moral Deduction Work

so I give him two dollars. Why do I do this? Because I have induced the notion of generosity and applied it to this specific situation.

We need to introduce a finer distinction. In his discussions on moral reasoning, Aristotle occasionally distinguishes between what we can call **inductive virtue** and what we can call **deductive wisdom**. He writes '[inductive] virtue makes us aim at the right mark, and [deductive] wisdom makes us take the right means'.[137] 'Inductive virtue' is able to come up with the right moral ideas; 'deductive wisdom'

is able to figure out the best way to put these ideas into practice. We need both these abilities if we are to succeed at morality. We may then picture Aristotle's general account of moral reasoning as in Figure 5.6. The basic idea is very straightforward. We first induce the principles of moral goodness, then we use deduction to put them into practice. (Keep in mind that Aristotle believes that moral decision-making is a kind of rationality. It is not simply that we 'internalize' any set of values; we possess a critical capacity that is able to discern

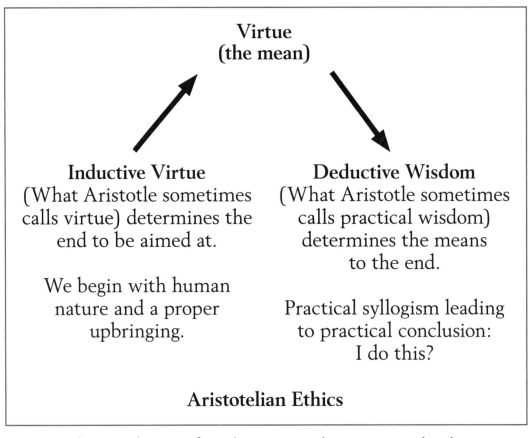

**Virtue
(the mean)**

Inductive Virtue
(What Aristotle sometimes
calls virtue) determines the
end to be aimed at.

We begin with human
nature and a proper
upbringing.

Deductive Wisdom
(What Aristotle sometimes
calls practical wisdom)
determines the means
to the end.

Practical syllogism leading
to practical conclusion:
I do this?

Aristotelian Ethics

Figure 5.6 The General Pattern of Moral Reasoning: Inductive Virtue and Deductive Wisdom

the difference between right and wrong. What we moderns call 'conscience' is a capacity for intelligent discernment, not a vague feeling.)

Deductive wisdom is a more specific manifestation of something Aristotle calls cleverness (*deinotes*). Successful business people, politicians, military commanders, and administrators are clever. They know how to get things done. They make good decisions so as to achieve their ends. They have a target and they 'hit it'.[138] Aristotle views cleverness as a necessary but insufficient condition for moral wisdom. Moral people cleverly choose effi-

cient means to moral ends, but clever people are not always moral. Aristotle writes, 'Now if the mark is noble, the cleverness is laudable, but if the mark is bad, the cleverness is mere smartness'.[139] Immoral people who cleverly achieve their ends—like the organized crime boss who stays out of jail—are merely 'smart'; they are not practically wise. They choose the right means to their goals, but they choose the wrong goals.

Note the relationship between three practical states: cleverness, deductive wisdom, and good deliberation. All three states are

---

✎ Applied Philosophy Box 5.9 ✎

Tough Love Finds a Way to Beat Heroin

Pam North . . . used what she now refers to as 'tough love' with her 25-year-old son, Craig. Initially, she didn't suspect he was taking heroin. . . . When they found out, Pam and her husband continued to support Craig, giving him money and clothes.

'Then there was this point where I realised where the money was going. But it's part of the mother's problem—I couldn't accept that the responsibility for the problem was his and not mine. . . .'

The crunch came when Craig stole money from his brother, and Pam threatened to call the police if it happened again. It did; she reported her son, and he went to court. 'It was the hardest thing I ever had to do,' she says. 'Here was a boy with no previous criminal record—someone I thought could be so kind and loving—and I was getting him into trouble.' . . .

Pam says, 'Mothers are used to making things right when their children do wrong. But children have to work it out for themselves. You can't do it for them.' . . .

Tessa [a former heroin addict from another family] is sure that her parents made the right decision [when they forced her to leave home]. 'It's easier to do the caring thing. It could be seen as heartless to throw me out but it was a fairer option. "Tough love" is saying, "We love you." But it's also saying, "You've got the final choice".'

The debate about 'tough love' is not about 'inductive virtue' but about 'deductive wisdom'. Everyone believes in the virtue of good parenting. Everyone knows that good parents should love their children. The question is: 'What should you do if you have heroin addicts for children?' 'Tough love' is one answer. Being tough on your children is proposed here as the most efficient means to the right end—good parenting. What do you think is the best way to deal with this kind of situation? (It may be, of course, that different approaches work best in different situations, something Aristotle would readily agree with.)

Source: Emma Cook, 'Tough Love Finds a Way to Beat Heroin.' *The Independent*, www.independent.co.uk/arts-entertainment/tough-love-finds-a-way-to-beat-heroin-1173764.html, Monday, 24 August 1998.

---

about successfully choosing a practical means to an end. Agents revert to cleverness to get things done; they revert to deductive reason to get *moral* things done; and they revert to good deliberation to *weigh alternatives* to get *moral* things done. Deductive wisdom is a more specialized form of cleverness; good deliberation is a more specialized form of deductive wisdom. (Deductive reasoning might involve a very quick mental movement, whereas good deliberation seems to require some conscious to-and-fro between competing alternatives.)

Mistakes arise in moral reasoning because people have the wrong moral ideas or because they are unable to put the right ideas into practice. There may involve a failure of inductive virtue or of deductive wisdom. These are not entirely separate issues, however, for even when we choose our means, we must be guided by the right moral ideas. Aristotle (like Socrates) insists that we can never choose an evil means to a good end. We cannot rob the local grocery store to give money to charity, for the means employed—robbery—is itself incompatible with virtue.

Sometimes we may fail to achieve moral ends through lack of knowledge. Suppose the pilot of the plane I am in has a sudden heart attack. I jump to the controls but am unable to save myself and the other passengers because I do not know how to fly a plane. I did not act immorally. This tragedy cannot be traced to any moral fault. I suffered from a lack of knowledge, that is all. If, of course, this lack of knowledge could be traced back to immoral behaviour, this would make me morally culpable. (Suppose, for example, I happened to be the co-pilot and was unable to save the plane because I was too lazy to study carefully at flight school. My ignorance would, in these circumstances, be immoral.) We will discuss these issues further in the next chapter.

On Moral Approximation

Aristotle believes that we can reason about morality. It is important, however, to emphasize that he views moral reasoning as a more *approximate* form of reasoning. Aristotle advises: 'We must be content, then, in speaking of [ethical] subjects . . . to indicate the truth roughly and in outline.'[140] The problem is *not* that there is no definite right and wrong; it is that reliable standards of right and wrong have to be applied to the variable conditions of human life. Aristotle claims that when it comes to 'matters concerned with conduct and questions of what is good for us [there is] no fixity, any more than matters of health'.[141] We cannot make a simple rule: everyone should eat more. What good health requires changes according to the circumstances. In some situations, we should eat more; in others, we should eat less. And so it is with morality. There are no hard and fast rules when it comes to applying morality to the myriad circumstances of human life.

Aristotle writes, 'It is the mark of an educated man to look for precision in each class of things just so far as the nature of the subject admits'.[142] Morality requires knowledge; it must be reasoned about, but it is not *exact* theory in the way that mathematical physics is. We cannot measure good or bad behaviour the way a physicist measures the movement of a pendulum. We cannot determine morality to the fifth decimal place. If, however, moral knowledge does not admit of exactitude; it is accurate enough for what we need. Aristotle compares carpentry to geometry: 'A carpenter and a geometer investigate the right angle in different ways; the former does so in so far as the right angle is useful for his work, while the latter . . . is a spectator of the truth.'[143] The carpenter wants to *do* something; he wants to build a table. If, however, the carpenter wants to build something; in our role as moral agents, we want to construct a life of worthwhile achievement. Aristotle believes that we have more than enough moral knowledge for that.

Aristotle claims that we should not teach ethics to young people: because they are inexperienced and emotional, they cannot master the capacity for approximation necessary for ethics. Morality requires balancing and making sense of many variables all at the same time. Aristotle writes, 'Young men [can] become geometricians and mathematicians . . . [but] a young man of practical wisdom cannot be found. The cause is that . . . a young man has no experience, for it is length of time that gives experience'.[144] One has to be older and have a developed sense of judgement to be a good moral reasoner. (Note that Aristotle concedes that it is not the student's chronological age but the level of maturity that matters.)

(More) On First Moral Principles

We need to say a few more words about moral first principles. Clearly, we do not derive the first principles of morality from sense perception. We do not *see* the most basic moral truths the way we see physical objects. We access moral principles, first of all, through an intuitive understanding. But there is more to the story.

As mentioned, Aristotle stresses the importance of good upbringing. He believes that students need to be properly raised *before* studying moral philosophy: 'anyone who is to listen intelligently to lectures about what is noble and just and, generally, the subjects of [morality] must have been brought up in good habits'.[145] Whereas moral philosophy extends our moral understanding in a consistent and comprehensive manner, we need to start with correct moral principles. Aristotle writes, 'the man who has been well brought up has or can easily get starting points'.[146]

In contemporary society, we have transferred the role of moral education to the private family. Although Aristotle grudgingly accepts that in households, 'the injunctions and the habits of the father' may aid in moral education, mostly, he thinks that legislation is necessary.[147] Law is a necessary tool for encouraging and teaching virtue. Aristotle believes that the community should play a role as moral teacher, inculcating moral values and enforcing them whenever necessary. Because 'most people [respond to] punishments rather than the sense of what is noble', we need to legislate extensively.[148]

In a discussion of the opinions of his contemporaries, Aristotle reports, 'Now some think that we are made good by nature, others by habituation, others by teaching'.[149] Aristotle thinks there is an element of truth to all three opinions. Nature gives us a mental eye so that we can recognize and respect the most basic moral truths of all. Habit, in accordance with morality, preserves and extends the fund of moral knowledge we begin with. Teaching encourages morality through arguments, examples, reward, and punishment. Aristotle writes, 'we ought to have been brought up in a particular way from our very youth . . . so as both to delight in and to be pained by the things that we ought; for this is the right education'.[150] Virtuous individuals (as opposed to the merely continent) enjoy virtue. They will find morality pleasant and immorality painful. They will naturally find their way to the good.

If morality begins with the right kind of upbringing, we might ask how moral philosophy develops. What can we use for the starting points of our philosophical arguments? Aristotle suggests that we begin with what he calls **endoxa**, that is, with moral opinions 'which are accepted by everyone, by the majority or by the wise'.[151] For example, it is commonly understood that stealing is wrong, that justice demands fairness, that we shouldn't tell lies, that children should obey parents, and so on. Such beliefs are the starting of moral philosophy. Each culture has a repository of revered practical wisdom passed on in great literatures or through oral traditions that can function as a starting point for deeper investigation.

But this is only a beginning. We need to use keen observation and logic to correct and refine and render consistent with our own experience what we have already received from the wise and from tradition. As Aristotle puts it, 'the truth in practical matters is discerned from the facts of life; for these are the decisive factor. We must therefore survey [moral opinion], bringing it to the test of the facts of life, and if it harmonizes with the facts we must accept it, but if it clashes with them we must suppose it to be mere theory'.[152]

Aristotle believes that moral inquiry is a community-based endeavour. In discussing prominent moral opinions, Aristotle insists, 'Now some of these views have been held by many men and men of old, others by a few eminent persons; and it is not probable that either of these should be entirely mistaken, but rather that they should be right in at least some one respect or even in most respects'.[153] Moral wisdom, as enunciated by the wise and by the many, must carry at least a grain of truth. The astute moral philosopher does not repudiate everything that went before but uses it as a starting point for moral inquiry.

Aristotle does not believe, however, that we must treat all moral opinions with equal respect. 'To examine all the opinions that have been held [is] perhaps somewhat fruitless,' he advises. It is 'enough to examine those [opinions] that are most prevalent or that seem to be arguable'.[154] Indeed, Aristotle is unfashionably blunt about disqualifying the moral opinions of the depraved or the immature. 'To examine all the views about happiness is superfluous,' he says, 'for children, sick people, and the insane all have views, but no sane person would dispute over them, for such persons need not argument but years in which they may change, or else medical or political correction—for medicine, no less than whipping is a correction'.[155] Aristotle also dismisses the views of the morally mediocre and uncritical, who are swayed by the vagaries of popular opinion. 'Similarly', he continues, 'we have not to consider the views of the multitude (for they talk without consideration about almost everything, and most about happiness); for it

is absurd to apply argument to those who need not argument but experience.'[156]

Keep in mind that Aristotle believes that there is a right answer to moral questions. If the morally mediocre do not recognize or acknowledge the correct answer, it is because they possess a skewed moral judgment. So the mere fact that someone has an opinion does not settle the matter; it is the opinions of the practically wise that matter. Determining who is practically wise is a matter for careful discernment.

On Slaves and Friends

We must finish this chapter on Aristotle by touching on a low point and a high point of his theory. On the negative side of things, Aristotle, a Greek aristocrat, defended slavery. On the positive side, he develops a remarkable account of friendship. Consider these issues in turn.

It is distressing to think that Aristotle entertains arguments in favour of slavery, but such is as it is. In the *Politics*, Aristotle claims that the natural master is superior in intelligence to the natural slave and that natural slaves are suited for menial physical tasks whereas natural masters are better suited for ruling. For those who 'are by nature slaves . . . it is better to be ruled by a master'.[157] Aristotle claims that masters must take good care of their slaves. Indeed, they must treat them as friends. He writes, 'The wrong exercise of his authority by a master is a thing which is disadvantageous for both master and slave. . . . There is . . . a community of interest, and a relationship of friendship, between master and slave'.[158] The relationship between a master and slave is more like the relationship between a parent and a child that never grows up than the relationship between say an oppressive tyrant and a prisoner.

Still, Aristotle does argue that 'someone who is thus a slave by nature is capable of becoming the property of another'.[159] He sometimes talks as if the relationship between master and slave is akin to the relationship between farmer and farm animals, which seems to ignore the obvious fact that master and slaves belong to the same human species (an important issue for a biologist). He also compares the slave to a garden tool the master owns. But we need not explore his bad arguments here. Indeed, Aristotle's arguments are so weak that some commentators suggest that he himself does not take them seriously. Whatever his personal views, do note that Aristotle left instructions that his own slaves be freed after his death. His last will and testament stipulates: 'Do not sell any of the slaves that served me, but employ them; and when they come of age, send them away free men as they deserve.'[160]

On a more encouraging note, Aristotle develops a rich account of friendship as one of the most important virtues. What is friendship? Aristotle defines it in terms of mutual care and concern: 'Goodwill when it is reciprocal [is] friendship.'[161] This is why we can't be friends with physical objects. I cannot be a friend of this bottle of chocolate milk because (1) the milk cannot love me in return, and (2) my concern for the milk is only a disguised concern for myself. It is not the milk I care about; I am only using it as a means to quench my thirst.

If we cannot befriend inanimate objects, can we be friends with an animal, say a pet dog? Certainly, you can like your dog and perhaps your dog can 'like' you, but Aristotle would not think that this is friendship in the truest, most perfect sense, 'for friendship is said

to be equality'.[162] A dog is not capable of the kind of equal-to-equal communication and intellectual sharing that marks true human friendship. Aristotle does admit that 'there is another kind of friendship, . . . which involves an inequality between the parties, e.g. that of father to son and in general of elder to younger, that of man to wife and in general that of ruler to subject'.[163] But friendship in the most proper sense is between two human beings who form a bond that brings them together as equals. Aristotle observes: 'loving seems to be the characteristic virtue of friends . . . It is in this way more than any other that even unequals can be friends; they can be equalized.'[164] You may be more powerful, richer, stronger, smarter than I am. If, however, we are to be true friends, this disparity needs to be set aside in a mutual meeting of wills, affections, and world views.

Aristotle claims that there are 'three kinds of friendship' based respectively on *utility, pleasure*, and *virtue*.[165] Two people may form a bond in order to be useful to one another, to take pleasure in one another's company, or to achieve virtue. In each case, there is a reciprocity at work. In friendships based on utility, each participant provides some kind of service or practical advantage to the other; when they are no longer useful to each other, the friendship breaks up. In friendships based on pleasure, each participant provides an occasion for pleasure for the other; when their company stops being enjoyable to each other, the friendship breaks up. In friendships based on virtue, each participant encourages the other in virtue; insomuch as true virtue lasts, this kind of friendship endures forever.

Consider first, an example of friendship based on utility and second, on pleasure. Aristotle writes, 'those who love each other for their utility . . . love each other . . . in virtue of some good which they get from each other'.[166] Fellow employees at the same workplace have a friendship based on utility. Usefulness forms the basis of their association. This does not mean that they should unfairly take advantage of one another, but this is not the deepest form of friendship. Aristotle writes, 'the useful . . . is always changing. Thus when the motive of the friendship is done away, the friendship is dissolved, inasmuch as it existed only for the ends in question'.[167]

Aristotle thinks that old people are inclined towards utility but that 'the friendship of young people seems to aim at pleasure'. [168] He points out that romantic and sexual pleasures play a large role in these types of friendships. Young people, he observes, 'live under the guidance of emotion, and pursue above all what is pleasant to themselves and what is immediately before them. . . . This is why they quickly become friends and quickly cease to be so; [for] such pleasure alters quickly'.[169]

Aristotle believes that friendships based on utility or pleasure are not truly friendships for they are inevitably self-centred. He explains, 'Those who love for the sake of utility love for the sake of what is [useful] for themselves, and those who love for the sake of pleasure do so for the sake of what is pleasant to themselves, and [only] in so far as [the other] is useful or pleasant'.[170] People involved in these derivative kinds of friendships are, on closer inspection,

seeking their own advantage. The best type of friendship, virtuous friendship is, in contrast, an association between people who care principally for the good of the other.

Virtuous friendship is based on a shared concern for human excellence. This type of friendship is useful and pleasurable in addition to being moral. 'Good people too are pleasant to one another.'[171] 'And the good are also useful to one another.'[172] This type of friendship makes one morally better. If an association 'of bad men turns out [to be] an evil thing, . . . the friendship of good men is good, . . . [for they] become better too by their activities and by improving each other'.[173]

Aristotle believes that friendship is a key ingredient in a happy life. 'For without friends no one would choose to live, though he had all the other goods; even rich men and those in possession of office and of dominating power are thought to need friends most of all.'[174] How many friends should one have? Not too many, it seems. Aristotle observes, 'it would seem actually impossible to be a great friend to many people'.[175] Living with other people is the best way to become true friends. Aristotle explains, 'friendship requires time and familiarity; as the proverb says, men cannot know each other till they have eaten salt [i.e., shared meals] together'.[176] True friendship takes time. Indeed, it may require a lifetime of loyal companionship.

❧ Questions for Study and Review ❧

1. What does the term *Peripatetics* mean?
2. How is Aristotle's method in his ethics influenced by his biological interests?
3. How do Aristotle's ethics differ from a rule-based morality?
4. Relate the modern English word *happiness* to Aristotle's concept of happiness (*eudaimonia*).
5. According to Aristotle, could dead people be unhappy? (Hint: explain in terms of *eudaimonia*.)
6. Explain what virtue ethics is.
7. What is the difference between plants, animals, and human beings, according to Aristotle?
8. In Aristotle's system, self-esteem is a good thing, but the point of morality is not quite self-esteem. Explain.
9. How could Aristotle defend his moral theory against complaints that it is speciesist?
10. Does Aristotle think that self-love is a bad thing? How does Aristotle describe the difference between good and bad self-love?
11. Explain Aristotle's notion of morality as self-realization.
12. Using a concrete example, explain and illustrate the difference between means and ends.
13. Why does Aristotle believe that ends are more important than means?
14. Explain the term 'external goods'.
15. What are the three basic lives Aristotle mentions? Which one is preferred? Why?
16. How does the cowardly person view the mean of courage? Explain this person's mistake. What does this tell us about the mean?
17. Give an example of an involuntary act. Are we responsible in such cases?
18. When does ignorance excuse acts with unfortunate consequences? Elaborate on some examples.
19. 'Ignorance is bliss.' Explain this statement in connection with Aristotle's theory.
20. List and define the six character types Aristotle outlines, from worst to best. Use examples to illustrate.
21. Explain what Aristotle means by the minor virtues of good deliberation and untheoretical wisdom.
22. Why does Aristotle think that ethics is an approximate discipline?
23. Make up a specific example showing how we move from moral deduction to moral induction. Use your example to explain Aristotle's theories.
24. Describe Aristotle's theory of moral education.
25. Explain the use of *endoxa* in moral philosophy.
26. Explain the three types of friendship Aristotle mentions and give an example of each. Which is the best type of friendship? Why?

❧ Suggestions for Further Reading ❧

- The most important text remains Aristotle's *Nicomachean Ethics*. David Ross, trans., revised by J. Ackrill and J.O. Urmson (Oxford, UK: Oxford, 2000).
- One may also consult: Aristotle, *Politics*, Ernest Barker trans., revised by R.F. Stalley (Oxford, UK: Oxford, 1998).
- And for what is usually considered a more minor work, see: Aristotle, *Eudemian Ethics*, available at the Perseus website mentioned previously. (The electronic version is from Aristotle, *Aristotle in 23 Volumes*, Vol. 20, H. Rackham, trans. (Cambridge, MA: Harvard University Press; London: William Heinemann Ltd., 1981).

Chapter Six

Understanding Moral Theory: Thomas Aquinas

❧ Chapter Objectives

After reading this chapter you should be able to:

- Explain and apply Thomas's account of the cardinal virtues (and the theological virtues).
- Explain and apply Thomas's theory of natural law.
- Explain and apply the doctrine of double-effect.
- Describe Thomas's model for the structure of human action and his threefold criteria of a good act.
- Differentiate between voluntary, involuntary, and non-voluntary acts as well as between several different categories of human ignorance.

Introduction

Given the honorific title 'the Angelic Doctor' by the Roman Catholic Church, Saint Thomas Aquinas (1225–74) was a philosopher and a theologian who spent his life as a Dominican Friar, teaching at the University of Paris and the University of Naples and playing an important public role in the religious and political events of the day.

Three quick anecdotes may indicate the mood of Thomas's life. The first anecdote is about how Thomas, something of a rebellious teenager, was determined to join the religious congregation known as the Dominicans (also known as the Order of Preachers or as simply the Blackfriars because of their black cloak and hood). This was a new organization of 'urban monks' who lived off charity. Thomas's wealthy, aristocratic mother, who was not impressed by such wild ideas, sent soldiers after him and had him imprisoned in the family castle for over a year. There is even a story that his brothers sent a prostitute to lure him away from his priestly vocation, but Thomas persisted in his resolve and was eventually allowed to leave home and join the Dominicans.

The second anecdote has to do with Thomas's way of doing philosophy. Nicknamed 'the Dumb Ox' as a student because of his large build and his absent-minded, methodical mindset, Thomas very quickly matured into a renowned scholar and teacher and was widely recognized as a philosophical genius. It was said that the mature Thomas came up with arguments so quickly that it would take four scribes (or secretaries) to record the movement of his mind. The scribes would sit in a circle around him; he would dictate to them in sequence so that by the time he finished with the fourth scribe, the first one would have finally finished the first passage and be ready to begin writing afresh. It has been suggested that the learned scholar could, in this way, work on four different arguments or even books all at once.

Although we tend to think of Thomas as a writer and philosopher, we should not underestimate his life of intense religious experience. The third anecdote is about how the saint gave up writing at the end of his life in response to some mysterious mental event that happened during prayer. Asked why he refused to take up philosophy again, Thomas allegedly replied, 'I have seen things which make all my writings like straw'.[1] We need not assume that he meant that his philosophical writings had no value but that the intensity of his mystical experience so surpassed ordinary thought as to be inexpressible.

Thomas wrote copiously. His most famous and important work is the **Summa Theologiae** (Latin for 'summary of theology').[2] Intended as a comprehensive introduction for theology students, the *Summa* is organized according to the debating techniques of the time in a rigorously formalized prose style called 'disputed questions' or *disputatio* (a Latin abbre-

viation for *quaestiones disputatae*). The treatise is, in effect, a long collection of questions and answers. Each section begins with a question. The answer to the question is subdivided into four separate parts: first, a list of possible 'objections' to the conclusion Thomas will eventually support; second, a list of contrary opinions that often includes quotations from diverse authorities; third, Thomas's own position with supporting arguments, which begins with the phrase 'I answer that'; and fourth and finally, a list of responses to any leftover objections. Each part and section is meticulously titled and numbered. This formalism may seem somewhat forbidding and dry, but it provides an efficient and thorough way of dealing with philosophical issues. As we shall see, Thomas writes in a plain, technical style with little literary flourish.

On Religion and Morality: The Euthyphro Problem

It will come as no surprise that many modern philosophers are hostile to religion. This is not a book on religious ethics or moral theology. We take no position on these issues here. It seems important then, from the outset, to explain why the work of a Christian theologian deserves a place of note in a book on contemporary moral philosophy.

The idea that religion adds little and indeed can be opposed to secular morality is not new. As mentioned in an earlier chapter, Plato famously and succinctly brings up the problem in his short dialogue entitled *The Euthyphro*, in which Socrates and Euthyphro have a very unsatisfying discussion about ethics. Plato depicts Euthyphro as a pious young man who, motivated by an excess of religious zeal, is bringing his father to court for murder. This is a very serious (and, as it turns out, exaggerated) charge. The idea of prosecuting (rather than defending) your father would be, for the Greeks, the height of immorality. So Euthyphro is doing something immoral for religious reasons because he believes that the gods will approve of his piety.

Prodded by a relentless Socrates, Euthyphro defines true piety (or holiness) as 'that which is pleasing to the gods'.[3] But this is an empty definition. Piety, however pleasing, cannot be pious *because* it pleases the gods. As Socrates puts it, 'The gods love piety because it is pious, . . . it is not pious because they love it'.[4] Even if morality is based on piety and even if the gods love piety, the moral philosopher, who is in the business of explaining morality, ought to analyze the nature of piety. Questions about likes and dislikes of the gods seem irredeemably after the fact.

This problem has come to be known as the **Euthyphro problem**. Religious people often suggest that something is moral because God commands it. But surely it can't be the fact that God commands something that makes it moral? Opponents of this divine command approach ask a pointed question: If God commanded you to murder your children (as in the story of Abraham and Isaac), would this act of murder suddenly become moral? No doubt, the religious believer will insist that God would not command anything so dreadful. God will take care only to command what is good. If, however, even God must be good, why not investigate the nature of the good without bothering about God? Naturalistic ethics—i.e. ethics without the supernatural—seems to be more than sufficient.

Some modern moralists have argued, along these lines, that religion has nothing to bring to ethics. But there are various ways of meeting this challenge. First, this criticism of religious morality largely misses Plato's point. Plato is not criticizing *all* religious belief but the simple-minded religious belief of a fanatical young man. As we have already explained, Socrates himself is a deeply religious person. What Plato targets is *uncritical* religious belief, the kind of overbearing self-righteousness that stands in the way of careful philosophical analysis. Whatever our personal religious views, Plato's criticisms simply do not apply to a thinker like Thomas. Thomas cannot be accused of *uncritical* religiosity. A close reading of page after page of the *Summa* reveals a sensible, moderate mind, patiently and consistently working through the myriad details of his religious and philosophical convictions. Readers may, of course, take issue with Thomas's religious convictions, but Thomas is no Euthyphro. Even a brief look at the several thousand pages of his *Summa* should put suspicions of *hasty* reasoning definitively to rest.

Second, Thomas believes that we can also learn about morality by studying human nature. Some religious authors (such as the medieval philosopher William of Ockham and a number of contemporary Protestant authors) argue for an exclusive sort of **divine command morality** based on a single principle: that something is right solely because God commands it. This is the position the Euthyphro problem is intended to refute. Thomas, in sharp contrast, revisits Aristotle's virtue ethics and goes on to elaborate a 'natural law' morality. He believes, of course, that in obeying moral law, we are also obeying the laws of God. But he also believes that Aristotelian ethics is largely sound and true. Like Aristotle, he bases his own ethics on a careful study of human nature, weaving together empirical, anthropological, sociological, and psychological insights to produce an ethical perspective that has been unfairly neglected in recent treatments. As we shall see, Thomas has a legal mind; he produces a systematic account that organizes a wealth of Aristotelian theory in an unprecedented way.

As a third way of meeting the challenge that religion brings nothing to ethics, note that Thomas does not believe that religion contradicts natural morality. He believes, rather, that religion provides an additional source of moral wisdom. As we explained in the previous chapter, Aristotle thinks that moral reasoning begins with *endoxa*, celebrated or proverbial sayings that have found a place in the collective memory of peoples. It would be unfair not to acknowledge that some religious thinkers make comments about morality that are widely regarded (even by people who are not religious) as truthful and profound. It would be an unusual person, for example, who would say that Jesus's teachings about love lacked any moral credibility. Even if one wants to argue that the *Sermon on the Mount* has a uniquely human (as opposed to divine) source, it (like many other religious sources) provides starting points, or *endoxa*, for moral theory.

Or consider something like the Ten Commandments, the principles of religious law passed to a wider audience by the Judaic tradition. Thomas believes that we can use natural reason to arrive at morality, but he also believes that religiously ordained law, what he calls **Divine Law**, can act as an aid to moral thinking. He writes, '[because] of the uncertainty of human judgment, . . . [so] that man may know without any doubt what he ought to do, . . . it was necessary for man to be directed in his proper acts by a law given by God, [for] such a

law cannot err'.[5] We are fallible reasoners who fall, at times, into confusion, disagreement, and error. Divine Law explicitly states correct moral conclusions. Using natural reason, we can, in hindsight, see that these conclusions were correct. This is to use Divine Law as an aid to natural reason. Something like the Ten Commandments has a place even in secular ethics.

In Western society, religious and secular discourse overlap to such an extent that it sometimes becomes difficult to draw any sharp distinction between them. In discussing the virtue of mercy, Thomas approvingly quotes St. Augustine's *City of God*. Augustine in turn quotes the pagan Roman philosopher Cicero: 'Of all [of the king's] virtues none is more marvelous or more graceful than [his] mercy'.[6] The king in question is the very non-Christian Augustus Caesar. The Christian Thomas uses, then, a citation originally used within an ancient Roman political context as an argument in favour of the virtuousness of mercy. So there is a mixing here of Christian, non-Christian, and non-religious sources.

Thomas does argue that natural morality is not enough. Religious law is also necessary for personal salvation: 'Since man is ordained to an end of eternal happiness . . . therefore it was necessary that, besides the natural and the human law, man should be directed to his end by a law given by God.'[7] Divine law adds religious duties to our usual moral responsibilities. And it also demands a *higher* degree of moral conduct. One has to aim at moral perfection. But the general content of natural morality and religious morality remains very much the same: don't lie; don't cheat; don't steal; don't murder; help the widow and the orphan; forgive those who offend you; work for peace, practise responsible sexuality, and so on.

On Virtue: Theological and Cardinal

Most contemporary textbooks that discuss Thomas's ethics focus on his conception of the natural law. We do discuss this important element of his theory here. If, however, the truth is to be told, the vast majority of Thomas's moral philosophy does not focus on natural law but on a remarkably Aristotelian notion of virtue. There is only one short section in the *Summa* on the natural law, but pages and pages on the subject of virtue. Thomas is, first and foremost, a virtue ethicist like Aristotle.

Thomas's teacher, the scientifically minded St. Albert the Great (1206–80), was particularly instrumental in spearheading an Aristotelian revival, of which Thomas came to play a large role. (Albert, for all his trouble, has been derogatorily referred to as 'Aristotle's ape'.) These were newfangled ideas at the time and Thomas (and his religious order, the Dominicans) ran into some serious opposition in church circles for their innovative approach. Nonetheless, Thomas does not repudiate his pagan predecessor Aristotle, building instead on Aristotelian foundations.

Although much of Thomas's work is theological and metaphysical (in the technically refined style known as medieval scholasticism), the largest part of his enormous *Summa* is devoted to virtue ethics. Thomas identifies two essential characteristics of virtue. First, virtue requires the successful actualization of a potential. It is the 'perfection of a power'.[8] We are born with powers (or abilities) that need to be developed through proper training. Second, virtue is a reliable disposition to act in the right way. It is, in Thomas's stock phrase, 'a habit by which we work well'.[9] Human beings possess, for example, the power of language. Honesty is a perfection of this power. Honesty, the habit of telling the truth, is a virtue. Dishonesty, the opposite vice, is a habit that develops in the other direction.

Thomas believes that we can distinguish between good and bad habits by evaluating them in light of what we know about human nature. Human beings are, according to the traditional definition, rational animals. Virtues are developed habits that facilitate intelligent action, whereas vices are developed habits that hinder such action. But virtue requires something more than raw intelligence. It also

---

◌ Applied Philosophy Box 6.1 ◌

How Lying Starts

It's like lying. People begin by lying to others; then start lying to themselves; soon, they don't know what's true and what's false any more. And the ensuing moral rot can corrode you from the inside out.

Thomas, like Aristotle, would agree with this description of the vice of dishonesty. Explain.

Source: David Eddie, 'Response to "I made plans with a friend".' *David Eddie's Damage Control, The Globe and Mail*, www.theglobeandmail.com, 18 September 2009.

requires **good will**. Thomas observes: 'If a man do well, this is because he has a good will'.[10] This is why Thomas does not consider intellectual abilities, such as superior understanding, knowledge, cleverness, science, and art, to be *moral* virtues. These are excellent human traits to have, but they do not qualify as moral virtues until someone wills a good end.

Thomas also distinguishes between the *good taken relatively* and the *good taken absolutely*. He explains, 'Through being gifted in science or art, a man is said to be good, not simply, but relatively; for instance, a good grammarian or a good [black]smith.'[11] If the 'good' blacksmith skilfully produces swords and spears to help in criminal activity, he can be a 'good blacksmith' but a bad man. He may be good relatively—i.e., relative to the art of iron-working—but he will be bad absolutely—i.e., relative to human nature.

Thomas thinks that although we may be good grammarians, blacksmiths, business executives, politicians, chemists, football players, cooks, or interior decorators—the more fundamental issue is this: are we good human beings? Morality looks at the big picture. It situates our life within a general framework that explains which things contribute to or detract from a good human life. Morality evaluates our actions and character from the viewpoint of the most important virtues and vices.

Thomas simplifies Aristotle's list of virtues. Instead of a miscellaneous grouping, he identifies seven principle virtues. Every positive human quality is, one manner or another, a variation on one of these seven principle character traits. He further divides the seven principle virtues into three theological and four cardinal virtues. The difference between cardinal and theological virtues is, roughly, the difference between natural and religious

morality. The **theological virtues** are faith, hope, and charity (or love); the **cardinal virtues** are prudence, temperance, justice, and fortitude. Basically, the cardinal virtues can be accounted for by the ordinary workings of human nature. The theological virtues, in Thomas's mind, require a direct infusion of God's grace. We cannot achieve faith, hope, and charity through our own unaided, ordinary efforts. We need some kind of supernatural help. It is as if God directly intervenes and gives us an extra push.

While the object of the cardinal virtues is a moral life, the object of the theological virtues is union with God in Heaven. But Thomas believes that we cannot get to heaven by ourselves. He explains,

> Because [heaven] surpasses the capacity of human nature, man's natural principles . . . do not suffice to direct man [there]. Hence it is necessary for man to receive from God some additional principles, whereby he may be directed to supernatural happiness. . . . Such like principles are called 'theological virtues': first, because their object is God, inasmuch as they direct us aright to God: secondly, because they are infused in us by God alone: thirdly, because these virtues are not made known to us, save by Divine revelation, contained in Holy Writ.[12]

We will, for the most part, examine Thomas's account of the cardinal virtues. But we need to consider, at least in passing, the role that virtues such as faith, hope, and charity play in Thomas's ethics. Let us very briefly consider his account of charity (or love), the most important theological virtue. Thomas observes that 'Charity is more excellent than faith or hope, and, consequently, all the other virtues'.[13] He formally defines charity as 'the friendship of man for God'.[14] But the term has a much wider scope than may first appear. Thomas thinks that anyone who aims at the good is trying to move closer to God. So charity, aspiring to a proper relationship with God, includes other kinds of virtuous love: 'The habit of charity extends not only to love of God, but also to the love of our neighbor.'[15] And it does not stop there. In addition to our neighbours, we are obliged to love ourselves, to love our bodies, to love (what is good in) sinners, and to love angels. Thomas even suggests that we can, after a fashion, love irrational creatures (plants and animals).[16] So charity, friendship with God, opens outward to embrace all that is good in Creation.

Under the topic of charity, Thomas discusses seven different subtopics:

1. The internal effects of love (joy, peace, mercy)
2. The external effects of love (beneficence, almsgiving, fraternal correction)
3. The major vice that is directly opposed to love (hatred)
4. The minor vices opposed to the internal effects of love (melancholy, envy, discord, contention, war, quarrelling, sedition)
5. The minor vices opposed to the external effects of love (scandal)
6. Wisdom, a further effect of love
7. The opposite of wisdom, folly

This is a lot of ground to cover![17] Clearly, morality has a lot to do with charity, even construed in a narrow sense. And that is not all. Thomas believes that charity (or love) is the underlying cause and a necessary precondition for all the other virtues: 'Whoever has charity must necessarily have all the other virtues as well.'[18] He continues: 'Charity inclines us toward all virtuous acts'[19] and 'No true virtue is possible without charity'.[20]

Notice what Thomas is doing. He believes that in the ordinary realm of natural moral striving, prudence (what Aristotle calls practical wisdom or *phronesis*) is the chief virtue; it directs and regulates all the other natural virtues. Charity plays the same role in the religious realm—it directs and regulates the other theological virtues. But that is not all. Because the religious realm is both superior and more basic, charity becomes a kind of superior practical wisdom (*phronesis*). Considered from a higher perspective, it becomes the thing that regulates and orders *all* the virtues. It becomes, so to speak, the *higher* prudence that directs the *lower* prudence.

Thomas aims to correct Aristotle in an interesting way. As we have already seen, Aristotle posits friendship as a virtue. In his explanation of love, Thomas explicitly borrows from Aristotle's definition of friendship as a kind of mutual well-wishing. This is, for Thomas, what love is: a mutual caring, in the highest instance, between God and creature. But in Thomas, this notion of love *qua* friendship becomes *the principle virtue*; it becomes the new practical wisdom (*phronesis*). Love of God, but also of his creatures and of everything good that comes from Him, comes to prevail, so to speak, over practical smartness. It is in this (non-denominational) sense that Thomas (assisted by many medieval colleagues) introduces a Christian revolution in ethics. In this account of virtue, love becomes the engine and the guiding force for all human morality.

Thomas recognizes that there is something transcendental in love. It is as if love is a **supererogatory act**, an act of moral heroism that exceeds the bounds of what is humanly possible. This is why when we have selfless love for others—i.e., when we truly love them for their own sake—we need some sort of direct infusion of grace, some sort of supernatural push in order to be able to move outside the confines of our all-too-natural self-ishness. Aristotle recommends love between friends but Thomas, following Jesus, extends the scope of moral love to include neighbours, strangers, even enemies, and ultimately, by way of extension, to everything that is good in Creation. In Thomas, the universe, created by a God who is love, is itself an expression and embodiment of that love. So love of God and love of everything good besides becomes the universal, underlying principle of morality. Jesus's many sayings about love are the *endoxa* that eventually give rise to Thomas's reformulation of Aristotle.

The idea that morality is, at its deepest, an attitude of beneficence and loving care directed toward other people elicits an almost universal consensus. Even in a secular age, to be moral is to have regard for others; it is to be other-centred, rather than self-centred. Hence, the usual contrast drawn between self-interest and morality. As we examine Thomas's ethics, keep in mind that the idea of an all-comprehensive love is always in the background. We will not focus on Thomas's theological notion in the present chapter, but it is always there, between the lines so to speak. Thomas would agree with the popular attitude that morality, in the final analysis, boils down to something like love for others. But the general idea of love has to be analyzed and applied in a rigorous and thorough manner to the many different aspects of human behaviour—hence the need for concepts like virtue and natural law.

Although we will not explore these issues further here, note that Thomas's account of the theological virtues of faith and hope also have ramifications for morality. Faith has to do with issues about what we should and should not believe: clearly, an important issues in ethics. Hope, on the other hand, as the opposite of despair, seems a necessary component of any happy, healthy, virtuous life. But we will not try to sort through these interesting issues here. Let us turn next to Thomas's account of the cardinal virtues.

On the Cardinal Virtues

If Aristotle's approach to the virtues is somewhat helter-skelter, Thomas provides a masterful synthesis of the cardinal virtues in one over-arching scheme. The idea that there are four major virtues originates in Plato, who divides the soul into three parts: mind, will, and appetites. Plato associates a different virtue with each part: wisdom with the mind (the thinking part of the soul), courage with the spirit (the enthusiastic, wilful part of the soul), and temperance with the appetites (the animal desires). Plato adds to this triad a fourth virtue, justice, which represents the right relationship between these three different parts of the soul, with the mind, aided by the spirit, ruling the appetites. After Plato, the Stoics (Zeno of Citium, Chrysippus, Cicero, Seneca), the early Christian Fathers (Ambrose, Jerome, Augustine, Gregory the Great), and later theologians (Peter Lombard, Philip the Chancellor, Albert the Great) develop these ideas further. But we will turn now to Thomas's account.[21]

Think of the cardinal virtues as a kind of pivot-point around which the moral life revolves. Thomas explains, 'The term cardinal is taken from [the Latin] *cardo*, the hinge on which a door turns. . . . Therefore we call those virtues cardinal . . . through which as through a door one proceeds. . . . [and] on which the whole moral life . . . turns, and on which . . . it is founded'.[22] There are, so to speak, four hinges to morality, i.e., four cardinal virtues. We can think of them as (1) isolated traits of character or (2) as the four contributing features present in each and every instance of moral behaviour. We will consider each virtue, first on its own, and second, as a contributing cause present in any moral act. But before we do that, a word about moral psychology.

Thomas points to the passions as the affective or emotional engine of human endeavour. He distinguishes broadly between two types of passions: the **concupiscible** and the **irascible**. The concupiscible passions involve desire. They push and pull us, on many different levels, toward what seems good and away from what seems evil. (The name comes from the Latin term *concupisco*: 'to long for', or 'to be very desirous of', or 'to covet'.) The irascible passions, in contrast, involve activity, exertion, or effort expended in the overcoming of opposition or difficulty. They serve the concupisciple passions, coming to the surface when our desires are thwarted and frustrated by circumstances. (The word *irascible* comes from the Latin term *ira*: 'anger', 'wrath', 'rage', or 'ire'.) Thomas explains, 'Since the soul must, of necessity, experience difficulty or struggle at times, in acquiring some such good, or in avoiding some such evil, . . . [this] good or evil . . . [which is] of an arduous or difficult nature, is the object of the irascible faculty'.[23]

We have, then, two kinds of human passions. The concupiscible passions involve straightforward attraction and, to a lesser extent, aversion. The irascible passions involve the determined overcoming of obstacles that stand between us and our goals. Thomas associates human traits such as love (inclination toward), hatred (inclination away from), desire (movement toward a good), aversion (movement away from an evil), joy (possession of a good), and sorrow (possession of an evil) with the concupiscible passions. He associates qualities such as hope (of overcoming obstacles), despair (at overcoming them), fear (of difficulty), daring (in the face of difficulty), and anger (reaction to obstacles) with the irascible passions.[24]

Now let us turn to the two moral virtues Thomas calls **temperance** and **fortitude**. Temperance (or moderation) is the virtue associated with the concupisible passions; fortitude (courage, perseverance) is the virtue associated with the irascible passions. Temperance principally keeps our pursuit of natural goods within reasonable bounds; it moderates our overenthusiasm 'in accord with . . . reason'.[25] Fortitude, 'on the other hand, bestows firmness', and 'is chiefly concerned with . . . flight from bodily evils, and consequently with daring, which attacks the objects of fear in the hope of attaining some good'.[26] To be temperate is to practise proper self-restraint when enjoying those things we are attracted toward; to possess fortitude is to persevere in the midst of hardships that threaten to defeat our (good) purposes. Thomas believes that both these virtues require the adherence to the Aristotelian mean discussed in Chapter 5. In the case of temperance, reason traces a middle path between the extremes of excess and insensibility; in the case of fortitude, reason traces out a middle path between rashness and cowardice. Thomas brings his own originality to the study of morality without, however, discarding what is useful in what went before.

Underneath the rubric 'temperance', Thomas considers diverse topics such as abstinence, sobriety, chastity, virginity, decency (honesty), gluttony, drunkenness, lust, incest, rape, adultery, studiousness, modesty, humility, anger, clemency, meekness, continence, incontinence, and so on. Underneath the rubric 'fortitude', he considers such topics as fear, fearlessness, daring, pusillanimity (cowardice), perseverance, effeminacy, patience, martyrdom, presumption, and vainglory. This method of identifying variations of the principle virtues allows Thomas to bring some order to the bewildering complexity of human psychology. It provides a basic skeleton for his account of virtue and vice.

If temperance and fortitude are self-regarding virtues, **justice**, the third cardinal virtue, provides a different vantage point for moral evaluation. Justice has to do with our relationships with other people. It 'joins [us] together in equity with others'.[27] While temperance and fortitude involve the *interior* passions of the person, justice has to do with whether the *external* actions of an agent satisfy an objective criterion of fairness, proportionality, or decorum that varies with individual circumstances. Thomas writes, 'It pertains to

---

೫ Applied Philosophy Box 6.2 ೬

Gluttony

'Mulloverthis' is a female, black, Christian blog writer. She is complaining here that religious people who emphasize the importance of temperance (self-control) when it comes to issues such as sexuality and drug addiction overlook similar problems with overeating:

Can we talk? One of the greatest displays of what can be safely dubbed a Jerry Springer experience in an actual church setting was when I witnessed a diatribe against 'nasty' church folks who were 'hoes' and 'not saved'. . . . The speaker's apparent mission [in] explicitly addressing sins of perversion, . . . adultery, fornication, masturbation, pornography, bestiality, seductiveness, homosexuality [etc.] was to bring those in bondage to these sins and strongholds into a place of liberty and freedom . . . There was only one major problem. The speaker had to be tipping the scale at about 450–500 pounds.

Lack of temperance and self-control through over-eating . . . is not pleasing to God. [If] it is sinful to give heed to temptation to the lusts of the flesh and have sex outside of the marital covenant, [it is just as sinful] to over-indulge in riotous eating to appease our own lust and fleshly desires. We are to eat and enjoy nourishing and enriching our bodies, but *we cannot lick our fingers to the grave*. . . . So then, overeating and its resultant effects that in many cases mirror what drug addiction does to our bodies—due to our own choices—is not acceptable. . . .

Since Christians are motivated in life by what we know pleases God, . . . the growing trends of obesity in the United States should be recognized and curtailed by . . . nutritional knowledge, athletic activities and teams, health screenings [etc.]. . . .

Please be careful to note that *all obesity does not stem from gluttony, or because of a lifestyle of sin.* Some obese people have glandular or other medical issues that impose massive weight gain.

Do you agree with this author? Temperance has been typically associated with self-control when it comes to drinking alcohol. (Hence the old 'temperance societies' that combated the use or availability of alcohol.) Thomas would extend temperance to all 'concupicible passions'. Explain why this is an instance of temperance rather than fortitude. Name another domain of human endeavour where temperance is needed.

Source: Mulloverthis's Weblog, 'Gluttony,' http://mulloverthis.wordpress.com/category/gluttony, 20 December 2007.

justice that a man give another his due. [But] the thing due is not [always] of the same kind . . . for something is due to an equal in one way, to a superior, in another way, to an inferior, in yet another; and the nature of a debt differs according as it arises from a contract, a promise, or a favor already conferred'.[28] In other words, what is justice in one situation may be injustice in a different situation. It will follow, then, that justice can be divided into all sorts of subordinate virtues. Thomas explains: 'Corresponding to these various kinds of debt there are various virtues: e.g. "Religion" whereby we pay our debt to God; "Piety", whereby we pay our debt to our parents or to our country; "Gratitude", whereby we pay our debt to our benefactors, and so forth.'[29]

We have now identified three of the cardinal virtues: temperance, fortitude, and justice. Thomas does insist on the distinction between these different virtues, while at the same time, recognizing that they may, in a sense, overlap. A medieval logical distinction may be of help here. The scholastics (medieval philosophers) differentiated between distinctions made according to the mind (*secundum rationem*) or according to the reality of the thing (*secundum rem*).[30] We could say, for example, that murder understood as an outburst of anger and the murder understood as a breach of justice are the same *according to the reality of the thing* but differ according to the *idea* of virtue invoked. Considered from the perspective of temperance, the murderer is unable to restrain himself; the problem is a lack of self-control. Considered from the perspective of justice, the murderer transgresses fair standards of human interaction. Still, this is the same bad act and the same bad person, considered however from two different perspectives. There is a single act, not two acts. When we analyze human behav-

iour we can use our terminology to focus on one particular aspect of the person or act, but we must keep in mind that the distinctions we make are aids to understanding, not references to different metaphysical realities. Thomas himself explains in slightly technical prose,

> In operations which are directed to another [person], [badness may result] by reason of some inordinate passion of the soul. In such cases justice is destroyed in so far as the due measure of the external act is destroyed: while some other virtue is destroyed in so far as the internal passions exceed their due measure. Thus when, through anger, one man strikes another, justice is destroyed in the undue blow; while gentleness [a form of temperance] is destroyed by the immoderate anger.[31]

It almost goes without saying that justice is the virtue embodied in law, the court system, the police, and the judiciary. It is the legal virtue. (The word *justice* comes from Latin term *justitia*; *jus* = 'what is binding or obligatory', 'rights', 'justice', 'duty', 'having to do with a court of justice, authority, power, permission'.) In a just society, law properly regulates what people can and cannot do to one another. It acts as a referee, surveying, evaluating, and even forbidding certain interactions among individuals. In Thomas's account, law is so closely linked to justice that an unjust law is not truly a law. It only has the appearance not the reality of law. Unjust law is not law the way a vase that has been shattered on a marble floor is no longer a vase. Why? Because it cannot function the way it must be able to function to qualify as a proper law. (We will discuss further the connection between the law and morality in Chapters 9 and 10.)

In a very large section on justice, Thomas discusses a vast array of topics, including honour, obedience, friendliness, gratitude, truth-telling, equity, murder, assault, thefts, robbery, quarrelling, imprisonment, false witness (in court), vengeance, tale-telling, cheating, usury (lending money on excessive interest), lying, hypocrisy, fanaticism, superstition, and true religion (proper relation to God). In every case, justice represents conformity to an external (or objective) measure of proper proportion; injustice represents a violation of that measure. Why, for example, is robbery unjust? Because it takes from others what belongs to them. It violates the bond of ownership between individuals and their possessions. It does not give to proper owners their due; indeed, it takes away what is their due. Why is dishonesty (i.e., purposeful deception) unjust? Because, in withholding the truth, we deprive other humans of that which they have a natural aptitude to know. We violate their natural right to know the truth; we do not give these rational beings their due. Why is hypocrisy unjust? Because it violates the moral standards we impose on other people. When I act hypocritically I do not give society what is its due. And so on. In all these cases, we fail in our relationship to other people. Our acts do not properly correspond to the circumstances.

Let us turn finally to the fourth and final cardinal virtue, **prudence** (from the Latin *prudentia* or *providentia*: 'seeing ahead').[32] Prudence plays the same role within the cardinal virtues that charity plays within the theological virtues. Thomas writes, 'prudence is the virtue which commands'.[33] It is the chief virtue, the guiding light, the commanding intelligence that orders our acts with an eye to our future moral and practical well-being. Just as Divine Providence benevolently orders the events of the world, so prudence, from a human perspective, watches over our actions and orders them to our future happiness.

Thomas defines prudence as 'right reason applied to action'.[34] We cannot be moral without prudence. 'It belongs to the ruling of prudence to decide in what manner and by what means man shall obtain [virtue] in his deeds.'[35] If, however, prudence is the supreme virtue, prudence itself depends on a prior mental ability that Thomas calls **conscience**. Although 'prudence is more excellent than the moral virtues, and moves them; yet [conscience] moves prudence'.[36] Think of a line of dominoes. You push the first domino and the others fall over, one by one, in sequence. When it comes to moral deliberation, conscience is the first domino in the line. It begins the process of moral thinking. With conscience we start to know the most basic moral ideas and the most basic moral laws. Although conscience is accompanied by strong feelings (at least in a healthy individual), it is more than an emotion: for Thomas (as for Aristotle), it is a basic form of intelligence. (In Thomas's system, 'conscience' plays the same role that moral understanding plays in Aristotle.)

Thomas derives the term *conscience* from a Latin phrase: *cum alio scientia*, which means 'knowledge applied to an individual case'.[37] This moral knowledge arises, in the first instance, from an intuition Thomas calls **synderesis**. (The term comes from St. Jerome's interpretation of Ezekiel's mystical vision of four angelic figures, each with four faces: a human face representing reason, a lion's face representing strong emotion, an ox's face representing appetites, and an eagle's face representing *synderesis*, the spark of transcendental moral knowledge that comes directly from God.) What is important for our purposes is that Thomas believes that morality starts in a direct awareness of the most basic moral principles, *not* in a type of argument. We begin with an immediate understanding of right and wrong, a divinely inspired intuition of good moral sense, that prudence then applies to the individual circumstances of our lives.

Thomas sets down moral conscience as the prior condition for prudence. He then distinguishes between three types of prudence: individual, domestic, and political. Individual prudence is 'directed to one's own good', domestic prudence 'is directed towards the common good of the home [or family]', and political prudence is 'directed to the common good of the state or kingdom'.[38] Thomas also differentiates between false, imperfect, and perfect prudence:

1. **False prudence** is a practical cleverness that aims at bad ends. Thomas claims, 'whoever [aims at an] evil end has false prudence . . . Thus a man is called a good robber, and in this way we may speak of a prudent robber . . . Because he devises fitting ways of committing robbery'.[39]
2. **Imperfect (or incomplete) prudence** is deficient in one of two ways:
    a. In the first case, imperfect prudence is a specialized kind of prudence that, although not wicked, is not enough, by itself, to constitute complete morality. Thomas explains, 'The good which it takes as an end is not the common good of all human life, but of some particular affair: thus: when a man devises fitting ways of conducting business or sailing a ship, he is called a prudent businessman or a prudent sailor'.[40]
    b. In the second case, imperfect prudence involves someone who knows how to achieve an end but somehow fails to put it into practice. This imperfect prudence involves right opinions but does not result in right action.
3. **Perfect prudence** is the action of good decision-making which 'judges and commands

aright in respect of the good end of man's whole life'.[41] In other words, perfect (or moral) prudence successfully puts into practice the kinds of decisions that turn us into good human beings, and it orients us properly within the framework of the most important virtues and laws that regulate basic human decency.

Thomas has much more to say about prudence. For example, he divides it into its various parts, according to three different schemas. Just as a room is composed of roof, floor, walls, windows (and so on), prudence, he says, is composed of the following eight integral parts:

1. Memory is necessary so that we can learn from past experience.
2. Understanding (or conscience) is necessary so that we can know what moral requirements should guide our actions.
3. Docility is necessary so that we learn from other (more experienced) people.
4. Shrewdness is necessary so that we can quickly size up the situation we are confronted with.
5. Reason (understood as penetrating inquiry) is necessary because we sometimes have to think hard about puzzling situations.
6. Foresight (knowledge about the future) is necessary because sound decision-making has to result in good consequences.
7. Circumspection (proper appreciation of the circumstances) is necessary because we have to tailor our acts to specific situations.
8. Caution is necessary because 'evil [often] has the appearance of good'.[42]

These are all integral aspects of perfected decision-making, and Thomas explains these issues at length. Why, for example, is 'docility' a necessary part of prudence? Thomas responds:

৯৹ Applied Philosophy Box 6.3 ৯৹

Dumb Criminals

Jarell Arnold, 34, in line at the Alaska USA Federal Credit Union in Anchorage in August, showed his ID in order to check his balance, took the account slip from the teller, wrote his holdup note on it, gave it back and escaped with $600 (but only briefly).

Lonnie Meckwood, 29, and Phillip Weeks, 51, were arrested in Kirkwood, N.Y., in June after allegedly robbing the Quickway Convenience Store. Their getaway ended about a mile from the crime scene as their car ran out of gas, even though the Quickway is also a gas station.

Admitted gang member Alex Fowler, 26, of Jasper, Texas, was arrested in July and charged with an attempted home-invasion robbery that went bad. Tough-guy Fowler, who has the words 'Crip for Life' tattooed on his neck, was chased from the house by the 87-year-old female 'victim' pointing a can of Raid insect repellant at him, threatening to spray.

'Dumb criminals' is a familiar trope (or theme) in the news media. Popular culture often glamorizes criminal or immoral behaviour. These news features are intended as a response to this romanticization of immorality. What is going on here is a kind of moral exhortation: 'Look how stupid criminals are! You wouldn't want to be associated with this kind of lifestyle.' To say that criminals are 'dumb' is to say, in Thomas's language, that they lack prudence. One needs prudence—i.e., practical intelligence—to live a successful life. Thomas believes that smart, successful decision-making is inseparable from morality.

Sources: 'Name, Date, Threat.' *Anchorage Daily News*, 12 August 2009. [Online source: *News of the Weird*, www.trutv.com/weird/really-stupid-robberies/index.html].
'Slowway.' WMAR-TV (Baltimore), AP, 30 June 2009. [Online source: *News of the Weird*, www.trutv.com/weird/really-stupid-robberies/index.html].
'Squashed Like a Bug.' *Beaumont Enterprise*, 20 July 2009. [Online source: *News of the Weird*, www.trutv.com/weird/really-stupid-robberies/index.html].

Prudence is concerned with particular matters of action, and since such matters are of infinite variety, no one man can consider them all sufficiently; nor can this be done quickly, for it requires length of time. Hence in matters of prudence man stands in very great need of being taught by others, especially by old folk who have acquired a sane understanding of the ends in practical matters. . . . Now it is a mark of docility to be ready to be taught: and consequently docility is fittingly reckoned a part of prudence.[43]

Thomas further divides prudence into three sequential steps: we inquire, we judge, and we command ourselves to act. Commanding 'is the chief act of . . . prudence'.[44] A good ruler of a country commands; he or she makes citizens do what is right or best. In the same way, prudence rules over the individual, commanding all talents and aptitudes, making them do what is right or best. The prudent individual is the do-er, i.e., the person who gets the job done, not so much the thinker.

Interestingly, Thomas does not divide prudence into more specific virtues. He considers instead its parts, its different applications in ordinary life and in politics, its opposites (imprudence and negligence), and the vices that may, at first glance, look like prudence (guile and solicitude or worry). We could perhaps try to divide prudence into more specific virtues, such as leadership (the capacity for social direction), or business smarts (efficiency in money matters), or decisiveness. But Thomas would say that these are all imperfect (or incomplete) kinds of prudence. Prudence presupposes all the other virtues. Or, rather, they presuppose it. Everything depends upon prudence. The prudent individual, the individual who commands well, is the virtuous individual. Without prudence, virtue is impossible.

As mentioned, we can consider the four cardinal virtues as separate human traits, or as 'certain general conditions of the human mind, to be found in all the virtues'. When Thomas takes this latter approach, viewing each moral act as a combination of all four cardinal virtues, he links each individual virtue to one of the four human powers that, seen from a medieval perspective, motivate and manifest themselves in human action.[45] These four powers are (1) the **intellect**, (2) the **will**, (3) **desire**, and (4) **emotion**. Thomas believes, then, that each capacity has its own peculiar excellence, as designated by the corresponding virtue. Prudence relates to the intellect; justice, to the will; temperance, to desire; fortitude, to the emotions. In moral behaviour, four things happen simultaneously:

1. Prudence, *in the intellect*, directs all acts in accordance with reason.
2. Justice, *in the will*, orders all the acts according to what is due or fitting.
3. Temperance, *in the desires*, sees to it that the agent does not give in to unruly appetites.
4. Fortitude, *in the emotions*, strengthens the individual in spite of fear, fatigue, toil, etc.

Thomas writes, 'Four things—rational direction [i.e., prudence], correctness [i.e., justice], resolution [i.e., fortitude], and moderation [i.e., temperance]—are required for any virtuous action'.[46] All four aspects of a human being—the mind, the will, the desires, and the emotions—have to work together harmoniously to produce moral action.

Understood either way, the concept of the four cardinal virtues provides a useful model for good human behaviour. Thomas's account represents the culmination of a lengthy discourse on virtue and vice that had been largely forgotten until recent efforts to bring this important part of ethics back into prominence. The theme of the four cardinal virtues is not only an important tool for moral analysis; it is part of the cultural tradition in the Western world. Consider Renaissance artist Raphael's depictions of the cardinal virtues (painted about 1511). (See Figures 6.1 and 6.2.) Raphael presents the virtues as four muses. (You should be able to identify each virtue from the appearance of each figure.) In Figure 6.1, we have three young women seated on a series of steps. The highest virtue—i.e., the muse seated on the highest step—is, of course, Prudence. Prudence is thoughtfully looking at herself in a mirror. In other words, prudence requires accurate introspection: self-knowledge of a clear, thoughtful sort. The emblem on her blouse seems to be an old man (age = wisdom) with a painful expression, a symbol perhaps of the relationship between bitter experience and practical wisdom. The two lower figures represent Fortitude dressed in armour (a symbol of military strength and readiness), who is petting a docile panther (like a lion, a symbol of obedient strength) underneath an oak tree (another symbol of strength). Across from her, Temperance holds up reins (a tool for restraining the desires) that visually link to an open, burning torch (hot fire being a symbol of hot desire). The lone, crowned figure in Figure 6.2 is Justice. She is brandishing a sword, for

Figure 6.1 Raphael's Fresco Mural of the Three Cardinal Virtues—Prudence, Fortitude, and Temperance

Source: http://en.wikipedia.org/wiki/File:Raffael_054.jpg

Figure 6.2 Raphael's Ceiling Mosaic of the Fourth Cardinal Virtue—Justice

Source: http://commons.wikimedia.org/wiki/File:Raffael_053.jpg

justice is upheld by the law and has recourse to imprisonment and punishment. She also holds a balance, representing an objective criterion of fairness. The inscription on the tablets is *Ius suum unicuique tribuit*: 'She gives to each one his own right/due.' (Note that three of the cherubs in the first panel represent the theological virtues: Charity is harvesting acorns from the oak tree [i.e., bringing human life to fruition], Hope is holding up the torch that lights up the darkness of despair [the torch having two meanings], and Faith is pointing skyward.)

On the Definition of Law

But we must now turn to Thomas's new formulation of the old idea that morality is abiding by the right rules or laws. Thomas's famous account of natural law has come, through a series of transformations, to represent our usual or familiar way of thinking about ethics. Although it is unfortunate that so much of the earlier tradition of virtue ethics was lost in the process, the idea of moral law is a legitimate and insightful way of looking at morality.

We can consider virtue ethics and moral law ethics as two contrasting but complementary approaches to moral thinking. On the one hand, virtue ethics pushes us to develop good character; on the other hand, moral law pushes us to conform to external, objective standards of right and wrong expressed in rules. Whereas virtue ethics focuses on what kind of person we become, moral law focuses on individual actions. And whereas virtue ethics evaluates the cause, moral law evaluates the effect. The moral law approach reduces morality, in effect, to a species of justice: we are obliged to conform to an external standard of what is due, fair, or fitting. As Thomas points out, the Latin word for law, *lex*, 'is derived

from '*ligare*' [to bind], because it binds one to act'.[47] It follows, he writes, that 'Law is a rule and measure of acts, whereby man is induced to act or is restrained from acting'.[48]

Before considering particulars, Thomas considers the general case. And so, before examining the nature of moral law, he elaborates a fourfold definition of law in general. According to this key definition, law 'is nothing else than (1) an ordinance of reason, (2) for the common good, (3) made by him who has care of the community, and (4) promulgated'.[49] Let us consider each aspect of this definition in turn:

1. Law is an ordinance of reason. Why? Because law has to make sense. The nonsense phrase 'Higgledy-piggledy-squiggledy' cannot be a law. Why? Because it is unintelligible. In the same way, if the track coach were to make a rule that his sprinters must run at the speed of light, this could not be a law. Why? Because reason (i.e., physics) tells us that no physical mass can travel at the speed of light. And law is an ordinance of reason. Any demand, then, that students run faster than the speed of light is irrational; it is nonsense, not law.

2. Law is for the common good. The common good is not, however, the good of the majority. The common good is that which is good for *everyone*. Thomas does not believe, as many do today, that people's interests are truly at odds with each other. In a true community, we all will care for one another. The point of law is to regulate relationships and interactions in a way that makes us all better off. Thomas thinks of society as a team: we are all in this together. A law that is not for the betterment of everyone, then, is not really a law. A greedy dictator could perhaps establish a law that forces everyone to pay

the dictator all their money. But this would not be law; it would be tyranny.

3. Law is made by him who has care of the community. Suppose I decide to make new traffic laws for all of Brazil. This would not be a law, according to Thomas. Why? Because I, an ethics professor in North America, do not have the proper authority to make laws in Brazil. Those in charge of the Brazilian system of government could make such laws because they have been entrusted with the care of that community. Perhaps I could make a rule that applies to how I shall test my students at the university because what happens in my class has been entrusted to my care. But I cannot make a law that relates to that which is outside the limits of my own 'jurisdiction'. Such a thing would not be a law; it would be at most an opinion.

4. Law must be promulgated. Law must be made public; it must be published, displayed, distributed. Law-makers must make sure that all citizens have access to the content of the law. If a government passed secret laws, citizens could not be expected to obey these hidden laws which they did not know about. And they could not be (fairly) punished for breaking such laws. Law becomes law only when it becomes public knowledge. A secret law is no law at all. This, then, is what law requires.

On the Four Kinds of Law

Thomas distinguishes between eternal law, natural law, human law, and divine law. All these laws obey the above definition; they derive from or complement one another. Let us consider them in order:

1. **Eternal law** is, in short, the orderly plan that pervades the universe. Thomas writes, 'the whole community of the universe is governed by Divine Reason'.[50] Thomas believes that God designed the world according to certain basic principles. The laws of chemistry, physics, and biology, which originally derive from the will of an all-wise God, are part of the eternal law. The laws of logic and mathematics, which originate in the mind of God, are also part of the eternal law. And finally, the laws of morality, devised since all eternity for the betterment and welfare of humanity, are part of the eternal law. These laws are promulgated, not in mere words, but in the very existence of the universe; they are an ordinance of 'Divine Reason' ordered to the common good of all things (for God is benevolent). The eternal law is the most fundamental law of all. All other forms of law (including moral law) have their origin in eternal law.

2. **Natural law** is the morality God has enclosed in the human heart. It is 'the rational creature's participation [in] the eternal law'.[51] In other words, it is God's eternal law seen from a human perspective. Just as God takes care of the world, morality is the authoritative rule within human nature that tells us how to take care of ourselves and the world. Thomas writes, 'the rational creature is subject to Divine providence in the most excellent way, in so far as it partakes of a share of providence, by being provident both for itself and for others'.[52] In effect, God shares the government of the universe with us. He gives us intelligence so that we can promulgate and respect the laws that should control our interactions with the world and with other people.

   Thomas describes the natural law in two related ways. First, he declares that it is inscribed in the human heart. When we look inside ourselves, we can find the basic principles of right and wrong written out inside our psychology. Second, Thomas describes natural law as something revealed by the natural light of human reason. This natural light derives from God. Thomas explains, 'the light of natural reason, whereby we discern what is good and what is evil, . . . is nothing else than an imprint on us of the Divine light'.[53] Like Aristotle, Thomas situates the source of morality in human nature, but, unlike Aristotle, he traces it further back, to its ultimate origin in a moral, benevolent God.

Natural law complies with the four criteria outlined in the general definition of law mentioned earlier: (1) It is an ordinance of reason: it derives from our rational nature. (2) It is for the good of all, i.e. for the common good. (3) It is *promulgated*, not in mere words, but in the fact of human conscience. And (4) it is directed towards those who rule over the world, i.e., to human beings. Hence the famous passage from *Genesis*: 'God said to them, "Be fruitful and multiply, and fill the earth, and subdue it; and rule over the fish of the sea and over the birds of the sky and over every living thing that moves on the earth."'[54] (Although this passage is sometimes interpreted negatively as providing a justification for raping and pillaging nature, it can be read as a call to good stewardship over all of God's creation.)

3. **Human law** is, according to Thomas, the body of rules or conventions enforced by judicial decision that regulate a particular community. It is what we, in ordinary conversation, refer to as law. Although Thomas believes that morality, when it comes to fun-

---

ᶜᵒ Applied Philosophy Box 6.4 ᵒᵛ

Martin Luther King, Jr

'Letter from a Birmingham Jail,' 16 April 1963

You express a great deal of anxiety over our willingness to break laws. This is certainly a legitimate concern. Since we so diligently urge people to obey the Supreme Court's decision of 1954 outlawing segregation in the public schools, at first glance it may seem rather paradoxical for us consciously to break laws. One may well ask: 'How can you advocate breaking some laws and obeying others?' The answer lies in the fact that there are two types of laws: just and unjust. I would be the first to advocate obeying just laws. One has not only a legal but a moral responsibility to obey just laws. Conversely, one has a moral responsibility to disobey unjust laws. I would agree with St. Augustine that 'an unjust law is no law at all'.

Now, what is the difference between the two? How does one determine whether a law is just or unjust? A just law is a man-made code that squares with the moral law or the law of God. . . . To put it in the terms of St. Thomas Aquinas: An unjust law is a human law that is not rooted in eternal law and natural law.

Martin Luther King, Jr, borrows from Thomas the basic idea that human law must be an expression of higher law. Explain.

Source: Martin Luther King, Jr, 'Letter from a Birmingham Jail,' 16 April 1963, African Studies Center, University Of Pennsylvania, www.africa.upenn.edu/Articles_Gen/Letter_Birmingham.html.

damental issues, is the same for everyone, he accepts that particular nations, states, provinces, and municipalities may regulate human interaction in an individual manner. These individual arrangements are not, in principle, immoral; they are just different. Different communities have different traditions, customs, and ways of doing things. For example, people may work from nine-to-five here; they may take an afternoon siesta there. The age of majority may be 18 here, but 21 there. While people may stand stiffly at funerals here, they may wail and shout and dance over there. These differences may be translated into statutes, customs, and expectations that vary from society to society. Thomas thinks that such differences are permissible and legitimate just so long as they do not involve any serious breach of universal morality.

Thomas explains that 'from the [general] precepts of the natural law . . . human reason needs to proceed to the more particular determination of certain matters. These particular determinations, devised by human reason, are called human laws'.[55] There is, then, a chain of logical derivation: human law derives from natural law and natural law derives from eternal law. It follows that in order to qualify as law, human law must respect natural law; it must be moral. Thomas writes, 'Every human law has just so much of the nature of law, as it is derived from the law of nature. But if in any point it deflects from the law of nature, it is no longer a law but a perversion of law'.[56] Thomas believes that an immoral human law does not have to be obeyed; it is not even a law. We should generally avoid breaking the law so as not to set a bad example for other people. Nonetheless, obeying a seriously unjust law would be a sin.

4. **Divine law** is, finally, the law directly revealed by God in Revelation or Scripture. It would include, for example, the Ten Commandments, the spiritual advice of Jesus, and even the laws of the Church as an expression of God's will. Thomas believes, of course, that divine law must be in accordance with morality. Although divine law may require more than ordinary morality—for example, religious observances of a particular type—it cannot contradict natural (or moral) law. Thomas believes, as we have already explained, that religious law can be used to clear up moral confusion that derives from the uncertainty of human judgment. But let us turn, now, to Thomas's account of natural law.

On Natural Law in Particular

First Rule, Connatural Knowledge

Thomas writes, 'this is the first precept of [natural] law, that *good is to be done and pursued, and evil is to be avoided*'. This is how moral law begins—with a broad and blindingly obvious rule of thumb: Do good! Don't do evil! There is no use complaining that we already knew this, for Thomas would respond, 'Of course, you did'. Thomas is not trying to invent a new theory or understanding of morality. Nor is he trying to prove the existence of morality. He is, rather, trying to express what we already know about morality. He maintains that we cannot even begin to act morally unless we first try to conform to one basic principle that is at the root of natural law: do good and avoid evil! In the contemporary period, many tend to think of morality in subjective terms. In this account (which we discuss in Chapter 7), we tend to call what we like 'good' and what we don't like 'bad'. To tell someone to 'do good and not do evil' is to tell them to do what they like and not do what they don't like! But clearly, this is *not* what Thomas has in mind.

Thomas believes, like Aristotle, that conscience is a form of intelligence. We are not just a bundle of emotions; we can move beyond our personal likes and dislikes to some rational understanding of what is objectively right or wrong of its own accord. Conscience is not perception, but Thomas thinks it operates in a somewhat analogous way. Just as we do not decide the colours of things on a whim, we do not decide 'right' and 'wrong' on a whim. We are forced to see red as red and blue as blue. Just so, we are 'forced' to see serial killing as wrong and love for our children as right. Thomas is confident that if only we strive to be fair and objective, we will be able to accurately tell the difference between right and wrong. Morality is, then, more than subjective preference. Indeed, one of the most common human experiences is the clash between personal preference and morality, when we stop ourselves from doing something we would prefer to do because we know that it is wrong.

Thomas thinks that we all possess an inner sense of right and wrong. If some present-day authors embrace moral skepticism, Thomas goes to the other extreme. It is not simply that we have an inner moral sense; we could not get rid of this deeply ingrained moral sensibility even if we tried. Thomas writes, 'there belong to the natural law, first, certain most general precepts, that are known to all; . . . [these] can nowise be blotted out from men's hearts'.[57] We are stuck, so to speak, with a basic awareness of the difference between good and bad inside us, whether we like it or not. We can lose sight of the details of the moral law, what Thomas loosely calls the secondary rules; we can even lose sight of the basic difference between right and wrong in

a fit of anger or in the heat of passion. But the basic distinction between right and wrong is so firmly embedded in our rational nature that we cannot permanently lose them without pathology or mental defect.

Contemporary readers of Thomas may run up against a second source of confusion. If 'do good, avoid evil' is the first rule of natural law, do not think of it as a sequence of words inside our heads. It is a natural inclination. Someone who has never read Thomas or taken a course in ethics, someone who is inarticulate or verbally deficient, can still be moral. Such people can still follow the natural law enshrined in their hearts.

Modern Thomist Jacques Maritain makes a useful distinction between theoretical and **connatural** knowledge of morality. Someone who has theoretical knowledge can make a good argument; someone who has connatural knowledge knows virtue through lived experience. Maritian explains,

> we can possess . . . conceptual and rational knowledge of the virtues. . . . Then if we are asked a question about fortitude, we shall give the right answer by merely . . . consulting . . . our concepts. [Or] we can possess [virtue] in our own powers of will and desires, [and] have it embodied in ourselves. . . . Then, if we are asked a question about [say] fortitude, we shall give the right answer, no longer through science, but through inclination, by looking at and consulting what we are and [our] inner bents or propensities. . . . A virtuous man may possibly be utterly ignorant in moral philosophy, and know as well—probably better—everything about the virtues, through connaturality.[58]

Thomas claims likewise that there is a 'twofold manner of [moral] judging, . . . a man may judge in one way by inclination, . . . in another way, by knowledge'.[59] We may learn about morality through 'rectitude of the will which tends naturally to good' or by theorizing about morality.[60] In the normal course of things, moral knowledge first arises in lived experience. The important point is that we do not have to repeat philosophical arguments inside our heads in order to gain ethical knowledge.

Thomas believes that there is a basic goodness to humanity. So, acting in accordance with our best inclinations is equivalent to morality. The critic may protest that morality acts as a brake on inclination, that it restrains many drives and impulses that naturally arise in us. Suppose I have a bad temper. When I lose my temper, I may seem to be acting in accordance with my nature, but this is clearly immoral. So, the critic may claim, morality must mean something more than acting in accordance with my own nature. This is, however, to misconstrue Thomas's meaning.

Thomas accepts Aristotle's definition of human beings as *rational* animals. This is the special characteristic that makes us human beings. Thomas explains, 'Thus I might say that fierceness is, in a way, the law of a dog, but against the law of a sheep or another meek animal. And so the law of man, which, by the Divine ordinance, is allotted to him, according to his proper natural condition, is that he should act in accordance with reason'.[61] When we allow unreasonable emotions to engulf us, we are swept away, not by reason but by unthinking passion. Anger, for example (generally speaking), involves a loss of our rational self. (There may, in fact, be times when it is moral to be angry, but mere anger—i.e., anger that is simply a loss of self-control—is not moral.) Thomas would argue that when I lose my temper, I am not acting as a rational animal; so I am not acting morally.

Secondary Rules of Natural Law

Morality means, for Thomas, following our basic inclination to do good and avoid evil. This is what natural law obliges us to do. In the modern era, we often think of moral law as a series of prohibitions: 'Thou shalt not do this; thou shalt not do that. . . .' Thomas, however, puts moral law in a more positive light. He explains the details of natural law in terms of what we *should* do. (Obviously, if people should do certain things, this presupposes that they should refrain from doing other, contrary things. Still, when it comes to moral law, Thomas's emphasis is clearly on what we should do. He is influenced, here, by virtue ethics.)

Thomas subdivides the primary rule of natural law, 'do good and avoid evil', into three more specific rules. In presenting these secondary rules, Thomas starts again with the *more general* and moves to the *more specific*. He begins, first of all, by describing what human beings are like, and second, by drawing out a moral lesson from this observation. Let us consider, then, his three secondary rules in turn.

The first of the secondary rules of natural law has to do with preservation of human life. Thomas observes, in nature, an *inclination to self-preservation*: 'Inasmuch as every substance seeks the preservation of its own being, . . . whatever is a means of preserving human life . . . belongs to the natural law.'[62] Thomas claims that human beings have a basic inclination they share with other 'substances' in the world. (The word *substance* is metaphysical terminology for a 'thing': for our [nontechnical] purposes, think of it as an independent whole composed of different parts bound together into a tight unity.) Thomas points out that substances, which are made up of interlocking parts, have a cohesive force that keeps them in existence. This tendency to self-preservation runs throughout the universe. It pertains to both living and non-living things. Imagine a large marble boulder, held together by its molecular structure.[63] Winds lash against it; maybe waves crash against it; snow and ice piles up against it in the winter. But the boulder perseveres as a single marble block. Can we destroy it? Perhaps, using a sledgehammer or even dynamite. But doing so will require enormous energy and effort. Even an inert thing like a marble pillar resists its own disintegration; the chemical bonds that cement it together are the means (so to speak) of its self-preservation.

Human beings, Thomas says, share 'an inclination to good in accordance . . . with all substances'.[64] In other words, human beings share this basic inclination toward self-preservation. We do not want to die; we cry at funerals; we pay large amounts of money for medical care; we fear personal annihilation. There may be unusual cases of severe trauma and acute suffering where pain looms so large it eclipses or masks the natural desire to stay alive, but that desire is a basic trait of human nature. In trying to preserve human life, we follow our natural inclinations. But, on the natural law model, this is what morality requires. Therefore, it is moral to preserve human life.

The first of the secondary rules of natural law could be expressed like this: strive so as to preserve, protect, and enhance human life. However, the exact wording does not matter. Human beings, as rational animals, find within themselves a natural inclination to

---

◆ Applied Philosophy Box 6.5 ◆

Woman Survives 5 Days after Car Crashes Near Central City

A news item in the *Denver Post* (18 September 2009) reported on the case of Cindy Hoover, who survived five days of rain, freezing rain, and near-freezing conditions in the Colorado mountains after a single-vehicle car accident.

The article opens with the reaction of local fire chief Gary Allen, who commented, "She had a heck of a will to live.' The article then reports on Hoover's condition when she was finally found:

> Hoover's face was purple, her mouth covered in dirt. She said everything hurt and especially painful were her bare feet . . . Hoover used half a golf club that was in her car to help her crawl. She also was going to use it to fend off any animals, but none attacked her. . . .
>
> That Hoover is a survivor is not a surprise to people who know her. She is described as upbeat, outgoing and a very strong woman. . . . Officials at the hospital said today that Hoover . . . is listed in fair condition. [One rescuer] is still amazed by Hoover's endurance: 'It is absolutely amazing'.

When we think of the moral injunction to preserve human life, we tend to focus on the law against murder: 'Thou shalt not kill.' But it is also moral to save your own life. What this woman did was morally heroic. It should be celebrated—as it was in this prominent newspaper piece. Which of the cardinal virtues did Cindy Hoover display? Explain.

Source: Howard Pankratz, 'Woman Survives 5 Days After Car Crashes Near Central City.' *Denver Post*, www.denverpost.com, 18 September 2009.

self-preservation that can serve as a basis for moral decision-making. When someone rescues a drowning stranger, when someone protects a child from harm, when soldiers bring food to the starving, when a doctor saves a life through surgery, these are moral acts. On the other hand, murder is an evil act. Why? Because it violates the first of the secondary precepts of natural law—the injunction to preserve human life.

The second of the secondary rules of natural law concerns sexuality, reproduction, and family life. Thomas observes, in humans, an inclination they share with other animals to procreation: 'there is in man an inclination to things that pertain to him more specially, according to that nature which he has in common with other animals: and in virtue of this inclination, those things are said to belong to the natural law, which nature has taught to all animals such as sexual intercourse, education of offspring and so forth.'[65]

Clearly, Thomas's views about sex are not as permissive as those of many modern readers, but the stereotypical idea that he, as a medieval person and a celibate priest, is against all sex does not survive fair examination. Thomas thinks that sexuality, properly understood, is good. Why? Because it is a natural inclination. If, as we have seen, human beings share a natural inclination to self-preservation with other things (inert and living), they also share with other animals a natural inclination to sexuality and to family life. Animals have sexual intercourse and they care for their offspring, but they do it out of instinct, not from moral motives. Human beings, who possess reason and free will, can *thoughtfully* find this inclination inside themselves. So part of morality includes such things as falling in love, courting, enjoying physical intimacy, having chil-

dren, raising a family, and so on. (Thomas would, of course, condemn certain forms of sexuality, co-habitation, and child-rearing as immoral. But unlike certain older thinkers, he is not against physical sexuality. He believes that such activities are, in principle, an expression of moral goodness.)

Obviously, Thomas does not think that everyone has to get married and have children. One can, for example, forego marriage for the sake of a life of religious or public service, for a life of study, or even for a life of artistic creation. Still, marriage, sexual intercourse, and family are good things. In choosing this path, individuals are obeying the natural law. They are engaging in moral conduct. Even those who do not themselves marry have mothers and fathers, siblings, aunts and uncles, and so on. There are duties of gratitude, affection, and mutual support that bind together family members. Thomas would argue that respecting and preserving these relationships is a part of morality.

The third of the secondary rules of natural law has to do with those inclinations that are exclusive to human beings as rational animals who can discover and communicate truth through language. Thomas observes in human beings an inclination toward knowledge (including religious knowledge) and community life. He observes this:

> Thirdly, there is in man an inclination to good, according to the nature of his reason, which nature is proper to him: thus man has a natural inclination to know the truth about God, and to live in society: and in this respect, whatever pertains to this inclination belongs to the natural law; for instance, to shun ignorance, to avoid offending those among whom one has to live, and other such things regarding the above inclination.[66]

Let us divide this third secondary rule into two subrules:

1. To begin with, as mentioned, as thinking animals we have an inclination toward the truth. Understanding, learning, inquiring into the truth is a good thing. Education (including religious education) is, then, something that should be promoted and permitted. Because we are beings that are able to know, the pursuit of knowledge is a virtuous activity; to extend our knowledge is to act in accordance with our natures.
2. Thomas thinks (like Aristotle) that we are social animals. Rationality includes the capacity for language, and the purpose of language is moral co-operation with others. We have, then, as 'languaged' animals, an inclination toward community living. So anything that promotes civil order and social harmony is good. (Remember that Thomas thinks of friendship, or charity, as the highest virtue. Citizenship, solidarity, community loyalty are kinds of friendship. Our inclinations push us in this direction, and following these inclinations is part of morality.)

In summary, Thomas's account of natural law moves from more general principles to more specific principles. The first rule, 'do good, avoid evil', is the most general principle of all. The three secondary rules are more specific. They are arranged in order of increasing specificity. The first is about an inclination to self-preservation, something all substances (things) share. The second is about family life, something all animals share. And the third is about knowledge and social co-operation, something all human beings as rational animals share. So Thomas moves methodically, in his analysis, from all things, to all animals, to all rational animals.

Although Thomas's introduction to natural law ends with these three secondary rules, it is important to point out that this is not enough for a complete moral theory. We need to adapt natural law to still more specific circumstances. We can envisage then a limitless number of tertiary rules that deal with narrower concerns such as 'Don't lie', 'Don't steal', 'Don't murder', 'Take care of your children', 'Respect your parents'. And we can derive these tertiary rules from the secondary rules discussed above. Why is telling lies is wrong? Because it violates the third secondary rule: lies provide an obstacle to knowledge while undermining social trust. Why should we take care of our children? Because this is in accordance with the first and second secondary rules: procreation is a natural inclination and children cannot survive by themselves. And so on. In this way, we can derive very specific laws from the more general principles Thomas outlines. (Note that the same act may violate or conform to more than one secondary rule at the same time. If I murder my father, this act violates the first rule about preserving human life; it violates the second rule about respecting family obligations, and it violates the third rule about good citizenship. So it violates all three secondary rules at the very same time. We leave it to the reader to derive other familiar moral laws from these general notions.)

Individual Cases, Casuistry

Although the majority of cases involving the moral evaluation of individual acts are straightforward, this is not always the case. Thomas affirms, 'the natural law, as to general principles, is the same for all . . . but as to certain matters of detail, . . . it is the same for all in the majority of cases, . . . and yet in some few cases it may fail'.[67] In other words, the rules we have been discussing do not apply in any straightforward or routine way to odd or complicated cases. Let us begin with an obvious example: the first of the secondary rules of natural law tells us to preserve human life. But what about killing someone in self-defense? This act of killing seems to violate the first precept of natural law; but surely, self-defense is moral. So how can we make sense of this exception? In fact, Thomas uses a special principle called 'the principle of double-effect' to explain the moral legitimacy of self-defense, a topic we investigate below. Simply note, for starters, that the application of general rules to specific situations can call for some very precise reasoning.

Thomas writes, 'although there is necessity [in natural law] in the general principles, the more we descend to matters of detail, the more frequently we encounter defects. . . . In matters of action, [morality] is not the same for all, as to matters of detail, but only as to the general principles'.[68] There are two issues here. First, there are exceptional cases that seem to diverge from the usual rules; second, it is easier to make mistakes when applying general rules to complicated cases. This is where moral philosophy can help.

Casuistry is the technical name given to the science or art of applying general moral rules to specific cases. Unfortunately, the term has taken on pejorative connotations. According to an unfair caricature, casuists are mostly looking for ways to excuse morally dubious behaviour. Rather than taking the moral law in its plain sense, they play tricks with words, using over-subtle distinctions to 'water down' the requirements of morality. This caricature overlooks the genuine difficulty that arises when one is faced with broad rules that must be applied to perplexing human situations. Laws are a moral abbreviation, a useful way of reminding ourselves of the basic principles of moral behaviour. But the complexity of human life is at odds with the inevitable simplicity of moral law. Once the moral law approach becomes the predominant way of thinking about morality, casuistry inevitably follows. Judaism, which places great emphasis on religious law, is particularly famous for its casuist traditions.

Consider a concrete case as an illustration of the way casuistry is intended to operate. Jean Valjean, the hero in Victor Hugo's famous novel *Les Misérables*, steals bread for his poor, starving family and is subsequently caught and imprisoned for stealing. What are we to make of this kind of action? Surely, there is a moral precept: 'Do not steal'. Thomas himself concludes that '*every* theft is a sin'.[69] On the other hand, the natural law tells us to care for our children. The Jean Valjeans of this world are faced with a dilemma: they must either break the moral law against stealing or break the moral law about providing for our children. What should they do? Can starving people steal to feed themselves? What does morality require in such puzzling individual situations?

In consulting natural law, we can reason from the first, most general rule—'Do good, avoid evil'—to the more specific secondary rule—co-operate with others in society—to the even more specific tertiary rule—'Do not steal'. We might envisage these three levels of natural law, as shown in Figure 6.3.

Assume, as Thomas argues, that stealing is wrong because respecting other people's property contributes, in necessary ways, to the harmonious well-being of society.[70] He advises that *every* case of theft is a sin. Is, then, stealing bread when you (or your children) are starving immoral? This seems like a cruel conclusion. But, in fact, Thomas claims that the starving person taking the bread *is not*

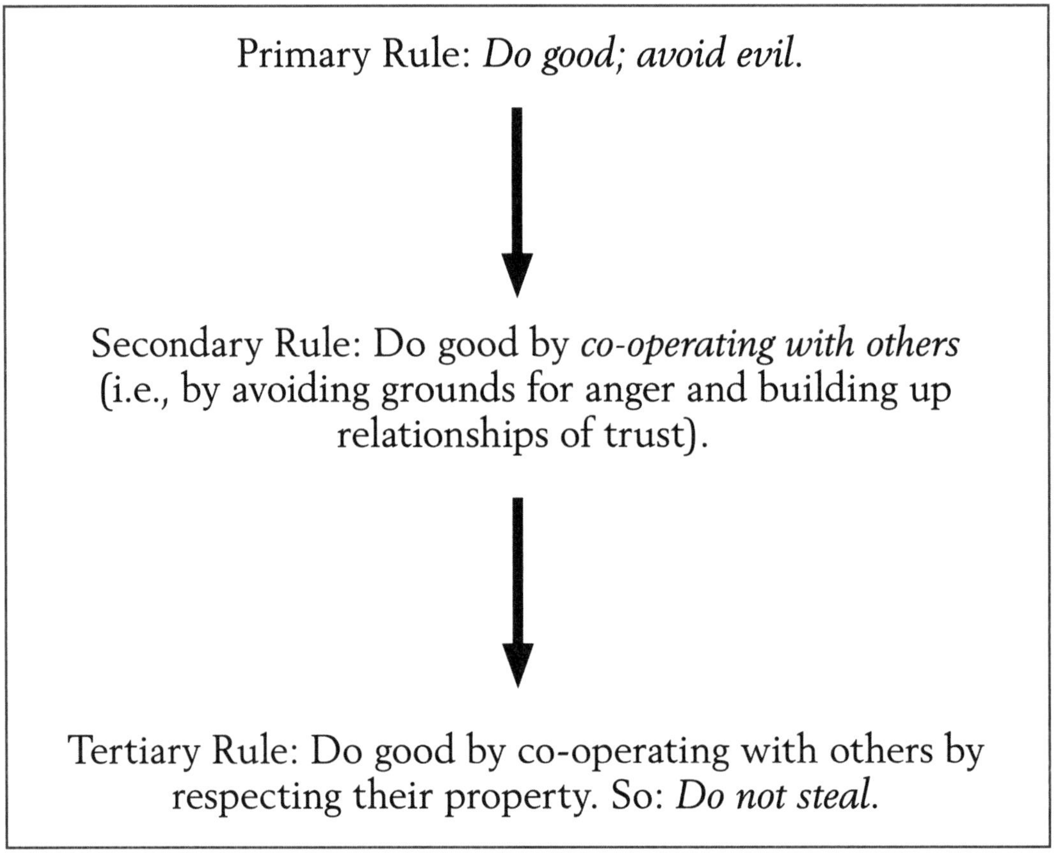

Primary Rule: *Do good; avoid evil.*

Secondary Rule: Do good by *co-operating with others*
(i.e., by avoiding grounds for anger and building up
relationships of trust).

Tertiary Rule: Do good by co-operating with others by
respecting their property. So: *Do not steal.*

Figure 6.3 Different Levels of Natural Law

stealing. He observes, 'If the need be so manifest and urgent, that it . . . must be remedied by whatever means be at hand . . . then it is lawful for a man to succor his own need by means of another's property, by taking it either openly or secretly: nor is this properly speaking theft or robbery'.[71] If someone can only save themselves (or their children) by taking bread that 'belongs' to someone else; this is their right and their prerogative. So, according to Thomas, Jean Valjean did not do anything wrong. He did not even steal.

Thomas claims that 'stealing' to save oneself from 'imminent danger' is not stealing.

Consider then a second example. Suppose I am being chased by a murderer and I happen upon a parked car with the keys in the ignition. I jump inside and use it to escape my pursuers. Normally, taking someone else's car would be stealing. In this case, however, I have a right to the car because it is the only way I can save my life. Taking it is not stealing. Strange circumstances may call for exceptional measures. This is what casuistry is about: applying general rules to very specific and sometimes perplexing cases.

Thomas isolates and identifies a mental capacity that he calls equity as the virtue associated with casuistry. Borrowing an example from Plato, he explains that:

[s]ince human actions, with which laws are concerned, are composed of contingent [circumstances that] are innumerable in their diversity, it was not possible to lay down rules of law that would apply to every single case. Legislators in framing laws attend to what commonly happens: . . . if the law be applied to certain cases it will frustrate the equality of justice and be injurious to the common good. . . . Thus the law requires deposits to be restored, because in the majority of cases this is just. Yet it happens sometimes to be injurious—for instance, if [as Plato suggests] a madman were to put his sword in deposit, and demand its delivery while in a state of madness, or if a man were to seek the return of his [sword] in order to fight against his country. On these and like cases it is [as Plato points out] bad to follow the law, and it is good to set aside the letter of the law and to follow the dictates of justice and the common good. This is the object of . . . equity. Therefore it is evident that [equity] is a virtue.[72]

Thomas readily makes use of examples and arguments from earlier philosophers such as Plato and Aristotle. In a discussion of legal matters, Aristotle had already acknowledged the need for a recognition of exceptions to the letter of the law. Aristotle explains, 'all law is universal but about some things it is not possible to make a universal statement which shall be correct. In those cases, . . . the law takes the usual case, though it is not ignorant of the possibility of error. . . . And this is the nature of the equitable, a correction of law where it is defective owing to its universality'.[73]

We should emphasize that Thomas does not believe that moral laws are truly defective. It is not that there is something wrong with moral law; it is that morality applies to endlessly diverse human experience. Knowing how to

properly apply moral law to peculiar circumstances is not the same as breaking it. Think of each moral rule as an abbreviation. A law like 'keep your promises' is a terse expression of a large and subtle moral understanding that has been poured into only three words. This is useful; it is easier to remember three words than to remember a technical treatise about the nature and limits of promise-keeping. But moral law cannot stand on its own; it must be backed up by some wider understanding. In unusual cases, this may lead to behaviour that appears, at first glance, to break the moral law. Such violations of moral law are, according to Thomas, only skin-deep. A proper understanding of the moral law leaves room for unusual situations. It is not enough to know what we are to do; we need to know when and how we are to do it.

Thomas views equity as a part of prudence. He borrows the technical term *gnome* from Aristotle, to refer to this specific virtue. Whereas Aristotle uses this term to refer to the sound but untheoretical judgment of old people, Thomas uses it to refer to that good discernment 'which concerns judgment in matters of exception to the law'.[74] There is, of course, a connection between the two uses of the term. Older people have a lot of experience. They are more practised at adapting the requirements of morality to diverse and even extreme situations. So it makes sense to say that the moral wisdom they possess is what is needed for equity.

What should we do when we find ourselves in situations we are uncertain about? Thomas recommends that we should return to the very first principles of natural law. He observes, 'Now it happens sometimes that something has to be done which is not covered by [more specific] rules of actions. . . . Hence it is necessary to judge of such matters according to

---

✒ Applied Philosophy Box 6.6 ✒

Traffic Signs Can Make Streets Dangerous

This article was written after a cyclist in Toronto was killed in an altercation with a motorist.

Here's what's scary. The North American approach to regulating traffic, rules that are supposed to ensure safety, may do just the opposite . . . Compared with most places in Europe, North American cities are crammed with traffic lights and signs telling us what we can and can't do . . .

That's the subtext every time a driver races through the intersection on a green light and honks loudly at any pedestrian who has lingered too long in crossing.

It's there when a cyclist blocks an entire lane or a pedestrian marches onto a crosswalk without checking to see whether an oncoming car or cyclist can safely stop in time.

John Staddon, a professor of psychological and brain sciences at Duke University who's lately been turning his attention to traffic, argues that the plethora of signs is actually the key reason North American roads are more dangerous than European ones. We look to signs to give us instruction . . . rather than making decisions based on the actions of other drivers, pedestrians and cyclists. . . .

An experiment now sweeping Europe is the removal of as many signs as possible, and sometimes even sidewalks. It seems to be working. In some neighbourhoods that have tried this approach, pedestrian accidents have fallen by 40 per cent . . .

Would Toronto's streets be safer and more civil with fewer signs and a greater reliance on the collective judgment of drivers, cyclists and pedestrians? It's possible.

This editorialist is arguing that a mechanical reliance on traffic laws and signs leads to more accidents. Instead of teaching people to mechanically apply traffic laws as expressed on road signs, we should cultivate a sensitivity to individual circumstances. This is to argue for a greater reliance on the virtue of 'equity'. Explain.

Source: Kenneth Kidd, 'Traffic Signs Can Make Streets Dangerous.' *Toronto Star*, http://thestar.com/, 5 September 2009.

---

higher principles'.[75] Higher principles here means more general principles. Thomas is recommending that we return to the secondary rules or even the first rule of natural law to clear up confusion. Whatever happens, we must always act in accordance with the first and most general rule of all: 'Do good and avoid evil'. This one rule has primacy.

Can Natural Law Change?

We need to explore one final issue relating to natural law: can natural law change? Is morality fixed forever, or can it morph into differ-

ent and perhaps even contradictory forms, as some relativists would have it? Thomas distinguishes between two possible kinds of changes. He believes that although we cannot *subtract* anything substantial from the content of morality, we can, over time, come to a better understanding of the difference between right and wrong. So we can *add* new moral rules to natural law.

Thomas explains:

A change in the natural law may be understood in two ways. First, by way of addition. In this sense nothing hinders the natural law from being changed: since many things for the benefit of human life have been added over and above the natural law, both by the Divine law and by human laws. Secondly, a change in the natural law may be understood by way of subtraction, so that what previously was according to the natural law, ceases to be so. In this sense, the natural law is altogether unchangeable in its first principles: but in its [tertiary] principles, which . . . are certain detailed proximate conclusions drawn from the first principles, . . . it may be changed in some particular cases of rare occurrence, through some special causes hindering the observance of such precepts.[76]

Thomas's basic intuitions here seem plausible. Let us consider an obviously immoral act, say torturing people for the fun of it. We all agree that this is wicked behaviour. Let us express this consensus as a moral rule: 'Don't torture people for the fun of it'. It does not seem possible that this moral law could ever change. This is what Thomas means when he claims that substantial moral principles cannot, for the most part, be subtracted from moral law. On the other hand, there can be progress in moral understanding. If slavery was once widely accepted, civilization has come to a general consensus (for good reasons) that slavery is immoral. We could articulate this insight as a moral rule: 'Don't keep slaves.' So there is a new moral intuition, now obvious, but which was not obvious at a certain point in history. This is what Thomas means when he claims that new moral truths can be added to the natural law. (It would, in fact, be better to say that we are not adding to moral law but recognizing something that was overlooked by previous generations.)

Thomas believes that morality derives ultimately from a perfectly good, unchangeable God. Even if human nature were to change, this would not alter the first principles of morality. If human beings were to evolve into cruel animals that mistreat one another—this would not make cruelty moral. It would only turn human beings into an immoral species. (Such speculation does not, in any case, seem germane to the present task, which is development of a morality for human beings.) Thomas's general point is that the most fundamental principles of natural law, as we know them, cannot conceivably change.

Modern Thomist Jacques Maritain, who played a role in formulating the United Nations' Universal Declaration of Human Rights (1948), provides a new exegesis of Thomas's original doctrine intended to leave room for the idea of progress in morals. Maritain posits an intermediary category of moral law between natural law and human law that he calls *jus gentium* or the common law of nations. Maritain writes, 'The natural law is known through inclination; the law of nations is known through the conceptual exercise of the human reason (considered not in such and such an individual, but in common civilized humanity)'.[77] Maritain explains, in an interesting way, how something could be added to our shared moral consciousness. Theoretical discussion among different ethnic or religious groups can lead to a better recognition of aspects of natural law that were overshadowed or overlooked in the past such as the injustice of slavery, the equality of women, the importance of individual freedom, the necessity of environmental protection, and the like.

I have provided an overall view of Thomas's account of natural law. Recent writers in the Thomist tradition such as Germain Grisez, Joseph Boyle, and John Finnis replace Thomas's original account of the primary and secondary inclinations with seven self-evident human goods. These include, in Finnis's formulation, life, knowledge, play, beauty (aesthetic experience), sociability, practical reasonableness, and religion. On this revised account, to do good and avoid evil is to promote *all* these incommensurable values, all of which are considered necessary for human flourishing.

On the Principle of Double Effect

Let's turn now to a more specialized aspect of Thomas's moral theory. What has been called 'the principle of double effect' is not restricted to natural law theory. It has been used by moralists of all stripes. Still, Thomas is credited with introducing this way of thinking in his discussion of self-defense in the *Summa*. We will use the term 'mortal self-defense' to describe the case where someone kills someone else (or at least tries to kill someone else) in self-defense. As we have already seen, mortal self-defense is a problematic issue in morality. In cases of extreme duress, either I kill my assailant or my assailant kills me. Either way, someone dies. There is an uncontroversial moral rule: 'Thou shalt not kill' (which can be derived from the value of human life, the need for peaceful co-existence, and other requirements about justice). Still, mortal self-defense requires that we deliberately kill someone else to save ourselves. Is this wrong? Does this deliberate destruction of a human life run counter to the natural law? How are we to make moral sense of such situations?

Only an extreme passivist would consider mortal self-defense immoral. The idea that one would accept violent death without protecting oneself is usually regarded as a either a supererogatory act, an act of nonobligatory moral heroism, or, at the other extreme, as a blameable act of quietism (the 'doing nothing' syndrome). The overwhelming majority of thoughtful people would consider mortal self-defense an acceptable act and perhaps even a moral obligation. Thomas agrees, suggesting that such acts are permissible (and obligatory), granted that certain conditions are met.

What happens in the criminal courts when it comes to self-defense is instructive in this connection. Courts generally rely on some sort of 'reasonable man' criterion to identify acceptable acts of self-defense. In short, we can do what a reasonable person would do to defend ourselves but no more. In other words, we can meet force with similar force. If you hit me with a sledgehammer, I can defend myself with a sledgehammer; if, however, you hit me with a feather, I cannot defend myself with a sledgehammer. I must use only 'reasonable force' in defending myself. Thomas, who has a legal mind, invokes a similar principle. He explains, 'An act may be rendered unlawful, if it be out of proportion to the end. Wherefore if a man, in self-defense, uses more than necessary violence, it will be unlawful: whereas if he repel force with moderation his defense will be lawful'.[78] If killing my assailant is the only way to save my life, this is permissible. But if some less forceful response will work just as well—e.g., maiming him, frightening him, running away—I must use one of these alternative methods. I must try, if possible, not to kill my assailant. But mortal self-defense is, as a last resort, morally acceptable.

Thomas believes that we have a special responsibility for preserving our own lives. (We are most responsible for what belongs to us.) Thomas advises, 'Nor is it necessary for salvation that a man omit the act of moderate self-defense in order to avoid killing the other man, since one is bound to take more care of one's own life than of another's'.[79] Assuming that we are innocent, we have at least some reason to prefer saving our lives over that of an assailant, for the assailant is doing something seriously wrong. Still, this does not change the fact that the act of self-protection will necessitate an act of deliberate killing. How is this excusable?

In arguing for self-defense, Thomas elaborates, in seminal form, the **doctrine of double-effect**. He explains: 'Nothing hinders one act from having two effects, only one of which is intended, while the other is beside the intention. . . . Accordingly the act of self-defense may have two effects, one is the saving of one's life, the other is the slaying of the aggressor. Therefore this act, since one's intention is to save one's own life, is not unlawful, seeing that [self-preservation] is natural.'[80] In other words, if you kill your assailant unwillingly—as a necessary but intrinsically repugnant last resort—we should consider this, first and foremost, as an attempt to save your life and only incidentally as an act of homicide. It is as if you were forced *against your will* to kill another human being. We should not hold this against you because this is not what you wanted to do. What you wanted—saving your life—was a moral, indeed commendable, act, which is how we should interpret your actions.

Clearly, this case calls for some subtle casuistry (in the technical, nonpejorative sense). Thomas's original approach has been formalized in a list of five conditions that an act with two effects must be morally acceptable. An act that has both good and bad effect is moral if:

1. the main action (understood as an intention directed toward a goal) is good or at least morally acceptable;

2. the good effect, not the bad effect, is the one that is truly intended;

3. there is a serious enough reason for allowing the bad effect to happen;

4. there is no other better way of solving the problem; and

5. the bad effect is not used as a means to the good effect.

As we shall see, these conditions overlap somewhat. Let us apply, then, these five formal criteria to an act of mortal self-defense:

1. Thomas believes that the main goal of the agent determines the nature of the act. If you are principally intent on saving yourself, this defines the act. What kind of act is it? It is an act of self-defense. But the act of defending yourself in order to save your life is moral. So the act passes criterion 1.

2. You must intend the good effect, not the bad effect. Assuming that you are not using the situation as an excuse to kill someone else, that the death of the assailant really is a regrettable side-effect, that you really are focused on saving your own life, then the act passes criterion 2.

3. There has to be a serious enough reason for allowing the bad effect. In the case of mortal self-defense, your life is in imminent danger, so you have a serious enough reason for permitting the bad effect, the killing of another person. So the act passes criterion 3.

4. There must be no better way of resolving the situation. Assuming that this is a last resort, that there is no other way of saving yourself, that you must kill the assailant or die, the act passes criterion 4.

5. You cannot use the bad effect as a *means* to the good effect. This is a more complicated requirement. We explain the issue further below. For the moment, simply note that chronology is important. The bad effect can

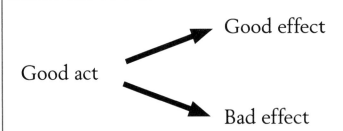

Good act

Good effect

Bad effect

A: The structure of an act that *obeys* the fifth criterion of the doctrine of double effect.

Bad 'effect'   Good 'effect'

B: The structure of an act that *violates* the fifth criterion of the doctrine of double effect. The bad 'effect' (not really an effect) becomes a means to the good effect.

Figure 6.4 Doctrine of Double Effect, Fifth Criterion

not precede the good effect. We cannot use a *prior* bad effect as a means to a *subsequent* good effect. The good and bad effect must both happen *after* the main aact (what the person is trying to do). In the case of mortal self-defence, however, I defend myself (a good act)—and the good effect that follows. But this good effect is regrettably accompanied by a bad effect—the assailant dies. One is not using a bad act here as a means to a good end. One is using a good act (of self-preservation) as a means to a good end, which is accompanied by a bad effect.

This is a quick example of how to calculate the moral permissibility of an act with a bad effect using the doctrine of double-effect. Because mortal self-defense satisfies all five criteria, a philosopher such as Thomas would deem it morally acceptable even though it produces the bad effect of homicide.

But we need to examine, more closely, the all-important fifth criterion of the doctrine of double effect. Thomas (like other mainstream philosophers) believes that we are not permitted to use a bad means to a good effect. Suppose, to use a conspicuously different example, I hear a rumour that you want to kill me. So I plot your murder in order to protect my life. I hide in a grocery store and shoot you as you are buying milk for your children. In this case, I am using a bad act—your murder—as a means to a good effect—the preservation of my life. The bad 'effect' precedes the good effect. So the act conforms to alternative B rather than to alternative A in Figure 6.4. It violates the fifth criterion of the doctrine of double-effect and is, thus, morally unacceptable.

Let us compare, more closely, morally acceptable and unacceptable acts of lethal self-defense. In the first case, I am forced to kill someone when I am defending myself. In the second case, I kill someone beforehand because I think they *may* kill me. I never get to the point where self-defense is needed. I act in anticipation so as to avoid any situation that would require mortal self-defense. These are obviously not equivalent situations. Defending myself is morally good. Committing murder beforehand is evil. We can use vigorous self-defence but not murder as a means to a good effect. Vigorous self-defence may result in the assailant's death. But it is not a bad means. It is a good means that produces (a good and) a bad effect.

The final, fifth criterion of the doctrine of double effect relies on a familiar moral idea: *the end does not justify the means*. If we were to permit individuals to use immoral means to good ends, moral havoc would ensue. We can always find a way to justify our immoral acts, large and small, by positing some attractive future consequence. This is a favourite ploy of Aristotle's self-indulgent man. Imagine the following brief conservations:

1. Question: Why are you always late for work?
    Answer: Scientific studies show that we all need our sleep. I have bad nights. If I don't come to work rested, there may be an accident. Safety comes first.

2. Question: Why did you steal the money?
    Answer: I thought it was important that he learn, once and for all, that he can't leave his wallet unattended. It's better for him that he learns his lesson now. I didn't really want the money. The important things was to teach him something.

3. Question: Why did you murder him?
    Answer: He was a criminal; he would have inevitably killed more people. Society is better off rid of him. People will thank me. Think of all the innocent lives I have saved!

You will note that the same strategy is at work in each case. The agent justifies something inherently wrong (tardiness, stealing, assault, murder) by pointing to some attractive future consequence. But this is a facile way of justifying immoral actions, a handy way of excusing ourselves. If we accept this kind of reasoning, the clever arguer will be able to justify any immoral action by pointing to some possible good result. This would be tantamount to getting rid of morality altogether. (We will revisit this issue when discussing utilitarianism.) The final, fifth criterion of the doctrine of double-effect provides an obstacle to this kind of rationalization. No doubt, it would be so much easier if we were able to make exceptions for ourselves and act immorally on this or that occasion. But Thomas, like the earlier tradition, argues that we must always act morally. As we have already mentioned in connection with Aristotle, individuals under duress may resort to immoral means. We may be able to forgive such behaviour, but it is not, strictly speaking, moral. We discuss this issue further in Chapter 9.

If Thomas believes that mortal self-defense, within reasonable limits, is morally legitimate, he also believes that police officers and soldiers who kill others in the line of duty are a special case. They are engaged in a legitimate form of self-defense on behalf of community as a whole. Police officers and soldiers are blameless as long as they are acting reasonably, for a just cause, and not out of private animosity. Here again, we could use a formal method like the principle of double-effect to explain the moral permissibility of police or military actions. As long as law enforcement is not an excuse to kill people (in some countries it is), as long as these representatives of the state really are enforcing the law (a moral act), their behaviour is morally acceptable. We leave it to the reader to apply the doctrine of double effect to such situations.

The doctrine of double-effect does not only apply, of course, to cases of mortal self-defence. Consider, very briefly, other examples of acts with bad consequences that would be permitted by the doctrine of double-effect. Suppose a soldier in wartime deliberately falls on a grenade to protect his companions. This is almost the opposite of self-defence. There is an obvious good effect here—the companions are saved—and an obvious bad effect—the solider dies (from self-inflicted wounds). Is this a moral act according to the principle of double-effect? Consider it in light of all five criteria.

1. This is not an act of suicide. The soldier's principle aim is not to kill himself but to save his comrades. But saving other people's lives is a morally good act. So the act passes the first criterion.
2. The soldier does not want to die. The good effect is the one intended. So the act passes the second criterion.
3. Clearly, saving lives is a serious enough reason. So the act passes the third criterion.

4. Presumably, there was no alternative solution. So the act passes the fourth criterion.
5. (One cannot use the bad 'effect' as a *means* to the good effect.) A good act—trying to protect others—was *followed* by a good and a bad effect—saving the bystanders' lives and the soldier's death. So the act passes the fifth criterion. (Note that this is not the same as a soldier who commits suicide and inadvertently saves lives. How one defines the act is crucial. More on this below.)

So the act is a morally permissible act.

One often encounters double-effect reasoning in the field of medicine, which regularly deals with life-and-death situations. If, for example, your leg is infected with flesh-eating disease, doctors may have to amputate. This surgical intervention has a good and bad effect: the disease is cured but you lose your leg. We will leave it to the reader to apply the double-effect procedure to this morally acceptable case. In a more controversial vein, it is generally accepted in debates over euthanasia that there is a difference between giving someone medication to ease pain even though it shortens their life span and killing them to ease the pain. In the first case, we use a good means (medically easing pain) that produces a good effect (elimination of pain) and a bad effect (a shorter life-span for the patient). In the second case, we use a bad means (killing another human being) to produce a good effect (ending suffering). Again, readers can apply the five-step approach to such issues on their own.

On the Internal and External Structure of Voluntary Action

Virtue ethics evaluates the whole person. A Greek concept like *eudaimonia* proposes a value judgment about an entire life. A law-like approach to morality, on the other hand, forces us to consider discrete acts as the unit of evaluation. This is inevitably artificial. The individual acts that make up a human life are not marbles in a bag; they are beads on the same string, or, better yet, they are the string. They are connected to one another in some seamless fashion. If then we are to use a moral law approach, we must first divide a human life into individual acts for evaluation.

Let each human act correspond to an individual act of intention. In effect, one decision = one act. Obviously, larger decisions may be composed of countless smaller ones. If, for example, someone were to commit premeditated murder, the murderer would have to select the victim, decide when and where to commit the murder, determine what weapon to use, how to dispose of the body, what alibi to use, and so on. Nonetheless, these smaller acts would all be joined into a single act characterized, so to speak, by one over-arching (or *under*-arching) intention: the act of murder in question. This evil aim would set in motion a whole series of decisions that could all be considered together for the purposes of moral evaluation. The one decision—to murder *X*—would join all these individual acts together into a single, unified episode.

Thomas believes that morality is ultimately about intention: 'Good and evil are essential[ly] differences . . . of the will.'[81] He elaborates a general theory of human action, distinguishing first between human and animal behaviour. Thomas believes that only human beings can be moral because they possess 'perfect knowledge' of their own intentions. Animals, he claims, possess only 'imperfect knowledge' of what they are doing.[82] This description of human knowledge seems an exaggeration. We

do things for many different reasons, some of them obscure and inaccessible. Gaining perfect knowledge of why we do things would be a daunting task. Suffice it to say that human acts are *sufficiently* voluntary to qualify for moral status in so far as they involve a conscious decision by an agent who has the mental capacities for distinguishing between right and wrong. Because animals (presumably) do not understand the difference between right and wrong and because they act on instinct, their acts are insufficiently voluntary to be evaluated morally.

Thomas goes on to distinguish between **human acts** and 'acts by human beings'. Human acts involve deliberate choice. Acts made by a human being may or may not involve choice. For example, when you digest your dinner, this is the act performed by a human being, but it is not a 'human act'. Thomas writes, 'If [the act] does not proceed from deliberate reason . . . as when a man strokes his beard, . . . such an action, properly speaking, is not moral or human. . . . It will be indifferent, as standing apart from . . . moral actions'.[83] It goes without saying, then, that morality only pertains to human acts that require choice. We will restrict our present discussion, then, to 'human acts'.

Thomas organizes discussion about human acts into two separate orders or categories. Issues connected with the agent's purpose belong to the **order of intention**; issues connected with what physically happens belong to the **order of execution**. An example may help. Suppose you watch a lumberjack as he chops down a tree. There are two distinguishable aspects to this act. On the one hand, you can see what is physically happening: someone of a certain shape and size is swinging an axe until the tree falls to the ground in a certain way. Everything observable here relates to the order of execution. On the other hand, you cannot see the intention of the man with the axe. You can surmise what his motivation is, but you cannot observe his intention directly. All that is going on inside the man's mind relates to the order of intention. To fully understand what is happening, we need to evaluate both aspects of human behaviour.

Understanding the order of execution is a matter of careful observation. When it comes to knowing what someone's intention is, the situation is more complicated. For Thomas, only God knows for sure what goes on inside the mind: 'Man looks at the outward appearance, but the Lord looks at the heart.'[84] All we can do is observe what other people do and *infer* their intentions. We must, like detectives, reconstruct on the basis of the physical evidence the reasons behind the act. We can make a more than reasonable conjecture, but

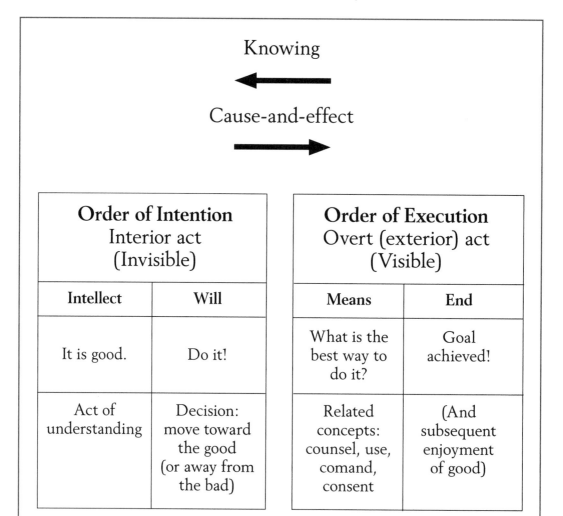

Figure 6.5 The Internal and External Structure of a Human Act

we can never know for sure. That is just the way things are; as human beings, we must rely on our best knowledge of other people's intentions, not on absolute certitude.

Thomas models the structure of human action. In the case of voluntary acts, intention comes before execution. We settle on a goal, then try to achieve it. When it comes to moral evaluation, however, we must move in the opposite direction. First, we observe what is physically happening; and second, we infer the intention. The direction in action is from intention to execution; the direction in evaluation is from execution to intention. Figure 6.5 depicts the structure of a human act; the reader can consult the diagram whenever helpful.

The order of intention has to do with what happens inside the mind. Thomas divides the mind into two parts. The *intellect* is the power of understanding that evaluates of things; the *will* is a rational power that is able to initiate and sustain action in a chosen direction. In any voluntary act, two things must happen: the intellect first identifies something as good; the will then pushes the subject toward the good. If the will provides the impetus for movement, the intellect determines where that movement is directed. Thomas regards the activity of the intellect and the will as two necessary components that, taken together, constitute an intention. In other words, an intention = an act of intellect + a movement of will. We cannot have a moral or an immoral act without intention.

Thomas further distinguishes between **volitions** and 'intentions'. A volition is an act of intellect minus an act of will. On their own, volitions are not morally culpable. Suppose, for example, that someone hurts me, and I spontaneously think to myself, 'I would kill him if I could!' This is a simple volition; Thomas would

not consider it as an immoral act, for it is missing an act of will. If, on the other hand, I were to run out and buy a gun to accomplish this goal, this would be an immoral act because the thought has been translated into action by a (culpable) act of will. In Thomas's system, volitions do no qualify as actions. Action requires an exercise of will. When we start to put our ideas into practice, this demonstrates that we have *decided* on a course of action. And this is where moral evaluation (usually) begins.

Consider next, what Thomas means by 'the order of execution'. Thomas, like Aristotle, divides the physical execution of an act into means and end. We implement the means so as to achieve and enjoy the end. Suppose I decide to have a glass of chocolate milk. I identify chocolate milk as good (an act of intellect) and so I *decide* to get a glass from the refrigerator (an act of will). Taken together this is an **intention**. My actual getting up out of my chair, opening the refrigerator door, and pouring out a glass: these are the means to my end. In drinking the chocolate milk, I attain my end. Take this example as an illustration for a successful human act. First, the intellect identifies something as good: chocolate milk. Then the will initiates action. I *decide* to have a glass of chocolate milk. Then I do whatever is necessary to achieve my goal. And finally, I enjoy the result. Thomas believes that this basic pattern applies to all successful human acts: the intellect understands the value of things; the will decides the goal; we act to implement the means and so come to enjoy the goodness of the end.

In the example of the glass of chocolate milk, the means are straightforward. But sometimes, there may be many ways of achieving one's purpose. Thomas writes that **counsel** (good deliberation) helps us choose the right means. (Think of high school *counsel*lors; their role is to help students choose the right *means* to their future success.) If we follow good counsel, we will choose the best, most efficient strategy for accomplishing our purposes.

Thomas also points out that we *use* many things as instruments in accomplishing our goals. If I am attacked by a rabid dog, I may use a stick to beat it off. If I am lost in the wilderness, I may use my memory to find my way home. In the first case, I use something physical as an instrument; in the second case, I use my memory, something purely mental. Thomas points out that we use our minds, our bodies, our possessions, our material objects, our friends, money, technology—indeed, anything in our power—to achieve our ends. He defines *prudence* as the art of commanding all the instruments at our disposal so as to achieve a morally good end.[85]

In his discussion of moral psychology, Thomas also discusses the role of **consent**. He is not concerned here with agreements between human beings but with the ways in which we consent to (or co-operate with) evil. He argues, most importantly, that we cannot use a bad means to a good end (the fifth criterion of the doctrine of double-effect) because anyone who chooses a bad means has already consented to evil. Morality requires that we never consent to immorality; that is, that we never choose bad means to a good end. Thomas's probing analysis of the structure of human actions provides the descriptive basis for a more in-depth moral evaluation.

On the Three Moral Criteria of a Good Action

Thomas believes that human acts are basically good. He identifies four sources of goodness in a successful human act. The first source of goodness is metaphysical rather than moral. Thomas believes that existence, in any shape or form, is better than nonexistence. Even immoral acts exist. So even they possess a certain metaphysical goodness. But this is not enough to qualify as *moral* goodness. Let us turn, then, to Thomas's threefold criteria of moral goodness.

Thomas writes that a moral act has goodness (1) 'according to its species' (i.e., it must be the right kind of act); (2) 'from its end' (i.e., it must be an expression of good intention); and (3) 'from its circumstances'[86] (i.e., it must provide a proper fit with the specific context). Fully moral behaviour must be good in all three ways. Immorality happens when something goes wrong, when something breaks down in the normal machinery of human behaviour. An immoral act is, then, a defective act. A single defect makes for a morally imperfect act. Let us consider then each criterion of moral goodness separately.

1. A Moral Act Must Belong to the Right 'Species'

Thomas thinks we can identify the *species* of an act much like a biologist identifies species of living things. The species of an act is not solely determined by the agent's intention (although this plays a role). What is objectively going on has to do with the way the precise physical gestures fit together into a coherent whole. People do many different things: they write books, play checkers, go fishing, give to charity, cheat on exams, commit arson, and so on. These acts are organized in characteristic ways. Suppose you are knitting a sweater. Even if you can knit while asleep or in a trance, what your hands are busy about is producing a sweater. This, then, is the species of this act: knitting a sweater. Determining exactly what an agent is doing may require detailed observation.

If there are many species of human action, Thomas does not set out to provide a complete taxonomy of possible acts. (This may be impossible, given the limitless variety of human behaviour.) He is content to point out that the moral evaluation of individual acts must always include an appraisal of the species of the act. Some species of acts are good; some are bad. Consider the act of nursing the sick. This is a good thing to do. Perhaps there are circumstances or intentions that could conceivably make nursing the sick immoral, but there is something good about the act to start with. Considered in and of itself, it is a good act. There are, on the other hand, acts that are, from the outset, inescapably bad. Consider rape. Intentions or circumstances could never turn rape into a good act. Rape is a bad species of act. Once you identify an act as rape, you have already condemned it. In morally evaluating individual acts then, we must include some consideration of whether the species in question is good or bad (or morally neutral).

Thomas observes that determining the species of an act is not a matter of degree or quantity: 'More or less does not change the species.'[87] Consider stealing. Stealing is stealing. Thomas writes, 'Wherefore to take what belongs to another in a large or small quantity, does not change the species of the sin'.[88] Stealing $5 from a woman's purse may be a lesser sin than stealing $1,000, but both acts belong to the same species. The difference is a matter of degree, not of *kind*. Thomas continues: 'Nevertheless [the quantity stolen] can aggravate or diminish the sin.'[89] Any act that belongs to a bad species, then, is a bad act. It may be a more or less serious instance of bad-

ness, but nothing can turn a bad species of act into a good species of act.

2. A Moral Agent Must Have a Good Intention

As we have already explained, we can divide the structure of an act into an internal and external component. The internal structure of the act, what happens inside the mind, is composed of the intention; the external structure of the act, what happens outside the mind, is composed of a physical event in the world. Thomas's second criterion, that a moral agent must have a moral intention, has to do with what is happening inside the mind. Let us consider, then, the role of *intention* as the second source of moral goodness.

We cannot fully evaluate an act by examining only outward appearances. We also have to evaluate the internal motivation. Thomas brings up an example of what he calls 'a truthful lie.' Suppose someone sets out to deliberately tell a lie, which, by pure accident, turns out to be the truth. Suppose, for example, I were to tell my next-door neighbour that you stole her bicycle, believing this was untrue and hoping to cause a ruckus, but my allegation turned out to be true. Would this still be a lie? Thomas claims that it still counts as a lie: 'Even if what one says [in such circumstances] be true, . . . [the act still has] the specific nature of a lie'.[90] I told a lie because I *meant* to tell an untruth. We might argue here about what kind of act this was. Considered in light of what actually happened, it was an instance of truth-telling. Considered in light of my intention, it was a lie. Suffice it to say that a moral act must satisfy all three criteria of moral goodness. A single defect produces a bad act. But an act with a bad intention already has one defect and, by that very fact, is less than fully moral.

Agents with good intentions already do something right; agents with bad intentions already do something wrong regardless of the circumstances or what physically happens. Except for special cases, such as negligence, unintended acts are, so to speak, morally neutral. (Even in the case of negligence, however, one could argue that there is an intention to carelessness, which is tantamount to an inclination to immorality.)

3. A Moral Act Must Fit the Specific Context

Thomas further believes that to be fully moral, the act must fit the context. A good act is a proportionate response to individual circumstances. Any failure to respond to events in the world in an appropriate way will detract from the goodness of human action. Thomas writes, 'If something [is] wanting that is requisite as a due circumstance the action will be evil'.[91] We might compare a moral act to first aid. First aid is only successful when care-givers adapt their actions to the precise nature of the emergency that arises. One does not apply a tourniquet to someone who needs mouth-to-mouth resuscitation. Moral acts, in a similar way, must take into account the needs and challenges posed by the individual circumstance.

In contemporary moral philosophy, some authors have emphasized the moral importance of the consequences that follow an act. (We discuss this modern view in Chapter 9.) Thomas believes that human acts must be evaluated in light of what happens both *before* and *after* the event. Suppose someone were to drive home drunk. The immorality of this act could be linked to a failure to appreciate the bad consequences of drinking and driving. After all, there may be a serious accident. But it could also be linked to a previous event. It is what happened prior to driving the car— this individual's heavy drinking—that makes this an inappropriate and immoral act. Clearly, knowledge of both past and future circumstances plays an important (and overlapping) role in moral evaluation. Suffice it to say that we must consider all relevant circumstances when appraising specific human acts.

On Voluntary, Involuntary, and Non-Voluntary Acts

In moral evaluation, we have to judge, not just the act itself, but the person doing the act. As medieval philosophers and theologians began to realize, we cannot assume that everyone who does a bad act is a bad person, for there are occasions when good people, *because of circumstances beyond their control*, do bad acts. We need to examine, then, the issue of moral responsibility. When can we hold agents responsible for a bad act they have performed?

Contemporary authors often seem to assume that morality is mostly about catching people doing the wrong things. It is about blaming wrongdoers, about holding bad people accountable for the bad they do. But morality, so to speak, goes both ways: it is as much about congratulation and praise as it is about blame. If we blame, condemn, criticize, and even punish those who are responsible for bad acts, we credit, applaud, praise, and congratulate those who are responsible for good acts. There are also instances when individuals *wrongly* feel guilt or shame. In these cases, morality is about lifting the burden of shame; it is about excusing instead of blaming. Thomas provides a carefully thought-through method for ascertaining the degree to which someone can be held accountable for good and bad acts.

We will examine, then, his account of moral responsibility.

Thomas divides things in the world into three categories: (1) inanimate objects that blindly obey the laws of physics, (2) animals who act on instinct, and (3) rational beings (human beings) who choose freely. He explains: 'Some things act without judgment; as a stone moves downwards; and . . . some act from judgment, but not a free judgment; as brute animals. For the sheep, seeing the wolf, judges it a thing to be shunned . . . from natural instinct . . . But man [alone] acts from judgment, . . . not from a natural instinct, but from some act of . . . reason.'[92]

Like the stone, human beings must obey the laws of physics. And like the sheep, humans also (at least sometimes) act on instinct. But humans are also able to reflect about what they do and direct their actions accordingly. This may involve lengthy premeditation, but not always. Deliberate acts may also be done on the spur of the moment. A person who decides to ride a horse does not have to think, 'I will ride a horse'. No, that person simply has to get on the horse and ride. All things being equal, this is a free will decision.

Although we cannot determine all the circumstances of our lives, Thomas believes that we can, to a very large extent, choose how we react to those circumstances. Our lives are filled with free, deliberate, conscious intention. Thomas distinguishes, then, between three kinds of human acts: (1) voluntary acts, (2) involuntary acts, and (3) non-voluntary acts. Most of the time, we are engaged in **voluntary acts**. We choose what we do. This is why it is appropriate to hold agents, who have reached the age of reason, responsible for their behaviour. Unless there is some serious obstacle to free choice, mature agents must be credited or blamed for what they do. There

are, however, exceptional circumstances in which we should not hold such agents responsible for their acts.

Involuntary acts are unintended. This may come about in three different ways: (1) through physical force, (2) through ignorance of the circumstances, and (3) through some mental incapacity. Let us consider each possibility in turn.

1. We may be physically forced to do something we do not want to do. If, for example, you were to hold me down, put a gun in my hand, and force me to pull the trigger, I would not be responsible for any resultant injury. This would be an involuntary act outside my control.

2. Or again, we may be ignorant—not morally ignorant, but ignorant of the circumstances through no fault of our own—and end up doing something we never intended. For example, suppose I was to give your sick mother her daily medication without realizing that you, the beneficiary of her will, had mixed it with deadly poison. I would be ignorant—through no fault of my own—as to what was really going on. If your mother dies as a result, this would not be my fault. My killing your mother would be an involuntary act. I could not be held responsible.

3. Finally, we may be ignorant because our mental or psychological state has been incapacitated—*through no fault of our own*—so as to obscure either the moral knowledge and/or the factual awareness we ordinarily possess. We can call this condition 'induced moral ignorance'. Induced moral ignorance may arise through neurosis, brainwashing, extreme fatigue, narcotics, medication, even sleepwalking. Suppose, to use another simple example, you are a nondrinker unaccustomed to alcohol. And suppose I secretly

---

✍ Applied Philosophy Box 6.7 ✎

Date Rape Drugs

The term 'date rape drug' usually applies to the drugs Rohypnol, Gamma Hydroxy Butyrate (GHB) and Ketamine Hydrochloride. . . . There are many factors that make these drugs desirable to sexual predators. . . . Date rape drugs are easily slipped into drinks and food and are very fast acting. . . . The drugs also make the victim act without inhibition, often in a sexual or physically affectionate way. Like most drugs, date rape drugs render a person incapable of thinking clearly or of making appropriate decisions. This makes for a very passive victim, one who is still able to play a role in what is happening but who will have no clear memory of what happened after-the-fact.

Explain in relation to the three categories of involuntary acts.

Source: 'Date Rape Drugs,' http://teenadvice.about.com, 1 October 2007.

---

spike the nonalcoholic punch at a party with hard liquor so that you end up drunk and fall through the front window. This would have to be classified as an involuntary action, outside your control. I put you in this altered state and I, not you, must bear responsibility for breaking the window.

However they occur—through force, through ignorance, or through mental disturbance—involuntary actions absolve the agent of the moral condemnation that usually attaches to such behaviour because the agent performing them does not intend what happens. Thomas believes, however, that there is a related, third category of acts that we will call **non-voluntary acts**. Non-voluntary acts are blameworthy *even though they are performed in ignorance*. Non-voluntary acts are caused by either (1) negligent ignorance, (2) self-induced ignorance, or (3) concomitant ignorance. Let us consider these three possibilities in turn.

Negligent Ignorance

Negligent ignorance seems self-explanatory. It does not arise from any precise motivation to do wrong, but from a blameworthy carelessness. Suppose, for example, my unattended three-year-old were to fall in the backyard swimming pool and drown. Obviously, I would have saved her had I known she was drowning. She drowned because I did not know what was happening. But this is culpable (i.e., blamable) ignorance. I was ignorant of her plight because I did not take proper care of her. Responsible parents do not leave three-year-olds unattended beside a swimming pool. They make it their business to know, at all moments of the day, what their young children are doing and where they are. I must, therefore, be held responsible for my daughter's death. (This is, to use theological nomenclature, a sin of omission, not a sin of commission. But it is not morally permissible to omit or ignore certain responsibilities. This is then a *non-voluntary* not an involuntary act.)

Negligent ignorance may be a mitigating factor, however, when it comes to the attribution of moral blame and punishment. In the case of negligence, harm happens through inattention or carelessness. Because there is no direct attention to harm, negligence is a lesser degree of immorality than deliberate evil. A person who lets her child drown through negligence is less evil than someone who would *deliberately* drown her child. This is why the criminal courts grant shorter sentences to those guilty of negligent manslaughter than to those guilty of murder.

In some cases, negligence occurs when someone impairs their own mental judgement through voluntary action. When individuals are intoxicated, high on drugs, under medication, or even excessively tired, they may be careless or inattentive in a morally blameworthy way. Someone who knowingly puts themselves in such a state without taking necessary precautions is responsible for any negative consequences that result. Suppose I am a truck driver. I go 14 hours without sleep. I am so tired, I can't think straight. I end up driving the wrong way down a one-way street and run over a child. I didn't mean to hurt the child but I was too tired to pay close attention to the map and the road signs. This is a form of self-induced negligence. My condition of extreme fatigue (produced by my own voluntary actions) reduced my ability to safely navigate the city streets. If I had been wide awake, I would have seen where I was going and made a better decision. This is not a case of immoral motives but of negligence. Although I did not consciously intend to kill the child, I *am* morally responsible for its death as a result of my negligent behaviour. (Obviously, anyone who encourages other agents to put themselves in a morally negligent situation is also responsible, to some degree, for the harmful consequences that occur. If you are my boss, and you threaten to fire me unless I drive for 14 hours straight, you also share some moral—and perhaps some criminal—blame for the accident that results. This does not, however, excuse my giving in to your threats.)

Self-Induced Ignorance for Ulterior Motives

The second category of non-voluntary acts involves a more disturbing form of mental incapacitation: what we can call 'self-induced ignorance for ulterior motives'. In these cases, agents themselves alter their own psychological or mental state so as to *remove* the moral restraints that ordinarily hold them back from any active involvement in evil. The nervous murderer who 'liquors himself up' so that he can accomplish the lethal act would be an example of induced *voluntary* ignorance. Or consider a real and woeful example: the ingestion of mood-altering drugs by soldiers in Africa to remove the usual human inhibitions on savage behaviour (see Box 6.8). Any soldier who voluntarily takes drugs for this purpose is guilty of an induced form of direct voluntary ignorance. (Obviously, individuals who would force, encourage, or facilitate such practices would also be guilty of grievous moral harm, even if they themselves did not individually participate in such acts. We have a responsibility to encourage moral behaviour in other agents, as well as a responsibility to do what we can to prevent, not encourage, the commission of serious evil.)

In the examples of self-induced ignorance for ulterior motives cited in Box 6.8, there is a degree of intention: the agent uses drugs *in order to* facilitate the commission of evil. Agents purposely numb their minds so that evil may follow. Those who act in an addled state are not quite themselves (which is why we have not classified this kind of case as a directly voluntary act). They have deliberately, however, put themselves in a state where they

---

✍ Applied Philosophy Box 6.8 ✍

Child Soldiers in Africa

Children come out of the armed forces scarred and battered all over—both mentally and physi-cally. . . . They have experienced horror beyond belief as well as committed unbelievable atrocities. . . . Addicted to drugs by being forced to use heroin, marijuana, alcohol, and cocaine before battles in order to ward off fear and inhibitions, . . . the physical problems that they suffer are nothing compared to the results of the atrocities that they have committed. What they have done haunts them for the remainder of their lives:

'Before a battle, they would make a shallow cut and put powder in. Afterward, I didn't see any human being having value.' — Alleu Bangaru, 14

'When we caught kamajors (pro-government militiamen) we would mutilate them by parts and dis-play them in the streets. When villagers refused to clear out of an area we would strip them naked and burn them to death. Sometimes we used plastic and sometimes a tire. Sometimes they would partially sever a person's neck and then leave them on the road to die slowly. . . .We gang-raped women, some-times six people at a time. I didn't feel much because I was drugged and was just there for sex.' — Abdul Rahman Kamera, 15

'The (older rebels) would (impale people) when the drugs had taken hold and they wanted to play wicked games.' — Zakaria Turay, 14

There are many such reports. Why are these child soldiers being made to take drugs? Relate to different notions of ignorance. Is this voluntary or involuntary behaviour? Explain.

Source: Carolyn Muir web page, 'Child Soldiers in Africa.' New Trier Township High School, IL, http://nths.newtrier.k12. Il.us/academics/ faculty/muir/africa_project/p7/ChildSoldiers/index.htm, 6 August 2010.

---

are, so to speak, 'out of their minds'. So they must be held accountable for their acts. This is *non-voluntary*, not involuntary behaviour.

Concomitant Ignorance

The third category of non-voluntary acts involves the even more unusual case of **con-comitant ignorance**. We invoke this some-what makeshift category when we want to recognize the role that *involuntary* ignorance plays in an act without, however, excusing or softening our moral condemnation of the participating agents. In such cases, agents are not responsible for their own ignorance, but we still want to hold them responsible for the bad effects that thereby result. There are vari-

ous ways in which this kind of situation can come about.

Thomas brings up the example of parricide: the crime of killing one's father. For Thomas, parricide is even worse than ordinary murder; it is the murder of someone to whom you owe special loyalty. Parricide is a conspicuously vile sort of murder. Suppose then that some-one kills his father without knowing that it is his father. (This is what happens to Oedipus in Sophocles's play, *Oedipus Rex*.) Does the man who kills his father without knowing that it is his father commit murder or parricide? Thomas believes it depends on the criminal's state of mind. If he would have refrained had he known, then he is not guilty of parricide.

If, however, '[his] will be so disposed that he would not [have] restrained from the act . . . even though he recognized his father',[93] he is guilty of parricide. Thomas claims that, in this latter case, the man's ignorance is 'concomitant with the sin'.[94] It accompanies the sin without diminishing his guilt. Such a man is a father-killer. His ignorance is no excuse, for had he known that the victim was his father, he would have killed him anyway.

The issue of concomitant ignorance is complicated by the fact that we cannot see inside the minds of other people. It is not easy to know what someone's intentions would have been under different circumstances. Still, it is important to recognize that there are cases when the ignorance accompanying an act does not eliminate moral responsibility. If, for example, someone kills someone accidentally during the commission of a crime, that person is often held legally responsible for the homicide. Suppose a gang of robbers use dynamite to explode their way into a bank and inadvertently kill the janitor in the process. Perhaps the robbers did not know that the janitor was on the premises. Perhaps they did not intend to kill anyone. In many criminal jurisdictions, this would not be accepted as a sufficient excuse. The robbers would be charged with murder, the underlying idea being that those who deliberately break the law forfeit their right to use ignorance as an excuse. (The message here is clear: don't break the law!) Readers may think of other cases involving concomitant ignorance.

A Thomistic Account of Ignorance

Authors sometimes claim that a *subjectively* moral act may be *objectively* immoral. This is a confusing use of terminology, but these authors do have a point. Suppose, for example, the agent gives the loaded gun to the criminal, thinking that he is an undercover police officer. Although this agent does the objectively wrong thing, one could say that the subjective (or internal) part of the act—the intentions—are above moral reproach. A well-intentioned agent may, through ignorance, unwillingly do wrong. (A moral agent would not knowingly do wrong.) Sometimes we hold agents responsible for not knowing what to do: we say, 'they should have known!' Other times, we do not hold them responsible for their ignorance; we pity them instead. We need to consider, then, the moral status of different types of human ignorance.

Thomas provides a detailed and comprehensive taxonomy of human ignorance, labeling and classifying the different ways in which a human can fail to possess knowledge. His classification scheme, which is depicted in Figure 6.6, is like a detailed, comprehensive map of the different categories of ignorance. Although he may seem, at first glance, to posit a bewildering number of subtle distinctions, each new level of logical analysis follows in a straightforward manner. Keep in mind, Thomas's system has a practical purpose; this is not an exercise in mere theory. The goal is to be able to accurately evaluate specific situations we meet with in our daily lives. We may sometimes find it difficult, due to lack of information, to insert a particular act into one precise category or another. Still, even problematic cases can be situated, in a general way, within Thomas's overall system.

Ignorance and Nescience

When we evaluate an individual act with respect to the voluntary-involuntary-non-

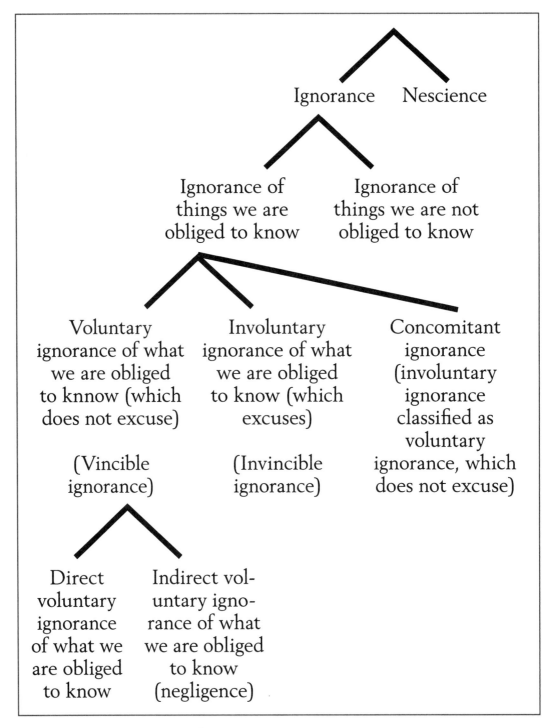

Figure 6.6 Thomas's Account of Ignorance

voluntary distinction (as in the last section), we are trying to answer certain type of question: Did this person freely choose? Was this person forced to act a certain way? Was this a case of voluntary behaviour? In distinguishing between different kinds of ignorance, we are asking a different type of question: What was the mental state of this particular agent? Did some identifiable lack of knowledge play a significant role in the agent's conduct? Can the agent be fairly described as 'not knowing'? What produced this present state of 'not knowing'? Let us turn our attention, then, to this second set of questions.

Thomas, following Aristotle, recognizes the importance of different mental states. In the following treatment, we will focus, like Thomas, on those types of ignorance that are morally blameworthy. Let us begin, then, by defining our terms. Thomas defines human ignorance as a defect (not necessarily a moral defect) in human understanding. Ignorance happens when our human intelligence, for some reason or another, does not know what it can know.

Thomas begins his treatment of different types of ignorance with a broad distinction between (1) ignorance and (2) **nescience**. 'Ignorance differs from nescience', he writes, 'in that nescience denotes mere absence of knowledge. . . . [whereas] ignorance denotes privation of knowledge, i.e. lack of knowledge of those things that one has a natural aptitude to know'.[95] Thomas believes, for example, that human beings cannot access all the knowledge possessed by angels or by God. Not possessing this knowledge is not a defect. It does not count as ignorance but only as nescience. To use a nonreligious example, consider a dog whistle that makes a high-pitched tone the human ear cannot hear. The fact that we cannot hear a dog whistle is not defect in human hearing, for such a feat is beyond the limits of human nature. This is what nescience is like. There are, no doubt, principles and facts beyond any human capacity. Not knowing these things— whatever they are (no one knows!)—is not ignorance. The term *ignorance* refers to not knowing what we have a natural capacity to know. It represents a defect in proper human judgment.

Morality is about what is humanly possible. Nescience is about the humanly impossible. So nescience has no bearing on morality. We cannot be held morally responsible for not knowing what we cannot know. Let us turn now to a consideration of those things we *are* obliged to know.

Ignorance of Things We Are Obliged or Not Obliged to Know

Among those things we can know, Thomas makes a distinction between (1) things 'we are under an obligation to know', and (2) things we are 'not bound to know'.[96] (See the second row in Figure 6.6.) Things we are obliged to know include basic moral principles as well as the necessary practical and theoretical principles that pertain to our station in life. Things we are not obliged to know include certain specialized moral principles as well as the specialized practical and theoretical principles that do not pertain to our own station in life. Let us consider these two categories of obligatory and non-obligatory knowledge in turn.

Thomas thinks we have an obligation to know the most basic moral (and religious) truths. For example, we are all obliged to know that the preservation of human life is good, that charity is a duty, that telling lies is wrong. But we are also obliged to know the moral principles that pertain to our particular station in life. If I am an accountant, a stock-broker, a lawyer, a priest, a prison guard, a parent, or a volunteer on a suicide hotline, I am obliged to know and master the moral requirements that pertain to this special role in society. I may also be morally obliged to know particular theories and facts that pertain to my occupation. If, for example, I were an engineer, I would be *obliged* to know the differential calculus. (Otherwise, how could I be a good engineer?) Or if I were a professor of Russian literature, I might be obliged to know the plot sequence in Tolstoy's *War and Peace*. (Otherwise, how could I be a good professor of Russian literature?) And so on.

The range of things we are obliged to know extends to some perhaps surprising concrete details. Suppose you are driving a car down the street. You are obliged to know if there are cars in front of you or beside you; if there is a light turning yellow; if there is a pedestrian crossing the street. You would be a public menace if you did not make it your business to cultivate knowledge of your physical surroundings. We are not only obliged to know moral principles; we are obliged to know whatever is fitting to the detailed, concrete circumstances of our lives.

Deliberate ignorance of what we are obliged to know is already immoral. But there are great swaths of knowledge we are *not* obliged to know. Thomas sets out the boundaries of what it means to be a minimally decent person. He identifies forms of ignorance that are seriously immoral. It may be good to know many things we are not bound to know, but it is not morally required. Someone who knows all sorts of wonderful facts about the Australian Outback, about ice fishing, about nuclear physics, about Egyptian pharaohs, or French cathedrals may be intellectually or practically virtuous, but

this is not required as a moral minimum. So let us move on and take a brief look at the moral status of different cases of ignorance of things *we are obliged to know*.

Involuntary Ignorance of What We Are Obliged to Know (Which Excuses)

The next three subsections all relate to the third division in Figure 6.6. What we can call 'involuntary ignorance' comes about through no fault of the agent—it is forced on the agent by external circumstances or by other agents. An agent may be blamelessly ignorant for a variety of reasons: insufficient education, neurosis, extreme fatigue, a lack of time for proper decision-making, miscommunication, deception, drugs or alcohol (which have not been misused by the agent), brainwashing, and so on. In the case of involuntary ignorance, when individuals are ignorant *through no fault of their own*, we cannot hold them morally responsible for their condition or for the negative consequences that arise from this condition. (Traditional moralists sometimes referred to involuntary ignorance as 'antecedent ignorance' because it happens *before* the act and not as an outcome of the act. It is a prior condition of the circumstances and is not caused by the actions of the agent. This is why we cannot blame these agents for their ignorance.)

Concomitant Ignorance (Which Does Not Excuse)

We have already discussed concomitant ignorance in our discussion of non-voluntary acts. Concomitant ignorance is a specialized species of involuntary ignorance that, in effect, we decide to treat as a case of blame-worthy voluntary ignorance. (It is an odd, in-between category—hence, its location at one extreme of the third row in the diagram.) Concomitant ignorance accompanies an act without reducing the level of moral blame. We morally condemn the agent even though his or her ignorance is involuntary. Moral theorists usually rely on the concept of concomitant ignorance when dealing with thoroughly evil individuals. We do not allow individuals who actively participate in evil to benefit from the kind of moral reprieve we normally grant individuals who suffer from involuntary ignorance. In cases of concomitant ignorance, we deal with such agents as if they were committing a deliberate act with full knowledge of what they were doing. Unlike usual cases of involuntary ignorance, concomitant ignorance does not eliminate moral blame. And it does not lessen the moral fault. We have already discussed such cases.

Voluntary Ignorance of What We Are Obliged to Know (Which Does Not Excuse): Direct and Indirect

Unlike involuntary ignorance, voluntary ignorance *is* morally culpable. (This is the first category at the third level in the diagram.) This is a vice, a character flaw, and it represents an appropriate occasion for moral blame. (Traditional moralists sometimes called voluntary ignorance 'consequent ignorance' because it is caused by and therefore *consequent* to our own deliberate acts.)

Thomas distinguishes between direct and indirect voluntary ignorance (as in the fourth level of Figure 6.6.) As he explains, 'ignorance is voluntary, either directly, as when a man wishes of set purpose to be ignorant of certain things that he may sin the more freely; or indirectly, as when a man, through stress of work or other occupations, neglects to acquire the knowledge which would restrain him from sin'.[97] We will consider first, the case of direct

voluntary ignorance; and second, indirect voluntary ignorance.

Direct Voluntary Ignorance of What We Are Obliged to Know

Direct voluntary ignorance arises from some purposeful attempt to hide incriminating knowledge from ourselves. We purposely avoid pertinent issues or avert our eyes from important moral or factual questions that naturally come to the surface. Deliberately keeping ourselves in a state of ignorance about things we are obliged to know in this way is itself immoral. Suppose, for example, I decide to go fishing and choose not to inform myself about catch limits so that if I am caught by the game warden with too many fish, I can respond, 'It's not my fault, I didn't know what the limit was'. A sharp-thinking game warden will retort, 'Well, you should have known'. Thomas believes that morality operates on a similar principle. The onus is on us. We are obliged to inform ourselves of both the general and specialized requirements of morality. Any failure to do so is already immoral. If, for example, I strongly suspect that my employees are involved in dishonest business practices, I am obliged to inquire into the matter. If I purposely look the other way, I am directly cultivating a kind of moral ignorance. This strategy of avoidance is itself immoral. Human beings are distressingly capable of avoiding hard questions when their self-interests are at stake.

The case of self-induced moral ignorance for ulterior motives discussed in the previous section would be another example of direct voluntary moral ignorance. When agents take drugs *in order to* obliterate their sense of right and wrong, they are purposely doing something to makes themselves morally ignorant.

Indirect Voluntary Ignorance of What We Are Obliged to Know: Negligence

As we pointed out, direct voluntary ignorance involves a deliberate attempt to avoid moral knowledge. *Indirect* voluntary ignorance, on the other hand, involves negligence or inadvertent ignorance. This happens through laziness, through tiredness, through substance abuse, or through simple inattention. As Thomas explains, 'Sometimes . . . the ignorance . . . is not directly voluntary, but [arises] indirectly or accidentally, as when a man is unwilling to work hard at his studies, the result being that he is ignorant, or as when a man willfully drinks too much wine, the result being that he becomes drunk and indiscreet'.[98] The man who does not study is not aiming at ignorance. He is just lazy. The *indirect* result is ignorance. Again, the man who drinks too much wine is probably not trying to be rude and indiscreet; he is simply enjoying the sensation of being drunk. The *indirect* result is momentary ignorance of etiquette and polite social convention.

Incidents of moral and factual ignorance may result in harmful consequences even when they are not directly willed by the agent. An engineer designing a bridge, for example, may make a mistake that kills many people, not because he planned to kill them but because he neglected his studies and ends up being professionally incompetent. Likewise, the drunkard may assault a stranger, not because he planned to beat up someone but because he was too intoxicated to distinguish between right and wrong. These are ignorant agents in that they do not know what they are obliged to know. The engineer had a professional duty to know about the strength of building materials; the drunkard should have known, in the heat of the moment, about the moral law that forbids

harming other people. Neither the engineer nor the drunkard can legitimately protest, 'It's not my fault; I didn't know'. They *should* have known. We hold such individuals responsible for the harm that inadvertently results from their ignorant behaviour. (The case of driving fatigue discussed in the previous section also involves negligent ignorance. Readers can situate the example within Thomas's theory of human ignorance on their own.)

Indirect voluntary moral ignorance does not excuse. At the same time, it is important to repeat that ignorance due to negligence is less blameworthy than ignorance that is purposefully cultivated. Moral ignorance that arises out of negligence involves an act of omission rather than an act of commission. In the case of direct voluntary ignorance, the agent *deliberately* cultivates moral ignorance in order to participate in evil. This is very bad. In the case of indirect voluntary ignorance, evil arises as an undesired byproduct of other voluntary actions. This is bad, but quite as bad. As Thomas explains, the indirect nature of the condition 'diminishes voluntariness and consequently alleviates the sin'.[99]

Vincible and Invincible Ignorance

Thomas makes a further distinction between **vincible** and **invincible moral ignorance**, which we should briefly mention here. (These categories are not included in the previous diagram.) Although this distinction plays a role in moral theology, we will only consider its moral aspect here. *Vincible moral ignorance* is defined as ignorance that can be overcome through diligence, effort, or study. *Invincible moral ignorance*, as ignorance that 'cannot be overcome', '[that] is not in our power to be rid of'.[100] Thomas believes, perhaps surprisingly, that invincible moral ignorance is not blameworthy. As he observes, 'no invincible igno-rance is a sin'.[101] (We can, more or less, equate 'vincible ignorance' with 'voluntary ignorance' and 'invincible ignorance' with 'involuntary ignorance', in the third level of Figure 6.6.)

Despite his firm religious convictions, Thomas is more tolerant than some of his harsher critics acknowledge. The concept of invincible moral ignorance makes us less judg-mental and more tolerant of other ages and cultures. Suppose someone from the ancient world, let us call him Demetrius, believed in slavery. Does Demetrius's support for slavery count as invincible ignorance? Was it beyond Demetrius's capacities to conceive of the immorality of slavery? This is a good and puz-zling question. Suppose Demetrius was used to slaves; suppose he was not terribly bright; suppose that trusted moral authorities told him slavery was right and good; suppose he treated slaves humanely, and so on. Is this enough to absolve Demetrius from moral guilt? Or should we say that if only he had examined his conscience more rigorously, he would have discovered the moral truth about slavery con-tained in his own heart? Did Demetrius and his fellow ancients deliberately overlook the injustice of slavery, perhaps out of economic self-interest? Was their moral ignorance vin-cible or invincible? We will leave it to readers to puzzle over this conundrum. Keep in mind that although Thomas accepts the reality of invincible moral ignorance, he is not a moral relativist. It is important to emphasize that *invincible ignorance does not turn immorality into morality*. It does *not* lessen the objective immo-rality of the practice under consideration. Any failure to appreciate the evil of slavery counts as moral blindness, even if it is a case of invin-cible blindness. The issue here is should we hold these individuals accountable for their moral ignorance? A moral acceptance of slav-ery remains a glaring defect in moral under-standing even if we accept that some historical individuals were incapable of rising above the prejudices of their age.

✎ Questions for Study and Review ✎

1. What is the Euthyphro problem?
2. Seen from a religious perspective, how does theology reinforce ordinary, secular morality?
3. What is Thomas's definition of virtue? (There are *two* components to his definition.)
4. Thomas believes that all morality begins in and is dependent on which virtue? Explain.
5. Thomas moves from a consideration of each principle virtue to the more specific manifestations of that general character trait. Name three more specific manifestations of the virtues of temperance and fortitude and explain how they differ (slightly) from each other. Do the same for corresponding vices of 'excess' and 'cowardice'.

6. According to Thomas, how are justice and the law related?
7. What are the eight integral parts of prudence? What role does each play?
8. What is Thomas's definition of law? Explain each of the (four) necessary components.
9. What is the relationship between human law and natural law?

10. Does Thomas think that human nature is evil? Explain.
11. List the five criteria that an action must satisfy in order to qualify as legitimate under the doctrine of double effect. Apply to the case of mortal self-defence.
12. What is the 'reasonable man' criterion in law and morality?
13. Using the principle of double effect, explain why Thomas believes that we have the right, when our lives are in danger, to kill someone in self-defense.
14. Evaluate an immoral and moral act according to Thomas's threefold criterion of moral goodness.

15. What is a voluntary act? Give an example.
16. What, in general terms, is an involuntary act? Give an example.
17. What, in general terms, is a non-voluntary act? Give an example.
18. What are the three types of involuntary acts? Give an example of each.
19. What are the three types of non-voluntary acts? Give an example of each.
20. What is the difference between nescience and ignorance?
21. Explain the concept of 'invincible ignorance' using a concrete case that would (in your mind) qualify as an example.

ᕦ Suggestions for Further Reading ᕤ

- Perhaps the best way for the general reader to access the *Summa Theologica* (or, more rigorously, the *Summa Theologiae*) is through the internet version published online by the New Advent site: www.newadvent.org/summa/. This is the Second and Revised Edition, 1920, translation by the Fathers of the English Dominican Province (Online Edition Copyright © 2008 by Kevin Knight).
- For a more recent translation see the bilingual Blackfriars edition: Thomas Aquinas, *Summa theologiae*, 60 volumes, translation, glossaries, etc., Blackfriars (Cambridge, UK; New York: McGraw-Hill, 1964–70s). At the time of writing Alfred J. Freddoso is preparing a new, complete translation of the *Summa* for St. Augustine's Press.

- For a shorter selection of passages from the *Summa* discussing virtue, see: Thomas Aquinas, *Treatise on the Virtues*, John A. Oesterle, trans. (South Bend, IN: University of Notre Dame Press, 1966).
- Jacques Maritain, Natural Law: Reflections on Theory and Practice, edited by William Sweet (South Bend, IN: St. Augustine's Press, 2001).
- For a more technical, specialized but still readable discussion (not from the *Summa*), one could consult: Thomas Aquinas, *Disputed Questions on the Virtues*, E.M. Atkins, Thomas Williams, eds., E.M. Atkins, trans. (Cambridge; New York: Cambridge University Press, 2005).

Chapter Seven

The Contractarians: Thomas Hobbes, John Locke, Jean-Jacques Rousseau, and Karl Marx

> ✏ **Chapter Objectives**
>
> After reading this chapter you should be able to:
> - Explain, in general, what contractarianism is.
> - Describe, compare, and evaluate the specific contributions of the anonymous ancient author, Hobbes, Locke, Rousseau, and Marx to the contractarian tradition.
> - Explain, in relation to individual authors, key concepts such as the social contract, the state of nature, the right of nature, the law(s) of nature, hypothetical agreement, sovereignty, private property, *amour-propre*, natural pity, the general will, alienation, and so on.
> - Explain, in particular, how Hobbes reconciles self-interest and morality; explain the difference between exclusive and two-tiered contractarianism; explain natural duties and obligations.
> - Describe key virtues necessary for a contractually-based morality.

Introduction

In the next three chapters we consider philosophers and theories from the early modern and modern periods: roughly, from 1500–1900. In this chapter, we begin with Thomas Hobbes's account of contractarianism; in the next chapter, we will focus on Immanuel Kant's account of deontology, and finally, in the chapter after that, we will consider versions of utilitarianism and liberalism associated with John Stuart Mill. Authors like Hobbes, Kant, and Mill are Enlightenment (or post-Enlightenment) thinkers, impressed by science, who often denigrate and dismiss—while frequently misunderstanding—the work of previous philosophers. They sometimes assume or imply that earlier ways of looking at morality were superstitious, illogical, or otherwise flawed, and that the old ways of virtue ethics must be replaced with a markedly superior version of moral law theory. Many of these ethnocentric attitudes are reflected in popular culture today.

Modern philosophers, such as Hobbes, Kant, and Mill tend to conceive of morality as a system of strict rules and even, in some cases, as a mathematical calculation. Heavily influenced by the scientific temper of the time, they privilege explicitly stated logical principles or laws that are to be used, in an almost mechanical manner, to *calculate* the demands of morality. A growing number of contemporary philosophers now believe that this moral law approach has produced an impoverished account of morality that cannot capture, in sufficient detail, what human aspiration and behaviour is about. If, however, some proponents of virtue ethics are intensely critical of all moral law approaches, we should not be too quick to dismiss what is truly good and innovative in this Enlightenment approach to morality.

In the present chapter, we will consider **contractarianism**, the idea that morality is fundamentally a social contract, an agreement between members of a society to co-operate with one another. Contemporary authors John Rawls, Robert Nozick, James Buchanan, David Gauthier, and Jan Narveson have developed different versions of contractarianism. Here, we will principally focus on Thomas Hobbes (1588–1679), the most famous historical proponent of contractarianism in the English-speaking world. We then go on to briefly mention major contributions by John Locke, Jean-Jacques Rousseau, and Karl Marx, finishing the chapter with a discussion of contemporary issues and contractarian perspectives on virtue.

Contractarians trace morality back to agreement. They usually view morality as a social contract or agreement between consenting parties to live peaceably together in society. We cannot expect other people to agree to treat us morally unless we agree to treat them morally. In effect, I agree to be moral to you and you agree to be moral to me in return. In contractarian accounts, it is the fact of our mutual *agreement* that is somehow at the origin of morality. We will discuss different aspects of this idea in detail. But first, it is important to note that there are contractarian accounts that predate Hobbes.

Ancient Contractarianism: The *Anonymous Iamblichi*

We can find an ancient version of contractarianism in a minor author, one whose name has been lost to future generations. This fifth-century BC Sophist has been dubbed 'the Anonymous' by later scholars because his unattributed words were found among the work of the later Pythagorean philosopher Iamblichus (245–325 AD).[1] One contemporary scholar complains that the author of this collection of passages, now known as the *Anonymous Iamblichi*, 'shows himself . . . to be . . . a champion of law and order, whose virtues he sings at length, in awkward Greek, and in a very derivative fashion'.[2] The judgment is a little harsh. While the Anonymous is not a great thinker, his short discourse does provide a revealing glimpse into the contractarian mindset of at least some ancient Greek intellectuals.

The first thing to notice is that the Anonymous is, like other Greek thinkers, a virtue ethicist. He writes, 'The final completion and perfection of anything [is dependent upon] natural ability, and while one may think that this is due to fortune [i.e., luck], the following qualities are up to the individual himself: he must be eager to achieve noble and admirable things, work hard at them, learn them as quickly as possible, and persevere at them for a long time'.[3] To summarize, the Anonymous believes that positive character traits or virtues such as nobility, enthusiasm, industriousness, alertness, and perseverance lead to success in any field. In line with his contractarianism, however, he also emphasizes the importance of positive social interaction with other people.

The Anonymous describes the human predicament in a way that reminds us of the Greek Sophist Protagoras. He observes this:

> Since men are constitutionally incapable of living alone and have been compelled to join together with one another, . . . and since it is impossible for them to live with one another without law (which would be an even worse penalty for them than living alone), it is these necessities that have enthroned law and justice as kings over men, and they will never be dislodged, because they have been bound securely in place by nature.[4]

The Anonymous believes that justice is a matter of nature (*physis*), not of social convention (*nomos*). We cannot survive on our own—the hermit is a rare and impoverished individual— and so, we need to peacefully co-exist with our neighbours. Nature pushes this obligation on us. It follows that an agreement to collectively abide by the law is at the very centre of the moral project.

Could individuals flagrantly violate their moral obligations to their neighbours and live happily, doing as they choose? This question is a central issue in ancient Greek philosophy. In one of Plato's dialogues (the *Gorgias*), Plato mentions a character called Callicles, who argues that if someone were powerful enough, he could manage to break out of the social straitjacket of morality and rule over others, doing whatever he pleased, by force and wit alone. (The German philosopher Nietzsche was powerfully influenced by such thoughts.) The Anonymous, however, disagrees. He pens a resolute response to such arguments:

> Now, if a person were born who was invulnerable, enjoyed nothing but good health, never suffered any setbacks, had a supernatural constitution, and was physically and mentally as hard as nails, one might perhaps think that the power that accompanies advantage over the others would be alright for such a man, because he could get away with refusal to obey the law. But one would be wrong to think that, because if (what is impossible) there were to be such a man, it is only by allying himself with the laws and justice, and by confirming them, and by using his strength to reinforce them and their supports, that he could be safe. Otherwise, he would never survive, because it is likely that everyone would come out against such a man, and because of their conformity to the law and numbers their skill or power would be superior to his, and they would get the better of him. It therefore turns out that power . . . is maintained by law and justice.[5]

The Anonymous believes that any individual can be overpowered, injured, and enslaved by a greater number of people. Everyone is vulnerable; the strongest man cannot defend himself effectively against a more numerous enemy. It follows that morality, understood as a friendly contract between neighbours, is our only salvation. We must all agree to honestly and fairly interact with each other; this is the only way to save ourselves from discord and war with others.

The Anonymous views morality as an agreement between individuals to respect the law. He identifies lawfulness and lawlessness, respectively, as the most important virtue and the most important vice. Lawfulness leads to 'trust, which brings enormous benefits for everyone and is one of the great blessings of the world'.[6] Lawlessness, in contrast, 'make[s] both war from abroad and internal discord more likely to occur'.[7] It also produces the 'unspeakably terrible evil' of tyranny, allowing a small group of accomplices to take control over a divided populace. Wise individuals will do everything in their power to promote lawfulness as a means to a tolerable and even pleasant existence among equals. Morality, then, is a useful tool that brings peace to naturally competitive beings. It is better to be moral and accept restrictions on our own (and other people's actions) so as to avoid living in a lawless city.

Thomas Hobbes, the most prominent modern contractarian, takes up these same themes 20 centuries later. Hobbes believes that humans are, by nature, egotistical beings. We need social and moral rules to prevent the outbreak of a natural war of everyone against everyone. In the absence of authoritative restraints, human society would be reduced to continual conflict and chaos. Like the Anonymous, Hobbes believes that morality is a rational strategy based on common agreement designed to prevent such social upheaval.

Thomas Hobbes and the Beginnings of Modern Contractarianism

The British philosopher Thomas Hobbes of Malmesbury, whose life spanned the sixteenth and seventeenth centuries, lived in turbulent times. In his autobiography—written in verse!—he recounts that he was born prematurely because his mother took fright at the news that the powerful Spanish Armada, intent on invasion, was approaching the English coast:

> For fame had rumour'd that a fleet at sea,
> Would cause our nation's catastrophe.
> And hereupon it was my mother dear
> Did bring forth twins at once, both me and fear.[8]

Hobbes's repeated insistence that fear was his natural-born twin provides a way into his philosophical mindset. As many commentators have observed, Hobbes's contractarianism can be viewed as a stern reaction to the bloodshed and civil unrest that divided British society during his lifetime. In Hobbes's mind, morality is necessary as a way of securing public order and safety.

Hobbes came from a contentious lineage. His father, a small-town vicar, fled to London after being involved in a brawl outside his own church, leaving his young son to be raised by a wealthy uncle. After graduating from Magdalen College (Oxford), the young man went on to work as a private tutor to the wealthy in England and abroad. He was eventually caught up in the political troubles that gave rise to the English Civil War (1642–51). A man of outspoken and controversial opinions, Hobbes managed to offend both sides in the conflict. After fleeing to France to escape the wrath of parliamentarians who objected to his support for an absolute monarchy, he returned to England 11 years later to escape the wrath of exiled Royalists who objected to what they saw as his anti-religious secularism. Later in life, he was accused of promoting atheism and blasphemy. Derided as the 'Monster of Malmsbury' and 'the bug-bear of the nation', his books were publicly burned at Oxford. He was, however, protected by the king and granted a generous pension, becoming an established if contested figure in English intellectual society. He lived an exceptionally long life, dying at the age of 91.

Hobbes ventured strong opinions on such diverse topics as morality, metaphysics, epistemology, geometry, physics, psychology, and history. He also produced several translations of the Greek classics. He is, however, mostly remembered for the political and legal views set out in three works: *Elements of Law* (1640), *De Cive* (*Of the Citizen*, 1642, 1647), and *Leviathan* (1651). We will consider the latter text here.[9]

Leviathan: *Human Nature*

Unlike many contemporary liberal authors, Hobbes does not distinguish sharply between politics and morality. *Leviathan* is both a political and a moral work. As this is a book on ethics, however, we will pass quickly over his political views to focus on his historically influential contractarian account of morality.

It may seem somewhat odd that Hobbes would entitle a political and moral tract *Leviathan*, an old Hebrew term for 'whale'. (The Hebrew term can be literally translated as 'the great sea monster'). But Hobbes's metaphor is strikingly apt. During that era of seafaring, when navies ruled the world, the whale was familiarly known as the most powerful creature on earth. Hobbes compares the modern nation-state to an artificial, man-made animal of terrifying power and size. He writes, 'the multitude so united in one person is called a COMMONWEALTH; in Latin, CIVITAS. [Such] is the generation of that great LEVIATHAN . . . to which we owe, under the immortal God, our peace and defence'.[10] Considered individually, human beings are a puny, frail, clawless, hairless species, among the weakest animals of all. When humans join together to form a political state, however, they are able to produce the largest and most powerful entity on earth, an artificial whale or Leviathan, in effect, a benevolent monster that is armed and vigilant, that keeps the peace and defends citizens. Hobbes views morality as the cement that holds the state together; it is the bond that turns vulnerable individuals into an invincible community.

Hobbes proposes a purely materialist account of human nature. There is no room in his metaphysics for immaterial souls or angels or ghosts or other non-physical beings. As a vocal proponent of the new physics, Hobbes maintains that the universe is uniquely composed of physical objects, and that human beings are like mechanical clocks or windup toys who move themselves: '[Human] life is but a motion of limbs, the beginning whereof is . . . within.'[11] Although Hobbes does appeal to the traditional idea of God in his political theory, this is strangely at odds with the materialist bias of his moral project.

Hobbes uses the term 'endeavour' to describe human behaviour. There are two opposed emotions that motivate human agency: desire and aversion. Desire pulls us toward some things; aversion pushes us away from other things. Hobbes believes that the whole of human life is trying (or endeavouring) to move closer to what we desire and further away from what we feel aversion to.

Hobbes believes that humans are, by nature, egoists—they always act in their own self-interest. He writes, 'All the voluntary actions of men tend to the benefit of themselves'.[12] And again, he assures us, 'Of all voluntary acts the object is to every man his own good'.[13] This inborn egoism is the key to human behaviour. We all want happiness *for ourselves*. This is, at the deepest level, what motivates us. Happiness, what Hobbes calls 'felicity', means getting as much as possible of what we want.

Hobbes defines *power* as a means to our ends. **Original power** derives from what we are, from our inborn talents. Some people are naturally strong, attractive, intelligent; and so on. Such people can use these natural abilities to get what they want. But there is also a second kind of power that Hobbes calls **instrumental power**. This power derives from acquired, external goods, such as money, property, friends, political station, reputation, or even (as Machiavelli points out) good luck. In a competitive world, we need to use original power and instrumental power to obtain what we want. This is why we are all so power-hungry.

Hobbes famously writes, 'So that in the first place, I put for a general inclination of all mankind a perpetual and restless desire of power after power, that ceaseth only in death'.[14] So, how much power do we desire? As much as possible! We are never satisfied with the amount of power we have. Why? First, to be alive is to experience desire and aversion. If we were to ever reach the point of being without desires or aversions—we would be dead! Hobbes writes, 'life itself is but motion, and can never be without desire, nor without fear'.[15] Second, Hobbes thinks we 'cannot assure the power and means to live well . . . without the acquisition of more [power]'.[16] We must struggle against many forces that are always beating us back, plotting our ruin and destruction. We intuitively understand that we must keep on increasing the power we have in order to protect and maintain what we already possess. We are like a man in a boat, rowing upstream. As soon as he stops rowing, he forfeits whatever distance he has gained. The individual who stops accumulating more power immediately starts losing the power he already has.

Earlier moralists such as the ancient Stoics, the skeptics, or even the Epicureans would argue that Hobbes unwittingly perpetuates unhappiness by ignoring the path of self-restraint that leads to true tranquility of spirit. Hobbes, however, pays little attention to the early theorists, who recommend temperance. In this new mechanical picture of human nature, we are like perpetual motion machines. The wheels within us never stop turning. We are egotistical and power-hungry and restless and we will always endeavour to get more and more and more. We cannot extinguish human desire. That is just the way we are.

Leviathan: *The State of Nature*

Hobbes believes that human desire is never satisfied; we always want more. The moral law, on the other hand, limits desire and restricts our behaviour. Submitting to morality is, then, an onerous task because it goes against the grain of human nature. The point of Hobbes's theory is to give us a reason to be moral.

Hobbes proposes what is called a **negative theory of freedom**. 'A freeman,' he writes, 'is he that . . . is not hindered to do what he has a will to'.[17] On this negative account, freedom is a matter of removing positive obstacles that stop us from doing as we will. It is a matter of opening up space for personal initiative. But this seems to clash with moral standards that resrict our freedom. Moral law draws a line in the sand and tells us not to step over it. It tells us, 'Don't steal'; 'Don't lose your temper'; 'Don't be a racist'. Moreover, it instructs us not to do these things even when we feel like doing them. So why should we give up our freedom in order to be moral? Why not leave morality aside and do whatever we want?

Like the Anonymous discussed previously, Hobbes believes that morality, understood as co-operation among individual human beings, is essential to our own well-being. Hobbes proposes the following thought experiment. Suppose we all lived in an uncivilized state without any organized government to enforce morality, what he calls the **state of nature**. Suppose we let people do what ever they wanted. What would happen? Hobbes believes that this absence of law and order would lead to a state of all-out war. In perhaps the most famous passage from the *Leviathan*, he makes a terrifying prediction:

> Hereby it is manifest that during the time men live without a common power to keep them all in awe [of morality], they are in that condition which is called war; and such a war as is of every man against every man. . . . There is no place [here] for industry, because the fruit thereof is uncertain: and consequently no culture of the earth; no navigation, nor use of the commodities that may be imported by sea; no commodious building; . . . no knowledge of the face of the earth; no account of time; no arts; no letters; no society; and which is worst of all, continual fear, and danger of violent death; and the life of man, solitary, poor, nasty, brutish, and short.[18]

Hobbes believes that a permissive state of nature would be a terrible free-for-all marred by continual discord and struggle. Because individual human beings are more or less equal in talent and power, we all believe that we have as much right as anyone else to whatever goods are available. He explains, '[because] NATURE hath made men so equal in the faculties of body and mind [it follows that] the difference between man and man is not so considerable as that one man can thereupon claim to himself any benefit to which another may not pretend as well as he'.[19] Because the

world has scarce resources, conflict will inevitably erupt over the little that is available'.[20] Hobbes continues: 'And therefore if any two men desire the same thing, which nevertheless they cannot both enjoy, they become enemies; and in the way to their end (which is principally their own conservation, and sometimes their delectation only) endeavour to destroy or subdue one another.'[21]

Hobbes believes that there are 'three principal causes of quarrel' in the world: the desire for gain, the desire for safety, and the desire for reputation or honour.[22] Without some governing power that is able to forcibly temper our appetites and referee conflicts, civilization will be destroyed. A person of superlative strength, intelligence, and determination (like Callicles's 'great man') could perhaps prevail in a state of nature, but Hobbes thinks this is impossible for even 'the weakest would only have strength enough to kill the strongest, either by secret machination or by confederacy with others'.[23] Conditions in a state of nature would be like an ongoing feud between families, different sides would periodically win or lose without any ultimate victory. Hobbes concludes that in a state of nature there will be no end to war. Even if there are momentary interludes of relative peace, the ever-present threat of violence will be such as to approximate a state of war:

> For war consisteth not in battle only, or the act of fighting, but in a tract of time, wherein the will to contend by battle is sufficiently known: and therefore the notion of time is to be considered in the nature of war, as it is in the nature of weather. For as the nature of foul weather lieth not in a shower or two of rain, but in an inclination thereto of many days together: so the nature of war consisteth not in actual fighting, but in the known disposition thereto during all the time there is no assurance to the contrary.[24]

We should be clear. Hobbes believes that there is no place for morality in the state of nature. He explains: 'To this war of every man against every man, this also is consequent; that nothing can be unjust. The notions of right and wrong, justice and injustice, have there no place.'[25] Because the state of nature results in total war, moral law does not apply. As Hobbes points out, 'Force [i.e., violence] and fraud are in war the two cardinal virtues'.[26] When your life is at stake, you would be foolish not to resort to violence or deceit so as to preserve yourself. Such behaviour is not 'immoral' but 'amoral'. The state of nature is like a moral vacuum. Hobbes believes, however, that immorality means breaking the law. One cannot break the law when there is no law to break. As Hobbes expresses the thought, 'Where there is no [government], there is no law; where no law, no injustice'.[27]

Although contemporary contractarians insist that Hobbes intends his account only as a thought experiment, he himself points to three historical circumstances that come close to a state of nature: (1) Aboriginal self-government in North America, (2) civil war, and (3) international politics. Although his reference to Aboriginal forms of government is simplistic, his comments on the British civil war and the problem of international warfare are more to the point. But Hobbes is primarily a philosopher. He wants to demonstrate, *in principle*, what would happen in the absence of law and morality. Even if there never was a time when the state of nature existed in any pure form, he paints a compelling picture.

Leviathan: *How to Escape from the State of Nature*

Hobbes is convinced that the biggest danger confronting humanity is the state of chaos and perpetual war that is inevitably precipitated when we all follow our desires without the restrictions of morality. How do we avoid this state of nature? By agreeing with one another to act in a moral manner. For example, if I agree to act morally toward you, and you agree to act morally toward me and we both abide by our agreements, we can be reconciled with one another. Morality, understood as a com-

---

ꙮ Applied Philosophy Box 7.1 ꙮ

No Rules: Internet Security a Hobbesian 'State of Nature'

Nate Anderson

> Life in cyberspace can be nasty, brutish, and short. So says a new report on international cyber-security, which argues that the Internet is a Hobbesian 'state of nature' where anything goes. . . . The report . . . paints a stark picture of the security problems faced by major enterprises and infrastructure groups, and some of the statistics are downright shocking.

This article goes on to cite statistics concerning the alarming frequency of cyber attacks on the Internet. Explain the reference to Hobbes.

Source: Nate Anderson, 'No Rules: Internet Security a Hobbesian State of Nature.' *Ars Technica*, http://arstechnica.com/tech-policy/news/2010/02/no-rules-internet-security-a-hobbesian-state-of-nature.ars, 1 February 2010.

✑ Applied Philosophy Box 7.2 ✑

Chaos as Water Reaches Shattered City

Port-Au-Prince, Haiti — Precious water, food, and early glimmers of hope began reaching parched and hungry earthquake survivors today on the streets of this shattered city, where despair at times turned into a frenzy among the ruins.

'People are so desperate for food that they are going crazy,' said accountant Henry Ounche, in a crowd of hundreds who fought one another as U.S. military helicopters clattered overhead carrying aid.

When other Navy choppers dropped rations and Gatorade into a soccer stadium thronged with refugees, 200 youths began brawling, throwing stones, to get at the supplies.

This news report describes the situation in Haiti after the catastrophic 2010 earthquake. Hobbes would see this as an example of society reverting to the state of nature. Explain.

Source: 'Chaos as Water Reaches Shattered City.' *New York Post* (Associated Press), www.nypost.com/, 16 January 2010.

---

mon agreement to treat one another fairly and respectfully, is, thinks Hobbes, the only way to ensure a safe and prosperous existence for all.

Hobbes believes that the basic human predicament is to be understood in terms of a moral liberty and a moral obligation. The **right of nature** is the freedom to do whatever is necessary to preserve our lives; other people must allow us to defend our lives and well-being, with whatever force is necessary. The **law of nature** is the moral *obligation* to refrain from harming ourselves and to undertake whatever means is necessary to preserve our own lives. These two principles form the very basis of Hobbes's system. In his words, 'THE right of nature, which writers commonly call *jus naturale*, is the liberty each man hath to use his own power as he will himself for the preservation of his own nature; that is to say, of his own life; and consequently, of doing anything which, in his own judgment and reason, he shall conceive to be the aptest means thereunto'.[28] On the other hand, 'A law of nature [or]

lex naturalis is a precept, or general rule, found out by reason, by which a man is forbidden to do that which is destructive of his life, or taketh away the means of preserving the same, and to omit that by which he thinketh it may be best preserved'.[29]

In other words, Hobbes believes that intelligent individuals will (1) demand and insist on the freedom to do whatever is needed to defend their lives and (2) seek out the best means for protecting their lives. The first principle, the right of nature, *frees* us from any restrictions or even agreements that threaten our survival. The second principle, the law of nature, *obliges* us to save our lives in any way we can. Hobbes complains about those who confuse rights and laws: 'They that speak of this subject . . . confound . . . right and law, yet they ought to be distinguished, because right consisteth in liberty to do, or to forbear; whereas law determineth and bindeth to one of them: so that law and right differ as much as obligation and liberty, which in one and the same matter are inconsistent.'[30] Hobbes views the *law* of nature (not the right of nature) as the ultimate source of moral obligation.

Hobbes's new 'law of nature' is a revised version of natural law. Whereas an earlier author such as Thomas presents morality as the voice of God within us, Hobbes presents morality as the voice of reason telling individuals to do what is good for them. As we progress forward into the secular modern age, a Christian morality based on selfless charity gives way to a morality of prudential calculation based on self-interest. Hobbes's emphasis on the natural egoism of human beings is excessive. Perhaps there are occasions when we should break his law of nature and sacrifice our own lives to a greater cause. If my daughter is about to be run over by a car, perhaps I ought to give up my life to save her. Perhaps I should push her out of the way even if I will be killed in the process. Hobbes embraces a purely self-interested account of human nature. This is a caricature. Nonetheless, there is an important lesson to be learned here. Hobbes sets out to demonstrate that even a purely self-interested person should be moral. Even when we consider the issue uniquely from the view point of self-interest, we can find good reasons to be moral.

Hobbes sets out to prove that morality is also for the selfish. As we have seen, the state of nature is a dangerous, brutal place. Those who are sane will do everything they can to avoid ending up there. This is the purpose of morality. Morality is a doorway out of all-encompassing warfare. We must accept the constraints of morality in order to save our lives.

Just as Thomas derives secondary moral principles from the very first principle of natural law, Hobbes derives more specific moral rules from the law of nature. The first and most important application of the general law of nature is that we must endeavour to maintain peace with our neighbours (because it is safer) without, however, giving up the right of nature. Hobbes writes, 'every man ought to endeavour peace, as far as he has hope of obtaining it; and when he cannot obtain it, [he] may seek and use all helps and advantages of war'.[31] In short, we must try to live peacefully with others while remaining vigilant and ready to protect ourselves by any means necessary if they respond in a hostile manner.

Hobbes believes then that morality starts with agreements between individuals not to harm one another. The second application of the general law of nature is 'that a man be willing, when others are so too, . . . to lay down this right to all things; and be contented with so much liberty against other men as he would allow other men against himself'.[32] If we are to escape the state of nature, we must all agree (1) to respect each other's property and (2) to respect each other's right to do as we will within reasonable limitations. In other words, we must agree not to steal and to accept—with some qualifications—equal amounts of individual freedom.

The third application of the general law of nature is 'that men perform their covenants made'. [33] We must keep our agreements if we hope to live in peace with one another. When individuals do not do what they have agreed to do, there is inevitably anger, resentment, revenge, and mistrust. Broken agreements produce conflict and discord. If we hope to stay out of the state of nature, we must keep all the agreements we enter into.

Hobbes goes on to formulate a long list of moral rules, all derived from the general law of nature: 'that such things as cannot be divided be enjoyed in common'; that a man 'ought to pardon the offences past of them that repenting, desire it'; 'that every man acknowledge another for his equal'; that 'all men that mediate peace be allowed safe conduct'; 'that every man strive to accommodate himself to the rest'; and so on.[34] The specific formulation of each individual law is not so important. Hobbes' general recommendation is what matters. If we all agree to obey some common-sense rules of morality, this will foster trust and good will among individuals. We can, in this way, reconcile with our neighbours and escape from the condition of war in the state of nature.

Hobbes even claims that these individual applications of the law of nature, taken together, add up to nothing more than the familiar Golden Rule of Scripture, which he views as a simplified version of his own moral philosophy. As he explains,

> though this [precise formulation of the laws of nature] may seem too subtle a deduction of the laws of nature to be taken notice of by all men, whereof the most part are too busy in getting food, and the rest too negligent to understand; yet . . . they have been contracted into one easy sum, intelligible even to the meanest capacity; and that is: Do not that to another which thou wouldest not have done to thyself.[35]

The devout Christian may understandably protest that Hobbes's self-centred morality does not live up to the exalted standards of Jesus of Nazareth. Still, Hobbes's basic point is that morality is reducible to mutual good will or reciprocity. If we all agree to treat others in the way we would wish to be treated—a genuinely Christian ideal—we can live together in peace and harmony and escape from strife and turmoil in the state of nature.

Although Hobbes believes that he is advancing a new, scientific explanation of morality, he also believes that he is reaffirming traditional virtue ethics. To obey a moral rule is, for Hobbes, to exhibit a corresponding virtue; to disobey that rule is to exhibit an opposing vice. For example, Hobbes tells us that 'gratitude . . . is the fourth law of nature'[36] and that 'The breach of [this fourth] law is called ingratitude'.[37] And again, that 'the observers of [the fifth] law may be called sociable, [whereas breakers of the law may be called] stubborn, insociable, forward, intractable'.[38] Hobbes concludes, more generally, that

> The science of virtue and vice is moral philosophy and . . . [that] all men agree on this, that peace is good, and therefore also the way[s], or means of peace, which . . . are justice, gratitude, modesty, equity, mercy, and the rest of the laws of nature, [all these] are good; that is to say, [all believe that] moral virtues [are good]; and their contrary vices, evil.[39]

Hobbes thus reconciles contractarianism with virtue ethics. On his account, a morality of agreed-upon rules is ultimately equivalent to a morality of good character traits.

Leviathan: *The Sovereign*

Hobbes believes then that we must abide by moral law so that we can live in peace with one another and escape from the state of nature. Except that Hobbes lacks confidence in human nature. He is no sentimentalist, no bleeding heart. He does not believe that good intentions are enough. Hobbes comments, 'Covenants without the sword, are but words and of no strength to secure a man at all'.[40] Hobbes insists that agreements must be physically enforced or they will not be respected. Without the sword, men will not keep their word. There must be a higher authority that can promulgate laws and, more importantly, punish those who break them.

If then we are to emerge from the state of nature, we must join together with others so as to institute a government ruled by a **sovereign** (a monarch or a small group of people) equipped with sufficient power to frighten the populace into submission. This is the very purpose of a political state: to force people (for their own good) to be moral. Hobbes observes, 'before the names of just and unjust can have place, there must be some coercive power to compel men equally to the performance of their covenants, by the terror of some punishment greater than the benefit they expect by the breach of their covenant'.[41] We need the spectre of harsh punishment to overcome the violent egoism of human nature and force compliance with morality.

Hobbes believes, therefore, in an authoritarian state. His argument for the sovereign is, in fact, a thinly-veiled argument for the British monarchy. Hobbes believes that everyone should obey the king and that the king must have final say in all important decisions. There are no limits to his earthly power. As 'God's lieutenant who hath the sovereignty under God',[42] the ruler is above human law and cannot be constrained by the laws he himself makes. At the same time, he is subservient to God. Hobbes explains: 'The office of the sovereign, be it a monarch or an assembly, consisteth in the end for which he was trusted with the sovereign power, namely the procuration of the safety of the people, to which he is obliged by the law of nature, and to render an account thereof to God, the Author of that law, and to none but Him.'[43]

Hobbes suggests, in short, that a ruler that abuses his power will be harshly punished in the after-life by God, Who will, on the Day of Judgment, hold any earthly king accountable for his actions toward his subjects. The king, so to speak, enters into an agreement—i.e.,

a contract or covenant—with God. In giving the king his earthly power, God demands, in return, wise government over others. Still, Hobbes believes that only God has any authority over the sovereign. Mere citizens cannot limit his powers in any way.

Hobbes's portrait of the ideal king as an absolute monarch who demands complete submission from all his objects offends our contemporary sensibilities. But Hobbes thinks that absolute power in an earthly sovereign is necessary to ensure peace in the land. The human propensity toward selfishness and partiality is too strong. We will not act morally unless we are actively restrained by the threat of severe punishment: 'For the laws of nature, as justice, equity, modesty, mercy, and, in sum, doing to others as we would be done to . . . without the terror of some power to cause them to be observed, are contrary to our natural passions, that carry us to partiality, pride, revenge, and the like.'[44]

Hobbes describes the rationale behind the moral restraint forced on individuals when a sovereign is instituted to dispense law and order. As he explains,

> THE final cause, end, or design of men (who naturally love liberty, and dominion over others) in the introduction of that restraint upon themselves, in which we see them live in Commonwealths, is the foresight of their own preservation, and of a more contented life thereby; that is to say, of getting themselves out from that miserable condition of war [the state of nature] which is necessarily consequent . . . to the natural passions of men when there is no visible power to keep them in awe, and [to] tie them by fear of punishment to the performance of their covenants, and observation of [the] laws of nature.[45]

Hobbes accepts that the enforcement of morality by the sovereign in a civilized society limits our individual freedoms. At the same time, he believes that this limitation can be reconciled with the previously explained concept of negative liberty. It may seem strange to think that the idea that freedom means doing what you want can be reconciled with the heavily authoritarian view of government Hobbes champions. But Hobbes is a contractarian; he believes that morality is something we *agree* to. There may have been no decisive, historical moment when everyone sat around and actually signed a formal agreement, but Hobbes believes that all clear-thinking individuals would agree to this social contract if they were given the opportunity to express themselves. This is why abiding by the rules of the social contract is not adverse to individual freedom—we are only agreeing to what we, as rational persons, would agree to do if we were formally asked to give an opinion. The resultant constraints on our freedom are, in this sense, self-chosen and not at odds with human freedom.

Hobbes goes even further, suggesting that when we obey the sovereign, we are obeying ourselves. On his account, the sovereign (a monarch or a small, powerful elite) represents the collective will of the people. The political state begins when individual citizens collectively agree, for their own safety and security, to hand over all authority to the sovereign. Hobbes writes this:

> A COMMONWEALTH is said to be instituted when a multitude of men do agree, and covenant . . . that to [the sovereign] shall be given . . . the right to present the person of them all, . . . to be their representative; . . . [that same multitude] shall authorize all the actions and judgments of that [selected] man, or assembly of men, in the same manner as if they were [their] own, to the end to live peaceably amongst themselves, and be protected against other men.[46]

In obeying the sovereign, citizens are fulfilling the conditions of the (implicit) agreement that holds society together. Strictly speaking, this is not a restriction on their negative liberty, for they have already agreed to this.

In sharp contrast to most contemporary authors, Hobbes believes that the political state serves a moral purpose. This is why it was created—or rather, this is why it would have to be created if it were not already in place. We cannot live unmolested by our neighbours without morality. We cannot get out of the state of nature without an exchange: we have to give something away in order to gain something in return. What we give away is any claim to that absolute freedom of action that exists in a lawless state of nature; what we receive, in return, is peace, security, and the possibility of a prosperous existence that accompanies morality. This is a reasonable exchange. Except in unusual situations, any rational agent would do the same. Obeying the law, which Hobbes equates with morality, turns out to be the most advantageous course of action, *even for the self-interested agent.*

Most modern contractarians think of the initial agreement that brought individuals together in society as a hypothetical occurrence, as something that does not correspond to an exact historical event. (Hobbes is not entirely clear on this point.) Seen from this perspective, the state of nature is not an actual episode from human history, but a thought experiment that demonstrates how self-interested decision-making would lead inevitably to morality. Morality is an implicit or **hypothetical agreement** that represents what rational individuals would agree to. Moral rules are the product of *reasonable* argument. When we obey the law, we succeed at rationality.

Hobbes does recognize, however, one important limitation to law-abiding behaviour. If society turns against you for any reason—if the state, for example, threatens your life (or even seriously curtails your freedom)—you can break the law. Hobbes writes, 'A covenant not to defend myself from force, by force, is always void. For . . . no man can transfer or lay down his right to save himself from death, wounds, and imprisonment'.[47] Hobbes believes that we embrace morality to escape the state of nature. In effect, each citizen makes the following exchange: I will agree not to hurt others as long as the rest of society agrees not to hurt me. If then society threatens my life (even by seriously undermining my freedom or prosperity), it defaults on its side of the agreement. So the contract is now null and void. Because society is not keeping up its end of the bargain, I don't have to keep up my end. I can do anything I have to do in order to save my own life, even if this means hurting others.

We must not jump to conclusions. Hobbes is not arguing against capital punishment. Hobbes believes that the state *can lawfully execute a criminal*. The king has every right to hunt down serious criminals and kill them. Still, Hobbes believes that society can never take away the criminal's right to resist or escape. Whenever society threatens your life, you are thrown back into a state of war against other citizens. You are pushed back, in effect, into the state of nature, and so the most fundamental moral principle, what Hobbes calls the right of nature, reasserts itself. You can do whatever you must do to save your life. You can never give this up right.

Hobbes writes,

> The laws of nature oblige *in foro interno*; that is to say, they bind to a desire they should take place: but *in foro externo*; that is, to the putting them in act, not always. For he that should be modest and tractable, and perform all he promises in such time and place where no man else should do so, should but make himself a prey to others, and procure his own certain ruin, contrary to the ground of all laws of nature which tend to nature's preservation.[48]

In other words, we should try to be as moral as we can, but when others treat us immorally, when our own lives are in danger, we are justified in pushing aside moral requirements.

In a legal context, this Hobbesian line of reasoning is familiarly known as the defence of necessity. Most criminal courts accept that citizens can act in a manner that would normally be considered illegal if this is the only way they can protect themselves. In extenuating circumstances, for example, you can steal to save your life; you can break into someone's house to save your life; you can kill another human being to save your life, and so on.

Leviathan: *Amoral Nature*

As mentioned, Hobbes's 'law of nature' is a reworking of Thomas's account of 'natural law'. But there is an important difference. Hobbes wants to re-establish morality on a new contractarian basis. Morality, he thinks, comes from political agreement. It follows that there can be no moral obligations prior to the establishment of a social contract when people gather together under a lawful ruler. Hobbes assures us: 'The desires and other passions of man, are in themselves no sin. No more are the actions that proceed from those passions, till they know a law that forbids them; which till laws be made they cannot know: nor can any law be made, till they have agreed upon the person that shall make it [i.e., the sovereign].[49] First, there must be a ruler. Second, the ruler must decide what the laws are. Third, the ruler must make sure the people know what the laws are. Only subsequently do moral obligations appear.

This brings into focus one crucial way in which Hobbes's morality differs radically from previous theories. Most traditional philosophers would argue that we should agree to those things that are right because they are right; they are not right simply because we agree to them. Morality is more than mere agreement. In contrast, Hobbes believes that morality means keeping your agreements. This is why there is no immorality in the state of nature— because there is no agreement. Hobbes writes, 'where no covenant hath preceded, . . . every man has right to everything and consequently, no action can be unjust. But when a covenant is made, then to break it is unjust and the definition of injustice is no other than the not performance of covenant'.[50]

Although he is not entirely clear, Hobbes seems to be arguing for an *exclusive* contractarianism, as if to suggest that agreement is the *only* source of morality. Some contemporary contractarians follow suit. Canadian philosopher David Gauthier, for example, has entitled an important book on the subject *Morals By Agreement*.[51] He means to suggest that there is no objective morality to be found in the world, in human nature, in reason, in practical circumstance, in tradition, or in religion (etc.). Morality can be found only in agreement. But even Hobbes himself (somewhat inconsistently) suggests that there is more to morality than mere agreement.

After listing the moral requirements the social contract places on individuals, Hobbes moves on to acknowledge that morality is a broader aspiration. 'There be other things tending to the destruction of particular men', he writes, '[such] as drunkenness, and all other parts of intemperance, which may therefore also be reckoned amongst those things which the law of nature hath forbidden, but are not necessary to be mentioned, nor are pertinent enough to [any discussion of the social contract]'.[52] If agreement were all there is to morality, it would be hard to explain how drunken behaviour could be considered immoral even when the drunk in question has not broken any agreements made with other people. But Hobbes himself recognizes that excessive drinking is immoral, even if it lies outside the scope of a narrow contractarian conception of morality. He hints here that contractarianism tells only one part of the moral story.

The idea that morality derives solely from agreement seems too narrow to account for all moral obligations. Consider briefly three possible exceptions: (1) What about our moral obligations to ourselves? It seems odd to say that we enter into agreements with ourselves, but most moral theorists would claim that we do have moral obligations to ourselves. (For example, we have an obligation to refrain from suicide and to oppose degrading treatment.) (2) Suppose you are shipwrecked alone on a deserted island. Many people would claim that morality has a place even on a deserted island, although there is no one else there to enter into an agreement with. (3) Finally, what about beings that cannot consciously agree to anything: human babies, the insane, plants, animals, ecosystems, even works of art? Does the fact that we cannot enter into agreements with these beings mean that there are no moral standards that regulate how we should treat them?

We will leave it to readers to explore such issues on their own. Suffice it to say that seen from the perspective of virtue ethics it is a mistake to identify morality solely with social agreement. Virtue theorists argue that moral obligations are anchored in human nature, that we only have to consult our consciences to determine the fundamental principles of morality. These principles follow us around (so to speak), inside and outside the state of nature. Hobbes may believe that anyone who is naive enough to act in a 'moral' manner in the state of nature will be quickly destroyed. But morality does not require one to underestimate risks to one's own well-being. On the virtue ethics model, defending oneself can be construed as a moral requirement. Morality has to be adapted, in any case, to the precise context. What we are required to do in times of peace is different from what we are required to do in a state of war.

Hobbes is not consistent on these issues. As we have seen, he argues that we are *required* to do what is needed to preserve ourselves (the law of nature). But to say that we are required to do something, that we *ought* to do something, sounds a lot like morality. But this universal requirement *predates* the social contract. It is an agreement-independent 'moral' injunction that is inherent in the nature of things. So Hobbes himself suggests then that morality originates in something more fundamental than human agreement.

Leviathan: A Subjective Theory of the Good

In sharp contrast to most mainstream historical thinkers, Hobbes proposes a *subjective* theory of the good. He explains:

> whatsoever is the object of any man's appetite or desire, that is it which he for his part calleth good; and the object of his hate and aversion, evil. . . . For these words of good, evil, and contemptible are ever used with relation to the person that useth them: there being nothing simply and absolutely so; nor any common rule of good

and evil to be taken from the nature of the objects themselves.[53]

In Hobbes's account, human beings have different likes and dislikes—hence, different conceptions of good and evil. Moral language is, at best, disguised preference. To say that something is good is equivalent to saying, 'I like it'. To say that something is evil is equivalent to saying, 'I dislike it'. But this account of moral language does not withstand close scrutiny.

Here again, Hobbes is inconsistent. He writes as if human tastes and preferences vary widely from individual to individual, as if different individuals want very different things. In the state of nature, however, people want the same things: according to Hobbes, it is our competition for the *same* goods that produces an all-out war. Suppose, to use a very simple example, we all lived in an orchard. And suppose you wanted only oranges; I wanted only apples; and Mary-Jane, only cherries. There would be no reason for us to fight with one another. You could have all the oranges; I could have all the apples, and Mary-Jane could have all the cherries. The problem, according to Hobbes, is that there are only apples and we all want apples. It is the competition for the very same goods that produces inevitable conflict.

Surely, it makes good sense to suggest that humans commonly judge some goods to be worthwhile and desirable. While it is true that individual tastes differ—I prefer chocolate ice cream; you prefer strawberry—on closer inspection, these desires are not so very different. In the case of the ice cream, we both want food; we both want food that tastes good; and presumably, we both want the money we need to buy this food. Viewed on a micro level, then, there is considerable variation in individual preference. But viewed on a macro level (from the viewpoint of the big picture), we share desires for similar things. This is hardly surprising. If we all share the same human nature, why wouldn't we, more or less, want the same things? Food, health, safety, peace of mind, happiness, friendship, and so on.

Morality, then, is the same for everyone. Why? Because, deep down, we all share similar aspirations. Hobbes himself argues that although individual human desires differ, every rational agent properly desires 'peaceable, sociable, and comfortable living'. He complains that 'the writers of moral philosophy, though they acknowledge the same virtues and vices; yet, not seeing wherein consisted their goodness, [they do not see] that they come to be praised as the [necessary] means of peaceable, sociable, and comfortable living'.[54]

The suspicion that morality is little more than self-centred rationalization abounds in contemporary culture. According to a pervasive popular account, good and evil are issues of desire, not reason. There are no objective standards by which to judge our actions, only values that change arbitrarily. This world view derives, in part, from Hobbes. But even Hobbes accepts that moral laws and virtues retain a fixed value in every place and time. Again, he writes, 'the laws of nature are immutable and eternal, for injustice, ingratitude, arrogance, pride, iniquity, acception of persons [favouritism], and the rest, can never be made lawful. For it can never be that war shall preserve life, and peace destroy it'.[55] Hobbes himself does not believe that morality can change on a whim or in some arbitrary fashion.

Hobbes's equation of our subjective desires with the good is too simple. Hobbes claims that the statement 'X is good' is equivalent to the statement 'I desire X'. But suppose you were to ask someone, 'why do you desire X'? A rational agent would have to respond, 'I desire X because X is good'. But this is equivalent, in Hobbes's theory, to saying that 'I desire X because I desire X'. At the very least, such answers are uninformative.

In Hobbes's theory, moral evaluation comes to an end in our desires. But it is solipsism to think that it is the fact that I desire something that makes it valuable. We may have bad desires, even evil desires, and we may experience guilt or shame about what we desire. So we cannot simply assume that whatever we desire is good. If we wish to provide a foundational account of what morality and human aspiration are about, we need to go beyond a mere description of subjective desire. We need to evaluate desire in light of an objective description of human experience and nature considered more broadly. Desire is one thing; moral judgment is another. Morality proposes external standards of human excellence; it distinguishes between good and bad desires.

Contractarianism does not provide an answer to every moral question. At the same time, Hobbes proposes a powerful new model for understanding morality, one that has had an immense (if sometimes uncritical) influence on modern ways of thinking about ethics. Hobbes effectively demonstrates that even if human agents are inevitably irascible and self-interested, we can still make a convincing case for morality.

John Locke and Two-Tiered Contractarianism

Thomas Hobbes is the most famous early modern contractarian. But there are other early modern philosophers who offer competing contractarian accounts of morality. John Locke

(1632–1704), the prominent British philosopher, is particularly deserving of note. Although politics and morality inevitably overlap in contractarian theory, we will focus primarily on the moral ramifications of Locke's account.

Locke is sometimes identified as the first liberal thinker. His philosophy is, in many ways, the original inspiration for the American political system. A secretary to the Whig politician the Earl of Shaftesbury and a champion of British empiricism, Locke advances, in determined opposition to Hobbes, a rival interpretation of social contract theory. In his *Second Treatise on Civil Government*, he describes the state of nature as a place of plenty regulated by tacit moral laws, shifting the emphasis in his own contractarian account to notions of equality and property.[56]

As we have seen, Hobbes claims that there is no morality in the state of nature. In the ensuing war of everyone against everyone, behaviour of any sort is permissible. Locke argues, in contrast, that there is morality in the state of nature, a morality that derives from the natural law God has placed in human minds. He observes:

> Though [the state of nature] be a state of liberty, yet it is not a state of licence. . . . [It] has a law of nature to govern it, which obliges every one: and reason, which is that law, teaches all mankind, . . . that being all equal and independent, no one ought to harm another in his life, health, liberty, or possessions: for men being all the workmanship of one omnipotent, and infinitely wise maker; . . . sent into the world . . . about his business; they are [God's] property, . . . made to last during his, not one another's pleasure. . . . There cannot be supposed any such subordination among us, that may authorize us to destroy one another, as if we were made for one another's uses, . . . Every one . . . [must endeavour] as much as he can, to preserve the rest of mankind, and may not, unless it

be to do justice on an offender, take away, or impair the life, or what tends to the preservation of the life, the liberty, health, limb, or goods of another.[57]

Like Hobbes, Locke takes the idea of a social contract very seriously. But Locke does not go so far as to suggest that morality comes into existence with the establishment of the political state. He believes that the same fundamental standards of justice must be maintained inside and outside the state of nature. There are so-called natural rights, moral rights that exist prior to or outside of any formal jurisdiction such as the right to life, the right not to be physically molested, the right to property, the right to choose for ourselves (within reasonable limits), and so on. These rights derive, not from the nature of the political process but from the nature of the world. Even in the absence of organized methods of law and order, even in a state of nature, we cannot treat other human beings in any way we please. A properly ordered political society must respect and embody a prior morality inherent in human reason. On Hobbes's account, agreement *makes* morality. On Locke's account, moral agreement must correspond to a more fundamental standard.

Locke believes that a just political state is better than the state of nature because it is able to dispense justice in a coordinated, regular, and impartial manner. There is no judicial apparatus, no central authority, no police force in the state of nature to take up the business of enforcing justice on recalcitrant individuals. It falls then on individuals to administer justice on their own, outside of any formal framework, a less reliable process. Still, Locke insists that, 'EVERY MAN HATH A RIGHT TO PUNISH THE OFFENDER, AND BE EXECUTIONER OF THE LAW OF NATURE' in the state of nature.[58] (The capitalization comes from

Locke.) In the absence of government, we all have the right—indeed, the obligation—to administer justice. We may punish or even execute the offender, but only in accordance with independent moral standards of fairness and proportionality. Locke explains:

> In the state of nature, [a] man [has] no absolute or arbitrary power, to use a criminal, when he has got him in his hands, according to the passionate heats, or boundless extravagancy of his own will; but only to retribute to him, so far as calm reason and conscience dictate, what is proportionate to his transgression, which is so much as may serve for reparation and restraint. . . . which is [what] we call punishment.[59]

The difference between the political state and the state of nature is, in Locke's mind, the difference between justice administered formally and informally (or collectively and individually). *But it is the same justice.* It nowise follows, as Hobbes suggests, that an individual can do anything to another individual in the absence of a government. (Locke believes that a properly organized judiciary provides a neutral umpire for resolving conflicts, but the same morality applies inside and outside the court system.)

Locke, like Hobbes, argues for 'the right of nature'. He, too, insists that individuals have the right to defend their lives and security by any means necessary, even to the point of killing aggressors: 'It being reasonable and just, I should have a right to destroy that which threatens me with destruction.'[60] But Locke does not appeal here, like Hobbes, to naked self-interest. He believes that the right of nature is secured through morality. In killing a hostile party, we do what is right; in defending ourselves, we obey moral law.

Locke advances two *moral* arguments in favour of our right to lethal self-defence. First, he claims that 'the safety of the innocent is to be preferred and [so a man] may destroy [any one] who makes war upon him'.[61] What Locke means is that it is morally better that the innocent victim survives and the aggressor, being the guilty party, dies. Second, Locke believes that criminals or 'outlaws' separate themselves from the human community and

---

ঙ Applied Philosophy Box 7.3 ঙ

Citizen's Arrest? Leave Policing to the Police

Alan Shanoff

> There was a time when society encouraged citizen's arrests but that time has long passed as David Chen, owner of a Toronto grocery store, can attest. Chen and two of his employees chased a man they observed stealing from the store. When they caught him, they tied him up and placed him in the back of their van. . . . Chen and his employees were charged with assault, kidnapping, forcible confinement and carrying a concealed weapon, namely a box cutter.

This is the opening paragraph to an editorial about a Chinese grocery store owner who, after catching a thief, faced criminal charges in Toronto. Would Locke agree with the man's actions or not? Why?

Source: Alan Shanoff, 'Citizen's Arrest? Leave Policing to the Police.' *Toronto Sun*, www.torontosun.com/comment/columnists/alan_shanoff/2009/06/07/9703121-sun.html, 7 June 2009.

thus lose their moral status as fellow human beings. In effect, they transform themselves into wild animals. So it is not immoral to kill them (in self-defence). A man can kill a hostile aggressor 'for the same reason that he may kill a wolf or a lion; because such men are not under the ties of the common law of reason, have no other rule, but that of force and violence, and so may be treated as beasts of prey'.[62] Keep in mind that Locke believes that morality is the final authority in human decision-making, *even in the state of nature.*

We can compare Hobbesian and Lockean contractarianism. Hobbes strongly suggests that morality resides uniquely in human agreement. Although Locke acknowledges the importance of agreement, he claims that agreement must also conform to a higher moral standard. In his two-tiered approach, morality stands on two pillars or steps: agreement **and** moral conscience. The social contract arises from an agreement (first tier) that corresponds to natural law (second tier). Mere agreement, then, is not enough for morality; agreement must also correspond to a (properly formed) moral conscience.

In Locke's theory, social arrangements have to satisfy two criteria: (1) we must agree to them, and (2) the content of these agreements must respect the basic requirements of morality. This two-tired contractarian approach represents a more subtle version of contractarianism but one that is, perhaps, less appealing to the purist. Locke accepts that morality has an inevitable social dimension—it is the glue that joins us to the rest of humanity—but we cannot agree to just anything. Morality requires *reasonable* agreement: agreement in accordance with human nature, with the nature of the world, and with the nature of God.

On Equality

Locke, the Parliamentarian, and Hobbes, the Royalist, disagree in a second important way. Hobbes believes we agree to submit to a sovereign in order to escape from the state of nature. Once the political state has been established, this sovereign can rule without the consent of subjects. Locke has more democratic sensibilities. Although people must occupy positions of authority in any society, Locke believes that human beings are fundamentally equal and that representative democracy provides a mechanism for rule through consensual arrangement. He observes, 'MEN being . . . by nature, all free, equal, and independent, no one can be put out of this estate, and subjected to the political power of another, without his own consent'.[63] Hobbes argues that the sovereign is above the law; Locke believes that even the king is subject to the law. Whereas Hobbes believes that the sovereign can rule without the further consent of subjects, Locke believes that political legitimacy requires the continued consent of citizens who retain the right to overthrow a bad ruler. (We will not explore the details of Locke's political views here. Simply note that this emphasis on consensual agreement comes to the fore in the moral philosophy of later liberal thinkers such as John Stuart Mill, whom we discuss in Chapter 9.)

Locke's position on slavery illustrates, in an edifying way, not merely his political convictions, but his moral indignation at the very idea of human inequality. Locke does not merely argue that it is wrong to enslave other people. He argues that individuals cannot willingly enslave *themselves*: 'A man . . . cannot, by compact, or his own consent, enslave himself to any one, nor put himself under the absolute, arbitrary power of another.'[64] Suppose I were to agree to become your slave if you pay my son $3 million. Even if we both consent—in full knowledge of what this agreement entails—Locke thinks this would still be an immoral (and illegal) arrangement. It is not that I did not agree to being enslaved. It is that slavery clashes with the law of nature enshrined in human reason. Slavery, even by agreement, violates fundamental human equality. In eliminating consent, it undermines the egalitarian basis for moral interaction between human beings.

On Property: The Virtue of Industriousness

We would be remiss if we were to omit mention of Locke's influential views on private property. Locke justifies the institution of private ownership through an appeal to the Protestant virtue of industriousness. He claims (like Hobbes) that there was no private property in the original state of nature:

> The earth, and all that is therein, is given to men [by God] for the support and comfort of their being. . . . All the fruits it naturally produces, and beasts it feeds, belong to mankind in common, as they are produced by the spontaneous hand of nature; and no body has originally a private dominion, exclusive of the rest of mankind, in any of them, as they are thus in their natural state.[65]

How, then, did property arise? Locke points to the example of someone who gathers fruit for his own sustenance in the state of nature:

> He that is nourished by . . . the apples he gathered from the trees in the wood, has certainly appropriated them to himself. No body can deny but the nourishment is his. I ask then, when did they begin to be his? When he digested? Or when he eat? Or when he boiled? Or when he brought them home? Or when he picked them up? And it

is plain, if the first gathering made them not his, nothing else could. That labour put a distinction between them and common: that added something to them more than nature, . . . and so they became his private right.[66]

This, then, is the origin of property. When we use the raw materials of nature, we somehow add our work to them and make them a part of ourselves. Locke explains, 'every man has a property in his own person. . . . The labour of his body, and the work of his hands, we may say, are properly his. Whatsoever then he removes [from] nature, . . . [and] hath mixed his labour with, . . . that is his own, and thereby makes it his property'.[67] For example, when you pick apples, the apples are yours because you picked them; when you grow cabbages, the cabbages are yours because you grew them; when you build a house, the house is yours because you built it; when you write a poem, the poem is yours because you wrote it; and so on. It is your industry mixed with the physical objects of the world that is at the origin of private ownership.

Locke explains the original human acquisition of land through farming. He continues, 'God and his reason commanded [man] to subdue the earth, i.e. improve it for the benefit of life, [through] . . . his labour. He that in obedience to this command of God, subdued, tilled and sowed any part of it, thereby [made it his own]'.[68] This is, for Locke, a fair exchange. By improving the world through his virtuous industry, the farmer justly enriches himself in the process: 'As much land as a man tills, plants, improves, cultivates, . . . so much is his property. He by his labour does, as it were, inclose it from the common.'[69] Locke sets two limits on how much property individuals can own. First, he argues that we can only acquire goods for ourselves, '*where there is enough, and*

ᶜᵒ Applied Philosophy Box 7.4 ᵍᵛ

You Don't Need That!

Abby Williamson

An epidemic has swept the nation. It has been growing for some time. It has to do with American consumerism. . . . It is hoarding. Hoarding of magazines, birthday cards, old notes, Virgin Mary candles, all the T-shirts you wore when you were still in high school and all the free jive from student fairs. Despite our lack of active use of these things, we keep them because they mean something to us, or we fool ourselves into thinking we'll maybe use them someday. However, because the magazines are out of date, the cards cannot be reused, the notes are no longer relevant to current classes, and the wicks on those candles were lost to a wax-pool long ago, we buy up-to-date products, clothes and new notebooks for our new classes. The storage space dwindles and thus begins the cycle of hoarding. . . . Go through your stuff. I guarantee you will find loads of needless articles of clothing, papers, letters, knickknacks, and broken this or that. Get rid of them either by taking it to a thrift store, throwing them in the trash, or recycling them properly.

Locke argues that we are allowed to accumulate property but only to the point that there is enough left over for other people. One could argue that there are people who need any excess possessions: the homeless, welfare mothers, the unemployed, the mentally ill. Is hoarding a vice? What would Locke think? Do you agree or disagree? Why?

Source: Abby Williamson, 'You Don't Need That!' *The Oklahoma Daily* (University of Oklahoma newspaper), www.oudaily.com/news/2010/feb/03/column-you-dont-need/, Wednesday, 3 February 2010.

---

as good, left in common for others'.[70] In short, we cannot take more than our fair share. We must leave the same opportunities for acquiring property to others.

Second, Locke believes that we cannot waste the riches of creation. That is, we cannot hoard for ourselves so much of nature's goods that they begin to spoil. He advises, 'God has given us all things richly. . . . But how far has he given it us? To enjoy. As much as any one can make use of to any advantage of life before it spoils, so much he may by his labour fix a property in: whatever is beyond this, is more than his share, and belongs to others. Nothing was made by God for man to spoil or destroy'.[71]

As explained earlier, Hobbes believes that individuals in the state of nature must compete with one another for the same goods. This natural scarcity leads to a war of all against all. Locke, in comparison, optimistically argues that original nature produces goods in such abundance that there will be more than enough for everyone. He explains that the appropriation of farmland by the first enterprising landowners did not injure anyone else, as there was plenty of land left over for others:

Nor was this [individual] appropriation of any parcel of land, by improving it, any prejudice to any other man, since there was still enough, and as good left. . . . So that, in effect, there was never the less left for others because of his enclosure for himself: for he that leaves as much as another can make use of, does as good as take nothing at all. No body could think himself injured by the drinking of another man, though he took a good draught, who had a whole river of the same water left him to quench his thirst: and the case of land and water, where there is enough of both, is perfectly the same.[72]

Not surprisingly then, Locke does not envision a war of all against all in the state of nature. In Locke's mind, the only real difference between the state of nature and the civilized state is the presence of a judiciary and a formal agency for law-enforcement in the latter. Civilization is a more efficient and reliable means to peace and prosperity, but peace and prosperity are, to a limited extent, possible in the state of nature.

Locke believes that the acquisition of private property is a moral endeavour. The industrious improve the world through their labour and end up owning what rightfully belongs to them. In theory, it is only the lazy and the useless that end up without possessions. This conception of property provides a plausible new basis for making moral judgments about other people. Locke's ideas are abundantly referenced in everyday attitudes. In the minds of many, virtue and financial success go together; and vice and financial failure go together. Wealth requires hard work, individual initiative, discipline, perseverance, frugality, temperance, and so on. Wealth, then, is evidence of virtue. The poor and needy may be that way because they were lazy, intemperate, self-centred.

Locke's account of private property provides a cogent rationale for more specific value judgments. It explains, for example, why gambling—at least to any excessive degree—was traditionally held to be wrong. If I buy a lottery ticket and 'accidentally' win $7 million, I become instantaneously wealthy—not through hard work, not because I improve the world, but through sheer luck. I acquire private property without deserving it. Those who gamble aim to acquire wealth without the accompanying virtue of industriousness. One could extend this moral criticism to other activities such as stock-market speculation.

Or consider the wrongness of stealing. Locke views private property as an extension of the owner. Suppose you make something with your hands. This finished product could be considered as an extension of your hands. Just as your hands belong to you, we could argue that the finished product (which, so to speak, came from your hands) belongs to you. This is, according to Locke, why stealing is wrong. You rightfully own whatever comes about, directly or indirectly, through your labour. You extend, so to speak, through your possessions. They are as much a part of you as your body. Stealing your possessions would be like making off with a part of your body.

Locke's account of private property is, of course, open to valid criticism. Locke himself observes that individuals in the state of nature began to collect and store precious metals, such as gold and silver. This led to the invention of money. As Locke himself acknowledges, hoarding became much easier once money was invented. Money also seems to seriously undermine the intimate connection between virtue and wealth. A money economy permits further accumulation of wealth through speculation and investment. You can make more money, not because you work but because you have money to start with. (This was the traditional sin of usury.) The wealthy also tend to pass on their wealth to their children, which further complicates the connection between work and virtue. If I inherit large sums from my hard-working father, I can be utterly lazy yet wealthy. Private ownership also seems to lead to an unequal distribution of wealth in society, which seems at odds with

Locke's egalitarianism. As we discuss in the next section, a later contractarian such as Jean Jacques Rousseau attacks the resultant consolidation of wealth in modern society.

In this era of looming ecological disaster, we could also take issue with Locke's attitude toward nature. Locke believes that bare nature is not very valuable. It is the investment of human labour in nature that produces value. This is in line with attitudes stemming from the Industrial Revolution. Locke writes,

> It is labour indeed that puts the difference of value on every thing. . . . I think it will be but a very modest computation to say, that of the products of the earth useful to the life of man nine tenths are the effects of labour: nay, if we will rightly estimate things as they come to our use, and cast up the several expences about them, what in them is purely owing to nature, and what to labour, we shall find, that in most of them ninety-nine hundredths are wholly to be put on the account of labour.[73]

This human-centred approach to value underestimates the value of the natural world. Locke assumes that human intervention always improves nature, which, sadly, is not always the case. Nature can be depleted and corrupted by excessive development, and human economic interests may harm the world instead of improving it. We should also point out that nature is not, despite Locke's naive enthusiasm, an inexhaustible source of natural resources. Morality requires a judicious and frugal use of nature.

Jean-Jacques Rousseau and the State of Nature

Jean-Jacques Rousseau (1712–78) was an influential French intellectual, a political philosopher, novelist, essayist, musician, and composer, who developed a great following in Enlightenment Europe. As a celebrated and eccentric personality, his multifaceted and perhaps contradictory views cannot be easily summarized. Still, his ethical sympathies fall clearly within the contractarian camp. His account of the social contract presents a conspicuous foil to Locke. If Locke has been thought to appeal to conservatives who cherish freedom from government intervention, Rousseau has been thought to appeal to those who lean toward government intervention, toward socialism, or even toward Communism. But beware! Although these political generalizations contain a grain of truth, they are overly simple and liable to mislead.

Rousseau was a popular author who produced many well-known texts, including *Emile*, a combined treatise and novel on education; the *Confessions*, his autobiography; *Julie, or The New Heloise*, a sentimental novel; *The Discourse on the Origin of Inequality*, an important essay on moral themes; and finally, an influential political tract entitled *The Social Contract*, where he describes the transition from the state of nature to the political state. Rousseau, like other contractarians, views morality and politics as overlapping aspirations. He argues, first, that progress and civilization are the cause of moral decay; and second, that morality results from a social contract where individuality gives way to a larger collective identity. Let us consider these two ideas in order.

On Progess and Civilization as the Cause of Moral Decay

In *The Discourse on the Origin of Inequality*, Rousseau argues that the steady advance of science and civilization has had disastrous moral consequences.[74] Rousseau believes that the modern society has corrupted the original goodness of human nature. We make money from other people's misfortunes. We compete for financial success. We gain more power when other people have less. Despite surface appearances of camaraderie, loyalty, and harmony, modern individuals are, according to Rousseau, motivated by a selfish concern for individual advancement at the expense of other people. It is hard to overstate the intensity, not to say the ferocity, of Rousseau's rhetoric. Playing the modern role of the angry social critic, he writes this:

> There may be no well-off man whose death is not secretly wished by his grasping heirs, often his own children; no ship at sea whose wreck would not be welcome news for some merchant; no place of business that some debtor would not like to see burn up with all its papers in it; no nation that does not gloat at the disasters of its neighbours. . . . We each find our profit at the expense of our fellows, and one man's loss is nearly always someone else's gain. Public disasters are looked forward to and hoped for by a multitude of individuals. Some wish for diseases, others death, others war, and still others famine. I have seen despicable men weep with sorrow at the prospect of a good harvest; and the deadly Great Fire of London, which claimed the lives of so many ill-fated victims, made the fortunes perhaps of more than ten thousand persons.[75]

Rousseau inverts the Hobbesian formula. Hobbes argues that nature is hostile and that civilization is good. We need morality to escape from nature. Rousseau argues, in sharp contrast, that the state of nature is benevolent and that civilization is bad. We need morality to reform society. In direct opposition to Hobbes, Rousseau claims that 'man is naturally good'.[76] Whereas Hobbes had described human life as 'a ceaseless striving for power

after power until death', Rousseau believes that this condition of 'always wanting more' is an artificial by-product of modern civilization. He compares the free 'savage' in the state of nature to the obsessive civilized man:

> The savage man breathes only peace and freedom; he wishes only to live and remain idle, and even the serenity of the Stoic does not approach his profound indifference. . . . The ever-busy civilized man, in contrast, sweats, scurries about, and constantly frets in search of more laborious occupations; he toils until death. . . . He pays court to great men he loathes and rich men he holds in contempt; he spares nothing to gain the honour of serving them; he delightedly boasts of his own humble station and of their protection, and, proud of his slavery, he speaks patronizing of those who have not the honour of sharing it.[77]

In a kind of amateur history, Rousseau traces out the evolution of the happy-go-lucky savage in the state of nature into the dissatisfied, envious, modern individual. He suggests that it is rivalry for social approval that produced the first seeds of injustice and inequality. This rivalry emerged in primitive gatherings in small villages. Rousseau explains:

> [As] the human race became more sociable. . . . people developed the habit of gathering together in front of their huts or around a large tree. . . . Each person began to gaze on the others, and to want to be gazed on himself and what came to be prized was public esteem. Anyone who best sang or danced; he who was most handsome, the strongest, the most skilful, or the most eloquent came to be the most highly regarded, and this was the first step toward inequality and also toward vice.[78]

Rousseau suggests that this village competition for the attention and adulation of others 'eventually led to concoctions [of negative and positive emotions] ruinous to happiness and innocence'.[79] Those who gained the attention of others became vain and scornful. Those who were ignored came to feel 'shame and envy'. As the desire for social attention and approbation supplanted more natural desires for food, sleep, sexuality, and shelter, people came to view social recognition as the essential ingredient of happiness. Competition for this scarce commodity pitted individual against individual and group against group.

Rousseau believes that the 'savage' in the state of nature lived a largely solitary existence without seeking out the approval of others. This is in complete contrast to the modern world where everyone yearns madly for public recognition and status. Rousseau attributes atrocities, calamities, and wars to this inveterate and jealous competition for social esteem. He maintains that the modern habit of seeking attention from others is dangerous for at least three different reasons. First, we are never satisfied with the attention we receive; we always want more. Second, we are inevitably jealous of the social admiration other individuals receive. And third, when we do not receive social approbation, we take it as a sign of disrespect and even as a matter for violent dispute. Rousseau explains:

> Once men learned to appraise one another and formed the idea of esteem, everyone claimed a right to it, and no one could then be denied it without taking affront. . . . Henceforth every intentional wrong became a grave offence, for along with the harm resulting from the affront, the offended person often saw an insult to his person as more intolerable than the harm itself. Thus, . . . revenge became terrible, and men bloodthirsty and cruel.[80]

As we have explained, Locke associates private property with virtue. Rousseau, in sharp contrast, identifies private property with vice. He observes:

> The true founder of [corrupt, modern] society was the first man who, having enclosed a piece of land, thought of saying, 'This is mine' and came across people simple enough to believe him. How many crimes, wars, murders and how much misery and horror the human race might have been spared if someone had pulled up the stakes or filled in the ditch, and cried out to his fellows: 'Beware of listening to this charlatan. You are lost if you forget that the fruits of the earth belong to all and that the earth itself belongs to no one!'[81]

Rousseau believes that the idea of private property is entirely artificial and disruptive. And that the Lockean view of the world has spawned an inevitable competition to see who can possess the most. He reports on the present-day moral decay that has resulted:

> In all men [we now find] a consuming ambition, the burning passion to increase one's relative fortune, . . . to make oneself superior to others, [which] inspires a dark propensity to harm each other [and] a secret jealousy; . . . in short we have competition and rivalry . . . and always the hidden desire to gain some advantage at other people's expense. All these evils are the first effects of property.[82]

Although Rousseau does not denounce the virtue of industriousness, he believes that the institution of private property championed by philosophers such as Locke has undermined social unity. The resultant accumulation of wealth in the hands of private individuals has fuelled an excess of greed, selfishness, and enmity so as to produce what Rousseau identifies as the most basic injustice of all—inequality in terms of wealth, power and social privilege between classes and individuals. No one can deny the huge gap that separates rich from poor in present-day society. Rousseau believes (like his opponent Locke) that human beings are naturally equal and that the inequality that

---

❧ Applied Philosophy Box 7.5 ❧

The Wealth Divide, The Growing Gap . . . Between the Rich and the Rest

Edward Wolff

The most common measure [of economic inequality] used . . . is: what share of total wealth is owned by the richest households, typically the top 1 percent. In the United States, in the last survey year, 1998, the richest 1 percent of households owned 38 percent of all wealth. . . . The top 5 percent . . . owned 59 percent of all wealth. Or to put it another way, the top 5 percent had more wealth than the remaining 95 percent of the population, collectively. The top 20 percent owns over 80 percent of all wealth. . . . The bottom 20 percent basically have zero wealth. They either have no assets, or their debt equals or exceeds their assets. The bottom 20 percent has typically accumulated no savings.

Relate this article to Rousseau's notion of justice.

Source: Interview with Edward Wolff, *The Multinational Monitor*, 'The Wealth Divide, The Growing Gap in the United States Between the Rich and the Rest,' 24 (5), www.multinationalmonitor.org/mm2003/03may/may03interviewswolff.html, May 2003.

---

disfigures society is deeply immoral. Surely, he has a point.

On Pity and Vice

Rousseau positions himself, from the outset, as an outspoken critic of European society. Before considering his precise take on contractarianism, let us first consider his theory of virtue and vice. Rousseau believes that virtue originates in a natural aptitude for pity and that vice originates in conceit or vanity, what he calls *amour-propre*. We will examine these two ideas next.

Morality Originates in Pity

When it comes to the topic of private property, the difference between Rousseau and Locke could not be greater. When it comes to the topic of virtue, the difference between Rousseau and Hobbes is just as conspicuous. As we have seen, Hobbes views humans as naturally self-interested, whereas Rousseau believes they are naturally disposed to feel pity. Borrowing an example from Bernard Mandeville (an 'immoralist' political thinker and author of *The Fable of the Bees*), Rousseau proposes the following thought experiment. Suppose (to cite from Rousseau's florid prose) a stranger were 'compelled to behold, from a place of confinement, a wild beast tear a child from his mother's breast, crushing the child's fragile limbs with its murderous fangs and ripping out the quivering entrails with its claws'.[83] How would the stranger feel? What would be the effect of this pathetic sight on any normal human being?

Rousseau thinks that any human would be shaken to the core at the contemplation of such a terrible sight. He exclaims excitedly, 'What terrible agitation must be felt by this witness of an event in which he has no personal stake! What agony he must suffer at seeing the sight, and being unable to do anything to help the fainting mother or the dying child!'[84] Strangers would feel pity, not because they felt personally threatened, but because we naturally feel empathy for others. Self-interest would play no role in their resulting emotional turmoil. Rousseau insists that Mandeville's example reveals what all human beings feel *before rational thought*. He states, 'Such is the pure movement of nature, prior to all reflection, such is the force of natural pity, which the most vicious immortality still finds hard to overcome'. [85]

Rousseau, who was influenced, no doubt, by the central Christian emphasis on the theological virtue of love, substitutes pity as the root source of all morality. He claims that without pity, the other virtues would not be possible, for specific virtues such as generosity, mercy, humanity, kindness, and friendship are only more specialized expressions of pity:

> Men, despite all their ethics, would never be anything but monsters if nature had not given them pity to bolster their reason. . . . This trait alone is the source of all the social virtues. . . . Indeed, what are generosity, mercy and humanness if not pity accorded to the weak, the guilty, the human race in general? Kindliness, even friendship, correctly understood, is only the outcome of an enduring pity for a particular object. [86]

Rousseau advances a compelling picture of human nature. Contrary to Hobbes's suggestion, he insists that human beings are naturally sympathetic. People feel *more* sympathy for their fellows in the state of nature than in the civilized world. Modern society inevitably blunts and attenuates the original good impulse of nature. Rousseau goes so far as to argue that reason, knowledge, and even philosophy, in separating us from our feelings, tend to undermine the original moral impulse toward pity:

> Pity becomes stronger as the animal looking on more closely identifies itself with the animal suffering. Clearly, this identification must have been immeasurably more powerful in the state of nature than in the state of reasoning. It is reason

that breeds vanity and reflection that strengthens it; reason that turns men inward; reason that separates man from everything that troubles or afflicts him. It is philosophy that isolates him and prompts him secretly to say at the sight of the person suffering: 'Perish if you will, but I am safe'. [87]

Properly construed, Rousseau's attack on moral philosophy is of a piece with his opposition to modern civilization. Cleverness, a civilized trait, undermines our natural goodness. The inhabitants in the state of nature are simple-minded but in touch with themselves. We moderns, on the other hand, are able to use a spurious logic to distance ourselves from the original good impulse of benevolence inside us. Rather than listening to feelings or intuitions, Rousseau believes that modern philosophers use fancy reasoning to excuse their own self-interested behaviour. He complains:

> Now only dangers to society as a whole will disturb the tranquil sleep of the philosopher and yank him from his bed. Someone may with impunity slit the throat of a fellow man under the philosopher's window, and the philosopher need only put his hands over his ears and argue a bit with himself to prevent nature, which is rebelling inside him, from making him identify himself with the man being murdered. The savage man does not have this commendable talent, and for lack of wisdom and reason he always yields impetuously to the first impulse of human feeling. In riots and street brawls, the crowd always gather round and the cautious man departs; it is the ill-bred rabble, the market-women, who separate the scufflers and prevent decent people from tearing one another to pieces. [88]

Rousseau believes that pity replaces moral reason or conscience in the state of nature. He writes that:

> Pity is a natural sentiment moderating the action of self-love in each individual. . . . It is pity that sends us unreflecting to the aid of those we

see suffering; [and] it is pity that in the state of nature takes the place of laws, moral habits, and virtues. . . . It is pity that, in place of that sublime maxim of rational justice, 'Do unto others as you would have them do unto you', inspires in all men that other maxim of natural goodness, much less perfect but perhaps more useful 'Do what is good to yourself with as little possible harm to others'.[89]

Vice Originates in Amour-Propre

If Rousseau identifies pity as the ultimate source of virtue, he traces vice to *amour-propre*. Translated literally, this French term means 'own-love' or 'love directed towards oneself'. Although some translators render the phrase as 'self-esteem', Rousseau uses it in a distinctly pejorative manner to designate an unhealthy vanity or conceit that thrives off partisan comparisons with other people. Individuals motivated by *amour-propre* seek to be the centre of attention, place themselves on a pedestal, act condescending toward others, and jealously disparage and undermine the status of their imagined rivals.

Rousseau condemns *amour-propre* as 'a relative, artificial sentiment born in society, a sentiment that prompts each individual to set greater store in himself than by anyone else'.[90] He carefully distinguishes between *amour-propre* and what he calls **amour de soi-même** or love of oneself. 'One must not confuse vanity [*amour-propre*] and self-love [*amour de soi-même*]', he explains, for these are 'two very different passions in their nature and their effects. Self-love is a natural sentiment that prompts every animal to watch over its own preservation and that, guided in man by reason and modified by pity, produces humanity and virtue'.[91] It is not self-love but *amour-propre* that leads to the unhealthy

rivalry that Rousseau identifies as the source of modern social injustice. The problem is not that people love themselves; as already explained, the problem is that civilized society transforms a legitimate and healthy concern for the self into a rancorous vanity that pits citizens against one another, producing competition and even open hostility between individuals who should naturally treat one another as colleagues or even as friends. We have already discussed the social ills that result in the previous section.

On the Social Contract, the General Will

We will not focus on the political aspects of Rousseau's controversial views here. As we have seen Rousseau believes that modern, industrialized, commercial society perpetrates vast inequalities in wealth, power, social standing, and privilege. In an influential political tract entitled *The Social Contract*, he proposes, as a contractarian solution to these problems that involves the creation of a new kind of political state.[92] Let us consider the moral ramifications of his account.

Like Hobbes and Locke, Rousseau views morality, in contractarian terms, as an agreement that takes us out of the state of nature. We must leave the state of nature, not to escape open warfare with others but to fully realize ourselves as moral beings. This is a noble destiny. Rousseau explains:

This passage from the state of nature to the civil state produces in man a very remarkable change, replacing instinct by justice in his behaviour, and conferring on his actions the moral quality that they lacked before. It is only now as the voice of duty succeeds to physical impulse and right to appetite, that man who had previously thought of nothing but himself, is compelled to act on other principles, and to consult his reason before he attends to his inclinations. Although in the civil state, he deprives himself of a number of advantages which he has by nature, the [moral advantages] are so great, so greatly are his faculties exercised and improved, his ideas amplified, his feelings ennobled, and his entire soul raised so much higher, that if the abuses that occur in his new condition did not frequently reduce him to state lower than the one he has just left, he ought constantly to bless the happy moment when he was taken from it forever, and which made of him, not a limited and stupid animal, but an intelligent being and a man.[93]

Rousseau believes that morality, understood in contractarian terms as an agreement to co-operate among individuals, elevates human nature, allowing individuals—in the traditional virtue ethics sense—to fully realize their human potential. In establishing a true community, the social contract transforms largely solitary animals in the state of nature into interconnected moral agents who, in submitting to the collectivity, realize themselves as virtuous individuals. Rousseau claims that humans are incapable of rational, thoughtful behaviour if left to their own devices in the state of nature. Morality means obeying the social contract. Without a social contract there is no morality. Virtues such as duty, justice, generosity, friendship, equality, or love are only possible when we live in society in close association with other people.

Rousseau proposes then a revolutionary new contractarian society ruled by a **general will** (*volonté générale*). This general will is composed of the individual wills of citizens joined together into some larger unity. It is an expression of the common good, the embodiment of some shared judgment. Rousseau seems to believe that a just society will not be ruled by particular members but through some sort of consensus-like agreement. Instead of a state ruled by a single ruler, or by partisan politics, Rousseau envisions an almost mystical blending of individual human interests into the larger, purposeful whole. Think of a raindrop falling into a lake. In Rousseau's theory, something similar happens when individual human beings enter into society: they merge with the rest of humanity. Once we have all joined together in a social contract, there is no longer any distinct boundary between separate citizens. From that point forward, we must all be understood as indivisible parts of a larger whole represented by a general will that specifies our communal needs and desires.

Rousseau argues that the social contract that brings the state into existence begins with a radical act of loyalty that requires 'the complete transfer of each associate, with all his rights, to the whole community'.[94] There are two sides to the contract: (1) the state accepts each individual citizen as an equal, indivisible part of itself; and (2) each individual citizen, in turn, agrees to submit to the general will. The result is a transformation of a group of separate individuals into an organic whole that is greater than the sum of its parts. 'In place of the individual persons,' who first came together, there is now a political state, 'a moral and collective body, . . . endowed with its unity, its common self, its life, and its will'.[95]

Rousseau is disturbingly vague when it comes to determining what the general will entails. He assumes that true leaders will know through some sort of moral insight what is best for everyone. They will discern what the general will—which is not always the will of the majority—requires. But this leaves us in a quandary. How are we to know whether leaders are telling the truth when they claim that their decisions and policies represent the general will? Rousseau provides no clear answer to this question. This is particularly troubling as, in Rousseau's account, we are obliged to obey the general will at all times. In return for social acceptance, each citizen agrees to do whatever the general will commands: 'Each [individual] puts his person and all his power in common under the supreme direction of the general will.'[96]

If this seems like a recipe for totalitarianism, Rousseau does not retreat from the disturbing conclusion. He writes, 'If anyone refuses to obey the general will he will be compelled to do so by the whole body'.[97] If citizens do not do what the general will commands, they will be forced to do so against their will. In Rousseau's system, *this counts as freedom*. In

obeying the state, you are obeying your larger self. (Remember, once you have been joined to the rest of society in the social contract, you are no longer a separate individual but a mere extension of the state.) Rousseau goes so far as to insist that when a citizen is 'compelled' to do something against his will by the whole community, this 'means nothing else than that he will be forced to be free'.[98]

Being 'forced to be free' is a worrisome concept. Rousseau's contractarianism is extreme: we become free *when we are ruled by the political state*. Rousseau disagrees with Hobbes's negative notion of freedom. Freedom does not mean doing what we feel like doing; it means obeying a higher moral law. This is in line with earlier moral theories, *except* that Rousseau identifies moral law with the general will. To be free is to submit to the public good as expressed and embodied in the laws and

---

❧ Applied Philosophy Box 7.6 ❧

From a Review of *The Rise of Totalitarian Democracy,* by J.L. Talmon

Irving Kristol

There are, according to Talmon, three stages in the development of 'totalitarian democracy' in the French Revolution. First, there was the Rousseauist intellectual background, which rejected all existing institutions as relics of despotism and clerical obscurantism, and which demanded a complete renovation of society so that it would be an expression of the General Will—this last being no mere consensus but an objective standard of virtue and reason that imperfect humanity must be coerced into obeying. . . . Second, there was the Reign of Terror, when an 'enlightened' vanguard of Jacobins undertook to impose the General Will—when Robespierre acted out his role as 'the bloody hand of Rousseau', as Heine called him. Third, there was the post-Thermidorean conspiracy of Babeuf and his associates, which added to political messianism the doctrine of economic communism, thereby pointing the way to Marx.

J.L. Talmon argues that Rousseau's vague notion of a general will that we must all obey leads inevitably to totalitarianism. This is a common criticism. Do you agree? Is the idea of a 'general will' morally and politically useful?

Source: Irving Kristol, 'Review of *The Rise of Totalitarian Democracy*, by J.L. Talmon.' *Commentary Magazine*, www.commentarymagazine.com/viewarticle.cfm/the-rise-of-totalitarian-democracy--by-j--l--talmon-1568, September 1952.

policies of the reigning political authority. In transforming us into moral beings, the social contract frees us from our brutish self-absorption, making moral achievement possible through submission to the political state. Citizens realize their potential as virtuous human beings only in submitting to the political will of society. But this seems to be a recipe for authoritarianism. It is not simply that Rousseau's use of the term 'general will' is ambiguous and open to variable interpretation. The very idea that we are free only when we do what we are told to do leaves room for enormous abuse. Not surprisingly, perhaps, Rousseau's political and moral ideas took a turn toward a radical collectivism in communism, a political system with deeply moral undertones.

Karl Marx: Rousseau's Legacy

Rousseau's influence on European intellectual society was far-reaching, but it played a particularly prominent role in the work of Karl Marx (1818–83) and his associate and patron, Friedrich Engels (1820–95). We will consider briefly the *moral* content of Marxism here.[99]

Marx and his followers were fond of making comments to the effect that communism entails the abolishment of bourgeois morality. But Marx's campaign against capitalism depends upon an appeal to justice understood as equality. Marx argues, in short, that the capitalist system of private property is morally wrong. Why? Because it unfairly divides citizens into *unequal* classes: the owners (the bourgeoisie) and the workers (the proletariat). The former are wealthy and powerful; the latter are poor and powerless. Like Rousseau, Marx believes that something has gone disastrously wrong with modern

civilization. If, however, Rousseau attributes inequality in society to individual vice, Marx transforms Rousseau's moral complaint into a larger attack on capitalist society as a whole. Injustice is not, rigorously speaking, a matter of individual behaviour but a matter of systemic or structural injustice. It is the organization of the whole 'political economy' that leads to abuse.

Marx claims that capitalist society is organized so as to unfairly impoverish the workers and enrich the business classes. Human labour, in a capitalist economy, creates a basic dichotomy:

> [It] produces for the rich wonderful things—but for the worker it produces privation. It produces palaces [for the rich]—but for the worker, hovels. It produces beauty [for the rich]—but for the worker deformity. It replaces labor by machines [so the rich don't have to work], but it . . . turns . . . workers into machines. It produces intelligence [for the rich]—but for the worker stupidity, cretinism [i.e., extreme stupidity].[100]

Things have gotten so bad, Marx thinks, that armed revolution is the only answer. Workers must violently overthrow the capitalist status quo. They must *force* the capitalist classes at gunpoint to surrender their power and their wealth.

Marxism can be viewed as a forward-looking rather than a backward-looking contractarianism. Marx situates the hypothetical consensus that justifies the political order in the future rather than in the past. Whereas Hobbes, Locke, and even Rousseau claim that society begins with a social contract that brings morality into existence, Marx believes that society begins in oppression with one class lording it over the other. He views capitalist society as little more than a thinly disguised state of nature (a sugges-

---

◈ Applied Philosophy Box 7.7 ◈

The Legacy of Karl Marx

Duncan Hallas

[Actually, Marxism] is about . . . how working men and women can create a truly free society in which all contribute according to their ability and receive according to their needs—a society free from exploitation, free from oppression, free from racism, from unemployment, from war, from poverty and inequality. Is all this pie in the sky? The early Christians had just such a vision. Except that they saw it coming in an (imaginary) world above the sky, and they looked to a savior, Lord Jesus, to get them to it. Marx showed how it could be gotten in this world—and not by a supernatural savior, but by the collective efforts of working people themselves.

This is Marx viewed by a Marxist. Do you agree or disagree? Why? Explain how this represents a chronological inversion of the usual contractarian scheme.

Source: Duncan Hallas, 'The Legacy of Karl Marx.' *Socialist Worker*, http://socialistworker.org/2002-2/423/423_08_HallasOnMarx.shtml, 27 September 2002.

---

tion first found in Rousseau). In Marx's account, the goal of political activity is to escape *organized* injustice through violent revolution. Consensus is possible, but only at some future date in a classless utopia when individuals live in solidarity. It is this *future*, not past, agreement that legitimizes the political state.

It may seem odd to base the legitimacy of a political view on a tentative agreement that will (allegedly) happen in the future, but as we have seen, most contemporary contractarians accept that the agreement that legitimizes society cannot be traced to an actual historical event. The social contract is an in-principle theoretical event; an hypothesis that puts on display what ideally rational agents would agree to. If, however, the social contract is only hypothetical, it should not matter whether it is located in the past or future. If rational agents would agree, either in the past or the future, this should be enough to establish the legitimacy of the resulting political regime.

Marx, who argues for the abolition of private property, is usually thought of as an inveterate opponent to Locke. But this is overly simple. In *The Communist Manifesto*, Marx addresses an imaginary member of the bourgeoisie:

> You are horrified at intending to do way with private property. But in your existing society private property is already done away with for nine-tenths of the population. . . . You reproach us, therefore, with intending to do away with a form of property the necessary condition for whose existence is the non-existence of property for the immense majority of society.[101]

This is, however, to make a *Lockean* argument. As we have already seen, Locke himself sets strict limits on private property. An individual can own property *just so long as there is enough left over for everyone else*. This is, according to Marx, why capitalism is wrong. Because the bourgeoisie have such a monopoly on private property, there is none left over for workers.

According to Marx, capitalism is little more than theft, for it is the workers in the factories who have mixed their labour with the finished products. When the owners sell these products and keep the profits for themselves (without providing equivalent remuneration to the workers) they are stealing what does not belong to them. Marx calls this economic arrangement, where owners unfairly expropriate the value of the workers' labour for themselves, **exploitation**. Justice requires that the workers rise up and forcibly re-appropriate what has been taken from them. Notice, again, that Marx relies here on a Lockean explanation of property.

Marxism has spawned innumerable and often conflicting interpretations. Marx champions historical determinism, the idea that history marches forward in some unalterable pattern. This leaves little room for free choice. At the same time, he repeatedly appeals to a sense of moral outrage, to an ideal of justice and fairness, and even to a sort of virtue ethics. Although his stance is deeply inconstant, his moral ideas are provocative and, in their own way, insightful. His description of the **alienation** of modern workers is particularly powerful.

In a discussion of alienation, Marx claims that capitalism turns human beings into brutes, dehumanizing them and separating them from their own human nature. (Workers become an alien object to themselves; hence, their *alien*ation.) Marx comments:

> In his work [the labourer] does not affirm himself but denies himself, does not feel content but unhappy, does not develop freely his physical and mental energy but mortifies his body and ruins his mind. . . . As a result, therefore, man (the worker) only feels himself freely active in his animal functions,—eating, drinking, procreating, or at most in his dwelling and in dressing-up etc.; in his human function he no longer feels himself to be anything but an animal.[102]

Marx identifies an apparent paradox in the industrial world. As the quality of marketable goods improves, working conditions deteriorate to a corresponding degree:

> The more the worker produces, the less he has to consume; the more value he creates, the more valueless, the more unworthy he becomes; the better formed his product, the more deformed the worker; the more civilized his object, the more barbarous becomes the worker; the more powerful labor becomes, the more powerless becomes the worker; the more ingenious labor becomes, the less ingenious becomes the worker.[103]

Marx claims that the capitalist economy is organized so as to facilitate the mass production of marketable goods at the expense of the labourer: 'The worker becomes a slave of the object.'[104] What is human—the worker—is subjugated to the object, which is bought and sold. Workers are removed from the arena of human achievement and treated like animals, or worse, like machines. They are deprived of any opportunity for human self-fulfillment, self-realization, or moral happiness. Thus, it becomes impossible for workers to achieve human self-realization—i.e., to lead virtuous lives—in a capitalist economic environment. It goes without saying that Marx's theories had an explosive effect on modern history, an issue we will not explore here.

On Hypothetical Agreement

Contractarianism represents an influential episode in the history of moral philosophy. To equate morality with what sensible people would agree to is an effective way of illuminating what is morally acceptable. Suppose you are considering entering into some arrangement. You can always ask yourself, 'What would rational agents do in this circumstance?

Would sensible people agree to this?' This is, in effect, what is going on in contractarianism. Contemporary contractarians, such as John Rawls, Gauthier, Narveson, and Hampton, further develop these ideas in various ways.

There are two kinds of contractarianism: what we have already called exclusive contractarianism and two-tiered contractarianism. Exclusive contractarianism attempts to derive all morality from agreement; two-tiered contractarianism recognizes the existence of a prior moral sense that provides criteria for judging whether agreement is morally legitimate or not. Hobbes often writes as if he is championing exclusive contractarianism; Locke argues for two-tiered contractarianism. In Rousseau and Marx, the emphasis is on a hypothetical agreement that is self-evidently moral. So they could be said to embrace a two-tiered model as well. We have suggested that the two-tiered model is, epistemologically, more plausible.

We will discuss the role of consent more fully when we consider liberalism. For the moment, simply note that although specific obligations arise through consent, moral standards exist prior to agreement. Contemporary philosopher Michael Sandel decisively makes this point in a discussion of contractarian John Rawls's theory of liberal justice. Rawls draws a distinction between **natural duties** and **obligations**. As Sandel explains,

[There are] two ways in which persons may be bound—as a matter of natural duty or of obligation. Natural duties are those moral claims that apply to persons irrespective of their consent, such as the duties to help others in distress, not be cruel, to do justice, and so on. Such duties are 'natural' in the sense that they are not tied to any particular institutions or social arrangements but are owed to persons generally. Obligations, by contrast, describe those moral ties we voluntarily incur, whether by contract or promise or other expression of consent. The obligations of public office voluntarily sought are one such example. But even with obligations, consent is not sufficient to create the tie. A further condition is that the institution or practice agreed to be just.[105]

Rawls himself illustrates the point with a useful example:

Thus we have a natural duty not to be cruel, and a duty to help another, whether or not we have committed ourselves to these actions. It is no defense or excuse to say that we have made no promise not to be cruel or vindictive, or to come to another's aid. Indeed, a promise not to kill, for example, is normally ludicrously redundant, and the suggestion that it establishes a moral requirement where none already existed is mistaken. Such a promise is in order, if it ever is so, only when for special reasons one has a right to kill, perhaps in a situation arising in a just war.[106]

The contractarian conceit that society is based on some logically prior agreement is a useful way of isolating the basic moral requirements necessary for a just and prosperous community. It does not follow, as some theorists (like Hobbes) imply, that the bare fact of agreement is enough for morality. Morality is not restricted to what we have formally or specifically agreed to. The nature of some bad (or good) acts is enough to 'impose' moral obligations on me whether I agree to them or not. (Hence Locke's condemnation of even consensual slavery.) If I do not agree to do morally required acts, I am a bad person. That is all. Some acts are morally required whether I agree to them or not.

A moderate contractarianism recognizes these limitations. In focusing on *hypothetical* agreement, it widens the scope of moral interaction to include whatever rational agents would freely agree to if they were fully informed. It is not whether a particular living individual has actually consented. The question is this: Would these agents consent if they were fully informed and rational? This is a useful way of approaching moral questions.

On Contractarian Virtue

Philosophers in the modern world have developed separate, competing schools of moral philosophy. This is not the approach taken here. Contractarianism is not often associated with virtue, but this is short-sighted. It is not mere agreement but agreement backed up by reliable character that matters. Consider what a virtuous person would look like viewed from a contractarian perspective. There are three different approaches we might take to this problem.

A Hobbesian/Lockean/Rousseauian Approach

Hobbes lists the virtues he associates with contractarianism. We could, to begin with, provide an updated list. To wit:

1. Contractarianism requires agents who keep their promises. Agreements mean nothing if they are not upheld. Call this reliability, honesty, trustworthiness, integrity, justice.
2. Contractarianism requires good will. Individuals have to be willing, at least initially, to join in agreements with others. Call this optimism, affability, openness, optimism, even hope.
3. Contractarianism requires ideally rational agents, agents who are knowledgeable enough to make good decisions. Call this prudence.

4. Contractarianism presupposes fundamental human equality. Call this recognition of the most basic human equality: civility or impartiality.
5. Contractarianism treats law as a moral imperative. Call the virtue of obeying (legitimate) law: due diligence, lawfulness, or law-abidingness.
6. Contractarianism requires that authority be wielded in a manner that rational agents would agree to. Call this ability: fairness, justice, or reasonableness.
7. Contractarianism does not disparage self-love, properly understood. Call 'good self-love': self-respect or self-esteem.
8. Contractarianism generally presupposes a realm of private life free from interference. Call this respect for individuality, tolerance.
9. Contractarianism, of a Lockean sort, proposes an ideal of hard work. Call this industry, self-discipline, initiative, proper ambition.
10. Contractarianism, of a Lockean sort, requires that we leave enough for others. Call this humanity, selflessness, concern for others.
11. Contractarianism, of a Rousseauian sort, requires that we do not lose touch with deep moral feeling. Call this authenticity.
12. Contractarianism, of a Rousseauian sort, requires that we do not abuse philosophy by inventing clever arguments to excuse our indifference to other people. Call this sincerity.

And so on.

The exact terminology we use to describe each character trait is not so important. The purpose here is not to compile any exhaustive, definitive list of contractarian virtues but only to show the kinds of character traits a contractarian would value. Clearly, the idea that morality is best represented as a contract is compatible with the idea that virtues are a necessary part of morality.

The Traditional Cardinal Virtues Approach

A second way of examining the relationship between contractarianism and virtue is to review the traditional schedule of cardinal virtues, applying them to the notion of moral agreement. We could define *justice*, in contractarian terms, as keeping our agreements. But we also ne need *prudence* to determine which agreements we should consent to; we need *perseverance* to keep to our agreements, and we need *temperance* because intemperance often causes us to break our agreements. (We could even extend this analysis to include the theological virtues of faith, hope, and charity. Seen from the perspective of moral agreement, we need to have *faith* in people before we can make agreements with them; we need *hope* to prompt agreement; and we need *love* or co-operation to keep to our agreements with others.)

The Virtue through Concrete Example Approach

Finally, we could describe contractarian virtue through concrete example. What virtues, for example, would you look for in a good business partner? Surely, you would not go into business with just anyone. If you were going to depend upon someone else for your livelihood, you would demand and expect certain attitudes, commitments, and dependable positive behaviour. You would want to be sure the person was honest, reliable, thorough, courteous, frugal, prompt, and so on. Insomuch as morality is based on agreement with other people, these are the virtues any moral person should exhibit.

❧ Questions for Study and Review ❧

1. Define contractarianism.
2. According to contractarianism, how does morality begin?
3. What does the 'Anonymous' identify as the most important virtue and the most important vice? Why?
4. Why did Hobbes entitle a book on moral and political philosophy *Leviathan*? Relate to his contractarianism.
5. Explain succinctly Hobbes's psychology. How does he explain the origin and the intent of human behaviour?
6. How would Hobbes respond to ancient thinkers such as the Stoics, who emphasized virtue such as temperance and ascetic practices? How would those ancient thinkers respond to Hobbes, in turn?
7. Hobbes identifies three main sources of human quarrels. Identify each and explain.
8. In the contractarian account, what is the relationship between self-interest and morality?
9. Compare Locke's account of the state of nature with Hobbes's account of the state of nature. How do they differ? How are they the same?
10. Locke subscribes to a 'two-tiered' contractarianism. Compare with Hobbes's 'exclusive' contractarianism.
11. Locke believes in democracy and that democracy is a moral requirement for justice. Explain.

12. Compare Rousseau's account of the state of nature with Hobbes's account of the state of nature. Who do you agree with? Why?

13. Compare Locke's and Rousseau's views of private property.

14. Compare *amour-propre* ('own love') to *amour de soi-même* ('self-love').

15. What, according to Rousseau, is the primary purpose of the social contract?

16. In what sense does Marx share Rousseau's moral disdain for modern society? (Hint: think of his notion of economic class.)

17. Marx proposes a forward-looking contractarianism. Explain. Compare to Hobbes, Locke, and Rousseau.

18. What does it mean to say that the social contract is a *hypothetical* contract (either in the past or the future)?

19. Describe at least four virtues that a contractarian account of ethics presupposes.

20. Explain the relationship between the cardinal virtues and contractarianism.

✍ Suggestions for Further Reading ✍

- Thomas Hobbes, *Leviathan*, John Gaskin, ed. (Oxford, UK: Oxford, 1998).
- For another easily available edition, consult: Thomas Hobbes, *Leviathan*, Edwin Curley, ed. (Indianapolis, IN: Hackett Publishing, f1994).
- Thomas Hobbes, *The Elements of Law, Human Nature, and De Corpore Politico*, John Gaskin, ed. (Oxford, UK: Oxford, 1999).
- John Locke, *Two Treatises of Government*, Peter Laslett, ed. (Cambridge, UK: Cambridge University Press, 1961).
- Jean-Jacques Rousseau, *Discourse on Inequality*, Patrick Coleman, ed.; Franklin Philip, trans. (Oxford, UK: Oxford, 1999).
- Jean-Jacques Rousseau, *Discourse on Political Economy*, *The Social Contract*, Christopher Betts, trans. (Oxford, UK: Oxford, 1999).
- Karl Marx, Friedrich Engels, *The Communist Manifesto*, David McLellan, ed. (Oxford, UK: Oxford, 1998).
- Freidrich Engels, *The Condition of the Working Class in England*, David McLellan, ed. (Oxford, UK: Oxford, 1999).

Chapter Eight

Kant:
Duty and Moral Law

Introduction

Immanuel Kant (1724–1804) was a German philosopher from Königsberg in Prussia, a medium-sized city on the Baltic Sea that is now called Kaliningrad and located in Russia. Kant is generally regarded as a leading representative of German philosophy and one of the most influential philosophers of the European Enlightenment. He wrote many influential works. We will discuss, in particular, his *Groundwork for the Metaphysics of Morals*.

Kant's life was remarkably uneventful. He was raised in a Pietist household. The **Pietists** were zealous, biblically oriented Lutherans who were suspicious of the established Church and ecclesiastical hierarchy. They were stern, rigid, and somewhat anti-intellectual, avoiding all theological speculation and stressing a personal relationship to God. They were, in effect, German Puritans. Although Kant's own moral philosophy is determinedly secular in its orientation, as we shall see, he could not escape the influence of this earlier religious formation or of the historical influences of his time.

Kant and the Enlightenment

We cannot properly appreciate Kant's moral philosophy without placing him within his historical context. Kant was, first, a self-conscious spokesman of the European Enlightenment, and second, a child of the **Protestant Reformation**. Let us begin by considering how these events influenced his philosophical perspective and thought.

The *Oxford English Dictionary* defines the **Enlightenment** as 'the 18th Century philosophical movement in Europe in which reason and individualism were emphasized at the expense of tradition'. The imagery here is important. Thinkers of the En*light*enment thought of themselves as agents of progress, 'lighting' up the darkness of an old and stultified civilization. (The Enlightenment was referred to in French as *le Siècle des Lumières*, which means 'the Century of Light'.) This wide-ranging group of cutting-edge intellectuals heralded the dawning of a new age. Filled with almost missionary zeal, they enlisted in an ideological cause: the overthrow of the establishment; of traditional ideas; of the political, religious, and philosophical status quo. Their philosophy expresses immense energy, supreme self-confidence, a belief in progress, and a deep optimism that, over time, becomes tempered by darker skepticism. Still, Enlightenment thinkers, especially in its early stages, see themselves as bold adventurers travelling down an uncharted road that leads from a dogmatic, religious, and unscientific past to a new age of tolerance, reason, liberty, and empirical science.

Kant closely identified himself with the aspirations of his generation. In a famous essay entitled 'What Is Enlightenment?' he, rather typically, presents this historical movement as a brave step forward from a childish, unthinking reliance on religious and **secular** authority to intellectual freedom. Here is how his essay begins:

> Enlightenment is man's emergence from his self-incurred immaturity. Immaturity is the inability to use one's own understanding without the guidance of another. This immaturity is self-incurred if its cause is not lack of understanding, but lack of resolution and courage to use it without the guidance of another. The motto of enlightenment is therefore: *Sapere aude*! [Dare to know!] Have courage to use your own understanding![1]

In Kant's mind, the Enlightenment is about intellectual and moral self-affirmation. What matters is taking charge of our own lives and minds and daring to think for ourselves, outside the box of prior thought and tradition. (There is an echo here of the sentiment that motivated the Protestant Reformation.)

Kant's 'beware of outside authority!' stance may sound radical, but the German philosopher is quite conservative by contemporary standards. Kant does not believe in political revolution. He believes that moral and political progress is a gradual thing. 'A revolution . . . will never produce a true reform in ways of thinking,' he writes.[2] And again, 'A public can only achieve enlightenment slowly'.[3] Kant believes that we must change our fundamental ways of thinking, moving gradually, in an orderly manner, from an exaggerated adherence to traditional ways of thinking to a new rationalism that operates, not out of an uncritical deference to what went before but on the basis of evidence and logic. Even Kant's moral philosophy is, as we shall see, an attempt to be strictly logical.

On Reformation Theology

Kant's moral philosophy is resolutely secular. Enlightenment thinkers generally distrusted religion because they saw it as superstitious and authoritarian. In his Enlightenment essay, Kant writes, 'I have portrayed matters of religion as the focal point of enlightenment, i.e. of man's emergence from his self-incurred immaturity. This is . . . because religious immaturity is the most pernicious and dishonorable variety of all'.[4] Kant is worried that unquestioning, docile believers forfeit their reason for a blind adherence to inflexible **dogma**. After early schooling in a strict religious environment, he vowed never to set foot in a church again, a promise he apparently kept.[5] This does not mean that Kant had no religious convictions; indeed, his own position on religion and on the deep nature of morality is heavily influenced by the Protestant Reformation. Nonetheless, Kant strives to present morality as an expression of secular reason, not as a series of commands from God.

Kant's emphasis on individual conscience, his distrust of religious authority, and his objection to unchanging dogma is clearly influenced by the Protestant emphasis on the unfettered individual interpretation of Scripture. Reformation thinkers, influenced by Saint Augustine, emphasize the utter sinfulness of human nature. They elaborate, in extreme terms, the theological doctrine that man is so wicked that he cannot merit heaven by his own efforts. The intent of this theological speculation is to give all glory to God and to emphasize our utter dependence the free gift of God's undeserved grace. But the reverse side of the coin is an extremely negative picture of human nature. Kant, despite his reservations about traditional religion, is deeply affected by this negative picture of human nature.

A religious theme that haunts Reformation theology is the story of the original fall from grace of Adam and Eve, the parents of humanity, in the Garden of Eden. There are two things to notice about the story. First, the fall of our original parents stains human nature, indelibly marking it with **Original Sin**, and leaving us forever tainted with a proclivity toward sinfulness. Second, Adam and Eve are driven out of the Garden into a harsh new world of 'thorns and thistles', 'sweat', 'painful toil', and 'pain in childbearing'.[6] This is a world where husbands dominate wives, where childbirth comes about through labour, where harsh nature grudgingly gives up her food and shelter, where humanity has to work hard to survive, and where human life ends in death and decay. Both of these themes—that life is hard and that human beings are unworthy—surface in Kant's work. They provide a way into his thought.

On Duty

In a treatise on international relations, Kant laments the difficulty—indeed, the impossibility—of constructing a lasting peace between nations. Why? Because 'from such crooked wood as man is made of, nothing perfectly straight can be built'.[7] We cannot achieve political peace, Kant believes, because human nature is deeply flawed. It has been warped and twisted as if by Original Sin. Left to their own inclinations humans give themselves over to the pursuit of their own self-indulgent, capricious needs and pleasures. They ignore the moral imperative. This leads, naturally enough, to conflict between different groups.

Kant's view of humanity represents a major shift in philosophical anthropology. As we have seen in the earlier chapters, Aristotle, and early Greek thinkers in general, situate morality in human nature. So do the Stoics and Thomas (and other natural law thinkers). In this earlier account, morality comes naturally. And while we are all capable of immorality, it is inevitably seen as a deviation from human nature. In this traditional view, morality results when we allow our own natures to unfold according to their inner proclivities. Kant, in sharp contrast, cannot situate morality in human nature, for he seems to accept that the original goodness in humanity has been bent out of shape by the sinfulness of the Original Fall; we are made of twisted timber. We must force ourselves to be good against the grain of nature. This is why Kant stresses the importance of will. He proposes a kind of 'clenched-teeth-in-spite-of-everything-else-I-will-force-myself-to-do-what-is-right' morality. Morality depends upon sheer willpower.

This is the best we can do. We cannot change human nature; we can, however, dominate and control it in line with correct moral thinking.

Kant proposes a **deontological ethics**, that is, an ethics based on duty, on a strong sense of moral obligation. Kant defines **duty** as 'the necessity of an act done out of respect for the law'.[8] Dutiful people do the moral thing, not because they feel like doing it, not because it comes easily, but solely because it is their duty, i.e., because the moral law requires them to do it. To act out of duty is to do what is required independent of our feelings, desires, personal inclinations, or even the consequences. To act out of duty is to do what is right simply because it is right and for no other reason.

The word *duty* has a harsh ring to it. For example, the expression 'doing your duty' can signify the completion of an onerous, difficult, arduous task: it can be an achievement that takes effort, blood, sweat, and tears. This is, in Kant's mind, how it must be. If human nature has been corrupted, morality will require, of course, a lot of hard work and self-denial. In the Kantian view—in comparison to, say, the natural law view—we have to erase inclination from the moral equation. *Our inclinations push*

ᴥ Applied Philosophy Box 8.1 ᴥ

Ohio Teen Sentenced 2 Years for Baby's Rat Bites, Loss of Toes

Waverly, Ohio —An 18-year-old Ohio man has been sentenced to two years in prison for his role in an infant's loss of two toes to rat bites inside a filthy mobile home. . . . Authorities discovered in July that the 6-week-old girl had been seriously injured by rats. . . . Child endangering charges are still pending against . . . the mother.

The problem here is that the mother and her boyfriend did not do their duty. Explain.

Source: Associated Press, 'Ohio Teen Sentenced 2 Years for Baby's Rat Bites, Loss of Toes.' *Fox News*, www.foxnews.com, Tuesday, 6 October 2009.

us in the wrong direction. Kant writes, 'The only thing that could be an object of [moral] respect . . . [is] something that does not serve my inclination but overpowers it or at least excludes it entirely from my decision-making—consequently, [it must be] nothing but the law itself'.[9] Kant believes that the moral person acts out of respect for the moral law, that is all. Morality is not about emotion; it is not about doing what comes naturally; it is not about following temperament or inclination. This results in a very cold, cerebral account of moral behaviour. In the perfectly moral person, nothing else remains in the mind but the logic of the moral law, independent of inclination, temperament, or feeling as the motivating force or engine of action.

As we have seen, truly moral action origi-nates in good will, that is, in having the right intention. But how can we know if someone has the right intention? Kant explains:

> Out of charity I am willing to grant that most of our actions are in accord with duty; but if we look more closely at the devising and striving that lies behind them, then everywhere, we run into the dear self which is always there; and it is this and not the strict command of duty (which would often require self-denial) that underlies our intentions. One need not be an enemy of virtue but only a dispassionate observer . . . to become doubtful at certain moments whether any genuine virtue can really be found in the world. (Such doubts occur particularly as one grows older and experience renders one's power of judgment and observation shrewder and more discerning.)[10]

Kant believes that the mere fact that we do what is right is not enough. We may be doing what is right for the wrong reasons. Indeed, he suspects that we mostly do what is right, not because it is right but because it is in our self-

interest, because it is to our own advantage. In other words, we do the right thing because moral behaviour is rewarded or because we are afraid to act immorally, not because it is the right thing.

Kant proposes a morality for the pure-in-heart. He identifies four categories of human behaviour:

1. **Blatant immorality:** One can break the moral law; one can lie, cheat, steal, murder, and so on. Such acts are unambiguously evil.
2. **Self-interested 'morality':** One can act in conformity with the moral law for self-inter-ested reasons. Kant points to the example of the shopkeeper who is honest with his customers, not out of respect for the moral law, not because dishonesty is immoral, but because he knows that if he gains a reputa-tion for dishonesty, his customers will stop buying at his store. This individual obeys the moral law about telling the truth for self-interested reasons; therefore, he is not truly moral.
3. **Morality by inclination:** One can act in conformity with the moral law and in conformity with direct inclination. Kant mentions two examples. There is a moral law that requires us to preserve human life. If, however, we protect ourselves, not because it is the moral law but because we are afraid to die, we act 'in conformity *with duty* but not *out of duty*'.[11] Preserving our life merely because we are frightened is not a truly moral act. Again, Kant points out that 'it is a duty to help others where one can'.[12] If, however, we help others because we 'find an inner pleasure in spreading joy, . . . taking delight in the contentment of others, [our behaviour] still has no genuinely moral worth'.[13] Why? Because these charitable acts are done for our own self-gratification,

because we *enjoy* doing them. We are acting out of personal inclination, not out of duty. These acts may look like moral acts from the outside, but they are expressions of psychological egoism, not morality.

4. **Genuine morality:** One can act in accordance with the moral law *against* self-interest and *against* inclination. This is, for Kant, what true goodness entails. He mentions two examples of genuine morality. Suppose someone is subject to such misfortune that she wishes she were dead. Yet this person refrains from suicide out of a sense of moral duty. Kant writes that if 'disappointments and hopeless misery have entirely taken away someone's taste for life; if that wretched person, strong in soul and more angered at fate than faint-hearted or cast down, longs for death and still preserves life without loving it—not out of inclination but out of duty—then indeed that person's [motivation] has moral worth'.[14] Moral individuals preserve their lives because it is the right thing to do—not because they are enjoying life or are afraid of death.

The second example of genuine moral behaviour involves people who give to charity, not because they are so inclined but solely because it is the right thing to do:

> Suppose . . . the mind [of the charitable person] were overclouded by sorrows of his own which extinguished all compassion for the fate of others, but that he still had the power to assist others in distress; suppose that . . . no longer moved by any inclination, he nevertheless tears himself out of this deadly apathy and does the action without any inclination, solely out of duty. Then for the first time his action has genuine moral worth . . . It is precisely in this that the worth of character begins to show—a moral worth, and incomparably the highest—namely that he does good, not out of inclination, but out of duty.[15]

Kant seems to limit moral achievement to cases of genuine morality. We are moral when we force ourselves to do our duty against the pull of self-interest and inclination. Kant concedes that we could, in principle, conceive of someone who would possess a **holy will** like a saint or an angel or Jesus. This perfectly virtuous person would automatically do what is right without any internal struggle. But Kant believes that the behaviour of someone with a holy will is above morality; it has no relevance to the human condition. The activity of morality, as he conceives of it, is a distinctly human pursuit undertaken by flawed natures. Morality is a matter for ordinary human beings, not perfect saints.

If morality means acting out of duty, duty arises out of obligation. Obligation comes into existence when a flawed nature sees the necessity of acting in a certain way. To be obliged is to be *forced*—not physically forced, but forced by the requirements of reason—to act accordingly. As Kant, somewhat cumbersomely, explains, 'The dependence of a will not absolutely good on the principle of . . . moral necessitation is *obligation*'.[16] In this account, the concept of moral obligation could not apply to someone with a holy will: 'A will whose [decisions] necessarily agree with [moral] laws is a holy, absolute good will. . . . Obligation can thus not apply to a holy being.'[17] Those who have a holy will do not need to be pushed to do what is good; they do what they should do automatically, effortlessly. They do not do what is right from moral obligation but from nature.

In fact, a human being with a holy will is, for Kant, a pure impossibility. As human beings, we must experience morality as constant warfare between our better judgment and our natural inclinations. This is the human predicament. Imagine a situation in which doing the right thing does not feel good; where it causes personal pain, produces loss, leaves one open to persecution, and puts one at a disadvantage. You must do the right thing regardless. Why? Because it is your duty! Kant believes that anything other than a mental determination to do your duty because it is your duty is less than moral. We must do what is right simply because it is right; that is all.

Needless to say, Kant sets a very high standard for moral behaviour. Still, some virtue ethicists criticize the narrowness of the Kantian approach because this is not what *all* of moral life is about. Suppose you were to tell your spouse, 'I love you but only out of duty'. Your spouse would not be impressed! We must love our partners even when we do not feel like it—even when we are too tired, or sick, or burnt out, or poor, or disappointed to derive any pleasure from the relationship. And in those instances, the Kantian formula— to do what is good because it is good—rings true. Still, in the best marriages, love is not a burden. Happiness and inclination and morality and even self-interest come together. But marriage is a moral aspiration. It follows that morality is not always an onerous burden, nor should it be.

Kant's approach, despite its strengths, is unnecessarily narrow. It leaves little room for the person with a good character who enjoys doing what is right in accordance with rightly formed desires. Kant is convinced that the most we can hope for is to be able to resist our thoroughly bad natures. Aristotle's continent man, then, becomes the new moral ideal: even when we are good, we must suffer through constant temptation. There is no room here for virtuous individuals who only experience good desires they enjoy satisfying in the performance of their moral acts.

Kant's morality has a Puritan tone. It is a morality of obeying strict rules regardless of our feelings. This conception of right and wrong is not without value; in fact, in a world where we all struggle against temptation, it strikes a deep cord. On the other hand, Kant's purist approach seems very limited. No human being is perfectly good, but there are times and occasions when individual human beings *desire* the good and act accordingly. The person who has come to enjoy helping others through volunteer work is one such example. This is a real possibility—indeed, an ideal we should strive toward.

Morality Derives from Pure, A Priori Reason

Kant narrows down the moral focus in another way. Like earlier authors in the philosophy tradition, he believes that morality means acting in accordance with reason. But Kant, who does not have an adequate conception of practical reason, bases morality on pure cerebral reason. In this regard, Kant is more like Plato than Aristotle. If human beings are inescapably corrupt, what saves us is our cerebral intellect, for it is this intellectual, rational part of us that is most removed from our inclinations, emotions, and desires.

In Kant's account, morality cannot be traced back to human nature; it is not enshrined in the human heart; it does not derive from particular human experience or from the world as a whole. Kant wants to move beyond psychology, beyond feelings, beyond temperament, but also beyond science, beyond religion, beyond culture, beyond historical tradition. He wants to develop a morality based purely on the nature and structure of logic itself. 'The ground of [moral] obligation must be sought,' he writes, 'not in the nature of human beings or in facts about the way the world is, but solely *a priori* in concepts of pure reason'.[18] Pure **a priori reason** is reason *prior* to sense experience, prior to desire and emotion. It is reason as it exists inside our heads prior to our experience of the world and prior even to our experience of ourselves. Kant claims,

> all moral concepts have their seat and origin in reason completely *a priori*. . . . Moral principles cannot be abstracted from any empirical, and therefore merely contingent, cognition. Their worthiness to serve as supreme practical principles lies precisely in [the theoretical] purity of their origin. It is of the utmost necessity [and] also of the utmost importance for action, that we derive these concepts and laws from pure reason, enunciating them pure and unmixed.[19]

Kant believes that 'pure reason'—reason unmixed with sense perception, feeling, desires, self-interest, history, religion, science, or culture—is the only thing that can save us. His cerebral approach turns moral philosophy into a kind of moral mathematics. It is not observation, i.e., what we see happening out in the world, that yields moral insights; it is critical philosophy understood as an inquiry into the limits of logic. We fail at morality when we do not think straight, when we do not follow theoretical reason sufficiently.

Kant aims to uncover a logic of morality that moves beyond psychology (which studies human nature), anthropology (which studies human history and culture), and hedonism. Morality is *above* human nature, he believes. To situate morality in human nature would be to 'anthropologize' it, to turn it into one curious artifact of one curious species on one curious planet. Kant writes, 'We must not make [moral] principles depend on the particular nature of *human* reason. . . . Since moral laws must hold for every rational being as such, our principles must instead be derived from the universal concept of a rational being as such'.[20] Kant believes that morality is the same for *all* rational beings. If, to use a far-fetched example, we were to meet rational beings from another solar system, these extraterrestrials would have to come to the same conclusions about the content of morality. As rational beings, they would have to think about morality the

---

✎ Applied Philosophy Box 8.2 ✎

Crime and Alcohol

The U.S. Department of Justice Report on Alcohol and Crime found that alcohol abuse was a factor in 40 percent of violent crimes committed in the U.S. . . . Two-thirds of victims who suffered violence by an intimate (a current or former spouse, boyfriend, or girlfriend) reported that alcohol had been a factor. Among spouse victims, 3 out of 4 incidents were reported to have involved an offender who had been drinking.

How would an author such as Kant explain the correlation between drinking and violent crime (i.e., immorality)? Remember that the Prohibition was motivated, in part, by Puritan beliefs.

Source: U.S. Justice Department, Bureau of Justice Statistics, 'Alcoholism.' *About.com*, http://alcoholism.about.com/, April 1998.

way we do, for the logic of morality follows necessarily.

Like other Enlightenment thinkers, Kant views Newtonian physics as the crowning intellectual achievement of the age. 'Everything in nature', he believes, 'works in accordance with laws'.[21] Kant divides philosophy then into the study of different kinds of laws. **Material philosophy** is that field of philosophy that investigates the laws governing all material things. It can be divided into **physics** and **ethics**. Physics elaborates the laws governing nonrational beings; ethics elaborates the laws governing rational beings. Kant calls the laws of ethics the **laws of freedom**. He continues, '[the] laws of nature are laws according to which everything happens; [the] laws of freedom are laws according to which everything ought to happen. . . . In this way there arises the idea of a twofold metaphysics—*a metaphysics of nature* and *a metaphysics of morals*'.[22] If the physicist can discover and explain the logic of the physical world, the moral philosopher can discover and explain the logic of morality. If Isaac Newton discovered a universal law of gravitation that holds for all physical objects, Kant aims to discover a universal moral law that 'hold[s] for all rational beings'.[23]

On Happiness

Like his philosophical predecessors, Kant concedes that all human beings do, in fact, aim at happiness. As he puts it, 'there is one aim which . . . we can assume with certainty that [all rational beings] *do* have by a necessity of nature and that aim is *perfect happiness*. . . . We can presuppose . . . with certainty [that this orientation is] present in everyone because it belongs to the essence of human beings'.[24] If, however, we all aim at happiness, Kant views happiness as something separate from morality. Whereas earlier philosophers, such as Aristotle and Thomas, identify happiness and morality, Kant pushes them far apart. In Kant's account, 'making people happy is quite different from making them good'.[25]

Kant, perhaps unwittingly, subscribes to a new definition of human happiness. His view is closer to Hobbes's position than to the traditional account. Kant believes that autonomy matters. What distinguishes humans is the capacity to decide for themselves. In this new understanding, successful decision-making means, more or less, getting what you want. This is what modern thinkers such as Kant and Hobbes associate with happiness. But getting what you want is not always the same as 'being moral'. Seen from this modern perspective, we are left with an inevitable dichotomy: happiness is getting what you want; morality is doing what you ought to do. Happiness is about self-satisfaction, whereas morality is about duty.

Remember that Kant views morality as a logical aspiration. As we will discuss, he believes that we can have a 'science' of morality. He does not think, however, that human happiness is open to the same kind of logical investigation. Yes, we can come up with makeshift generalizations about what people want, but Kant dismisses this kind of rough-and-ready approximation as empirical 'anthropology', a subordinate kind of knowledge that depends on familiarity and anecdote rather than on rigorous logic. Kant claims that 'all the elements that belong to the concept of happiness are empirical'.[26] There is, according to Kant, no universal law of happiness. To come up with a logical or scientific description of happiness would be like trying to come up with a logical account of high fashion. It simply is not possible. Why? Because fashion is not a matter of logic; it changes according to whim and fancy. Kant thinks that this is what happiness is like. Happiness means getting what we want. But our actual desires are capricious; they change like the weather. So we cannot come up with a scientific, law-like answer to questions about happiness. Happiness depends on the contingent, the changeable, the particular.

Kant is not satisfied, furthermore, with the thought that we cannot know what we really want. Whereas earlier philosophers identify happiness with morality, Kant, in effect, views happiness as if it were something bad. Why? Because it distracts us from our duties. Kant writes, 'Human beings feel within themselves a powerful counterweight opposed to all the commandments of duty, which reason portrays as so worthy of esteem: the counterweight of needs and inclinations, whose total satisfaction people sum up under the name happiness'.[27] In Kant's account, the desire to be happy—to get what we want—pulls us away from duty. Although good people manage to focus their efforts on morality, the desire for happiness is an ever-present temptation that distracts the weak.

The Kantian notion of duty emphasizes what is sometimes called the over-riding nature of morality. Morality comes first. We must do what is right because it is right whatever the personal cost. Earlier philosophers would have agreed with Kant that moral considerations over-ride other considerations but, unlike Kant, they did not define happiness as unqualified desire-satisfaction but as the sense of self-esteem that accompanies virtue. They did not view happiness as a moral distraction. They would have viewed Kant's reduction of happi-

ness to the satisfaction of desire as narrow and unsatisfying. Still, as we shall see, Kant's bold approach does serve to illuminate some aspects of moral decision-making.

On Good Will

As previously discussed, earlier philosophers recognize the importance of good intentions. Kant, however, in an excess of enthusiasm, wants to trace *all* moral value to good intentions. He dismisses the moral importance of the consequences of our actions and tries to reduce morality to nothing but good will. Kant insists that the consequences of our moral decision-making have *no* bearing on the moral worth of our own behaviour. It is what happens inside the mind, not what happens in the outside world, that matters morally. The precise nature of the physical act that results from an act of will is morally unimportant; what the agent *intends* is the crucial issue. Kant explains:

> A good will is not good because of its effects or accomplishments, and not because of its adequacy to achieve any proposed end; it is good only by virtue of its willing—that is, it is good in itself. . . . Even if it were to happen that, because of some particularly unfortunate fate or the miserly bequest of a step-motherly nature, this [good] will were completely powerless to carry out its aims; if with even its utmost effort it still accomplished nothing, so that only good will itself remained (not, of course, as a mere wish, but the summing of every means in our power), even then it would still, like a jewel, glisten in its own right, as something that has its full worth in itself. Its utility or ineffectuality can neither add to nor subtract from this worth.[28]

Kant's almost rapturous praise of good will indicates the single-mindedness of his ethical thought. Kant's moral philosophy is about intentions, not consequences. If morality is about duty, duty means *intending* to obey the moral law. It is not enough to do what the moral law requires by accident, instinct, or blind chance, or because one has been forced or coerced to act in such a manner. Morality requires a conscious, deliberate decision. In Kant's eyes, good will is not simply the seed from which all morality grows; it is the whole plant.

Kant points out that without good intentions, the best possibilities go bad. Even good things can be turned to evil ends. For example, I can use intelligence—intelligence is a good thing—to become a clever criminal. I can use physical strength—physical strength is a good thing—to intimidate you. I can use friends—friends are a good thing—to gain an unfair advantage. Intelligence, strength, and friends are all valuable. But evil intentions can make them bad. A good will, on the other hand, is always good. Kant writes, 'It is impossible to imagine anything at all in the world, or even beyond it, that can be called good without qualification—except a good will'.[29] Only a good will is, in every instance, worthwhile. Even if people with good intentions are unable to accomplish very much, the fact that they are trying already counts as a moral achievement.

Kant correctly emphasizes the importance of good intentions, but he simplifies these issues. Is it true that good will is the only thing that is without qualification valuable? This seems an exaggeration. One can plausibly point to other intrinsically valuable things: love, honesty, beauty, pleasure, knowledge, etc. As we have seen in the previous chapter on Plato, older philosophers accept that things in the world can be intrinsically *and* instrumentally valuable at the same time. If then intelligence, strength, and friends can be turned to good or evil ends, if they possess instrumental value for good and bad agents alike, this does not detract from the fact that such things are valuable in and of themselves, that they are worthy of respect and admiration simply because they are what they are. So good will does not seem to be the only thing in the world that has intrinsic value.

Kant assumes that good will is the only thing in the world that can never be a means

---

⌒◎ Applied Philosophy Box 8.3 ◎⌒

Art

Clive Bell

> Art is above morals, or, rather, all art is moral because . . . works of art are immediate means to good. Once we have judged a thing a work of art, we have judged it ethically of the first importance and put it beyond the reach of the moralist. . . . The forms of art are inexhaustible; but all lead by the same road of aesthetic emotion to the same world of aesthetic ecstasy.

Kant claims that 'good will' is the only thing in the world that is good in an unqualified sense. British aesthetician (philosopher of art) Clive Bell disagrees. Bell argues that great art (or the appreciation of great art) is, without qualification, valuable.

Source: Clive Bell, 'Art and Significant Form,' from *Art*, 1913. Available at denisdutton.com, www.denisdutton.com/bell. htm.

to an immoral end. But this is not quite accurate. Kant neglects to point out that immoral individuals can use someone else's good intentions as a means to do evil. Suppose I know that you are a compassionate person. I lay down at the side of the road pretending I am hurt. When you stop to help, I rob and murder the rich passengers in your car. You had good intentions. You stopped in order to help a stranger in distress just as I knew you would. But I used your invariable good will as a means to my immoral ends. So an instance of 'good willing' can, in this sense, be a means to evil. You are not, of course, guilty of anything, but surely, something has gone morally wrong. One could argue that you were stupid to stop and that stupidity and good intentions are not enough for morality. Kant assumes that if you had good will, if you—in stopping—intended to respect the moral law, then you are morally perfect. But, as we have discussed in a previous chapter, this is not true in cases of negligence or culpable ignorance. Although we cannot, of course, use our own good intentions to deliberately achieve evil, negligent or ignorant individuals who display good will may still do something wrong by not knowing something they are morally obliged to know. Although we admire their good will, we may still protest that there is something morally lacking in their overall behaviour.

The single-mindedness of Kant's focus on good will has spawned a long-standing (and largely unresolved) dispute in modern ethics between **deontologists**—largely Kantians, who emphasize the importance of good will—and **consequentialists**—largely utilitarians, who emphasize the importance of consequences. (We discuss utilitarianism in Chapter 9.) Deontologists and consequential-

ists offer contrasting base criteria for morality. Seen from a deontological perspective, moral behaviour requires good intentions. An action is good if the agent means well. Seen from a consequentialist perspective, moral behaviour requires good consequences. An action is good if, for example, it makes the world a happier place. Both positions have their shortcomings. Surely, intentions and consequences are *both* important; it is not a matter of choosing between them. The intentions and consequences of a moral act are not separate things; they are two parts of one and the same thing like two sides of a single coin. It is not as though the insides of the act (the intentions) have value and the outside of the act (the physical event and all it entails) is worthless. That would be like saying that only one side of a coin is valuable. As we discussed in Chapter 6, on Thomas, a perfect moral act will be motivated by good will *and* produce good consequences. If there is something wrong with either the intentions or the consequences, this will result in a moral imperfection. The act will not be as good as it should be.

If the deontology vs. consequentialism debate has generated considerable heat, it also muddies certain issues. Consequentialists sometimes talk as if Kant leaves no room in his theory for a careful consideration of consequences. This is plainly false. The difference between deontology and consequentialism is that the deontologist emphasizes the importance of the *intended* over the actual consequences. Kant believes that if agents strive with all their heart—or, better yet, with all their willpower—to achieve good consequences, this is enough. In a fallen world, where the best intentions go astray, it is not what results that matters but what the agent is trying to make happen. When you stop to help a stranger in distress, you are trying to preserve that person's life. So this is, for Kant, is a moral act. Whatever results, it is your good intention that determines the moral status of the act. As we saw in the chapter on Thomas, however, an act begins in some kind of understanding, and this understanding includes an orientation toward the eventual consequences. If there were no good consequences, there could be no good intentions.

On Imperatives: Categorical and Hypothetical

Kant conceives of morality as an **imperative**. As we know from basic English grammar, an imperative is a sentence that expresses a command: 'Bring me the pipe wrench'. 'Turn off the TV'. 'Don't take drugs'. The moral law is, however, a special kind of imperative. Not only does it tell you what to do, it tells all of us what to do. It applies to all rational beings, in every circumstance.

Kant distinguishes between hypothetical and categorical imperatives. A **hypothetical imperative** tells us what we need to do if we aim at a particular goal. Suppose I want to build a table for my kitchen. I must draw a plan, cut the wood, assemble the pieces, sand the pieces, and then stain and varnish the finished product. This collection of imperatives—'Draw the plan! Cut the wood! Assemble each surface! Sand them! Stain and varnish!'—apply to me in those circumstances. They hold hypothetically—that is, they hold if I want to build a table. But I am not obliged to build a table. I can buy one at the furniture store if I want. Hypothetical imperatives only apply *hypothetically*; they only apply *if* the agent decides to do some optional task. Moral imperatives, on the other hand, apply *necessarily*. Everyone has to act morally. So, all human agents *must* obey moral imperatives whatever their personal aspirations and decisions.

We could say that Kant thinks that of morality as an 'unhypothetical' imperative, one that applies to everyone in every circumstance. Consider the moral commandment, 'Thou shalt not murder'. The content of this moral rule is intended to be taken categorically; that is, without exception. Every human being in every circumstance must obey the moral law, 'Thou shalt not murder.' Although we can be moral without following the hypothetical imperatives that regulate the construction of a kitchen table, we cannot be moral and decide to murder people. Kant insists that categorical imperatives *never* admit exceptions. Moral laws are, in this sense, absolute.

Kant thinks that hypothetical imperatives regulate what we may or may not decide to do, but moral imperatives apply without exception. This is precisely what makes morality, morality: because it is logically forced on us *regardless of our desires* and because the content of moral law follows logically from the nature of the situation, not from how we may feel about it. The difference between hypothetical and categorical imperatives can be traced to a difference in logical form. A hypothetical imperative has the following logical form:

If you want A, then you must do X.

This 'if–then' sentence is called a conditional statement in logic; we can call it a **practical conditional**. The second part of the sentence stipulates what must be done if the first part of the statement relating to your desires holds. If you desire A; well, then, you must do X. You desire to make an omelette; well, then, you must first break some eggs.

A categorical imperative holds *regardless of the desires of the agent*. It has the following logical form:

> Whatever your desires are, you must do X.

Or, more simply,

> Do X.

This is sheer, unqualified affirmation; we can call it a **practical affirmation**. In the hypothetical case, you must have the proper desires for the imperative to hold. In the latter case, it does not matter what your desires are. You must do X. (Morality is, in this sense, above desire; it derives from logic. Indeed, logic tells you which *desires* you ought to have.) Kant believes that morality is about acting on the right principles. If one's motivation fits into the right logical form, it does not matter what the results are. What matters is that the intention follows a certain logical pattern—the agent must deliberately act so as to obey a *categorical* imperative. Kant observes, 'There is one imperative which commands a certain line of conduct directly, without assuming or being conditional on any further goal to be reached by that conduct. That imperative is categorical. It is concerned not with the material of the action and its anticipated result',—i.e., it is not concerned with the consequences of the act—'but with its [logical] form and with the principle from which the action itself results'.[30] Kant's prose is difficult at the best of times but his point can be readily summarized. Moral law fits a strict logical pattern. It does not require a specific material result but a specific state of mind. In short, it demands that the moral agent obey compulsory laws that apply at all times to everyone. Obeying these exceptionless laws is, for Kant, what morality is all about.

Kant's account of the categorical imperative has its uses. Nonetheless, his one-sided emphasis on logic is excessively narrow. We can all agree that moral behaviour should be (in some sense) logical. Except that Kant reduces logic here to a recognition of universal grammatical form. But this is not enough for moral discernment. Suppose I were to insist, 'Everyone must, in every circumstance, slice carrots into three equal parts before they eat them'. This affirmation has the same logical form as a categorical imperative, but it would be ridiculous to accept it as a moral principle. So it is not the logical form of a statement that makes it a genuine moral law.

Kant's approach is legitimate in that we are able to distill from human experience principles of behaviour that are much more fundamental than others. Kant equates these principles with morality. The problem is that Kant does not explain how we are able to distinguish these principles that are legitimately moral from those that are not. Everyone immediately recognizes that the principle 'You must slice carrots into three equal parts before you eat them' is not a moral law, and that the principle 'you must keep your promises' *is* a moral law. Kant, however, acts as if we know this because of the logical form of the sentence when, in fact, we know this through moral induction, through conscience, or through some kind of carefully considered practical judgment. Unlike earlier authors such as Aristotle or Thomas, Kant does not provide any proper account of this moral intuition. He wrongly assumes that logic alone can do the work of distinguishing between moral and non-moral principles. Kant fails to recognize that a moral law must satisfy two conditions: (1) it must be universally applicable, and (2) it must coincide with reliable moral judgment. Satisfying condition (1) is not

---

☙ Applied Philosophy Box 8.4 ❧

Ethics as Obedience to Duty and God

Deontological moral systems are characterized by a focus upon adherence to independent moral rules or duties. . . . When we follow our duty, we are behaving morally. When we fail to follow our duty, we are behaving immorally. Typically in any deontological system, our duties, rules, and obligations are determined by God. Being moral is thus a matter of obeying God.

This author, who describes himself as an 'atheism guide' misses the point, at least when it comes to Kant. Kant, the most famous deontologist, would have no problem equating morality with the will of God. But he believes that our duties, rules, and obligations are, in the first instance, determined by secular reason. Logic speaks inside us, showing us what is moral. Religious and logical morality may coincide, but pure a priori reason is enough for morality.

Source: Austin Cline, 'Deontology and Ethics: What is Deontology, Deontological Ethics?' http://atheism.about.com/od/ethicalsystems/a/Deontological.htm, 9 November 2010.

---

enough. If genuine moral principles are universal, it does not follow that any universal practical rule pronounced by anyone is, ipso facto, a moral principle.

On the Categorical Imperative: Five Universal Formulations

Kant sees himself as a champion of morality in a secular age. He sets out to rescue morality from 'those scoffers' who would 'mock all morality as a mere phantom of the brain, [as] an illusion with which, out of vanity, the human imagination puffs itself up'.[31] His strategy is not to turn to God or to human nature but to logic. Moral knowledge does not correspond to anything we can observe; it cannot be identified with an inclination or an emotion; it is not important because religion or tradition or because society tell us so. No, Kant believes that morality is inherent in the very structure of reason. We cannot be logical without it.

For Kant moral behaviour is logical behaviour. Logic applied to human action produces the categorical imperative. After identifying morality as a categorical imperative, Kant moves on to consider the specific content of morality. He proposes several different formulations of the categorical imperative, all of which are, according to Kant, different ways of expressing the very same underlying principle. We will let the reader determine exactly how similar or dissimilar different formulations of the categorical imperative really are. They do add up, however, to a largely consistent theory.

Formulations 1 and 2: The Universal Formulations

Kant writes, 'If I think of a categorical imperative, I know right away what it contains. . . . The maxim of action should conform [to] the universality of a law as such'.[32] Kant believes that moral laws apply to everyone who finds themselves in the same situation without exception. He expresses this basic belief in his first two formulations of the categorical imperative: (1) *'Act only on that maxim by which you can at the same time will that it should become a universal law'*;[33] and (2) *'Act as though the maxim of your act were to become a universal law of nature'*.[34] As these two formulations of the categorical imperative are almost identical, we shall consider them together.

Kant's various formulations of the categorical imperative are addressed to the agent: this is how you must act if you want to be moral. The first two formulations tell us that we are only to act on those **maxims** that apply equally well to other people. What is a maxim? One dictionary defines a maxim as 'a principle or rule of conduct'. An example will help. Surgeons wash their hands when they are on duty. Why? To prevent the spread of germs. We might express the maxim behind their act: 'Wash the germs off your hands after touching a sick patient so as to prevent the spread of disease.' This is the rationale behind the surgeon's act. It is the maxim they are following every time they wash their hands. Kant declares that we are only to act on that 'maxim' or through that 'maxim' that is universalizable. We can know that we are acting morally when we can consistently apply the rationale behind our acts to all other agents. Kant presents four examples to illustrate his meaning:

1. Suppose someone who is on the verge of bankruptcy is tempted to borrow money although he knows he will never be able to pay it back. Kant identifies the following as the maxim of this act: 'When I believe myself short of money, I will borrow money and promise to pay it back, even though I know that this will never be done.'[35] Is it moral to act on this idea that I can make promises I know I cannot keep? Kant believes that we cannot will that other people break their promises to us, so we cannot will that this

maxim of human conduct be a universal law of nature. So this is an immoral act.

Kant believes that a mistake in moral reasoning is a mistake in logic. If the worst logical mistake is a contradiction, immoral agents inevitably contradict themselves. Kant comments,

> [We] then see immediately that this maxim [of making a promise we do not intend to keep] can never qualify as a self-consistent universal law of nature but must necessarily contradict itself. For the universality of a law that permits anyone who is in need to make any promise he pleases with the intention of not keeping it would make promising, and the very purpose one has in promising, itself impossible.[36]

Think of what promising entails. To promise is to guarantee delivery of whatever is promised. If then I make a promise I know I cannot keep, I am guaranteeing delivery of what can never be delivered. But this is impossible. So we cannot will that everyone act in this manner. (Indeed, we cannot even will that a single person act in this logically incoherent manner.) As Kant points out, if we were to allow people to make promises they did not intend to keep, this would make promising a 'hollow pretence' and, indeed, a logical absurdity.

Another way of thinking about this reveals the contradiction involved in making a promise we cannot keep. Kant believes that there will be no inconsistency between what immoral agents expect of themselves and what they expect of others. When we act immorally, we are making, in effect, an exception for ourselves. But this involves a contradiction. I cannot consistently will that other human beings refrain from making promises they cannot keep while making an exception for myself, for I, too, am a human being—so I must do what other human beings must do. If other human beings must keep their promises (because they are logical beings), then I must keep my promises (because I am a logical being).

2. Kant proposes a second example. Suppose a prosperous individual sees someone who needs help but decides not to help this person. Is this a moral act? In Kantian terms, can we turn the maxim of this act—do not help others when they are in distress—into a universal law? Kant concedes that we could, in theory, act according to this maxim. Nonetheless, we cannot *will* that it be made into such a law. Why? Because we would have to will that no one help us when we are in distress and we want other people's help when we need it. (Kant thinks this is just a natural fact about human beings.) To will this maxim to become a universal law, then, would be impossible. I cannot simultaneously will that others help me in distress and that they rigorously follow the maxim 'don't help others in distress' for that would involve a contradiction; it would require willing, at the same time, two mutually incompatible options. As Kant explains, 'It is impossible to *will* that such a principle [to not help others in distress] should hold everywhere as a law of nature. For a will that intended this would be in conflict with itself, since many situations arise in which [a] man needs love and sympathy from others, and . . . such a law of nature . . . would rob himself of all the hope of the help he wants'.[37]

3. Let us next consider Kant's third example. In Kant's own words, suppose someone 'finds in himself a talent that, with a certain amount of cultivation could make him a useful man for all sorts of purposes. But he sees himself in comfortable circumstances, and he prefers to give himself up to pleasure rather than to bother about increas-

ing and improving his fortunate natural aptitudes'.[38] We can identify the maxim of this act as 'Neglect one's useful talents for the sake of amusement'. Kant, once again, concedes that we *could* follow such a rule but claims that none of us could *will* that such a rule of conduct be a universal law. Why? Kant believes that it is a natural fact that 'a rational being . . . necessarily wills that all his powers should be developed'.[39] It is illogical to neglect talents for frivolous reasons. Perhaps because this would be to settle for less good instead of more good, which would be irrational. To will that human beings 'neglect their talents' would mean willing that rational beings live irrationally. This would be like willing that fish live like birds or, better yet, that circles be squares. But to will that fish be birds or that circles be squares is to will a contradiction in terms. Likewise, to will that rational beings not strive to better themselves is, according to Kant, to will a contradiction in terms. It is to decide that rational agents should be something they are not which is illogical.

There is a second way to see the logical contradiction that results from such immoral action. If everyone were to neglect their talents, there would be no doctors, no airplane pilots, no mechanics, no engineers, no scientists, no novelists, and so on. The good life as we know it would collapse. If, for example, your orthopedic surgeon were to neglect her talents, she would no be able to repair your knee so that you could walk again. To will that 'neglecting one's talent' become a universal law would be to will that your knee not be properly repaired. But you cannot will this. So when you give in to laziness and neglect your talents, you are not acting in the way you want others to act. But the first two formulations of the categorical imperative tell us that if one cannot will that the maxim 'neglect your talents' be applied to every human being, it is immoral to act on this maxim.

Again when people decide to neglect their talents, the truth is that they want to make an exception for themselves. They simultaneously believe that other human beings should develop their talents and that they should not develop their talents. If, however, human beings should develop their talents, they themselves—being human beings—should develop their own talents as well. What this shows, according to Kant, is that such behaviour is illogical and therefore immoral. (Note, in a general way, how similar to virtue ethics all this is.)

4. Finally, Kant considers the case of someone who, beset by misfortune and despair, is tempted to commit suicide. Kant identifies this as the maxim of this act: 'I make it my principle out of self-love to shorten my life if its continuance threatens more evil [to myself] than it promises advantage'.[40] Kant believes that we cannot will that this maxim become a universal law. Some scholars have disputed his conclusion, but his reasoning is often misconstrued. (Kant's argument here is more complicated than in the previous two examples. The case of suicide is, he believes, more like the first example of promise-breaking.) For Kant, the important issue here is the focus on self-interest. One is not, for example, losing one's life in defence of others. One is losing one's life 'to avoid future misery' because one loves oneself. Kant writes, 'that the very same feeling [of self-love] meant to promote life should actually destroy life would contradict itself'.[41]

Kant believes that we cannot will that the maxim behind suicide-as-misery-relief become a universal law. It is not simply that

making this a universal law would depopulate society of many useful, productive individuals. The problem is more fundamental. Kant thinks that suicide cannot be a categorical imperative because it is not even logical. Consider an obvious case of something logical. The arithmetical formula $2 + 2 = 4$ must hold in every instance (whatever our feelings). The categorical imperative is like this: it must apply in every case. Kant believes that the maxim 'commit suicide when you are unhappy' is a moral and logical mistake. It is like the erroneous formula $2 + 2 = 3$, which is not universalizable because it cannot hold in a single case. This is what suicide is like. It cannot hold in every case because it cannot hold in a single case. It is incoherent to start with.

Some readers may object that if suicide is what the person wants to do, it must be a rational course of action. But this is to confuse what Kant is saying with a contemporary emphasis on consent. (Something we discuss in Chapter 9.) Seen from a Kantian perspective, the fact that someone consents to a contradiction does not make it any less of a contradiction. Suppose I were to agree to $2 + 2 = 3$. This is still a contradiction. We may agree to illogical behaviours in order to satisfy our capricious, contingent, ephemeral feelings. And we may consent, out of misguided feelings of self-love, to suicide. But this is beside the point. Kant believes that suicide is illogical and therefore immoral, whatever our feelings are.

Why, then, does suicide involve a logical contradiction? Kant believes that those who kill themselves out of self-love are acting on the following maxim: 'I have decided I must kill myself because I love myself.' Kant believes that the maxim 'destroy what you love' cannot be universalized because it is contradictory. We cannot logically will to destroy what we truly love. Suppose you own a wonderful piece of art. You reason that because you love this painting by Vincent van Gogh, you will destroy it. That would be illogical. The maxim of your act, 'I destroy what I love', is illogical. You might complain, 'The painting has no feelings, whereas I feel discouraged'. But to commit suicide because one *feels* discouraged is to give into mere sentiment over logic.

Kant believes then that people who commit suicide make a logical mistake. They are doing the exact opposite of what a rational person would do. It would be illogical to refuse to eat because you are starving. In the same way, Kant argues that rational people cannot kill themselves because they love themselves. Indeed, Kant is convinced that self-love has a specific logical purpose: self-preservation. This is what he means when he writes that 'that very same feeling [of self-love] meant to promote life should actually destroy life would contradict itself'.[42] To kill yourself out of self-love would be like closing your eyes in order to see. It would be to use some aspect of human nature in a contradictory way.

Consider a sports analogy. Killing yourself out of self-love would be like a football team using their very good quarterback to lose the game. It is a possible to do this; but it is illogical. The point of football is to win games; the point of self-love is self-preservation. Self-love drives us to preserve ourselves so that we can, according to Kant, do our duty. In destroying yourself, you render yourself unable to do your duty. (Remember, to do your duty is to have good intentions. You can't have good intentions once you are dead!) So Kant would consider suicide the height of immorality. No single act of suicide can ever be justified. Because suicide is illogical, we cannot make it a universal law for humanity.

Narrow versus Wide, Perfect versus Imperfect Duties

More could be said but let's review Kant's four examples. Kant's methodology is largely negative. These are all bad acts, they all involve things we ought not do; we know that they are bad acts because they cannot be expressed in a categorical imperative. The first two formulations of the categorical imperative teach us this: (1) that we should not break our promises, (2) that we should not neglect those who need our assistance, (3) that we should not neglect our own talents, (4) that we should not commit suicide. We could, of course, express these truths in a more positive vein. We should, as it turns out, (1) keep our promises, (2) help those in need, (3) develop our talents, (4) preserve ourselves. (We could even express these principles as virtues: (1) we should be trustworthy; (2) we should be charitable; (3) we should be industrious; (4) we should be prudent.) Still, Kant is mostly concerned about formulating strict rules of conduct that warn us away from the immoral behaviours that our fallen natures are prone to.

Kant believes that moral rules such as (1) 'Keep your promises' and (4) 'Do not commit suicide' are **perfect duties** or duties in a strict sense. These rules admit of no exceptions. Because promise-breaking and suicide (out of self-love) are contradictory acts, they cannot be logical in even a single instance. On the other hand, Kant believes that the moral rules such as (2) 'Help others' and (3) 'Perfect your talents' are **imperfect duties** or duties in a loose sense. These acts are not logically contradictory. We can even imagine circumstances in which not helping others or not perfecting your talents is morally acceptable. If you are busy providing for your family, you may not be able to develop particular talents. If you cannot swim, you may not be obliged to help a drowning stranger. And so on.

Kant writes,

> Some acts are so constituted that we cannot *conceive* without a contradiction that their maxim be a universal law of nature . . . In other cases, we do not find this inner impossibility, but it is still impossible to *will* that their maxim should be raised to the universality of a law of nature, because such a will would contradict itself. We see readily that the first kind of action is opposed to strict or narrow duty; the second only opposed to wide (meritorious) duty.[43]

The difference between narrow and wide duty is the difference between perfect and imperfect duty. As we will discuss, this distinction does not resist closer analysis. Nonetheless, it is an important aspect of Kant's original treatment. It can serve, for the moment, as a rough-and-ready indication of how duty applies in more or less restricted circumstances.

In the case of both perfect or imperfect duties, we are dealing with a categorical imperative. Why? Because desires play no role. Because both kinds of duties apply regardless of temperament or inclination. In the case of perfect duties, the logical form of the maxim behind the act will be:

In all circumstances, do (or do not do) X.

So, in all circumstances, keep your promises. Or, more simply, keep your promises. And, in all circumstances, do not commit suicide. Or, more simply, do not commit suicide.

In the case of imperfect duties, the logical form of the maxim behind the act will be:

In these (objective) circumstances,
do (or do not do) X.

So, when you are able, help other people. When you are able, develop your talents. Note that desires (or emotions) play no role even in the case of imperfect duties. It is the (objectively measured) conditions that determine what is morally required, not our own feelings. In both cases, the moral rule is: disregard your feelings, do *X*!

Is Kant Reinventing the Golden Rule?

The reader may have noticed that Kant's categorical imperative resembles the traditional Golden Rule aptly expressed by Jesus: 'Do onto others what you would have them do onto you.' In a footnote, Kant (somewhat testily) denies any close resemblance, going so far as to claim that negative-formulations of the Golden Rule (Do not do onto others . . .) are in fact derived from and inferior to his own account of the categorical imperative! A fairer description of the difference between Kant and Jesus is that Kant is a philosopher in a modern, post-Enlightenment sense, whereas Jesus is a religious prophet. Kant wants to derive morality from logic, whereas Jesus speaks out of a sense of supernatural religious authority.

Kant writes, 'If we now look at ourselves whenever we transgress a duty, we find that we do not in fact intend that our maxim become a universal law. . . . We only take the liberty of making an *exception* to it, for ourselves (of course just this once) to satisfy our inclination'.[44] Consider stealing. What is going on inside the mind of someone who steals? They are motivated by greed, not logic. They want one standard of behaviour to apply to human beings generally and a different standard of behaviour to apply to themselves. If I steal money from your purse, I steal this money from you even though I do not want other people stealing money from me. But this violates the Golden Rule. I am making an exception for myself. I am not treating you the way I would like to be treated. Both the Golden Rule and the first two formulations of the categorical imperative tell us not to make exceptions for ourselves. Kant's protestations notwithstanding, his account is more aptly described as a philosophical reworking of the much earlier Golden Rule.

Criticisms of the First Two Formulations

Some authors criticize Kant's universal formulations of the categorical imperative. Some of these complaints are unfair; others raise legitimate concerns. Let us consider these criticisms in turn.

Kant's Logic is Too Narrow to Account for All Morality

Kant, as an Enlightenment thinker, wants to propose a progressive system that will render older systems obsolete. Most importantly, he wants to set morality on a logical, scientific basis, to make it intellectually respectable. Sometimes, Kant goes so far as to suggest that his concept of a categorical imperative is enough to account for all morality. Such claims are overly ambitious. As we have already mentioned, we cannot make sense of the categorical imperative unless we assume some deeper level of moral intelligence. It would be better to consider the categorical imperative as a heuristic device that pushes us to apply our moral intuitions more consistently.

Seen from a virtue ethics perspective, the categorical imperative operates in the way Aristotle's mean works or the way the Golden Rule of Jesus works. It should not be approached as a proof of morality directed toward the moral ignoramus but as an instructive way of focusing and critically gathering our thoughts so that we can ascertain if we are acting morally. Once we have followed through the thought experiment to see if our acts are universalizable, we should end up with a conclusion that strikes us as morally accurate.

Kant wants to emphasize the logical nature of morality, but logic must be understood here as *more* than someone's willingness to insist on the universal application of some arbitrary principle. A crazy person could insist that everyone act consistently with a crazy principle. This is not enough for morality. If, for example, a serial killer thought that 'murder whenever you can get away with it' was a categorical imperative, this individual could not use the categorical imperative to any proper effect. Serial killers lack the most basic moral judgment. Their ideas are simply outrageous. (One can question whether any sane person could really think like this. Kant assumes that we will be honest about our deep convictions. Someone who flippantly proposes serial killing as a categorical imperative is most likely insincere or seriously misguided.)

Practical rationality must accomplish two different tasks. First, it must be able to secure *consistency* in decision-making. This is what the first two formulations of the categorical imperative are about. They provide a useful test of consistency. Second, practical reason must be able to make sense of the world in a reasonable way. It must be able to separate out what should be admired, preserved, cherished, or treated with respect, from what should be criticized, eliminated, despised, or condemned. As we shall see, Kant goes on to devise other formulations of the categorical imperative that do address, in an insightful way, the specific issue of moral evaluation.

Kant Ignores Casuistry and Particular Context

Although earlier authors acknowledge the validity of general moral principles, they accept that they must be continually tailored to specific circumstances. Kant provides no proper account of how we are to adapt general moral principles to individual cases. Mostly he asserts the importance of willpower: do what is right regardless of the circumstances. But this is hardly enough. As we have seen, Thomas goes a long way to developing a subtle casuistry that deals with unusual situations. Kant does not provide any equivalent analysis.

Because Kant wants to produce a Newtonian physics of morality, he favours a moral law conception of ethics. Roughly put, he claims that morality reduces to the assertion that we should treat everyone the same. (This is, certainly, how some contemporary authors understand Kant's message.) But suppose I were to tell you that you should treat your mother the same as everyone else. It would be callous—indeed *immoral*—to treat your mother the same as everyone else. You owe her a special debt of gratitude, devotion, and loyalty. So any attempt to consider morality solely in terms of universal rules that apply to anyone is bound to be problematic.

Contemporary Kantians (such as Thomas Nagel and Susan Wolf) try to restrict the sphere of morality to purely universal rules of conduct. The proper response to such criticisms is not the rejection of what is truly worthwhile in Kant but a return to the moral wisdom of earlier moral philosophers who elaborate an account of human excellence that is sensitive to specific circumstance. Any account of

ethics that refuses to take into consideration the *particular* identity of your mother—that she is your very own mother!—provides an inadequate guide to morality. One of the Ten Commandments expresses a timeless, cross-cultural moral truth: 'Honour thy mother and thy father.' Insensitivity to specialized moral obligations is itself immoral.

Kant proposes a moral law ethics, but moral laws are abbreviated statements of moral obligation that enclose a much larger understanding that must be teased out of them. There are issues of interpretation, of definition, of consequences, of intention, of double-effect, of means-to-end reasoning, and so on. Consider a specific example. We all know this moral rule:

1. 'Thou shalt not kill.'
   But what exactly is this law telling us to do? Most of us think that it is moral to kill animals (and plants) for food. If we want to be technically rigorous, we must reword the law:

2. 'Thou shalt not kill *human beings*.'
   But here, again, this wording is not precise enough. Most of us believe that self-defence is justified. So we must rewrite the rule:

3. 'Thou shalt not kill human beings *except in self-defence*.'
   But this is, again, less than exact. Sometimes self-defence—if, for example, it involves excess force—is unjustified. So we must again, rewrite the rule:

4. 'Thou shalt not kill human beings except in *justified* self-defence.'
   Leave aside the criteria we would need to measure whether a particular case of self-defence is 'justified'. But suppose someone kills a human being by accident. This is another exception, so again, we must rewrite the rule:

5. 'Thou shalt not kill human beings except in justified self-defence, *but this rule is not broken when homicide is accidental.*'

But this is not exact, either, for accidental deaths due to negligent behaviour are morally blameworthy. So we must once more rewrite the rule:

6. 'Thou shalt not kill human beings except in justified self-defence, but this rule is not broken when homicide is accidental *unless this is because of negligence.*'

But neither is this exact. It turns out that negligence might be an excuse if I am not of sound mind—if, for example, I am mentally ill. So we must, yet again, rewrite the rule:

7. 'Thou shalt not kill a human being except in justified self-defence, but this rule is not broken when homicide is accidental unless this is because of negligence *unless the agent is not of sound mind.*'

Leave aside the criteria we would need to measure whether a particular agent is of sound mind. If I am not of sound mind through my own fault—because I am drunk or high on drugs—this excuse is no longer acceptable. So we must rewrite the rule again:

8. 'Thou shalt not kill human beings except in justified self-defence, but this rule is not broken when homicide is accidental unless this is because of negligence unless the agent is not of sound mind *through no fault of her own.*'

Again leave aside further criteria we would need to measure whether it is a particular agent's fault that she is of unsound mind. Still, this is not enough, *even in Kantian terms.* As it turns out, Kant believes in capital punishment. He would claim that the moral injunction 'thou shalt not kill' does not preclude capital punishment. Assuming he is correct, we must yet again reword the rule:

9. 'Thou shalt not kill a human being except in justified self-defence, but this rule is not broken when homicide is accidental but not because of negligence unless the agent is not of sound mind through no fault of her own. *One can also kill human beings in cases of capital punishment.*'

But, of course, capital punishment—even if it is sometimes justified—is only legitimate when used in certain circumstances, which need to be specified. And so on.

Much more could be said, but the general point is clear. Encapsulating a moral understanding in a short, pithy, universal rule such as 'Thou shalt not kill' is a worthwhile device. It provides a conspicuous moral landmark we can use to orient ourselves morally. At the same time, moral rules are only abbreviations. Although they provide a useful guide for behaviour, we should not lose sight of the way they depend on an underlying understanding that determines precisely how they should be applied in individual circumstances. Think of a moral rule like the tip of an ice-berg. The tip floats because of the bulk of underwater ice that holds it up. In the same way, moral rules depend on an unspoken understanding that allows us to adapt our application of the law according to specific circumstances. Applying rules to puzzling cases—what we have called casuistry—is an essential aspect of moral reasoning. Kant, in his enthusiasm for the moral law, overlooks and misunderstands the way in which the categorical imperative depends on local circumstances. He writes as if there was no need for casuistry, as if the memorization of a few succinct rules and their mechanical application to uncomplicated cases was enough for morality.

Kant's discussion of perfect and imperfect duties only confuses the issue. As previously discussed, Kant claims that although a perfect duty applies in all circumstances, an imperfect duty applies only in *some* circumstances. His doctrine of perfect duties is really a restatement of an earlier idea—found in authors such as Socrates and Thomas Aquinas—that some acts are intrinsically bad: they are not bad for their effects; they are bad in themselves. The internal structure of these acts is so flawed that their performance can never be moral. Kant labels the moral obligation to refrain from such internally disordered acts a '*perfect* duty'. Examples of perfect duties include prohibitions against suicide, against breaking promises, against telling a lie, against cheating on your spouse, and so on. Kant would say that it is *never* right to commit suicide, break a promise, tell a lie, or cheat on your spouse. *Imperfect* duties, in contrast, admit of exceptions. They apply only in *most* circumstances. Kant points out that we have a duty—in *most* circumstances—to 'help strangers in need' and to 'develop our talents'. But there may be unusual circumstances in which these duties do not apply.

Kant does not elaborate any definitive list of perfect and imperfect duties; he does not tell us how to determine which applications of a moral rule are the most correct or authoritative or how to distinguish between competing moral rules. As we have seen, the moral rule 'do not kill' is an imperfect duty. There are special circumstances in which one human being can morally kill another human being. But what about the moral rule 'Do not kill innocent strangers for the fun of it'? Or the moral rule 'Capital punishment for crimes one did not commit is wrong'? Or 'killing women because they are women is wrong'? One cannot imagine *any* circumstances where such behaviour would be permissible. So these seem to be perfect duties. Or are they be considered only

as more specific or incomplete expressions of the same *imperfect* duty: 'do not kill.' Kant does not tell us. For the most part, he overlooks such complications. As it turns out, we can easily modify a moral law in order to turn an imperfect duty into a perfect duty.

Kant does not come close to sorting out the complexities involved in moral judgment, but his theory has a saving grace. It reduces moral obligation to an easily-remembered and comprehensive logical rule of thumb. Remember, Kant wants to be a moral scientist; Newton is his model. Kant aims to discover the moral equivalent of the universal law of gravitation. So, instead of proposing a carefully detailed system of moral rules, he proposes one fundamental rule that, in effect, includes all the others. There is *one* categorical imperative that applies across the board: *Act so that you can will that the maxim of your act become a moral rule for all human beings.* Kant assures us that as long as we follow this one rule, we will end up doing what is morally required.

Kant's genius is to see that who we are holds no moral weight unless it significantly changes what is actually happening. His basic argument is: don't make exceptions! If duty commands Paul to do (or not do) *X*, and if Leo and Aisha find themselves in exactly the same situation, Leo and Aisha must do (or not do) *X*. Anything else would be illogical. To say that Paul, Leo, and Aisha do not have to obey the same moral laws would be to turn morality into an arbitrary pastime. Kant believes: similar circumstances require similar actions. Call this (to borrow from the German philosopher Leibniz) the **principle of the indiscernability of moral cases**. If morality is to be consistent, then the moral law must be the same for everyone.[45] Remember, for Kant, morality is logical, like arithmetic. If Paul holds three oranges in his right hand and three oranges in his left hand, it follows that he holds six oranges in his hands. Likewise, if Leo and Aisha each hold three oranges in their right hands and three oranges in their left hands, it necessarily follows that they must each hold six oranges in their hands. The fact that it is Paul or Aisha or Leo holding these oranges cannot change what logically follows. Kant believes that this is what morality is like. The *same* situation must be treated in the *same* way. So the same moral laws must apply to different individuals. Kant's

basic argument could be easily summarized: hold yourself to the same moral standards to which you hold other people. (What Kant fails to recognize, however, is that we sometimes need help in understanding how a moral rule applies to the specific circumstances of our lives—we need casuistry.)

There are also limitations to Kant's methodology. As we have seen, he identifies morality with good intentions. To act morally is to intend to obey the categorical imperative. But how do we truly judge the intentions of

---

✆ Applied Philosophy Box 8.5 ✆

Indianapolis Robbery Suspect Who Prayed with Victim Surrenders

Gregory Smith, 23, turned himself into police Tuesday after his mother saw him on television, police said.

Smith, of Indianapolis, faces a preliminary charge of robbery for the stick-up at Advance America Monday afternoon.

Police said Smith apologized to the cashier for his actions but went ahead with his robbery even after praying with her.

'He said that he hated to have to do this, but times were hard and he had no choice,' cashier Angela Montez, 43, told police, according to a police report.

Montez began crying when she realized Smith's intentions, she told police. She began to talk to him about God, she said, telling him he still had a chance to refrain from committing the crime.

Smith told Montez he had a 2-year-old child to support and then asked her to pray with him about overcoming his hardships. The two got down on their knees and prayed, remaining there for nearly 10 minutes, police said.

In response to the woman's kindness, Smith took a bullet out of his handgun and gave it to her, according to the report, telling the clerk it was his only bullet and promising not to hurt her. He then asked Montez for a hug.

Despite the heart-to-heart talk, Smith was not dissuaded from his plans. He took Montez's cellphone and told her to go into the restroom and to refrain from calling police for 20 minutes.

Smith took $20 in $5 bills from the cash drawer, according to the report, leaving the rest of the cash in the drawer.

Stealing is wrong, but this is an unusual case. Should this bank robber be shown mercy? Is his crime less than that of an unrepentant, unfeeling bank robber? Kant gives us no clear way of sorting through such issues.

Source: Bill McCleery, 'Indianapolis Robbery Suspect Who Prayed with Victim Surrenders.' *USAToday.com*, www.usatoday.com/news/offbeat/2009-10-20-gunman-prayer_N.htm, 20 October 2009.

ourselves and other people? We have discussed these issues at some length already. As we have seen, someone may be well-intentioned and act immorally. Again, as Aristotle powerfully argues, agents sometimes do wrong things and yet deserve mercy instead of punishment. Kant provides no precise way of sorting through these complicated issues.

And there is one final issue. Kant views mortality as a matter of strict obligation. But there are circumstances in which we must choose between diverse alternatives that are all morally acceptable. Suppose, for example, I can choose to donate to either charity *A* or charity *B*. Kant's categorical imperative seems to provide little guidance here. Either action is a good action. Still, it might be that one is better than the other. Sometimes, it is not enough to know what strict moral law prohibits or requires. Sometimes, we want to go beyond the bare minimum that can be expected of everyone. Sometimes, we want to aim at the best outcome, at heroism, at virtue. Kant's first formulations of the categorical imperative also fall short on this score.

Kant Insists All Lies Are Equally Immoral

We turn now to the most common criticism of Kant. A steady stream of philosophers (beginning with the Swiss philosopher Benjamin Constant) have decried Kant's alleged absolutism. They have argued that there are exceptions to moral laws. If, however, we can point to authentic exceptions, it will follow that the moral laws only hold in *some* conditions. This would clash with Kant's conviction that morality must be rigorously universal. It would undermine his pivotal distinction between hypothetical and categorical imperatives. It would also detract from the authority of morality. It would give us a reason to be suspicious

of the moral generalizations and the possibility of an objective ethics.

There is a minor industry in academic philosophy that advances thought-experiments designed to undermine the universality conditions of Kant's categorical imperative. Let us consider what we will call the **rigid counterexample** to Kant's moral system. As we will discuss, the rigid counterexample raises legitimate but not unanswerable questions about his theory. To use a version that is popular in graduate schools, let us suppose that members of the Nazi Gestapo are looking for your grandmother. They believe that she is Jewish and have decided to torture her and murder her. The Gestapo come to your door and ask if your grandmother is inside. It just so happens that she is in the living room, reading. What should you do? Tell the truth, that she is in the living room? But then they will capture and kill your grandmother. So should you tell a lie, that she is somewhere else? Most readers will say yes, of course, tell a white lie and save your grandmother! Kant believes, however, that the moral law 'do not tell lies' is a perfect duty. It admits of no exceptions. Furthermore, he is a deontologist: it is the intentions of an act that matter, not the consequences. A lie is a purposeful deception. Viewed from a Kantian perspective, we can never deliberately do wrong, no matter how bad the consequences.

It may seem inhumane to suggest that moral people must tell the truth and allow the blatant murder of a loved one. We should point out, however, that Kant himself responded to this kind of criticism at the end of his life in an essay entitled, 'On a Supposed Right to Tell Lies from Benevolent (or Altruistic) Motives'. Confronted with just this kind of glaring counterexample, he does not budge. Kant continues to claim that one cannot tell a lie *under any circumstances*. (He appeals, in fact, to a notion not unlike Thomas's account of nonvoluntary action, but we will not consider his precise response to his critics here.) Many scholars dismiss Kant's approach as mere stubbornness, as a wilful refusal to come to grips with a potentially fatal weakness in his theory. If, however, his response is not as insightful or as temperate as it should be, closer inspection shows that his overall attitude is consistent.

Before analyzing this 'can-I-tell-a-lie-to-save-granny' counterexample, we need to understand why Kant believes that lying is always wrong. Because Kant equates morality and logic, he must accept that all lies are equally bad. Every lie is a perversion of reason, for every lie entails a contradiction. If I say that granny is not in the living room when I know that she is in the living room, I simultaneously deny (inside my mind) and affirm (aloud) the claim that 'she is in the living room'. But affirming and denying the same claim is a contradiction. It follows that telling lies is illogical and hence immoral. Circumstances are irrelevant. It is the internal nature of the act that is wrong.

In the Gestapo scenario, one might argue that lying is permissible for telling a lie is a very small evil given the circumstances. (Thomas Aquinas, for example, distinguishes between lies that are venial, or small, sins and lies that are mortal, or large, sins.) But Kant does not believe that we can justify a lie by claiming that it is 'a small lie'. Every lie involves an implicit contradiction and contradictions do not come in degrees. One contradiction is as much a contradiction as any other. Because a 'small lie' is as much a contradiction as a 'big lie', it is equally immoral.

One can propose various responses to the rigid counterexample. But the first thing to notice is that this is an extremely problematic situation. Human life is messy; this kind of context poses a difficult question, for which there is no nice, easy, straightforward answer. Let us call the first way of dealing with the situation the 'sneaky solution'. Suppose that you could manage to divert these murderers from their task without telling an explicit lie. For example, suppose these members of the Gestapo ask if Granny is in the house and you respond, 'I saw her at the grocery store 15 minutes ago'. And suppose that you did see her at the grocery store 15 minutes ago. Is this a lie? It seems to be a deliberate attempt to mislead. On the other hand, you did not say anything that was actually false. Some ethicists would say that this is the ideal way out of this situation. As long as you tell the strict truth, you have done nothing wrong. You outsmarted the Gestapo officers by telling a literal truth. You did not tell a lie and you did not help them murder Granny. In the end, this seems the best course of action. All is well.

One problem with the sneaky solution is that it does not always work. For example, what if the Gestapo officers were to respond, 'I didn't ask about 15 minutes ago, I asked if she is in the house *now*. Answer yes or no. Any refusal to answer will be taken as a "yes"'. What do you do in that situation? You can only save your grandmother by reassuring them that she is not in the house. Only lying will save her.

Seen from a Kantian perspective, when you tell a lie to save your grandmother's life, you do something evil, tell a lie, to prevent a larger evil, the murder of your grandmother. In short, you use an evil means to achieve a good end. As explained in Chapter 7, we can use Thomas's criterion of double effect to demonstrate the permissibility of some evil consequences. But this is of no help here. In this kind of case, we are obliged to use *immoral* means to achieve a good end which sins against the fifth rule of the principle of double effect. Even if we achieve genuinely good consequences, we must perform an intrinsically bad act in order to achieve them.

One straightforward response to the rigid counterexample is to simply concede that in extreme circumstances we can sometimes use an immoral means to achieve a beneficial effect. In the Gestapo case, for example, you should tell a lie, which is only a small evil, in order to prevent the painful death of your grandmother, a much greater evil. We will call this strategy, which permits the performance of a lesser evil for the sake of preventing a greater evil, **preventive evil**.

Preventive Evil as a Moral Immoral Strategy

Lying to save you grandmother from the Gestapo is a clear case of preventive evil. One permits a lesser evil—telling a lie—to prevent a greater evil—her torture and murder. The justification is obvious. Although you shouldn't be enthusiastic about the prospect of telling a lie, there are extreme occasions where one must do something slightly *evil* in order to prevent a far greater evil. This, then, is the rationale behind the moral strategy of preventive evil: very small evils are to be preferred over very large evils.

It should be clear that Kant would not think that 'preventive evil' is a valid moral approach. He has such rigorous moral standards, he cannot countenance any possibility of evil. This seems stubbornly heroic but also heartless and unhelpful. We can posit three basic criteria we can use to make sense of preventive evil as a tolerable but morally imperfect response to extreme situations:

1. The first evil must be very small. You can imagine telling a lie to save your grandmother's life because this is a very small moral mistake.
2. The second evil must be very serious. Telling a lie to save your mother from going to the hairdresser is not acceptable because the 'evil' of going to the hairdresser is hardly a serious enough negative consequence.
3. Preventive evil must be a last resort. If there are other ways of preventing the evil without resorting to evil, these are clearly preferable.

When we analyze a case of preventive evil, we must not be distracted by the complexity of the situation. There are many things going on in the Gestapo example. Suppose you tell the lie, 'She is not in the house'. We may admire your courage in standing up to the Gestapo; we may admire your love for your grandmother; we may admire your steely self-possession under duress. It is the lie *qua* lie that is not good. As Kant *correctly* insists, there is always something wrong about lying. This is why Kant does not accept preventive evil as a moral strategy. Someone who argues that preventive evil is an appropriate response to the Gestapo situation accepts that telling a lie is wrong but claims that it is nonetheless a legitimate strategy if it prevents a very great evil.

It must be emphasized then that anyone who argues for preventive evil acknowledges that this response is not perfectly moral. When we use a small evil to prevent a large evil, the small evil is not in itself a good. It is, rather, the *consequences* of the first evil that are good. Because Kant does not sufficiently recognize the importance of consequences, he does not fully appreciate the moral problem that arises in such circumstances. As Thomas indicates, the ideal moral act will have good intentions *and* good consequences. To fail to appreciate the importance of either intentions or consequences is a grave mistake.

If we are going to accept preventive evil as a morally acceptable strategy, even in rare cases, we need to find some way of weighing alternative evils. Individual philosophers have elaborated various 'priority rules' as a way of ranking competing moral demands. (These are controversial; we will not consider them here.) Thomas, more simply, proposes love (charity) as an ultimate criterion of how good or bad something is. Lies that seriously sin against love are a major evil; lies that do not are a minor evil. Kant, however, does not offer any explicit method for distinguishing between major and minor evils. In his other formulations of the categorical imperative, he does offer a suggestion as to what could be used as a criterion for distinguishing between greater and lesser evils. We discuss this approach below. The important point here is that anyone who wants to defend a case of preventive evil will have to think about what is more or less evil and why. And there are various ways of going about this.

We should emphasize that the rigid counterexample poses a serious problem for people who want to be moral, but it does not show that there is anything wrong with Kant's universal formulations of the categorical imperative. Philosophers like Kant, Thomas, Aristotle, and Socrates all find lying intrinsically repugnant. Human intelligence is the ability to discover and communicate truth. This capacity for revealing the truth goes to the very heart of what it means to be human. To use our ability to discover the truth to purposely deceive is inevitably, in the minds of most older philosophers, a perversion of our own basic natures. Preventive evil can only be invoked as a last resort in very unusual circumstances. The rigid counterexample does not show that lying is good; the most it shows is that life is sometimes very complicated. Preventive evil is never, strictly speaking, properly moral,

---

ഇ Applied Philosophy Box 8.6 ക

Eight Dead in Suicide Attack on ANP Rally

Daily Times (Pakistan)

> *Miranshah*: A suicide attack on a public meeting in North Waziristan on Monday left at least eight people dead . . . including a candidate for the National Assembly. According to sources, the bomber blew himself up at an Awami National Party (ANP) gathering in Aidak, some 15 kilometres east of Miranshah. . . . The attack was a suicide car bombing. . . . [The report] said eight people were killed and 13 others sustained critical wounds. . . . The incident was the second such attack on an ANP public meeting in the past three days. On Saturday, a bomb ripped through a similar gathering in Charsadda district.

Is suicide bombing a case of the doctrine of double effect or preventive evil? Can this strategy be justified either way?

Source: Staff Report, 'Eight Dead in Suicide Attack on ANP rally.' *Daily Times* (Pakistan), www.dailytimes.com.pk/, 12 February 2008.

but it may be tolerable—even required—in extreme circumstances. Contemporary political philosophers such as Michael Walzer refer to the preventive evil strategy as the 'dirty hands dilemma': can we dirty our hands (by doing something immoral) in order to avoid extreme (political) evil?

A Modern Alternative to Kant: Ross's UnKantian Quasi-Categorical Imperative Theory

In response to these kinds of problems, more recent authors, notably W.D. Ross (1877–1971), have tried to dilute the universality requirement for the categorical imperative.[46] They argue for a softened version of deontology, for a **quasi-categorical imperative**. Ross, in a particular, distinguishes between **prima facie** duties and actual duties. Prima facie duties include such basic values as fidelity reparation, gratitude, non-injury, harm prevention, beneficence, self-improvement, and justice. (The list could be expanded in various ways.)[47] But Ross (unlike Kant) believes that all these duties are **defeasible**; in other words, they can be 'defeated' or overridden by other pressing concerns depending upon the circumstances. So we begin with a list of prima facie duties and then, relying on something like Aristotelian practical judgment, choose which duties have priority in these precise circumstances.

The concept of prima facie duties is intended to resolve situations when two (or more) duties compete for our allegiance. Louis Pojman describes the kind of problem Ross's theory is intended to solve:

> Suppose you have promised your friend that you will help her with her ethics homework at 3:00 PM. While you are on your way to meet her, you encounter a lost, crying child. There is no one else around to help the little boy, so you help him

find his way home. But, in doing so, you miss your appointment. Have you done the morally right thing? Have you broken your promise? It is possible to construe this situation as constituting a conflict between two moral principles: (1) We ought always to keep our promises. (2) We ought always to help people in need when it is not reasonably inconvenient to do so. In helping the child home you decided that the second principle overrides the first. This does not mean that the first is not a valid principle—only that the ought in it is not an absolute ought. The principle has objective validity, but it is not always decisive, depending on which other principles may apply to the situation.[48]

The idea here is that we are caught between competing duties: (1) keep your promises and (2) help people in need. If these moral duties are absolute (as Kant allegedly believes), there is no way to settle the conflict. In this situation, we cannot comply with both duties at the same time. If, on the other hand, these duties are defeasible, we can solve the problem by saying that the second duty defeats the first duty in this kind of circumstance. We can then go for help without worrying about breaking our promise.

But this seems to be much ado about nothing. When you promised your friend to help her with her homework, you presumably did not mean, 'I will be there at three o'clock sharp even if I come across a homeless child who needs my urgent help'. What you meant was something along the lines of 'Assuming there are no dire emergencies, I will be there at three'. Any other interpretation reads into the promise something no reasonable person would promise. These kinds of problems arise because commentators oversimplify what the moral law stands for, because they mechanically apply moral law without taking into account unusual circumstances, and because they do not acknowledge the role of casuistry.

To the extent that Kant's theory is mistaken, it is only because he fails to adequately comment on these considerations.

Some authors use the term 'escape clauses' to refer to the idea that moral laws have built into them certain unspoken restrictions which only apply in unusual circumstances. This terminology may mislead. It is not as if moral laws have a series of invisible restrictions corresponding to this or that odd situation attached to them. As we have already explained, general moral rules are abbreviations; they always need to be interpreted in the light of good judgment. They enclose a wider moral understanding that has to be sensitively applied to the particularities of an individual life. One never knows what unexpected circumstances may arise and force some new and perhaps surprising application of even the most familiar moral laws. In addition to virtuous laws, we need wise people to interpret them.

Kant would complain that any suggestion that laws against lying, murder, and promise-breaking (etc.) are only *prima facie* duties would risk weakening morality. It is one thing to say that moral rules need to be applied carefully to circumstances; it is quite another to say that it is alright to violate them. If morality is to be consistent, then as the principle of the indiscernability of moral cases indicates, moral law must be the same for everyone. Kant's ethics is all about consistency. Problems only arise from his unwillingness to consider the role of specific circumstances. But let us turn now to a consideration of Kant's other formulations of the categorical imperative.

Formulation 3: The Legislative Formulation

In the first and second formulations of the categorical imperative, Kant focuses on the universal content of the moral law; in his third formulation, he focuses on a method of decision-making that would produce the categorical imperative. Imagine you are given a country to rule. As supreme ruler, you take on, in effect, the role of the legislative branch of government. Imagine, too, that your commands will become laws governing the actions of every citizen. And that every citizen will dutifully obey these laws. If you decree that a person should do Y in situation X, every citizen will do Y in situation X. In this circumstance, you would be responsible for the behaviour of everyone. Your every decree would take on tremendous importance. Kant claims, however, that the moral person acts like a supreme ruler in devising moral laws. When we consciously act in accordance with the categorical imperative, we conform to a law that applies to all human beings. In formulating moral rules we ourselves must respect, we formulate moral rules everyone must respect. So we become, in Kant's mind, like a supreme ruler.

Kant believes that morality requires decision-making from an objective, i.e., a universal point of view. It demands that we act according to rules that have authority over everyone. Hence, his third formulation of the categorical imperative: '[the] *Idea of the will of every rational being as a will that legislates universal law.*'[49] Usually, when we decide to act, we imagine that we only need to think about ourselves. Carlos only needs to think about Carlos; Marie-Hélène only needs to think about Marie-Hélène; Huy-Dang only needs to think about Huy-Dang. Kant strongly disagrees. When we decide to act, we must decide what everybody should do (in like circumstances) and act accordingly. We must base our decisions on logical laws that can serve as an obligatory model for all rational agents.

Hence, Kant's comparison of the moral agent to a supreme ruler.

Kant's third formulation of the categorical imperative follows logically from his first two formulations. If moral agents must act according to maxims that are universal laws for all rational beings, they must first determine what these maxims are. Moral behaviour takes place in two stages, so to speak. First, moral agents must determine what should be done, and second, they must act accordingly. The first two formulations of the categorical imperative focus on the second task: we are to *act* in accordance with the content of universal laws. The third formulation focuses on the first task: we are to devise good laws using our very best judgment. We are to consider carefully what all rational beings, i.e., what the citizens of a hypothetical rational kingdom, would do in this situation. We are to act as legislators for a kingdom composed of rational beings, coming up with the very best laws for everyone.

Kant writes, 'in willing something just out of duty, the renunciation of interest is the specific mark distinguishing a categorical from a hypothetical imperative'.[50] Moral law holds back our self-interested desires so that we can act in a logical (as opposed to an 'interested') manner. Morality restrains our all-too-natural tendency to act out of our own self-interest. But a legislator who properly *acts as a legislator* acts in a disinterested manner. Kant (along with authors such as Plato, Aristotle, or Thomas) would believe that those who use their positions as legislators to further their own interests are acting *as private citizens*, not as true legislators. True lawgivers make decisions that promote the common good. And this is what moral agents do every time they act morally. They do not act in a self-interested way; they act in a way that takes the good of everyone into account.

There is a second reason Kant believes that the moral individual must act as a supreme ruler. Supreme lawgivers do not obey any outside authority. In their own jurisdiction, they possess all authority. To be a supreme ruler is to be the final link in the chain of command. So in obeying the law, supreme rulers obey a law they give themselves. A religious believer might protest that earthly rulers must obey a higher law given by God, but Kant wants to produce a secular moral system. Even if God exists, He is in charge, so to speak, of a different jurisdiction. Here on earth, moral law has to end somewhere. Kant believes that it ends with the moral person acting as supreme lawmaker.[51] Our status as supreme rulers makes us very special. It gives us more authority and, conversely, more responsibility than other (non-rational) beings.

Kant calls this legislative formulation of the categorical imperative the 'autonomy formulation'. The word *autonomy* comes from two Greek words: *auto*, meaning 'self'; and *nomos*, meaning (as we have seen) 'law' or 'convention'. To be autonomous is to be self-ruled; it is to act according to a law you give yourself. Moral people are autonomous because, in their role as supreme lawgivers, they act according to a moral law they give themselves. The moral law has to conform to reason, but reason is implanted deep within us; hence to obey the biding of reason is to obey a call that emanates from our very own natures. It is to act according to a law human nature gives itself.

Like other Enlightenment thinkers, Kant wants to emphasize the difference between his theory and previous theories. He writes,

> If we look back on all the previous efforts to discover the principle of morality, it is no wonder that they have all had to fail. One saw that human

beings are bound to laws by their duty, but it never occurred to anyone that they are subject only to *laws which they themselves have given* but which are nevertheless *universal* and that people are only bound to act in conformity with a will that is their own but . . . that gives a universal law.[52]

Kant's observation here that the moral law is an extension of human nature and therefore something people give themselves is not nearly as new an idea as he suggests. Kant is, not surprisingly, a very poor historian. In fact, most authors in the Western tradition describe morality in somewhat similar terms. Earlier philosophers such as Thomas Aquinas, the Stoics, the Epicureans, Aristotle, Plato, and early Greek thinkers generally trace morality back to human nature and, ultimately, to human reason. In each case, morality is seen as something that comes from inside the individual. Kant's account of autonomy presents an insightful twist on this idea of moral self-government—he highlights the importance of will and logic—but it is historically unsound to think that it is at odds with what all that went before.

In Kant's account, we have value, not only as beings who submit to morality, but as beings who make moral law. Having morality inside us endows us with great dignity. In everyday life, we do treat rulers, legislators, heads of state with great deference. These are very important people after all! Kant believes that the ordinary person is likewise deserving of respect. This is a momentous destiny: to legislate rules that every rational being must follow. Indeed, morality is more fundamental than politics. Being a moral lawgiver is a more impressive and important role than being, for example, president of the United States or queen of England. Kant, throughout his work, emphasizes the moral dignity of ordinary

human beings. This emphasis on individual human dignity is expressed, in a particularly conspicuous way, in Kant's fourth formulation of the categorical imperative.

Formulation 4: The Means–End Formulation

The previous three formulations of the categorical imperative all appeal to the notion of universal law. A universal law posits a uniform standard of behaviour for all agents. In the fourth formulation of the categorical imperative, Kant takes a different approach: he focuses on human nature as the ultimate source of human value. As we have already seen, earlier authors in the mainstream tradition recognize that some objects, properties, and/or activities are intrinsically valuable; that is, such things are valuable, not simply as a means to something else, but merely because they are what they are. Kant goes one step further and identifies human individuality as intrinsically valuable. Kant believes that all humans deserve respect for their own sake, merely because they are human beings. He uses the traditional distinction between means and ends to express this idea.

We value something as a means when we value it for the sake of something else; we value something as an end when we value it for its own sake. Kant writes: 'Now, I say, a human being, and in general every rational being, does exist as an end-in-himself, *not merely as a means* to be used by this or that will as it pleases. In all his actions, whether they are directed to himself or to other rational beings, a human being must always be viewed *at the same time as an end*.'[53] Kant believes that although we can value humans as a means to a larger goal—say, the way a volleyball coach values her players as means to a regional championship—we must at the same time value them for their own sakes, solely because they are who they are. He articulates this line of thought in his fourth formulation of the categorical imperative: 'Act in such a way that you treat humanity, whether in your own person or in any other person, always at the same time as an end, never merely as a means.'[54] Let us consider, then, in closer detail, what this fourth formulation entails.

To value something is to treat it like a treasure; it is to seek to guard, protect, enhance, and preserve it; it is to respect or admire its nature. To value something as an end-in-itself is to value it because it is what it is.

Kant claims that we ought to value people as ends-in-themselves. To say that you are valuable as an end-in-yourself is to say that you have intrinsic worth apart from other people's desires or purposes. It doesn't matter how useful you are to other people—you are valuable solely because you are you. Nor does your value change; it is not dependent on other people's judgments and perceptions or on circumstances: you are valuable as yourself. It is your unique individual identity that is valuable. Kant explains this by means of a comparison between objects and persons.

Kant Distinguishes Between Objects and Persons

Kant believes that objects and persons do not possess the same moral value. Objects—non-human things we buy and sell, like tables, houses, cars, vegetables, works of art (etc.)—have instrumental value. In the case of objects, our attachment to them endows them with value. Because we are attached to them, and (only) to the extent that we are attached to them, they possess value. Their value comes from us. They are valuable inso-much as they provide us with a means to our ends. Human persons are not like this, at least not according to Kant. In the case of human persons, our attachment to them is after the fact. We should be attached to them but this is not why they have value. Their value is derived from their own nature. Even if we were not attached to them, they would still possess value. Indeed, Kant believes that human persons are so valuable, they have something more than ordinary value: they have dignity.

Kant sharply distinguishes between (1) economic value and (2) dignity. Objects have a price; human persons have dignity. Objects can be bought, sold, traded for, or replaced with one another; their value can be measured and compared according to some common scale. Kant believes that each human person, in contrast, is unique; so the value of one cannot be measured in terms of the value of another. Each human person, he believes, possesses absolute or infinite value, value that is beyond measurement. Kant writes, 'Everything has a price or a dignity. Whatever has a price can be replaced by something else as *equivalent*. Whatever by contrast is exalted above all price and so admits of no equivalent has dignity'.[55]

So, Kant believes, there is a divide, a great chasm that separates the economic rationality of the marketplace from morality. We can have a marketplace for objects because (1) the value of objects can be measured (in terms of some shared monetary scale) and (2) objects can be replaced by other objects. We cannot have a marketplace for persons because (1) we cannot measure the value of persons and (2) individual people, being unique, are irreplaceable. This is why slavery—the buying and selling of persons—is wrong. It requires putting a price

---

❧ Applied Philosophy Box 8.7 ❧

Human Face to Sex Slavery in Toronto

Toronto's first human trafficking charges since Canada's human trafficking legislation came into effect November 2005 [have been laid]. Many experts pointed to the case as the tip of the iceberg for the ever lucrative flesh trade moving into our borders. Though no one really knows the statistics, two years ago, the RCMP estimated 600 to 800 people are trafficked into Canada for modern day [sex] slavery every year. . . . [Detective Randall] Cowan estimates there are 'hundreds' of domestic trafficking victims in the Greater Toronto Area alone, forced to satisfy every fetish and fantasy in the sex industry.

Contrary to what we often assume, human slavery is not a thing of the past. From the viewpoint of the human traffickers, what is the value of these sex slaves? Why are they valuable? Explain and critique in Kantian terms.

Source: Tamara Cherry, 'Human Face to Sex Slavery in Toronto.' Sun Media, *The Toronto Sun*, 2008/02/10; posted at 'Holly's Fight to Stop Violence,' http://fighttostopviolence.blogspot.com/2008/02/human-face-to-sex-slavery-in-gta.html.

---

on the value of a human being. It means treating individual human beings as if they could be replaced by an object of equal value. As Kant clearly states, each human person is 'an end such that no other end can be substituted for it'.[56] To treat humans as replaceable objects is a category mistake; it is to misunderstand what morality is all about.

Kant argues that ownership is not an appropriate model of human relationship. You are not even the property of yourself. You do not own yourself; you *are* yourself. If you owned yourself, you could sell yourself or rent yourself the way people sell or rent out property. You could do this to make a financial profit. But Kant would consider such behaviour flagrantly immoral. This would be to treat yourself as a *means* to financial gain, not as an end-in-itself. It would be to turn yourself into a commodity, something with economic instead of moral value. This is why Kant would believe that activities like prostitution or selling your organs for money are immoral, because we are persons, not objects. In Kant's system, moral-

ity is bigger than the marketplace. Economic transactions are driven by self-interest. Buying and selling is, roughly put, a matter of the buyer and the seller getting what they, respectively, want. Individuals involved in business make use of hypothetical, not categorical, imperatives: 'If you want *A*, do *B*.' Kant thinks that morality overrides economic considerations; it puts a brake on self-interest; it supplies a standard of right conduct that transcends economics. The categorical imperative applies inside and outside the marketplace without exception.

Morality Means Treating Persons as Ends-in-Themselves

As we have seen, the fourth formulation of the categorical imperative tells us to treat human beings as ends-in-themselves. Kant is, however, rather vague when it comes to explaining what it means to treat people as ends-in-themselves. Mostly, he is content to say we should not *use* other human beings solely as means to our own purposes. He writes, 'Rational beings . . .

are called persons because their nature already marks them out as ends in themselves—that is, as something which ought not to be used merely as a means'.[57] To use other people merely as means is to value them only to the degree to which they contribute to our own projects and personal goals. To use a familiar example, when a man *uses* a woman for his sexual pleasure—we say things like 'he was just using her'—we mean that he was using her solely as a means to something he wants—pleasure—without caring about her needs, her happiness, her future. He was too interested in satisfying his own sexual desires to care about any negative effects the experience might have on her.

To treat other people as ends is, on the other hand, to treat them in a way that promotes *their* welfare. It is to do what is good for *them*, not just what is good for us. It is to value their needs and aspirations as much as our own. Suppose I hire you to build a house. You are the means to my desired end: a house. This is not necessarily immoral. Suppose, however, I pay you an unfair wage. Or suppose I make you work in dangerous conditions. Or suppose I refuse to give you any holidays to rest and recuperate from your work. This would be immoral for I would be treating you *only* as a means to my own ends; I would be ignoring your own well-being.

Kant says that we cannot use other people *solely* as means. If I hire you to build my house, I must make building the house good for you as well as for me. The building of the house must not only serve as a way for me to achieve my ends; it must also serve as a way for you to achieve your ends. We must *both* benefit. Morality requires that I treat your aims and aspirations as deserving of serious consideration. When we interact with other people, we must respect their legitimate concerns and needs.

This ends-formulation of the categorical imperative places the value of other human beings out of the reach of changing circumstances. Sometimes other people contribute to our purposes; sometimes they hinder our purposes. If I want to build a table, a carpenter will contribute to my purposes. If I want to fix my lamp, an electrician will contribute to my purposes. Kant argues that the value of other human beings does not depend on these changing circumstances. Considered from a moral point of view, we must consider the carpenter and the electrician as valuable as ever, even when we do not need their services. Other human beings are not mere appendages to our own desires and dreams. They possess an intrinsic value of their own, simply because they are human beings. Their goals are important simply because they are the goals of another human being.

Kant believes that each instance of humanity constitutes something of value for its own sake. Pedro is valuable because he is Pedro. Aiko is valuable because she is Aiko. To say that we must treat Pedro and Aiko as ends-in-themselves is to say that we must behave toward them in ways that promote their preservation and well-being. We all suffer from a kind of self-centredness that makes us value everything in the world—including other persons—in the light of our own personal designs and aspirations. Kant warns us against this all-too-familiar tendency. He reminds us that other people are valuable independent of their usefulness. To treat human beings as ends-in-themselves is to accept that their value derives from their own (logical) nature, not from the degree to which they help us achieve our own ends.

❧ Applied Philosophy Box 8.8 ❧

Suicide: A Civil Right?

To these statements of support for the right to commit suicide, I will add my own: In a truly free society, *you own your life.* . . . I believe everyone is entitled to be treated as the sole owner of himself or herself and of his or her own life. Accordingly, I think a person who commits suicide is well within his or her rights. . . . In a free society where self-ownership is recognized, 'dangerousness to oneself' is irrelevant. In the words of the title of a movie starring Richard Dreyfuss: 'Whose Life Is It, Anyway?' The greatest human right is the right of self-ownership, one aspect of which is the right to life, but another aspect of which is the right to end one's own life.

Kant would disagree wholeheartedly with such sentiments. Why?

Source: Lawrence Stevens, 'Suicide: A Civil Right.' *antipsychiatry.org*, www.antipsychiatry.org/suicide.htm, n.d.

It is important to emphasize again that Kant believes that we have duties to ourselves as well as to other people. If we are to be consistent—i.e. if we act logically—we must treat *ourselves* as ends-in-ourselves. This is, according to Kant, why suicide is wrong. Kant writes, 'I cannot dispose of a human being in my own person, by maiming, corrupting, or killing him'.[58] Someone who commits suicide deliberately destroys something irreplaceable, something of infinite worth. This is, for Kant, plainly wrong. Unhappiness as a motive for suicide would be tantamount to a justification for unhappiness as a motive for murder. It is not just that suicide sets a dangerous precedent. In Kant's mind, using ourselves solely as a means to pleasure is as bad as using someone else solely as a means to pleasure. Kant claims that human beings possess absolute value. Our humanity is still valuable even when we are unhappy. People who commit suicide because they feel unhappy only value themselves in certain circumstances. When circumstances change, they destroy themselves. This is, for Kant, to turn a person into an object, into something that has contingent, not absolute, value.

Formulation 5: The Kingdom of Ends Formulation

Morality is not just about individual behaviour. It is also a group project. It requires social interaction. Kant proposes, then, a fifth and final formulation of the categorical imperative: *'Every rational being must act as if he were always by his maxims a lawgiving member in [a] universal kingdom of ends.'*[59]

Kant devises the concept of a universal kingdom of ends to refer to humanity considered as an all-encompassing moral community composed of individual persons who treat one another as ends-in-themselves. The basic idea here is that moral law obliges us to act as if we were members of a prefect society where everyone aims at morality. We are to act as if we are united with all human beings in a common project: the organization and maintenance of a just way of life that respects people as ends-in-themselves. This is, in principle, what happens in a kingdom of ends. There is 'a systematic union of rational beings through shared objective laws'; i.e., through a common adherence to the various versions of the categorical imperative.[60] This fifth version of the categorical imperative, like the third version, proposes a way of making decisions that, Kant believes, will lead to morality. He advises: act as if you are a member of this kind of community and you will act morally.

We must emphasize four aspects of Kant's notion of a kingdom of ends:

1. This ideal society cannot exclude any rational being It must be made up of all rational beings taken together and considered as a community.
2. Every person in a kingdom of ends must treat everyone else as an end.
3. A kingdom of ends must be composed of persons whose everyday existence is organized around objective moral laws, summed up in various formulations of the categorical imperative.
4. Kant suggests that rulers in a kingdom of ends will enact the very same laws citizens would posit for themselves. In obeying this higher authority, citizens are simultaneously obeying themselves. In this ideal community, self-rule and submission to a higher authority come together. There is no room for oppression or tyranny.

Kant's conception of 'kingdom of ends' is only intended as a thought-experiment. It is, he quips, 'only an ideal'.[61] It is a vision of an earthly heaven, a place where *everyone* behaves morally. Unfortunately, no society is like this. The communities we live in are composed of good and bad people and all degrees in-between; so they do not correspond precisely to what Kant means by a kingdom of ends. We can, however, conceive in our minds what it would be like to be part of a fully moral community.

Kant points out that if we always act as if were part of such a community, we will inevitably act morally—hence, his second wording of this formulation of the categorical imperative: '*Act on the maxims of a . . . member of a . . . kingdom of ends.*'[62] Do what a member of a perfectly moral community would do. In other words, act, not according to the laws in present-day society, but according to those laws that would exist in a perfectly moral society.

It is not entirely clear whether the kingdom of ends formulation of the categorical imperative adds new content to the picture of morality Kant has already sketched. Kant seems to think it has inspirational value; it is an edifying thought to think that we can work together toward the establishment of an ideal community. At the very least, the kingdom of ends formulation gives us another way of thinking about morality. Do you want to know if you are acting morally? Ask yourself, am I doing what someone in a perfectly moral community would do? If you act according to the laws that would be enacted and observed in an ideal society, you can know you are acting morally.

A Summary of the Five Formulations of the Categorical Imperative

We can now list Kant's five formulations of the categorical imperative:

1. 'Act only on that maxim by which you can at the same time will that it should become a universal law.'[63] In other words, always act in the same way you want everyone else to act.
2. 'Act as though the maxim of your act were to become a universal law of nature.'[64] In modern terms, always act so that you could, in principle, oblige everyone else (as a matter of universal moral law) to act on the same intentions you act upon.

3. '[The] idea of the will of every rational being as a will that legislates universal law.'[65] In other words, always act as if you were a supreme ruler and the intentions expressed by your acts were to be made into universal laws.

4. 'Act in such a way that you treat humanity, whether in your own person or in any other person, always at the same time as an end, never merely as a means.'[66] That is, human beings have dignity, infinite value. Always consider other people's goals as equally deserving of respect. Never use others as objects.

5. 'Every rational being must act as if he were always by his maxims a lawgiving member in [a] universal kingdom of ends.'[67] Here, Kant means that we must always act as if we were part of a perfectly moral community that treated all citizens with adequate dignity, as ends-in-themselves.

Kant suggests that all these different versions of the categorical imperative 'are basically only so many formulations of the same law'.[68] At the same time, he seems to believe that the first universal formulations of the categorical imperative must be taken as the most fundamental expression of the moral impetus. The universal consistency requirement of morality set out in the first three formulations of the categorical imperative is not logically equivalent to the value requirement set out in the final two formulations. The first formulations tell us to act consistently—act the way you would want others to act. The last formulations tell us that human beings are of inestimable value. Suffice it to say that all these different formulations reinforce and complement one another. Taken together, they constitute a coherent, moral world view.

On Autonomy

As the reader will have noticed, Kant proposes a 'muscular' morality. To be moral is to ignore the incessant pull of desire, interest, and inclination. It is to force oneself to do what is right because it is right. It is to muster up all one's willpower and do the right thing, even though it goes against the grain of human nature. Seen from this perspective, morality may seem to be a restraint, a chain, something that limits our freedom. But in fact, Kant claims just the opposite: he believes that rather than chaining us down; morality liberates us. Morality is a part of ourselves—the most important part. We cannot be ourselves without being moral. If we are moral, then we are free.

Kant joins the three deepest human aspirations—rationality, morality, and freedom—together into a single concept, what he calls **autonomy**. According to Kant, these three human qualities do not clash; they coincide. We can express his idea in a simple formula: reason = morality = freedom. In words, to be rational is to be moral is to be free. When we act rationally (i.e., logically), we act morally, and when we act morally, we act according to laws we give ourselves. This is the meaning of freedom. Morality means obeying our own rational (human) nature. And this, according to Kant, is what it means to be free.

Kant then distinguishes between autonomy and the opposite condition, which he calls **heteronomy**. Heteronomous agents desire licence, not true freedom. They act immorally because they are distracted by momentary feelings, by vacillating wants and wayward inclinations. Kant believes that they are less than free, for they are ruled by something outside themselves—i.e., they are ruled by the superficial goodness they mistakenly see in the objects they pursue rather than by their own inner worth. In his words, 'If the will . . . goes outside itself and seeks [the] law [that regulates its behaviour] in a property of any of its objects—the result is always *heteronomy*. In that case the will does not give itself the law; rather the object gives the law to it'.[69]

Kant identifies 'autonomy of the will' as 'the supreme principle of morality'.[70] 'Heteronomy of the will' is, in contrast, 'the source of all the spurious principles of morality'.[71] Kant believes that we cannot achieve autonomy if we submit our will to anything other than logic. He complains that earlier philosophers mistakenly situate the moral impetus in something other than our logical nature: in anthropology, psychology, emotion, local custom, religion, or prejudice. His criticism presupposes, however, a misunderstanding of earlier philosophy. As we have seen, moral philosophers before Kant focus likewise on the rational element in human nature. True, they propose a wider notion of rationality, one that includes a practical and a psychological aspect. But this is a positive not a negative thing. Kant's unduly narrow view of moral reason leads to difficulties which we will consider next.

Criticisms of Kant's Deontological Approach

Let us now consider some basic criticisms of Kant's deontological approach.

Anti-Morality: Nietzsche and the Anti-Kantian Backlash

The narrowness of Kant's deontological method has serious drawbacks. Kant locates morality in the head rather than the heart: he asks us to act out of strict duty; to deny the demands of inclination, feeling, temperament, and personality in favour of the demands of pure logic. But this aloof, cerebral, almost mathematical account of morality has precipitated an equally extreme reaction in the other direction. It has led to the rise of a kind of anti-morality in modern culture, philosophy, and public thinking. In extreme cases, these anti-moralists go so far as to champion the advantages of immorality over morality. These anti-moralists trumpet their choice of immorality over morality as a reaffirmation of all that is human: feelings, desire, emotion, temperament, individuality, inclination. They present blatant immorality as authenticity, as a noble struggle against the inhumane and limiting structures of an overly cerebral, deontological conception of moral reason.

The reaction against Kantian ethics culminates in the extreme anti-moralism of authors such as the German existentialist Friedrich Nietzsche, the Marquis de Sade (from whom we derive the word *sadism*), and the popular novelist Ayn Rand. These anti-moralists denounce morality as an outdated convention that drags down the free human spirit, restricting heroic individuality, and enforcing social conformity. More moderate authors also denounce, in gentler terms, the rule-bound morality of Kant as a recipe for conformism and mediocrity. We encounter this anti-morality sentiment in media depictions of moral people as 'square', dull, and uninteresting; in heroic or flamboyant accounts of sometimes heinous criminals and outlaws, and in a sometimes frenzied public appetite for anything having to do with extreme forms of sex, drugs, power, crimes, and violence.

John Stuart Mill, the famous British liberal (whom we discuss in the next chapter), criticizes the whole deontological approach. Mill takes a swipe at 'Calvinistic' (or Puritan) theories of ethics and, without a doubt, at Kant himself, caricaturing his deontological account, Mill writes, 'According to Kant, . . . all the good of which humanity is capable, is comprised in obedience. . . . "Whatever is not a duty is a sin." [Because] human nature being radically corrupt, there is no redemption for any one until human nature is killed within him.'[72] This is ferocious satire but Mill does not pull his punches: 'To one holding this theory of life, crushing out any of the human faculties, capacities, and susceptibilities, is no evil.'[73]

Mill's plea for the goodness of the human personality is really a distant echo of the much richer virtue ethics found in an earlier author like Aristotle. If Kant tells us to deny our personalities for morality, Mill tells us to develop our personalities to the utmost. He continues, 'There is a different type of human excellence from the Calvinistic; a conception of humanity as having its nature bestowed on it for other purposes than merely to be abnegated. "Pagan self-assertion" is one of the elements of human worth, as well as "Christian self-denial."'[74]

We will discuss Mill's moral philosophy in the next chapter. But the most conspicuous anti-Kantian is, doubtless, Friedrich Nietzsche (1844–1900), a less than systematic theoretician but a superb writer, who opposes morality as an artificial brake on the virile, life-affirming instinct to domination that, he thinks, motivates great men and women. Whereas Kant denies nature and affirms morality, Nietzsche affirms nature and denies morality. A master of hyperbole, he denigrates standard moral values as nothing more than a quaint and curious custom of a diseased and decadent Christian society. Conformist Christian European morality tells us (according to Nietzsche) to be

nice to others. It commands us to refrain from harming our neighbours and our enemies, to treat them as equals, to be submissive and subservient to secular and religious authority.. Influenced by Darwinian ideas of biological evolution, Nietzsche argues that human life is a competitive struggle to dominate rivals and that any morality that condemns such tendencies constitutes a rejection of life itself. He identifies *the will to power* as the basic instinct that expresses itself in all human achievement. In his sometimes extravagant work, the German philosopher claims that we always want more power and endeavour to dominate others and our environment: this is the real goal of our efforts. Nietzsche insists, 'Life is simply will to power . . . which is simply the will to life'.[75]

Nietzsche, whose all-consuming fascination with power is reminiscent of Hobbes, turns morality upside-down. Indeed, he champions immoralism. Human life, at its core, is about subjugating and exploiting others. To deny this is to take refuge in sentimentalism, artificial convention, and pious falsehood. Nietzsche believes that such attitudes constitute a denial of nature. He writes, 'To refrain from injuring, abusing, or exploiting one another; to equate another person's will with our own [may be] good manners. . . . But if we try to take this [moral understanding] further and possibly even make it the *basic principle of society*, it would immediately be revealed for what it is: a will to *deny* life, a principle for dissolution and decline'.[76] To be true to human nature is then to embrace the eternal project of dominating and using others. Nietzsche comments, 'life itself *in its essence* means appropriating, injuring, overpowering those who are foreign and weaker; [it means] oppression, harshness, forcing one's own forms on others, incorporation and . . . exploitation'.[77]

Nietzsche does not point to logic as a guide to greatness, providing instead a description of the great man, whom he calls the *ubermensch* (German for 'the overman' or 'the superman'). Nietzsche's *ubermensch* will break with mediocre convention, living according to a set of values he *creates* for himself. He will be a warrior, an aristocrat, a commander, a 'blond beast of prey'. He will love his friends and hate his enemies with an astonishing inventiveness. Nietzsche *enthusiastically* paints a picture of the *ubermensch* as a conquering hero subjugating foreign peoples with savage intensity:

> [Overmen will] behave towards the outside world—where the foreign, *foreigners* are to be found—in a manner not much better than predators on the rampage. There . . . [they will] regress to the innocence of the predator's conscience, as rejoicing monsters, capable of high spirits as they walk away without qualms from a horrific succession of murder, arson, violence, and torture, as if it were nothing more than a student prank, something new for poets to sing and celebrate for some time to come.[78]

There are endless variations on this anti-morality motif. In the works of an author like the infamous Marquis de Sade, this exaltation of power is added to a libertine caricature of human nature as a bottomless pit of carnal appetites devoid of any spark of moral decency. In the works of popular novelist Ayn Rand (who fled Communism), it is joined to an enthusiasm for free-market capitalism. In the works of French social critic Michel Foucault, power becomes the dominating force in a sociological account of knowledge. Anti-moralists argue that *immorality* is the only way to be true to yourself. Authenticity is more important than morality. Morality is too cramped, too narrow an ideal to fully count as human flourishing.

There is a deep irony in all of this bold, antimoralist rhetoric. Although Nietzsche writes as if he is against all morality, he is as much a moral philosopher as Kant. Think about it. Nietzsche condemns and praises certain kinds of behaviour; he champions specific values; he has an account of human perfection; he substitutes an ethics of warrior virtue for Kant's morality of lawful constraint. Nietzsche replaces the Kantian emphasis on duty with a preoccupation with individual greatness. It is not enough to do what everyone else must do. It is not enough to make decisions based on some internalized logic like a computer. A valuable human life requires spontaneity, great feeling, activity, absolute freedom, individual accomplishment.

If, however, Nietzsche criticizes Kant mercilessly, he remains unwittingly a Kantian, at least in some important sense. Nietzsche's account of 'the will to power' is a reduction—some would say a **reductio ad absurdum**—of Kant's view that willpower matters most of all. Nietzsche unwittingly adopts the Kantian emphasis on will. He champions the idea of a heroic will that affirms itself in spite of endless suffering. In Kant's theory the will must be directed toward the good, whereas in Nietzsche's theory, it can be directed anywhere, just so long as it operates robustly, vehemently, heroically, and so long as it as a matter of individuals choosing for themselves. But, surely, this is to turn Kantian morality into a caricature of itself.

The Problem of Moral Motivation

We can criticize the narrowness of Kant's approach. But the biggest problem with Kant's theory concerns moral motivation. While Kant can explain what the moral law is, he is unable to explain why people act morally. To understand how this problem arises, we need to briefly consider his metaphysical views.

Kant divides human beings in two, distinguishing between an empirical, physical part that belongs to the world of experience and an invisible part that we can conceive of only through philosophy. We can know the first part, what he refers to as the-thing-as-it-appears-to-us, but the second part, what Kant calls the thing-in-itself (*Ding an sich*), is an impenetrable mystery. He explains:

> behind appearances we must admit and assume something else which is not appearance—namely, things in themselves. . . . This thought must yield a distinction, however rough, between a *sensible world* and the *intelligible world*. . . . Beyond [a sensible] constitution of himself . . . compounded of nothing else but appearances, [a human being] must assume that there is something else that is [his] foundation—namely his ego, however it may be constituted in itself. [On the one hand,] he must count himself as belonging to the world of sense; [on the other hand] he must count [himself] as belonging to the *intellectual* world. Of that [intellectual] world, however, he knows nothing.[79]

According to Kant, reason 'goes far beyond anything [perception and experience] can offer'.[80] Beyond what we perceive or experience, there is a conscious mental capacity all human beings encounter in themselves. As Kant puts it, 'a human being actually finds in himself a power by which he distinguishes himself from all other things . . . that power is *reason*'.[81] Kant uses this two-tiered metaphysical schema to account for the possibility of free will. Freedom is possible because there are two levels of personhood. Insofar as a human being belongs to 'the world of sense-experience', he must submit to the deterministic laws of nature; insofar as he belongs to 'the intelligible world', he must submit to 'laws

that are not empirical but, being independent of nature, are founded on reason alone'.[82]

Kant believes that reason 'must regard itself as free'.[83] We all know that we are free, for 'it is impossible to conceive of a power of reason that consciously regards its own judgments as directed from the outside'.[84] So we inhabit a world with two kinds of laws: physical laws, which science elucidates; and moral laws, which (according to Kant) logic or reason elucidates. The 'idea of freedom' is 'inseparably attached' to the concept of morality, which 'is the ground of all the actions of rational beings, just as the law of nature is the ground of all appearances'.[85]

Kant unsurprisingly believes that our intelligible selves are superior to our empirical selves. Every human being knows that 'he is [in] his true self, an intelligence only'.[86] This, then, is the human predicament. We are caught in a constant tug-of-war between two hostile possibilities: whereas our physical, biological, emotional, psychological, and anthropological selves push us uncritically toward pleasure and self-interest, our rational, logical, intelligible selves tell us what we *ought* to do, directing us toward morality. To live according to our empirical selves is heteronomy; to live according to our logical, intelligible selves is autonomy. Only autonomous agents are truly free, for they alone act according to an internal law that derives from their true nature.

Kant, for understandable reasons, wants to unhook morality from desire, inclination, self-interest, or emotion. But a problem immediately surfaces: how can desire be inevitably evil? After all, good people *desire* to be moral. Good people *feel* the need to act decently. They are *inclined*, psychologically and socially, toward virtue. They believe that it is in their *self-interest* to act morally. Is this a terrible thing? If morality were to exist independently of all desire, emotion, inclination, and self-interest, what in the world could make anyone *want* to be moral? It is not enough to say (like Kant and his followers) that we should act morally out of respect (or reverence) for the law. Unless we accept that an attitude of respect for the moral law includes a psychological push in the right direction, we cannot use it to explain why people are motivated to act morally. In undertaking his unrelenting moral criticism of the empirical aspects of the human personality, Kant unwittingly eliminates the grounds for moral motivation. He cannot explain why anyone would want to be moral. This is why the anti-moralists, with some justification, react so strongly against his account.

Kant sometimes writes as if the idea of morality and immorality produce *feelings* of pleasure and displeasure in the mind of the moral person, but it is hard to reconcile such notions with his moral philosophy as a whole. Kant himself admits that he is at a complete loss when it comes to the question of what motivates us to be moral. At the very end of his *Groundwork*, he asserts that questions about moral motivation are unanswerable. He comments: 'how pure reason can supply a motive and create an interest which could be called purely *moral*; . . .—all human reason is totally incapable of explaining this, and all the pains and labor to seek such an explanation are wasted.'[87] But, surely, this is an inadequate response to a legitimate philosophical question. To simply state that the mystery of moral motivation 'is the supreme limit of all moral inquiry'[88] is not very helpful.

Kant claims that explanations of the need to act morally lead us astray in one of two ways. Either (1) they force us to give an empir- ical, self-interested reason for morality, which will turn morality into a type of economics—what's in it for me?—and obscure the severe but noble voice of duty, or (2) they force us to delve into the unknowable realm of metaphysics. We must give up the search for an explanation of moral motivation, so that (1) 'reason may not . . . hunt around in the sensible world, to the detriment of morality, for the supreme motive [in] some comprehensible but empirical interest'; and (2) 'so that [reason] will not [in attempting the inexplicable] . . . impotently flap its wings in the . . . empty space . . . of transcendent [or metaphysical] concepts . . . losing itself among the phantoms of the brain'.[89] Kant's morality is, in some sense, a motivation-less morality, a morality for the pure of heart, a strict and austere call to a kind of logical selflessness. He does not, in the final analysis, give us an emotional, flesh-and-blood reason to be moral.

We have come full circle. We have surveyed Kant's major contributions to ethics and returned to the basic problem with his theory. In his haste to come up with a new theory that breaks with the past, Kant overlooks the rich resources of history. If Kant cannot give us a reason to be moral, earlier authors, ancient and medieval, identify happiness (properly defined) with morality. It does not follow (as some contemporary analysts claim) that morality becomes thereby a self-centred preoccupation, for earlier authors identify happiness with noble achievement, with human flourishing, with good reputation, with subservience to nature, with religious devotion, with friendship, with love. If, however, we identify morality with happiness, this gives us a reason to be moral.

Almost all philosophers, like Kant, trace morality to the power of reason, but earlier authors view reason, in larger terms, as an ability for clear thinking which includes a cosmic and an anthropological aspect. The earliest philosophers find morality in the workings of nature considered as a harmonious whole. Plato situates morality in ontological ideas that are everlastingly beautiful. Aristotle situates morality, more specifically, in the goodness of human nature. Thomas likewise believes in human goodness but also appeals to a notion of supernatural grace that can overcome the lasting effect of original sin. Hobbes locates morality in self-interest. In sharp contrast, Kant wants to erect a logical morality separate from tradition, from nature, from Platonic metaphysics, from human psychology, from God. He emphasizes duty, the need to resist the pull of fallen nature, while trying to develop a purely selfless, secular alternative to theological ethics. Although his theory highlights the logical nature of morality, it seems largely incomplete.

Other philosophers do provide answers to questions about moral motivation. The earliest philosophers believe that nature pushes us in the direction of morality. Hedonists such as Epicurus believe that the intelligent pursuit of pleasure can make us moral. Plato thinks morality is based on knowledge. Epistemology saves us: if we set out to know—using philosophy—we will come to see what is good and act accordingly. Aristotle focuses on habit: if we keep acting charitably, we will become charitable people. Thomas argues for habit and grace: everything is based on divine love, and whenever mere natural inclination is not enough, God (so to speak) gives us an extra push in the right direction. Even a modern author like Hobbes believes that self-interest can give us a good reason to act morally. Whichever answer (or answers) we prefer, there are ways to account for moral motivation that Kant overlooks or dismisses.

Kant's approach has an undeniable grandeur, but it is also extreme. Disembodied reason, the power of logic, may be an important part of what we are—indeed, it may be one of the most important parts of what we are—but it is not the whole human being. Earlier authors did not separate reason from the rest of the human person; they came up with an account that merged the empirical, biological, and psychological aspects of the human personality with practical reason. In so doing, they give us various reasons to be moral. Without denying what is insightful about Kant's work, we need to develop a more three-dimensional explanation of what moral striving is all about. Virtue ethics, joined to legitimate conceptions of universal moral law, can provide such an account.

∾ Questions for Study and Review ∾

1. Explain how Enlightenment thinkers such as Kant viewed tradition. What were the values and attitudes of the Enlightenment?
2. Relate the biblical story of Adam and Eve to Kant's ethics.
3. Define *deontology*.
4. Define *duty*.
5. Kant views Isaac Newton as a model of intellectual achievement. How is this admiration expressed in his moral philosophy?

6. What is the *new* definition of happiness that comes to the fore in the Enlightenment? How, in Kant's mind, does it change the relationship of happiness to morality?

7. Kant refers to the 'categorical imperative'. What is a categorical imperative?

8. Describe the difference between hypothetical and categorical imperatives. Present an example of each.

9. What is Kant's argument against suicide?

10. How are the Golden Rule of Jesus and Kant's categorical imperative similar?

11. Kant wants to emphasize *universal* moral law. But Kant provides an inadequate account of casuistry. This is a weakness in Kant's system. Explain.

12. Why, according to Kant, is telling a lie immoral?

13. What are the three criteria for preventive evil? Explain each criterion in turn.

14. In what sense, according to Kant, is every human being a 'supreme ruler'?

15. Kant believes that human beings are valuable even when they are not useful. Explain.

16. Explain, according to Kant, the difference between an 'object' and a 'person'.

17. Compare 'autonomy' and 'heteronomy'.

18. Describe 'anti-moralism', understood as a fierce reaction against Kant's moral philosophy. What did anti-moralists propose in the place of conventional morality?

19. In what sense is Nietzsche still a Kantian?

20. Kant divides the human self in two. Explain.

✍ Suggestions for Further Reading ✍

• Immanuel Kant, *Groundwork for the Metaphysics of Morals*, Arnulf Zweig, trans., Thomas E. Hill, Jr., and Arnulf Zweig, eds. (Oxford; New York: Oxford University Press, 2002).

• For another, very readable translation see: Immanuel Kant, *Groundwork of the Metaphysics of Morals*, H.J. Paton trans. (New York: Harper Torchbook, 1964).

• See also 'Kant and Kantian Ethics', maintained by Lawrence Hinman for an excellent and extensive website with links to many sources, historical and contemporary: http://ethics.sandiego.edu/theories/Kant/index.asp.

• Friedrich Nietzsche, *A Nietzsche Reader*, selected, translated with an introduction by R.J. Hollingdale (London: Penguin Books, 1977).

Friedrich Nietzsche, *The Birth of Tragedy*, Douglas Smith, trans. (Oxford: Oxford University Press, 2000).

Chapter Nine

Utilitarianism and Liberalism: Jeremy Bentham and John Stuart Mill

ꙮ Chapter Objectives

After reading this chapter you should be able to:
- Explain and critique the two main forms of historical utilitarianism, the first associated with Bentham, the second with Mill.
- Analyze and critique the following concepts and theories: Godwin's Famous Fire Cause, impersonalism, consequentialism, act and rule utilitarianism, the great evil strategy, harm reduction, the no-harm principle, communitarianism, the life of rational freedom.
- Describe moral liberalism and major objections to this position.
- Describe Mill's account of genius, individuality, and virtue and explain how it relates to his view of the role of women in society.
- Compare and contrast utilitarianism, liberalism, and virtue ethics, and evaluate attempts at reconciliation.

Introduction

In this chapter, we will begin by investigating utilitarianism, an influential moral theory that came to the fore in eighteenth- and nineteenth-century Britain. Although utilitarianism is associated with many well-known authors, we shall focus on the two most famous and important utilitarians in the history of philosophy: Jeremy Bentham and John Stuart Mill. As we shall see, Bentham enthusiastically presents a seriously flawed theory that the later Mill tries to correct and bring into line with a more tradi-

tional understanding of ethics. We will finish the chapter with a careful look at Mill's views about liberalism, virtue ethics, and feminism.

We should make something clear from the beginning: seen from the perspective of the virtue ethics tradition, utilitarianism is, at least in its usual manifestations, a deeply problematic theory. Contemporary philosophers, such as G.E.M. Anscombe, Alasdair MacIntyre, Joseph Raz, Bernard Williams, Derek Parfit, and Charles Taylor, have effectively criticized

---

∽ Applied Philosophy Box 9.1 ∾

Political Animals Owe Each Other Political Altruism

The revival of the principle of a communal life got a big boost, when anti-government individualism turned out to be inadequate to the inequality and harrowing working conditions created by the Industrial Revolution. At that point thinkers like Jeremy Bentham and John Stuart Mill developed the western secular philosophy we call utilitarianism. In utilitarianism, people are understood not as all different and separate but as similar and equal, capable of feeling pleasure and pain. These understandings give rise to some moral obligation to reduce the pain and maximize the pleasure of other humans.

This is a journalist's account of utilitarianism.

Source: Linda Hirshman, 'Political Animals Owe Each Other Political Altruism.' *The Huffington Post*, www.huffingtonpost. com/linda_hirshman/ liberal_principles_ii_b_110160.html, 1 July 2008.

---

one or more aspects of the theory. It is important to review these acknowledged criticisms here. Still, utilitarianism focuses attention on larger aspects of moral practice that were sometimes overlooked in the past, and it can be seen as a common-sense response to legitimate concerns that have come to the fore in the modern age. It also provides a useful moral perspective in some situations. Although utilitarianism no longer holds the pride of place it once held among professional philosophers, it still plays a central role in public policy and deserves close scrutiny. In this chapter, we will try to reconcile utilitarianism and virtue ethics. Suitably modified, utilitarianism can be used to address important moral problems.

Jeremy Bentham: Original Utilitarianism

While there are a number of moral philosophers associated with utilitarianism—including William Paley, James Mill, William Godwin, and more recently, Henry Sidgwick, R.M. Hare, and Peter Singer—Jeremy Bentham (1748–1832), a legal commentator and a radical political reformer in Great Britain, is often pointed to as the founder of the system.

In his scattered and vast work, Bentham argued for such diverse causes as animal welfare, women's equality, the end of slavery, the separation of church and state, freedom of expression, the abolition of retributive punishment, the right to divorce, the right to sexual privacy, free trade, and usury (interest paid on a loan). He was influential in intellectual circles of the day and became something of an icon among progressive intellectuals. Although most of his work remained unpublished at his death, Bentham was a prolific, even compulsive, author and was reputed to spend eight to twelve hours a day writing.

Bentham is an odd character. He sincerely devoted himself to socially progressive causes but was, at the same time, an ideologue and a highly partisan voice in British politics. His most important book, *The Introduction to the Principles of Morals and Legislation* (1789), introduces, in grandiose, sweeping prose, the theory behind utilitarianism.[1] Still, Bentham is not a sophisticated philosophical theoretician. He clearly read Lucretius (the Roman Epicurean), but he does not display any breadth of scholarly understanding when it comes to other authors in the moral philosophy tradition. He has an unbounded but naive enthusiasm for science and arithmetic; he leaps to premature conclusions, and he is a very partial commentator on specific issues. On the whole, he is more comfortable with law than philosophy. Indeed, much of the book is taken up with a largely mechanical exercise in psychological, ethical, and legal taxonomy. Bentham, for example, wants to divide the different aspects of human behaviour into their basic kinds, an essential task for the legal arena. In a plodding way, he sets about constructing an enormous classification system that, he hopes, can be applied to every odd case imaginable.

Bentham's mindset must be placed against the backdrop of his age. Like Kant, he sees himself as a representative of rational, scientific, Enlightenment thinking. But he lacks the philosophical depth and the metaphysical acumen of the German master. A product of the new optimistic Industrial Age, Bentham has a practical cast of mind. He stands for common sense and solid observation; in fact, he reduces morality to counting, to mere arithmetic. In his mind, society is like one big machine, producing happiness or pleasure for all. Morality is mostly a matter of more efficient production.

In recent years, Bentham has gained some notoriety as the inventor of the infamous 'Panopticon', an 'all-seeing' circular prison that would allow prisoners to be observed at all times by hidden guards. Later authors (such as Michel Foucault) point to the Panopticon as the physical embodiment of the repressive principles that regulate the modern totalitarian state. Bentham did believe that one could control the behaviour of prisoners through the ever-present threat of pervasive surveillance by an invisible, centralized authority. At the same time, he had a generally enlightened view of criminal punishment, believing that its main purpose was rehabilitation rather than retribution. His project for a centralized prison was at least intended as a practical contribution to social progress in industrialized Britain.

At his death, Bentham's estate was used to finance University College London, a new educational venture supported by Bentham that made a point of admitting students regardless of religion, political persuasion, ethnic background, or social class. (This meant accepting 'nonconformist' Protestants, Catholics, and Jews.) In his will, he made the strange request that his preserved corpse be mounted, dressed, and seated—like a stuffed animal—on a chair in a wooden closet (dubbed his 'Auto-icon'). This artifact, complete with lifeless body, is now kept on public display in University College London. (The body has a wax head; the real head, kept in a glass jar, was damaged in the embalming process.) An odd man, indeed.

On the Pleasure Calculus

Although Bentham's *Introduction* is, truly, more a book about the nature of legislation than morality, he begins by laying out a moral theory on which to base good government. We shall mostly concern ourselves with the first chapters.

The first thing to notice is that Bentham is an out-and-out **hedonist**. In a throwback to earlier philosophers, like Democritus and the Epicureans, Bentham (who only seems vaguely familiar with the moral philosophy tradition) adopts a rather crude hedonism. What is valuable is pleasure and what matters is producing as much pleasure as possible. This includes, of course, as a necessary condition, producing as little pain as possible. Bentham begins his book with a famous assertion:

> Nature has placed mankind under the governance of two sovereign masters, *pain* and *pleasure*. It is for them alone to point out what we ought to do, as well as to determine what we shall do. . . . They govern us in all we do, in all we say, in all we think: every effort we can make to throw off our subjection, will serve but to demonstrate and confirm it. In words a man may pretend to abjure their empire: but in reality he will remain subject to it all the while.[2]

Grand-sounding phrases indeed, but the astute philosophical reader should immediately see that Bentham is making two incompatible claims: (1) that we *ought* to act so as to produce pleasure, and (2) that this is already the case, regardless. Hedonists argue that we *ought* to strive for pleasure. This logically implies that there is at least a possibility that this is something we will not do. Bentham wants to say that we always act for pleasure and that we ought to act for pleasure but, at the very least, the second part of the claim is redundant. And the first part is highly suspect. In fact, we often act (stupidly perhaps) in ways that produce more pain than pleasure. If our acts were predetermined—if we were slaves to pain and pleasure—this would leave no room for praiseworthy or blameworthy choice; i.e., no room for morality or immorality. If one wants to opt for hedonism, it would be better to argue that we will be happier and better people if we single-mindedly pursue pleasure, something we often fail to do, either because we are ignorant or because we are (in some manner that needs to be explained) weak-willed.

If we are to defend a consistent hedonism, we first need to know what pleasure is. Bentham explains, 'Pains and pleasures may be called by one general word, interesting perceptions'.[3] Unfortunately, this is not the most helpful way of putting it. We do not perceive pleasures and pains with the five senses: 'sight, sound, touch, taste, feel'. What Bentham presumably means is that we become aware of pleasures and pains; this is the sense in which we 'perceive' them. Pleasures and pains are 'interesting'—worthy of attention—either because we want to hold onto them or because we want to be rid of them. As Hobbes might have said, we call feelings we want to possess pleasures; and feelings we want not to possess, pains.

Bentham does not elaborate any rigorous account of the precise nature of pleasure and pain. He does, however, supply a list of the most basic pleasures:

> The several simple pleasures of which human nature is susceptible, seem to be as follows: 1. The pleasures of sense. 2. The pleasures of wealth. 3. The pleasures of skill. 4. The pleasures of amity. 5. The pleasures of a good name. 6. The pleasures of power. 7. The pleasures of piety. 8. The pleasures of benevolence. 9. The pleasures of malevolence. 10. The pleasures of memory. 11. The pleasures of imagination. 12. The pleasures of expectation. 13. The pleasures dependent on association. 14. The pleasures of relief.[4]

His list, however, seems (to put it bluntly) muddled and superficial. For one thing, he seems to confuse the opportunity for pleasure with the nature of pleasure itself. Those who possess more wealth, power, skill (etc.) may have more opportunities for pleasure, but it does not follow that their experience of pleasure is any different from the rest of humanity. Again, it does not seem that the pleasures associated with wealth and the pleasures associated with power are of different kinds. We can avail ourselves of the very same pleasures, either because we possess political power or because we possess wealth. Indeed, one could even argue that wealth is power. These are, at the very least, overlapping conditions. Again, to define pleasures and pains, not by reference to some internal psychological or physiological state but by reference to external circumstances seems to miss the point. Construed charitably, Bentham's position reduces to the idea that we all know what pleasures and pains are. What matters is not coming up with a precise metaphysical or biological definition of pleasure and pain, but the practical business of increasing pleasure and reducing pain for all of us.

If Bentham does not provide much of a definition for pleasure and pain, he also fails to distinguish between pleasure and happiness. Indeed, he uses the terms interchangeably. As we have seen, earlier philosophers strenuously argue that pleasure—the tickling of nerves, agreeable feelings, the experience of sensual gratification, etc.—is not enough for happiness. Happiness is more complex concept: it includes an idea of self-esteem, of self-fulfillment, of good reputation, and of worthwhile moral achievement. In Bentham's account, to aim at pleasure is to aim at happiness; to aim at happiness is to aim at pleasure. But this is oversimplification.

Bentham's moral philosophy is called utilitarianism because it measures the goodness of individual actions in terms of their **utility** or usefulness when it comes to producing pleasure. As Bentham, who can be rather wordy, explains: 'By utility is meant that property in any object, whereby it tends to produce benefit, advantage, pleasure, good, or happiness, (all this in the present case comes to the same

thing) or (what comes again to the same thing) to prevent the happening of mischief, pain, evil, or unhappiness.'[5] In short, the utility of an action is its propensity to increase pleasure (and reduce pain). A moral action must have some utility; it must be a useful way of increasing pleasure and decreasing pain. Immoral actions are either useless ways of increasing the amount of pleasure in the world or, in more serious cases, actually *decrease* pleasure and *increase* pain.

As the leading light of utilitarianism, Bentham introduces the **utility principle** as the ultimate foundation of morality: 'By the principle of utility is meant that principle which approves or disapproves of every action whatsoever according to the tendency it appears to have to augment or diminish the happiness of the party whose interest is in question.'[6] He reformulates the utility principle, in more exact terms, in his preface to *A Fragment on Government* (1776), proposing 'the greatest happiness of the greatest number' as 'the [ultimate] measure of right and wrong'.[7] This particular wording of the utility principle, which came to be known as the Greatest Happiness Principle, was the motto and the rallying cry of the radical, 'progressive', Benthamite side in British politics.

Utilitarianism is then a universalistic hedonism. Bentham believes that we should strive to promote the happiness (or pleasure) of everyone, not only ourselves. In his words, 'A man may be said to be a partizan of the principle of utility, when the approbation or disapprobation he annexes to any action, or to any measure, is determined by and proportioned to the tendency which he conceives it to have to augment or to diminish the happiness of the community'.[8] This is the ultimate goal of utilitarian morality: the promotion of happiness for the community as a whole or, at least, for as many people in the community as is humanly possible.

Bentham claims that the principle of utility does not stand in need of proof. He writes, 'Is [the principle of utility] susceptible of any direct proof? It should seem not: for that which is used to prove every thing else, cannot itself be proved: a chain of proofs must have their commencement somewhere. To give such proof is as impossible as it is needless'.[9] He further claims that we rely on the principle of utility without thinking about it and that philosophical attacks on its soundness are self-defeating: 'When a man attempts to combat the principle of utility, it is with reasons drawn, without his being aware of it, from that very principle itself. His arguments, if they prove any thing, prove not that the principle is *wrong*, but that, according to the applications he supposes to be made of it, it is *misapplied*. . . . To disprove the propriety of it by arguments is impossible.'[10]

This, then, is the basic message of utilitarianism: increase pleasure, decrease pain *as much as possible*. More formally, always act so as to increase the total amount of happiness in the world. This seems, charitably construed, a laudable (if obvious) project. It is hard to imagine that anyone would disagree. But Bentham is highly partisan. He identifies and loudly denounces an opposing principle to the utility principle, the **principle of asceticism**, which he associates with 'moralist and religious types'.[11] Bentham explains:

> By the principle of asceticism I mean that principle, which, like the principle of utility, approves or disapproves of any action, according to the tendency which it appears to have to augment or diminish the happiness of the party whose

interest is in question; but in an inverse manner: approving of actions in as far as they tend to diminish his happiness; disapproving of them in as far as they tend to augment it.[12]

According to Bentham, traditional 'moralist and religious types' want people to be *as unhappy as possible*! As fervent adherents of the ascetic principle, they want to create *more suffering and pain* in the community. This, they perversely believe, is the goal of morality.

But, whatever one thinks of utilitarianism, this is blatant, vehement caricature. Bentham does not strive toward the neutrality displayed by the best members of the tradition. He sees himself as arguing against a pernicious social conservativism for a progressive morality. But Bentham's allegations are little more than a wild misrepresentation. As discussed in Chapter 3, asceticism had its roots in ancient philosophy in the ethical practices of philosophers like the Stoics and the Cynics. These earlier authors proposed asceticism as *a means to happiness*. They believed that human life is inevitably difficult and filled with suffering; one needs to harden oneself, to develop willpower and emotional self-mastery. But this takes training—hence the need for asceticism. Ancient authors believed that asceticism builds character so that we can achieve happiness, understood as peace of mind.

Like other **Enlightenment** authors (David Hume comes to mind), Bentham provides a **straw man**, a caricature of what traditional asceticism is about. But it is not simply that Bentham misinterprets the ancients. There is a deeper problem here. Bentham makes happiness sound easy. If we procure as many pleasurable sensations as possible, we will be happy. But life is not so simple. Even a hedonist like Democritus argues that it is better not to have too much pleasure. Why?

৹ Applied Philosophy Box 9.2 ৹

Childhood Obesity Threatens the Nation's Health

Lafayette: About 12 million kids are overweight, and 12 million more are at risk of becoming overweight. The obesity epidemic has serious effects, including asthma, diabetes, and heart trouble. Rising levels of overweight and obese children are at risk for serious health problems.

'Childhood obesity I hate to say is a growing problem. When I was growing up, type 2 diabetes occurred in middle age adults now it's occurring in adolescents. These adolescents all have at least one more risk factor for cardiovascular disease,' said Dr. Debbie Wright, a Sigma cardiologist.

Wright said children are eating too much junk food and not enough fruits and vegetables. She said parents can help change those habits.

'We can involve our kids in better diets. We can make it more fun to have good food and make that food available. We can go into the pantry and throw away the junk foods, so that some of us who have very little self control, are not tempted,' she said.

Wright said kids spend most of their time sitting, so parents should find ways to get the family more active.

'They can involve their children in activities, find things to do, go for walks, go to the park. Our communities have beautiful parks. . . .' she said.

Wright said early intervention is important, because obese children are likely to become obese adults.

There are, no doubt, many factors at play here. In a society that focuses on the maximization of pleasure, it is easy to overindulge. But the pleasures or comforts of overeating come with a 'heavy' price. The good doctor proposes different strategies for dealing with this problem: have more fun eating good food and walking in the park; make bad food less accessible. She does not suggest a moral solution: working on increasing our self-control. Does asceticism understood in the original sense as training in self-discipline have a role to play here? Discuss from an ancient hedonist and a modern utilitarian perspective.

Source: 'Childhood Obesity Threatens the Nation's Health.' WLFI-TV, www.wlfi.com/Global/story.asp?S=843 6206&nav=menu591_3, 5 June 2008.

Because people who are accustomed to too much pleasure are unable to cope with inevitable pain and disappointment. The ancients understood something a 'progressive' thinker like Bentham overlooks. It may very well be that aiming at more and more pleasure fosters impatience, a sense of entitlement, softness, self-indulgence, a lack of appreciation for the little things in life, and an inability to cope with sorrow and despair when faced with life's inevitable hardships. It is a simplistic and self-indulgent moral psychology that assumes that we can produce happiness without cultivating self-restraint. If we want to be happy, we also need strength of character. And asceticism is all about developing strength of character.

Bentham simply assumes that there is little to be learned from this earlier moral tradition. He is convinced that modern thinkers have science on their side. Indeed, he seemed obsessed with the idea that we can and should measure accumulated happiness in a scientific way. He writes as if morality was a simple exercise in bookkeeping, devising his own **felicific**

calculus to precisely measure the total amount of pleasure or pain produced by a particular act:

> To take an exact account then of the general tendency of any act [to produce pleasure or pain] . . . proceed as follows. Begin with any one person of those whose interests seem most immediately to be affected by it: and take an account[:] 1. Of the value of each distinguishable *pleasure* which appears to be produced by it in the *first* instance. 2. Of the value of each *pain* which appears to be produced by it in the *first* instance. 3. Of the value of each pleasure which appears to be produced by it *after* the first [pleasure]. . . . 4. Of the value of each *pain* which appears to be produced by it after the first [pain] . . . 5. Sum up all the values of all the *pleasures* on the one side, and those of all the pains on the other. The balance, if it be on the side of pleasure, will give the *good* tendency of the act upon the whole, with respect to the interests of that *individual* person; if on the side of pain, the *bad* tendency of it upon the whole. 6. [Then] take an account of the *number* of persons whose interests appear to be concerned; and repeat the above process with respect to each. *Sum up* the [pleasures] . . . with respect to each individual. . . . Do this again with respect to [the pains experienced by] each individual. . . . Take the *balance* which if on the side of *pleasure*, will give the general *good tendency* of the act, with respect to the total number or community of individuals concerned; if on the side of pain, the general *evil tendency*, with respect to the same community.[13]

Bentham based his moral calculations on a unit measure of pleasure and pain he called the 'utile': hence the term 'Utilitarianism'. He evidently believed that utiles would eventually be subject to physical measurement. One of his later followers, economist Francis Edgeworth (1845–1926), went so far as to propose the construction of a 'hedonimeter', a psycho-physical apparatus that would precisely measure pleasure and pain the way a thermometer measures hot and cold. But such suggestions seem plainly preposterous. Ask yourself, how much pleasure are you experiencing now? Can you come up with a precise number? Are you feeling 11.65 utiles of pleasure? Or only 9 utiles? Or perhaps 200.6 utiles? Although we do distinguish between more and less pleasure (or pain) as a matter of practical judgment, there is no precise, black-and-white way of measuring such things.

Bentham simply *assumes* that we can measure pain down to the last degree. But there are too many obstacles to assert this with confidence. To begin with, our experience of pleasure or pain is an intensely private affair— it is not publicly accessible. As well, different individuals experience significantly different degrees of pleasure or pain and may react to the very same circumstances in unique ways. And pleasure itself is a multi-faceted phenomenon. Bentham himself identifies seven separate characteristics of pleasure:

1. the intensity,
2. the duration,
3. the number of people affected (the 'extent'),
4. the likelihood of its occurrence,
5. the time the pleasure takes to come into effect (its 'propinquity'),
6. its tendency to produce associated pleasures (its 'fecundity'), and
7. the likelihood of it *not* being followed by pain (its 'purity').[14]

Similar issues of ambiguity and imprecision attend the measurement of each one of these different facets of the pleasure phenomenon.

Like a number of other modern philosophers, Bentham tends to assume that happiness means 'getting what you want'. Following faithfully in his footsteps, some leading contemporary utilitarians define happiness in terms of **preference-satisfaction** understood as the satisfaction of as many preferences as possible. (Neo-classical economists notably make calculations on the basis of preference-satisfaction. What people do with their money is taken as a final measure of what their preferences are.) But this preference-hedonism is as problematic as simple pleasure-hedonism. Let us leave aside the fact that we can seriously question whether people's preferences are so straightforward. (You bought the new TV—perhaps you would have *preferred* to spend your money on something else but your wife insisted; perhaps a smooth salesperson got you to make a thoughtless purchase you will later regret; perhaps you have been socially conditioned to think that life is impossible without television, and so on.) Even if we *could* accurately and precisely evaluate our individual preferences, this would not solve a deeper problem.

So-called preference-utilitarians reinterpret the utility principle, substituting preference-satisfaction for the experience of pleasure. In their account, the most general moral directive is something along the lines of this: 'make sure that you act in such a way that people get as much of what they want as possible.' But this particular directive is not, on closer inspection, a moral principle. Giving people what they want may or may not be moral; *it depends on what they want*. If we are talking about good people, then perhaps we should give them what they want. If, however, we are talking about bad people, it may be that we should do everything we can to make sure we don't give them what they want!

The basic utilitarian directive: 'give people what they want, what gives them pleasure— *as much as possible*', is not a moral principle.

We cannot determine whether this would be a good thing without appealing to an external criterion of right and wrong to determine whether the desires or preferences in question are morally acceptable. As Aristotle argues, the difference between the immoral and the moral person is *not* that one experiences more or less pleasure than the other. The difference is that the moral person feels pleasure at the right things; the immoral person feels pleasure at the wrong things. Historical authors in the moral philosophy tradition formulate objective criteria for determining whether particular desires or preferences are moral. They variously appeal to a theory of human nature, to a more penetrating description of happiness, to a critical account of rationality, to notions of fairness or justice, to practical human experience, to the idea of God, and so on. Utilitarians, in turn, need to produce, at the very least, some theory of human nature and moral epistemology if they hope to establish a deeper criterion of morality. (A contemporary utilitarian such as David Braybrooke does address such issues. Braybrooke argues, surprisingly, for a natural-law utilitarianism.)

Utilitarianism may be, in its rough outlines, correct. We have a duty to improve the world we live in, to reduce overall suffering and increase happiness for everyone. Most importantly, we have larger moral responsibilities that go beyond the realm of our personal interests and preoccupations. In some real sense, Bentham's infatuation with the pleasure calculus is beside the point. We do not need a finely tuned pleasure calculus to understand that morality requires serious attempts to ameliorate the condition of disadvantaged people. The idea that public social problems are an important moral concern that should be rigorously approached in a constructive way is a fundamental moral insight. Although Bentham does not provide anything close to an adequate theoretical account of morality, he is, in all fairness, more interested in issues of public policy than moral theory. In the case of industrialized England, his reforming theory may have played an enlightened role politically and legally.

John Stuart Mill: Moral *and* Political Philosophy

John Stuart Mill (1806–73) was one of the most prominent public intellectuals in England during the nineteenth century. In fact, his influence is still felt today. As a proponent of empiricism, radicalism, liberalism, utilitarianism, and romantic individualism, there is no easy way to reconcile the various tensions between his different theoretical positions. His published works include *A System of Logic* (1843), *The Principles of Political Economy* (1848), *On Liberty* (1859), *Utilitarianism* (1861), *The Subjection of Women* (1869), *Autobiography* (1873), and *Three Essays on Religion* (1874).[15] We shall chiefly consider *Utilitarianism* here and will comment briefly on *On Liberty* at the end of the chapter.

Mill was not a university professor but a civil servant. He held a well-paid position as a chief examiner at the famous East India Company (1826–57), contributing to the company's policies in India. On his retirement, he served one term as a Member of Parliament. Toward the end of his life, he spent considerable time in France, where he is buried.

Touted as a child prodigy, Mill was homeschooled by his father, James Mill, a colleague and a collaborator of Bentham. Under his father's strict tutelage, he studied Greek at age three, Latin at eight, and moved in his child-

hood to a comprehensive curriculum, including world history, classics, logic, math, science, politics, economics, legal philosophy, and eventually metaphysics and epistemology. He was required to teach his younger siblings and was tested daily by his father. He also spent a year in France, where he learned to speak French fluently. As Mill grew older, his father employed him as an editor and gradually initiated him into the intellectual life and politics of the time.

But the strenuous course of early studies was too much. In 1826, Mill suffered a fit of depression or perhaps a nervous breakdown. He later commented that his one-sided academic education had fostered his logical and analytical skills while ignoring the proper development of sentiment and feeling. In his *Autobiography*, he writes,

> For I now saw . . . that the habit of [logical] analysis has a tendency to wear away the feelings . . . Analytic habits . . . are therefore . . . favourable to prudence and clearsightedness, but a perpetual worm at the root both of the passions and of the virtues; above all, [they] fearfully undermine all desires, and all pleasures. . . . My education, I thought, had failed to create these feelings in sufficient strength to resist the dissolving influence of analysis.[16]

Mill complains that under the microscope of objective philosophical scrutiny, feelings, affections, and commitments may evaporate. Much like the novelist Charles Dickens, he criticizes the one-sided emphasis on science, facts, and practicality in Victorian education, recommending a steady diet of music, poetry, and art as a way of reviving and sustaining wholesome feeling. As we shall see, Mill's bout with depression had an influence on his ideas, leading him to reconsider certain aspects of the original utilitarian doctrine.

Mill's relationship with his eventual wife, Harriet Taylor, needs to be mentioned. Mill fell in love with Taylor in 1830 while she was married to another man. With the consent of her husband, the two engaged in an intimate but platonic relationship that scandalized polite London society. They were eventually married in 1851 after Harriet's husband's death. She herself died seven years later, to Mill's great sorrow. Although the precise extent of Harriet's influence on Mill's writing is vigorously debated, it seems clear that she was an intellectual partner and critic and that she had some influence on his thought, particularly in the realms of political, moral, and social philosophy. Mill heaps extravagant praise on her, identifying her as his helper and a major influence on his thought.

On Utilitarianism

As we shall see, Mill is a moderate voice, a sophisticated and urbane commentator who tends to seek out the middle road of common sense and consensus. He is a more polished and erudite writer than Bentham. Embarrassed by the rhetorical excesses of early utilitarianism, he sets out to rehabilitate Bentham's theory in the eyes of the general thinking public. But there is a catch. Although Mill insists on his loyalty to reform-minded utilitarianism, he changes the theory so much that his new, improved 'utilitarianism' is arguably no longer utilitarianism, at least not in the original, Benthamite sense. With Mill we get a more plausible theory but a theory that is less than true to its original roots.

In 1861, Mill published an extended essay entitled 'Utilitarianism' in *Fraser's Magazine*, a nontechnical trade publication for a wide readership.[17] This famous essay has come to be recognized as the canonical expression of the school. An eloquent prose stylist, Mill spends much time toning down Bentham's rhetoric and reconciling the original utilitarian doctrines to common-sense moral intuitions. Mill's analysis is intended, however, as a partisan political defense of utilitarianism rather than as an objective exploration of the theory's strengths and weaknesses. While Mill has interesting ideas, he is less than rigorous. Throughout his essay, he modifies his stance depending on the criticisms of utilitarianism he is currently addressing. A careful reading does not reveal a consistent line of doctrine but, rather, an attempt to defend a cherished theory through a series of responses to objection after objection. Mill continually shifts his position, changing his terms, his emphasis, and his arguments as he moves along. We are left, not with a rigorously consistent moral theory, but with the edifying reflections of an ethical and eminently reasonable man. Mill is able to salvage utilitarianism but only insomuch as he appeals to a surreptitious kind of virtue ethics.

Quantities and Qualities of Pleasure

Mill defines *utilitarianism* as 'the creed which accepts as the foundation of morals, Utility, or the Greatest Happiness Principle, [and] holds that actions are right in proportion as they tend to promote happiness, wrong as they tend to produce the reverse of happiness'.[18] Initially, he seems to reassert the universalistic hedonism espoused by Bentham, defining *happiness* as 'pleasure, and the absence of pain'; and *unhappiness*, as 'pain, and the privation of pleasure'.[19] But Mill immediately distances himself from Bentham, insisting that what matters is not just the *quantity* but also the *quality* of pleasure. We need then to incorporate qualitative— i.e., nonmathematical—distinctions into our moral thinking. We need to promote the qualitatively higher pleasures at the expense of the qualitatively lower pleasures. Mill concludes, 'it would be absurd that while, in estimating all other things, quality is considered as well as quantity, the estimation of pleasures should be supposed to depend on quantity alone'.[20]

Mill, in contrast to Bentham, claims that 'some kinds of pleasure are more desirable and more valuable than others'.[21] For Mill, it is not enough to increase the amount of pleasure in the world; we need to promote intellectual pleasures and even, perhaps, suppress the lower, physical pleasures. Mill envisages a progressive society that values the enjoyment of educated pleasures over the animal pleasures associated with the lower appetites. Like Bentham, he believes in political reform, but it is reform through general education so that ordinary people can derive pleasure from nobler human pursuits: poetry, art, philosophy, classical music, etc.

As we have seen, Bentham based morality solely on quantitative considerations. Mill, in highlighting qualitative concerns, is responding to period critics who claimed that utilitarians, like Bentham, in proposing the 'quantity of pleasure' as the sole criterion of a successful life, were slipping back into the 'pig philosophy' the ancients associated with Epicureanism. If, as Bentham insists, the quantity of pleasure is the only thing that matters, if we are to aim at as much pleasure as possible, why not settle for a life of libertine dissipation and sensual enjoyment? Why not gorge ourselves with physical pleasure while ignoring intellectual and artistic achievement? Mill thinks he has an answer: 'Pleasures of the intellect, of the feelings and imagination, and of the moral sentiments, [have] a much higher value as pleasures than [do] those of mere sensation.'[22] In other words, these intellectual, imaginative, moral pleasures are qualitatively better and therefore more important than physical pleasures, so they deserve more intense cultivation.

If, however, we are going to incorporate some measure of the quality of a pleasure into our utilitarian calculus, how are we to determine which pleasures are better or worse, of higher or lower quality? Mill offers what may seem, at first glance, to be a sensible answer:

> If I am asked, what I mean by difference of quality in pleasures, or what makes one pleasure more valuable than another, merely as a pleasure, except its being greater in amount, there is but one possible answer. Of two pleasures, if there be one to which all or almost all who have experience of both give a decided preference, irrespective of any feeling of moral obligation to prefer it, that is the more desirable pleasure. If one of the two is, by those who are competently acquainted with both, placed so far above the other that they prefer it, even though knowing it to be attended with a greater amount of discontent, and would not resign it for any quantity of the other pleasure which their nature is capable of, we are justified in ascribing to the preferred enjoyment a superiority in quality, so far outweighing quantity as to render [quantitative considerations], in comparison, of small account.[23]

In short, Mill claims that we can determine which of two pleasures is of superior quality by asking those who are well-acquainted with both. A consensus of those in the know strongly in favour of one or the other settles the question. Mill goes on to argue (quite unconvincingly) that those who are well-acquainted with intellectual pleasures and the pleasures of higher moral feeling inevitably prefer them over lower animal pleasures associated with sensual activities, such as eating, drinking, and sexuality. 'It is an unquestionable fact,' Mill writes

> that those who are equally acquainted with, and equally capable of appreciating and enjoying, both, do give a most marked preference to the manner of existence which employs their higher faculties. Few human creatures would consent to be changed into any of the lower animals, for a promise of the fullest allowance of a beast's pleasures. . . . A being of higher faculties . . . can never really wish to sink into what he feels to be a lower grade of existence. . . . It is better to be a human being dissatisfied than a pig satisfied; better to be Socrates dissatisfied than a fool satisfied. And if the fool, or the pig, are of a different opinion, it is because they only know their own side of the question. The other party to the comparison knows both sides.[24]

Mill's approach begs the question. To argue that everyone who has adequate knowledge of two pleasures always chooses the higher pleasure is, charitably construed, a stretch. Is it never the case that someone chooses the pleasures of drink, or drugs, or promiscuity over intellectual and moral pleasures? Mill himself admits as much, offering an explanation as to why some people seem to choose lower pleasures over higher pleasures: 'Men lose . . . their intellectual tastes, because they have not time or opportunity for indulging them; and they addict themselves to inferior pleasures, not because they deliberately prefer them, but because they are either the only ones to which they have access, or the only ones which they are any longer capable of enjoying.'[25] This is to acknowledge that knowledgeable people sometimes do choose lower over higher pleasures, but to explain away the phenomenon by simply assuming that such individuals have been forced into this alternative. Mill does not come close to proving what is largely a contentious assumption.

Mill wants a more refined utilitarianism in line with common moral intuitions. His revised utilitarianism has its attractions. But is it really utilitarianism? Mill seems to substitute a new *virtue ethics* for Bentham's original utilitarianism. What Mill (correctly) values is not happiness understood in terms of number or intensity of pleasant sensations, but happiness understood as a generalized sense of well-being and self-esteem that accompanies healthy human achievement. This is more like Aristotle than Bentham. In this virtue account, intellectual, imaginative, and moral pleasures are more valuable—not because they feel good, but because perfecting our higher capacities is intrinsically valuable. The life of a 'discontented Socrates' is a more desirable fate—even if it involves serious unpleasantness—because Socrates is realizing his intellectual nature and achieving something noble.

And Mill and Bentham differ in another way. Remember: Bentham's goal was the precise measurement of pleasure. Mill seems, inconsistently, to claim that we can and cannot measure the moral worth of pleasure. On the one hand, he takes almost for granted the Benthamite doctrine that we can have an arithmetic of pleasure and so figure out the total amount of pleasure produced; on the other hand, he claims the moral worth of pleasure depends on quality, not just quantity. If, however, this latter claim is to have any weight, qualities of pleasure cannot be reduced to mere differences in quantity; they must be numerically incommensurable. This seems to deal a definitive blow to any but the most approximate attempts to measure pleasure. Indeed, it suggests that utilitarianism—as understood in the original Benthamite sense as an attempt to increase the total *quantity* of pleasure in the world—is fundamentally misguided. Mill claims to be a faithful utilitarian, but his theory is more than a minor revision of the earlier one Bentham and his colleagues elaborated.

Suppose Mill is right. Suppose there are different qualities of pleasures. Quality is not quantity. To use an analogy: the sensation 'red' is not quantitatively but qualitatively different than the sound of a clarinet playing B-flat. In other words, redness is not more or less than B-flat; it is a completely different thing. To claim likewise that there are different kinds of pleasure is to accept that pleasures are incommensurable (something contemporary philosopher Joseph Raz contends). If we take qualitative distinctions seriously, it will follow that desirable human experiences cannot be measured in terms of one another. Bentham wants to reduce all human experience to a common mathematical standard so that we can devise a quantitative basis for preferring some behaviours over others. Mill eschews Bentham's reductionism and proposes an entirely new basis for the evaluation of human experience.

It is not clear that hedonism can survive Mill's concession that there are qualitative differences between pleasures. Suppose it really is the case that ignorance is bliss. Mill argues that it does not matter how much pleasure one derives from ignorance; a cultivated person will never prefer ignorance to knowledge. Better to be a dissatisfied human being than an ignorant pig. In other words, it is better to experience much *less* pleasure when acting like a human being than to experience much *more* pleasure when acting like an animal. But this seems to be just the reverse of hedonism! Hedonism is just this: the moral doctrine that more pleasure is better and less pleasure is worse. Mill proposes, at the very least, a strange hedonism!

Mill is a fierce champion of intellectual, 'highbrow' pleasure. He attributes the justifiable human preference for higher pleasure 'to a sense of dignity'.[26] Losing oneself in stupefying pleasure—drunkenness, drugs, gross sexuality—is undignified and therefore unacceptable to any self-respecting human being. It is better to experience less pleasure and preserve our dignity. But this means that pleasure is not the highest value. If we should accept less pleasure for the sake of dignity, it must be the case that dignity is more valuable than pleasure. So pleasure is not the supreme value, and hedonism must be wrong. (If pleasure were the supreme value, we would have to give up our dignity for the sake of pleasure, not the other way around.)

Mill is caught on the **horns of a dilemma**. He thinks we should prefer small amounts of high-quality pleasure over large amounts of low-quality pleasure. There are only two possibilities, and both are fatal to his own theory. Either (1) we should prefer high-quality pleasure because it is more enjoyable; or (2) we should prefer it even though it is not more enjoyable. If alternative (1) is correct, Mill's account is no different than Bentham's. All his talk of higher qualities of pleasure is mere camouflage, a disguised way of talking about larger quantities of pleasure. If, on the other hand, alternative (2) is correct, hedonism is wrong; pleasure is not the supreme value.

To be fair, Mill's qualitative account of pleasure rings true. People do tend to admire or respect higher forms of pleasure. And they feel ashamed about very base pleasures. Why, for example, is the intellectual pleasure of reading a good book of poetry better than, say, the pleasure of getting 'stinking drunk'? One important difference is that reading a good book of poetry requires thought and imagination. It exercises our mental capacities and develops emotional intelligence. Losing yourself in drink means forfeiting your rationality and any capacity for high-minded thought. It is not that Mill's account is wrong; it is that his view is at odds with straightforward hedonism. We value the so-called higher pleasures because we admire the associated character traits, not simply because they produce more pleasure.

Is Mill a Hedonist?

Given his loyalty to the utilitarian cause, Mill is forced to argue for hedonism. But it does not seem philosophically precise to call him a hedonist. Mill argues that we should pursue pleasure, but he uses the term *pleasure* as a vague, catch-all word for almost any kind of positive human experience. Indeed, he widens the definition of *pleasure* so as to include any morally positive experience—*even those entailing a great deal of pain*. This is not so much to provide an argument for hedonism as to define rival theories out of existence. The fact that moral agents pursue positive human experience does not, in and of itself, provide any strong support for hedonism, rigorously construed.

Mill, like Bentham, uses the words *pleasure* and *happiness* interchangeably. To cite only one example from his essay, *Utilitarianism*, he moves from the claim that we 'desire nothing which is not either a part of *happiness* or a means of *happiness*' to the claim (two sentences later) that we 'do desire nothing for [ourselves] but that which is a *pleasure* [etc.]'.[27] It is absolutely clear from the context that Mill considers the pursuit of happiness and the pursuit of pleasure as identical pursuits. As we have seen, 'happiness' is not, however, mere 'pleasure'. Pleasure is 'enjoyable sensation'. Happiness is a condition of moral and intellectual well-being

and self-esteem associated with virtue. Self-esteem and enjoyable sensation may overlap, but they are not the same thing.

Mill argues, like Bentham, for hedonism because he believes that desiring anything other than pleasure is logically impossible. In his words, '[all] sources of evidence impartially consulted, will declare that desiring a thing and finding it pleasant . . . are phenomena entirely inseparable, [that is, these are] two different modes of naming the same psychological fact: *that to think of an object as desirable . . . and to think of it as pleasant, are one and the same thing*'.[28] Mill's argument leads to psychological egoism (which we have already criticized in Chapter 2). In any case, the statement seems empirically inaccurate. As Aristotle points out, courage is by nature unpleasant. It means facing up to unpleasant situations. Nonetheless, the noble person 'desires' courage. Suppose I am a member of the French Resistence caught by Nazi forces. If I tell them what they want to know, they will stop torturing me. But I *pleasure* not to talk. I want to remain true to the cause. This is what I *desire*. Human history is marked by heroes who desire moral accomplishment that leads to martyrdom. It does not always follow that we desire things because they are pleasant.

Contemporary American philosopher Robert Nozick devises an apposite thought-experiment we can use to test Mill's claim that people want enjoyable sensations most of all.[29] Imagine that 'super-duper neuro-psychologists' have invented a pleasure-machine to hook up to your brain. All you have to do is lie on a bed and expert doctors will turn a knob so that you feel as much pleasure as possible. Nozick points out that if we were all hedonists, we would want to live a life hooked up to the machine, for this alternative is guaranteed to produce the most pleasure. But this is not, in fact, what people would choose. People do not want give up their present life (with all its inevitable ups and downs) in order to be hooked up to a pleasure machine. Why? Because they don't just want to be passive receptacles for enjoyable sensations; they want to live a life filled with real accomplishments. It is not just disembodied pleasure but human achievement, what Aristotle would have called a life of virtue, that most people are after. We discuss Mill's account of virtue ethics below.

Godwin's Mother

Mill, like Bentham, believes that a moral agent must care about the welfare of the entire community. These are noble sentiments, in line with the moral tradition. Indeed, Mill himself goes so far as to compare utilitarianism to Christianity. He observes, 'In the golden rule of Jesus of Nazareth, we read the complete spirit of the ethics of utility. To do as you would be done by, and to love your neighbour as yourself, constitute the ideal perfection of utilitarian morality'.[30]

But there are important differences between Christianity and utilitarianism. Jesus's command is people-oriented: love *other people*! The original utilitarians were concerned with increasing the total amount of pleasurable feeling in the world. The motivating ideal is to 'multiply pleasures', as if we are to be loyal, not to individual people, but to an emotional property of people. This is not the same thing. People naturally care about other people, not about pleasure in the abstract. Motivating individuals to love their spouse, their grandchildren, their next-door neighbours, children, even strangers, is in line with human nature. Commanding people to devote themselves to an ideological ideal of more enjoyable sensa-

tion seems unnatural and unconvincing. It is also dangerous.

Utilitarianism reduces a rich account of interpersonal concern to a preoccupation with an abstract goal: the greatest pleasure for the greatest number. In the Christian (and Kantian) account, we love people for their own sake. In the utilitarian account, we love them as a *means* to the realization of this abstract ideal. This is different. In the first case, we are caring about persons because of who they are; in the second case, we are caring about them in so much as they contribute to an ideological cause: the successful production of pleasure. In the first case, we are loving people as people; in the second, we are using them as a means to greater quantities and/or qualities of pleasure.

Utilitarianism takes such an anonymous, 'scientific' view of moral duty that it leaves no or little room for the personal attachments and special obligations that characterize any normal human life. Mill writes: 'As between his own happiness and that of others, utilitarianism requires [that the moral agent] be as strictly impartial as a disinterested and benevolent spectator.'[31] But this utilitarian notion of impartiality also demands that we give no special consideration to the happiness of family members or close friends or loyal colleagues. William Godwin, another champion of utilitarian impartiality (1756–1836), brings home the point in an example that came to be known as the 'Famous Fire Cause', which caused a great outcry in social and intellectual circles at the time.

In his book *Enquiry Concerning Political Justice* (1793), Godwin asks us to imagine that a palace is on fire and that two people are trapped inside: Archbishop Fénelon, who, as a writer of important moral treatises, is a benefactor to the entire human race and a lowly chambermaid. You are able to save only one person. Who should you save? Godwin thinks that the answer is straightforward. Utilitarianism tells you, in no uncertain terms, that you should save the archbishop because his future works of moral prose will do more to promote the overall good than anything that can be accomplished by a humble chambermaid. Suppose, however, that the humble chambermaid turns out to be your very own mother? What then? Godwin reasoned, to great scandal, that one should still save the archbishop. If the educated, powerful, intelligent archbishop can do more good for society, he is the one whom morality obliges you to save. We must act *impartially* for the greater good. End of story. Godwin comments:

> Supposing I had been myself the chambermaid, I ought to have chosen to die rather than Fénelon should have died. The life of Fénelon was really preferable to that of the chambermaid . . . Suppose the chambermaid had been my wife, my mother, or my benefactor. That would not alter the truth of the proposition. The life of Fénelon would still be more valuable than that of the chambermaid; and justice—pure, unadulterated justice—would still have preferred that which was most valuable. Justice would have taught me to save the life of Fénelon at the expense of the other. What magic is there in the pronoun 'my' to overturn the decisions of everlasting truth? My wife or my mother may be a fool or a prostitute, malicious, lying, dishonest. If they be, of what consequence is it that they are mine.[32]

The popular uproar occasioned by Godwin's comments focused on his seeming indifference to the prospect of leaving his mother to die. Godwin seemed almost proud of the fact that he could (in theory) follow through the utilitarian doctrine to this extreme. In his mind, this unswerving devotion to the greatest happiness principle was a sign of progressive, new moral righteousness; it meant overcoming the old, sentimental ways and being moral in a bold, unflinching, scientific way. But, surely, this utilitarian line of argument is out of touch with deep moral intuitions. We naturally feel that our own mother deserves special respect, that we owe her a special debt of loyalty, affection, and gratitude. Whatever the philosophical explanation, there seems to be something decidedly cold and unnatural about leaving your own mother behind to burn while you save someone else—even if it could be shown that this other person might contribute more to universal happiness.

Godwin does pose an interesting dilemma. We may wonder what individuals caught in this fanciful situation should do: save their mother or save the archbishop? The rigorous moral answer seems to be that either option is moral. Saving anyone from a burning building, whether it be your mother or an archbishop, is a heroic feat. Not being able to save the other person is not an immoral act. You are not deliberately killing someone; you are—against your will—being forced to leave them behind. This is a tragedy, but it is not a crime. (The careful moral thinker might legitimately complain that we cannot decide what to do based on the information Godwin gives us. The wag might respond, 'save whoever is closer'. This is not a silly answer. In this kind of extreme situation, there might be innumerable issues to consider. Practical considerations play a large role.)

One could even disagree with Godwin's recommendation that we should save the archbishop on utilitarian grounds. After all, a society composed of children who did not feel a special connection to their mothers would be a very unhappy society. Normal psychological development depends, to a large extent, on a certain mutual exchange of affection and loyalty between children and parents. Godwin's apparent indifference to this family bond seems to cut at the very roots of society.

Even if Godwin's suggestion that we should save the archbishop because he is more useful to society were true, utilitarianism supplies the wrong rationale for such decision-making. We are not saving the archbishop because we love him but in order to increase the happiness of the greatest number. We are *using* the archbishop as a means to greater pleasure; he is a more efficient tool than the chambermaid.

That is all. If someone else was more useful, we would not save the archbishop. Godwin's concern for the archbishop's welfare depends solely on the calculation of expected utility. He does not value the archbishop for who he is but for what he can do for the rest of us. This is, in Kantian terms, to treat a human being as a means to an end.

Although utilitarianism seems, at first glance, a benevolent doctrine, it provides a convenient rationale for the mistreatment of specific individuals. If the ultimate goal is producing as much pleasure as possible, then getting rid of

---

৵ Applied Philosophy Box 9.3 ৵

German Euthanasia 1938–45

Italy's Parliamentary Affairs minister, Carlo Giovanardi, said during a radio debate: 'Nazi legislation and Hitler's ideas are reemerging in Europe via Dutch euthanasia laws and the debate on how to kill ill children.'

Unsurprisingly, the Dutch were outraged . . . Dutch Prime Minister Jan Peter Balkenende [responded], 'This is scandalous and unacceptable'.

The seeds of German euthanasia were planted in 1920 in the book *Permission to Destroy Life Unworthy of Life* (*Die Freigabe der Vernichtung lebensunwerten Leben*). Its authors were two of the most respected academics in their respective fields: Karl Binding was a renowned law professor, and Alfred Hoche, a physician and humanitarian.

The authors accepted wholeheartedly that people with terminal illnesses, the mentally ill or retarded, and deformed people could be euthanized as 'life unworthy of life'. More than that, the authors professionalized and medicalized the concept and, according to Robert Jay Lifton in *The Nazi Doctors*, promoted euthanasia in these circumstances as 'purely a healing treatment' and a 'healing work' justified as a splendid way to relieve suffering while saving money spent on caring for the disabled.

Over the years Binding and Hoche's attitudes percolated throughout German society and became accepted widely. These attitudes were stoked enthusiastically by the Nazis so that by 1938 the German government received an outpouring of requests from the relatives of severely disabled infants and young children seeking permission to end their lives.

The disabled are particularly vulnerable to the utilitarian analysis. Explain the reasoning at work here. (Note the twofold rationale: (1) to eliminate suffering, and (2) to save money. Relate this to utilitarianism.)

Source: Wesley J. Smith, 'German Euthanasia 1938–1945.' From: 'Killing Babies, Compassionately, The Netherlands Follows in Germany's Footsteps.' *Weekly Standard*, www.weeklystandard.com/Content/Public/Articles/000/000/012/003dncoj.asp, 27 March 2006.

suffering is more important than respecting individual persons. As any student of modern history will know, the 'scientific' experts in charge of the social project are sometimes all too willing to take it upon themselves to determine which lives should be snuffed out for the greater good. The disabled are an easy target: handicapped individuals who do not enjoy a sufficiently high 'quality of life' (whatever that means) decrease the total amount of happiness in a society. Utilitarianism seems to provide a justification for their (painless) removal. At the very least, it lends credence to this kind of thinking.

Impersonalism versus Personalism

We will call the belief that morality requires *strict* impartiality **impersonalism**. We will call a belief in the moral importance of particular relationships **personalism**. One can perhaps link the growth of impersonalism in utilitarianism and in modern ethics generally, to the influence of the scientific method. Utilitarians settle on the Greatest Happiness Principle as the moral equivalent to Newton's universal law of gravitation. (Kant considers the categorical imperative in a similar light.) These philosophers present a view of moral obligation from a universal perspective. They favour a moral law approach over virtue ethics, aiming to explain in one brief, sweeping, over-arching principle all the intricacies of moral behaviour. Every circumstance is evaluated in the same way, in relation to the same fundamental formula. Although there are specialized circumstances in which this approach provides an effective, unsentimental, objective methodology, there also occasions when it seems an aberration.

In the case of early thinkers such as Socrates, Jesus, Aristotle, and Thomas, moral duties grow naturally out of our everyday obligations.

We begin with familiar requirements of parenthood and kinship and hospitality and are called to strive toward some higher, individualized ideal of virtue. Philosophers push these moral intuitions outwards, further than we are accustomed to. Nonetheless, in the main, morality builds upon what we already know. Authors such as Aristotle and Thomas, in particular, emphasize casuistry; moral agents must be able to efficiently adapt abbreviated, large-scale principles to changing circumstances. One problem with the top-down method of impersonalism is that it rides roughshod over ordinary morality and over particular obligations. There is a reason for this.

Mill describes Bentham, in glowing terms, as a negative philosopher and a skeptic, calling him 'the great subversive', and, again, 'the great questioner of things established'.[33] (In truth, Bentham is only selectively skeptical. He does not question hedonism, for example.) Early utilitarians, like Bentham, were infected with a kind of triumphalism, an unshakable belief that their own systematic thought represented the way forward. This attitude of 'manifest destiny' made them largely impervious to the kind of philosophical correction that comes from attentive observation of everyday feelings and behaviours. (All philosophers believe in their ideas; otherwise they would not argue for them, but there is a matter of degree.) Authors such as Bentham and Godwin set out to 'scientifically' correct everyday morality. If, however, it is a mistake to *uncritically* acquiesce to everyday practice, it is equally wrong to ignore it all together. Mill tries, with only partial success, to reconcile utilitarianism with everyday moral belief.

Mill draws a parallel between Jesus's command to love one another and utilitarianism. If, however, strict utilitarianism is a form of impersonalism, Jesus does not command us to be impartial to everyone. He commands us, in contrast, to be *partial* to everyone. His teaching is not that we should treat *no one* as our brother, sister, mother, etc., but paradoxical as that may sound, that we should treat *everyone* as our brother, sister, mother, etc. Dealing out this kind of special attention to everyone—treating everyone as a brother (to use the traditional phrase)—is humanly impossible, but the command to love everyone is not a law in the usual sense. It is not intended as a *minimum* that we have to measure up to but as a *maximum* we are morally obliged to strive toward. It is a lofty ideal, an aspiration that we can never fully achieve. It functions, nonetheless, as an authoritative, ever-present ideal that directs moral striving toward those that are nearby, those we connect with in our particular circles and daily occupations.

Impersonalists tend to emphasize the virtue of justice and focus on cases of excess partiality, such as favouritism. As anyone with even a modicum of common sense knows, there are many situations in which we need to push aside particular loyalties. A judge in a court must make a decision based on broad principles of jurisprudence, not on the basis of her relationship to a particular plaintiff. A professor marking an exam should not assign a grade on the basis of his relationship to a particular student. But it would be absurd to model all forms of human behaviour on these specialized situations.

Not every display of special attention is wrong. Human children need enormous attention and care, so the fact that parents naturally focus their attention on their own children is fitting and appropriate. Friendship, as Aristotle points out, carries with it particular obligations. Even the mere fact of physical proximity plays a role in moral reasoning. Those people right beside us have a more momentous claim to our attention as we can hurt or help them in an especially intense way. I am morally obliged to help the man who has a heart attack in front of me at the supermarket, but I am not morally obliged to help the person who has a heart attack on the streets of Calcutta. Again, if I am an officer in the military, or a nurse, an airplane pilot, a teacher, a defense attorney, or a dentist, I will have moral responsibilities to care for a specific group of people under my charge. And so on. The general principles of morality remain the same, but as Aristotle insists, ethics has to be applied to the specific contexts of our lives. The same holds true for moral law. We need to develop moral judgment so as to properly apply moral law to individualized cases.

It is important to note that the moral obligations that derive from special relationships with other people do not turn immoral acts into moral acts, but they do define and orient the nature of moral obligation. Special relationships are *additive*, not subtractive. The fact that someone is my wife, my brother, my student, my patient, my boss (etc.) *adds* to what I am obliged to do, but it does not cancel out the more basic demands of morality. If my brother is guilty of a crime, it would be wrong to tell lies to get him out of prison. Still, I have special duties or obligations to my brother. I cannot do anything immoral, but I may have a special duty to visit my brother in prison, to financially contribute to his defense, to watch over his wife and children, and so on.

If utilitarians argue for strict impersonalism, some modern philosophers and theologians explicitly identify themselves as personalists. We will discuss personalism and some related strands of feminist thought in the next chapter.

Utilitarianism Is Consequentialism

Mill, like Bentham, is a **consequentialist** (a term coined by Anscombe). He claims that it is the *consequences* of an act that matter. If an act has good consequences—if it *increases* pleasure—it is a moral act. If an act has bad consequences—if it *decreases* pleasure—it is a bad act. This is in direct contrast to Kant, who claims that the agent's intentions determine the morality or immorality of a particular act. In Mill's consequentialist account, the difference between right and wrong boils down to how much or what quality of pleasure is produced. In Kant's deontological account, it boils down to whether or not the agent had a good will. These are deeply contrasting views.

The debate between utilitarian consequentialists and Kantian deontologists has monopolized the discussion in modern moral philosophy. Clearly, both consequences and intentions matter; it is not an issue of choosing between them. Still, Mill goes so far as to claim that the motives behind an action—why someone does something—play absolutely no role in distinguishing between right and wrong actions. If an act produces pleasurable consequences, it must be good. If it produces painful consequences, it must be bad. The motive is irrelevant.

Mill enthusiastically reports, 'utilitarian moralists have gone beyond almost all others in affirming that the motive has nothing to do with the morality of the action, though much with the worth of the agent. He who saves a fellow creature from drowning does what is morally right, whether his motive be duty, or the hope of being paid for his trouble'.[34] Mill's point is that this act has the same good consequences—a drowning individual is saved—regardless of whether the agent is acting on selfless or self-interested motives. What is going on inside the mind of the rescuer does not alter the effect of the intervention. A person is saved from drowning, and this is morally what matters. One life is saved; there is more happiness in the world; so this is a good act, regardless.

Mill goes out of his way to detach the morality of an act from the character of the doer. Good utilitarians, he reports, 'do not allow their judgment respecting the rightness or wrongness of an action to be influenced by their opinion of the qualities of the person who does it'.[35] Again, Mill claims that 'no known ethical standard decides an action to be good or bad because it is done by a good or a bad man, still less because [it is] done by an amiable, a brave, or a benevolent man'. Considerations of character, Mill claims, 'are relevant, not to the estimation of actions, but of persons'.[36]

The utilitarians were initially attracted to consequentialism as an empirical, scientific point of view. Intentions are invisible; we cannot observe what is going on inside someone's head. We can, it seems, observe what the consequences of an act are. To focus uniquely on consequences is, in some sense, to de-mystify what morality is all about. Mill, however, misconstrues these issues. Consider, in turn, four objections to Mill's consequentialism.

The first problem is that consequentialism, taken to its logical extreme, does not respect the distinction between moral and amoral or non-moral acts. What if there is an act that has good consequences without any intention behind it. For example, suppose I am carrying AIDS medication to missionaries and when a rock rolls down a mountain and kills an attacking bandit, saving my life so that I can deliver medical supplies and save thousands of people. A strict consequentialist might have to declare this a good act: after all, it had good consequences! Granted, there was no intention. But consequentialism tells us that intention does not matter. Presumably, no contemporary consequentialist would declare this a good act but the difficulty is in explaining why this is so if intentions really do not matter morally.

Second, Mill is himself inconsistent in his defence of consequentialism. There are situations in which we cannot begin to determine the moral status of an act without considering intention. Suppose someone dies falling from a great height. We cannot sort out whether this was a (blameless) accident, culpable negligence (manslaughter), murder, or suicide, without considering the issue of intentions. So the same result may be produced by morally different acts. Mill, in a response to such criticisms, distinguishes intention from motive, defining *intention* as 'what the agent wills to do' and *motive* as 'the feeling that makes him will so to do'.[37] Mill claims that intention but not motive may change the moral status of an act, but this is to concede the critic's point. (Mill's distinction is, in any case, questionable. Intention and 'motive' are not easily separated. Feeling may play an uncontroversial role in moral evaluation. If, for example, I feel angry because I have gotten into the habit of feeling superior, this 'motive' undermines the moral status of my act.)

Third, Mill, like other consequentialists, seems to rely on an artificial division. It is as if he wants to look at the external features of the act, rather than examining the movement of willpower the act expresses. But the same act has two inseparable aspects. As an author like Thomas points out, a thorough investigation of human behaviour requires a consideration of the whole act, its internal features along with its external features.

Fourth, Mill seems to overlook the fact that immoral acts are an expression of a bad character. Conduct originates in who and what you are. Wicked people do wicked acts because of greed, pride, anger, intemperance, incontinence, moral ignorance, etc. Good character, in contrast, produces good acts.

And there is still a further problem with consequentialism. Mill claims that moral acts have good consequences, but it is sometimes impossible to predict what the actual consequences of an act will be. Suppose I tell my family to take the seven o'clock instead of the six-thirty flight from Philadelphia. The first plane arrives safely but the second plane crashes, killing my family. I caused the death of my family. This is clearly a bad consequence. But this is not an immoral act, for the bad consequence was not intended. Human acts may have unintended consequences, good or bad. When we evaluate the moral status of an act, it is not just the consequences but also what was intended by the agent that matters.

And there is another complication when it comes to unintended consequences. Individual acts affect other acts. Think of a line of dominoes. When a domino falls, the whole line falls, one domino after another. But how can we know that the present pleasure produced by an act is not cancelled out by a future sequence of pain-producing effects? How can we know that any present *increase* in pleasure is not outweighed by a larger *decrease* over the longer term? As Mill sensibly points out, the future consequences of an act are often minimal. But this is not always the case. Suppose a stranger attacks you in a bar, and as a result you spend the rest of your life avoiding bars and dangerous places and thereby enjoy

❧ Applied Philosophy Box 9.4 ❧

Couple Pay Another Table's Tab, and Chain Reaction of Generosity Lasts Hours

Danielle Johnson

Philadelphia — It played like a scene from a holiday movie—a mystery couple, who didn't leave their names or numbers, walked into a restaurant, finished their meal and then set off a chain reaction of generosity that lasted for hours.

That's just what employees at the Aramingo Diner in the Port Richmond section of Philadelphia said a man and a woman did during their breakfast shift Saturday morning. . . .

Willard and other waitresses told NBC Philadelphia that the couple started the chain reaction by paying double: for their own meal and for the tab of another table of diners at the restaurant.

There's no evidence that one group of diners knew the others.

'I could not believe it. And it continued and continued—it was very nice,' said Willard. 'They asked us not to say anything until they left, say, "Merry Christmas, that person picked up your check."'

For the next five hours, dozens of patrons got into that same holiday spirit and paid the favour forward. . . .

'It was a surprise to all of us; the girls were even taken aback,' said the diner's manager. 'Those who took the check also tipped the waitress. So nobody had to do anything other than pass it on, and that's what they did. They just passed it forward.'

It's a true holiday story that proves how a small gesture of kindness can create some magic.

This is a nice example of good consequences. The anonymous couple in question deserve some credit for this display of holiday giving. On the other hand, suppose their action did not produce this 'chain of generosity'. Suppose they paid for another person's dinner and that was the end of it. Would that make their original act less moral? What should a consequentialist say? What do you think?

Source: Danielle Johnson, 'Mystery Pair at Diner Spark Cascade of Giving: Couple Pay Another Table's Tab, and Chain Reaction of Generosity Lasts Hours.' *NBCPhiladelphia.com*, (MSNBC.com), www.msnbc.msn.com/id/34420892/ns/us_news-giving/, 14 December 2009.

a long and healthy life. This original assault had a major effect on your life, a beneficial effect. Would it follow that that your assailant should be credited with a good act? Surely not. Suffice it to say that consequentialism cannot be rigorously applied because individual acts may have unintended and largely unpredictable consequences. Morality is about praising or blaming people for what they choose to do. We cannot praise or blame someone for things that happen unintentionally or accidentally.

Utilitarianism does rest on a fundamental moral intuition. Moral agents must consider the foreseeable consequences of their acts. An individual who deliberately acts in such a way so as to engender good future consequences deserves at least some credit for the goodness that results. Someone who does the opposite deserves at least some blame for the bad future consequences that result. Still, morality has to do with more than consequences. Any exclusive consequentialism is seriously problematic.

To ignore the original intentions of an agent (or the intrinsic worth of an act) is to miss out on an important part of what morality is all about.

Acts versus Rules

Debate revolving around the issue of unpredictable consequences has spawned two competing interpretations of utilitarianism. Proponents of act utilitarianism focus on individual acts; proponents of rule utilitarianism focus on rules as they apply to groups of acts. Act utilitarians claim that we should always do whatever produces the most utility; rule utilitarians claim that we should act in accordance with that set of rules that will, in most cases, maximize utility. To see the difference between these two theories, consider the familiar example of lying. Telling lies is usually bad. So a moral rule against lying is a good rule, and a rule utilitarian may claim that we should *never* lie. In odd circumstances, where lying happens to have good consequences, act utilitarians will claim that lying is not wrong; indeed, they may claim that we have *a moral obligation to tell a lie*. Rule utilitarians argue that trying to figure out the morality of each individual act is too time-consuming and complicated. It is best to teach people a few basic rules about morality and have them act accordingly. Act utilitarians, on the other hand, are sticklers about general principles. One must always act—in each instance—in accordance with the Greatest Happiness Principle.

Act utilitarianism seems problematic. If, for example, it sounds inoffensive to suggest that there may be morally legitimate cases of lying, what about murder? Do we have to consider each murder as morally neutral—that is, as neither moral nor immoral—until we look at its precise consequences? Surely, it makes sense to posit a general rule against murder. Rules are, after all, a useful guide to moral conduct. And they can be sensibly adapted to specific circumstances, as we saw in the earlier discussion of casuistry.

Mill, who does not use this terminology, takes a middle position. On the one hand, he suggests that moral rules inevitably have exceptions. In a discussion of the interdiction against lying, he writes, 'even this rule, sacred as it is, admits of possible exceptions'.[38] On the other hand, he argues that we need 'intermediate moral rules', secondary rules that prohibit or encourage specific kinds of behaviour—such as 'Don't kill!' or 'Don't steal!' or 'Always tell the truth!' It would be absurd, he suggests, 'to pass over [these] intermediate generalisations entirely, and endeavour to test each individual action directly by the [utility] principle'.[39] His advice seems to be that we should rely on moral rules most of the time but in strange circumstances revert to the utility principle. This is not unlike the advice given by other authors in the tradition. In hard cases, retreat to the most fundamental moral truths. In other words, go back to the basics!

Does the End Justify the Means?

Utilitarians, in contrast to the overwhelming majority of mainstream historical philosophers, argue that the end justifies the means, then an agent can use evil means to achieve a good aim as long as the amount of happiness produced is large enough to offset any pain or suffering associated with the evil means. Although Mill does not consider this issue in sufficient depth, he seems to suppose that we can do whatever is needed (as in the lying case) to produce the greatest amount of pleasure. Any such suggestion is, however, highly implausible. This is the general gist of much contemporary criticism of utilitarianism. Let us consider, then, a well-known critique of utilitarianism borrowed largely from contemporary philosopher Bernard Williams. Williams proposes a thought experiment in order to demonstrate how utilitarianism conflicts with our deepest moral intuitions.

Suppose that you are a diplomat visiting an evil regime. General X, a murderer and a tyrant, invites you to his palace. He ushers you into a large bull-fighting ring, where you see 21 men lined up against a concrete wall, tied to posts and blindfolded. A firing squad marches in. The General, it seems, wants you to watch an execution of rebel peasants. You are obviously disturbed at the slaughter you are about to witness, but the General, noticing your discomfort, winks and smiles. 'I will make a deal', he says. 'In your honour, I will halt the execution and let 20 prisoners go free if, for your part, you will be gracious enough to shoot just one of these evil prisoners.' He hands you a rifle: 'Just a little co-operation, please. Shoot any one of the prisoners and the rest go free.'

This is a devilish predicament. You know that every prisoner is innocent. If you kill any one of them, you will be shooting an innocent man. Deliberately doing so is tantamount to murder, and murder is a great evil. If, however, you refuse to murder one prisoner, all 21 will be executed. That seems a worse consequence. It seems, then, a cruel dilemma. What should a moral agent do?

If you are a utilitarian, you must shoot one of the prisoners. Utilitarianism accepts the use of evil means, as long as the eventual good consequences outweigh the evil consequences. Having one innocent person die is clearly a better result than having 21 innocent people die, whoever does the killing. So

you should kill the one of them and be done with it. We will call this the **great evil strategy**. Murder is acceptable if it has sufficiently good consequences, i.e., if it leads to a great increase in happiness. (Some rule utilitarians might disagree with the great evil strategy, but this seems to be one of those exceptional cases Mill talks about, where the true utilitarian will have to consult the utility principle. And the utility principle tells us to do what produces the greatest happiness. In other words, shoot the prisoner.)

Non-utilitarians may complain that murdering the prisoner will make them feel queasy, but consistent utilitarians will respond that visceral responses are not arguments. The 'squeamish factor', they typically respond, has no moral weight. The fact that killing another person is an unsettling emotional experience is irrelevant. Indeed, they will argue that a moral agent is *obliged* to kill the innocent prisoner. Moral agents must do whatever it takes to produce happiness for the greatest number. In this unfortunate situation, they will kill a third party, not because they enjoy killing human beings, but because it produces more happiness. In the utilitarian account, this is what morality is all about.

As we have already discussed in previous chapters, the virtue ethics tradition does not condone the use of immoral means to achieve good ends. The great evil strategy is not equivalent to the traditional doctrine of double effect (discussed in Chapter 6 on Thomas). Nor is it equivalent to the doctrine of 'preventive evil' (discussed in Chapter 8 on Kant), which allows a small evil for the sake of a greater good. Utilitarianism permits the commission of a *great evil* just as long as it is outweighed by a greater good. You can do something very bad as long as the good effects are large enough.

Most authors in the moral philosophy tradition would condemn any such suggestion as outrageously immoral.

We could critique the utilitarian strategy in various ways. For his part, Williams complains that utilitarians lack integrity. You owe it to your own sense of self-respect not to participate in evil. If the General and his soldiers shoot 21 innocent men, *they* shoot them. If you shoot 1 innocent man, *you* shoot him. In the first case the General and his soldiers do something very wrong; in the second case *you* do something very wrong. It is true that your refusal to participate in evil will result in the death of 21 men. This would be terrible. Still, if you shoot the innocent man, *you* (not the General) are choosing to do evil. You *collaborate* with evil. Because utilitarianism is a form of impersonalism, it focuses on the total result, overlooking the issue of individual responsibility. But your first obligation as a moral agent is to refrain from evil yourself.

The great evil strategy is insidious. Once the use of great evils becomes a morally required option, morality slowly unravels. It is not simply that consistent utilitarians must kill 1 innocent prisoner to save 20. If the General promises he will let 1 innocent prisoner go free if you accept to kill 100 others, utilitarianism tells you that you are morally *obliged* to execute 100. Why? Because saving 1 life is better than saving none. Because this is the best possible result and because—according to utilitarianism—the end *does* justify the means.

And there is a second, related problem. Utilitarianism sets a dangerous precedent. Clever agents can always find ways to justify evil through some appeal to a future good. Suppose I embezzle money in order to save my bankrupt business. I can argue that stealing is, in this case, justified, for many people would lose their jobs if my company went out of business. Or suppose I cheat on my medical exam. I can argue that dishonesty is usually immoral, but in this case, it will allow me to become a doctor who will be able to move to rural Quebec and help the sick. And so on. Utilitarianism, in legitimizing evil as a means to an end, gives everyone an alibi.

It might be true that many people faced with the firing-squad scenario would feel compelled to shoot the innocent prisoner to save the others. It does not follow that this is, as utilitarians suggest, a moral course of action. Aristotle's account of mixed acts fits this situation well. Aristotle tells us to pity people who find themselves in such predicaments. They deserve clemency and forgiveness, not harsh condemnation. If someone were to shoot an innocent prisoner, we can fully understand their motives. We ourselves might do the same thing. Still, this is not, strictly speaking, a moral act. (Utilitarians act as if the present killing of an innocent man can somehow be cancelled out by a subsequent good. But morality is not like this. Good future consequences cannot change the bad nature of what has already happened. The future good does not cancel out the present evil. Forgiveness does not turn the first bad act into a good act.)

Morality-For-Its-Own-Sake?

As we have seen, mainstream authors in the moral philosophy tradition argue that morality is valuable for its own sake. Utilitarianism, on the other hand, does not value morality for morality's sake, but for the sake of something else, namely, pleasure. For utilitarians, morality has instrumental rather than intrinsic value; it is only valuable for its consequences, as a means to larger doses of pleasure.

Following in Bentham's footsteps, Mill criticizes asceticism, distinguishing between two kinds of martyrs who sacrifice themselves for morality. Good martyrs 'abnegate for themselves the personal enjoyment of life, when by such renunciation they contribute worthily to increase the amount of happiness in the world'.[40] Bad martyrs practise renunciation for the sake of morality even when this does not increase the total amount of pleasure in the world They are 'no more deserving of admiration than the ascetic mounted on his pillar'.[41] Their acts of self-sacrifice are pathetic and ridiculous, not sublime.

Utilitarianism cannot, in principle, cope with situations where there are no discernible consequences. Other moral philosophers would argue, for example, that telling the truth is good, simply because telling the truth is valuable. It is intrinsically valuable, regardless of the consequences. Even if there were no consequences, telling the truth would still be a good act. Mill claims that moral heroism without good consequences is patently ridiculous, even perverse. Does this follow? Suppose I am being tortured to death because I believe *X*. The executioner asks me, once again, if I believe in *X*. I know that if I tell the truth, it will be worse for me. Yet I courageously say, 'I believe *X*'. Is this, as Mill would have it, a morally perverse act? Shouldn't I tell the truth simply because telling the truth is something good thing to do? Most earlier philosophers would argue that this is a noble and virtuous act simply because I am telling the truth *regardless of the consequences*.

In the utilitarian account, it is not, strictly speaking, the act under consideration that is right or wrong. In a sense, the act is morally neutral. It is, more precisely, the consequences of the act that are right or wrong. So the same act can become right or wrong depending on the consequences. It is not surprising, then, that utilitarianism overlooks, not only the intrinsically good nature, but also the intrinsically evil nature of certain acts. As we have seen, utilitarianism accepts the doctrine that the end justifies the means. It will follow, on the utilitarian scheme, that an intrinsically evil act will be justified if it leads to good enough consequences. Mill adds further considerations about the quality of the resultant pleasures, but this will not solve the basic problem. Suppose, for example, that someone were to discover that playing on violin strings made from human intestines cut out of living children sounded better than playing a Stradivarius. It would not follow—no matter how heavenly the sound produced—that this would be a good thing to do. In these cases, talk about increasing happiness of the greatest number magnificently misses the point. This act is blatantly, fundamentally, irrevocably immoral. Measuring how much pleasure or what quality of pleasure is produced is supremely irrelevant. Because utilitarianism reduces morality to some kind of pleasure calculation, it cannot adequately address these serious issues. We need to be wary of bold, new, 'scientific' theories that ask us to ignore our deepest moral intuitions.

Mill adamantly criticizes the emphasis Kant places on duty. He comments, 'No system of ethics requires that the sole motive of all we do shall be a feeling of duty; on the contrary, ninety-nine hundredths of all our actions are done from other motives'.[42] But Mill misunderstands the Kantian concept of duty. To act out of duty is, for Kant, to have the right intentions. It is to act morally for the sake of morality, not from ulterior motives. Utilitarianism, in effect, in valuing morality as a means to pleasure, could be said to value morality for ulterior motives. This does not mean that the Greatest Happiness Principle has no merit. It only means that utilitarianism is an incomplete theory. It needs to be enlarged, supplemented by other theories.

Egalitarian Principles I

Utilitarians, past and present, often try to shore up utilitarianism through an appeal to **egalitarianism**, the idea that people should be treated equally. Mill, at the end of his essay on utilitarianism, cites Bentham's maxim 'everybody to count for one, nobody to count for more than one'.[43] He claims that the Greatest Happiness Principle would be 'a mere form of words without rational signification, unless one person's happiness . . . is counted exactly as much as another's'.[44] But this stipulation (or assumption) that the pleasures (or preferences) of each individual have equal value cannot solve deeper problems with the theory.

Utilitarianism proposes an egalitarianism of pleasure, not an egalitarianism of persons. It is not people that have to be valued to the same amount. It is every unit of pleasure that has to be valued to the same amount. If the total amount of happiness is what matters, it need not follow (as Mill somewhat disingenuously implies) that every person will count for as much as any other in society. Mill puts it, 'equal amounts of happiness are equally desirable, whether felt by the same or different persons'.[45] The idea here is that we are to produce as much pleasure as possible. It will follow that people who can experience more pleasure, those with more nerve endings and more sensitive dispositions, will deserve special treatment, whereas those who have a diminished capacity for pleasure—babies, the handicapped, the sick, the depressed, even the

temperamentally morose—will not warrant the same attention. They cannot add much to the total. If there is anyone who feels little or no pleasure, their desires and needs can mostly be neglected. So an egalitarianism about units of pleasure reduces, in principle, to *unequal* treatment of different people.

Utilitarians turn human beings into pleasure-producers. The person who produces the most pleasure is the most valuable. Mill's concession that the quality of pleasure must also be considered cannot disguise the fact that it is the pleasure—quantity or quality—not the person that matters. Seen from a utilitarian perspective, what is important about you as a human being is not your humanity, your intelligence, your capacity for truthfulness, virtue, or wisdom. What matters is how much pleasure you produce.

Egalitarian Principles II

And there is a second problem with utilitarian egalitarianism. Suppose we were to assume, against the empirical evidence, that we all possess the very same capacity for pleasure. Still, utilitarianism is a community-minded theory. What matters is the *total* amount of pleasure produced. But the total amount of pleasure produced will be a function of population. This gives rise to two different problems.

As Derek Parfit has pointed out, utilitarianism seems to favour the endless multiplication of a barely happy people.[46] He calls this puzzle the 'mere addition paradox'. As a moment's reflection makes clear, the total amount of pleasure produced by vast numbers of *barely* happy people will dwarf the total amount of pleasure produced by a much smaller number of very happy people. Compare two different worlds. In the Stingy World, 300 billion people each experience one unit of pleasure. In the Ample World, 1 million people each experience 100 units of pleasure. So the Stingy World produces 300 *billion* units of pleasure; the Ample World produces only 100 *million* units of pleasure. Parfit calls this the **repugnant conclusion**. He means this as a comment on nagging worries about overpopulation. Whatever one thinks about the overpopulation issue, there is something seriously wrong with the idea that multiplying the number of barely happy people makes for a better world.

Public Policy

Mill does his best to reconcile utilitarianism with common-sense morality. But utilitarians are caught in something of a bind. Mill writes as if we have been intuitively following the utilitarian doctrine all along. But previous generations were not, except in some very loose sense, utilitarians. If then previous generations could succeed at morality without modern utilitarianism, why do we need it now?

This is the dilemma. Insomuch as the moral recommendations of utilitarianism depart from everyday norms, they strike us as implausible. If, on the other hand, utilitarianism reduces to the everyday principles of morality, why do we need the theory? Many contemporary utilitarians have come to accept that people are not consciously motivated by utilitarian considerations. Authors such as Bentham and Mill substitute universal hedonism for more familiar concepts, such as (moral) happiness, virtue, conscience, friendship, love, peace of mind, and duty. It is not clear, however, that most people believe in universal hedonism. This is a problem for theorists.

Still, the utilitarian approach does have a positive side. Mill writes of 'a world in which there is so much . . . to correct and improve'.[47]

Because the utilitarians believed in political and scientific progress, they were peculiarly sensitive to the future consequences of human behaviour. Equipped with a vision that looked forward, they *correctly* saw that moral agents must take into account the future consequences of their actions. Much public policy still follows a utilitarian model; it takes as the most important social goal, the maximization of happiness in a traditional utilitarian sense. This has advantages and disadvantages. Let us consider one concrete example of the way utilitarianism has been applied to social policy: the **harm reduction** approach to the drug issue.

It goes without saying that the use of hard drugs, such as cocaine, heroin, and amphetamines, is a serious problem in contemporary society. Advocates of harm reduction argue that the decriminalization of drugs, needle exchange programs, medically supervised injection sites, and even the (free) medical prescription of heroin to 'needy' individuals reduces the incidence of hepatitis, venereal disease, and AIDS, the rate of fatal overdoses, the level of criminality and prostitution in drug ghettoes, and so on. They propose a consequentialist strategy: society must implement non-judgmental programs so as to reduce the bad consequences of hard drug use. Opponents of harm reduction, on the other hand, argue that drug use is a moral evil, that decriminalizing such activity, handing out clean needles, prescribing heroin (etc.) is to aid and abet immoral behaviour. (The end does not justify the means.) A moral society cannot condone or encourage the use of hard drugs by the implementation of such policies even if they would have good consequences. Readers can consider these issues futher on their own.

ᴈ Applied Philosophy Box 9.5 ᴇ

'World Banker to the Poor'

Muhammad Yunus is often referred to as 'the world's banker to the poor'. . . .

His revolutionary Grameen (Village) banking system is estimated to have extended credit to more than seven million of the world's poor, most of them in Bangladesh, one of the poorest nations in the world.

The vast majority of the beneficiaries are women.

Mr Yunus came up with the idea in 1976 while professor of economics at Chittagong University in southern Bangladesh.

The first loans he issued had a value of $27 (£14.50). Their recipients were 42 women from the village of Jobra, near the university.

The women had relied until then on local money lenders who charged high interest rates. The conventional banking system had been reluctant to give credit to those who were too poor to provide any form of guarantee.

The success of Mr Yunus' scheme exceeded all expectations and has been copied in developing countries around the world.

His 'micro finance' initiative reaches out to people shunned by conventional banking systems—people so poor they have no collateral to guarantee a loan, should they be unable to repay it. . . . Even beggars have been able to borrow money under his scheme.

The actions of Muhammad Yunus are just the kind of thing that utilitarianism succinctly and accurately identifies as moral behaviour. Note that the 'Micro-financing' or 'Micro-credit' movement is all about creating opportunity; it gives people a chance to better themselves. It is about increasing happiness not merely pleasure. How does this initiative fit into the larger utilitarian mindset? Discuss.

Source: 'World banker to the poor.' BBC NEWS, http://news.bbc.co.uk/go/pr/fr/_/2/hi/south_asia/6047234.stm, 13 October 2006.

Despite its shortcomings, utilitarianism articulates key ideas that are worthy of inclusion in any moral almanac. Looking at the big picture; increasing happiness for all; battling against all types of suffering, disease, hunger, oppression; improving the world for future generations: these are important aspects of morality. Insomuch as utilitarianism takes our responsibility to wider society and future generations seriously, it adds something worthwhile to moral discourse. But it cannot stand on its own. Considered rigorously, it is a seriously problematic theory that needs to be supplemented.

Revising Utilitarianism

The most recognizable feature of utilitarian theories is the calculation of the total amount of happiness or harm produced by an action. Leaving aside the unrealistic hope of contriving any exact pleasure calculus, we can often measure, roughly, how much harm or how much good is caused by an action. This loosely utilitarian way of thinking can be incorporated into moral decision-making.

Traditional utilitarians wanted an algorithm that one could use mechanically—like a machine—to find out whether an action is right or wrong. This is an impossibility. Ethics is not as easy as counting. There is no simple algorithm that can replace practical judgment. Still, we can itemize some useful moral criteria we can take away from a *modified* utilitarian approach. The following list reflects an *enlarged* utilitarianism, one that incorporates constructive responses to the different problems we have been discussing throughout this chapter. Taken together, these criteria might be seen as offering a methodology for evaluating individual acts. We must do the following then to succeed at morality:

1. We must think carefully about the (future) consequences of our decisions.
2. We should recognize that happiness is more than so many units of pleasure; it is a sense of self-fulfillment that legitimately accompanies the realization of human potential.
3. We should recognize that more happiness (properly understood) is better than less happiness.
4. We should care about the happiness of other people. (Self-centredness, self-absorption are moral faults.)
5. We must accept that suffering is an intractable aspect of finite human existence. Suffering may build character, but it is the building of character that is to be valued, not the bare fact of suffering. Pain or suffering, for the sake of pain or suffering, is an evil.
6. We should recognize that the end does not justify the means whatever the consequences.
7. We should recognize that good intentions are an essential aspect of morality.
8. We should understand that the people that surround us, our families, our friends, our dependants, have a particularly momentous claim on our attention.

We can reduce these concerns to a series of informative questions:

1. Does the act have good consequences?
2. Does it produce human fulfillment in the very best sense?
3. Does it produce more or less happiness?
4. Does it help other people?
5. Does it avoid unnecessary suffering?
6. Does it employ evil means to a good end?
7. Is it an expression of good intentions?
8. Does it respond to particular duties and obligations?

When we are asking these kinds of questions, we are already engaging in the kind of moral reflection authors in the virtue ethics tradition recommend.

Consider some very quick examples:

(Ex.1) Suppose I have to kill animals (for food, for fur, because they are old, diseased, whatever). It is morally preferable if I can accomplish this task painlessly (criterion #5). All things being equal, if I have a choice between using two efficient methods, I should use the one that is less painful.

(Ex. 2) Suppose I manufacture baby clothes that are flammable because it is cheaper to do so. Clearly, this is a bad act. It has bad future consequences (criterion #1), and produces unnecessary suffering (criterion #5) and less happiness (criterion #3).

(Ex. 3) Is binge-drinking moral? This is not producing happiness in the very best sense (criterion # 2); in fact, it produces unnecessary suffering (criterion #5); it destroys character (criterion #6), and it arguably produces less happiness (criterion #3).

(Ex. 4) Suppose I do something thoughtlessly, without weighing the negative consequences. This sins against criterion #1. It is a refusal to even consider the question.

(Ex. 5) Suppose I make a promise I know I will be unable to keep. This is to use an evil means to my end. Whatever the other harmful consequences, it violates criterion #7. And so on.

These helpful moral principles are no substitute for practical wisdom. They must be interpreted wisely, adjusted and tailored to specific circumstances, and so on. Still, they provide a useful way of initiating critical reflection about moral problems.

On Liberalism

We have been discussing Mill's famous defense of utilitarianism. But Mill was also a political philosopher. We cannot finish any adequate treatment of his thought without briefly looking at one of the most famous political tracts of all time, Mill's stirring defense of individual freedom, *On Liberty*.

Mill is, at the same time, a utilitarian, a liberal, and—as we shall see in the next section—a virtue ethicist. His extended essay *On Liberty* (1869) is probably the most influential liberal manifesto in the English language.[48] Obviously, the term 'liberal' is ambiguous. This is because political commentators, who often nurse ideological agendas, use the terms *liberal* and *liberalism* in many different ways. Unfortunately, no one been able to come up with a universally agreed-upon definition of the theory. Let us begin, then, with an uncontroversial approximation: **liberalism** is the idea that individual liberty, understood as the freedom to do as one wants, is the most important value. Or, at the very least, it should be given priority in political life. This is certainly how Mill understands the theory.

The No-Harm Principle

Mill, following Hobbes, defines *political freedom* as an absence of restrictions. He sets out the basic doctrine of liberalism in his famous **no-harm principle**, which might be considered as the canonical (or authoritative) account of the contemporary liberal view. Mill declares,

> [The] only purpose for which power can be rightfully exercised over any member of a civilized community, against his will, is to prevent harm to others. . . . [A citizen] cannot rightfully be compelled to do or forbear because it will be better for him to do so, because it will make him happier, because, in the opinions of others, to do so would be wise, or even right. These are good reasons for remonstrating with him, or reasoning with him, or persuading him, or entreating him, but not for compelling him, or visiting him with any evil in case he do otherwise. To justify that [his] conduct . . . must be calculated to produce evil to some one else. The only part of the conduct of any one, for which he is amenable to society, is that which concerns others. In the part which merely concerns himself, his independence is, of right, absolute. Over himself, over his own body and mind, the individual is sovereign.[49]

This, then, is the no-harm principle: that we can only stop other people from doing what they want when their actions harm other people. In their private lives, people are free to do what they will. Mill writes, 'The only freedom which deserves the name, is that of pursuing our own good in our own way, so long as we do not attempt to deprive others of [their liberty to do the same]'.[50] (We should point out that Mill's no-harm principle has historical precedents. The ancient Greek philosopher Epicurus writes that 'Natural justice is a symbol or an expression of expediency, to prevent one man from harming or being harmed by another'.[51] This Epicurean no-harm principle is not unlike Mill's principle: we are to enjoy freedom to do whatever we want to do, a freedom that is insured by a mutual agreement not to harm each another. One could find other historical influences.)

The Don't-Impose-Morality-on-Me School

It is not surprising that a political emphasis on individual liberty should clash with morality. What morality does, at first glance, is impose values on people. Mill insists, 'liberty consists in doing what one desires'.[52] But morality may mean '*not* doing what one desires'. Because morality removes some options from the list of things we can do, it is easy to view it as the enemy of liberty understood as the freedom to do what we want. Call this negative approach to morality, which is pervasive in popular culture, the 'don't-impose-morality-on-me' school. Champions of the don't-impose-morality-on-me school propose a milder form of the anti-morality world view discussed in the last chapter. This is dangerous. In a liberal society, those who seek to divest themselves of the burdens of morality can rationalize their behaviour by claiming that they wish to broaden the scope of freedom. This rhetorical trope provides a familiar but facile argument against moral responsibility. Let's consider, very briefly, the problems with this approach.

The first and most fundamental problem with the 'don't-impose-morality-on-me' attitude is that it misconstrues the origins of morality. Morality is not imposed on us by outside forces; we impose it on ourselves. Put another way, morality comes from the inside; it is not an artificial restraint imposed from the outside. It is human nature that imposes moral standards on us. We cannot escape moral responsibility as long as we are human. This is, briefly stated, the answer given by the long line of moral philosophers already presented in previous chapters.

The second problem with this approach is that it overlooks, ignores, or minimizes the role of moral reasoning. As this survey of moral philosophy has demonstrated, historical authors view morality as a form of intelligence. Members of the 'don't-impose-morality-on-me' school argue for freedom and against morality, but this is like saying we want to be freer so we can be less intelligent. Yes, intelligence imposes restraints on human behaviour, but this is not a restriction on human flourishing. As we have seen, earlier philosophers, as a rule, do not define freedom in terms of doing *anything* we want to do but in terms of self-realization or the possession of what is truly good.

In his political writing, Mill (who is not a consistent philosopher) legitimizes this interpretation of morality as unreasoned choice by reducing morality to personal preference and social convention and also by encouraging moral skepticism. Mill writes: 'To an ordinary man, . . . his own preference, thus supported [by others], is not only a perfectly satisfactory reason, but the only one he generally has for any of his notions of morality, taste, or propriety.'[53] Mill also suggests that morality is to be traced to power structures that subjugate minorities: 'Wherever there is an ascendant class, a large portion of the morality of the country emanates from its class interests, and its feelings of class superiority.'[54] He concludes that many moral opinions held by past generations are 'not only false but absurd'[55] and 'now known to be erroneous'.[56] Our own opinions, he assures us, will be 'rejected by future ages'.[57]

We have already discussed some of these epistemological issues in previous chapters. Mill's attitude is deeply problematic. If ordinary people do not elaborate long philosophical arguments, it does not follow that they are acting on mere preferences or 'likings'. It is one thing to complain that many people are not reflective enough about conventional moral beliefs (which is often quite true); it is quite another thing to equate their deepest moral beliefs—about fairness, honesty, respect for life, friendship, and so on—with personal preferences. Generally speaking, people know the difference between personal desire and distinctions between right and wrong. Moral errors do not usually arise because individuals have no grasp of first principles, but because they apply these principles inconsistently.

Again, if we sometimes make mistakes, it is a leap to embrace moral skepticism, the idea that we cannot have any knowledge. (If we were to consistently embrace skepticism, we would have to doubt liberalism itself which is, after all, only another point of view like all the others.) The appropriate response to human fallibility past and *present* is not to abandon rigorous thought altogether, but to retrieve what is valuable from past and present thought while correcting mistakes and inconsistencies. The familiar suggestion that moral thinkers down through the ages never agreed with on another does not stand up to close scrutiny. Indeed, it is odd that Mill, who identifies Jesus as a utilitarian and who claims that enlightened moralists in previous ages were all (unknowingly) utilitarians, should be so quick to discount the soundness and relevancy of previous moral teaching. Although political and economic regimes may encourage certain moral beliefs, the best moral thinking is driven by logic and attentive observation and often serves as a criticism of conventional ideas. Without objective morality, we would have no grounds for criticizing those in power.

A third problem with the 'don't-impose-morality-on-me' school is the way it uncritically divorces morality from politics, social policy, and the law. We moderns all believe in a large sphere of individual liberty. No one believes that we can outlaw all immorality. Still, why shouldn't society impose some basic elements of morality on its citizens? Plato and Aristotle assume the purpose of good government is turn citizens into virtuous people; Thomas argues that positive human law is only a more localized expression of morality; Hobbes views morality as a matter of social contract; and so on. Utilitarianism was itself a reformist political movement fueled by moral indignation at social mores and legal conventions that were viewed as inhumane, unfair, unequal, or just plain vicious. It was a moral theory replete with political implications. Insomuch as politics and law invoke or appeal to ultimate questions about what has value or how human beings should live together, they will inevitably have some sort of moral content.

Moral Liberalism I

The 'don't-impose-morality-on-me' approach overlooks the fact that liberalism itself imposes strict limits on individual freedom, i.e., the no-harm principle. Some liberals go so far as to propose this principle as the basic axiom of morality. Call this view **moral liberalism**, a phrase taken from contemporary libertarian Jan Narveson. As we shall see, moral liberalism begins with Mill. It is as important an aspect of his moral thought as utilitarianism. Whatever the inconsistencies this shift of focus reveals in Mill's work as a whole, moral liberalism needs to be studied because it has been, in the final analysis, deeply influential.

Moral liberals propose what is called a **thin theory of the good**. They say very little about what counts as true happiness, the good life, virtue, duty, natural law, etc. Mostly, they avoid taking a substantive stance on such issues and point to individual freedom as an ultimate good that needs to be respected.

They do this deliberately so as to preserve as much room for individual choice as possible. But what should we choose? Moral liberalism leaves it up to us: we can choose whatever we want just as long as we do not interfere with the lives of others.

Moral liberalism, which is as much an attitude as a theory, is fueled by a loss of confidence in traditional morality. It is a morality of last resort. In the alleged absence of moral consensus and objective moral standards, moral liberals propose a minimalist standard of acceptable behaviour. Narveson writes, 'the very best we can do is to agree to let each other do as he pleases, so long as he does not thereby inflict costs or losses on others'.[58] Narveson intends this colloquially expressed version of the no-harm principle as a *moral*, not just a political principle. On this theory, your personal, private life is your own business. It is a morality-free zone. Only public faults, errors that harm other people, are, in any rigorous sense, immoral.

Moral liberalism is deliberately a minimalist theory. It offers us very little help in determining what kind of life we should live. As long as we don't cross over the line and harm other people, we are free to do as we want. Narveson comments on this:

> Now there may be cases where I want to do something but realize that it would be silly or too expensive. If so, that too implies a reason for me not to do it. But it implies a different sort of reason from the moral type. It may not matter to the public what I do, or it may be none of their business. The moral rule may be: 'So, go ahead dummy!' Morals may leave the decision up to you, but that doesn't mean there is no further question whether you should do it. Of course there is, but it goes beyond the limited realm of morals into the much wider one of how to live one's life.[59]

Narveson tells us that morality cannot give us any guidance when it comes to the question, 'how should I live my life?' In the mind of most historical authors, however, this is precisely what morality is all about! Telling people to do what they want is little help to reflective individuals who want to investigate what it means to be a good human being. The goal of traditional moral philosophy is to provide wise counsel for human action, and to do so fairly, objectively, without hiding the difficulties. Historical sources, however imperfect, provide a very good starting point for any such project. It is not a matter of social coercion. It is a matter of following, without being partisan, where the moral reasoning leads us. Moral liberalism, pursued single-mindedly, seems to empty morality of much of its content.

We should point out that these attitudes can be traced all the way back to Mill. As we have already seen, earlier philosophers distinguish between four cardinal virtues: temperance, fortitude, prudence, and justice. (Thomas adds, of course, the three theological virtues—faith, hope, and love—to the list.) Moral liberalism, in contrast, comes to equate morality with a single virtue: justice. Mill explicitly defends this view. In his essay on utilitarianism, he writes this:

> I account the justice which is grounded on utility to be the chief part, and incomparably the most sacred and binding part, of all morality. Justice is a name for certain classes of moral rules, which [are] of more absolute obligation, than any other rules for the guidance of life. . . . The moral rules which forbid mankind to hurt one another (in which we must never forget to include wrongful interference with each other's freedom) are more vital to human well-being than any [other] maxims. . . . Thus the moralities which protect every individual from being harmed by others, either directly or by being hindered in his freedom of

pursuing his own good, are at once those which he himself has most at heart, and those which he has the strongest interest in publishing and enforcing by word and deed . . . Now it is these moralities primarily which compose the obligations of justice.[60]

Mill explicitly identifies morality here with the no-harm principle. What morality is chiefly about is justice and what justice is about, on the liberal view, is not harming other people.

Mill reiterates this point in *On Liberty* when he advises his readers that negative behaviours or character traits that do not obstruct the freedom of others are *not* moral faults. Such 'self-regarding qualities or deficiencies', he writes, '. . . are not properly immoralities, and to whatever pitch they may be carried, do not constitute wickedness. They may be proofs of any amount of folly, or want of personal dignity and self-respect; but they are only a subject of moral reprobation when they involve a breach of duty to others'.[61] Immorality, according to the *liberal* Mill, is a matter of hurting other agents; whatever else you do with your life, however flawed or ill-conceived, is your business.

Moral Liberalism II

Moral liberalism bases moral judgment on the no-harm principle. Different commentators interpret the no-harm principle in different ways, but successive generations of philosophers have come to a consensus that a consistent liberalism must construe the phrase 'do no harm' as a command to leave other people free from unwelcome restriction. To harm other individuals is to force them to do something against their will. **Consent** becomes here the ultimate criterion for morality. If people consent—what they are doing is moral. But if some do not consent—what they are doing is immoral. For moral liberals, uncoerced mutual agreement is, in principle, the basis for moral behaviour.

We have already discussed the problematic issue of consent in our previous discussion of contractarianism. The difference between contractarianism and moral liberalism is that contractarianism traces all morality to a social contract, whereas moral liberalism applies the consent criterion on a case-by-case basis. (Clearly, the two views overlap.) One might think that the case-by-case consent criterion is a good guide to morality as human beings will not consent to immoral treatment. But human beings are fallible. It does not necessarily follow from the fact that a *fallible* human being consents to an arrangement that such an arrangement merits consent. Individuals may agree to all sorts of things that are, in hindsight, unjust, foolish, demeaning, repugnant, or unfair. In responding to such criticism, moral liberals often claim that the proper criterion for moral behaviour is not actual consent, or what is technically called **occurrent consent**, but hypothetical consent.[62] What matters is not so much what this or that individual *actually* agrees to, but what rational agents would hypothetically agree to. (This strategy is again reminiscent of contractarianism.)

There are many problems with moral liberalism as an ethical theory. The first problem is that human beings sometimes do seem to consent to things that many of us see as immoral: prostitution, sadomasochism, spousal abuse, drug addiction, assisted suicide, incest, over-eating, extreme risk-taking, and so on. We may argue that such people are mentally deranged, or depressed, or less intelligent, that these activities are not moral because a rational agent would not consent to them. This is to adopt hypothetical rather than occurrent consent as the base criterion of morality. If, however, this seems a sensible suggestion, it crucially undermines the insight at the very heart of moral liberalism. We are left with a moral theory that imposes certain restrictions (like other moral theories) on acceptable decision-making. The difficulty is in seeing how this reliance on *hypothetical* consent counts as liberalism understood as the theory that favours maximum free choice.

A related problem with moral liberalism is its uninformative approach to moral questions. To say that X is moral because people consent to X tells us little. Surely, the important question is this: Why do they consent? And: should they consent? To tell me that what I consent to is moral does not tell me what I should consent to. Moral liberals emphasize the supposed failure of traditional moral philosophy. We are to rely on consent because this is all we have left. But we cannot determine what a rational human being would agree to without returning to just the kind of investigation authors in the moral philosophy tradition were involved in.

We should add that Mill himself places restrictions on free choice. Like Locke, he argues that it is wrong for people to sell themselves into slavery. Why? 'By selling himself for a slave, [a person] . . . is no longer free.'[63] We can all agree with Mill's conclusion: it is wrong to sell oneself into slavery. Still, Mill believes that the institution of slavery is an intrinsic wrong, even if someone were to agree to it. This is not liberal thinking. In Mill's mind, the *objective* value of liberty clearly overrides the importance of consent. But this is to disapprove of slavery on independent moral grounds even if there is consent. It follows that consent cannot be the sole basis for moral decision-making.

A third problem with moral liberalism is its largely passive approach to moral behaviour. The no-harm principle doesn't tell us to help other people; it only tells us not to interfere with them. This makes for a very weak moral imperative. Authors in the virtue ethics tradition came to see morality as epitomized in selfless generosity. Inside the political realm, such moral aspirations may be excessive. But once we turn liberalism into a moral doctrine, we need something more robust than an aloof doctrine of simple non-interference. We need a morality that pushes us beyond an ideal of mere mutual tolerance, toward an ideal of solidarity, caring, brotherhood, and love. Liberal notions of non-interference fall far short of these aspirations. (Note that Mill himself seems to inconsistently champion two divergent theories. Utilitarianism tells us that we are morally obliged to help other people; that government should be run on the Greatest Happiness Principle. Moral liberalism, in contrast, tells us that we are free to do what we want as long as we don't interfere with other people. Many commentators have tried to reconcile these aspects of Mill's thought.)

A fourth problem that arises with moral liberalism involves self-regarding duties. The no-harm principle sets out our duties to other people—we are not to interfere with their freedom—but what about our duties to ourselves? Consider an epidemic of suicide among young people. One would think that preserving our lives and our health, treating ourselves with dignity, and developing self-esteem are all part of the moral equation. But telling us not to harm others does exclude us from killing ourselves. Moral liberalism considers how you treat yourself a private matter, but this is to overlook a significant aspect of morality. Mill claims that we cannot be held socially accountable for 'what are called duties to ourselves . . . unless circumstances render them at the same time duties to others'.[64] Understood politically and/or legally, this may or may not make sense. Considered from a moral point of view, however, some things are wrong, not merely because they harm others, but because they harm ourselves.

A fifth problem of moral liberalism is the way it misconstrues and exaggerates the specific role of consent in moral decision-making. Clearly, consent is important. At the same time, as we explained in the previous discussion on contractarianism (Chapter 7), not every moral obligation derives from consent. As has already been suggested in the previous section on impersonalism, consent is better construed as an additive factor in moral decision-making. It brings into existence new moral obligations that did not exist until the moment of agreement. For example, if I sign a piece of paper saying that I agree to pay you $500 for your old car, I have, by this act of consent, incurred a moral obligation. I am morally (not just legally) obliged to pay you $500. I did not have this obligation before I signed the piece of paper. Consent narrows down our moral duties to specific responsibilities and agreements. Formal, written contracts have a particularly decisive moral force, but a verbal contract is still a contract.

We will not develop any detailed moral account of contracts or agreements here. Suffice it to say that we have a prima facie obligation to keep our agreements. On the other hand, we cannot simply assume from the mere fact that two parties have agreed to something that the resulting agreement is therefore moral. People are fallible; they make mistakes; they agree to things that, in hindsight, they should not have agreed to. Morality requires that we enter into fair agreements. This is a matter of justice, 'of giving each man his due'. Morality also means, in specific circumstances, respect-

ing someone's freedom not to choose, but we will not explore these issues here.

It goes without saying that moral agreements must exist within the limits of what is morally acceptable. Some things are by their nature immoral and can never be consented to. There may be special circumstances in which we cannot keep agreements we freely enter into. Mill (influenced no doubt by his relationship with Harriet Taylor) fervently argued for a liberalization of divorce laws. He claims, with some heat, 'that [marital] obligations [do not] extend to requiring the fulfillment of the contract at all costs to the happiness of the reluctant party'.[65] Narveson makes the same point in a discussion of contemporary sexual morality: 'Having marriages that are undoable [i.e., dissolvable] at the insistence of both parties,' he claims, 'seems the minimum condition for a reasonable marital institution.'[66] And what if only one person wants the divorce? Narveson asks and speedily answers the question: 'This, too, seems reasonable, for one person surely should not be able to keep another in unhappiness.'[67] Whatever one thinks about this issue, it is odd to hear both Mill and Narveson argue that happiness is more important than consent. This is utilitarian not liberal thinking! Both authors claim that someone can break their agreement to their spouse because they are unhappy. This suggests that, in this situation at least, happiness is more significant than consent. Such inconsistencies suggest that moral liberalism is not a viable moral theory, at least not on its own.

Turning liberalism into a moral theory produces a very impoverished account of morality. Liberalism, understood as a political or legal theory, is a different sort of issue. Suffice it to say that, in a pluralist society, we need to respect and tolerate what we do not agree with. The no-harm principle serves, roughly, as a reminder to keep our noses out of other people's business. It supplies one way of drawing lines between what must be left alone and what can be interfered with. At the same time, there are limits to what we can morally tolerate. Insomuch as morality is at the origins of our ideas about the common good, about human happiness and achievement, it inevitably becomes a matter of public concern. How, then, do we reconcile apparently opposing goals: giving everyone as much freedom of choice as possible while living in a civilized society that nurtures the weak, encourages human achievement, and minimizes evil? Presumably, we need to have some kind of equilibrium that acknowledges, to some predetermined degree, both considerations. This is not an easy thing to do; ideologically, it is simpler and rhetorically more effective to militate for one extreme than to proceed cautiously in a balanced, attentive way on a case-by-case basis.

There is something right about liberalism. Individual liberty is an important ground condition for morality and happiness. We all need room to make important personal decisions according to our own conscience. We can use the no-harm principle as the prima facie rule of thumb. The default position is to let people do as they want, to only intervene in response to some serious issue.

Without inquiring into these political issues any further, we can concede that there are two issues that need to be addressed: what we can call them the freedom issue and the harm issue. We want as much freedom as possible and as little harm as possible. When there is very serious harm, egregious harm, we may have to intervene. (Note that harm is not solely physical.) This is, however, an issue of casuistry and of practical wisdom. There is no overarching, rule-in-the-sky to appeal to here. We have to do our best in light of what we know about morality and human nature at this point in history.

On Mill's Virtue Ethics

We discussed, first, Mill's account of utilitarianism; and second, his account of liberalism. It is hard to fully reconcile these two philosophical viewpoints. But there is a third Mill that is often overlooked in the academic literature. Mill subscribes to the Romantic notion of genius: he proposes a virtue ethics that idealizes the legendary great man who is able to rise above the mediocre masses to fashion for himself a life of original and heroic accomplishment. This was a common theme in the eighteenth and nineteenth centuries.

Heroic Individuality

Kant had earlier formulated a concept of genius to refer to an unteachable mental aptitude that Kant saw expressed in the work of great artists who move beyond the mechanical application of the established rules to produce artworks that are uncannily original. The great Renaissance sculptor Michelangelo— referred to as 'the divine Michelangelo' during his own lifetime—would be a good example of the artistic figure Kant had in mind. This archetype of the eccentric but brainy genius takes a darker turn in literary figures, such as Milton's Lucifer, Goethe's Faust, Mozart's Don Giovanni, Lord Byron's collection of 'Byronic heros', and, in a more philosophical vein, in Nietzsche's overman (the *ubermensch*). Mill tones down some of the more disturbing and nihilistic aspects of this literary type, proposing genius-like individuality as an ideal of character development. Although he displays only passing knowledge of the earlier virtue ethics, Mill reaffirms, in a provocative way, the importance of virtue to morality.

Mill entitles the third chapter of his political treatise *On Liberty*: 'Of Individuality, As One of the Elements of Well-Being'. A treatise within a treatise, the chapter proposes an account of virtue ethics that is difficult to reconcile with both Mill's utilitarianism and his liberalism. Mill begins by quoting leading German intellectual Wilhelm von Humboldt (1767–1835) to the effect that each human being must strive, first and foremost, toward 'the highest and most harmonious development of his powers', and that the goal 'towards which every human being must ceaselessly direct his efforts . . . [is] individuality of power and development.' Each individual agent needs, however, 'freedom, and a variety of situations', to achieve, 'individual vigor and manifold diversity' and ultimately, 'originality'.[68] This short passage already contains, in embryonic form, a basic theory of character development.

To begin with, note the supreme importance Mill attaches to ideas of self-actualization and individual self-expression. He observes, 'Among the works of man, which human life is rightly employed in perfecting and beautifying, the first in importance surely is man himself'.[69] Mill claims that each human individual should 'become a noble and beautiful object of contemplation'[70] and that 'it really is of importance, not only what men do, but also what manner of men they are that do it'.[71] Although these sentiments are reminiscent of earlier philosophers in the moral tradition, Mill seems to situate virtue and personal achievement in a realm of human endeavour that is somehow outside of morality. At the same time, he writes with an urgency and conviction that is the hallmark of moral expression. He does not refrain from using a language of

wide normative reach and ultimate obligation. In effect, he treats the pursuit of virtue both as if it was and was not a major component of morality.

If the utilitarian Mill focuses on pleasure and the liberal Mill focuses on freedom, the romantic Mill concedes that human achievement is, first and foremost, a matter of successful character development which Mill associates with genius. He does not mince his words: 'I insist thus emphatically on the importance of genius', he writes, 'and [on] the necessity of allowing it to unfold itself freely both in thought and in practice'.[72] Mill complains that although people pay lip service to the idea of genius, 'almost every one, in reality, is totally indifferent to it'.[73] They view it, in purely instrumental terms, as a means to art: 'People think genius a fine thing if it enables a man to write an exciting poem, or paint a picture. But in its true sense, that of originality in thought and action, . . . nearly all, at heart, think they can do very well without it.'[74]

Mill is not denigrating artistic creation. He believes that we are all in need of a sentimental education through art and poetry. But he is more interested here in elaborating a general theory of virtue or human excellence. Mill maintains, 'Human nature is not a machine to be built after a model, and set to do exactly the work prescribed for it, but a tree, which requires to grow and develop itself on all sides, according to the tendency of the inward forces which make it a living thing'.[75] Artistic genius provides an illustrious example of what we should all be striving toward, the actualization of those 'inward forces' that make us uniquely what we are.

Mill sounds rather like Aristotle. What matters is not restraint but self-realization and the development of human potential.

The problem, in Mill's words, is that 'the men and women who at present inhabit the more civilized parts of the world . . . are but starved specimens of what nature can and will produce'.[76] Mill castigates the Calvinists (and Kant), who insist on believing that 'human nature being radically corrupt, there is no redemption for any one until human nature is killed within him'.[77] Mill argues, in contrast, that human nature is fundamentally good and needs to be developed by rigorous exertion. In a broad reference to Greek philosophy, he makes an urgent appeal to the virtue ethics tradition:

> There is a different type of human excellence from the Calvinistic [one], a conception of humanity as having its nature bestowed on it for other purposes than merely to be abnegated. 'Pagan self-assertion' is one of the elements of human worth, as well as 'Christian self-denial'. There is a Greek ideal of self-development, which the Platonic and Christian ideal of self-government blends with but does not supercede. It may be better to be a John Knox [the Protestant reformer] than an Alcibiades [Socrates's student, who became a traitor to Athens], but it is better to be a Pericles [the Athenian statesman] than either; nor would a Pericles, if we had one in these days, be without anything good which belonged to John Knox.[78]

Mill does not dismiss the importance of Christianity. He contends, rather, that the correct interpretation of Christianity supports his own account. If many Christian enthusiasts champion self-discipline against human nature, Mill makes a sensible theological argument that a good God must welcome human achievement:

> If it be any part of religion to believe that man was made by a good Being, it is more consistent with that faith to believe, that this Being gave all

human faculties that they might be cultivated and unfolded, . . . and that He takes delight in every nearer approach made by his creatures to the ideal conception embodied in them, [and in] every increase in any of their capabilities of comprehension, of action, or of enjoyment.[79]

Self-realization is, then, for Mill, a religious as well as a secular value.

Mill argues against any kind of enforced conformity, proposing an ideal of human achievement that celebrates robust individuality. 'Persons of genius,' he notes, 'are . . . more individual than any other people'.[80] As he points out, 'No one's idea of excellence in conduct is that people should do absolutely nothing but copy one another'.[81] Mill believes that a good society made up of healthy individuals will leave plenty of space for eccentricity and odd behaviour. 'That so few now dare to be eccentric,' he opines, 'marks the chief danger of the time'.[82] Why? Because eccentricity is a sign of genius and character. 'Eccentricity has always abounded, when and where strength of character has abounded,' Mill reports, 'and the amount of eccentricity in a society has generally been proportional to the amount of genius, mental vigor, and moral courage which it contained.'[83]

Mill enlists these ideas in support of his argument for liberalism. Human beings need a large amount of individual freedom to be able to cultivate, on their terms, their own special talents and personalities. This is why enforced conformity on unconventional or nonconformist members of society is so troubling. Because this 'tyranny of the majority' extinguishes the possibility for virtue: 'It is only the cultivation of individuality which produces, or can produce, well-developed human beings.'[84]

Mill, much like Hobbes and Kant—and in a milder way than Nietzsche and his followers

—views strength of character as the essential ingredient in human development. Mill insists that 'desires and impulses are as much a part of a perfect human being, as beliefs and restraints',[85] and that 'strong impulses are only perilous when not properly balanced'.[86] Noteworthy human beings must possess 'great energies guided by vigorous reason, and strong feelings strongly controlled by a conscientious will'.[87] Mill continues:

> Strong impulses are but another name for energy. Energy may be turned to bad uses; but more good may always be made of an energetic nature, than of an indolent and impassive one. . . . The same strong susceptibilities which make the personal impulses vivid and powerful, are also the source from whence are generated the most passionate love of virtue, and the sternest self-control. . . . A person whose desires and impulses are his own . . . is said to have a character. One whose desires and impulses are not his own, has no character, no more than a steam-engine has a character. If, in addition to being his own, his impulses are strong, and are under the government of a strong will, he has an energetic character.[88]

To have an 'energetic character' used in the right way is, in Mill's mind, to achieve supreme human excellence, i.e., it is to possess what the tradition means by virtue.

Mill is careful to point out that, despite his belief in the importance of robust individuality, he is 'not countenancing the sort of "hero-worship" which applauds the strong man of genius for forcibly seizing on the government of the world'.[89] Still, a critic could complain that there is something here akin to hero-worship in the way that Mill lionizes the nonconformist figure of the powerful man, who, with original ideas, huge appetites, powerful feelings, and an iron will, reshapes the world for the better. Mill comments, 'If [men of genius] are of a

strong character, and break their fetters, they become a mark for the society which has not succeeded in reducing them to common-place. [The rest of us] point at [them] with solemn warning as "wild", "erratic", and the like; much as if one should complain of the Niagara river for not flowing smoothly between its banks like a Dutch canal'.[90] This is eerily similar to Nietzsche and some of the ancient Greek Sophists.

Mill's Utilitarianism, Liberalism, and Virtue Ethics: Consistencies and Inconsistencies

Mill is obviously a complex figure, someone who conspicuously embodies the contradictions inherent in our present ways of thinking. There is no fully satisfactory way to reconcile the different elements of his philosophy. Utilitarianism, liberalism, and virtue ethics make for an explosive marriage. Let us consider, briefly, the connection between Mill's virtue ethics and his political and moral views.

Mill's argument in favour of a Romantic notion of heroic individual virtue may seem like a watertight argument in favour of the liberal no-harm principle. Mill proposes two requirements for the fostering of virtue: (1) freedom of choice, and (2) variety of situations. In his account, strength of character can be learned only through the exercise of free choice in diverse circumstances. When we give individuals a large sphere of individual freedom, we give them the opportunity to develop their moral muscles and thus aid them in their personal development. Mill writes,

> The human faculties of perception, judgment, discriminative feeling, mental activity, and even moral preference, are exercised only in making a choice. . . . The mental and moral, like the muscular powers, are improved only by being used.

. . . He who lets the world, or his own portion of it, choose his plan of life for him, has no need of any other faculty than the ape-like one of imitation. He who chooses his plan for himself, employs all his faculties. He must use observation to see, reasoning and judgment to foresee, activity to gather materials for decision, discrimination to decide, and when he has decided, firmness and self-control to hold to his deliberate decision.[91]

We might, then, try to reconcile Mill's utilitarianism, his liberalism, and his romantic ideal of heroic individual virtue in the following way. The liberal no-harm principle, in preserving individual freedom, allows agents to develop their own individual capacities through practice and experience and thus become more virtuous human beings. Presumably, virtuous individuals will make felicitous moral choices that benefit themselves and therefore society as a whole. In this way the utilitarian goal of greater overall happiness can be reached. It seems then, that all three theories can work together, complementing one another to produce virtue, happiness, and freedom all at the same time. Except that this imagined scenario seems a very hopeful caricature of what happens in real life. Liberals, traditionally, had a very optimistic view of human nature; conservatives, in contrast, had a much more pessimistic view. Who is right? These deep views will influence our political and moral opinions. Realism demands that we leave at least some room for human error and even turpitude.

Does it really follow that placing people in diverse situations and allowing them the freedom to do as they will is enough for virtue? This is, in Hobbes's account, what produces the most brutally imaginable state of nature! As authors in the moral tradition argue, virtue is a product of a good upbringing, of habit, of knowledge, of willpower, and of good intentions. It seems naive to suggest that leaving people to their own devices in a complicated world full of alluring temptation will automatically produce the most virtuous results. As we have pointed out throughout this text, people do in fact do stupid, unsafe, self-destructive, angry, and shameful things, things they will later regret. Should we stop them? If everyone always made the right decisions, liberal freedom and utilitarian happiness would inevitably coincide. It is abundantly clear, however, that this is not always the case. What if I am about to make a bad decision? Should the rest of you restrain me? This is a very difficult question.

Some liberal authors (like Mill himself) argue that we should be free to criticize people who make immoral decisions but we should not be able to intervene. But mere criticism may be a woefully ineffectual way of changing behaviour. An ancient author such as Aristotle argues explicitly and forcefully that we need to use laws and sanctions to force people to be moral. This may seem like an outmoded way of thinking, but similar concerns (in a watered-down form) surface in modern discussions. Let us consider some contemporary issues.

We can ask some pertinent questions: Should the mentally ill be *forced* to take their meds? Should people on welfare be *forced* to work? Should pedophiles be *forced* into rehab? Should recreational drug users be *forced* off drugs. And so on. All these practices could perhaps be justified using a utilitarian calculus. But they run directly counter to the liberal emphasis on allowing people to do as they want. And how do we inculcate virtue?

Ancient philosophers, such as Plato and Aristotle—obviously not liberals in the modern sense—wanted a society that would produce virtue. But they enthusiastically embraced coercion, authoritarian political structures, strict laws, and generous punishments as means for teaching the recalcitrant human animal. Mill asks a rhetorical question: 'What more or better can be said of any condition of human affairs, than that it brings human beings themselves nearer to the best thing they can be? Or what worse can be said of any obstruction to good, than that it prevents this?'[92] In more modern language, what situation could be better than one that promotes virtue? Or what situation could be worse than one that prevents virtue? Mill is surely correct: abject authoritarianism drains away the individual initiative that is necessary for the widespread development of robust virtue. But a lack of moral guidance that comes from shared community values is also a problem. Herein lies the dilemma.

Communitarianism as a Response to Mill

Contemporary criticisms of Mill's liberalism are, broadly speaking, **communitarian** in scope. Modern-day communitarians argue that individuals can only be properly understood in terms of their relationships to other people. What makes life worth living is not bare freedom but a sense of belonging and loyalty to others. It is not enough to refrain from harming other people; we need to identify with our neighbours and actively help them. This often politicized debate has important moral implications. The disagreement is not just about government policy. It is about the key values that should direct our personal lives, about moral education, and, ultimately, about the meaning of virtue.

The communitarian label has been pejoratively used as a catch-all term to refer to political systems (like communism) that value the collectivity at the expense of legitimate expressions of individual freedom. There is some truth to this kind of criticism when it is directed against historical authors such as Jean-Jacques Rousseau (1712–78), Georg Wilhelm Hegel (1770–1831), and Karl Marx (1818–83), who—sometimes to an alarming degree—subjugate the individual to the interests of the wider community. It does not follow, on the other hand, that there is nothing of worth in their writing. And there are moderate communitarians.

Leading contemporary communitarian Amitai Etzioni criticizes an exaggerated liberalism that uncritically denounces the combined forces of tradition, religion, law, custom, public opinion, and conventional morality, viewing them, without sensitivity, as so many fetters on individual liberty. This is surely a one-sided view of how human nature operates. Someone who breaks with their childhood religion makes a choice, but someone who conscientiously decides to adhere to their childhood religion is also making a choice. It is uncharitable and one-sided to suggest that everyone who follows tradition, custom, authority, religion, and so on, does so in a robot-like fashion without thinking about what they are doing. Freedom means assenting to and acting upon those principles that we come to cherish. A doctrinaire decision to 'reject all tradition' would be as much an obstacle to self-fulfillment as a doctrinaire decision to 'always submit to tradition'. Critical individuals cannot unthinkingly subscribe to either principle. Communitarians, for their part, argue that liberal society, in rejecting tradition and social authority, is moving toward what the sociologist Emile Durkheim (1858–1917) called **anomie**, a condition of normlessness, an absence of meaningful standards that drains life of significance and leads, in extreme cases, to suicide. Human beings need values, limits, and shared markers to guide them through the dark night.

Etzioni explains the historical roots of a modern alienation of the individual from the larger community in terms of relentless attack on a medieval authoritarianism. He suggests that it is a case of the pendulum swinging too far in the opposite direction. Yes, medieval societies and values were too restrictive, but the resulting reaction against these antiquated power structures has been so successful as to undermine even legitimate authority. Etzioni explains, 'After the forces of modernity rolled back the forces of [an unnecessarily restrictive] traditionalism, . . . they pushed ahead relentlessly, eroding the much weakened foundations of social virtue and order while seeking to expand liberty ever more. As a result, . . . [Western] societies . . . are [at present] heavily burdened with the anti-social consequences of *excessive* liberty'.[93] Etzioni argues for a re-evaluation of contemporary liberalism, pushing for 'a carefully crafted equilibrium' between social order and individual autonomy.[94] As he sees it, people need large amounts of individual freedom, but they also need some robust sense of shared morality to give meaning and structure to their lives.

As this is not a textbook in political philosophy, we will not discuss a host of attendant political issues here. When it comes to morality, however, two points are in order. First, communitarians argue that liberalism itself is not morally neutral. It encourages certain values and discourages others. For example, it proposes a negative conception of freedom; it pushes virtues like tolerance; it champions diversity; it penalizes discrimination; and so on. These may all be positive results, but they are not morally neutral.

Second, communitarians argue that politics itself is inherently moral. We cannot have a good society without morally good people to run it, and we cannot have good moral people unless society, as a group, *encourages* morality. This is what is missing, communitarians allege, from the standard liberal account. It is not enough to leave people, without morality, to do whatever pleases them. A society that does not provide moral education, however rudimentary, is not a good society. This means, however, that a good society cannot be morally indifferent.

Contemporary liberalism proposes a morally neutral state. As Ronald Dworkin reports, the 'constitutive morality' at the heart of liberalism 'requires official neutrality amongst theories of what is valuable in life'.[95] It follows that society as a whole should not support any moral view. It should treat all moral alternatives equally, brokering a kind of public ceasefire between warring ideologies and belief systems within a pluralist society. Communitarians oppose this ideal of a morally-neutral state. As this is an ongoing debate, we will leave it for readers to further sort through these opinions on their own.

As this is a textbook on the long history of moral philosophy, it seems instructive to end this discussion of the liberal–communitarian debate with something of a warning. Communitarians and liberals spar over the concept of individuality. It has become something of a commonplace to speak as if a distinctive concept of human individuality is a modern invention, a product of the Enlightenment and the Protestant Reformation. The contemporary debate over the relationship between the individual and society seems to take it for granted that historical authors have little to contribute. The ancients and medievals, they allege,

---

✎ Applied Philosophy Box 9.6 ✎

Denver Library Secure for Kid Porn

Felisa Cardona

Investigators routinely use the Internet to capture sex offenders, but there's still a place where online traffickers of child pornography can escape the arm of law enforcement: the public library. Library computers have been used in Colorado and elsewhere as a distribution point for child pornography. Law enforcement officials believe that's partly because the users know the machines will be flushed clean by library officials as part of their security and privacy measures, making it impossible to track who is sending child pornography. . . . Colorado Springs police Detective Clayton Blackwell of Colorado's Internet Crimes Against Children Task Force . . . says detectives nationwide are frustrated by child pornography traders who use libraries, and he doesn't see an end to the problem given the concern about privacy.

'The only solution is legislative intervention requiring the (libraries) to keep logs,' Blackwell said. 'Where do we draw the line in protecting civil liberties and protecting children? Children should come first.'

Librarians say they are also sickened by child pornography but are concerned about maintaining privacy and freedom. . . . In Colorado, it's illegal for a public library to disclose information that identifies a person who has requested, used or obtained specific materials from the library. . . . Internet users often expect privacy at the library as they conduct banking online, order products with a credit card, learn about an unpopular religious or political belief, or look up information on a private medical condition.

'Our mission is to provide access to information, and we want people to feel comfortable to pursue intellectual interests whether they are popular or not,' (librarian) Garnar said.

Since 2002, there have been 17 child-pornography-trading cases with roots in Denver Public Library branches.

This might be a case that pits liberals against communitarians. Explain what might be their respective positions on this issue. What do you think? Is it privacy rights or the concerns about law enforcement that should prevail? Should government be morally neutral?

Source: Felisa Cardona, 'Library Secure for Kid Porn.' *Denver Post*, www.denverpost.com/ci_7494175, 18 November 2007.

---

had no sense of the importance of individual personality. However, this is, like many beliefs about historical authors that have gained popular credence, a misleading stereotype. Even the ancients had a strong concept of individual agency and heroic personality despite the emphasis they placed on social responsibility. To cite only one brief example, Marcus Tullius Cicero (106–43 BC), the Roman statesman and Stoic thinker, in a book dedicated to

his son, writes about how to choose a future career, indicating that we need to find something that suits our own unique talents and temperaments. He advises:

Nature has endowed us with [a specialized role] which is assigned uniquely to each individual, for just as there are great variations in physical attributes, . . . so our [individual] mental makeup likewise displays variations greater still. We should each of us stick close to the characteristics peculiar to us as long as they are not flawed . . . We must follow . . . our natural bent [and] the criterion of our own nature. It is pointless to go to war with nature. . . . We must therefore work hardest at the things for which we are best suited. . . . [We must] search for what is fitting by reference to our native endowments . . . In ordering our whole life, the greatest part of our concern must be directed at being able to be true to ourselves as long as we live.[96]

Much more could be said. Clearly, thinkers from other historical periods believed in individuality and in choice, even if they did view unswerving loyalty to the sate as a major aspect of citizenship. Individual choice has always played a role in moral philosophy.

On the Subjection of Women: Mary Wollstonecraft

We cannot finish this chapter on Mill without some comment on one final aspect of Mill's philosophical and moral platform, his arguments against the unequal treatment of women, a theme that has, of course, been expanded on by contemporary feminist authors. *The Subjection of Women*, Mill's aptly titled work on the issue, was written about the time of the publication of 'Utilitarianism' and published toward the end of the author's life (1869).[97] We cannot engage the details of the work here, but it is interesting to situate the underlying arguments in relation to Mill's larger world view.

Mill begins his text with an unequivocal affirmation:

The object of this Essay is to explain as clearly as I am able the grounds of an opinion which I have held from the very earliest period when I had formed any opinions at all on social political matters, . . . that the principle which regulates the existing social relations between the two sexes—the legal subordination of one sex to the other—is wrong itself, and now one of the chief hindrances to human improvement; and that it ought to be replaced by a principle of perfect equality, admitting no power or privilege on the one side, nor disability on the other.[98]

Mill's argument, which is largely political and legal, rests on a utilitarian basis. It will be better for everyone involved if women are given, as is their right as equal human beings, the freedom to make similar choices as men. As we shall see, however, Mill also integrates his account of sexual equality into his account of virtue ethics.

Mill was not, of course, the first modern author to argue for women's rights.[99] Mary Wollstonecraft (1759–97), in her well-known text *A Vindication of the Rights of Woman* (1792) makes arguments that closely foreshadow Mill. Wollstonecraft is particularly incensed at the way in which young women are educated in modern society. She takes conscious aim at the influential educational theories of Jean-Jacques Rousseau, claiming that women are encouraged to turn themselves into frivolous objects of romantic and sexual dalliance on the exclusive hunt for husbands as a means to fulfillment and financial security. She alleges that 'Rousseau declares that a woman should never, for a moment feel herself independent, that she should be governed by fear to exercise her *natural* cunning, and made a coquetish slave in order to render her a more alluring object of desire, a *sweeter* companion to man, whenever he chooses to relax himself'.[100]

Wollstonecraft's complaint is not simply that women are placed in a subordinate position with respect to men. She explains,

The most perfect education, in my opinion, is such an exercise of the understanding as is best calculated to strengthen the body and form the heart. Or, in other words, to enable the individual to attain such habits of virtue as will render it independent. In fact, it is a farce to call any being virtuous whose virtues do not result from the exercise of its own reason. This was Rousseau's opinion respecting men: I extend it to women.[101]

The problem, then, according to Wollstonecraft, is that young women, in being made into 'play-things' and 'slaves' for men, are robbed of the opportunity for moral self-realization.

Wollstonecraft compares modern women to birds in a gilded cage: 'Confined then in cages like the feathered race, they have nothing to do but plume themselves, and stock with mock majesty from perch to perch. It is true they are provided with food and raiment, for which neither toil or spin, but health, liberty, and virtue are given [away] in exchange.'[102] To bring her argument up-to-date: an education in designer clothes, cosmetics, and promiscuity is an obstacle that gets in the way of true achievement and human excellence.

Wollstonecraft roundly claims, in Aristotelian-sounding terms, that 'the grand end of [women's] exertions should be to unfold their own faculties, and acquire the dignity of conscious virtue'.[103] She forces the issue, setting out the dilemma in a simple disjunction (an either-or statement): 'Women are, therefore, to be considered either as moral beings, or so weak that they must be entirely subjected to the superior.'[104] But clearly, women are moral beings; they are capable of independence and are able decide for themselves; therefore, she concludes, they need and deserve a serious, substantial, moral education. Even 'if women [were] by nature inferior to men', she argues, 'their virtues must be the same in quality . . . consequently, their conduct should be founded on the same principles, and have the same aim'.[105] Wollstonecraft believes that men who

are sufficiently enlightened will agree with her observations. The proper cultivation of women as intellectual and moral beings will give them the benefit of friendship with an equal.

Wollstonecraft's personal life gave way to a complicated social scandal that tarnished her reputation among succeeding generations, but the basic structure of her arguments for a kind of quasi-feminism is repeated in Mill. Mill actively promotes female voting rights: 'Under whatever conditions, and within whatever limits, men are admitted to the suffrage, there is not a shadow of justification for not admitting women under the same.'[106] He also argues against traditional marriage, equating it with slavery: 'There remain no legal slaves, save the mistress of every house.'[107] He clamours against unexamined prejudice, for gender equality, for social progress, and so on. But he also insists, in line with Wollstonecraft, that women have the ability and the right to devote themselves to self-chosen pursuits of virtuous self-realization.

Toward the end of *The Subjection of Women*, Mill observes this:

> Thus far, the benefits which it has appeared that the world would gain by ceasing to make sex a disqualification for privileges and a badge of subjection, are social rather than individual. . . . But it would be a grievous understatement of the case to omit the most direct benefit of all, the unspeakable gain in private happiness to the liberated half of the species; the difference to them between a life of subjection to the will of others, and a life of rational freedom.[108]

What Mill means by a **life of rational freedom** is a life that permits the development of individual projects and personal talents without unnecessary interference. Mill believes that men will be better served by this new gender-equal arrangement. He predicts that women, once freed from the yoke of social expectation, will be able to aspire, as equal partners with men, toward the ideal of energetic individuality that he associates with virtue.

Mill continues with a resounding *plaidoyer* (or plea) in favour of the equality of women. Women deserve to be set free and treated as equals, he declares, because they are equally capable of the highest levels of virtue. As he assures the reader,

> Whatever has been said or written, from the time of Herodotus [the ancient Greek historian] to the present, of the ennobling influence of free government—the nerve and spring which it gives to all the faculties, the larger and higher objects which it presents to the intellect and feelings, the more unselfish public spirit, and calmer and broader views of duty, that it engenders, and the generally loftier platform on which it elevates the individual as a moral, spiritual, and social being—is every particle as true of women as of men.[109]

In his argument for equality between the sexes, Mill brings together elements of utilitarianism, liberalism, and virtue ethics. Freedom from subjection will, he believes, make women (and men) happier—so the utilitarian criterion for morality will be satisfied. Women (and men) will also be better able to do what they want—so the liberal criterion of justice will be satisfied. And women (and men) will be able to achieve virtue together—so the virtue ethics criterion of individual self-realization will be achieved. Again, this is a hopeful but not an uncontroversial picture. It raises a series of questions: Should a recalcitrant man (or a recalcitrant society) be *forced* to treat women equally? Are gender roles exactly the same or different? Should cultural and religious identities be allowed to structure or restrict male–female relationships? And so on.

Clearly, the individual striving after human excellence that authors in the moral tradition call 'virtue' is a pursuit that is open to both men and women. Mill deserves credit for emphasizing this fact. He focuses here on an important moral issue that had been overshadowed (though not entirely ignored) in past philosophy. This is a good example of the way in which Mill's sometimes conflicting moral ideas prefigured contemporary views.

✍ Questions for Study and Review ✍

1. What was Bentham's Panopticon?
2. Explain the origin of the term *utilitarianism*. What do utilitarians mean by 'utility'?
3. What does the Greatest Happiness Principle (the utility principle) tell us to do?
4. In what sense is utilitarianism a universalistic hedonism?
5. What is a hedonimeter? A 'utile'? What is the measurement problem that plagues utilitarianism?

6. Explain how Mill reforms Bentham's utilitarianism, adding to his quantitative measure of pleasure.
7. According to Mill, how can we distinguish between better and worse pleasures?
8. Critics of utilitarianism argue that different pleasures are qualitatively incommensurable. Explain. How does this undermine the original utilitarian project?

9. Describe the situation described by Godwin in his example known as the Famous Fire Cause. What was Godwin's recommendation? Do you agree? Why or why not?

10. Define *impersonalism* and *personalism*. Compare and contrast with an example.

11. The virtue ethics tradition grows out of a kind of personalism. Explain the relation between personalism and casuistry.

12. Was Jesus an impersonalist? One could answer both yes and no. Explain.

13. Are we responsible for the consequences of our acts? To what degree? What do you think? Explain and defend your point of view.

14. Explain the 'great evil strategy'. Use an example.

15. Utilitarians claim to be egalitarian. But strict utilitarianism does not guarantee equal treatment of individual people. Explain.

16. Apply harm reduction to a social problem, such as prostitution or teenage pregnancies. Would you agree with this strategy for dealing with this issue? Why or why not?

17. How do moral interpretations of the no-harm principle clash with the virtue ethics view of generosity?

18. How does Mill reconcile utilitarianism, liberalism, and virtue ethics? Is he successful? Critique his account. Use examples.

19. What is 'anomie'? Relate to debates about individual liberty as the main ingredient of virtue.

20. Relate Wollstonecraft's account of virtue to Mill's account of virtue.

✦ Suggestions for Further Reading ✦

- For an online electronic version of Bentham see: Jeremy Bentham, *An Introduction to the Principles of Morals and Legislation*, 1781 reprint edition (Kitchener: Batoche Books, 2000) at www.efm.bris.ac.uk/het/bentham/morals.pdf. There are many electronic and print editions available.

- John Stuart Mill, *Collected Works of John Stuart Mill*, J.M. Robinson, ed. (Toronto: University of Toronto Press, 1863f).

- For one web resource see: John Stuart Mill, *On Liberty* (London: Longman, Roberts & Green, 1869) elecronic reprint at Bartleby.com (1999): www.bartleby.com.

- John Stuart Mill, *On Liberty and Other Essays* (includes *On Liberty*, *Utilitarianism*, *Considerations of Representative Government*, *The Subjection of Women*) John Gray, ed. (Oxford, UK: Oxford, 1998).

- Mary Wollstonecraft, *A Vindication of the Rights of Men, A Vindication of the Rights of Women, An Historical and Moral View of the French Revolution*, Janet Todd, ed. (Oxford, UK: Oxford, 1999).

- For a very complete set of online texts for both authors see: The Online Library of Liberty, http://oll.libertyfund.org. This site also contains many other primary texts, particularly of a political nature.

- 'Utilitarianism Resources' provides an extensive and up-to-date online set of texts on utilitarianism: www.utilitarianism.com/.

Chapter Ten

Contemporary Moral Theory

∾ Chapter Objectives

After reading this chapter you should be able to:

- Describe and evaluate the basic thrust of four related theories: anti-theory, Kierkegaard's subjectivism, personalism, and Noddings's feminist ethics of care.
- Analyze and critique the moral role of rights-language in the contemporary world as well as specifying the five different justifications for punishment.
- Describe the ecumenical method of 'global ethics' and the arguments for and against divine command morality.
- Take a reasonable, historically informed, philosophically sophisticated stand on environmental ethics.
- Describe and critique contemporary contractarianism as represented by Rawls's theory of distributive justice and in the prisoners' dilemma situation.

In this final section, we will consider the present state of moral philosophy. We must accept from the outset that we live in **pluralistic** times and that there is no way to introduce competing philosophical viewpoints that will satisfy everyone. We will consider, then, nine influential ethical ideas that have sparked considerable interest both inside and outside the academy: (1) anti-theory, (2) Kierkegaard's transcendental subjectivism, (3) personalism, (4) a feminist ethics of care, (5) moral or human rights and related theories of punishment, (6) divine command theory, (7) ecumenical global ethics, (8) environmental ethics, and (9) contemporary contractarianism.

Anti-Theory: A Paradigm Shift in Ethics

The term *anti-theory* is used to describe a wide movement among contemporary academic philosophers who take issue with mainstream moral theory as it has been practised over the past three centuries at universities and in philosophical circles. Such diverse authors as Elizabeth Anscombe, Philippa Foot, Alasdair MacIntyre, Richard Rorty, Stuart Hampshire, Michael Stocker, Martha Nussbaum, Charles Taylor, Annette Baier, Bernard Williams, John McDowell, and Stephen Toulmin (along with many others) argue that modern theoretical attempts to fit ethics into a rigid straitjacket of unbending universal laws are misdirected in that they overlook the complexity of practical life, the limitless diversity in individual circumstances, and the importance of casuistry. As one text explains:

> The 'theory' that this movement opposes is modern moral theory, which takes . . . as its central task constructing and justifying a set of abstract universal moral rules and principles to guide and evaluate the moral behaviour of all rational beings. These principles are completely context-free and can be applied in an almost computational way to any particular case. Correct moral judgments and practices seem to be deducible from these timeless principles, and all moral values are commensurable with respect to a single standard. Any moral conflict can be solved in a rational way. The anti-theory movement claims that moral theory of this sort is unnecessary, narrow, and impossible, for it cannot specify moral norms embedded in cultural and historical traditions, it cannot account for virtue that is culturally informed and it is incompatible with the fact that there are irresolvable moral conflicts and dilemmas. In contrast, this movement suggests that ethics should return to Aristotelian

virtue ethics, claims the primacy of social moral practice over rational principles and the primacy of ethical perception over rules, and emphasizes the plurality of social conventions and customs.[1]

In the modern world, much mainstream moral philosophy has proceeded as though there are only two viable theoretical alternatives: **deontology**, which is associated with Kant; and consequentialism, which is associated with utilitarianism. (**Liberalism** has complicated the picture somewhat, but liberals themselves generally argue on deontological or consequential grounds.) Most mainstream moral philosophers have positioned themselves for Kant against utilitarianism or for utilitarianism against Kant. Anti-theorists dispute this way of setting out the problem, rejecting both modern alternatives as impoverished and ultimately flawed.

Anti-theorists raise five important objections to the deontology/utilitarianism account, objections that overlap with one another. Different authors make these points in various ways, some more felicitously than others. To begin with, anti-theorists argue that the complexity of real-world circumstances makes the straightforward, 'computational' application of moral rules—such as Kant's categorical imperative or the utilitarian rule about the greatest possible happiness—an impossible task. In response to the modern idea that one can produce laws that can be applied to every conceivable situation without any further thought, anti-theorists argue, in line with most of the historical authors presented in this text, that moral principles need to be adapted to particular circumstances through the practice of casuistry, i.e., through an individualized attention to specific cases. It is not enough to mechanically apply rules to the endlessly complex circumstances

◈ Applied Philosophy Box 10.1 ◈

Anti-Theory and the Uncodifiability of Ethics

In the first book of the *Nicomachean Ethics*, Aristotle warns us that the study of ethics is imprecise. Virtue ethicists have challenged consequentialist and deontological theories because they fail to accommodate this insight. Both deontological and consequentialist type of theories rely on one rule or principle that is expected to apply to all situations. Because their principles are inflexible, they cannot accommodate the complexity of all the moral situations that we are likely to encounter. . . . At best, for virtue ethics, there can be rules of thumb—rules that are true for the most part, but may not always be the appropriate response. . . . The idea that ethics cannot be captured in one rule or principle is the 'uncodifiability of ethics thesis'. Ethics is too diverse and imprecise to be captured in a rigid code, so we must approach morality with a theory that is as flexible and as situation-responsive as the subject matter itself. As a result some virtue ethicists see themselves as anti-theorists, rejecting theories that systematically attempt to capture and organize all matters of practical or ethical importance.

A contemporary scholar explaining the overlap between so-called 'anti-theory' and virtue ethics.

Source: Nafsika Athanassoulis, 'Virtue Ethics.' *Internet Encyclopedia of Philosophy*, www.iep.utm.edu/virtue/#SH2c, 28 August 2004.

of human life. We need to develop moral judgment, a capacity for intelligent discernment, if we are to successfully navigate the vicissitudes of moral life. Some of these authors also argue that there are real **moral dilemmas**, situations that are so problematic, it is very hard or even impossible (at least at the present time) to understand what the appropriate or best moral response is.

Anti-theorists object, secondly, to the deontology-utilitarianism account, because (they allege) it provides an inadequate explanation of the psychological aspects of morality. Both schools view morality as a matter of bloodless willpower, of forcing oneself to do what is logically required. Adumbrating abstract, theoretical reasons for morality is, however, hardly convincing. We also need an emotional or psychological push in the right direction. Anti-theorists point out that we need to supplement moral law treatments of

morality with some positive account of the emotional side of moral behaviour.

Anti-theorists object, thirdly, to the impersonal, anonymous nature of both deontology and consequentialism. They generally insist on a more personal approach to moral questions; they favour a philosophical method that addresses its arguments not to neutral, amoral agents who exist outside of any particular context but to situated agents who find themselves in concrete situations replete with historical, cultural, religious, and personal complications. They argue that ethics is not a matter of producing a formula that applies across the board but of meeting people where they are and of helping them work through the specific circumstances and personal loyalties that make them who they are individually.

Fourth, anti-theorists claim that moral individuals must be viewed in light of their relationship to larger communities and that this identification plays an important role in moral decision-making. They sometimes attack Enlightenment systems as overly Western and insensitive to cultural and historical context. Some of these authors do maintain that morality is objective; others seem to adopt a social relativism. Suffice it to say that one can acknowledge the pivotal role that ethnic, religious, and political allegiances can play in morality without abandoning an ideal of moral objectivity. Alasdair MacIntyre, in particular, sees morality as a cumulative development of a tradition, dependent on a historical process that progresses forward, building on previous insights and on the moral insights of former community members. Seen from this perspective, the generalized Enlightenment rejection of what went before is little less than moral forgetfulness.

Finally, anti-theorists contest the overly linguistic, theoretical preoccupations of modern moral philosophers and their somewhat skeptical focus on questions of moral epistemology. They generally believe that day-to-day experience demonstrates that we are moral beings and that there is no need to prove this is the case. These authors also tend to emphasize the practical, applied character of ethics. What matters is not the creation of a grandiose system so much as the solution of particular moral problems.

We have already discussed all these issues in this text. Indeed, the basic approach taken here could be described as anti-theory. Sadly some anti-theorists, despite good intentions, provide anachronistic and misleading interpretations of earlier authors. Others, while correctly objecting to the narrowness of moral law approaches, seem all to ready to jump to the conclusion that there is no place in ethics for moral law. This is, in turn, an exaggeration. In this textbook, we have tried to acknowledge what is good about the moral law approach without falling into the excesses anti-theorists rightfully criticize.

Kierkegaard's Transcendental Subjectivism: Becoming Yourself

The early modern Danish philosopher Søren Kierkegaard (1813–55) could be considered a precursor to anti-theory. A predominant influence on later thinkers in the Continental tradition such as John-Paul Sartre (1905–80) and Martin Heidegger (1889–1976), Kierkegaard is a complex thinker whose ideas are not easily summarized. Although his philosophy is intensely autobiographical, he writes using pseudonyms, placing his own thoughts into the minds of fictitious characters. His work is as literary as it is philosophical. He provides a penetrating account of a readily recognizable spiritual or psychological malaise that seems to grip modern society.

Kierkegaard is an overlooked resource for modern moral philosophy. He does not preach; his account of morality is neither didactic nor formulaic. Through a description of ordinary experience, he is able to sketch out a model of ethical aspiration and achievement that can be applied generally. He is a sincere religious believer who, nonetheless, offers a searing critique of institutional Christianity. Much as contemporary anti-theorists react against the comprehensive systems of Kant and the utilitarians, Kierkegaard can be seen as reacting against the abstract, excessively rationalistic, comprehensive metaphysical philosophy of Hegel.

In this section we will focus on two aspects of Kierkegaard's work: his subjective account of ethics and his probing analysis of immorality. Kierkegaard is often called an 'existentialist'. Although he himself never used the term, it is an appropriate label for a philosopher who does not believe we can to have a complete theory of anything. What matters is how we choose to live our lives. The proper subject for philosophy is lived *existence* rather than systematic science or metaphysics.

In an oddly-titled book *Either/Or*, Kierkegaard begins his probing analysis of the human condition with the commonplace experience of boredom. (The title *Either/Or* refers to the central issue of human choice in Kierkegaard's ethics.) A fictitious young author called 'A' explains the entire history of the world as advancing stages in boredom. The usual solution to boredom is something he calls 'the **rotation of crops**'. One must change what one is doing at regular intervals: 'One is weary of living in the country and moves to the city; one is weary of one's native land and goes abroad; one is *europamüde* [weary of Europe] and goes to America, etc.'[2] But *A* thinks this 'vulgar, inartistic' method cancels itself out and becomes boring in the long run. A better solution to boredom is not doing endlessly different things, but doing the very same thing in different ways. This involves, among other things, learning to recollect and forget. *A* tells the reader, 'No part of life ought to have so much meaning for a person that he cannot forget it at any moment he wants to; on the other hand, every single part of life ought to have so much meaning for a person that he can remember it at any moment'.[3] Through an intense concentration on such techniques and strategies of amusement, one can perhaps beat boredom and live esthetically. Life is like art!

Kierkegaard goes on to compare the esthetic and the ethical way of life. Another fictitious character, Judge William (also known as *B*) writes two long letters, telling him that he is so bent on choosing different crops that he has forgotten to make the most fundamental choice of all: he has forgotten to choose himself. The Judge posits a stark dichotomy: an esthetic person loses himself in distraction; the ethical person makes a commitment to a certain way of life. In committing oneself to a life-project, the person who operates at an ethical level 'becomes himself'.[4] Judge William writes, 'A human being's eternal dignity lies precisely in this, that he can gain a story'.[5] But before we can write the story of our lives, we must first choose what kind of character we will be. By losing himself in distraction, A is, so to speak, refusing to choose. Or, more accurately, he is sidestepping the main issue. The artistic way of life is not so much evil as 'indifferent'.[6] It is a life of missed opportunity.

This business of choosing to be oneself is at the heart of Kierkegaard's moral philosophy. Ethics is, in the first instance, a matter of choosing 'between choosing and not choosing'.[7] Before we can choose good over evil, we must make a more preliminary choice; we must choose to choose. Once we have chosen to become someone, once we have willed an identity, good and evil crystallize as alternatives. At the esthetic stage, we can only choose between interesting and boring. Once we make a commitment, we are suddenly confronted with good and evil. But we cannot even catch a glimpse of good and evil except from the viewpoint of commitment.

Kierkegaard's morality is not so much about telling us what we can and cannot do. He does not spend a lot of time telling us not to steal, not to tell lies, not to commit adultery. For him, morality does not mean obeying some external set of abstract standards; it means being true to oneself. Judge William writes, 'the richest personality is nothing before he has chosen himself; and on the other hand even what might be called the poorest personality is everything when he has chosen himself, for the greatness is not to be this or that but to be oneself, and every human being can be this if he so wills it'.[8] Commitment is what counts—not commitment to an abstract system of moral laws, but commitment to personal loyalties that surface in ordinary, everyday life. As his religious writing makes clear, Kierkegaard does not believe that morality requires stupendous achievements or exotic asceticism. Morality can be fully realized in daily life through a faithful attention to human decency.

It is important to emphasize that Kierkegaard does not view the leap from the esthetic to the ethical life as a further development of what went before; it requires a quantum jump to a new reality. (Kierkegaard writes about religion in similar terms, as a dark leap of faith from the ethical to the supernatural.) Judge William explains that the ethical, at the beginning, 'absolutely excludes the esthetic', but that once the individual had made a moral commitment, 'the esthetic returns in its relativity'.[9] If anything the ethical life enhances aesthetic appreciation. Still, one must begin with a decisive turn toward morality.

Kierkegaard thinks that most of us live hum-drum lives of mindless conformity. We avoid choice, live on autopilot, do what other people do, and think what other people think. Even when we believe we are being honest with ourselves, we may actually be fabricating lies to ease our conscience. If, however, Kierjegaard proposes an ethics of authenticity, many people use 'authenticity' as an excuse for bad behaviour: 'I can't help myself; I am just being me.' But Kierkegaard sees through these disguises.

Kierkegaard contrasts his position with that of Socrates. Socrates believes that evil is a result of ignorance; people choose to do wrong because they do not know any better. Kierkegaard believes that when we do something wrong, we go out of our way to hide this knowledge from ourselves. We are 'unwilling to understand'.[10] If Socrates believes that immorality arises from ignorance, Kierkegaard believes that it arises from *willed* ignorance. Through an incremental process of **rationalization**, evil people bring their consciences into line with a corrupted will. They blind themselves to their own shortcomings through excuses, qualifications, or rationalizations.

Kierkegaard explains the relationship between what the immoral person knows and what the immoral person wills:

> If willing does not agree with what is known, . . . willing allows some time to elapse, an interim called: 'We shall look at it tomorrow.' During all this knowing becomes more and more obscure . . . And when knowing has become duly obscured, knowing and willing can better understand each other; eventually they agree completely, for *now knowing has come over to the side of willing and admits what it wants is absolutely right*.[11]

Kierkegaard's account of what Aristotle called 'self-indulgence' provides a salient criticism of some trends in contemporary moral philosophy. We sometimes act as if arguments are the most important thing. Kierkegaard tells us that immoral agents are all too willing to use logical arguments that serve their purposes, not because they sincerely reflect the circumstances of human life but because they allow them to excuse their own immoral behaviour. We need to be on guard against such self-deception, in others and in ourselves.

Kierkegaard, like contemporary anti-theorists, is suspicious about philosophy. Judge William claims that 'German philosophers', for all their logical, argumentative prowess, are soul-sick. (Despair is, for Kierkegaard, the ultimate failure.) The problem is that logical philosophy approaches the riddle of human life from the outside. It is too impersonal to capture the transcendental subjectivity of ethics. Judge William writes, 'That is why I cling so firmly to the defining characteristic 'to choose'; it is my watchword, the nerve of my life-view, and that I do have, even if I can in no way presume a system'.[12]

One criticism that can be levelled against Kierkegaard's views is that the substantive content of his thought is too thin to provide adequate grounds for morality. Yes, one might agree, too many people act without thinking deeply about their choices. But an emphasis on authenticity may overshadow the need for objective standards of right and wrong. It is not enough to say that people must choose. People need guidelines, rules, principles to fill out the content of morality, to tell them what they can and cannot do. That is, for example, the purpose of moral law: it sets out clearly and succinctly guidelines that must be followed. Kierkegaard was writing, however, at a time when moral standards were clearer and more straightforward than they are today. Surely, there is room in moral philosophy for serious commitment *and* for robust moral standards. Except perhaps for the saintly, sincere choice is not enough of a guide for morality. The modern tendency to compartmentalize different aspects of the good life creates false oppositions. It is not a matter of being authentic *or* living up to independent, clear standards of moral achievement. One must do both together.

Personalism: Persons as the Most Fundamental Moral Reality

The world view of personalism resembles that of anti-theorists, existentialists, and feminists. Indeed, personalism could be considered, in many ways, as an earlier form of these later movements. Noteworthy personalists (or precursors of personalism) include the following (although there are many others we could list):

- French idealist and naturalist philosopher Charles Bernard Renouvier (1815–1903);
- American Methodist theologians Borden Parker Bowne (1847–1910), Edgar Sheffield Brightman (1884–1953) and Albert Cornelius Knudson (1873–1954);
- British atheist philosopher John M.E. McTaggart (1866–1925);
- Russian religious and political philosopher Nikolai Berdyaev (1874-1948);
- Jewish political commentator and theologian Martin Buber (1878–1965);
- German Catholic philosopher and prominent opponent of Nazism Dietrich von Hildebrand (1889–1977);
- French Catholic philosopher Emmanuel Mounier (1905–50);
- the late Pope John-Paul II, Karol Wojtyła (1920–2005).

Personalism was heavily influenced by Kant's description of human individuals as beings of supreme value. In his book entitled *Personalism* (1952), Mounier writes this:

Personalism is a philosophy not only an attitude. But its central affirmation being the existence of free and creative persons, it introduces . . . a principle of unpredictability which excludes any desire for a definitive system. Nothing can be more repugnant to it than the taste so common today, for an apparatus of thought and action functioning like an automatic distributor of solutions and instructions. . . . Also, although we speak, for convenience, of personalism, we ought rather to say that there is a plurality of personalisms. . . . A Christian personalism and an agnostic personalism, for instance, differ even in their intimate disposition. They would gain nothing by trying to unite in a middle way. Nevertheless, they confirm one another . . . in certain fundamental assertions and [practices] . . . concerning individual or collective order; and that is sufficient to justify their use of the same name.[13]

Personalism is a theology, a metaphysics, and an ethics. It conceives of a world where the most fundamental reality is 'the person', represented and embodied in God or in individual human beings. Each instance of personhood constitutes an irreducible, mysterious whole that cannot be explained in terms of something else. Once we arrive at the level of personhood, we are at the ground floor of reality, at least as it can be known to human cognition. Personalists believe that reality is composed of irreplaceable units, each possessing intrinsic value. Each individual unit retains its worth at all times. Because reality is, most fundamentally, composed of persons, morality is written into the very existence of things. There is no jump from 'is' to 'ought' in moving from a factual to a moral description of things. Existence is composed of persons and is essentially moral. Ethics is, at the deepest level, about establishing and maintaining a proper relationship between persons; ideally, these relationships involve respect and love.

In many individual cases, personalism was a philosophy embraced by activists who battled against totalitarianism and communism but also capitalism and excessive consumerism. Broadly speaking, these social critics resist

attempts to describe human beings as uniform, replaceable units whose behaviour is fully determined by physical, biological, psychological, or sociological laws. They argue that human beings are not purely physical; they are more than members of a collectivity, more than mere economic actors. Human beings possess inalienable dignity; they are free; they have rights that cannot be violated.

A Feminist Ethics of Care: Nel Noddings

Turn next to feminism. Nel Noddings is an educational theorist who has developed a moral voice that is closely attentive and true to the experience of women. This includes, for example, using the relationship between mother and child as an apt model for virtue and moral behaviour.

Noddings believes that all human beings, but particularly women, have a natural impulse to care for others. Morality builds on this natural tendency and is most accurately described, not in terms of dutiful submission to some abstract universal ideal, but in terms of an immediate, positive reaction to a perceived need in an adjacent other. To use one of Noddings's refreshingly ordinary examples, when babies cry, we see their discomfort and pick them up. We do this, not simply because we feel like doing it, but because it is the right thing to do. There is an internal awareness: not simply 'I want to pick up the baby', but 'I *must* pick up the baby'. In the ideally-ethical person, these two motivations, 'I want' and 'I must', may join into a seamless whole, but the moral sense that *this must be done* dominates and pervades the motivation of the moral person. We might prefer to sit on the sofa, turn up the TV, and ignore the crying baby, but we know we must respond to this person in need. This is, for Noddings, a paradigmatic example of moral behaviour.

Noddings makes a clear distinction between nonmoral or 'natural' caring and ethical caring. Natural caring just happens naturally, without any deep commitment to specific values. Moral caring, which builds on natural caring, has to do with living up to an ideal. Noddings explains it in this way:

> Genuine moral sentiment . . . arises from an evaluation of the caring relation as good, as better than, superior to, other forms of relatedness. I feel the moral 'I must' when I recognize that my response will either enhance or diminish my ethical ideal. . . . In a given situation with someone I am not fond of, I may be able to find all sorts of reasons why I should not respond to his need. . . . I am obliged then, to accept the initial 'I must' when it occurs and even to fetch it out of a recalcitrant slumber when it fails to awake spontaneously. The source of my [moral] obligation is the value I place on the relatedness of caring.[14]

Although Noddings does not dispute the usefulness of universal rules of conduct or moral principles, she insists that abstract moral principles derive from a prior experience of personal caring. The immediacy of caring comes first; rules always come second and are, at best, an attempt to make sense of morality after the fact. Authentic morality originates in a unique, face-to-face encounter between the 'carer' and the 'cared-for'. Suppose person *A* and person *B* interact. For this interaction to be a full-fledged instance of morality, three things must happen in sequence: (1) *A* must see that *B* needs care and turn toward *B* in an attitude of helpful concern; (2) *A* must translate that concern into a helpful act; and (3) *B* must acknowledge that *A* cares. All three steps are, for Noddings, a part of morality. It is the

resulting connection between the carer and the cared-for that is the ultimate source of all value.

To be a moral person, in Noddings's account, is to become a person who regularly establishes caring relations and maintains them over time. Caring requires 'motivational displacement'. Immorality results when we ignore or reject this internal call to care. The worst thing that can happen is to become a person who does not care. This is the essence of evil. Noddings thinks that social or educational institutions can be evil when, for example, they condition people not to care or they remove opportunities for caring. As she convincingly explains, anything that diminishes our ability to care is morally wrong. Whatever detracts from the personal ideal of being a caring person is to be avoided.

Noddings does not claim that we must help in every situation, which is a physical impossibility. She writes, 'We must acknowledge . . . that an ethics of caring places a limit on our obligation'.[15] In one controversial passage, she candidly states, 'I am not obliged to care for starving children in Africa'.[16] Philosophical opponents of utilitarian and Kantian ilk have seized on these comments to illustrate the moral advantages of impersonalism over any moral system based on personal friendships or relationships. Peter Singer, in particular, has argued that Noddings's feminist ethics of care ignores the pressing claims that those outside our small circle of acquaintance have on our sympathy. Singer and his allies claim that morality must be seen as a response to an *impersonal* imperative that tells us to treat everyone equally.

Although Noddings's explanation of her own position is less than felicitous, her opponents take her comments out of context. What Noddings wrote was 'I am not obliged to care for starving children in Africa because there is no way for this [kind of] caring to be completed . . . unless I abandon the caring to which I am obligated'.[17] Surely, she has a point. It is a moral truism that 'ought implies can'. In other words, we cannot be morally obliged to do the impossible. Moral obligations do not extend to events and situations outside our control. As much as possible, we ought to share our resources with those in need. But we cannot neglect our duty to care for those close at hand for the sake of some distant ideal. Our relationships to our parents, our children, our colleagues, our teammates, and so on, place an especially urgent demand on our attention.

Noddings makes a useful distinction between 'caring for' and 'caring about'. We care *for* individual people; we *care about* abstract causes. She argues, significantly, that the 'caring for' is morally prior to and more important than 'caring about'. She admits,

> [in my writing] I have brushed aside 'caring about'. . . . It is too easy. I can 'care about' the starving children of Cambodia, send five dollars to hunger relief, and feel somewhat satisfied. I do not even know if my money went for food, or guns, or a new Cadillac for some politician. This is a poor second-cousin to caring. 'Caring about' always involves a certain benign neglect. One is attentive just so far. . . . One contributes five dollars and goes on to other things.[18]

Noddings criticizes the 'Mr Jellybys' of the world (the name derives from an insufferable character from Dickens), for whom '"caring about" can deteriorate to political self-righteousness and to forms of intervention that do more harm than good'.[19] She concedes that 'caring about' can be the foundation for 'a sense of justice', and that justice is 'morally important because it is instrumental in establishing the conditions under which "caring for" can

flourish'.[20] Still, Noddings wants to emphasize the privileged nature of 'caring for' over 'caring about' and to focus on the personal encounter between carer and cared-for as the foundation of moral value. In her words, 'Theoretically, it is vital to place "caring for" over "caring about."'[21]

The best way to approach Noddings's thought is to view it as a phenomenological or descriptive account of an archetypical experience that gives value to things. In a world of blasé moral relativism, Noddings accurately and decisively discovers and shines light upon something no moral person can deny: caring is valuable. When someone helps another person and that other person acknowledges this outpouring of sympathy, this is humanly momentous. Noddings's theory is really a refreshing return to a much earlier philosophical idea that some things, in particular human relationships, have intrinsic value. They are valuable for their own sake. Suppose a machine—an arrangement of cogs and pulleys and electric switches without intentions, desires, or beliefs—was providing for the needs of a hospital patient; this would not be, on Noddings's model, a true instance of caring. What makes caring valuable is not merely the fact that someone's needs are met— this is good but there is something else which is good: the connection that joins two people together. Think of human relationships like a bridge. We can use a bridge to get places. This is well and good. But Noddings points out that when it comes to human relationships, the 'bridge' itself is valuable, indeed, intrinsically valuable.

Noddings's ethics of care may seem reminiscent of virtue ethics. But Noddings claims that caring is *not* a virtue. There seems to be a confusion here. Noddings is worried that virtue theories misplace the true origin of morality in virtue rather than relationship. Being a caring person is not, for her, the basis of morality; the actual back-and-forth encounter between carer and cared-for is instead the source of all moral value. This is why Noddings insists on the third step in her phenomenology of caring. It is not enough that the carer helps the cared-for. The cared-for has to acknowledge being helped. It has to be a two-way street. Both individuals have to turn and mentally and emotionally embrace the other. Otherwise, there is something flawed or incomplete in the instance of caring.

In line with this symmetrical depiction of caring, Nodding seems, implausibly, to propose the relationship between the carer and the cared-for, as a symmetrical relationship between equals. She writes, 'From the perspective of virtue theory, the carer gets the lion's share of moral credit. But from the care perspective, a huge thank-you goes to the responsive children, the students glowing with new learning, the feeble elderly who can do little more than smile a thanks for efforts at care. We know just how great these contributions are when they are withdrawn'.[22] No one disputes the importance of gratitude, but caring relationships are generally *asymmetrical*. There is a sense in which the carer contributes more, which is why that person takes on the initiative: because he or she is in a position to satisfy the needs of the person cared for. In most cases at least, it is unrealistic to suggest that the carer and the cared-for are able to contribute equal amounts to the situation.

Noddings's insistence that the two-way relationship we call caring is more successful when the cared-for exhibits some positive acknowledgement for the care received seems obviously correct, but this does not remove the need for a theory of virtue. To begin with, there would be no instances of caring unless we had caring people. Virtuous people are the cause of caring encounters. And that is not all. Noddings fails to acknowledge that the *virtue* of caring must take moral priority over an experience of caring. Someone who prioritizes the two-way emotional experience Noddings identifies with caring will not care for those who refuse to show gratitude. But it might be argued that the true test of morality is precisely whether someone continues to care for the ungrateful. (This is not to suggest that caring is appropriate in every situation—as feminists correctly point out, sometimes justice requires that an unacknowledged relationship of care be terminated. Nonetheless, there are clear cases where morality requires caring for those who are unable or unwilling to acknowledge help.)

There are different tasks that must be performed in moral philosophy. We may focus on the ultimate end of morality, what Aristotle calls good fortune (happiness) or **eudaimonia**. Or we may focus on the means to that end. Noddings, in focusing on the ideal experience of caring, is focusing on the ultimate end of morality; virtue ethicists who emphasize the virtue of caring are focusing on the means we must take to achieve that end. But one must master the virtue of care in order to achieve the experience of care. There is no real disagreement here. Except that morality is obviously about means as well as about ends. If we adopt the correct means and do not achieve the aimed-at end through no fault of our own, this is a disappointment but we cannot be morally faulted.

At its worst, Noddings's ethics of care collapses into an empty and even dangerous sentimentalism. An old man concerned about involuntary euthanasia once told me that he didn't want some *caring* nurse putting him out of his misery because she had decided he had suffered enough. Well-intentioned sympathy can lead one astray if it is not anchored to some wider understanding of morality. We can distinguish between two kinds of cases. There are instances where the injunction to care is clear and unmistakable. The woman on the bicycle is hit by a car right in front of me; I am a licensed paramedic. Of course, I must help! We can call such cases **lucid occasions**. But not every interaction with another human being results in a lucid occasion.

Sometimes it is difficult to determine how or to what degree we should help others. Let us call such instances **obscure occasions**. Suppose I am forced to choose between helping X or Y. I can only help one or the other. How do I decide? Or suppose I must decide between helping people right now or going to university so I can help them in the future? Or suppose that helping someone makes them dependent and unable to help themselves? And so on. To tell people that they should care for others is remarkably vague. We need a more precise forensic account of morality if we are to figure out what we should do on obscure occasions. (To be fair, Noddings is aware of some of these complexities.)

Even in the field of education, there is disquiet about some of Noddings's views. What does it mean to care for students? In the contemporary age, we are all too ready to translate discourse about caring into a demand to be *nice* to others. But niceness, soft sentiment, a warm glow is not the same as caring. Perhaps caring for individual students means failing them on their exams so they learn from their mistakes. Perhaps it means punishing those who lack discipline so that they learn that there are consequences to bad actions. Perhaps it means challenging them to work harder. Noddings cannot be faulted for popular misinterpretations or exaggerations of her views. But any single-minded emphasis on caring in education can be contested. The

---

✍ Applied Philosophy Box 10.2 ✍

'I Am Not a Caring Teacher'

Some days, I think that Nel Noddings is the most dangerous person in America, or rather, because others abuse her ideas, the common *image of Nel Noddings* is the most dangerous (imaginary) person in America. [Nodding's work on care] feeds into the historical rhetoric denigrating teaching as an intellectual occupation. Two hundred years ago, the primary qualification for teaching was virtue, not academics. When Mann and others encouraged the hiring of women as teachers, it was from the essentialist argument that women are more nurturing. While that was a shift from the predominance of men in teaching, it dovetailed with changing sex roles. We retain this legacy of seeing teachers as role models, with virtue and morals more important than skill.

This author, who is careful to distinguish between Noddings and her followers, argues nonetheless that an overemphasis on caring over intellectual achievement has been detrimental for education. Do you agree or disagree?

Source: Sherman Dorn, 'I Am Not a Caring Teacher.' *One-Blog Schoolhouse*, www.shermandorn.com/mt/archives/000458.html, 23 April 2006.

best way to care for students is perhaps to put 'caring for' in the background and to focus on the intellectual communication of knowledge, not on the multiplication of caring interactions. At least, this is what some of Noddings's opponents argue.

We have already discussed the importance of anti-theory. Noddings could be considered an anti-theorist. She describes her moral system as 'an inversion of Kantian ethics that recognizes the centrality of meeting others in caring relations and the futility of trying to solve moral problems completely and universally in abstract and codified schemes'.[23] This is fine as far as it goes, but one must be careful. Men and women *reason* about moral choices. (Not to accept this is to return to old stereotypes of women as irrational bundles of pure feelings.) An emphasis on raw, uneducated feeling will not suffice for careful moral deliberation. Concepts of practical judgment, of duty, of consequences, of moderation, of moral culpability, of logical cogency, etc., all play an important role in moral decision-making. They must be included in any complete system of ethics. Even Noddings's moral system can be codified in a universal and abstract law: *care for others*. Applying this axiom to the specific circumstances of a life requires, of course, a careful casuistry that depends on further concepts and principles in addition to Noddings's central notion of care.

One disappointing aspect of Noddings work is its scant recognition of the earlier tradition. Two modern religious figures, Edith Stein and Simone Weil, immediately come to mind as harbingers of her ethics of care: Stein elaborates a phenomenology of empathy; Weil writes about the importance of compassion. Although Noddings explicitly rejects Christian *agapism*, the idea that selfless love is the basis of ethics, her approach is, in many ways, a secularization of the key Christian value of love. At times, she comes close to reformulating, in modern, **secular** guise, the famous advice of St. Augustine: 'love and do what you will.' Noddings worries that an overemphasis on Christian love will lead to exaggerations of self-sacrifice and to the subservience of women. We need, however, an account of justice *in addition* to an account of caring to avoid such misunderstandings.

The idea that the mother-child relationship is an exemplary instance of morality is an abiding theme in earlier literature. One is reminded of the Hebrew psalm that describes, as a moral archetype, a similar caring relationship between God and the soul: 'as a child has rest in its mother's arms, even so my soul.'[24] Noddings's general focus on the importance of human relationships also harkens back to Aristotle's account of friendship for the moral life. Although Aristotle does refer to a mother's love for her children, he conceives of the best friendship as a relationship between equals. Noddings, interestingly and provocatively, widens the scope of moral friendship to include friendships between *unequals* as a model of the best ethical achievement. Still, an Aristotelian might complain that Noddings does not leave enough room for friendship between equals. Friendship may be as much a matter of felicitous adjacent equality as of need.

Human Rights: Looking at Duty Backwards, Punishment

Moral Rights

Human rights have been a subject of increasing attention in contemporary moral discourse. As of late, there has been a bewildering multiplication of rights-talk in both technical and wider circles. Individual authors variously refer to objective and subjective rights, active and passive rights, negative and positive rights, natural rights, human rights, civil rights, collective rights, group rights, minority rights, property rights, welfare rights, equality rights, animal rights, fiduciary rights, and so on. Some ways of talking about rights are misleading or worrisome, but there are also good reasons for making the concept an integral part of our moral vocabulary. We would be remiss not to consider the role of moral rights in contemporary ethics.

We cannot provide a history of 'rights-talk' here. If, however, we often assume that the concept of a right is a modern invention, it is important to note that the basic idea surfaces at the very beginnings of legal history. In about 1790 BC, Babylonian king Hammurabi had incised on a stone pillar a long list of laws, now known as the Hammurabi Code. Although the code never uses the term 'rights', it does contain a long list of *entitlements* for subjects and citizens. In a society based on agriculture, ordinary farmers had certain rights, including the right not to have their fields flooded by reckless or lazy neighbours. Here are two relevant laws from the code: #55: 'If any one open his ditches to water his crop, but is careless, and the water flood the field of his neighbor, then he shall pay his neighbor corn for his loss.' #53: 'If any one be too lazy to keep his dam in proper condition, . . . [and if] all the fields be flooded, then shall he be sold for money [to] replace the corn which he has caused to be ruined.'[25] The Code sets out what is in effect the right to compensation when one's fields are damaged by reckless flooding. This amounts to a formal acknowledgement of an entitlement that someone owes someone else.

Although these are *legal* rights, Hammurabi sets out a moral justification for them, claiming that God has set him up as ruler over the earth 'to bring about the rule of righteousness in the land [and] . . . to further the well-being of mankind'.[26] With time, such ancient notions evolved into our present concept of a 'right'.

Scholar Brian Tierney claims that the first explicitly modern use of the concept of a right surfaces in medieval church law (in what is called **canon law**) during the period from 1150 to 1250.[27] Early church lawyers wondered whether it was a sin for a starving man to steal food. After much discussion, a consensus grew that the starving man 'seems to use his right [to the food] rather than to plan a theft'.[28] To claim that someone is *entitled* to food is an explicit formulation of how modern authors have come to understand the notion of a right. This 'right to food' was eventually enlarged to include a general right to all the necessities of life, an idea Godfrey of Fontaines articulates in a particularly forceful manner when he declares that 'each one [of us] has a certain right (*jus*) in the common exterior goods of this world, and this right cannot be licitly renounced'.[29] We all have, in other words, a right to food, drink, shelter, security—in short, to what we need to survive. And we cannot relinquish that right under any circumstances. If, for example, I were to agree to not steal food when I am starving, this would be an immoral and therefore non-binding agreement.

William of Ockham and later Thomists, particularly in Spain, take up these issues in more detail. The discussion continues right up to the beginning of the modern period with the more familiar figure of John Locke, who writes that 'God, the Father of all, has given no one . . . such a Property . . . but that he has given his Brother a *Right* to Surplusage of his Goods; so that it cannot justly be denied him when his pressing Want calls for it'.[30] Locke recognizes then that those in need have a right to the surplus goods of others. Like earlier thinkers, he subscribes to the notion of a natural human right, a *jus naturale*, which comes to be understood as a moral entitlement that inheres in individuals simply because they are human.

We will use the expressions 'moral rights', 'natural rights', and 'human rights' interchangeably. A moral right is a moral obligation in reverse. It is something that is owed to you by nature because you are a human being, because of moral considerations. To say that starving individuals have a moral right to our surplus food is to say that we have to let them take it. The moral obligation is imposed on us; we have a *duty* to allow them to take the food. Contemporary philosopher Alan Gerwith sets out the general structure of a right as follows: *A* has a right to *X* against *B* by virtue of *Y* where: *A* is the person who has the right; *X* is whatever *A* is entitled to; *B* is whoever must provide *X* to *A*, and *Y* is the reason for the right.[31] With respect to the example we have been discussing, *A* = starving individuals; *X* = surplus food; *B* = ourselves; *Y* = morality requires human preservation. In other words, starving individuals have a right to our surplus food in virtue of the moral importance of preserving human life. Their right to surplus food is satisfied when they are allowed to take the food. If they were not allowed to take the food, this would be a violation or infringement of their rights. We will leave it to the reader to apply Gerwith's model to other cases. (One might begin by applying it to the implicit 'right' listed in the Hammurabi Code.)

Although the Universal Declaration of Human Rights adopted by the United Nations in 1948 provides a wide-ranging list of familiar rights, there is no single authoritative canon or codex of moral or human rights that everyone agrees upon. We can enumerate many universally recognized rights: the right to life, the right to freedom of conscience, the right not to be tortured, the right to property, the right to non-discrimination, the right to freedom of association, the right to privacy, the right to employment, the right to have a family, the right to education, and so on. If rights have traditionally been thought to inhere in human *individuals*, some recent theorists have tried to affirm various notions of group rights, claiming in particular that minorities have unique rights. Authors such as Peter Singer have also argued for animal rights.

Authors generally derive more specific rights from more basic rights. So, for example, your right to an ambulance might be derived from your right to proper medical care, which might be derived from your right to life. The most basic rights are typically invoked as a trump card that outweighs other moral (and political) considerations. Although these most basic rights are often thought to be inalienable, theorists usually concede that at least some rights can be infringed or ignored when they seriously detract from the common good. So, for example, the Canadian Charter of Rights and Freedoms has a provision that stipulates that all rights are subject to whatever is most conducive to a free and democratic society. It follows that the individual right to free speech or the right to free association could be suspended for the sake of civil peace in times of emergency or war.

Rights have a moral and a political dimension. We generally expect that the most basic rights will be enforced by legal authority. In political discussion, some authors distinguish between negative and positive rights. A **negative right** guarantees your freedom to do as you will. A **positive right** guarantees some positive good, either a service or a material benefit. Some **libertarian** commentators heavily favour negative interpretations of rights but we will not enter into these political disagreements here. Suffice it to say that law is not the same as morality. It traces and protects a freedom of choice that is inevitably larger than morality. Thomas Aquinas writes, 'Now human law is framed for a number of human beings, the majority of whom are not perfect in virtue. Wherefore human laws do not forbid all vices, from which the virtuous abstain, but only the more grievous vices, from which it is possible for the majority to abstain; and chiefly those that are to the hurt of others, without the prohibition of which human society could not be maintained: thus human law prohibits murder, theft and such like'.[32] Thomas argues here that we can curtail the freedom of individuals when their bad actions create enough evil so as to seriously disturb other citizens and the proper functioning of society. If, however, personal freedom provides an opportunity for virtuous self-realization, it does not follow that we must be free to do anything.

Some recent commentators such as Joseph Raz and Mary Anne Glendon have little patience for rights-talk. They complain that rights-claims are inevitably confrontational, that the concept of a right has come to monopolize moral discourse, and that this way of visualizing moral questions is often used by self-interested parties who make exaggerated claims against the collectivity. To claim a right to this or that is to claim, in effect, that *other* people owe something to us. This may be an insidious way of shifting moral responsibility away from ourselves onto other people.

Suppose, for example, I were to claim that I have a right to welfare payments. This claim could be a legitimate moral request for help or, perniciously, an artful way of evading the moral responsibility of providing for myself. In the latter case, the rights terminology disguises the moral vice of laziness. Although rights claims may direct attention to the plight of authentic victims, they are also an effective rhetorical tool for those who seek to profit from playing the role of victims. It goes without saying that moral obligations cannot be only composed of rights, for without duties, there would be no rights.

Punishment and Rights

Punishment places a curb or limit on our rights in the wake of immoral action. One might hastily assume that punishment is an infringement on our rights. If, however, we have a right not to be subject to cruel and unusual punishment, moral philosophers justify punishment in five different ways. Consider then five different reasons the moral individual could advance in support of just punishment: retribution, deterrence, reparation, shame, and rehabilitation. Describe punishment here as the deliberate causing of pain or discomfort or injury or disadvantage to another human being in the wake of wrong-doing. Punishment must have a moral basis or it would be nothing more than the stronger lording it over the weaker.

1. Retribution

Retribution is the idea that justice *requires* a proportional righting of wrongs. Someone who works hard and contributes to society deserves the fruits of his labours; someone who is guilty of a seriously immoral act *deserves* to be punished or harmed to an equivalent degree. The greater the wrong, the greater the required punishment. On this view, it is only just that the guilty must pay the price for their misdeeds. When an appropriate punishment is meted out, fairness is served. The fact that individuals do serious wrong and escape punishment would be a serious moral scandal. The most familiar example of this legal rationale is the *lex talionis* or 'law of retaliation' of the Old Testament: 'you shall give life for life, eye for eye, tooth for tooth, hand for hand, burning for burning, wound for wound, stripe for stripe'.[33] Authors who argue for retribution claim that punishment re-establishes moral harmony by visiting an equivalent degree of misfortune on those who deserve penalty. Those who argue for capital punishment often appeal to this rationale; hence the slogan 'a life for a life'.

2. Deterrence

Those who argue for **deterrence** claim that society has a right to self-defence. They believe that imprisoning or killing criminals reduces crime by removing dangerous individuals from society and by frightening them into submission. On this view, criminals justly lose the protection society normally grants its members. Such punishment secures our safety and dissuades offenders from further offences.

3. Reparation/Restitution

Reparation is motivated by the idea that wrong-doers must somehow repair the damage that has been caused by the initial offence. In contemporary society, reparation usually takes on a financial aspect through imposed fines or confiscation of property. What were formerly called 'road gangs' in North America and Great Britain were made up of inmates doing forced labour. The rationale was that criminals should be made to give something back to society through their hard labour. Even though restitution for specific loss, theft, or injury was not possible, there was still a symbolic sense in which benefits produced by inmate labour could be seen as satisfying the debt the offender owes the injured party.

4. Shame

Shame or dishonour can play an important role in punishment. Some recent authors argue that that punishment *should* place a social stigma on the individual, that those who commit serious offences *should* be made to feel the brunt of shame and ridicule. Not only because this is an effective deterrent, but also because it is morally right that people who do bad things suffer the emotional discomfort of social disapproval. Immorality *requires* a sense of guilt. If wrong-doers do not experience negative emotions on their own, we need to 'force' these emotions on them. Seen from this perspective, punishment may require a public shaming of the guilty. A famous (negative) example of public shaming is the scarlet letter *A* (for adultery) that Hester Prynne, the protagonist in Nathaniel Hawthorne's novel, was forced to wear on her bosom.

5. Rehabilitation

Finally, proponents of **rehabilitation** argue that punishment should transform a morally damaged person into a good citizen who can reintegrate into society. On this account, those who do bad acts need to be *forcibly* reformed through re-education or therapy. Incarceration must include some sort of positive behaviour modification. There is debate, however, over the question of whether rehabilitation works.

One does not have to propose a theory of punishment that focuses on a single explanation or justification. We can combine these different ideas to produce a viable theory. Historical philosophers touch on all these ideas. Aristotle, for example, recommends punishment as therapy and as a deterrence; Kant famously focuses on retribution, whereas Utilitarians emphasize deterrence and rehabilitation. Because this largely overlaps with political and legal issues, we will not enter into any closer analysis here. Suffice it to say that unbridled punishment can lead to abuses and the appropriate punishment of children adds other complications to any such discussion.

Divine Command Morality

A divine command morality stipulates that, in some essential way, morality consists of obeying the commands of God. God is sovereign over the world; God tells us to do certain things, and morality means doing what God tells us. Much philosophical ink has been spilled on whether this type of theory can be logically defended. Before discussing these views, however, consider what proponents find attractive in divine command theory.

Although the divine command perspective is often associated with evangelical thinkers and, more generally, with practising Christians who propose a biblical basis for ethics, the same view of morality arises in many other religious traditions. Not only are there Jewish and Islamic versions of divine command morality; the same basic idea that ethics requires submission to a divine law recurs in other religions, such as Hinduism, Buddhism, Jainism, and Sikhism. Ancient religions propose a similar line of thought. As we have already observed, Hammurabi's almost 4000-year-old code of Babylonian law is based on the same idea that God's decrees are the ultimate source of what is right and just. Of course, ordinary believers can accept this basic line of reasoning without engaging in further critical reflection. 'Divine command theory' is a philosophical attempt to justify and defend this view of morality.

An individual can philosophize from any set of (noncontradictory) premises. So, if we allow scriptural passages or religious truths to stand as premises, there is no reason why we cannot use them to construct logical arguments that produce clear conclusions about moral behaviour. This is, in large part, the motivation behind divine command theory. Thinkers who embrace this moral view generally find their inspiration in a scripture that they believe is divinely inspired. Disputes about the interpretation of sacred texts notwithstanding, this approach seems to offer clear, concise, objective standards for human behaviour. Consider the Ten Commandments. To the believer, the Decalogue offers universal laws that are timeless, authoritative, and surprisingly comprehensive. Many or most of these prescriptions are easily identifiable with widespread moral intuitions. They are set out in everyday, plain-language as practical directives to be put into practice. Even where application of the laws may seem uncertain or indecisive, divine command theorists would argue that the rest of scripture provides a good guide to the proper interpretation of these laws and that, all things considered, they present a better, clearer, and less corruptible ethical alternative than self-serving personal preference or even philosophical argument. It is, in large part, the desire for clear, unassailable guidelines that drives the interest in divine command morality. Divine command theorists believe that there is a great deal of straightforward moral content in religious traditions that can guide human behaviour.

Most objections to divine command theory derive from the so-called Euthyphro problem discussed in earlier chapters. According to these theorists, specific acts are right because God commands them; wrong because God forbids them. So the content of morality depends ultimately on God's commands. Opponents argue that acts cannot be right just because God commands them. Suppose—even if the idea is outlandish—that God were to command you to murder your next-door neighbour. If God commanded this, and doing what He commands is right, murdering your neighbour would be right. But that seems absurd. The divine command theorist will object that God would not command you to murder your next-door neighbour because that would be wrong. But this seems to indicate that God must consult some higher criterion of morality that is logically prior to what He commands. Critics argue that it must be this higher criterion—not the fact that God commands it—that makes something right. If God only commands people to do good things, this shows that God himself submits to an independent, non-religious criterion in decision-making.

Closer inspection of this criticism of divine command morality reveals, however, that it is a straw man. When we make a **straw man**, we simplify an argument to make it easier to refute (the idea being that it is easier to knock down a straw-man dummy than to wrestle with a real opponent). Whether we agree with religion or not, the usual dismissal of divine command theory does not take into account what proponents of the theory actually believe. Believers define God as a supremely good Being. But it is logically impossible for a supremely good Being to command someone to do something wrong. The very idea involves a contraction. It

is not even a real possibility. So proponents of divine command theory argue that the usual counterexamples to their theory miss the point. To say that divine command morality is wrong because God might command you to murder an innocent person is like saying that divine command theory is wrong because someone might discover a square circle. This is, from the believer's perspective, not a meaningful claim.

Opponents of the theory will respond that this defence does not deal with the essential problem with divine command theory: even if God only does what is right, there is still the problem that He must submit to a higher morality outside himself. But perhaps this way of explaining things turns morality upside down. Seen from a secular viewpoint, it may seem as if moral reason comes first; God, second. Viewed from the religious perspective, however, God is the source of moral reason. God comes first; moral reason, second. A thought-experiment may help. Suppose God were to make coins stamped with his image and suppose that the only thing that made these coins valuable was the fact that they bear God's image. This is how these theorists view human conduct. To the extent that an act bears, like the coin, the stamp of God's goodness, it is morally acceptable or virtuous. Critics talk as if secular or natural morality were a higher criterion above God that He must respect. In fact, proponents of this theory believe that the relationship is the other way around. What God commands is not perfect because it meets with human standards; rather, human standards are accurate insomuch as they approximate what God commands. Morality cannot be fairly construed as an independent or competing perspective from which to evaluate God.

Another problem with familiar criticisms of divine command theory is that they often focus on the most extreme versions of the theory imaginable. Few if any theists believe that human conscience can be ignored. It is rather that it needs to be instructed by and guided by divine revelation. For divine command theorists, all morality originates in God's commands. But God's laws needs to be interpreted and fitted to individual circumstances with the help of human reason. Theists do not believe that human conscience can be set aside, but that God is revealed both in his explicit commands and in the workings of human conscience. Sometimes, objections to the logical congruity of divine command morality can be traced to a disagreement with the content of religious morality. Opponents may dispute, for example, specific religious rules or laws about sexual behaviour. Even if specific interpretations of divine law can be faulted, it does not follow that the project of divine command morality is logically impossible. In such cases, it is better to explore the precise point of disagreement than to resort to a logical attack on the theory as a whole. Both secular thinkers and religious believers rely on moral argument. Even when agreement is not presently possible, there is ground for hopeful or at least informative dialogue between believers and nonbelievers.

Ecumenical Global Ethics: Agreement between Religions

One recent variation on religious morality is the attempt to devise an ecumenical, international, cross-cultural system of ethical belief by identifying universal, shared moral principles from all great religious traditions taken together. Theologian Hans Küng has established a prominent Global Ethic Foundation in Tübingen, Germany, which attempts to locate a moral consensus among all religions, including Christianity, Judaism, Islam, Unitarianism, Universalism, Buddhism, Hinduism, Jainism, Sikhism, Taoism, Confucianism, Baha'ism, Brahmanism, Zoroastrianism, Native and indigenous religions, and Neo-Paganism.[34] The participants in this broadly based movement aim to produce a shared morality that facilitates both a theoretical and practical response to global problems. In response to what they see as 'a crisis in global economy, global ecology, and global politics', they propose a shared set of broad moral principles that shed light on contemporary issues of world hunger, peace, poverty, health, education, women's rights, and so on.[35]

A manifesto sponsored by the movement and presented to the 1993 Parliament of the World's Religions, entitled 'A Declaration Toward a Global Ethic', explains:

> We are women and men who have embraced the precepts and practices of the world's religions: We affirm that a common set of core values is found in the teachings of the religions, and that these form the basis of a global ethic. We affirm that this truth is already known, but yet to be lived in heart and action. We affirm that there is an irrevocable, unconditional norm for all areas of life, for families and communities, for races, nations, and religions. There already exist ancient guidelines for human behaviour which are found in the teachings of the religions of the world and which are the condition for a sustainable world order.[36]

The goal of the global ethics movement is the development, through a series of shared reflections made by representatives of different religious groups, of a definitive set of objective, unchangeable, transcultural standards that can be used as clear signposts in a moral dialogue among world groups. The group points to the familiar Golden Rule as an 'irrevocable' basis for ethics:

> There is a principle which is found and has persisted in many religious and ethical traditions of humankind for thousands of years: What you do not wish done to yourself, do not do to others. Or in positive terms: What you wish done to yourself, do to others! This should be the irrevocable, unconditional norm for all areas of life, for families and communities, for races, nations, and religions. Every form of egoism should be rejected: All selfishness, whether individual or collective, whether in the form of class thinking, racism, nationalism, or sexism. We condemn these because they prevent humans from being authentically human. Self-determination and self-realization are thoroughly legitimate so long as they are not separated from human self-responsibility and global responsibility, that is, from responsibility for fellow humans and for the planet Earth.[37]

The group goes on to identify four common traits in religious ethics: a commitment to non-violence and respect for life, a commitment to social solidarity and a just economic order, a commitment to **tolerance** and truthfulness, and a commitment to equal rights and to fair partnership between men and women. They then apply these broad themes to more specific issues, following a common method: determine what the religions of the world say about a moral question, restate it forcefully as a law or 'directive', and then apply this directive to the specific circumstances of contemporary society. To cite only one brief examples of this approach, consider how the authors of a *Declaration Toward a Global Ethic* comment on the intensely immoral nature of genocide:

In the great ancient religious and ethical traditions of humankind we find the directive: You shall not kill! Or in positive terms: Have respect for life! Let us reflect anew on the consequences of this ancient directive: All people have a right to life, safety, and the free development of personality insofar as they do not injure the rights of others. No one has the right physically or psychically to torture, injure, much less kill, any other human being. And no people, no state, no race, no religion has the right to hate, to discriminate against, to 'cleanse,' to exile, much less to liquidate a 'foreign' minority which is different in behaviour or holds different beliefs.[38]

One familiar charge against religion is that it breeds fanaticism, the vice of excess or blind loyalty. Fanatics lose their capacity for self-criticism and the fair examination of opposing viewpoints. In fact, they may actively persecute other groups. Closer study shows that religious fanaticism is also driven by political divisions, ethnic rivalries, and economic injustices. Still, members of the global ethics movement recognize the problem of religious fanaticism while proposing interreligious ethics as a solution. The authors of the *Declaration* write this:

> Time and again we see leaders and members of religions incite aggression, fanaticism, hate, and xenophobia—even inspire and legitimize violent and bloody conflicts. Religion often is misused for purely power-political goals, including war. We are filled with disgust. We condemn these blights and declare that they need not be. An ethic already exists within the religious teachings of the world which can counter the global distress. Of course this ethic provides no direct solution for all the immense problems of the world, but it does supply the moral foundation for a better individual and global order: A vision which can lead women and men away from despair, and society away from chaos.[39]

Critics of the global ethics movement, some of them religious, argue that while this ecumenical work may constitute a gesture of goodwill, it produces directives that are too vague to be of much help in difficult situations, that consensus among everyone is not always a reliable indicator of what is moral, that the endeavour represents more an exercise in political diplomacy than moral reasoning, and that some of the opinions expressed correspond to politically acceptable ideology rather than to the orthodox views of different religions.

Environmental Ethics: Beyond Deep Ecology

There is no disputing the urgency of present threats to the environment: pollution, deforestation, rampant urban development of agricultural and wilderness lands, reckless mining and mineral extraction, overuse of pesticides and herbicides, overfishing, the extermination of species, global warming, and so on. Moral philosophers have responded in various ways to the environmental crisis. Beginning in the 1960s and 1970s, some philosophers have tried to erect entire systems of moral philosophy based on a commitment to environmentalism.

The 'deep ecology' movement associated with Norwegian philosopher Arne Næss (1912–2009) is a good example of the philosophical mindset that motivated an environmentalist critique of Western moral philosophy. Prominent spokesperson Warwick Fox captures the spirit of the movement in the following description of the difference between **shallow ecology** and **deep ecology**:

> The distinction between shallow and deep ecology was made in 1972 . . . by the distinguished Norwegian philosopher Arne Næss . . . Shallow ecology views human beings as separate from their environment. . . . Boundaries are sharply

drawn such that humans are perceived as the significant figures against a ground that only assumes significance in so far as it only enhances humans' images of themselves *qua* important figures. Shallow ecology thus views humans as the source of all value and ascribes only instrumental (or use) value to the nonhuman world. In short, it is anthropocentric, representing the attitude to conservation that says: 'We ought to preserve the environment . . . not for its own sake but because it has value to us . . .'. Deep ecology, on the other hand, rejects the 'human-in-environment image in favour of the relational total-field image'. Organisms are then viewed rather 'as knots in the biospherical net or field of intrinsic relations'. Figure/ground boundaries are replaced by a holistic or gestalt view. . . . This total field conception dissolves not only the notion of humans as separate from their environment but the very notion of the world as composed of discrete, compact, separate 'things'. When we talk about the world as if it were a collection of discrete, isolable 'things' we are, in Næss' view, 'talking at a superficial or preliminary level of communication'. Deep ecology thus strives to be non-anthropocentric by viewing humans as just one constituency among others in the biotic community, just one particular strand in the web of life, just one knot in the biospherical net. The intrinsic value of nonhuman members of the biotic community is recognized and the right of these members to pursue their own evolutionary destinies is taken as 'a clear and obvious axiom'. In contrast the idea that humans are the source or ground of all value ('the measure of all things') is viewed as an arrogant conceit of those who dwell in the moral equivalent of a Ptolemaic universe. Deep ecologists are concerned to move heaven and earth in this universe in order to affect a paradigm shift of comparable significance to that associated with Copernicus.[40]

In a book entitled *Communication and Argument: Elements of Applied Semantics* (1966), Næss recommends that those involved in public discussion should avoid the use of derogatory language and refrain from making straw-man caricatures of their opponents' positions. But the deep ecology movement sometimes seems to employ both tactics. The kind of activist rhetoric it indulges in seems deeply problematic. The very distinction these authors make between 'deep' and 'shallow' ecology is itself partisan. Is it better to have a deep or a shallow commitment to a good cause? Clearly, the word *deep* has many positive connotations; the word *shallow*, many 'negative' ones. The use of the deep–shallow distinction does not constitute a fair and even-handed use of terminology. We need to evaluate opposing views on environmental questions without resorting to loaded language.

Fox informs us that old authors believed that humans are the source of all value and that man is the measure of all things. Considered as an account of the history of moral philosophy, these allegations are wholly inaccurate. As previously discussed, the first moral philosophers argued that we must act 'according to nature'. This was a widespread intuition shared by most ancient philosophers. Protagoras was making a specific epistemological point when he claimed that 'man is the measure of all things'; he was not commenting on environmental ethics. And, in any case, most ancient authors *disagreed* with Protagoras's oracular pronouncement. It is simply incorrect to suggest that ancient philosophers such as the Stoics (or even the Epicureans) viewed human beings as isolated sources of value in a worthless universe. On the contrary, they taught that human beings were an integral part of the cosmos and that morality meant submitting to laws that regulate this greater whole. Ancient skeptics believed that one should refrain from imposing one's wants and desires on the world; ancient asceticism required that we moderate

our appetites and accept nature's ways; ancient cynicism taught that we should actually live like animals. Aristotle and the Medievals turned the focus on human nature but they never disputed its biological basis defining human beings as rational animals. And so on.

Western moral philosophy has consistently emphasized the moral grandeur of human beings as rational animals. But the anthropocentrism that deep ecologists critique is not a manipulative attempt to prop up the status of human beings. It is a frank acknowledgment of an obvious, unequivocal fact about the world. Disinterested observation demonstrates that human beings do have special abilities, that they are the smartest animals, that they have a capacity for language, moral discernment, and a level of abstract reasoning that sets them apart from other species. To make this acknowledgment a part of moral philosophy is not devious or dishonest; it is to deal with the natural facts as they present themselves to us. Deep ecologists, being human, engage in a level of moral reflection that is foreign to parrots and lions and tigers and salmon and salamanders and rose bushes. It does not follow that other animals and plants have no value, but only that human beings have special moral status. Human beings have a noble destiny as conscientious, reflective, self-aware, philosophically-capable agents. That one should have to remind modern readers of this point seems, at least, surprising.

Fox, following Næss, argues for a unified metaphysics that sees the distinctions between individual things as mere appearances that cloak a unified reality. Proponents of deep ecology discern a deeper, almost mystical connection between things. Although there are interesting metaphysical issues here, there is an obvious sense in which the world *is*

ᴥ Applied Philosophy Box 10.3 ᴥ

'All Animals Are Equal'

Peter Singer

The speciesist allows the interests of his own species to override the greater interests of members of other species. . . . Most human beings are speciesists. . . . For the great majority of human beings, especially in urban, industrialized societies, the most direct form of contact with members of other species is at meal-times: we eat them. In doing so we treat them purely as means to our ends. We regard their life and well-being as subordinate to our taste for a particular kind of dish. I say 'taste' deliberately—this is purely a matter of pleasing our palate. There can be no defence of eating flesh in terms of satisfying nutritional needs, since it has been established beyond doubt that we could satisfy our need for protein and other essential nutrients far more efficiently with a diet that replaced animal flesh by soy beans, or products derived from soy beans, and other high-protein vegetable products.

Why does Singer think that vegetarianism is morally required? What are the arguments on the other side of the issue?

Source: Peter Singer, 'All Animals Are Equal,' abridged from an essay first published in *Philosophic Exchange, 1* (5), www.fortunecity.com/emachines/e11/86/singer.html, Summer 1974.

composed of discrete, separate things. If you cut me with a knife, I feel pain; you do not. Your hand is not a part of me but a part of something else. This is not to discount the interconnectedness among things, something roundly acknowledged by older metaphysics. At the same time, we cannot deny the obvious fact of individuality. To argue that individual human beings are merely knots in a sea of tangled strands is to undervalue the uniqueness of individuals and their moral integrity as repositories of intrinsic value.

At the beginning of the movement, deep ecologists emphasized biological **egalitarianism**, the idea that all species having the same moral value. The term *speciesism* was used to condemn unequal treatment of nonhuman species. Peter Singer, in particular, used the concept to condemn meat-eating as immoral. We don't eat other human beings for

dinner. Why, then, he asked, do we have the right to eat other animals for dinner? Singer compares our attitude toward animals to discrimination practised against ethnic minorities. But the parallel Singer makes between speciesism and racism is not exact. Clearly, it is wrong for human beings of one race to treat members of another race as inferior. But speciesism has nothing to do with the unequal treatment of two groups of human beings. It has to do with two *different* species of unequal abilities. Is it unreasonable to suggest that species with clearly unequal abilities should be treated unequally? That seems to be a sensitive, rational response to the unalterable fact of biological difference.

As a society, we often practise discrimination in some morally neutral sense: We don't allow people without a driver's licence to get behind the wheel; we do not allow people who are not doctors to prescribe antibiotics; we do not allow children to vote, and so on. This is to exclude some people from certain privileges and activities. Such 'discrimination' is not immoral because it is based on a rational appraisal of agents' abilities. If we are going to base our moral philosophy on a sensitive reading of the book of nature, it would be inaccurate to overlook or ignore the fact of species differentiation. This is not to suggest that human beings should not care for nonhuman species, but it also means that there is nothing unnatural or unecological about human beings having a special concern for other human beings, a natural behaviour that characterizes other species as well. (The fact that human beings also care for non-human species in a prolonged, deliberate, and thoughtful manner derives from their particular status as reflective beings and contributes to their moral dignity.)

Valuing different species to unequal degrees depending upon their unequal abilities is not an absurd idea. Aristotle divides living organisms into plants, animals, and human beings. Plants metabolize and reproduce. Animals have additional capacities for perception and memory; they are capable of locomotion; they experience pleasure and pain. Only human beings are rational; they are capable of self-reflection and knowledge; they can distinguish between right and wrong. It seems a glaring error of omission to ignore this distinct human capacity when determining the degree to which human beings should be valued. It makes sense to claim that, for a wide variety of reasons, the distinguishing characteristics of humanity are morally momentous.

Singer's arguments notwithstanding, ecologists themselves propose an *unequal* approach to valuing things in the world, distinguishing between more and less valuable forms of life. Even vegetarians make a distinction between the moral status of plants and animals. They believe that plants are suitable for human consumption because they are incapable of perception and memory and because they do not feel pleasure and pain. But a similar type of moral gap arguably separates human beings from other animals. No one would argue that all forms of life ought to equally preserved or allowed to multiply to the maximum extent possible. So, for example, environmentalists in Australia have themselves advocated trapping and shooting feral cats because they eat large numbers of indigenous mammals and birds as well as called for the extermination of over-populating European rabbits that decimate and corrode the native vegetation and disrupt the original ecosystem.

Authors such as Næss and Fox argue that deep ecologists recognize the intrinsic value of nonhuman species and that shallow ecologists view nonhuman species as having instrumental value with respect to human purposes. In making the tendentious distinction between deep and shallow ecology, however, they ignore Plato's observation in the *The Republic* that the very same thing can have *both* intrinsic and instrumental value. We are not forced to choose between two mutually exclusive options. Animals may usefully contribute to human ends while being appreciated for their beauty, their conscious complexity, and their diversity. We can, at the same time, recognize the instrumental and the intrinsic value of nature. It is not wrong for humans to pursue their own survival in a wise and ethical manner. All living organisms exploit their environment in order to survive. If, however, the survival of humanity is a noble cause, this only adds force to the moral requirement that we be good stewards of nature. Ecological disaster, which is largely fuelled by the uncritical application of technology and by unbounded hedonism would be a moral as well as a natural catastrophe. The natural world plays an essential role in supporting both human and nonhuman life. We have a moral responsibility to preserve the natural world. As rational animals with the ability to foresee and correct ecological disaster, we are obliged to preserve the world for future human generations and for its own sake.

The ultimate moral solution for ecological problems can be found in perennial moral theories. The keen social observer cannot help but note that serious threats to the environment can usually be traced to ordinary vices such as greed, laziness, carelessness, waste, apathy, anger, pride, selfishness, and so on. Technological advances, economic pressures, political struggles, may combine to produce problems of calamitous proportions. Still, as Aristotle would have argued, morality requires virtue. We must change our habits. This is the fundamental solution to environmental questions.

Contemporary Contractarianism: Rational Agreement

John Rawls

John Rawls (1921–2002) has been credited with reviving academic interest in political philosophy in the later half of the twentieth century. In two influential books, *A Theory of Justice* (1971) and *Political Liberalism* (1993), he constructs a theory of justice that deeply marked several generations of Anglo-American political philosophers and ethicists.[41] At the end of his life, the Harvard professor turned to issues about international law and to critical reflections on the history of political thought. We briefly consider his account of distributive justice here. Although Rawls demonstrates a sincere commitment to individual freedom and social welfare, his ideas are open to serious criticism. They have had a restricting influence on the ethical debate in liberal society and can be seen as generally antithetical to any notion that government should promote virtue.

There are various ways of approaching the topic of justice. Retributive justice is about how we ought to punish people. Compensatory or restorative (or corrective) justice is about providing restitution to those who have been harmed by others. Procedural justice is about maintaining even-handed methods that efficiently apply the principles of good government. And, finally, **distributive justice** is about fairly dividing up goods and resources among citizens in a society. Although these categories overlap, Rawls is particularly concerned with the last question: how should we distribute goods among individual citizens in a just society?

Rawls adopts a social contract approach, proposing the following thought-experiment. Suppose we were to come together to determine how society should be organized. Rawls calls this the **original position**. People in the original position are unable to coerce each other. They exist as anonymous individuals in some timeless realm, waiting to decide which society to institute—like people waiting to vote in an election. But there is a problem.

Rawls believes that if we were to ask ordinary individuals how we should distribute goods, they would, in all likelihood, choose whichever system is to their own advantage. People who belong to a certain social class, ethnic group, political persuasion, religion, gender, or profession would likely favour the system that distributed the most goods to their own group. But we want individuals in the original position to choose the fairest method of distribution. Rawls suggests then that we must place these individuals behind a **veil of ignorance**. We must hide the specifics of their own personal identity from them. They cannot know who their family members are, what talents they possess, or anything about their ethnicity, gender, religion, and social class. They must choose without knowing which social arrangement will specifically favour them.

Rawls believes that individuals in the original position behind a veil of ignorance will agree to the safest arrangement possible. They will adopt (what is known in modern game theory as) a **maximin strategy**; they will choose the social structure that produces the maximum payoff for those in the most minimal positions. They will do this, not out of altruistic motives, but out of rational self-interest, because once the veil of ignorance is removed, they may discover that they themselves belong to the least favoured social group. They will agree then to whatever social arrangement produces the best results for the worst-off members of society.

More specifically, Rawls argues that individuals in the original position will choose a society that is regulated according two basic principles. The first and most important principle of justice is that 'each person is to have an equal right to the most extensive scheme of equal basic liberties compatible with a similar scheme of liberties for others'.[42] The second principle is that 'social and economic inequalities are to be arranged so that they are both a) to the greatest benefit of the least-advantaged and (b) attached to offices and positions open to all under conditions of equality and opportunity'.[43]

In short, we can summarize Rawls's theory by identifying three principles of good government. In light of some irregularity in accepted terminology, we will refer to these principles as follows:

1. The **liberty principle**—that everyone has as much freedom (understood as choice) as possible.
2. The **opportunity principle**—that everyone has equal, fair access to opportunity and positions of authority.
3. The **wealth principle** (usually called 'the difference principle')—that wealth be distributed in such a way that the poorest members of society benefit as much as possible.

Rawls makes a point of opposing utilitarianism in favour of liberalism. (Remember Mill had tried to be a utilitarian *and* a liberal.) Although Rawls qualifies his arguments in ways we cannot enter into here, his basic aim is to promote a socially-conscientious and prosperous liberalism. Rawls believes that if we allow people as much liberty and opportunity as possible, while refraining, as much as possible, from intervening with economic and social life, we can structure society so as to produce more prosperity for the least advantaged. Although Rawls would *not* express his preoccupations in these terms, we could say that he defends liberalism, understood as maximum free choice (the liberty principle), through a moral appeal to improvements in social welfare.

Viewed from the perspective of moral philosophy, there are two main problems with Rawls's theory of 'justice as fairness'. First, Rawls's account of justice seems theoretically inconsistent. Because of the lexical ordering of the three principles—liberty trumps opportunity, which trumps wealth—it seems to collapse inevitably into extreme libertarianism. Any government attempt to affect the distribution of opportunity or wealth will, it seems, violate the liberty principle. We cannot *force* people to act in a way that ensures there is equal opportunity or social welfare for everyone without restricting liberty. If liberty really does trump all other values, this leaves little room for the implementation of the other two principles. Any time there is a conflict between more liberty and more something else, we will have to choose more liberty. Despite his arguments to the contrary, Rawls's theory seems to collapse into a one-value system. What really matters is liberty. A rigorous Rawlsian might end up embracing libertarianism, but Rawls's three-valued theory seems to inadvertently disguise what is really going on.

The second problem with Rawls's theory is both theoretical and practical. Rawls claimed to base his notion of justice on **a thin theory of the good**. Because individuals in the original position would be placed behind a veil of ignorance, they would have no inkling of what they actually believed in terms of larger ideas about morality, religion, and even philosophy. So, Rawls reasoned, they would not choose a social arrangement that favoured any distinctive set of beliefs over any other. They would instead opt for a morally neutral government that did not attach itself to any 'comprehensive doctrine of the good'.

In Rawls's contractarian thought-experiment, agents in the original position can not make decisions based on any robust sense of morality. They base their choices uniquely on those instrumental goods that everyone has to value as a means to their own private aspirations. These instrumental goods include things such as health, money, power, political influence,

and so on. We all need health, for example, to accomplish our more specific goals and private aspirations, so it can operate as a universal good that everyone in the original position values. This way of setting out the original position makes a very minimal subset of instrumental goods—a thin theory of the good—the ultimate basis for political legitimacy.

Critics claim first, that Rawls is not as morally neutral as he claims, that his way of identifying primary goods and of determining the outcome of the selection procedure is heavily biased in favour of a pre-selected outcome. Second, they argue that it is impossible to establish justice on the basis of non-moral decision-making. Morality is an important value that should and would effect citizens entering into any kind of serious political and social arrangement.

To be fair, we should point out that Rawls introduces a useful notion of **overlapping consensus** in his later work, arguing that individuals who embrace different world views can still find enough common ground to produce a widely acceptable account of justice. But even this concession seems too narrow. Moral world views are not like shapes on a piece of paper that happen to overlap along their edges. They are more like irregularly shaped geometrical figures that turn, nonetheless, around the same centre. Different moral, religious, political, and even cultural traditions find their inspiration in a common fund of human experience: the individual lived experience of birth, death, love, hope, friendship, virtue, vice, happiness, unhappiness, and so on. Moral world views are not accidentally but essentially similar.

Authors like Rawls often exaggerate differences and minimize resemblances in moral beliefs. They focus on divisive issues (which do undoubtedly exist) and overlook a common fund of moral wisdom. To cite an example advanced by Amitai Etzioni, consider the virtue of honesty. Yes, there may be strange circumstances where truth-telling is problematic. Yes, there may be things we are not allowed to tell others. Nonetheless, we all acknowledge that truth-telling is an essential aspect of morality: it is good to tell the truth. Truth-telling can be a rallying point around which reasonable people in political society can gather. (Indeed, we could not have much confidence in public discussion that was not based on a fundamental commitment to truth-telling.)

Rawls goes on to propose a process of 'wide reflective equilibrium' as a method of reasoning about justice and ethics. Reasoners are to move back and forth between the different strands of moral belief until they achieve a coherent world view that logically supports or explains their views. The German philosopher Jürgen Habermas elaborates a somewhat similar theory he calls 'discourse ethics'. Suffice it to say here that although discussion provides an important resource for moral thinking, it is not enough that we act consistently with our own beliefs or even that we agree one another. We must also be attentive to a larger fund of moral knowledge and insight that has been recognized and examined by great thinkers in the past.

The Prisoners' Dilemma

Some contemporary decision-theorists have developed a mathematical analogue to contractarian arguments called the prisoners' dilemma. They attempt to use this thought experiment, which can be programmed in the form of a computer game, to demonstrate the rationality of morality. The issue has been much discussed and the approach to morality it repre-sents provides a useful foil to the virtue ethics account developed here.

Decision-theorists use applied mathematics to study and evaluate decision-making among interacting agents, often in a competitive context. This approach, which focuses generalized situations, is based on certain assumptions. It assumes that rational agents are self-interested, that we can know the consequences of decisions, and that these consequences can be quantitatively evaluated. Decision-theorists use an economic-like ranking of possible choices to evaluate how *rational* agents should act. The goal is to determine what behaviour most serves the agents' interests. Consider then the prisoners' dilemma.

The prisoners' dilemma can be explained in terms of a simple narrative. Suppose a crime has been committed. The punishment is 10 years in the local penitentiary. The police arrest the two suspects (who they know have committed the crime) and interrogate them separately. Because the police have only enough evidence to sentence each suspect to six months in jail for some minor charge, they encourage each to turn on the other. They separately offer each the following arrangement: Rat on your partner and we will see to it that it is to your advantage. If he remains silent, you will go free (as a reward) and he will receive a full 10-year sentence. Even if he rats on you, you will only receive 5 years with 5 years off for your confession. We can set out the possible choices and outcomes for each prisoner in the following decision-matrix:

The most important feature of the decision-situation is that self-interested thinking seems to lead to a less than optimal outcome. Analyze the circumstances from the viewpoint of

Prisoners' Dilemma

	A does not rat	*A* rats
B does not rat	*A* gets 6 months jail time *B* gets 6 months jail time	*A* gets 0 jail time *B* gets 10 years jail time
B rats	*A* gets 10 years jail time *B* gets 0 jail time	*A* gets 5 years jail time *B* gets 5 years jail time

prisoner *A*. *A* must consider two possibilities. Either his partner does not rat or he rats. If *B* does not rat, it is best for *A* to rat, for then he will get no jail time instead of 6 months. But if *B* rats, it is also best for *A* to rat, for then he will get 5 years jail time instead of 10 years jail time. So either way, it is best for *A* to rat. The very same reasoning holds true for *B*. It follows, then, that if the two prisoners act out of purely self-interested motives, they will both rat. This will result in a 5-year jail sentence for both suspects. Notice, however, that there is a better outcome! If neither prisoner rats, each will get only six months jail time. So it is better if the two prisoners co-operate with one another. It seems then that morality, understood as co-operation, is in our self-interest. If *A* promises *B* never to rat, and if *B* promises *A* never to rat, and if they both *keep* their promises, they will both be better off. Co-operation is better, it seems, than self-interest. So an exclusive focus on self-interest thinking is not, paradoxically, in our own self-interest. Contractarian decision-theorists use this example to argue that morality is, in an economic sense, rational—i.e., that it is in our self-interest for all of us to be moral.

We have already discussed contractarianism at length in an earlier chapter, but a few criticisms are in order here. First, note that the moral thing to do in the prisoner's dilemma situation is to co-operate with the police and confess everything regardless of the penalty. This is what honesty and moral responsibility require. It is at least odd to use a story about criminals getting away with crime to explain the rationality of morality. But overlook that sort of complication here. There is a bigger problem.

The prisoners' dilemma deals with criminals who have been caught by the police. But what about criminals who never get caught? Seen from a purely economic perspective, morality (understood as co-operation) is a better option than unsuccessful crime, but successful crime is still a better option than morality. As the ancient Greek Sophist Antiphon (about fifth century BC), explains, 'He who breaks the rules . . . and escapes detection . . . incurs no shame or penalty'.[44] Antiphon bluntly describes the most profitable way of life: 'A man will be just, then, in a way most advantageous to himself if, in the presence of witnesses he holds the laws of the city in high esteem, and in the absence of witnesses, when he is alone, [he holds] those of [his own selfish] nature in high esteem.'[45] The best way to be successful is, according to Antiphon, by making a public display of morality while reverting to whatever is to one's own advantage (even criminality) when there is no one around to see what one is doing.

Game-theorists, in response to worries about agents who cheat on their partners, have proposed an **iterated prisoners' dilemma**. This game-theory problem takes the formal structure of the prisoner's dilemma and turns it into a hypothetical competition that is played over and over again on a computer using the same players, choices, and outcomes. Two (or more) players interact, co-operating or not, and with input from this encounter, play again, again, and again. Studies show that although unco-operative players may take advantage of their playing partners at first, as the game progresses, victims quickly 'wise up' to their selfish motives and stop co-operating with them. Any player who hopes to gain the long-term benefits of co-operation with other players must co-operate regularly or they lose the opportunity for mutually beneficial co-operation. This is, as we have seen, the basic idea behind contractarianism. Accept basic limitations on your own actions so that you can benefit from the limitations other people place on their actions.

Although the iterated prisoners' dilemma reinforces the basic themes of contractarianism in a new, more rigorous way, it does not solve the problem of the successful cheater. *Successful* cheaters cheat in secret (maybe only once for a big payoff) and never get caught. We keep on co-operating with them because we do not realize that they are taking advantage of us. True, most criminals (we hope) do get caught. And if other people know that we are immoral, they will refuse to co-operate with us. Still, how can we show that even successful cheating, when it is possible, is not in our self-interest? There is a religious and a secular answer to this problem. Religion tells cheaters who think they will not get caught: you *cannot* escape detection from a vengeful God who functions, in part, as an all-knowing, all-powerful policing agency. In the religious

model, all cheaters get caught, for God enforces the social contract.

Contemporary philosopher David Gauthier suggests a secular alternative. If people feel guilty when they act immorally, this will be an obstacle to immoral impulses. Gauthier concludes that society should inculcate stringent moral values in all its citizens. If people who act immorally inevitably feel shame and guilt, even successful criminals will be punished by their own conscience. Conscience can be a powerful deterrent if, given the basic structure of human nature, remorse and shame arise not randomly but as a necessary consequence of seriously immoral behaviour. Presumably, except in the case of serious dysfunction, human nature recoils at the idea of serious evil.

We can compare the prisoners' dilemma situation to Rawls's account of the original position. In both cases, we have amoral or almost amoral agents (with a thin theory of the good) coming to an agreement on the basis of their own self-interest. This implicit contract is supposed to lead to a co-operative arrangement that these contractarian authors go on to associate with morality. But this can be questioned. Present-day communitarian author Michael Sandel points out that the mere fact that someone agrees to something does not make it moral.[46] It is not enough that agents agree to arrangement X. To show that this arrangement is moral, we must be able to show that they *should* have agreed to X. We cannot do this by pointing to the mere fact that they agreed. To say that they should have agreed is to say that X satisfies some higher standard of goodness, fairness, decency, benevolence, etc.

Sandel and his colleagues complain that contemporary contractarianism does not give us enough of a reason for morality. It is not enough to show that self-interested agents will consent to specific arrangements, that they have amoral preferences that result in certain amoral agreements. Because contemporary contractarians avoid any deep discussion of the virtues, of human nature, of duty, of moral intuition, of intrinsic value (etc.), they leave deeper questions largely unanswered. They simply assume that agreements are morally good because they are agreed to, but this is to beg the question.

Any contractarianism that relies exclusively on the prisoners' dilemma situation provides an impoverished or thin account of morality. An exclusive contractarianism reduces morality to prudential calculation. We are to do what is good for us economically. But this approach results in a pure consequentialism, in a moral theory that focuses exclusively on the predictable consequences of different choice patterns. And to self-interestedly pursue good consequences for oneself is to ignore much of what morality is about. Still, it seems better to view contractarianism as a helpful attempt to understand moral reasoning than to dismiss it out of hand. Although self-interest may not be an entirely noble way to convince someone to be moral, it is a beginning. Such considerations, at least, may give the morally lukewarm a good push in the direction of morality.

In an age fraught with **moral skepticism**, exclusive contractarianism may seem like an attractive alternative. When we are nervous about making robust moral claims, it seems easier to reduce morality to amoral agreement. We must resist such simplifications. Some adepts of the prisoners' dilemma scenario aim to produce morality out of amoral preference. There is nothing wrong with self-interest that is permeated with morality, but the project of creating morality out of amoral, self-interested preference comes up short. It misrepresents the human condition. Authors in the tradition would argue that an amoral human being is a contradiction-in-terms. We cannot eliminate morality from reflective human decision-making. That is not how healthy human beings operate. Human behaviour entails a search for deep consistency and moral ideals that transcends an amoral consequentialism.

Epilogue

Finishing up this book, the author met a young man on a train. He was terribly concerned about his future. He related to me how he had been home for a visit and how everyone had been asking him what he was going to do now that he was finishing his university studies and entering into the 'real world'. He had no idea, but we began discussing the importance of ethics as a guide to decision-making. The basic premise behind this book is that morality is the only reliable source of self-fulfillment and enduring happiness. These pages provide you with a large body of concepts, principles, arguments, insights, methods, and explanations built up over a long period of time by great thinkers. Hopefully, you can find here values you can believe in, values you can thoroughly and sensitively apply to the individual circumstances of your life, values you can defend through educated argument. Choice is both a responsibility and an opportunity. When I talked to the young man on the train, we did not come to any fixed conclusion about what he should do with the rest of his life. Finishing the conversation, he asked me for some advice. I told him, in effect, 'Be a good human being. If you can succeed at ethics, that is already a great accomplishment'.

ఴ Questions for Study and Review ఴ

1. Describe, in your own words, the basic principles of anti-theory. What are members of this loose movement in contemporary philosophy reacting against?
2. Briefly list five criticisms of modern moral theory made by anti-theorists.
3. How does Kierkegaard distinguish between the esthetic and the ethical?
4. Explain Kierkegaard's concept of 'willed ignorance'. How does Kierkegaard disagree with Socrates?
5. What is the basic metaphysical and moral idea behind personalism?
6. How does Noddings distinguish between 'caring for' and 'caring about'?
7. In Gerwith's formulation, 'A has a right to X against B by virtue of Y'. Explain with an example that has not been discussed in the text.
8. Describe the Medieval debate that gave rise to the modern notion of a right. What was the issue being discussed? Express that right in terms of Gerwith's formulation.
9. What is divine command morality?
10. Presumably God must always act in a way that discerning human beings recognize as moral. Religious thinkers claim, nonetheless, that it is technically, theologically, wrong to claim that God must conform to human morality. Why? Explain.
11. How do members of the global ethics initiative respond to the charge of religious fanaticism?
12. How do deep ecologists differentiate between 'deep ecology' and 'shallow ecology'?
13. Define the term *speciesism*.
14. Explain Rawls's account of the original position and the veil of ignorance. What is the point of this hypothetical scenario?
15. Describe the prisoners' dilemma scenario using a decision matrix to outline the different choices and outcomes. What is the moral of the story? What are these new contractarians trying to prove?

ఴ Suggestions for Further Reading ఴ

- Perhaps the most famous treatise in modern virtue-ethics and anti-theory: Alasdair McIntyre, *After Virtue* (Notre Dame, IN: University of Notre Dame Press, 1984).
- Søren Kierkegaard, *Either/Or*, Howard V. Hong and Edna H. Hong, trans., 2 vols. (Princeton, NJ: Princeton University Press, 1987).
- Nel Noddings, *Caring: A Feminine Approach to Ethics and Moral Education* (Berkeley: University of California Press, 1984).
- 'The Universal Declaration of Human Rights,' United Nations, 1948, available at the UN website: www.un.org/en/documents/udhr/index.shtml.
- 'Declaration Toward a Global Ethic,' Global Ethic Foundation, Tübingen, Germany, electronic source: www.weltethos.org/dat-english/index.htm.
- John Rawls, *A Theory of Justice* (Cambridge, MA: Belknap Press of Harvard University Press, 1971).
- Michael Sandel, *Liberalism and the Limits of Justice* (Cambridge, UK: Cambridge, 1998).
- Amitai Etzioni, *The New Golden Rule: Community and Morality in a Democratic Society* (New York: Basic Books, 1996).

ᗒ Glossary ᗕ

a priori reason the ability to know specific truths through reason alone, independent (or prior) to lived experience, sense perception, desire, or emotion.

absolute skeptic one who does not believe we can be certain about anything; he or she denies all definite claims to true knowledge, both practical and theoretical (compare mitigated skeptic).

actuality the condition of actually existing as fulfilled possibility (compare **potentiality**).

additive obligations obligations that are added onto more general moral duties because of the special circumstances of our lives; particularly because of personal relationships to other people or because of specific contractual (consensual) arrangements (see also obligations).

agent a being capable of acting under its own impetus; capable of initiating its own actions (from the Latin *agere*, meaning 'to do').

act utilitarianism focuses on the happiness produced by individual acts: we should always choose whatever act produces the most utility (see utilitarianism).

agnosticism refusing to pronounce for or against a belief, theory, or cause; associated with the skeptical view that we cannot know anything for certain; in a modern, religious context, professing neither belief nor disbelief in God.

akolasia a Greek word for self-excused excess, translated more specifically as self-indulgence or licentiousness.

akrasia Greek word for weakness of will (see **incontinence**).

alienation for Marx, the dehumanized condition of the oppressed workers who become strangers to their true human selves.

amoral having no moral standards or restraints; unaware of or indifferent to questions of right and wrong.

amour de soi-même for Rousseau, reasonable, natural love of oneself and concern for self-preservation.

amour propre for Rousseau, artificially-induced pride, competitiveness with others, a vicious, excessive self-love.

anachronistic out of proper or chronological order; reading modern ideas or themes into older texts.

ancient cynics a school of philosophy that proposes a positive ideal of animal-like behaviour that frees itself from what they see as the artificial impositions of polite society. Attacking social convention, they insist on a return to bare biological instinct for those who wish to be truly happy.

ancient skepticism a movement led by Pyrrho. Ancient sceptics valued scepticism as a means to happiness understood as freedom from anxiety (*ataraxia*).

angels in theology, pure spirits who, because they are more intelligent than human beings, are able to immediately intuit knowledge.

anomie a condition of normlessness; an absence of meaningful standards or ethical structure that drains life of significance and leads, in extreme cases, to apathy and suicide (from Greek *a-*, 'without', and *nomos*, 'law').

antecedent ignorance ignorance that cannot be traced to any act of will; it happens before one makes a decision and produces an involuntary act (see involuntary ignorance).

anti-morality to be against morality; the view that morality hampers the full expression of human potentiality, that it is opposed to freedom and therefore deeply inadequate, stultifying, or unsatisfying.

anti-theory a loose movement in contemporary ethics that argues (among other things) that the standard academic approach (involving deontology and consequentialism) is severely impoverished, that virtue is a more promising approach than moral law, that morality must be sensitive to individual context, and that individuals must be treated as part of communities.

antithesis opposition; contrast. The ancient sceptics tried to counterbalance every thesis with an antithesis to produce suspension of belief (*epoche*) as a means to peace of mind.

apathy from the Greek term *apatheia*, meaning without passion; lack of emotion or conviction (compare **stoic apathy**).

aphorisms short, pithy sayings or condensed thoughts that are sometimes difficult to decipher.

aporia Greek word for an insoluble paradox; when there is no conceivable answer to a puzzle.

appetites general, physical desires; for Plato, the

lowest part of the human constitution made up of biological, a-rational urges (*epithumetikon*) that produces unruly desire (compare **reason**, **spirit**).

arete Greek word for *virtue*, also translated more broadly as human 'excellence'.

argument a collection of one or more statements called premises that logically lead to and support another statement called a conclusion.

asceticism the deliberate practice of self-denial, abstinence, austerity to build character.

askesis from the Greek verb *askeo*, meaning exercise, practice, or training (hence asceticism).

asymmetry principle the idea that one should respond to evil in an asymmetrical way; e.g., by returning good for evil (associated especially with Socrates and Jesus).

ataraxia a Greek term for a stable mental condition of peace of mind or unperturbedness that was generally aimed at by early philosophers.

autonomy successful self-government or self-rule; for Kant, the condition of being in successful moral control of one's own actions that befits rational agents; in liberalism, autonomy (or 'personal autonomy') means possessing ultimate control over one's life and actions, freedom from external control or coercion.

bad faith (*mauvaise foi*) a chronic condition of insincerity or self-deception.

Beatitudes eight declarations of blessedness (or happiness) made by Jesus in the famous Sermon on the Mount.

beg the question to give no true support for a position; to assume the truth of a conclusion.

belief the second stage of learning in the Divided Line; referring to the strong conviction and confidence (*pistis*) we feel about the reality of sensible things and the truthfulness of our observations (see Divided Line).

blatant immorality one of Kant's four categories of human behaviour; an unambiguously evil situation in which one deliberately breaks the moral law.

bouleusis Greek word for *deliberation*; involves choosing a course of action as a means to the right end; skill at choosing the right course of action (hence *eubulia*, meaning good deliberation).

brutishness for Aristotle, the most ignoble state of morality; gross ignorance of morality or extreme wickedness, like an animal.

burden of proof to argue for the more controversial side of a dispute; to be logically required to establish one's point of view or lose the dispute.

cannon law body of laws adopted by (Christian) ecclesiastical authority for the government of the church.

cardinal virtues virtues relating to natural morality, the four cardinal virtues are prudence, temperance, justice, and fortitude. According to Thomas, they are the four necessary contributing factors for each and every instance of moral behaviour. The cardinal virtues relate to the ordinary working of human nature and have as their object a good life (compare **theological virtues**).

casuistry the technical term for the art of applying general rules to specific cases. Having taken on more negative connotations, the term sometimes refers to deceptive or over-subtle reasoning used by those looking to excuse morally dubious behaviour.

categorical imperative the moral law that must always be obeyed by everyone. Although Kant offers various formulations, it can be, most fundamentally, described as the ethical principle that one must do what all others should do under similar circumstances. Unlike **hypothetical imperatives**, the categorical imperative is a command that admits no exceptions.

choice for Aristotle, choice involves acts dignified by a certain intellectual intention. When one makes a choice one is morally aware of what one is doing and of alternative possibilities and therefore can be held accountable for one's actions; voluntary acts may or may not involve choice.

circular reasoning an argument in which a premise is used to support the conclusion and the conclusion is in turn used to support the premise.

communitarian someone who argues that individuals can only be properly understood in terms of their relationships to other people; what makes life worth living is not bare freedom but a sense of belonging and loyalty to others.

concomitant ignorance ignorance that accompanies an act without eliminating its badness, because the act is an expression of guilty intentions or the ignorance comes about through negligence.

concupiscible passions feelings that involve desires that push and pull us toward what seems to be good and away from what seems bad (compare **irascible passions**).

Confucianism moral system taught and practiced by Master Kong (Confucius) and his followers.

conjecture the first stage of learning in the Divided Line; knowledge of images (*eikasia*) and illusions, also called 'imagination' (see Divided Line).

connaturality knowing moral criteria, not through concepts or logic, but through inclination and lived experience.

conscience the inner sense of what is right or wrong in one's conduct or motives, the faculty of moral knowledge that also impels or thrusts one toward right action. Thomas sets down moral conscience as the prior condition for **prudence**.

consent voluntary agreement or knowledgeable voluntary agreement; in moral liberalism, the ultimate criterion for morality; for Thomas, we must consent, not only to our goals, but to the means we use to achieve those goals.

consequentialist someone who subscribes to 'consequentialism', the theory that the good or bad consequences of an act uniquely determine its moral status (coined by G. E. M. Anscombe). A good act is an act with good consequences; a bad act is an act with bad consequences.

contemplative life the life of study and thinking; for Aristotle, the most noble life; also Latin: *via contemplativa* (compare **life of enjoyment**, **political life**).

continence self-restraint; abstinence.

contractarianism generally, the view that morality is an obligation that arises from an implicit social contract or agreement between consenting parties (see exclusive contractarianism, forward-looking contractarianism, two-tiered contractarianism).

cosmopolitanism the belief that political and national distinctions are inconsequential or of secondary moral importance, that human beings are fundamentally all citizens of the same country sometimes understood as the universe as a whole.

counsel for Thomas, good deliberation; helps us choose the right means, the most efficient strategy, to accomplish our ends (compare *bouleusis*)

courage overcoming what is naturally repugnant, frightening, or unpleasant; for Plato, the virtue that principally characterizes the spirit. When the honourable part of the soul functions properly, it shows enthusiasm and determination about the right things, following the guide of reason (see spirit); for Aristotle, courage is unique among virtues in that it requires that one go against one's short-term inclinations.

Dao 'The Way'; how things must be according to nature, understood both in terms of the big pattern or structure that underlies surface-reality and in terms of the lives of moral individuals (Confucianism)."

deduction a form of reasoning that involves a movement from a general designation to particular cases (compare **induction**); e.g., All human beings are mortal; Socrates, Plato, and Aristotle are all human beings; therefore Socrates, Plato, and Aristotle are mortal.

deductive (practical) wisdom in Aristotle, the mental ability or cognitive faculty that moves from the general idea of virtue to the specific application (compare **inductive virtue**).

deep ecology school of environmental ethics that argues that nature has intrinsic rather than instrumental value, that humans are *not* more valuable elements of the ecosystem, and that Western ethics has been monstrously anthropocentric; coined by Arne Naess (compare **shallow ecology**).

defeasible in the case of duties, capable of being defeated or overridden by other pressing concerns.

defence of necessity in law, to justify an illegal act by pointing out that in the circumstances it was necessary to act in such a manner to save one's life (see right of nature).

deinotes Greek word for cleverness, quickness, or readiness of mind; *deinotes* is a natural intelligence that allows us to fit means to ends. **Deductive practical wisdom** is a more specific manifestation of the general ability of *deinotes* (see deductive practical wisdom).

deontological ethics school of ethics that defines right action principally in terms of duty; more broadly, any appeal to general or professional duties (see duty).

deontologists those who subscribe to deontology, largely Kantians, who emphasize importance of good will understood as the intention to do one's duty.

desire the appetite for something pleasant or good (biological and/or intellectual); for Thomas, one of four parts of human nature, associated with the cardinal virtue of temperance or self-restraint (compare **emotion**, **intellect**, **will**).

deterrence as a way to justify punishment, the idea that the threat of punishment deters crime and that incarcerating wrong-doers or executing them is a way to protect society.

différance the difference between the original meaning and later interpretations of a text that comes about because words and ideas are understood differently by different people in different historical periods (coined by Jacques Derrida).

distributive justice the aspect of justice that considers how to divide up goods and resources fairly among citizens in a society.

Divided Line a diagram composed of a vertical line divided into four sections used by Socrates to explain different stages of knowledge (see conjecture, belief, science, knowledge).

divine characteristic of or befitting the gods; of surpassing excellence.

divine command morality stipulates that, in some essential or exclusive way, morality consists of obeying the commands of God.

Divine Law religiously ordained law; Thomas believes that such law can act as an aid to moral thinking because it explicitly states correct moral conclusions that our natural reason can, in hindsight, confirm.

doctrine of double-effect when an act has a good and a bad effect, and the bad effect is not intended or used as the means to the good effect (and other conditions are met), the act is morally acceptable. Thomas explains that someone who kills in self-defence acts morally as long as his goal was not to kill but to defend his own life, which is a moral and commendable act.

dogma a settled or established opinion, belief, or principle deriving from a recognized authority.

duty generally, a task or function we are (morally) obliged to perform; for Kant, the sense that we must do what morality requires simply because morality requires it (regardless of one's feelings).

egalitarianism usually, the theory that people should be treated equally; in traditional utilitarianism, however, it is units of pleasure that must be valued equally.

egoism the notion that things have value only insofar as one's personal interests are concerned; thus, ethical self-centredness.

elenchus Greek word meaning cross-examination; the question-and-answer method of philosophical examination favoured by Socrates.

emotion in the modern sense, feeling or passion devoid of rationality; for Thomas, it includes the feelings of enthusiasm, drive, and dedication that allow us to persist in spite of obstacles (see irascible passions); thus, one of four parts of human nature, associated with the cardinal virtue of fortitude (compare **desire**, **intellect**, **will**).

empathy the experience of crossing over and entering inside someone else; identifying with someone else's feelings, thoughts, or attitudes.

endoxa proverbial, common-sense, or celebrated moral beliefs around which a consensus has

formed. For Aristotle, *endoxa* are a starting point in the development of moral reasoning.

Enlightenment the eighteenth-century philosophical movement in Europe in which reason and individualism were emphasized at the expense of tradition, established authority, and religion.

epicure a person who is excessively fond of sensual pleasure, of fine food and drink, and of luxurious living.

epicurean in ordinary usage, an epicure; in moral philosophy, a follower of Epicurus.

episteme Greek word for *knowledge*; for Plato, knowledge as opposed to opinion (*doxa*) or the highest stage of the Divided Line; Aristotle uses this term to describe rigorous, theoretical science in a broad sense including physics, chemistry, biology, and astronomy, as well as mathematics and even theology (see **science**).

epistemology branch of philosophy that inquires into the nature, limits, and requirements of knowledge (from Greek, *episteme*: knowledge).

epoche Greek term meaning suspension of judgment. Ancient sceptics aimed at *epoche* as a means to *ataraxia*.

esthetic life for Kierkegaard, an amoral (or pre-moral) condition that focuses on momentary amusement and avoids commitment (compare **ethical life**).

eternal law the most fundamental expression of law; the divinely-originated order that pervades the universe. Thomas believes all law has its origin in eternal law.

ethical life for Kierkegaard, the condition of morality that arises after the individual chooses and is true to their choice (compare **esthetic life**).

ethics for Kant, a branch of **material philosophy** that elaborates the laws of freedom that govern human behaviour.

eudaimonia a Greek word meaning happiness understood in terms of a fortunate life; to have a good fate; to be able to look back at your life with pride; literally to be watched over by a good spirit (compare **good reputation**, **happiness**).

Euthyphro problem the argument that religion cannot add anything to ethics because God's commands must satisfy a higher (secular) criterion of what is independently good; the idea that secular, unguided reason is enough to know what is morally good; named after Plato's character.

evil traditionally and for Augustine, the privation of the good.

exclusive contractarianism the idea that hypothetical agreement by itself is enough for morality (see contractarianism).

exploitation for Marx, the economic arrangement whereby owners underpay workers, keeping the value produced by their labour for themselves.

external goods goods that are outside of the body and the mind and therefore beyond our control. They depend on things that happen in the outside world and possess chiefly instrumental value (compare **internal goods**).

false prudence for Thomas, a practical cleverness that aims at a bad end (see prudence).

felicific calculus Bentham's (allegedly) precise method of measuring the utility, and so the total amount of pleasure or pain, produced by a particular act.

fortitude to be strong and resilient; for Thomas, a cardinal virtue associated with the **irascible passions**; fortitude, by its very nature, bestows firmness and perseverance.

forward-looking contractarianism situates the ideal (or hypothetical) social contract that justifies the social structure in the future (as in Marxism) rather than in the past (see contractarianism).

functional argument the idea that the function of something establishes the proper criterion of evaluation. Aristotle argues that if we can identify the function of a human being, we can determine the degree to which an individual succeeds at being a good human being.

general will (*volonté générale*) for Rousseau, the individual wills of citizens joined together into some larger unity; an expression of the common good; the embodiment of some shared judgment.

the gentleman According to Master Kong, the gentleman represents the highest level of moral success (compare **the small man**).

genuine morality one of Kant's four categories of human behaviour that involves acting in accordance with the moral law against self-interest and against inclination.

golden mean Aristotle's account of virtue as a middle between two extremes: excess and deficiency; a rule of thumb or measuring device for figuring out what virtue requires relative to varying circumstances and capabilities.

Golden Rule rule prominently formulated by Jesus of Nazareth to 'do unto others what you would want them to do unto you'. Intended as an encapsulation of the entire moral wisdom of the Judaic

tradition. Similar moral insights arise in many other traditions.

good life for Aristotle, the life that a rational person would choose to live if he or she had a choice.

good reputation for Master Kong, most perfectly, the enduring admiration that persists after the death of good people (compare *eudaimonia*).

good will deliberately intending the good; for Thomas, particular human traits do not qualify as moral virtues until someone wills a good end; for Kant, duty requires good will.

great evil strategy the notion that is it acceptable to commit a great evil in order to prevent an even greater evil; associated with utilitarianism.

habit a pattern of behaviour regularly followed to the point where it becomes your natural way of acting. Aristotle and Aquinas believe morality requires the habit of virtue.

happiness generally, the state of being content, satisfied; in a utilitarian sense, pleasure or, more recently, preference satisfaction; in direct contrast to earlier accounts of happiness focusing on self-esteem (compare *eudaimonia*).

harm reduction focussing, in a utilitarian sense, on the reduction of suffering in society; proponents argue that instead of trying to prevent morally problematic activities, we should focus on decreasing the negative medical, physical, and social consequences associated with such practices.

hedonism the belief that pleasure alone is ultimate source of value.

hermeneutics the art of accurately interpreting original texts.

heteronomy for Kant, the condition of being unfree; acting under the domination of that which is outside of one's logical and moral nature; acting under the excessive influence of desire, interest, or inclination.

holy will a will that exists independent of immoral desires and inclinations. Kant maintains that, strictly speaking, a being who possesses a holy will is not moral, only good.

horns of a dilemma to be caught on the horns of a dilemma is to be forced to choose between two equally unpleasant or illogical options.

human acts acts that involve deliberate (or rational) choice (see **choice**); Thomas distinguishes human acts from 'acts of human beings' that may or may not involve choice. Morality requires human acts that fully engage our capacity for free choice.

hydra a monster capable of growing multiple necks,

heads, and mouths of any size and shape symbolizing the unsatisfied, ever-growing craving that awaits the individual with unchecked **appetites**.

hypothetical agreement an agreement which is binding because this is, hypothetically, what rational agents would consent to, not because this agreement happened as an actual historical event.

hypothetical imperative tells us what we need to do in order to achieve a tentative goal; conditional on personal motive or desire (compare categorical imperative).

idea of the good (or **form of the good**) for Plato, the ultimate reality; the transcendent, unified, moral principle that is the source of all goodness in the world, which can be known through reason alone.

ignorance a failure to understand; misapplication of moral concepts or mental blindness; privation of knowledge of those things human beings have a natural aptitude to know; the condition of being uneducated, unaware, or uninformed. For Aristotle, people who suffer from ignorance are guilty of **vice**.

impartial spectator for Adam Smith, the hypothetical person inside us that judges our own acts from an objective distance.

imperative a sentence that expresses a command or an order.

imperfect duties duties in a loose sense; moral laws that admit of exceptions. Kant gives moral rules such as 'help others' and 'perfect your talents' as examples (compare **perfect duties**).

imperfect prudence for Thomas, a specialized kind of prudence which is (1) not enough to constitute complete morality by itself or which (2) involves knowing how to achieve a good end while failing to put it into practice (see prudence).

impersonalism the attitude that moral behaviour requires strict impartiality towards other people (compare **personalism**).

inalienable rights rights that cannot be taken away; those basic liberties, goods, or abilities that are said to be owed to someone (usually because of their human status) regardless of legal or political convention.

incontinence lack of willpower; inability to hold back when confronted with temptation. People who suffer **weakness of will** are guilty of incontinence.

indifferents for Stoics, ethically unimportant events, acts, or properties; those things that are morally indifferent, neither right or wrong.

indirect ignorance for Thomas, a type of voluntary ignorance, as when someone, through stress of work or other occupations, neglects to acquire the knowledge which would restrain them from immorality.

induction a form of reasoning that involves a movement from particular cases to a general designation (compare **deduction**); e.g., Socrates, Plato, and Aristotle are mortal; Socrates, Plato, and Aristotle are human beings; therefore all human beings are mortal.

inductive virtue for Aristotle, a mental faculty or cognitive ability that is able to induce the ideas of virtue (compare **deductive wisdom**).

instrumental power for Hobbes, the ability to get what we want that derives from acquired, external goods, such as money, property, friends, political station, reputation, or even (as Machiavelli points out) good luck (see original power).

instrumental value something has instrumental value insofar as it can be used as a means to attaining something else of value (compare **intrinsic value**).

intellect for Thomas, the power of first understanding that discerns the nature and value of things; more generally, one of the four parts of human nature, the guiding intelligence associated with the highest cardinal virtue of prudence (compare **desire**, **emotion**, **will**).

intellectual virtue in Aristotle, excellence in thinking (as opposed to doing); a human trait that illustrates some form of intelligence and generally comes about or is improved through education (compare moral virtue).

intrinsic value to have value as an end, not a means; to be valued for its own sake; that is, the value derives from the nature of the thing itself (compare **instrumental value**).

invincible moral ignorance a kind of ignorance which cannot be overcome due to historical circumstances, upbringing, and pre-conceived notions.

involuntary acts when one's acts do not correspond with their intentions; in such circumstances we do not hold the agent responsible for what happens because the agent never intended the result (compare **voluntary** and **non-voluntary acts**).

irascible passions feelings that produce activity, exertion, and effort in response to something unpleasant (compare **concupiscible passions**).

'is–ought' fallacy (or **naturalistic fallacy**) the (alleged) logical mistake of inferring an ought-statement from an is-statement in a moral argument.

iterated prisoners' dilemma a game-theory problem that takes the formal structure of the prisoner's dilemma and turns it into a hypothetical competition that is played over and over again on a computer using the same players, choices, and outcomes.

jus naturale a Latin term for 'natural law', sometimes used to designate a natural right.

justice the cardinal virtue that regulates relationships between people; justice posits an external criterion of what is appropriate, proportional, or decorous in a given circumstance; especially requiers fair treatment and due reward in accordance with honour, coherent standards, or law. For Plato, the ultimate human virtue, when the three different parts of the soul (reason, spirit and appetites) or the three parts of the city act harmoniously together.

knowledge generally true, justified belief; for Plato, the highest stage of learning in the Divided Line; knowing by reason or understanding alone (referred to alternatively as *episteme, noesis*) without the interference of sense perception.

law of nature for Hobbes, the moral *obligation* not to seriously harm ourselves and to undertake whatever means necessary to preserve our own lives.

law of three stages Auguste Comte's idea that history progresses in three distinct, chronological periods: the theological, the metaphysical, and the positive (or scientific).

laws of freedom Kant's term for the laws of ethics.

liberalism The idea that individual liberty, understood negatively, as the freedom to do as one wants, is the most important value. The meaning of the word is hotly disputed by some modern thinkers.

libertarian an extreme liberal; one who advocates drastically minimizing the role of the state (whatever the consequences) in order to maximize individual liberty.

liberty principle most important of three principles of justice in Rawls; that everyone should enjoy as much freedom (understood as choice) as possible (compare **opportunity**, **wealth principle**).

life of enjoyment for Aristotle, the life devoted chiefly to amusement, entertainment; a life of little human accomplishment (compare **contemplative life**, **political life**).

life of rational freedom for Mill, the life that permits the development of individual projects and personal talents without unnecessary interference.

logic the study and evaluation of arguments; that field of inquiry that elucidates the broad principles that govern reliable inferences.

logos root (Greek) word for 'logic'; the underlying logical pattern or structure that renders reality intelligible.

lucid occasions in Noddings's care ethics, cases where the injunction to care is clear and unmistakable.

maieutic having to do with midwifery; relating to Socrates' teaching method of assisting students in giving birth to ideas that come from themselves, not from the teacher.

makarios Greek term which means divinely happy or supremely fortunate (term used in the Beatitudes).

material philosophy for Kant, philosophy that identifies the laws governing material things. Kant divides material philosophy into **physics** and **ethics**.

maxim a principle or rule of conduct; the maxim behind an act is the basic idea of accomplishing something in some manner that motivates that particular action.

maximin strategy with respect to Rawls's theory of distributive justice, choosing the social structure that produces the maximum payoff for those in the most minimal positions.

misology Socrates's name for a hatred of arguments, logic, and philosophy that stands in the way of knowledge.

mitigated skeptic one who accepts that we can 'know' things in a practical everyday way, but doubts larger philosophical claims to metaphysical or rigorous truth (see also absolute skeptic).

mixed actions actions that seem both forced and voluntary; for Aristotle, extreme acts agents feel forced to choose in response to extreme circumstances; acts requiring forgiveness.

moderation avoiding blameworthy extremes in human character and behaviour (compare **golden mean**, **temperance**).

moral dilemmas situations that are so problematic, it is very hard or even impossible (at least at the present time) to understand what the appropriate or best moral response is; for some authors, situations in which it is impossible to satisfy all moral duties

moral egoist someone who believes that we should always act in our own self-interest.

moral liberalism the minimalist idea that consent provides the unique standard of moral behaviour.

moral philosophy an attempt to evaluate human behaviour at the most basic level possible; in older authors, a systematic attempt to understand and elucidate how we can best be happy.

moral right a right that is grounded, not in law or convention, but in the nature of morality (see right).

moral skepticism a radical rejection of moral values, ethical judgment, and moral arguments (see skepticism).

moral virtue in Aristotle, excellence in doing (as opposed to thinking); a human character trait that produces excellent, praiseworthy behaviour and comes about as a result of habit (compare intellectual virtue).

morality by inclination one of Kant's four categories of human behaviour, obeying the moral law out of inclination; in conformity with duty but not for the sake of duty. Although these acts may seem like moral acts, they are more appearance than reality.

natural duties obligations that arise whether or not someone specifically consents; e.g., the duty not to murder (compare **obligations**).

natural human right a moral entitlement that inheres in individuals simply because they are human. Natural rights, for an author like Locke, are moral rights that exist prior to or outside of any legal jurisdiction (see right).

natural law for the Stoics, divine order of the cosmos; for Thomas, the moral law God has enclosed in the human heart; so the morality inherent in the deep propensities of human nature; the **eternal law** applied to and seen from a human perspective.

nature principle the notion that good acts must be in harmony with nature, that the natural order of things provides the ultimate criterion of moral goodness.

negative rights those rights that guarantee our freedom to do as we will (compare positive rights).

negative theory of freedom the idea that freedom is a matter of removing those obstacles that stop us from doing as we will.

nescience absence of knowledge of that which human beings cannot know (e.g., human beings cannot know certain things higher intellects like angels can know; this is nescience); technically, *not* a form of human ignorance.

no-harm principle Mill's canonical (or authoritative) account of the contemporary liberal view that we should be free to do what we will as long as our actions do not harm others.

nomos Greek word for human law or custom; according to the Sophists the basis of morality (compare *physis*).

non-cognitivism a contemporary movement that argues that moral claims are not, rigorously speaking, true, that morality is not, strictly speaking, a form of logical knowledge. (Also called *emotivism* or *expressivism*.)

non-voluntary acts acts which are not voluntary and yet still deserve blame because they involve either culpable or concomitant ignorance (compare **voluntary** and **involuntary acts**).

nous Greek word for mind or understanding; intuitive reason.

obligations in a contractarian context, responsibilities that arise because we have consented to some specific arrangement; e.g., the obligation to respect the conditions of a contract voluntarily entered into (compare **natural duties, additive obligations**).

obscure occasions for Noddings, circumstances in which it is difficult to determine how or to what degree we should help others.

occurrent consent bare consent; agreement that qualifies as source of moral obligation, regardless of whether it fulfills some further criterion of morality or rationality.

opportunity principle one of three principles of justice in Rawls; that everyone should have equal, fair access to opportunities and positions in society (compare **liberty, wealth principle**).

order of execution for Thomas, issues connected with the observable, physical aspects of human acts.

order of intention for Thomas, issues connected with the agent's purpose, with what is mentally happening.

original position a hypothetical situation, proposed by Rawls, in which rational agents come together to voluntarily discuss how society should be organized. What they voluntarily determine is proposed as the ultimate criterion of distributive justice.

original power (or **natural power**) for Hobbes, the power to do as we will that derives from our inborn talents, from our own individual nature (compare instrumental power).

Original Sin a tendency toward evil believed to be innate in humankind as a consequence of Adam's sin in the Garden of Eden; the resultant privation of sanctifying grace.

overlapping consensus for Rawls, when individuals who embrace different world views can still find enough ethical common ground to produce a widely acceptable account of justice.

Panopticon Invented by the political philosopher Jeremy Bentham, the panopticon is an all-seeing circular prison that would allow prisoners to be observed at all times by hidden guards; used as a symbol of modern authoritarianism.

perfect duties   moral rules that admit of no exceptions. Among the perfect duties, Kant includes rules such as keeping one's promises and not committing suicide (compare **imperfect duties**).

perfect prudence   for Thomas, the practical virtue or reasoning that correctly judges and commands according to what is the true good o human life (see prudence).

Peripatetics   a term used to describe Aristotle's followers, derived from a Greek word meaning 'to walk up and down; to walk about' (because Aristotle allegedly walked up and down as he lectured).

personalism   the general attitude that accepts that particular relationships play an indispensable role in making moral judgments about how we should treat particular people (compare **impersonalism**); a twentieth-century movement in ethics that argues that morality should begin with a recognition of the supreme value of individual persons.

Phalaris   a Sicilian tyrant famous for burning people alive inside his bronze bull; for Aristotle, an example of brutish behaviour (see **brutishness**).

philosopher kings   for Plato, the ideal ruler who merits authority because he (or she) makes decisions for the common good based on the wisdom gained through philosophical training.

philosophia   perennis   perennial   philosophy; consideration of those deep questions repeatedly discussed through history.

phronesis   Greek word for practical wisdom or prudence; for Aristotle, wisdom in decision making; knowing how to choose means and ends; the means to wisdom or *sophia*.

physics   according to Kant, physics is a branch of **material philosophy** that elaborates the deterministic natural laws that govern physical bodies.

physis   Greek word for 'nature' from which we get the modern word physics (compare *nomos*).

Pietists   zealous, biblically-oriented Lutherans who distanced themselves from the established Church and ecclesiastical hierarchy. Stern, rigid, and anti-intellectual, they avoided excessive theological speculation and stressed a personal relationship with God; Kant's religious background.

pity   for Rousseau, a natural virtue, the sincere sympathy for others that arises when we see others suffer.

pluralistic (cultural pluralism)   the coexistence of diverse cultures that maintain their cultural differences within a society.

political life   for Aristotle, the noble life of active social involvement; a life spent doing as opposed to thinking; also Latin, *via activa* (compare **life of enjoyment**, **contemplative life**).

positive rights   those rights that oblige society to devote positive resources and services to improving or at least maintaining our well-being (see negative rights).

positivism   the idea that science, and science alone, produces true knowledge.

potentiality   an inherent capability or disposition not presently exhibited (compare **actuality**).

practical affirmation   a sheer, unqualified moral command; regardless of desires, one must carry out some particular task.

practical conditional   an 'if–then', or conditional statement; the second part of the sentence stipulates what must be done if the first part of the statement, relating to one's desires, holds.

practical reason   loosely, the kind of reasoning that stirs one to act; a capacity for judgment that motivates action; hence the ability to distinguish between good and bad.

practical syllogism   a deductive (logical) sequence of reasoning that ends in an action as opposed to a belief.

preference-satisfaction   getting what you want. Some contemporary utilitarians try to avoid the problem of measuring pleasure by defining happiness in terms of preference-satisfaction. An underlying idea is that if you want to know what someone wants you simply need to look at the choices they make.

pre-Socratics   the   first   Western   philosophers, so-called because they lived before Socrates. Nature philosophers, they tried to make sense of the cosmos in logical, scientific terms, but they also did moral philosophy.

preventive evil   moral strategy which permits a very small evil for the sake of preventing a greater evil. (Various conditions must be met.)

prima facie   at first appearance; before close investigation.

principle of asceticism   in direct contrast to the **utility principle**, the idea that we should increase pain and decrease pleasure. Bentham's blatant caricature of the ancient asceticism that viewed the formation of character as essential to happiness understood as peace of mind.

principle of sufficient reason explicitly formulated by Leibniz, it can be expressed in the general phrase, 'nothing happens without a reason'.

principle of the indiscernability of moral cases the same circumstances must require the same moral response; so the moral law must be the same for everyone.

prisoners' dilemma a hypothetical scenario involving prisoners, where the rational course of action, leading to the minimum penalty, requires trust and cooperation (compare **iterated prisoners' dilemma**).

property for Locke, those parts of nature we have an exclusive right to because they have been mixed with our labour or because they have, at some time, come to us through a consensual exchange with some antecedent owner.

Protestant Reformation a movement in Western Europe in the sixteenth century aimed at reforming some doctrines of the Roman Catholic Church, resulting in the establishment of Protestant churches, emphasizing human sinfulness, the need for grace, and individual freedom.

prudence a cardinal virtue Thomas describes as 'right reason applied to action'; caution with regard to practical matters; the chief cardinal virtue, it is the guiding light that orders our acts with an eye to moral and practical well-being (see also false prudence, imperfect prudence, perfect prudence).

psychological egoism a theory about human nature that assumes that, whatever appearances to the contrary, human beings always act self-interestedly, seeking out what is best for themselves.

punishment the deliberate causing of pain, discomfort, injury or disadvantage to someone in a measured response to an offense.

quality (of pleasure) for Mill, an experience of pleasure has more quality when it is preferred over other pleasures by knowledgeable subjects, not because it produces more pleasure, but because of the intrinsic desirability of the experience.

quasi-categorical imperative a duty that can be expressed in moral laws that hold most but not all the time; a duty that can be eclipsed by a competing duty; a mitigated deontology proposed by an author like Ross (compare **categorical imperative**).

quietism derived from a seventeenth century religious movement that preached passive withdrawal from the world, the term refers to those who evince a morally disturbing indifference to what is happening around them.

rational animal Aristotle's term for human beings who alone possess a conscience; because humans are unique in their ability to reason, they alone can tell the difference between right and wrong.

rationalization making excuses for bad behaviour; believing or arguing whatever is necessary to justify oneself.

reason for Plato, in the human constitution, the mental capacity for insight and logic (*logistikon*) that is naturally the highest and ruling part of the human constitution (compare **appetites**, **spirit**).

rectification of names the Confucian moral strategy of trying to live up to the true meaning of the term or title that describes our social or professional or family position.

reductio ad absurdum reducing an opponent's position to an absurdity; the refutation of a contrary view by demonstrating the inevitably absurd conclusion to which it would logically lead.

rehabilitation the idea that the goal of punishment is the transformation of a morally damaged person into a good citizen who can reintegrate into society.

relativism the view that different moral world views are equally true, and there is no way to settle deep disputes between them.

ren Chinese word that refers to the supreme moral virtue, variously translated as humanness, benevolence, reciprocity, mutuality, good-heartedness, or even love.

reparation the idea that wrong-doers must pay back or compensate the injured party to literally or symbolically repair the damage caused by the offense.

repugnant conclusion (mere addition paradox) the conclusion that seems to follow necessarily from utilitarianism that the existence of a much larger population in which the quality of life is lower will have higher overall happiness than a smaller population with a higher quality of life due to their greater numbers (Parfit's rendition of the mere addition paradox).

retribution the idea that justice *requires* that the guilty should pay with a punishment equivalent to the injury inflicted. So, in capital punishment, a life for a life.

Revelation the communication of divine truths through some sort of divine inspiration; revelation does not use logic to prove its points but operates through a kind of divine pronouncement; e.g., in the Christian and Judaic traditions, the Bible.

right a liberty, a good, a service, etc, owed to the

individual by society; an entitlement (see also inalienable rights, moral right, *jus naturale*, natural human right, right of nature, negative rights, positive rights).

right of nature   for Hobbes, the legal freedom to do whatever is necessary to preserve our lives and our essential well-being.

rotation of crops   the strategy of continually changing what one is doing to escape boredom; for Kierkegarrd, a feature of the esthetic way of life.

rule utilitarianism   focuses on rules: we should always act in accordance with the particular set of rules that will maximize utility (see utilitarianism).

sage   a moral teacher; having a prominent reputation for being wise and experienced.

science   for Plato, the third highest stage of learning in the Divided Line; knowing universal truths through discussion (*dianoia*) and logical argument (see Divided Line); for Aristotle, theoretical knowledge (*episteme*) of the most rigorous . . . range of cases (see *episteme*)."

secular   pertaining to worldly things or things that are not regarded as religious or spiritual; nonreligious or without reference to religion, as in 'secular morality' (compare **divine command morality**).

self-interested 'morality'   one of Kant's four categories of human behaviour in which one can act in conformity with the moral law for self-interested reasons; obeying the law for the wrong reasons and therefore not truly moral.

shallow ecology   a pejorative term referring to the (alleged) traditional view that human beings are separate from nature and that the natural world possesses value only insomuch as it serves human ends (compare **deep ecology**).

shalom   Hebrew term for peace; a state of completeness, wholeness, health, prosperity, harmony, and the absence of agitation or discord.

shame   a negative feeling of regret or unworthiness arising from a dishonourable or immoral act. Some argue that punishment should be designed to produce shame.

silver rule   the negative version of the Golden Rule: do not do to others what you do not want done to you.

skepticism   generally, the denial of the possibility of knowledge, or even rational belief, in some (see also absolute skeptic, ancient skepticism, mitigated skeptic, moral scepticism).

slippery slope problem   in Aristotle's virtue ethics, the problem of regressing into an ignorant or even

brutish state, moving from continence to incontinence to ignorance to brutishness.

sophia   Greek word meaning philosophical wisdom, which Aristotle believes is the highest intellectual virtue; 'intuitive reason combined with scientific knowledge of things that are highest by nature'. One who is philosophically wise is able to move from the most basic truths to the highest, most universal theoretical knowledge.

Sophists   itinerant Greek teachers, contemporaries of Socrates, skilled in the art of debate and persuasion. They were interested in politics and public life largely for reasons of personal gain; the movement fell into disrepute and they came to be seen as clever rather than wise.

sovereign   in Hobbes, a king or queen, or a small body of citizens, who make decisions on behalf of the entire community, who possess ultimate power and authority.

spirit   for Plato, in the human constitution, the middle element, the honourable passions (*thumoeides*), a capacity for honour and integrity mixed with and expressed through willpower (compare **appetites, reason**).

state of nature   the condition of human life before the institution of law and government. (Hobbes portrays this negatively, Locke and Rousseau, more positively.)

stoic   a philosophical adherent to ancient **Stoicism**; more generally, any one who is physically tough, self-controlled, and imperturbable, indifferent to joy, grief, pleasure, or pain.

stoic apathy   a disciplined, passion-less capacity for disinterested true judgment (compare **apathy**).

stoicism   The unofficial philosophy of ancient Rome, it maintains that the purpose of moral philosophy is happiness defined negatively as the absence of suffering, worry, bother, frustration and dissatisfaction.

straw man   a simplistic version of an opposing argument or theory; presented by opponents so that the more subtle original version can be more easily refuted or defeated (based on the idea that a straw dummy is easier to knock down than a live opponent.)

Summa Theologiae   Latin for 'summary of theology', the *Summa Theologiae* is Thomas Aquinas's most famous and important work, intended as a comprehensive introduction for theology students; sometimes called *Summa Theologica*.

supererogatory act   an act of moral heroism that

exceeds the bounds of what can normally be expected.

supervenience dependence of certain properties on other properties so that any change in the latter requires a change in the former.

synderesis Latin term in scholastic moral philosophy, the natural disposition of the practical reasons to intuitively or immediately apprehend the universal first principles of human action; the origin of conscience.

tautology a statement that must always be true; that which is true by definition.

techne Greek word for *art*, which includes the fine arts and in a broader sense, any instance of skilful or expert making. For Aristotle, art is an intellectual virtue that is fundamentally creative in nature.

temperance self-restraint, moderation, what the Greeks called *sophrosune*. For Plato, the virtue that characterizes the appetites when they submit to the guidance of reason; for Aristotle, an ideal moral state without temptation; for Thomas Aquinas, the cardinal virtue moderating the over-enthusiasm of the concupiscible passions in accord with reason. (compare **golden mean**, **moderation**).

theological virtues virtues relating to religious morality; the three theological virtues are faith, hope, and (the highest virtue of all) charity (or love), which all require a direct infusion of God's grace; we cannot achieve them through our own unaided efforts. Union with God in Heaven is their ultimate objective (compare **cardinal virtues**).

theoretical reason the cognitive faculty that thinks, speculates, and distinguishes between truth and falsity.

thin theory of the good the liberal notion that we should avoid adopting any precise, substantive account on what constitutes true happiness, the good life, virtue, duty, natural law, etc. so that individual freedom, understood as non-interference, can be respected.

thing-in-itself (*Ding an sich*) for Kant, the ultimate, impenetrable, unknowable nature of things.

tolerance the virtue (associated with a movement like Scepticism) of showing a wide respect for differing opinions.

two-tiered contractarianism in an author such as Locke, the idea that morality stands on two pillars or steps: social agreement and moral conscience (see contractarianism).

ubermensch (or overman) the heroic, non-conform-

ist individual Nietzsche presents as the epitome of human accomplishment.

understanding traditionally, the most basic operation of intelligence; the power of sheer mental insight; an immediate apprehension of truth that is prior to and gives rise to logic or argument. According to Aristotle, understanding is the root of all the other intellectual virtues. What Thomas sometimes refers to as intellect.

untheoretical judgement (*gnome*) for Aristotle, a sure capacity for accurate moral judgement unaccompanied by argument such as that displayed by wise older people.

utilitarianism an influential theory . . . number of people (see also act utilitarianism, rule utilitarianism).

utility Bentham defines the utility of an action as its usefulness in increasing pleasure and reducing pain.

utility principle later known as the Greatest Happiness Principle, Bentham's ultimate foundation of morality: in his words, 'the greatest happiness of the greatest number' is 'the [ultimate] measure of right and wrong'.

veil of ignorance (to be placed behind) to be ignorant of who you are; a condition imposed by Rawls on agents in the original position to ensure that their decision-making is impartial.

vice (*kakia*) immoral or evil habit or practice; in Aristotle, moral ignorance, not knowing the difference between right or wrong (compare virtue).

vincible moral ignorance ignorance that can be overcome through diligence, effort, or study (see invincible moral ignorance).

virtue (*arete*) human excellence, moral and intellectual, goodness, worth, superior functioning. Aristotle describes virtue as the mean between two opposing vices (compare **vice**).

virtue ethics term often used to describe Aristotle's approach to ethics. For Aristotle, the point of morality is the development of the best character traits. The morally good person successfully actualizes his or her talents, in the broadest sense possible, developing into an excellent human being.

volition for Thomas, an act of intellect minus an act of will.

voluntary acts acts that involve choice, a deliberate, conscious attempt to do right or wrong; hence, acts deserving of moral praise or blame; only human beings can act voluntarily (compare **involuntary** and **non-voluntary acts**).

weakness of will a lack of willpower which Aristotle

classifies as a temporary form of moral ignorance (see *akrasia*).

wealth principle   one of three principles of justice in Rawls; that wealth be distributed so that the poorest members of society benefit as much as possible (compare **liberty**, **opportunity principle**).

will   traditionally, a rational appetite or power that is able to initiate and sustain activity in the direction of the valuable; for Thomas, one of four parts of human nature associated with the cardinal virtue of justice, capable of ordering actions to a proper measure (compare **desire**, **emotion**, **intellect**).

will to power   for Nietzsche, the biological drive to dominate that is the root source of human striving.

wisdom   traditionally, the condition of being knowledgeable about fundamental or universal issues, including moral issues; the condition of knowledge and correct decision-making that results when reason fully governs human conduct; for Plato, the virtue that principally characterizes reason.

❧ Endnotes ❧

Throughout the text, I will use abbreviated citations whenever possible. For the most complete citations and helpful comments, check the chapter devoted to a particular figure and also the 'List of Further Readings' at the end of each chapter. When there are repeated citations from the same source, the first reference is generally complete, all others abbreviated. Names of translators are included in parentheses. Needless to say, most classical sources are widely available online and in numerous print editions.

Chapter 1

[1] Emily Post, *Etiquette: The Blue Book of Social Usage* (New York and London: Funk and Wagnalls Company, 1937), p. 5.

[2] Richard Duffy, 'Introduction' to *Etiquette*, p. xvi.

[3] Duffy, xv–xvi.

[4] Post, p. 2.

[5] *Nicomachean Ethics* (Ross) III.2, 111b11.

[6] John Milton, *Paradise Lost*, Book III, 98–9. In citing widely available canonical works (particular those originally in English), I will give a general citation where appropriate.

[7] *Nicomachean Ethics* (Ross) III.1, 1109b30–31.

[8] Viktor Frankl, *Man's Search for Meaning* (New York: Washington Square Press, 1963), pp. 211–13.

[9] Plato, *Ion* (Lane Cooper) 532e in: *The Collected Dialogues of Plato including the Letters*, Edith Hamilton and Huntington Cairns eds., (Princeton, NJ: Princeton University Press, 1963).

[10] Aristotle, *On the Parts of Animals* (Ogle) I.5.645a16.

[11] Thomas Aquinas *Summa Theologica* (English Dominican Province) II.II.49.1.

[12] Thomas Aquinas, II.II.49.1.

[13] Arthur Schopenhauer, *The Art of Literature* (T. Bailey Saunders), 'On Authorship,' eBooks@Adelaide 2004, http://etext.library.adelaide.edu.au/s/schopenhauer/arthur/lit/index.html.

[14] *Nicomachean Ethics* (Ross) I.3 1095a5.

[15] *Nicomachean Ethics* (Ross), II.2.1103b28.

[16] 'Amish Schoolgirl Hoped to Spare Others,' *New York Times* (Associated Press). 6 October, 2006, www.nytimes.com/aponline/us/AP_Amish_School_Shooting.html.

[17] Immanuel Kant, *Groundwork of the Metaphysics of Morals*. Translated by H. J. Paton (New York: Harper Torchbook, 1964), 403.23, pp. 72–3.

Chapter 2

[1] René Descartes, *Meditations on First Philosophy* (John Veitch English translation of 1901), Meditation 2.1, available online at www.wright.edu/cola/descartes/meditation1.html.

[2] Michael Ruse and E.O. Wilson, 'The Evolution of Ethics,' *New Scientist* 108 (1478), 1985, p. 52.

[3] Ibid.

[4] Randy Thornhill and Craig T. Palmer, 'Why Men Rape,' *The New York Academy of Sciences*, January/February 2000 (adapted from their book *A Natural History of Rape: Biological Bases of Sexual Coercion*, 2000).

[5] Ibid.

[6] A.J. Ayer, 'Language, Truth, and Logic,' p. 520, in W.T. Jones, Frederick Sontag, Morton O. Beckner, Robert J. Fogelin, *Approaches to Ethics* (New York: McGraw Hill, 1962), pp. 517–25.

[7] Ayer, pp. 532–3.

[8] David Hume, *A Treatise of Human Nature*, III.1.i: 'Moral Distinctions Not Derived from Reason'.

[9] Hume, III.1.i.

[10] J.L. Mackie, *Ethics: Inventing Right and Wrong* (Harmondsworth: Penguin, 1977), p. 38.

[11] Ibid.

[12] Hume, *Treatise*, III.1.i.

[13] Hume, *Treatise*, III.1.i.

[14] David Hume, *An Enquiry Concerning Human Understanding*, VIII.1, http://etext.library.adelaide.edu.au/ h/hume/david/.

[15] R.M. Hare, 'Universal Prescriptivism,' online edition accessible at www.philosophy.uncc.edu/mleldrid/SzCMT/HUP.htm. (Originally published in Peter Singer, *A Companion to Ethics* [Blackwell Publishers, 1991].)

[16] Hare, p. 145.

[17] Hume, *Treatise*, III.1.i.

[18] Hume, *Treatise*, III.1.ii.

[19] Aristotle, *Nichomachean Ethics*. Translated with an introduction by David Ross. Revised by J.L. Ackrill and J.O. Urmson (New York: Oxford University

Press, 1998), VI.2.1139a35.

[20]Thomas Hobbes, *Leviathan*, Edwin Curley, ed. (Indianapolis: Hackett Publishing, 1994), I.vi.7, p. 28.

[21]Michael Sandel, *Liberalism and the Limits of Justice* (Cambridge: Cambridge University Press, 1984), p. 165.

[22]Plato, *The Republic*, translated by Paul Shorey (London, UK: William Heinemann, 1956), Vi.508e.

[23]George E. Moore, *Principia Ethica* (1903), online edition: I §14; http://fair_use.org/g_e_moore/principia_ethica/.

[24]Augustine, *The Enchiridion; or On Faith, Hope, and Love*, translated by J. F. Shaw (New York: Philip Schaff, Christian Literature Publishing Co., 1886): 11; online edition available at www.leaderu.com/cyber/books/augenchiridion/enchiridiontoc.html.

[25]Augustine, 11, my italics.

[26]Adam Smith, *The Theory of Moral Sentiments* (London: A. Millar, 1790, 6th ed.; original ed., 1759), III.I.67, online edition available at *Library of Economics and Liberty*, www.econlib.org/library/Smith/smMS3.html.

[27]Edith Stein, *On the Problem of Empathy* (Washington: ICS Publications, 1989, original ed., 1917), p. 11.

[28]Jean-Paul Sartre, 'Bad Faith and Falsehood', From *Being and Nothingness*, translated by Hazel Barnes, in *Existing: An Introduction to Existential Thought*, Steven Luper, ed. (Mountain View California: Mayfield Publishing, 2000), p. 292.

[29]Outward Bound Canada, www.outwardbound.ca/.

[30]Ibid.

Chapter 3

[1]Cited passages taken from Confucius, *The Analects*, Raymond Dawson, transl. (Oxford: Oxford University Press, 2000).

[2](Dawson) 14.23.

[3](Dawson) 13.26.

[4](Dawson) 4.16.

[5](Dawson) 4.11.

[6](Dawson) 7.36.

[7](Dawson) 2.14.

[8](Dawson) 12.16.

[9](Dawson) 13.21.

[10](Dawson)15.2.

[11](Dawson) 16.8.

[12](Dawson) 12.19.

[13](Dawson) 19.13.

[14](Dawson) 14.42.

[15]He concludes, 'How true is this saying!' (Dawson) 13.11.

[16](Dawson) 12.19.

[17](Dawson) 15.22.

[18](Dawson) 15.37.

[19]Luke 6:31; Luke 10:27; Matthew 7:12. This has, of course, Old Testament antecedents.

[20](Dawson) 12.2.

[21]To cite the entire passage, 'Zigong asked: "Is there a single word such that one could practice it throughout one's life?" The Master said: "Reciprocity perhaps? Do not inflict on others what you yourself would not wish done to you".' (Dawson) 15.24.

[22](Dawson) 14.34.

[23](Dawson) 5.12.

[24](Dawson) 3.3.

[25](Dawson) 15.35.

[26](Dawson) 7.30.

[27]My italics. (Dawson) 7.6.

[28](Dawson) 13.19.

[29](Dawson) 13.19.

[30](Dawson) 19.19.

[31](Dawson) 12.11.

[32](Dawson) 13.21

[33]For example, Master Kong explains, 'When substance prevails over refinement there is churlishness, and when refinement prevails over substance there is pedantry. Only if refinement and substance are properly blended, does one become a gentleman'. (Dawson) 6.18.

[34](Dawson) 11.16.

[35](Dawson) 16.12.

[36](Dawson) 7.27.

[37](Dawson) 7.27.

[38] (Dawson) 7.27.

[39]*The First Philosophers: The Pre-Socratics and the Sophists*, Robin Waterfield, trans. (New York: Oxford University Press, 2000). Hence: Heraclitus (Waterfield) F22.

[40]Heraclitus (Waterfield) F23.

[41]Heraclitus (Waterfield) T10.

[42]*HERACLITUS: The Complete Philosophical Fragments*, translated by William Harris, http://community.middlebury.edu/~harris/Philosophy/Heraclitus.html. Hence: Heraclitus (Harris) 86.

[43]Heraclitus (Harris) 20.

[44]Heraclitus (Waterfield) F1.

[45]Heraclitus (Waterfield) F5.

[46]Heraclitus (Waterfield) F16.

[47]Democritus (Waterfield) F12.

[48]Democritus (Waterfield) T35 (from John of Strobi).

[49]Democritus (Waterfield) T36 (from Cicero).

[50]Democritus (Waterfield) F18.

[51]Democritus (Waterfield) F8. *My italics.*

[52]Democritus (Waterfield) F13.

[53]Democritus (Waterfield) F8.

[54]Democritus (Waterfield) F8.

[55]Democritus (Waterfield) T35 (from John of Strobi).

[56]Citations taken from Diogenes Laertius, *The Lives of Eminent Philosophers*, R.D. Hicks, trans. (Cambridge: Harvard University Press, 1931), Vol. II, Book vi ('Diogenes of Sinope'). So: (Hicks) II.vi.54.

[57](Hicks) II.vi.78.

[58]Cited in Donald R. Dudley, *A History of Cynicism': From Diogenes to the 6th Century* AD (Hildesheim: Georg Olms Verlagsbuchhandlung, 1967), p. 5. (An excellent scholarly introduction to Cynicism.)

[59](Hicks) II.vi.44.

[60](Hicks) II.vi.72.

[61](Hicks) II vi.78.

[62](Hicks) II.vi.23.

[63](Hicks) II.vi.37.

[64](Hicks) II.vi.37.

[65](Hicks) II.vi.73.

[66](Hicks) II.vi.40.

[67](Hicks) II.vi.28.

[68](Hicks) II.vi.70.

[69](Hicks) II.vi.49.

[70](Hicks) II.vi.71.

[71](Hicks) II.vi.20–1.

[72](Hicks) II.vi.71.

[73](Hicks) II.vi.58.

[74](Hicks) II.vi.63.

[75](Hicks) II.vi.72.

[76](Hicks) II.vi.38.

[77](My translation) II.vi.38.

[78](Hicks) II.vi.32.

[79](Hicks) II.vi.59..

[80](Hicks) II.vi.60.

[81](Hicks) II.vi.66.

[82](Hicks) II.vi.61.

[83](Hicks) II.vi.65.

[84](Hicks) II.vi.58.

[85](Hicks) II.vi.54.

[86](Hicks) II.vi.26.

[87](Hicks) II vi.76.

[88]The selections of Epicurus are taken from: Diogenes Laertius *Lives of the Eminent Philosophers* (Hicks), Vol. II, Book 10 ('Epicurus'), pp. 528–678. I give the title of original sources cited by Diogenes.

[89]*Letter to Menoeceus* (Hicks) 10.129.

[90]*Letter to Menoeceus* (Hicks) 10.129.

[91](Hicks) 10.137-8.

[92](Hicks) 10.4-9.

[93]www.thefreedictionary.com

[94]Cf. (Hicks) 10.136.

[95]*Sovran Maxims* 5 (Hicks) 10.19.

[96]*Letter to Menoeceus* (Hicks) 10.132.

[97]*Letter to Menoeceus* (Hicks) 10.127.

[98]*Sovran Maxims* 15 (Hicks) 10.144.

[99]*Letter to Menoeceus; Sovran Maxims* (Hicks) 10.129.

[100]*Letter to Pythocles* (Hicks) 10.123.

[101]*Letter to Pythocles* (Hicks) 10.123.

[102]*Letter to Herodotus* (Hicks) 10.64.

[103]*Sovran Maxims* 2 (Hicks) 10.139.

[104]*Letter to Menoeceus* (Hicks) 10.125.

[105]*Sovran Maxims* 27 (Hicks) 10.148.

[106]Thucydides, *History of the Peloponnesian Wars*, Rex Warner, trans. (New York: Penguin Books, 1954), 2.34–14.

[107](Hicks) 10.120.

[108](Hicks) 10.118–119.

[109]The citations from and about Epictetus are from *The Stoic and Epicurean Philosophers: The Complete Extant Writings of Epicurus. Epictetus, Lucretius, Marcus Aurelius*, edited with introduction by Whitney J. Oates (New York: The Modern Library, 1940), *Discourses* (translated by P. E. Matheson), pp. 223–457; *Fragments* (translated by P. E. Matheson), pp. 458–67; *Manual* (translated by P. E. Matheson), pp. 468–84. Hence *Discourses* (Matheson) III.xxii, p. 380.

[110]*Fragments* (Matheson) 10, p. 461.

[111]*Discourses* (Matheson) II.xix, p. 324.

[112]*Discourses* (Matheson) II.xix, p. 324.

[113]*Discourses* (Matheson) IV.v, p. 431.

[114]*Discourses* (Matheson) IV.v, p. 431.

[115]*Discourses* (Matheson) IV.v, p. 431.

[116]*Discourses* (Matheson) I.i, p.224.

[117]*Discourses* (Matheson) I.xxvi, p. 269.

[118]*Discourses* (Matheson) III.vi, p. 354.

[119]*Discourses* (Matheson) I.iv, p. 231.

[120]*Manual* (Matheson) 49, p. 482.

[121]*Fragments* (Matheson) 3, pp. 458–9.

[122]*Manual* (Matheson) 8, p. 470.

[123]*Discourses* (Matheson) I.xii, p. 248.

[124]*Manual* (Matheson), 1, p. 468.

[125]*Manual* (Matheson) 17, p. 472.

[126]*Manual* (Matheson) 1, p. 468.

127*Discourses* (Matheson) II.xix, p.323.

128*Discourses* (Matheson) II.xi, p. 300.

129*Manual* (Matheson) 43, pp. 480–1.

130*Manual* (Matheson) 26, pp. 474–5.

131*Manual* (Matheson) 26, pp. 474–5.

132*Manual* (Matheson) 46, p. 481.

133*Enchiridion*, 46 (Elizabeth Carter, trans.), *The Internet Classics Archive*, http://classics.mit.edu/Epictetus/epicench.html.

134*Manual* (Matheson) 5, p. 469.

135 *Manual* (Matheson) 20, pp. 472–3.

136*Manual* (Matheson) 5, p. 469.

137*Discourses* (Matheson) I.ix, pp. 239–40.

138*Discourses* (Matheson) I.ix, pp. 239–40.

319*Manual* (Matheson), 16, p. 472.

140*Manual* (Matheson), 3, p. 469.

141*Discourses* (Matheson) I.xi, pp. 243–6.

142*Manual* (Matheson) 12, p. 471.

143*Discourses* (Matheson) I.xix, pp. 258–9.

144*Discourses* (Matheson) I.xix, pp. 258–9.

145*Discourses* (Matheson) II.xx, pp.325–6.

146*Discourses* (Matheson) I.iv, p. 230.

147*Discourses* (Matheson) IV.i, pp. 407–8.

148*Discourses* (Matheson) IV.i, p. 406.

149*Manual* (Matheson) 19, p. 472.

150Selections about Pyrrho are from Diogenes Laertius, *Lives of the Eminent Philosophers* (Hicks), Vol. II, Book IX, Chapter 11, pp. 474–517. Hereafter (Hicks) 11.__.

151(Hicks) 11.71.

152(Hicks) 11.72. 'Plato, too, leaves the truth to gods and sons of gods, and seeks after the probable explanation.' This is a reference to so-called academic skepticism, i.e., the non-Pyrrhonean skepticism that later developed at Plato's academy.

153'A Pyrrhonean is one who in manners and life resembles Pyrrho.' (Hicks) 11.70.

154(Hicks) 11.61.

155(Hicks) 11.62.

156(Hicks) 11.62.

157(Hicks) 11.66.

158(Hicks) 11.108.

159(Hicks) 11.63.

160(Hicks) 11.68.

161The selections from Sextus Empiricus are taken from Sextus Empiricus, *Selections From the Major Writings on Skepticism, Man & God*, edited with introduction and notes by Philip Hallie; translated from the original Greek by Sanford Etheridge, Forward and Bibliography by Donald Morrison (Indianapolis: Hackett, 1985).

162(Etheridge) I.XII, p. 41.

163(Etheridge) I.XII, p. 42.

164(Etheridge) I.XII, p. 42.

165(Etheridge) I.XII, p. 42.

166(Etheridge) I.XII, p. 42.

167(Etheridge) I.XII, p. 41.

168(Etheridge) I.VIII, p. 37.

169(Etheridge) I.IV, pp. 32–3.

170(Hicks) 11.69.

171'Once he [Pyrrho] got enraged in his sister's cause (her name was Philista) and he told the man who blamed him that it is was not over a weak woman that one should display indifference'. (Hicks) 11.66.

172(Hicks) 11.76.

173(Hicks) 11.104.

174For example, Sextus is trying to convince other people that they should be skeptics, i.e., he is trying to construct an argument that will be satisfying to human beings in general.

175(Etheridge) I.XIII, p. 43.

176John F. Kennedy Presidential Library and Museum, www.jfklibrary.org/Historical+Resources/Archives/Reference+Desk/Dante+Quote.htm

177The selections on Protagoras are taken from *The First Philosophers* (Waterfield) The 'T' refers to the testimonal number in this text. Hence: T2 (from Plato, *Protagoras* (Burnet) 316b8–319a7).

178T2 (from Plato, *Protagoras* (Burnet) 316b8–319a7).

179T1 (from Diogenes Laertius, (Long) 9.51–3).

180T1 (from Diogenes Laertius, (Long) 9.51–3).

181T4 (from Aristotle, *Metaphysics* (Ross) 1062b13–19).

182Herodotus, *The Histories* (Godley) 3.38.1.

183T8 (from Plato, *Thaetetus* (Duke *et al.*) 161c2–e3).

184T5 (from Plato, *Euthydemus* (Burnet) 286b7–287a9).

185T8 (from Plato, *Thaetetus* (Duke *et al*) 161c2–e3).

186(Hicks) 11.69.

187T12 (from Plato, *Protagoras* (Burnet) 320c8-322d5).

188Compare John 1:1.

189John 8:28. Needless to say, there are many worthwhile and useful editions of the *Bible*; nothing said here hinges on disputed points of translation. I will cite in the traditional way. One consulted source: *The Bible: Authorized King James Version*, Robert Carroll and Prickett (New York: Oxford, 1997). For online editions see: www.biblegateway.com.

190Matthew 7:12.

191Matthew 7:12.

192For a contemporary account of the Golden Rule see: Jeffrey Wattles, *The Golden Rule* (New York: Oxford

University Press, 1996). There are many other scholarly treatments available. Cf. Harry J. Gensler, Q.C. Terry, Stephen J. Holoviak.

[193] Matthew 7:5.

[194] Luke 6:27–31.

[195] Matthew 5:38–42

[196] Matthew 5:27–36.

[197] Matthew 5:21–2; 27–8; 31–2; 33–4; 38–9; 43–4.

[198] Mathew 5:48.

[199] Matthew 22:35–40.

[200] Matthew 5:29–30.

[201] St. Matthew 5:3–10

[202] John 14:27.

[203] John 4:5–14.

Chapter 4

[1] Cf. Xenophon, *Symposium*, W.C. Guthrie, trans., 67–68 in *Socrates* (Cambridge: Cambridge University Press, 1971).

[2] Remember all of the Plato works are translated from Greek. Standard citations to Plato use the approximate Stephanus text numbers. The citations from the *Phaedo* are taken from: Plato, *Phaedo*, translated with introduction and notes by David Gallop (New York: Oxford University Press, 1993). Hence: *Phaedo* (Gallop) 118.a15.

[3] Plato, *Euthyphro* in: *Defence of Socrates, Euthyphro, Crito,* David Gallop, translation, introduction, notes (New York: Oxford University Press, 1997). Hence *Euthyphro* (Gallop) 10d5.

[4] *Euthyphro* (Gallop) 11a7.

[5] Plato *Defence of Socrates* (what is traditionally known as the *Apology*) in: *Defence of Socrates, Euthyphro, Crito.* Hence *Defence* (Gallop) 32a6–8.

[6] *Defence* (Gallop) 28ab6–c1.

[7] *Defence* (Gallop), 30e–31a7.

[8] *Defence* (Gallop) 30a7–b1.

[9] *Defence* (Gallop) 39d4–5.

[10] Plato, *Laches, Protagoras, Meno, Euthydemus* (Vol. 3 of Plato in Twelve Volumes), W.R.M. Lamb, trans. (Cambridge: Harvard University Press; London: William Heinemann Ltd., 1967). Hence *Protagoras* (Lamb) 358c–d.

[11] *Defence* (Gallop) 23b2–3.

[12] *Defence* (Gallop) 29b5–7.

[13] Cf. Iamblichus of Chalcis, *On the Pythagorean Life and; The First Philosophers: The Presocratics and the Sophists* (Waterfield), 'Empedocles of Acragas,' T1, F1, F3, F4.

[14] *Phaedo* (Gallop) 107b8–10.

[15] *Phaedo* (Gallop) 90b6–c5.

[16] *Phaedo* (Gallop) 90d–e2.

[17] *Phaedo* (Gallop) 90d–e2.

[18] Plato, *Theatetus*, Francis Conford, trans., in *The Collected Works of Plato* Hamilton and Cairns, 149; 150b5–150d10.

[19] *Theatetus* (Cornford) 149b5ff.

[20] *Theatetus* (Cornford) 149b5ff.

[21] Citations from the *Gorgias* from Plato, *Gorgias,* Robin Waterfield, Translation (New York: Oxford, 1994). Hence *Gorgias* (Waterfield) 471e–472c.

[22] *Phaedo* (Gallop) 68e6–69a5.

[23] *Phaedo* (Gallop) 69a6–b3.

[24] Cf. *Gorgias*, 494cff.

[25] *Gorgias*, 493 ff. This is a very famous passage.

[26] Plato, *The Republic*, Robin Waterfield Translation (Oxford: Oxford University Press, 1998) 488e–499e.

[27] *The Republic* (Waterfield) 586a–b.

[28] *Defence* (Gallop) 41c9–d2.

[29] *Gorgias* (Waterfield) 479b–c.

[30] *Crito* (Gallop) 49c10–d9.

[31] *The Republic* (Waterfield) 335d–e, my italics.

[32] *Crito* (Gallop) 49b7–10.

[33] *Crito* (Gallop) 53b7.

[34] *Crito* (Gallop) 50a9–b5.

[35] *Crito* (Gallop) 51b3.

[36] *Crito* (Gallop) 51b4–8.

[37] *Crito* (Gallop) 51a8–51c3.

[38] *The Republic* (Waterfield) 359d-360e.

[39] *The Republic* (Waterfield) 359d-360e.

[40] *The Republic* (Waterfield) 359d-360e.

[41] *The Republic* (Waterfield) 359d-360e.

[42] *The Republic* (Waterfield) 361c-362a.

[43] *The Republic* (Waterfield) 509c.

[44] *The Republic* (Waterfield) 506e.

[45] *The Republic* (Waterfield) 508a.

[46] *The Republic* (Waterfield) 508d.

[47] *The Republic* (Waterfield) 509b.

[48] *The Republic* (Waterfield) 509d.

[49] He presents two lists of terms at 511d and 534a. The terms representing the higher states of knowledge are not precisely the same.

[50] *The Republic* (Waterfield) 516b.

[51] *Phaedo* (Gallop) 64d.

[52] *Phaedo* (Gallop) 65b–d.

[53] *Phaedo* (Gallop) 65e5–66d5.

[54] *Phaedo* (Gallop) 83d4–8.

[55] See *Phaedo* (Gallop) 64a5. (This wording from *Phaedo*, translated by Sanderson Beck, www.san.beck.org/Phaedo.html.)

⁵⁶*The Republic* (Waterfield) 439b–439d.

⁵⁷*The Republic* (Waterfield) 439e–440a.

⁵⁸*The Republic* (Waterfield) 440b.

⁵⁹Plato, *Phaedrus*, Robin Waterfield, trans. (Oxford: Oxford University Press, 2002), 253d-e.

⁶⁰*Phaedrus* (Waterfield) 254e.

⁶¹*The Republic* (Waterfield) 571b–d.

⁶²*The Republic* (Waterfield) 368d.

⁶³*The Republic* (Waterfield) 433a.

⁶⁴*The Republic* (Waterfield) 433b.

⁶⁵*The Republic* (Waterfield) 588b–e.

⁶⁶*The Republic* (Waterfield) 589a–b.

⁶⁷*The Republic* (Waterfield) 589d–c.

⁶⁸*The Republic* (Waterfield) 589d.

⁶⁹*The Republic* (Waterfield) 591b–c.

⁷⁰*The Republic* (Waterfield) 590d–e.

⁷¹*The Republic* (Waterfield) 442e–443b.

Chapter 5

¹Remember that Aristotle wrote in Greek. All quotations, therefore, are translations. The standard way to quote from Aristotle is to use the 'Bekker numbers', which refer to the page and section in an original, complete German edition of Aristotle edited by August Immanuel Bekker. The Bekker numbers allow scholars using different editions of Aristotle's works to quickly find a common (approximate) point of reference. This is not an entirely felicitous device but it must do for the moment. Although many good translations of Aristotle are available, differences are largely a matter for specialized scholarly dispute. We will cite from the widely esteemed translation: Aristotle, *The Nichomachean Ethics*. Translated with an introduction by David Ross. Revised by J.L. Ackrill and J.O. Urmson. (New York: Oxford University Press, 1998). Any reference without a title is a reference to this edition of the *Nicomachean Ethics*. We will cite a few other Aristotlean sources with abridged bibliographical information.

²I.1.1094a1–3.

³I.7.1098a18.

⁴I.9.100a5–9.

⁵I.7.1097b22.

⁶I.7.1097b32.

⁷Aristotle, *Politics* (Ernest Barker), (Oxford: Oxford University Press, 1995), I.2.1253a15. All other references to the politics are to this edition.

⁸IX.8.68b9–10.

⁹IX.8.1169a11–12.

¹⁰IX.8.1169a18.

¹¹IX.8.1169a20–21.

¹²IX.8.1169a18.

¹³I.3.1095a5.

¹⁴ II.2.1103b28.

¹⁵I.7.1097a18.

¹⁶I.6.1096b14.

¹⁷I.5.109a6.

¹⁸I.7.1097a35–b7.

¹⁹I.10.1101a18.

²⁰I.1.21102a1.

²¹I.2.1094a19–22.

²²I.2.1094a19–22.

²³I.8.1098b11.

²⁴I.8.1099b1–5.

²⁵I.8.1099b6.

²⁶I.8.1099a32–33.

²⁷I.8.1099a33–b1.

²⁸I.10.1100b22–32.

²⁹I.10.1100b22–32.

³⁰I.10.1100b33–1101a7.

³¹Plato, *Selected Myths*, Robin Waterfield, Translation (Oxford: Oxford University Press, 2004), 618a ff.

³²IX.9.1170a8.

³³X.6.1176b28.

³⁴X.6.1176b33–35.

³⁵X.8.1178b21–23,32.

³⁶X.7.1177a32.

³⁷Philosophical "activity alone would seem to be loved for its own sake; for nothing arises from it apart from contemplating." X.7.1177b1.

³⁸X.7.1177a23.

³⁹*Politics* I.2.1253a7-8.

⁴⁰II.6.1106a3.

⁴¹II.1.1103a24.

⁴²II.1.1103a33.

⁴³II.4.1105b9. (Emphasis is ours.)

⁴⁴II.4.1105b12.

⁴⁵II.4.1105a28–b1.

⁴⁶II.4.1105b5.

⁴⁷II.2.1104a6.

⁴⁸*Eudemian Ethics* (Soloman), II.3.1220b35ff, from *The Complete Works of Aristotle*, J. Barnes, ed. (Princeton: Bollingen Press, 1984).

⁴⁹II.2.1104a11.

⁵⁰II.7.1107a33.

⁵¹II.7.1108a17.

⁵²*Eudemian Ethics* (Soloman), 2.3.1221a18.

⁵³II.6.1106b18.

⁵⁴II.6.1106a36.

55 II.9.1109a24.

56 II.6.1106b29.

57 II.9.1109b2.

58 II.6.1107a9.

59 *Eudemian Ethics* (Soloman), 2.3.1221b21.

60 VI.5.1140b22.

61 Cf. 3.8.1116a16.

62 Plato, *The Republic* X.617e.

63 *Politics*. VII.13.1332a25.

64 III.5.1113b14.

65 III.5.1113b23.

66 III.5.1113b21.

67 III.5.1113b7.

68 III.2.1111b7.

69 III.5.1114a23.

70 III.5.1113b29.

71 III.1.1109b35.

72 V.8.1135a27.

73 III.1.1110a1.

74 III.1.1111a3.

75 III.1.1111a15.

76 III.1.1111a21.

77 III.1.1110a18.

78 'E.g., 'if a tyrant were to order one to do something base, having one's parents and children in his power, and if one did the action they were to be saved, but otherwise would be put to death.' III.1.1110a5.

79 III.1.1110a23.

80 VII.2.1145b26.

81 VII.8.1151a6.

82 VII.8.1150b35.

83 VII.10.1152a20.

84 VII.10.1152a23.

85 VII.10.1152a20.

86 VII.8.1150b32.

87 X.9.1179b23.

88 III.11.1119a1.

89 III.11.1118b23.

90 III.12.1119b16.

91 Aristotle continues, 'any incontinent man is subject to regrets'. VII.8.1150b29.

92 VII.8.1150b33.

93 VII.8.1150b31.

94 VII.2.1146a26.

95 VII.1.1145a15.

96 VII.1.1145a18.

97 VII.1.1145a24.

98 VII.1.1145a28.

99 VII.1.1145a30.

100 VII.5.1148b20.

101 VII.5.1149a5.

102 VII.8.1151a15.

103 VI.12.1144a 35.

104 VI.12.1144a29.

105 VII.1.1145b12.

106 VII.2.1146a10.

107 VII.3.1147a12.

108 VII.3.1147b6.

109 VII.3.1147a22.

110 VII.3.1147a18.

111 II.3.1104b17.

112 I.13.1103a5.

113 II.1.1103a15.

114 VI.6.1141a8.

115 III.5.1114b6.

116 III.5.1114b9.

117 VI.6.1140b31.

118 VI.4.1140a7.

119 VI.4.1140a15.

120 VI.4.1120a11.

121 VI.4.1140a10.

122 VI.7.1141a12.

123 VI.7.1141a25.

124 VI.7.1141b4.

125 VI.12.1144a4.

126 VI.7.1141b2.

127 VI.5.1140b4.

128 VI.5. 1140a25.

129 VI.13.1145a1.

130 VI.13.1144b3.

131 VI.13.1144b7.

132 VI.13.1144b12.

133 VI.10.1143a7.

134 VI.13.1145a8.

135 VI.9.1142b34.

136 VI.9.1143b11.

137 VI.12.1144a8.

138 VI.12.1144a24.

139 VI.12.1144a24.

140 I.3.1094b19.

141 II.2.1104a1–5.

142 I.3.1094b23.

143 I.7.1098a25.

144 VI.8.1142a12.

145 I.4.1095b4.

146 I.4.1095b7.

147 X.9.1180a18.

148 X.9.1180a1.

149 X.9.1179b20.

150 II.3.1104b10.

151This quote is from one of Aristotle's logical works, *Topics* (Pickard-Cambridge), I.1.100a21–22.

152X.8.1179a19.

153I.7.1098b26.

154I.4.1095a29.

155*Eudemian Ethics* (Soloman), 1214b28–33.

156*Eudemian Ethics* (Soloman), 1214b33–1215a2.

157*Politics* I.5.1254b20.

158*Politics* I.6.1255b10.

159*Politics* I.5.1254b20

160From Diogenes Laertius, *Lives of the Eminent Philosophers*, (Hicks), V.11–16.

161VIII.2.1155b33.

162VII.5.1158a1.

163VIII.7.1158b12.

164VIII.8.1159a34.

165VIII.3.1156a7.

166VIII.3.1156a10.

167VIII.3.1156a22.

168 VIII.3.1156a31.

169VIII.3.1156a31.

170VIII.3.1156a10.

171VIII.4.1157a1.

172VIII.4.1157a3.

173 X.12.1172a3.

174VIII.1.1155a5.

175IX.10.1171a10.

176VIII.3.1156b26.

Chapter 6

1G.K. Chesterton, *St. Thomas Aquinas*, p. 61, A Project of Gutenberg of Australia ebook, available at: http://gutenberg.net.au/ebooks01/0100331.txt.

2Remember that all quotations are translated from Latin. I will use: St. Thomas Aquinas, *Summa Theologica*. Translated by Fathers of the English Dominican Province (New York: Benziger Bros. ed., 1947). This edition is readily available in print and online. Any reference without a title is to this edition. I will use standard notation, citing the numbered Part, the Question Number, and the number of the Article.

3*Euthyphro, Apology, Crito, Phaedo, The Death Scene*, F.J. Church, trans. (Indianapolis: Bobbs-Merrill, 1956), p. 7.

4*Euthyphro* (Church) 10d.

5I.II.91.4.

6II.II.30.4.

7I.II.91.4.

8I.II.55.1.

9I.II.56.4. Cf. I.II.55.3.

10I.II.56.3.

11I.II.56.3.

12I.II.62.1.

13II.II.23.6.

14I.II.23.1.

15I.II.25.1.

16Cf.I.II.25.

17With respect to the single issue of almsgiving, he mentions (1) corporal acts of mercy: feeding the hungry, giving drink to the thirsty, clothing the naked, giving refuge to the homeless, visiting the sick, ransoming prisoners, and burying the dead; and (2) spiritual acts of mercy: teaching the ignorant, counselling the doubtful, comforting the sorrowful, reproving sinners, forgiving injuries, bearing with those who trouble and annoy us, and praying for all. II.II.32.2.

18Thomas Aquinas, 'Disputed Questions on the Cardinal Virtues,' in: *The Cardinal Virtues*, R.E. Houser, trans. and ed. (Toronto: The Pontifical Institute of Medieval Studies, 2004), 157–205. Hereafter: 'Cardinal Virtues'. Cardinal Virtues, 2. Response.

19Cardinal Virtues, 2. Response.

20II.II.23.7.

21Cf. Cardinal Virtues. In an excellent introduction, Houser traces out ancient and medieval history of philosophy on the topic of the cardinal virtues.

22Cardinal Virtues. 1. Response.

23I.II.23.1.

24I.II.23.1.

25II.II.141.3.

26II.II.141.3.

27Cardinal Virtues, 1, Response.

28I.II.60.3.

29I.II.60.3.

30Thomas distinguishes between action and passion in this way. Cf. I.28.3.

31I.II.60.2.

32II.II.49.6.

33I.II.61.3.

34II.II.47.8.

35II.II.46.7.

36II.II.47.6.

37I.79.13. Thomas identifies conscience with the activity of *synderesis*. Synderesis is the cause; conscience is the effect. But Thomas concedes, 'sometimes the name conscience is given to the first natural habit—namely, *synderesis*. . . . For it is customary for causes and effects to be called after one another.' (I.79.12.) *Synderesis* is sometimes spelled with a *t* as *synteresis*.

[38]II.II.47.11.

[39]I.II.47.13.

[40]I.II.47.13.

[41]I.II.47.13.

[42]II.II.49.8.

[43]II.II.49.3.

[44]II.II.47.8.

[45]I.II.61.4.

[46]Cardinal Virtues, Art.1.

[47]I.II.90.1.

[48]I.II.90.1.

[49]I.II.90.4.

[50]I.II.91.1.

[51]I.II.91.2.

[52]I.II.91.2.

[53]I.II.91.2.

[54]*Genesis* 1:28.

[55]I.II.91.3.

[56]I.II.95.2.

[57]I.II.94.6.

[58]Jacques Maritain, *Natural Law: Reflections on Theory and Practice*, edited and introduced by William Sweet (South Bend, IN: St. Augustine's Press, 2001), pp. 14–5.

[59]I.1.6.

[60]I.II.62.3.

[61]I.II.91.6.

[62]I.II.94.2.

[63]Metaphysically, the boulder is not, in the most rigorous sense, a substance, but consider it *qua* substance (i.e., as a unity). There are metaphysical issues here we will not explore.

[64]I.II.94.2.

[65]I.II.94.2.

[66]I.II.94.2.

[67]I.II.94.4.

[68]I.II.94.4.

[69]II.II.66.4.

[70]II.II.66.2.

[71]II.II.66.7.

[72]II.II.120.1.

[73]V.10.1137b10.

[74]II.II.48.1.

[75]II.II.51.4.

[76]I.II.94.5.

[77]Maritain, *Natural Law*, p. 48.

[78]II.II.64.7.

[79]II.II.64.7.

[80]II.II.64.7.

[81]I.II.19.1.

[82]I.II.6.2.

[83]I.II.18.9.

[84]Samuel 16:7b.

[85]Note that Thomas himself uses the term *command* in a more restricted way.

[86]I.II.18.4.

[87]I.II.18.11.

[88]I.II.18.11.

[89]I.II.18.11.

[90]I.II.18.11.

[91]I.II.18.3.

[92]1.83.1.

[93]I.II.76.1.

[94]I.II.76.1.

[95]I.II.76.2.

[96]I.II.76.2.

[97]I.II.76.3.

[98]I.II.76.4.

[99]I.II.76.4.

[100]I.II.76.2.

[101]I.II.76.2.

Chapter 7

[1]We will cite from *The Anonymous Iamblichi* in *The First Philosophers*, (Waterfield), pp. 306–11. For an electronic translation see: 'Anonymous Discourse' in Iamblichus (Protrepticus XX), D.S. Hutchinson and Monte Johnson, trans., available through http://sites.google.com/site/montejohnson/protrepticus.

[2]Waterfield, introduction to the above, p. 301.

[3]Anonymous, p. 306.

[4]Anonymous, p. 309.

[5]Anonymous, p. 309.

[6]Anonymous, pp. 309–10.

[7]Anonymous, p. 311.

[8]Thomas Hobbes, *Leviathan*, Edwin Curley, ed. (Indianapolis: Hackett Publishing, 1994), *Hobbes Verse Autobiography*, p. liv.

[9]Many versions of Hobbes's *Leviathan* are available in print or online. See, for example Thomas Hobbes, *Leviathan*, J.C.A. Gaskin, ed. (Oxford: Oxford University Press, 1996). I will use Part, Chapter and paragraph number. For an electronic source, consult: http://oregonstate.edu/instruct/phl302/texts/hobbes/leviathan-contents.html.

[10]Hobbes, Introduction, 1.

[11]Hobbes, Introduction, 1.

[12]Hobbes, Part 1, Chap. 15.4.

[13]Hobbes, Part 1, Chap. 15.16.

[14]Hobbes, Part 1, Chap. 11.2.

[15]Hobbes, Part 1, Chap. 6.58.

[16]Hobbes, Part 1, Chap. 9.2.

[17]Hobbes, Part 2, Chap. 21.2.

[18]Hobbes, Part 1, Chap. 13.9.

[19]Hobbes, Part 1, Chap. 13.1.

[20]Hobbes, Part 1, Chap. 13.1.

[21]Hobbes, Part 1, Chap. 13.3.

[22]Hobbes, Part 1, Chap. 13.6.

[23]Hobbes, Part 1, Chap. 13.1.

[24]Hobbes, Part 1, Chap. 13.8.

[25]Hobbes, Part 1, Chap. 13.13.

[26]Hobbes, Part 1, Chap. 13.13.

[27]Hobbes, Part 1, Chap. 13.13.

[28]Hobbes, Part 1, Chap. 14.1.

[29]Hobbes, Part 1, Chap. 14.3.

[30]Hobbes, Part 1, Chap. 14.3.

[31]Hobbes, Part 1, Chap. 14.4.

[32]Hobbes, Part 1, Chap. 14.5.

[33]Hobbes, Part 1, Chap. 15.1.

[34]Hobbes, Part 1, Chap. 15.25, 18, 29, 17.

[35]Hobbes, Part 1, Chap. 15.35.

[36]Hobbes, Part 1, Chap. 15.16.

[37]Hobbes, Part 1, Chap. 15.16.

[38]Hobbes, Part 1, Chap. 15.17.

[39]Hobbes, Part 1, Chap. 15.40.

[40]Hobbes, Part 1, Chap. 17.2.

[41]Hobbes, Part 1, Chap. 15.3.

[42]Hobbes, Part 2, Chap. 18.3.

[43]Hobbes, Part 2, Chap. 30.1.

[44]Hobbes, Part 2, Chap. 17.2.

[45]Hobbes, Part 2, Chap. 17.1.

[46]Hobbes, Part 2, Chap. 18.1.

[47]Hobbes, Part 1, Chap. 14.29.

[48]Hobbes, Part 1, Chap. 15.36.

[49]Hobbes, Part 1, Chap. 13.10.

[50]Hobbes, Part 1, Chap. 15.2.

[51]This is, of course, the title of contemporary author David Gauthier's well-known book on contemporary contractarianism.

[52]Hobbes, Part 1, Chap. 15.34.

[53]Hobbes, Part 1, Chap. 6.7.

[54]Hobbes, Part 1, Chap. 15.40.

[55]Hobbes, Part 1, Chap. 15.38.

[56]Editions abound; for a complete electronic version consult: John Locke, 'The Second Treatise of Civil Government', 1760, *The Liberty Library*, www.constitution.org/jl/2ndtr02.txt. For an abridged version see:

John Locke, 'The Second Treatise of Government', in *Political Philosophy: The Essential Texts*, Steven M. Cahn, ed. (Oxford: Oxford University Press, 2005), pp. 246–273. I will cite in the usual way according to chapter and paragraph number.

[57]Locke, II.6.

[58]Locke, II.8.

[59]Locke, II.8.

[60]Locke, III.16.

[61]Locke, III.16.

[62]Locke, III.16.

[63]Locke, VIII, 95.

[64]Locke, IV.23.

[65]Locke, V.26.

[66]Locke, V.28.

[68]Locke, V.32.

[69]Locke, V.32.

[70]Locke, V.27. My italics.

[71]Locke, V.31.

[72]Locke, V.33.

[73]Locke, V.40.

[74]Jean-Jacques Rousseau, *Discourse on the Origin of Inequality*, Franklin Philip, trans., edited with an Introduction and Notes by Patrick Coleman (Oxford: Oxford University Press, 1994.) I will cite by part and page number. For an electronic version, see Jean-Jacques Rousseau, *Discourse On the Origin of Inequality Among Men, and Is It Authorised by Natural Law?* 1754; G.D.H. Cole, trans., rendered into HTML and text by Jon Roland. Available at: www.constitution.org/jjr/ineq.txt.

[75]Rousseau, *Inequality, Notes. I, pp. 94–5.*

[76]Rousseau, *Inequality, Part II, p. 94.*

[77]Rousseau, *Inequality, Part II, p. 83–84.*

[78]Rousseau, *Inequality*, Part II, p. 60–1.

[79]Rousseau, *Inequality*, Part II, p. 60–1.

[80]Rousseau, *Inequality, Part II, p. 61.*

[81]Rousseau, *Inequality, Part II, p. 55.*

[82]Rousseau, *Inequality, Part II. p. 66.*

[83]Rousseau, *Inequality*, Part 1 p. 46.

[84]Rousseau, *Inequality*, Part 1 p. 46.

[85]Rousseau, *Inequality*, Part 1 p. 46.

[86]Rousseau, *Inequality*, Part 1 p. 46.

[87]Rousseau, *Inequality*, Part 1, p. 47.

[88]Rousseau, *Inequality*, Part 1, p. 47.

[89]Rousseau, *Inequality*, Part 1, p. 47–8.

[90]Rousseau, *Inequality,* Notes O, p. 115.

[91]Rousseau, *Inequality,* Notes O, p. 115.

[92]Jean-Jacques Rousseau, *The Social Contract* (and *Discourse on Political Economy*), translated with

Introduction and Notes by Christopher Betts (Oxford: Oxford University Press, 1994). I will cite by chapter and page number. For an electronic version see: 'The Social Contract or Principles of Political Right,' by Jean-Jacques Rousseau, 1762. Translated by G.D.H. Cole, rendered into HTML and text by Jon Roland, at: www.constitution.org/jjr/socon.htm.

[93]Rousseau, Contract, viii, p. 59.

[94]Rousseau, Contract, vi. 55.

[95]Rousseau, Contract, vi, 56.

[96]Rousseau, Contract, vi, p. 55.

[97]Rousseau, Contract, vii, p. 58.

[98]Rousseau, Contract, vii, p. 58.

[99]We will cite from: Karl Marx, 'Economic and Philosophical Manuscripts of 1844,' reprinted in Steven M. Cahn, Political Philosophy (New York, Oxford: Oxford University Press, 2005), pp. 410–17.

[100]Marx, Economic, p. 412.

[101]Karl Marx and Friedrich Engels, 'Manifesto of the Communist Party,' In Cahn, pp. 423–35, p. 431.

[102]Marx, Economic, pp. 412–3.

[103]Marx, Economic, p. 412.

[104]Marx, Economic, p. 412.

[105]Michael Sandel, Liberalism and the Limits of Justice (Cambridge: Cambridge University Press, 1983), p. 110.

[106]John Rawls, A Theory of Justice (Oxford: Clarendon Press, 1972), I.19, p. 155.

Chapter 8

[1]Standard citation of Kant often includes page and line numbers to the German collection of Kant's works, Kant's Gesammelte Schriften, by the Königliche Preussische Akademie der Wissenschafaten (Berlin: Walter de Gruyter, 1908–13). Immanuel Kant, 'An Answer to the Question: "What is Enlightenment?"' 1784: Philosophy on the Eserver: http://philosophy.eserver.org/kant/what_is_enlightenment.txt.

[2]Kant, 'What is Enlightenment?'

[3]Kant, 'What is Enlightenment?'

[4]Kant, 'What is Enlightenment?'

[5]Kant, Groundwork for the Metaphysics of Morals, Arnulf Zweig, trans.; Thomas Hill and Arnulf Zweig, eds. (Oxford: Oxford University Press, 2002), p. 9. From this point forward, all unspecified citations are from this source.

[6]Genesis 3:19.

[7]Kant, 'Idea for a Universal History from a Cosmo-politan Point of View,' (1784), Lewis White Beck, trans. From Immanuel Kant, 'On History' (Indiana: Bobbs-Merrill, 1963), www.marxists.org/reference/subject/ethics/kant/universal_history.htm 1.10.200

[8](Groundwork) 1.12.202.

[9]1.12.202.

[10]2.17.209.

[11]1.10.199.

[12]1.10.199.

[13]1.10.199–200.

[14]1.10.199.

[15]1.10.200.

[16]2.38.240.

[17]2.38.240.

[18]Preface, 3.191.

[19]2.20.213.

[20]2.21.213–4.

[21]2.21.214.

[22]Preface, 2.189–90.

[23]2.30.226.

[24]2.22.217.

[25]2.39.242.

[26]2.23.219.

[27]1.16.206.

[28]1.7.195.

[29]1.7.195.

[30]2.22.217.

[31]2.17.209.

[32]2.25.222.

[33]2.25.222.

[34]2.26.222.

[35]2.27.223.

[36]2.27.223

[37]2.27.224.

[38]2.27.223–4.

[39]2.27.224.

[40]2.27.223.

[41]2.27.223.

[42]2.27.223.

[43]2.28.225.

[44] .29.225.

[45]Keep in mind that Kant conceives of 'doing' in terms of having the right intention.

[46]Cf. William D. Ross, Kant's Ethical Theory (Clarendon Press, 1954).

[47]Cf. Jan Garrett, A Simple and Usable (Although Incomplete) Ethical Theory Based on the Ethics of W. D. Ross, August 10, 2004, www.wku.edu/~jan.garrett/ethics/rossethc.htm.

[48]Pojman, *Ethics*, p. 134.
[49]2.34.232. (My italics.)
[50]2.34.232.
[51]Cf. 2.34.232.
[52]2.34.236.
[53]2.32.229.
[54]2.32.230.
[55]2.36.235.
[56]2.32.229.
[57]2.32.229.
[58]2.33.230.
[59]2.38.239.
[60]2.35.234.
[61]2.38.239.
[62]2.38.239.
[63]2.25.222.
[64]2.26.222.
[65]2.34.232.
[66]2.32.230.
[67]2.38.239.
[68]2.37.236
[69]2.38.241.
[70]2.38.241.
[71]2.38.241.
[72]John Stuart Mill, *On Liberty* (London: Longman, Roberts & Green, 1869); Bartleby.com, 1999 at: www.bartleby.com/130/, 'Chapter III: Of Individuality, as One of the Elements of Well-Being.'
[73]Mill, *On Liberty*, Chap. III.
[74]Mill, *On Liberty*, Chap. III.
[75]Nietzsche, *Beyond Good and Evil* (Faber), §259.
[76]Nietzsche, *Beyond Good and Evil* (Faber), §259.
[77]Friedrich Nietzsche, *Beyond Good and Evil*, Marion Faber, trans. (Oxford: Oxford University Press, 1998), §259.
[78]Nietzsche, *On the Genealogy of Morals*, Douglas Smith, trans. (Oxford: Oxford University Press, 1996), First Essay, §11.
[79](Kant) 3.44.250–1.
[80]3.44.251.
[81]3.44.251.
[82]3.44.252.
[83]3.43.248.
[84]3.43.248.
[85]3.44.252.
[86]3.46.257.
[87]3.48.260.
[88]3.48.261.
[89]3.48.261.

Chapter 9

[1]Unless otherwise noted, citations from Bentham have been taken from Jeremy Bentham, *An Introduction to the Principles of Morals and Legislation*, 1781, reprint, electronic edition (pdf file) (Kitchener: Batoche Books, 2000); available at: www.efm.bris.ac.uk/het/bentham/morals.pdf. There are many electronic and print editions available.
[2]Bentham, I.i, p.14.
[3]Bentham, IV.i, p. 35.
[4]Bentham, IV.ii, p. 35.
[5]Bentham, I. iii, pp. 14–5.
[6]Bentham I.ii, p. 14.
[7]Bentham, *A Fragment on Government; Being an Examination of What Is Delivered, on the Subject of Government in General in the Introduction to Sir William Blackstone's Commentaries* (1776), www.efm.bris.ac.uk/het/bentham/government.htm.
[8]Bentham I.ix, p. 15.
[9]Bentham, I.xi, p. 16.
[10]Bentham, I.xiii–xiv, p. 16.
[11]Bentham II.v, p. 20.
[12]Bentham, II.iii, p. 19.
[13]Bentham, IV.v, p. 32–3.
[14]Bentham, IV.ii–iv, pp. 31–2.
[15]One standard edition of Mill's works is: John Stuart Mill, *Collected Works of John Stuart Mill*, J.M. Robson, ed. (Toronto: University of Toronto Press, 1963ff). But there are innumerable editions of individual texts.
[16]John Stuart Mill, *Autobiography*, V: 'A Crisis in My Mental History. One Stage Onward' (1873), www.utilitarianism.com/millauto/five.html.
[17]Selections from 'Utilitarianism' from John Stuart Mill, *On Liberty and Other Essays*, edited with introduction and notes by John Gray (Oxford: Oxford University Press, 1998), 'Utilitarianism,' pp. 131–204. An electronic copy can be found at: *Utilitarianism*, University of Adelaide Library E_Books, http://etext.library.adelaide.edu.au/m/mill/john_stuart/.
[18]Mill, *U.*, I, p. 137.
[19]Mill, *U.*, I, p. 137.
[20]Mill, *U.*, II, 138–9.
[21]Mill, *U.*, II, 138–9.
[22]Mill, *U.*, II, p. 138.
[23]Mill, *U.*, II, p. 139.
[24]Mill, *U.*, II, pp. 139–40.
[25]Mill, *U.*, II, p. 141.
[26]Mill, *U.*, II. p. 140.

27 Mill, *U.*, IV, pp.172–3. The parallel structure of these two paragraphs shows that Mill is treating these concepts as synonymous.

28 My italics, Mill, *U.*, IV, pp. 172–3.

29 Robert Nozick, *Anarchy, State, and Utopia* (New York: Basic Books, 1974), pp. 42–5.

30 Mill, *U.*, II, p. 148.

31 Mill, *U.*, II, p. 148.

32 William Godwin, cited in Peter Singer, *One World, The Ethics of Globalization* (New Haven: Yale University Press, 2002), p. 155.

33 Mill, "Bentham," *London and Westminster Review*, Aug. 1838, revised in 1859, http://socserv.mcmaster.ca/econ/ugcm/3ll3/bentham/bentham.

34 Mill, *U.*, II, p. 149.

35 Mill, *U.*, II, p. 151.

36 Mill, *U.*, II, p. 151.

37 Mill, *U.*, II, p. 150, n. 1.

38 Mill, *U.*, II, p. 155.

39 Mill, *U.*, II, p. 156.

40 Mill, *U.*, II, p. 147.

41 Mill, *U.*, II, p. 147.

42 Mill, *U.*, II, p. 149.

43 Mill, *U.*, V, p. 199.

44 Mill, *U.*, V, p. 198.

45 Mill, *U.*, V, p. 199, n.1.

46 Cf. Derek Parfit, *Reasons and Persons*.

47 Mill, *U.*, II, p. 145.

48 Citations taken from John Stuart Mill, *On Liberty*, in John Stuart Mill, *On Liberty and Other Essays*, John Gray, ed., pp. 5–128. There are numerous editions readily available in print and online.

49 Mill, *L.*, I, p. 14.

50 Mill, *L.*, I, p. 17.

51 Diogenes Laertius, *Lives of the Eminent Philosophers*, R.D. Hicks, trans (Cambridge, MA: Harvard University Press, 1931), Vol. II, Book 10 ('Epicurus'), *Sovran Maxims* 31, 10.150.

52 Mill, *L.*, V, p.107.

53 Mill, *L.*, I, p. 11.

54 Mill, *L.*, I, p. 10.

55 Mill, *L.*, II, p. 23.

56 Mill, *L.*, II, p.24.

57 Mill, *L.*, II, p. 23.

58 'The Fox Guarding the Chicken Coop: An Interview with Jan Narveson,' by Alberto Mingardi, *The Laissez Faire City Times*, Vol 3, No 34, August 30, 1999. Cited in www.depressedmetabolism.com/the_fox_guarding_the_chicken_coop_an_interview_with_jan_narveson/.

59 Narveson, *Moral Matterss* (Peterborough, Ont.: Broadview Press, 1999, 2nd ed.), p.6.

60 Mill, *U.*, V, p.195.

61 Mill, *L.*, IV, p. 87.

62 I must thank Dr Malcolm Murray for informative discussion on these issues.

63 Mill, *L.*, V, pp. 113–4.

64 Mill, *L.*, IV, p. 87.

65 Mill, *L.*, V, pp. 115.

66 Narveson, *MM*, p. 252.

67 Narveson, *MM*, p. 252.

68 Mill, *L.*, III, p. 64. The quote is from *The Sphere and Duties of Government*.

69 Mill, *L.*, III, p. 66.

70 Mill, *L.*, III, p. 70.

71 Mill, *L.*, III, p. 66.

72 Mill, *L.*, III, p. 72.

73 Mill, *L.*, III, p. 72.

74 Mill, *L.*, III, p. 72.

75 Mill, *L.*, III, p. 66.

76 Mill, *L.*, III, p. 66.

77 Mill, *L.*, III, p. 68–9.

78 Mill, *L.*, III, p. 69–70.

79 Mill, *L.*, III, p. 69.

80 Mill, *L.*, III, p. 72.

81 Mill, *L.*, III, p. 64.

82 Mill, *L.*, III, p. 75.

83 Mill, *L.*, III, p. 74–5.

84 Mill, *L.*, III, p. 71.

85 Mill, *L.*, III, p. 66.

86 Mill, *L.*, III, p. 66.

87 Mill, *L.*, III, p. 77.

88 Mill, *L.*, III, p. 67.

89 Mill, *L.*, III, p. 74.

90 Mill, *L.*, III, p. 72.

91 Mill, *L.*, III, p. 65.

92 Mill, *L.*, III, p. 71.

93 Amitai Etzioni, *The New Golden Rule: Community and Morality in a Democratic Society* (New York: Basic Books, 1996), p. xvii.

94 Etzioni, p. 5.

95 Ronald Dworkin, 'Liberalism' (pp. 60–79), in *Liberalism and Its Critics*, Michael Sandel, ed. (New York: New York University Press, 1984), p. 77.

96 Cicero, *On Obligations*, Translated by P.G. Walsh (Oxford: Oxford University Press, 2000), pp. 37, 38, 39, 41.

97 Citations taken from John Stuart Mill, *The Subjection of Women*, in John Stuart Mill, *On Liberty and Other Essays*, John Gray, ed., pp. 471–582. There are

numerous editions readily available in print and on the net.

[98]Mill, *S.*, p. 471.

[99]Mary Wollstonecraft, *A Vindication of the Rights of Men, A Vindication of the Rights of Woman, A Historical and Moral View of the French Revolution*, Janet Todd, ed. (Oxford: Oxford University Press, 1993). All citations from this source.

[100]Wollstonecraft, II, pp. 91.

[101]Wollstonecraft, II, pp. 86–7.

[102]Wollstonecraft, IV, p. 125.

[103]Wollstonecraft, II, pp. 91–2.

[104]Wollstonecraft, II, p. 91.

[105]Wollstonecraft, II, p. 91.

[106]Mill, *S.*, IV, p. 527

[107]Mill, *S.*, IV, p. 558.

[108]Mill, *S.*, IV, p. 575–6.

[109] Mill, *S.*, IV, p. 577.

Chapter 10

[1]'Anti-theory', *The Blackwell Dictionary of Western Philosophy*, Nicholas Bunnin and Jiyuan Yu, eds., 2004, www.blackwellreference.com/.

[2]Søren Kierkegaard, *Either/Or* from: *Kierkegaard's Writings*, Howard and Edna Hong, eds. (Princeton, NJ: Princeton University Press, 1978–2000), hereafter E/O. E/O, 1, 263.

[3] E/O, 1, 265.

[4]E/O, II, 160.

[5]E/O, II, 224.

[6]E/O, II, 153.

[7]E/O, II, 161

[8]E/O, II, 160–1.

[9]E/O, II, 161.

[10]Søren Kierkegaard, *Sickness Unto Death* from: *Kierkegaard's Writings*, Howard Hong, Edna Hong, eds. (Princeton, NJ: Princeton University Press, 1978–2000), XI, 206.

[11]*Sickness*, 205.

[12]E/O, II,190.

[13]Emmanuel Mounier, *Personalism* (Notre Dame: University of Notre Dame Press, 2001), xv–xvi.

[14]Nel Noddings, *Caring: A Feminine Approach to Ethics and Moral Education* (Berkeley: University of California Press, 1984), pp. 83–4.

[15]Noddings, *Caring*, p. 86.

[16]Noddings, *Caring*, p. 86.

[17]Noddings, *Caring*, p. 86.

[18]Noddings, *Caring*, p. 112.

[19]Noddings, 'Two Concepts of Caring', *Philosophy of Education*, 1999, electronic source: www.ed.uiuc.edu/EPS/PES-yearbook/1999/noddings.asp.

[20]Noddings, 'Two Concepts'.

[21]Noddings, 'Two Concepts'.

[22]Noddings, 'Two Concepts'.

[23]Noddings, 'Two Concepts'.

[24]Psalm 133.

[25]*The Code of Hammurabi*, L.W. King, trans., Richard Hooker, ed. (1910), electronic source: www.wsu.edu/~dee/MESO/CODE.HTM.

[26]*Hammurabi*.

[27]Brian Tierney, *The Idea of Natural Rights* (Atlanta, Georgia: Scholars Press for Emory University, 1997).

[28]Tierney, p. 73.

[29]Cited in Tierney, p. 75.

[30]Tierney, pp. 75–6. (This is from Locke's *Two Treatises of Government* I.42. My italics.)

[31]Alan Gerwith, *Human Rights: Essays on Justification and Applications* (Chicago and London: University of Chicago Press, 1982), p. 2.

[32]*Summa Theologica* (Fathers of the English Dominican Province) First Part of the Second Part, 96.2, Whether it belongs to the human law to repress all vices? www.newadvent.org/summa/2096.htm.

[33]*Exodus* 21: 24–5.

[34]Global Ethic Foundation, Tübingen, Germany, electronic source: www.weltethos.org/dat-english/index.htm.

[35]*Declaration Toward a Global Ethic*, 'Principles of a Global Ethics,' Global Ethic Foundation website.

[36]*Declaration*, 'A. Introduction.'

[37]*Declaration*, 'A. Introduction.'

[38]*Declaration*, B.II.

[39] *Declaration*, III.1.A.

[40]Warwick Fox, 'Deep Ecology, A New Philosophy for Our Time', reprinted in *Environmental Ethics: An Anthology*, Andrew Light and Holmes Rolston, eds. (Oxford: Wiley–Blackwell, 2002), pp. 252–53.

[41]John Rawls, *A Theory of Justice* (Cambridge, MA: Belknap Press of Harvard University Press, 1971). Hereafter, *Theory*.

[42]*Theory*, p. 60.

[43]*Theory*, p. 83.

[44]Antiphon, fragment, cited in: John Robinson, *Introduction to Early Greek Philosophy* (Boston: Houghton Mifflin, 1968), p. 251.

[45]Antiphon, p. 251.

[46]Cf. Michael Sandel, *Liberalism and the Limits of Justice*.

꘎ Index ꘎

absolutism: Kant and, 318
Academy, 124, 147
acts: Aquinas and, 236–43, 246–9; Aristotle and,
175–7, 364; human, 237–9; 'by human beings',
237; involuntary, 176–7; mixed, 177, 364;
supererogatory, 208; unintended, 242, 243;
utilitarianism and, 359–66; voluntary, 175–7
actuality: Aristotle and, 151
act utilitarianism, 362
addiction, sex, 140
afterlife: Plato and, 136, 145; Socrates and, 121
agents, moral, 175–7
agnosticism, 93
agreement: enforcement of, 265–8; hypothetical, 267,
288–90; liberalism and, 376; morality as, 255–92;
rational, 414–20; see also social contract
akolasia, 179
akrasia, 178
Albert the Great, 206
alcohol: violence and, 300
Alexander the Great, 74, 147–8
alienation, 288
American Dissident, The, 171
Amis, Kingsley, 78
amour de soi-même, 283
amour-propre, 281, 283
Analects, The, 62, 64
ancient world: moral philosophy in, 60–110
Anderson, Nate, 262
angels, 25
animals: Aquinas and, 225; Aristotle and, 152, 154;
Singer and, 412, 413; speciesism and, 412; young
and, 33; see also rational animals
anomie, 382
Anonymous Iamblichi, 256–8
Anscombe, Elizabeth, 390
Anscombe, G.E.M., 339–40, 359
anthropological view, 45–7
anti-morality, 332–4, 371
Antiphon, 418
anti-theory, 389, 390–2, 401
antithesis: Pyrrho and, 94, 95; Socrates and, 118
apathy, 84, 96; Stoic, 84
aphorisms, 67
aporia, 180

appetites: Plato and, 136–41, 142
Aquinas, Thomas, 12, 25, 39, 109, 202–54, 404; law
and, 219–32
arete, 151–7, 162–3; see also virtue
argument: definition of, 24–5; functional, 151–2;
is–ought fallacy and, 43–51; Plato and, 135; 'from
queerness', 35–6; Socrates and, 118
Aristophanes, 113
Aristotle, 9, 12, 147–201, 364; anthropological view
and, 45, 46–7; Aquinas and, 204–5, 206, 207, 208,
209, 229; biology and, 31–2, 148–9; character
change and, 167, 185; criticism of, 153–7; ethics
of care and, 401; good life and, 163–4; imprecision
of ethics and, 391; inductive-deductive method
and, 192–6; punishment and, 406; purpose of
ethics and, 19–20; Socrates and, 177; Sophists
and, 98; speciesism and, 413; 'spirit of', 15–16;
three kinds of life and, 164–5; upbringing and,
192, 197
Arrian, 82
art: Aristotle and, 189; as valuable, 303
asceticism, 73; Bentham and, 344–5; Mill and, 365;
principle of, 344–5
askesis, 72–3
assistance: Kant and, 309, 311
asymmetry principle, 122–3
ataraxia: Epicurus and, 77, 78; skepticism and, 90–6;
Stoics and, 82, 84, 89
Athanassoulis, Nafsika, 391
atomism, 76
Augustine, 51, 205, 401
authenticity: anti-morality and, 334; Kierkegaard and,
394–5
authoritarianism: communitarianism and, 383;
Hobbes and, 267; Mill and, 382
autonomy: Kant and, 324, 331–2
aversion: Hobbes and, 259, 260
Ayer, A.J., 34

bad faith, 57–8
Baier, Annette, 390
Baranick, Alana, 150
Beatitudes, 107
beauty: Plato and, 128
begging the question, 100

beliefs, 37
Bell, Clive, 303
Bellah, Robert, 71
Bentham, Jeremy, 339–48; Mill and, 349, 350, 351, 352, 357, 366
Berdyaev, Nikolai, 395
Bett, Richard, 73
Bible, 102
Binding, Karl, 356
biology: Aristotle and, 31–3, 148–9
birthing metaphor, 118, 119
blindness, moral, 183
body: Plato and, 134–6, 145
bouleusis, 191
bourgeoisie, 286
Bowne, Borden Parker, 395
Boyle, Joseph, 231
Braybrooke, David, 347
Brentano, Franz, 10
Brightman, Edgar Sheffield, 395
brutishness, 181–2, 184, 185
Buber, Martin, 395
Buchanan, James, 256
Buddhism, 91, 104
Bunnin, Nicholas, and Jiyuan Yu, 390
burden of proof, 28–30

calculus: felicific, 345–6; pleasure, 342–8, 368–9
canon law, 402
capitalism: Marx and, 286–8; personalism and, 396
Cardona, Felisa, 384
care: ethics of, 389, 396–401; for/about, 398, 399; natural/ethical, 397
casuistry, 226–30, 357; anti-theory and, 390–1; Kant and, 314–18
categorical imperative, 305–31; criticisms of, 313–23; formulations of, 307–31; kingdom of ends formulation of, 329–31; legislative formulation of, 323–5, 331; means–end formulation of, 325–9, 331; quasi-, 322–3; single, 316; universal formulations of, 307–23, 330
caution: prudence and, 214
cave: analogy of, 133
character development: Mill and, 378–80, 381
character-states: Aristotle and, 181–7
charity: Aquinas and, 207–8, 213, 218
Charter of Rights and Freedoms, 403
cheating, 156
Chen, David, 273
children: obesity and, 345; as soldiers, 245, 246

chimera model, 141–3
choice: Aristotle and, 174–7, 237; Kierkegaard and, 393–5; Mill and, 375
Christianity: Kierkegaard and, 392; Mill and, 379; utilitarianism and, 354; *see also* religion
Cicero, Marcus Tullius, 81, 205, 384–5
circular reasoning, 99–100
circumspection: prudence and, 214
citizen's arrest, 273
civilization: Locke and, 277; Rousseau and, 278–81, 282
Civil War, English, 258
class: Marx and, 286
cleverness: Aristotle and, 194–5
coercion: Mill and, 381–2
commitment: Kierkegaard and, 393–5
communism, 286; Confucianism and, 63; personalism and, 396
Communist Manifesto, The, 287
communitarianism, 382–5
community: agreement and, 257–8; anti-theory and, 391–2; contractarian, 284; Kant and, 329–31; liberalism and, 382–5; natural law and, 225–6; retributive justice and, 414–17; Socrates and, 123–4; utilitarianism and, 366–7
compassion, 170
competition: Rousseau and, 279–80
Comte, Auguste, 18
conclusions: logic and, 24–5; repugnant, 367
Confucianism, 62, 63
Confucius (Master Kong), 61–7, 103; Heraclitus and, 67-8
connatural knowledge, 221–3
conscience: Aristotle and, 157, 213–14, 222; as deterrent, 419; divine command morality and, 408; Locke and, 274
consciousness, 10
consensus, overlapping, 416
consent: Aquinas and, 240; contractarianism, and, 289; hypothetical, 374–5; Kant and, 310; liberalism and, 374–5, 376; occurrent, 374-5
consequences: Kant and, 304–5, 320–1
consequentialism, 180, 359–62; anti-theory and, 390–1; Kant and, 304–5
conservatism: Confucius and, 63
Constant, Benjamin, 318
consumerism, 71; personalism and, 396
contemplative life, 164–5
contemporary contractarianism, 389, 414-20
contemporary moral theory, 389–421

context: Kant and, 314–18; moral act and, 242

continence: Aristotle and, 181, 183–4, 186, 187; incontinence and, 183–4

contractarianism, 47, 255–92; ancient, 256–8; contemporary, 288–90, 389, 414–20; exclusive, 289; Hobbes and, 258–71; liberalism and, 374; Locke and, 271–8; Marx and, 286–8; Rousseau and, 278–86; two-tiered, 274, 289; virtue and, 290–1; virtue ethics and, 265, 267–70

contradiction, 100–1; Kant and, 308, 309, 311, 319

controversy: ethics and, x–xi, 13–14

conventions: Diogenes and, 74–5

Cook, Emma, 195

co-operation: decision-theory and, 418, 419; Hobbes and, 261

Copeland, D.C., 3

cosmopolitanism, 73, 87

counsel: Aquinas and, 239–40

counterexample, rigid, 318–22

courage: Aristotle and, 168–70, 174; Plato and, 137, 209

cross-examination, 118

Csikszentmihalyi, Mihaly, 153, 160

culture: anti-theory and, 390–2; relativism and, 99–100

Curtis, Valerie, and Adam Biran, 48

Cynicism, 61, 70–5; as modern term, 73; Socrates and, 113

Dante, 95–6

Dao, 64

Day, Laura, 26

death: Epicurus and, 78–80

decision-making, 417–20; anti-theory and, 392; Aquinas and, 214–15; Kant and, 323–5, 330; utilitarianism and, 368–70

decision-theorists, 417–20

Declaration Toward a Global Ethic, 408–9

deduction: Aristotle and, 192–6

defense of necessity, 268

deinotes, 194

democracy: Locke and, 274; totalitarian, 285

Democritus, 61, 67, 90; hedonism and, 68–70, 341, 344

deontology, 296–338, 358; anti-theory and, 390–1; vs. consequentialism, 304–5; criticisms of, 313–23, 332–7; God and, 307

Derrida, Jacques, 19

Descartes, René, 28

desire: Aquinas and, 210, 216; Democritus and, 69–70; Epicurus and, 77–8; good and, 47; Hobbes and, 259, 260, 270–1; Kant and, 301–2, 305–6, 335–6; Plato and, 136–41

determinism, historical, 288

deterrence: punishment and, 405

différance, 19

dignity: Kant and, 326–7

Diogenes, 61, 70–5; Epictetus and, 89

disabled: utilitarianism and, 356–7

disagreement, moral, x–xi, 13–14, 30

'discourse ethics', 417

Discourse on the Origin of Inequality, The, 278–81

discrimination: speciesism and, 412–13

disgust, 48

disputatio, 203

Divided Line, 130–3, 135, 140, 144

divine command morality, 204–5, 389, 406–8

divine law, 205, 221

divinity: ancient philosophers and, 117; see also god(s)

divorce: Mill and, 376

docility: prudence and, 214–15

dogma, 295

dogmatism, 14; skepticism and, 92

Dorn, Sherman, 400

double-effect: principle of, 227, 232–6

drugs: child soldiers and, 245, 246; date rape, 244; harm reduction and, 367; responsibility and, 251

dualism: Plato and, 135, 145

Duclos, Susan, 96

Duffy, Richard, 6

Durkheim, Emile, 382

duty: actual, 322; defeasible, 322; imperfect, 311–12, 315–16; Kant and, 295–9, 301, 302, 303, 311–12, 315–16; Kant's definition of, 296–7; narrow, 312; perfect, 311–12, 315–16; prima facie, 322, 323; wide, 312

Dworkin, Ronald, 383

ecology, deep/shallow, 410–14

economic account: rationality and, 53–4

ecumenical global ethics, 389, 408–10

Eddie, David, 206

Edgeworth, Francis, 346

education: Aristotle and, 179; Epictetus and, 87; ethics of care and, 400–1; Plato and, 130–3; Socrates and, 119

egalitarianism: biological, 412; Mill and, 366–7

egoism: Hobbes and, 259–60, 264; Mill and, 353;

moral, 80–1; psychological, 54–5; Stoics and, 87–9
eidos, 128–9
Either/Or, 393
elenchus, 117–18, 119
Emerson, Ralph Waldo, 171
emotion: Aquinas and, 216; ethics and, 36–7; Kant and, 335–6
emotivism, 34
empathy, 56
Empedocles, 117
empiricism: ethics and, 39–41; Mill and, 348
endoxa, 197, 205
ends and means: Aquinas and, 235; Aristotle and, 158–62; ethics of care and, 399; Kant and, 325–9, 331; utilitarianism and, 362–4
ends-in-themselves, 325–9
Engels, Friedrich, 286
Enlightenment, 255–6; Kant and, 294–5
Enquiry Concerning Political Justice, 354–6
entitlements, 402; *see also* rights
environmental ethics, 389, 410–14
Epictetus, 61, 81–90
epicure, 76
Epicureans, 75–81, 341; as modern term, 76; Socrates and, 113
Epicurus, 61, 75–81, 370; Epictetus and, 89
episteme, 188
epistemology, 23–59
epoche, 91, 94
equality: contractarian, 290; global ethics and, 409; Locke and, 274–5; Marx and, 286; Mill and, 385–7; Rousseau and, 278–81; women and, 385–7
equity: Aquinas and, 228–9
'escape clauses', 323
eternal law, 219, 221
ethics: as agreement, 255–92; ancient world and, 60–110; anthropological view and, 45–7; as authoritative, 4–5; comprehensive, 4; contemporary, 390–421; definitions of, 7; discourse, 417; ecumenical global, 389, 408–10; as empirical discipline, 39–41; environmental, 389, 410–14; as evaluation, 2–8; as fundamental, 3–4; genuine, 298; history of ideas and, 16–19; imposed, 371–2; as instrumental, 364–6; introduction to, 1–22; as logical puzzle, 52 ; material philosophy and, 301; modern, *x–xi*, 2–7, 8; normative priority and, 5; as objective, 37–9, 55–8, 86; as obligatory, 2–3; purpose of, 19–22; as self-centred rationalization, 271; self-interested, 297; study of,

9–15; teaching of, *ix–xii*; as term, 1–2; traditional, *x–xi*, 2–3, 7–8; *see also* morality
ethics of care, 389, 396–401; as symmetrical/asymmetrical, 399
etiquette: ethics and, 5–7
Etzioni, Amitai, 382–3, 417
eudaimonia, 149–50, 399; *see also* happiness
euthanasia, 236, 356, 399–400
Euthyphro, 114
Euthyphro problem, 203–5, 407
evaluation: ethics and, 2–8; moral and non-moral, 2–3; non-moral, 2–3, 5–7; quasi-moral, 5–7
evil: enlarged utilitarianism and, 369–70; Epicurus and, 79–80; ethics of care and, 397; 'great', 363–4; Jesus and, 107; major/minor, 321; moral realism and, 50–1; preventive, 320–2; Socrates and, 116, 121; utilitarianism and, 363–4
execution: order of, 237–9
existentialism, 11, 393
exploitation, 288
expressivism, 34
external goods: Aristotle and, 162–3, 174

facts: values and, 34
faith: Aquinas and, 207, 209, 218; contractarian, 291
fallacy: 'is–ought', 43–51; naturalistic, 42
fallibility, human, 38–9
family: natural law and, 225
Famous Fire Cause, 354–7
fanaticism, religious, 409
faults: Aristotle and, 174, 177–81
favouritism: impersonalism and, 358
feelings: ethics and, 36–7; *see also* emotion
felicific calculus, 345–6
feminism, 389, 396–401
Finnis, John, 231–2
first moral principles: Aristotle and, 197–8
Fisher, Marian, 20, 21
fishing, 66–7
'flow', 153, 160
Foot, Philippa, 390
foresight: prudence and, 214
forms: Plato and, 128–9, 133
fortitude: Aquinas and, 207, 210–11, 212, 216
Foucault, Michel, 334, 341
Fox, Warwick, 410, 411–12, 413
Frankl, Viktor, 10–11
free choice: Mill and, 375
freedom: communitarianism and, 382; Epictetus and, 89–90; Hobbes and, 260, 264, 267; Kant and, 301,

331–2, 335; laws of, 301; liberalism and, 371, 372–3, 377; 'life of rational', 385–6; Mill and, 370, 381, 385–6; negative theory of, 260, 267; Rawls and, 414; Rousseau and, 285–6
free will: 9–10; Aristotle and, 174
friendship: Aquinas and, 208; Aristotle and, 198, 199–200; Epicurus and, 80–1; ethics of care and, 401; pleasure, 199–200; skepticism and, 94–5; Stoics and, 87–8; utility, 199–200; virtuous, 199–200
functional argument: Aristotle and, 151–2

gambling, 277
game-theorists, 418–19
Gassendi, Pierre, 75
Gauthier, David, 52, 256, 269, 289, 419
gender: global ethics and, 409; Mill and, 385–7
general will, 283–6
generosity: 'chain of', 361
genius: Mill and, 377–80
genocide, 409
'gentleman', 62–3
Gerwith, Alan, 403
Glaucon, 125–7, 143
Glendon, Mary Anne, 404
Global Ethic Foundation, 408
gluttony, 211
gnome, 229
god(s): Aquinas and, 207–8, 209; Aristotle and, 181; divine command morality and, 406–8; Epicurus and, 76, 78–9; Jesus and, 108–9; Socrates and, 113–15
Godfrey of Fontaines, 402
Godwin, William, 340, 354–7
Golden Mean, 167–74, 190, 210
Golden Rule, 63, 103–4, 265; global ethics and, 409; Kant and, 312–13
good: Aquinas and, 207; Aristotle and, 149–50, 161–3, 174; external, 162–3, 174; Hobbes and, 270–1; moral realism and, 47–51; Plato and, 127–30, 133; relative/absolute, 207; Socrates and, 116; subjective theory of, 270–1; 'thin theory of', 372–3, 416
good action: Aquinas and, 240–2
good deliberation: Aquinas and, 239–40; Aristotle and, 191, 194–5
good life: Aristotle and, 163–4
good reputation: Aristotle and, 150, 162; Confucius and, 64, 66
good will: Aquinas and, 207; contractarianism and, 290; Kant and, 297, 302–5

Gorgias, 256
Grameen banking system, 368
Grant, Jon, and S.W. Kim, 138
Greatest Happiness Principle, 343–4, 357, 362, 366; Mill and, 349
great evil strategy, 363–4
Grisez, Germain, 231
Groundwork for the Metaphysics of Morals, 293, 336
Gyges's ring, 125–7, 141, 143

Habermas, Jürgen, 417
Haiti, 263
Hallas, Duncan, 287
Hammurabi Code, 402, 406
Hampshire, Stuart, 390
hangovers, 78
happiness: ancient philosophy and, 61; Aristotle and, 149–50, 155, 161–2, 163, 190; Bentham and, 343–8; Confucius and, 66; Democritus and, 69, 70; enlarged utilitarianism and, 369; Epicurus and, 77; ethics and, 7–8, 40–1; ethics of care and, 399; Heraclitus and, 68, 70; Hobbes and, 260; Kant and, 301–2; Mill and, 349–58; modern account of, 153; science and, 301–2; Socrates and, 121–2; Stoics and, 81, 82–3, 84, 85–6; utilitarianism and, 343–8
'happy art/science', 7
Hare, R.M., 41–3, 340
harm reduction, 367; *see also* no-harm principle
Hawthorne, Nathaniel, 405
'hedonimeter', 346
hedonism, 68–70, 75–81; Bentham and, 341–8; Mill and, 352, 353–4; Plato and, 134–6; preference/pleasure, 347; Socrates and, 120–1; universalistic, 343–4, 367
Hegel, Georg Wilhelm, 382, 392
Heidegger, Martin, 392
Heraclitus, 61, 67–8, 90
hermeneutics, 17
Herodotus, 98–9, 100
heroic individuality, 377–80
heroism, moral, 113, 126, 129, 184, 208, 365
heteronomy, 331–2
Hildebrand, Dietrich von, 395
Hirshman, Linda, 340
history: anti-theory and, 390–2
hoarding, 276
Hobbes, Thomas, 47, 255–6, 258–71, 289, 290; Kant and, 301; Locke and, 274; moral rules and, 264–5; Rousseau and, 281

Hoche, Alfred, 356
holy will, 298–9
Homer, 90
homo economicus, 53
honesty, 171
hope: Aquinas and, 207, 209, 218; contractarian, 290, 291
Hrdy, Sarah Blaffer, 33
Hugo, Victor, 227
human act, 237–9
human behaviour: Aristotle and, 148–9; Bentham and, 341
human function: Aristotle and, 151–2
human law, 220–1
human nature: Aquinas and, 204–5; belief in, 154; Kant and, 295–6, 300–1, 325; Rousseau and, 282, 284; utilitarianism and, 347
'humanness': Confucius and, 65
human rights, 389, 401–6; as inalienable, 403; natural, 403
humans: deep ecology and, 411–14
human trafficking, 327
Humboldt, Wilhelm von, 378
Hume, David, 34, 36–7, 39–40; 'is–ought fallacy' and, 43–4, 46
hydra, 142
hypersexuality, 140
hypothetical imperative, 305–7

ideas: Plato and, 127–30, 133
ignorance: antecedent, 250; Aquinas and, 243–53; Aristotle and, 174, 176–82, 183,185–7; brutishness and, 182; concomitant, 246–7, 250–1; direct voluntary, 251; indirect voluntary, 251–2; induced moral, 243–4; invincible, 252–3; involuntary, 250; Kierkegaard and, 394; negligent, 244–5; nescience and, 246–9; obligation to know and, 249–50; Plato and, 112, 130; self-induced, 245–6; skepticism and, 92–3; Socrates and, 112, 116–17; veil of, 415, 416; vice and, 183; vincible, 252–3; voluntary, 251–2; weakness of will and, 185–7; willed, 394
immorality: blatant, 297; Hobbes and, 269; Kant and, 297; Plato and, 141–3; Socrates and, 116; Plato and, 134–6
impairment: responsibility and, 245–6, 251
impartial spectator, 56
imperatives: hypothetical, 305–7; Kant and, 305–31; *see also* categorical imperative
impersonalism, 357–8, 397

impulse control disorders, 138
inclination: Kant and, 296–8, 335–6; morality by, 297–8
incontinence: Aristotle and, 177–81, 182, 183–4, 186, 187; brutishness and, 182; will and, 185–7
indifference: skepticism and, 93–5
'indifferents', 86
indiscernability: principle of, 316–17
individualism: communitarianism and, 383–5; Mill and, 348, 377–80
induction: Aristotle and, 192–6
industriousness: Locke and, 275–8
injustice, systemic, 286
instrumental value, 158–62; deep ecology and, 413
intellect: Aquinas and, 216, 239
intelligence: Aquinas and, 206–7, 222; Aristotle and, 157, 187–91; ethics and, 9–10, 24–7
intention: Aquinas and, 237–9, 241–2, 245–6; enlarged utilitarianism and, 369; ignorance and, 245–6; Kant and, 297, 302–5, 317–18; moral act and, 241–2; order of, 237–9; utilitarianism and, 359–62, 369; volitions and, 239
intentionality, 10
Internet: as Hobbesian state of nature, 262
intrinsic value, 158–62; deep ecology and, 413
Introduction to the Principles of Morals and Legislation, The, 340–1
intuition, 25; Aristotle and, 188; Kant and, 306–7
intuitionism, 26, 34
involuntary acts, 242–4, 246–9
irrationality: ethics and, 9–10
Islam, 104
'is–ought fallacy', 43–51

James, William, 12
Jefferson, Thomas, 75
Jesus, 61, 63, 101–9; asymmetry principle and, 122–3; Kant and, 312; Mill and, 357–8; moral claims of, 103–6; other moralists and, 106–9; utilitarianism and, 354
Jewish religious tradition, 17, 102, 104
John-Paul II, 395
Johnson, Danielle, 361
judgment: Jesus and, 104–5, 106–7; rejection of, 27–8; suspension of, 91, 94; untheoretical, 191–2
jus gentium, 231
jus naturale, 403
just cause: natural law and, 236
justice: Anonymous Iamblichi and, 257; Aquinas and, 207, 211–13, 216, 218; compensatory,

414; contractarian, 290, 291; corrective, 414; distributive, 414–20; as fairness, 415–16; human rights and, 404–6; impersonalism and, 358; liberalism and, 373–4; Locke and, 272–3; Marx and, 286, 288; Plato and, 137, 139–41, 209; procedural, 414; restorative, 414

Kant, Immanuel, 7, 20, 255–6, 293–338; anti-theory and, 390; consistency and, 313, 323, 331; genius and, 377; lies and, 318–22; Mill and, 365–6; personalism and, 395–6; punishment and, 406; as secular, 295; 'supreme ruler' and, 323-5; utilitarianism and, 359
Kennedy, John F., 95–6
Kidd, Kenneth, 230
Kierkegaard, Søren, 389, 392–5
King, Martin Luther, Jr, 220
kleptomania, 138
knowledge: Aquinas and, 221–3, 225–6; connatural, 221–3; natural law and, 225–6; Plato and, 112, 130–3, 135; skepticism and, 91–3, 95; Socrates and, 112, 116–17; theoretical, 222
Knudson, Albert Cornelius, 395
Koster, Pepijn, 66
Kristol, Irving, 285
Küng, Hans, 408

labour: Locke and, 275–8; Marx and, 286–8
land: Locke and, 275–7
language: Aquinas and, 226
law: Aquinas and, 219–32; Aquinas's definition of, 218–19; canon, 402; common of nations, 231; divine, 205, 221; eternal, 219, 221; 'of freedom', 301; human, 220–1; justice and, 212; liberalism and, 372; 'of nature', 263–5, 268–70; Plato and, 143; religious, 205; rights and, 403–4; Socrates and, 123–4; see also moral law; natural law
Leviathan, 259–71
lex talionis, 105, 405
liberalism, 20; anti-theory and, 390; communitarianism and, 382–5; individualism and, 379; Mill and, 348, 370–7, 380–5; moral, 372–7; Rawls and, 415
libertarianism, 404, 416
liberty: retributive justice and, 415–16
liberty principle, 415
lies: Kant and, 318–22; 'truthful', 241
life: contemplative, 164–5; good, 163–4; of enjoyment, 164; political, 164–5
Lifton, Robert Jay, 356

Locke, John, 271–8, 289, 290; Hobbes and, 274; human rights and, 402–3; Marx and, 287, 288; Rousseau and, 278, 280–1
logic: ethics and, 55; Jesus and, 102-3, 106; Kant and, 299–302, 306–7, 316–17; Plato and, 135; reason and, 24–5; Revelation and, 102–3; Stoics and, 83–4; understanding and, 27; see also reason
logos, 67
love: Aquinas and, 208–9; Aristotle and, 199–200; contractarian, 291; ethics of care and, 401; Jesus and, 106, 108; Mill and, 357–8; Plato and, 144–5; Rousseau and, 283; Stoics and, 87–8; 'tough', 195
lucid occasions, 400
Lucretius, 75, 341
Lyceum, 147

McDowell, John, 390
MacIntyre, Alasdair, 339–40, 390, 392
Mackie, J.L., 35–6, 43
McTaggart, John M.E., 395
maieutic metaphor, 118, 119
makarios, 107
Mandeville, Bernard, 281
manslaughter: murder and, 245
Marcus Aurelius, 81
Maritain, Jacques, 222, 231
Marx, Karl, 286–8, 289, 382; legacy of, 287
Marxism, 286-8
Master Kong (Confucius), 61–7
material philosophy, 301
mathematics: decision-making and, 417; utilitarianism and, 342–8, 368–9
maxim, 308
maximin strategy, 415
means and ends: Aquinas and, 235; Aristotle and, 158–62; ethics of care and, 399; Kant and, 325–9, 331; utilitarianism and, 362–4
medicine: double-effect principle and, 236
memory: prudence and, 214
'mere addition paradox', 366–7
micro-financing, 368
Mill, James, 340, 348
Mill, John Stuart, 255–6, 274, 339, 340, 348–87, 415; acts and rules and, 362; inconsistencies and, 380–5; Kant and, 332–3
Milton, John, 9
misology: Socrates and, 118
mistreatment: utilitarianism and, 356–7
moderation: Confucius and, 64, 66

modus ponens, 80

modus tollens, 80, 107

money: Locke and, 277

monotheism: Socrates and, 113

Montaigne, Michel de, 94

Montessori, Maria, 119

Moore, G.E., 36, 50

moral approximation, 196

moral dilemmas, 391

moral egoism, 80–1

moral epistemology, 23–59; challenges to 27–58; definition of, 23-4

moral heroism, 126; Aquinas and, 208; Aristotle and, 184; Mill and, 365; Plato and, 129 ; Socrates and, 113

morality: genuine, 298; imposed, 371–2; 'muscular', 331; self-interested, 297; *see also* ethics

morality-for-its-own-sake, 364–6

moral law: Kant and, 293–338; utilitarianism and, 357, 358; virtue ethics and, 218, 256, 337

moral motivation: Kant and, 334–7

moral opinions: Aristotle and, 197–8

moral philosophy: as term, 1–2; *see also* ethics; morality

moral reasoning: approximate, 196; Aristotle and, 192–6

moral rights, 401–4; *see also* human rights

moral theory: Aquinas and, 202–54; Aristotle and, 147–201; contemporary, 389–421

Mounier, Emmanuel, 395–6

murder, 246–7; manslaughter and, 245

muses, 216

Næss, Arne, 410–11, 413

Nagel, Thomas, 314

narcissism, 156

Narveson, Jan, 52, 256, 289, 372–3, 376

natural duties/obligations, 289

naturalistic ethics, 204

naturalistic fallacy, 43

natural law, 204, 206, 218, 219–20, 221–32; change and, 230–2; exceptions to, 229; Hobbes and, 268; individual cases and, 226–30; Locke and, 272; secondary rules of, 223–6

natural rights: Locke and, 272

nature: amoral, 268–70; Confucius and, 64; Democritus and, 69; Diogenes and, 73, 75; Epicurus and, 76, 78–9; Heraclitus and, 68; law of, 263–5, 268–70; Locke and, 278; right of, 263–5, 273; Rousseau and, 279; Sophists and,

98; Stoics and, 84; *see also* human nature; state of nature

nature principle, 68; Jesus and, 108–9; Plato and, 127

Nazis: utilitarianism and, 356

negative rights, 402, 404

negligence, 242, 244–5, 252

Neo-Platonism, 124

nescience: ignorance and, 246–9

neutrality: skepticism and, 95–6

Newton, Isaac, 301

Nicomachean Ethics, 148, 149, 391

Nietzsche, Friedrich, 257, 332–4, 377, 379–80

Noddings, Nel, 396–401

no-harm principle, 370, 373–7, 380–1

nomos, 98, 99

noncognitivism, 33–43

non-violence: global ethics and, 409

non-voluntary acts, 242–9

normative priority, 5

Nozick, Robert, 256, 353

Nussbaum, Martha, 390

obesity: children and, 345

obituary, 150

objectivity: ethics and, 37–9, 55–8, 86

objects: persons and, 325–6

obligations: duty and, 298; utilitarianism and, 357, 358

occasions, lucid/obscure, 400

O'Connor, Flannery, 12

oneself: as life-project, 393–5

On Liberty, 370–7, 378

'open question test', 50

opinions: moral, 197–8

opportunity principle, 415–16

optimism: contractarian, 290

order of execution/intention, 237–9

original position, 414–15, 416, 419

Original Sin, 295–6

overeating, 211, 345

overman, 334, 377

pain: Bentham and, 342–8; enlarged utilitarianism and, 369; Mill and, 349

Paley, William, 340

Panopticon, 341

paradox: Aristotle and, 180–1; 'mere addition', 366–7

Parfit, Derek, 339–40, 366–7

Parliament of the World's Religions, 408

parricide, 246–7

passions: Aquinas and, 210

peace: Hobbes and, 264; inner, 107–8

peace of mind, 77; skepticism and, 90–6; Stoics and, 82, 89; *see also ataraxia*

pedophilia, 184

perception: Plato and, 134, 135

Pericles, 80

perseverance, contractarian, 291

personal achievement: Plato and, 141

personalism, 357–8, 389, 395–6

personality: Aristotle and, 151

persons: as ends-in-themselves, 325–9; Kant and, 325–9, 335; objects and, 325–6

Phaedo, 134–5

Phalaris, 182

Phidias, 82

philosopher kings, 140–1

philosophical wisdom, 189–90

philosophy, 24; material, 301; moral, 1–2; synoptic/ practical, 61; *see also* ethics; morality; practical philosophy

phronesis, 157–8, 173, 208

physics: Kant and, 301

physis, 98

Pietists, 293–4

pity: Rousseau and, 281–3

Plato, 90, 111–46, 163, 174, 256; appraisal of, 143–5; Aquinas and, 229; cave analogy and, 133; Diogenes and, 70, 72; Euthyphro problem and, 203–4; idea of the good and, 127–30, 133; moral realism and, 45, 50; self-interest and, 52; Sophists and, 97; value and, 413; virtues and, 209

Platonism, 124

pleasure: Bentham and, 342–8; definition of, 76–7; Democritus and, 68–70; egalitarianism and, 366–7; enlarged utilitarianism and, 369; Epicurus and, 75–81; as incommensurable, 352; Mill and, 349–58; Plato and, 134–6, 139; qualities of, 349–58, 365, 366

pleasure calculus, 341–8

pleasure-hedonism, 347

pluralism, 389

Pojman, Louis, 322

Political Liberalism, 414

political life, 164–5

politics: Aristotle and, 148; Hobbes and, 259; liberalism and, 372; morality and, 259; Plato and, 139–41; rights and, 403–4; Sophists and, 97

Politics, 152, 198

political state: Hobbes and, 259, 266–8; Locke and, 272–3; Rousseau and, 278–81, 283–6

pornography: libraries and, 384

positive rights, 402, 404

positivism, 18, 35

Post, Emily, 5–7

potentiality: Aristotle and, 151

power: Aquinas and, 206, 216; Hobbes and, 260; instrumental, 260; Nietzsche and, 333–4; original, 260; 'perfection' of, 206

practical affirmation, 306

practical conditional, 305–6

practical philosophy, 61; Diogenes and, 72; Epictetus and, 82, 86–7; Epicurus and, 78–9

practical reason, 37, 42, 46–7, 53; Aristotle and, 157–8; Kant and, 299, 313

practical wisdom, 173, 190–1, 208

preference, 42

preference-hedonism, 347

premise, 24–5; hidden, 45, 149

prescriptivism, 35; universal, 41–3

pre-Socratics, 67, 68

preventive evil, 320–2

price: Kant and, 326–7

principles: of aceticism, 344–5; asymmetry, 122–3; double-effect, 227, 232–6; first moral, 197–8; of the indiscernability of moral cases, 316–17; liberty, 415; moral, 4; nature, 68, 108–9, 127; no-harm, 370, 373–7, 380–1; sufficient reason, 28; utility, 343–7, 347; wealth, 415–16

prisoners' dilemma, 417–20; iterated, 419

private property: Locke and, 275–8; Marx and, 286–8; Rousseau and, 280

progress: Rousseau and, 278–81; utilitarianism and, 367

proletariat, 286

promise-making: Kant and, 308–9, 311

proof: burden of, 28–30

property: *see* private property

Protagoras, 61, 97–101, 257

Protestant Reformation, 294–5

prudence: Aquinas and, 207, 208, 213–16, 229, 240; contractarian, 290, 291; false, 214; imperfect/ incomplete, 214; integral parts of, 214–15; perfect, 214

psychological egoism, 54–5

psychology: ethics and, 391; happiness and, 153; moral, 210

public policy: liberalism and, 372; utilitarianism and, 347–8, 367–8

punishment: Aristotle and, 406; Bentham and, 341; capital, 268; Hobbes and, 265–6, 268; Kant and, 406; Locke and, 272–3; retributive justice and, 414; rights and, 404–6; Socrates and, 123, 143
Puritanism, 8, 299
Pyrrho, 90–6, 101, 109
Pythagoras, 117, 135

quasi-categorical imperative theory, 322–3
'queerness': argument from, 35–6
quietism, 95

racism: speciesism and, 412
radicalism: Mill and, 348
Rand, Ayn, 332, 334
rape, 32, 241, 244
Raphael, 216
'rational animal', 53–4, 151, 154, 411; Aquinas and, 206–7, 223
rationality: economic account of, 53–4; ethics and, 9–10
rationalization: Kierkegaard and, 394
Rawls, John, 256, 289, 414–17, 419
Raz, Joseph, 339–40, 352, 404
Read, Kimberly, and Marcia Purse, 140
realism, moral, 47–51
reality: Plato and, 112
reason: a priori, 299–301; Aquinas and, 205, 210; Aristotle and, 152; ethics and, 23–59; Hobbes and, 264; Hume and, 37; Kant and, 295, 298–301, 335, 336–7; moral, 83–4; Plato and, 136–41, 142; practical, 37, 42, 46-7, 53; 'principle of sufficient', 28, 29–30; pure, 299-301; skepticism and, 94; Stoics and, 82–4; theoretical, 37, 47, 83–4; *see also* logic; moral reasoning
'reasonable person', 232
rectification of names, 64, 65–6
reductionism, 31
rehabilitation, 405
reincarnation, 135–6, 163, 174
relativism, 98–100
religion, *xi–xii*; Aquinas and, 203–5; Confucius and, 64; divine command morality and, 406–8; ecumenical global ethics and, 408–10; ethics of care and, 401; Golden Rule and, 104; Jesus and, 102; Kant and, 293–4, 295; Kierkegaard and, 392, 394; Socrates and, 113–15
religious law, 205
ren, 64–5
Renouvier, Charles Bernard, 395

reparation, 405
reproduction: natural law and, 225
Republic, The, 125–7, 136, 139–41
repugnant conclusion, 367
responsibility: Aquinas and, 242–53; Aristotle and, 176
restitution, 405
retaliation, 404–5
retribution, 404–5, 406
Revelation, 102–3
revolution: Kant and, 294; Marx and, 286, 287
rhetoric: Sophists and, 97
right of nature: Hobbes and, 263–5; Locke and, 273
rights: natural, 272; negative, 402, 404; types of, 402; *see also* human rights
'rights-talk', 402, 404
rigid counterexample, 318–22
Rorty, Richard, 390
Ross, W.D., 322–3
rotation of crops, 393
Rousseau, Jean-Jacques, 278–86, 289, 290, 382; Marx and, 286–8; Wollstonecraft and, 385
ruler: Hobbes and, 265–9; Locke and, 274–5; Plato and, 140–1; *see also* sovereign
rules: anti-theory and, 390–2; Golden, 63, 103–4, 265, 312–13, 409; Hobbes and, 264–5; Mill and, 362; secondary, 223–6; Silver, 63–4, 103-4
rule utilitarianism, 362

Sade, Marquis de, 332, 334
Sandel, Michael, 48–9, 289, 419–20
Sartre, Jean-Paul, 11, 57–8
'savage': Rousseau and, 279, 280
scholasticism, 206, 212
Schopenhauer, Arthur, 16–17
science: Aristotle and, 188–9; Enlightenment and, 255–6; Epicurus and, 76, 78–9; ethics and, 35; is– ought fallacy and, 44–5; Rousseau and, 278
self-actualization: Mill and, 378–80
self-consciousness, 10
self-defence: mortal, 232–6; Hobbes and, 268; Locke and, 273–4; natural law and, 227, 232-6; unacceptable, 235
self-esteem, 55; contractarian, 290
self-indulgence, 179–80, 394
self-interest, 52–5; Hobbes and, 264; Kant and, 335–6; Plato and, 52; prisoners' dilemma and, 417–20; retributive justice and, 415, 416; Rousseau and, 281–2

selfishness: Aristotle and, 154–7
selflessness, 54
'self-love', 155–6; Kant and, 310–11; Rousseau and, 283
self-preservation: natural law and, 223–5, 232–6
self-realization, 420; Aristotle and, 154–7; Mill and, 378–80
Seneca, 81
Sextus Empiricus, 90–1, 93–4
sexuality: hyper-, 140; natural law and, 225; Plato and, 138–9, 140; Socrates and, 139
shalom, 107
shame: punishment and, 405, 419
Shanoff, Alan, 273
Shinto, 104
shrewdness: prudence and, 214
Sidgwick, Henry, 340
Silver Rule, 63–4, 103–4
simplicity: Diogenes and, 71–2
Singer, Peter, 153, 340, 397, 403, 412, 413
skepticism, *x–xi*, 14, 27–31; absolute, 91–2; academic, 95; ancient, 90–6; contractarianism and, 420; liberalism and, 372; mitigated, 91–2; moral, 27–31; Pyrrhonean, 95; Socrates and, 113, 118; Sophism and, 101
slavery: Aristotle and, 198; Kant and, 326–7; Locke and, 274–5; Mill and, 375
slippery slope problem, 187
Sloan, G. Tod, 171
'small man', 62–3
Smith, Adam, 56
Smith, Christian, 18
'sneaky solution', 319
social contract: contemporary, 414–20; future, 287; Hobbes and, 262–5, 265–70; Locke and, 272, 274; Marx and, 287; Rousseau and, 278, 283–6; *see also* agreement
Social Contract, The, 278, 283–6
society: *see* community
sociobiology, 31–3; is–ought fallacy and, 46
Socrates, 8, 11, 111–46, 203–4; asymmetry principle and, 122–3; birthing metaphor and, 118, 119; Diogenes and, 70, 72; Epictetus and, 89; execution of, 113, 116, 148; as gadfly, 115–16; ignorance and, 394; Jesus and, 102, 108, 109; as moral hero, 113; morality and, 115–16; as Plato's mouthpiece, 124–45; popular opinion and, 120; religion and, 113–15; sex and, 139; Sophists and, 97, 100–1; teachings of, 112–24
Socratic method, 117–18

soldiers: child, 245, 246
solidarity: global ethics and, 409
sophia, 189
Sophism, 61, 97–101, 180; skepticism and, 101
soul: Plato and, 135–41, 144–5, 164, 174; tripartite, 136–41
sovereign: Hobbes and, 265–9; Locke and, 274; *see also* ruler
species: moral act and, 240–1
speciesism, 153–4, 412–13
spirit: Plato and, 136–41
'squeamish factor', 363
state: *see* political state
state of nature: escape from 262–5; Hobbes and, 260–5, 269, 270; Locke and, 272–3, 275, 277; Marx and, 286–7; Rousseau and, 278–86, 283–4
stealing: Locke and, 277; natural law and, 227–8
Stein, Edith, 56, 401
Stocker, Michael, 390
Stoicism, 11, 61, 81–90; Socrates and, 113
straw man, 344, 407
Subjection of Women, The, 385–7
subjectivism: Protagoras and, 97–8; transcendental, 389, 392–5
subjectivity: ethics and, 37, 55–8
suffering: enlarged utilitarianism and, 369
suicide: Kant and, 310–11, 329
suicide bombing, 321
Summa Theologiae, 203, 204, 206
sunesis, 191
supererogatory act, 208
'superman', 334, 377
supernatural: Jesus and, 108–9; Pyrrho and, 109; Socrates and, 114
supervenience, 42–3
syllogism, practical, 192
Symposium, 128
synderesis, 213–14

talents: Kant and, 309–10, 311
Talmon, J.L., 285
Taoism, 104
tautology, 50
Taylor, Charles, 339–40, 390
Taylor, Harriet, 349
techne, 189
temperance: Aquinas and, 207, 210–11, 212, 216; Aristotle and, 183–4; contractarian, 291; Plato and, 137, 209; Socrates and, 120–1
texts: interpretation of, 16–19

theology, Reformation, 295

theory: Diogenes and, 72

Theory of Justice, A, 414

thing-as-it-appears-to-us, 335

thing-in-itself, 335

thin theory of the good, 372–3, 416

Thomists, 402

Thornhill, Randy, and Craig T. Palmer, 32

Tierney, Brian, 402

Tierney, John, 57

tolerance: contractarian, 290; global ethics and, 409

Tolkien, J.R.R., 127

totalitarianism: personalism and, 396; Rousseau and, 285

Toulmin, Stephen, 390

traffic signs, 230

transcendental subjectivism, 389, 392–5

triumphalism, 357

truth: as relative, 97–8; Sophists and, 97–8, 100–1

ubermensch, 334, 377

understanding, 25–7; Aristotle and, 188, 191; prudence and, 214; theoretical, 191

unfalsifiability, 29–30, 54

unhappiness: Mill and, 349; Socrates and, 121–2; Stoics and, 84

unintended acts, 242, 243

United Nations Universal Declaration of Human Rights, 403

universalizability, 41

universal prescriptivism, 41–3

University College London, 341

untheoretical judgment, 191–2

utile, 346

utilitarianism, 304, 339–48; act/rule, 362; anti-theory and, 390–1; Bentham and, 340–8; as consequentialism, 359–62; contemporary, 347; enlarged, 369–70; liberalism and, 375; Mill and, 348, 349–70; 380–5; natural-law, 347; original, 340–8; punishment and, 406; Rawls and, 415; revised, 368–70; women and, 385

Utilitarianism, 348, 349–70

utility principle, 343–4; preference-hedonism and, 347

utility, 343

Vadesolo, Piercarlo, and David DeSteno, 57

value: facts and, 34; human-centred, 278; instrumental, 326; intrinsic, 325–9, 398, 413; intrinsic/instrumental, 158–62; as relative, 159–60

veil of ignorance, 415, 416

vice: Aristotle and, 173, 178, 179, 181, 182–3, 186; Epictetus and, 86; Rousseau and, 281–3

viciousness, 177, 178

virtue ethics: Anonymous Iamblichi and, 256–7; anti-theory and, 390–1; Aquinas and, 206–9; Aristotle and, 148, 151–7; contractarianism and, 265, 267–70; ethics of care and, 398–9; Hobbes and, 265; Kant and, 299, 313; liberalism and, 375; Mill and, 351, 377–85, 380–5; moral law ethics and, 218, 256, 337; utilitarianism and, 339–40, 357; women and, 385

virtues, 2, 16; action and, 166-7; Aquinas and, 207–18; Aristotle and, 151–7, 162–3, 165–74, 181–7; cardinal, 207–18, 216, 291; Confucius and, 65; continence and, 183; contractarian, 290–1; Diogenes and, 72; Epictetus and, 86; as habit, 165–7; inductive, 193–4; intellectual, 187; Jesus and, 105–6; minor intellectual, 191–2; moral, 207; natural, 190–1; Plato and, 143–4, 209; principle, 207–9; Rousseau and, 281, 282; Socrates and, 121; 'in the strict sense', 190–1; superhuman, 181–2, 186; supreme moral, 173; theological, 207–8, 209; vice and, 182–3

Vlad the Impaler, 13

volitions: intentions and, 239

voluntary action: Aquinas and, 236–40, 242–3, 246–9; internal and external structure and, 236–40

Walker, Tim, 26

Walzer, Michael, 322

war: Heraclitus and, 67–8; Hobbes and, 261–2

'Way', 64, 65

weakness of will, 174, 177–81; ignorance and, 185–7

wealth: gap in, 281; Locke and, 277–8; Rousseau and, 280

wealth principle, 415–16

Weil, Simone, 401

'wide reflective equilibrium', 417

will: Aquinas and, 216, 239; Aristotle and, 174–81, 185–7; free, 9–10, 174; general, 283–6; holy, 298–9; Kant and, 296–9, 302–5; Nietzsche and, 333–4; 'to power, 333–4; *see also* good will

William of Ockham, 402

Williams, Bernard, 339–40, 363–4, 390

Williamson, Abby, 276

wisdom: Aristotle and, 189–91, 193–5; deductive, 193–5; philosophical, 189–90; Plato and, 137, 209; practical, 173, 190–1, 208

wisdom literature, 61
Wolf, Susan, 314
Wolfe, Alan, 53
Wolfe, Tom, 78
Wolff, Edward, 281
Wollstonecraft, Mary, 385–6
women: ethics of care and, 396–401; Mill and, 385–7

Xeophanes, 90

Yoruba, 104
Yunus, Muhammad, 368

Zeno of Citium, 81
Zeno of Elea, 90
Zoroastrianism, 104

☙ Credits ❧

Grateful acknowledgement is made for permission to reprint the following:

Page 3: Box 1.1 from D.C. Copeland, "Real Heroes vs. Sports Heroes," Aug. 31, 2006, http://ezinearticles.com/?Real-Heroes-vs.-Sports-Heroes&id-287017, EzineArticles.com.

Page 6: Box 1.2 from Emily Post, *Etiquette: The Blue Book of Social Usage* (New York and London: Funk and Wagnalls Company, 1937), p. 227.

Page 11: Box 1.3 from Viktor Frankl, *Mans Search for Meaning* (New York: Washington Square Press, 1963), pp. 122.

Page 13: Box 1.4 from "Vlad III the Impaler," Wikipedia, http://en.wikipedia.org/wiki/Vlad_III_the_Impaler.

Page 18: Box 1.5 from Christian Smith, *Moral Believing Animals* (Oxford: Oxford University Press, 2004), p.155.

Page 26: Box 2.1 from Tim Walker, "Intuitionist Laura Day predicted the credit crunch—now big business is paying her big bucks," *The Independent*, Thursday, 3 July 2008, from online edition at www.independent.co.uk/news/business/.

Page 30: Box 2.2 from The Ashley Madison Agency®, Affair Guarantee Program, online advertisement at: www. ashleymadison.com/app/public/guarantee/detailsform.p.

Page 32: Excerpt from Randy Thornhill and Craig T. Palmer, "Why Men Rape," The New York Academy Of Sciences, January/February 2000 (Adapted from their book, *A Natural History of Rape: Biological Bases of Sexual Coercion*.).

Page 33: Box 2.3 from "Animals that Kill Their Young," TIME (Magazine), Monday, Jan. 09, 1978; online edition at: www.time.com/time/magazine/article/0,9171,912086-2,00. html.

Page 34: Excerpt from A. J. Ayer, "Language, Truth, and Logic," p. 520, in W. T. Jones, Frederick Sontag, Morton O. Beckner, Robert J. Fogelin, *Approaches to Ethics* (New York: McGraw Hill, 1962) pp. 532–3; selection originally from A. J. Ayer, *Language, Truth, and Logic* (New York: Dover Publications, 1946), Chapter 6.

Pages 35–6: Excerpt from David Hume, An Enquiry Concerning Human Understanding, available online from ebooks@adelaide 2004 (from New York: P.F. Collier & Son, Harvard Classics 37, 1910), VIII.1, http://etext.library. adelaide.edu.au/ h/hume/david/.

Pages 36–7: Excerpt from David Hume, An Enquiry Concerning Human Understanding, available online from ebooks@adelaide 2004 (from New York: P.F. Collier &

Son, Harvard Classics 37, 1910), VIII.1, http://etext.library. adelaide.edu.au/ h/hume/david/.

Page 48: Box 2.5 from Curtis, Valerie and Adam Biran. Dirt, Disgust, and Disease: is hygiene in our genes? *Perspectives in Biology & Medicine* 44:1 (2001), 17-31. © 2001 by The Johns Hopkins University Press. Reprinted with permission of The Johns Hopkins University Press.

Page 53: Box 2.6 from Alan Wolfe, "The New Economics And The Pursuit Of Happiness," *The New Republic*, Wednesday, July 09, 2008, available online at: www.tnr.com/politics/story. html?id=3bc0e959-3b4e-440d-9b99-69078429b82c.

Page 56: Excerpt from www.tnr.com/politics/story.html? id=3bc0e959-3b4e-440d-9b99-69078429b82c.

Page 57: Box 2.7 from *The New York Times*, © July 1, 2008, The New York Times. All rights reserved. Used by permission and protected by the Copyright Laws of the United States. The printing, copying, redistribution, or transmission of the Material without express written permission is prohibited.

Pages 62, 63: Excerpts from *Confucius, The Analects*, translated by Raymond Dawson (Oxford: Oxford University Press, 2000), p. 14.42.

Page 66: Box 3.1 from Pepijn Koster. "Overfishing: A Global Disaster," http://overfishing.org/pages/what_is_overfishing.php.

Pages 70–1: Excerpt from Cited in Donald R. Dudley, A History of Cynicism" From *Diogenes to the 6th Century AD* (Hildesheim: Georg Olms Verlagsbuchhandlung,1967), p. 5.

Page 71: Box 3.2 from Robert Bellah, The Broken Covenant, 1975. From: Quotations on Consumerism/Overconsumption www.stthomas.edu/recycle/consume.htm.

Page 73: Box 3.3 from Richard Bett, *Melton Times*, 21 May 2008 www.meltontimes.co.uk/ news/John_Ferneley_visit_ to_Parliament.4104645.jp.

Page 78: Box 3.4 from Kingsley Amis (and David Lodge), *Lucky Jim* (Penguin, 1992), p. 61.

Page 78: Box 3.4 from Tom Wolfe, *The Bonfire of the Vanities* (Bibliolife, 2008), p. 165.

Page 83: Box 3.5 from DIGITALSPY.COM.

Page 96: Box 3.6 from DigitalJournal.com.

Pages 115, 116: Excerpts from Plato Defence of Socrates (what is traditionally known as the Apology) in: *Defence of Socrates, Euthyphro, Crito*; 30e-31a7 and 30a7-b1.

Page 186: Box 5.8 from the *Associated Press*, August 7, 2009.

Page 195: Box 5.9 from Emma Cook, "Tough love finds a way to beat heroin," *The Independent*, Monday, 24 August 1998.

Page 206: Box 6.1 from David Eddie, "Response to 'I made plans with a friend,'" David Eddie's *Damage Control*, Sep.18, 2009, The Globe and Mail.

Page 207: Excerpt from St. Thomas Aquinas, *Summa Theologica*. Translated by Fathers of the English Dominican Province (New York: Benziger Bros. edition, 1947). I.II.60.2.

Page 215: Box 6.3 from "Name, Date, Threat," News of the Weird, [*Anchorage Daily News*, 8-12-09] online source: www.trutv.com/weird/really-stupid-robberies/index.html.

Page 215: Box 6.3 from "Slowway," News of the Weird, [WMAR-TV (Baltimore)-AP, 6-30-09] online source: www.trutv.com/weird/really-stupid-robberies/index.html.

Page 215: Box 6.3 from "Squashed Like a Bug," News of the Weird, [Beaumont Enterprise, 7-20-09] online source: www.trutv.com/weird/really-stupid-robberies/index.html.

Pages 218–9: Excerpt from St. Thomas Aquinas, *Summa Theologica*. Translated by Fathers of the English Dominican Province (New York: Benziger Bros. edition, 1947). II.II.49.3.

Page 220: Box 6.4 from Martin Luther King, Jr., "Letter from a Birmingham Jail," April 16, 1963, African Studies Center—University Of Pennsylvania, online source: www.africa.upenn.edu/Articles_Gen/Letter_Birmingham.html.

Pages 225–6: Excerpt from St. Thomas Aquinas, *Summa Theologica*. Translated by Fathers of the English Dominican Province (New York: Benziger Bros. edition, 1947). I.II.94.2.

Page 229: Excerpt from St. Thomas Aquinas, *Summa Theologica*. Translated by Fathers of the English Dominican Province (New York: Benziger Bros. edition, 1947). I.II.94.2.

Page 230: Box 6.6 adapted from an article originally appearing in the *Toronto Star*, September 2009.Reprinted with permission—Torstar Syndication Services.

Pages 230–1: Excerpt from St. Thomas Aquinas, *Summa Theologica*. Translated by Fathers of the English Dominican Province (New York: Benziger Bros. edition, 1947). I.II.94.5.

Page 244: Box 6.7 © 2010 by Holly Ashworth (http://teenadvice.about.com) Used with permission of About, Inc. which can be found online at www.about.com. All rights reserved.

Page 246: Box 6.8 from Carolyn Muir web page, 'Child Soldiers in Africa.' New Trier Township High School, IL, http://nths.newtrier.k12.Il.us/academics/faculty/muir/africa_project/p7/ChildSoldiers/index.htm.

Page 256: Excerpt from The Anonymous Iamblichi in *The First Philosophers*, Robin Waterfield translator, (Oxford: Oxford University Press, 2000), pp. 309.

Page 256: Excerpt from The Anonymous Iamblichi in *The First Philosophers*, Robin Waterfield translator, (Oxford: Oxford University Press, 2000), pp. 309.

Page 258: Excerpt from Thomas Hobbes, *Leviathan*, Edwin Curley editor (Indianapolis: Hackett Publishing, 1994), Hobbes Verse Autobiography, p. liv.

Page 261: Excerpts from Thomas Hobbes, *Leviathan*, J. C. A. Gaskin editor, (Oxford: Oxford University Press, 1996), Part 1, Ch. 13.9 and Ch. 13.8.

Page 262: Box 7.1 from Nate Anderson, "No rules: Internet Security a Hobbesian State of Nature" updated February 1, 2010, electronic source: http://arstechnica.com/tech-policy/news/2010/02/no-rules-internet-security-a-hobbesian-state-of-nature.ars.

Page 263: Box 7.2 from "Chaos as water reaches shattered city," *New York Post* (Associated Press), January 16, 2010, from electronic edition: www.nypost.com.

Page 265–70: Excerpt from Thomas Hobbes, *Leviathan*, J. C. A. Gaskin editor, (Oxford: Oxford University Press, 1996), Part 1, Ch. 15.35 and Part 1, Ch. 15.40 and Part 2, Ch. 17.1 and Part 2, Ch. 18.1 and Part 1, Ch. 13.10 and Part 1, Ch. 6.7

Page 272, 273, 275, 276–8: Excerpt from John Locke, "The Second Treatise of Government," in *Political Philosophy: The Essential Texts*, Steven M. Cahn editor, (Oxford: Oxford University Press, 2005), pp. 246-273. Ch.II.6 and Ch.II.8 and Ch.V.26 and Ch.V.28 and Ch.V.33 and Ch.V.40.

Page 273: Box 7.3 Alan Shanoff, "Citizen's arrest? Leave policing to the police," *Toronto Sun*, June 7, 2009, electronic source: www.torontosun.com/comment/columnists/alan_shanoff/2009/06/07/9703121-sun.html.

Page 276: Box 7.4 from Abby Williamson, *The Oklahoma Daily Times*.

Page 279–80: Excerpts from Jean-Jacques Rousseau, *The Social Contract (and Discourse on Political Economy)*, translated with Introduction and Notes by Christopher Betts (Oxford: Oxford University Press, 1994). Notes, I, pp.94–5 and Part II, p.83–4 and Part II, p.60–1 and Part II, p.61 and Part II, p.55 and Part II, p. 66.

Page 281: Box 7.5 from interview with Edward Wolff, The Multinational Monitor, "The Wealth Divide, The Growing Gap in the United States Between the Rich and the Rest," May 2003—Volume 24—Number 5, www.multinationalmonitor.org/mm2003/03may/may03interviewswolff.html.

Pages 282-5: Excerpts from Jean-Jacques Rousseau, *The Social Contract (and Discourse on Political Economy)*, translated with Introduction and Notes by Christopher Betts (Oxford: Oxford University Press, 1994). Part I, p.46 and Part I, p. 47 and Part I, p.47 and Part I, p.47-48 and Ch.VIII, p.59.

Page 285: Box 7.6 from Irving Kristol, "Review of The Rise of Totalitarian Democracy, by J. L. Talmon," *Commentary Magazine*, September 1952, electronic reprint: www.commentarymagazine.com/viewarticle.cfm/the-rise-of-totalitarian-democracy-by-j-l-talmon-1568.

Page 286: Excerpt from Karl Marx, "Economic and Philosophical Manuscripts of 1844," reprinted in Steven M. Cahn, *Political Philosophy* (New York, Oxford: Oxford University Press, 2005), pp. 412.

Page 286, 287: Box 7.7 and excerpts from Karl Marx, "Economic and Philosophical Manuscripts of 1844," reprinted in Steven M. Cahn, *Political Philosophy* (New York, Oxford: Oxford University Press, 2005), pp. 412–3.

Page 296: Box 8.1 from Associated Press, "Ohio Teen Sentenced 2 Years for Baby's Rat Bites, Loss of Toes," Tuesday, October 06, 2009, Fox News, electronic source: www.foxnews.com.

Page 297: Excerpt from Kant, *Groundwork for the Metaphysics of Morals*, Arnulf Zweig, Translator; Thomas Hill and Arnulf Zweig editors (Oxford: Oxford University press, 2002), 2.17.209.

Page 298, 300, 302: Excerpt from Kant, *Groundwork for the Metaphysics of Morals*, Arnulf Zweig, Translator; Thomas Hill and Arnulf Zweig editors (Oxford: Oxford University press, 2002), 1.10.200 and .Part II, p.61 and Part II, p.55 and Part II, p. 66 and 1.7.195

Page 300: Box 8.2 from "Alcoholism, About.com, electronic source: http://alcoholism.about.com.

Page 303: Box 8.3 from Clive Bell, "Art and Significant Form," from Art, 1913, available electronically at: denisdutton.com: www.denisdutton.com/bell.htm.

Page 307: Box 8.4 from Austin Cline, "Deontology and Ethics: What is Deontology, Deontological Ethics?" electronic source: About.com.

Page 308: Excerpts from Kant, *Groundwork for the Metaphysics of Morals*, Arnulf Zweig, Translator; Thomas Hill and Arnulf Zweig editors (Oxford: Oxford University press, 2002), 2.27.223 and 2.28.225.

Page 317: Box 8.5 from Bill McCleery/*The Indianapolis Star*.

Page 321: Box 8.6 from Staff Report, 'Eight Dead in Suicide Attack on ANP rally.' *Daily Times* (Pakistan), www.dailytimes.com.pk/,12 February, 2008.

Page 322: Excerpt from Louis P. Pojman, *Ethics: Discovering Right and Wrong* (Belmont CA: Thomson, Wadsworth, 2006), p. 134.

Page 324–5: Excerpt from Kant, *Groundwork for the Metaphysics of Morals*, Arnulf Zweig, Translator; Thomas Hill and Arnulf Zweig editors (Oxford: Oxford University press, 2002), 2.34.236.

Page 327: Box 8.7 from Tamara Cherry, Sun Media, *The Toronto Sun* http://cnews.canoe. ca/CNEWS/Crime/2008/02/10/.

Page 329: Box 8.8 Lawrence Stevens, "Suicide: A Civil Right," www.antipsychiatry.org (electronic source) www.antipsychiatry.org/suicide.htm.

Page 330-1: Excerpt from Kant, *Groundwork for the Metaphysics of Morals*, Arnulf Zweig, Translator; Thomas Hill and Arnulf Zweig editors (Oxford: Oxford University press, 2002), 3.44.250-1.

Page 340: Box 9.1 from "Political Animals Owe Each Other Political Altruism," Linda Hirshman, *The Huffington Post*, July 1 2008, electronic source: www.huffingtonpost.com/linda_hirshman/ liberal_principles_ii_b_110160.html.

Page 342, 344: Excerpts from Bentham, *An Introduction to the Principles of Morals and Legislation*, 1781, reprint, electronic edition (pdf file), Kitchener: Batoche Books, 2000; I.i, p.14 and p. IV.ii, p.35 and II.iii, p. 19, available at: www.efm.bris.ac.uk/het/bentham/morals.pdf.

Page 345: Box 9.2 from "Childhood obesity threatens the nation's health," WLFI-TV, West Lafayette IN, June 5, 2008.

Page 346: Excerpt from Bentham, *An Introduction to the Principles of Morals and Legislation, 1781*, reprint, electronic edition (pdf file), Kitchener: Batoche Books, 2000; IV.v, p.32-33 available at: www.efm.bris.ac.uk/het/bentham/morals.pdf.

Page 350-1: Excerpts from Selections from "Utilitarianism" from John Stuart Mill, *On Liberty and Other Essays*, edited with introduction and notes by John Gray, (Oxford: Oxford University Press, 1998), II, p.139 and II, p. 139–140 "Utilitarianism," pp. 131–204. An electronic copy can be found at: Utilitarianism, University of Adelaide Library E_Books, http://etext.library.adelaide.edu.au/m/mill/john_stuart/.

Page 356: Box 9.3 from Wesley J. Smith, "German Euthanasia 1938-1945," From: "Killing Babies, Compassionately, The Netherlands follows in Germany's footsteps," *Weekly Standard*, 03/27/2006, electronic source www.weeklystandard.com/Content/Public/Articles/000/000/012/003dncoj.asp.

Page 361: Box 9.4 from Danielle Johnson, "Mystery pair at diner spark cascade of giving: Couple pay another table's tab, and chain reaction of generosity lasts hours," Dec. 14, 2009, NBCPhiladelphia.com (MSNBC.com), electronic source: www.msnbc.msn.com/id/34420892/ns/us_news-giving/.

Page 368: Box 9.5 from "World banker to the poor," BBC NEWS, 2006/10/13, electronic version: http://news.bbc.co.uk/go/pr/fr/_/2/hi/south_asia/6047234.stm.

Page 370: Excerpt from "On Liberty" from John Stuart Mill, *On Liberty and Other Essays*, edited with introduction and notes by John Gray, (Oxford: Oxford University Press, 1998), I, p. 14 "On Liberty" pp. 5–128. An electronic copy can be found at: Utilitarianism, University of Adelaide Library E_Books, http://etext.library.adelaide.edu.au/m/mill/john_stuart/.

Page 373: Excerpt from "Utilitarianism" from John Stuart Mill, *On Liberty and Other Essays*, edited with introduction and notes by John Gray, (Oxford: Oxford University Press, 1998), V, p.195. "Utilitarianism," pp. 131–204. An electronic copy can be found at: Utilitarianism, University of Adelaide Library E_Books, http://etext.library.adelaide.edu.au/m/mill/john_stuart/.

Page 379, 380–1: Excerpts from "On Liberty" from John Stuart Mill, *On Liberty and Other Essays*, edited with introduction and notes by John Gray, (Oxford: Oxford University Press, 1998), III, p. 69–70 and III, p. 69 and III, p. 67. "On Liberty" pp. 5–128. An electronic copy can be found at: Utilitarianism, University of Adelaide Library E_Books, http://etext.library.adelaide.edu.au/m/mill/john_stuart/.

Page 384: Box 9.6 from Source: Felisa Cardona, "Library secure for kid porn," *Denver Post*, 11/18/2007, electronic version: www.denverpost.com/ci_7494175.

Pages 384-6: Excerpts from "The Subjugation of Women," from John Stuart Mill, *On Liberty and Other Essays*, edited with introduction and notes by John Gray (Oxford: Oxford University Press, 1998), 575–6 and 577 "The Subjugation of Women" pp. 471–582.

Page 390: Excerpt from "Anti-theory," *The Blackwell Dictionary of Western Philosophy*, Nicholas Bunnin And Jiyuan Yu editors, 2004 www.blackwellreference.com/.

Page 391: Box 10.1 from Nafsika Athanassoulis, "Virtue Ethics," *Internet Encyclopedia of Philosophy*, August 28, 2004, www.iep.utm.edu/virtue/#SH2c.

Page 395-6: Excerpt from Emmanuel Mounier, *Personalism* (Notre Dame: University of Notre Dame Press, 2001), xv-xvi.

Page 397-8: Excerpts from Nel Noddings, *Caring: A Feminine Approach to Ethics and Moral Education* (Berkeley: University of California Press, 1984), p. 83–4 and p. 112.

Page 400: Box 10.2 from Sherman Dorn, One-Blog Schoolhouse, "I am not a caring teacher," April 23, 2006, electronic blog: www.shermandorn.com/mt/archives/000458.html.

Pages 408–9: Excerpts from Global Ethic Foundation, Tübingen, Germany. Declaration Toward a Global Ethic, II.B.1. Electronic source: www.weltethos.org/dat-english/index.htm.

Page 410: Excerpt from Warwick Fox, "Deep Ecology, A New Philosophy for our Time," reprinted in *Environmental Ethics: An Anthology*, Andrew Light and Holmes Rolston editors (Oxford: Wiley-Blackwell, 2002), pp. 252–3.

Page 412: Box 10.3 from Peter Singer, "All Animals Are Equal," abridged from an essay first published in *Philosophic Exchange* Vol. 1, no 5 (Summer 1974), online source: www.fortunecity.com/emachines/e11/86/singer.html.